Readings in criminal justice

Richter H. Moore, Jr.

Thomas C. Marks, Jr.

Robert V. Barrow

Readings in criminal justice

THE BOBBS-MERRILL COMPANY, INC.

Indianapolis

The Bobbs-Merrill Company, Inc.
4300 West 62nd Street
Indianapolis, Indiana 46268

First Edition
First Printing 1976
Design: Betty Binns

Library of Congress Cataloging in Publication Data
Main entry under title:

Readings in criminal justice.

   1. Criminal justice, Administration of—United
States. I. Moore, Richter H., 1928–   II. Marks,
Thomas C., 1938–   III. Barrow, Robert V.,
1936–
KF9223.R4   345′.73′05   75-38727
ISBN 0-672-61371-9

Contents

Contents   *vii*

Preface

Most Americans are mere spectators in the criminal justice arena. Many of us are too apathetic and too fearful of becoming involved to come to the aid of a neighbor in trouble. We fail to recognize the criminal justice practitioner as our neighbor and even as a member of our community. The criminal justice practitioner is considered as someone apart, a person to be feared rather than respected. We inculcate in our children prejudices toward the practitioner and the system. From us they learn it is alright to break a "little" law so long as we don't get caught. Repeatedly we demand law and order but for somebody else. We also fail to recognize the criminal justice practitioner as a professional. Only when we as citizens are willing to assume our responsibility for demanding and then supporting an effective, efficient single system of criminal justice will we have the type of justice we need and deserve.

Frequently those of us who are involved in some way with the criminal justice system close our eyes to corruption at the highest levels of government. Too often we ignore the improper infringement of the rights of American citizens by our criminal justice agencies. We are too willing to rationalize that such infringement was done in the name of national security or crime prevention. We have been unwilling to admit that the law must attach to law enforcers as well as law breakers. Repeatedly we criticize others for lack of concern with criminal justice and with law and order issues, yet oftentimes we as criminal justice practitioners are too apathetic to participate in the political arena. We tend to think of ourselves as being the system, forgetting that we are part of only one of the many *components of the system. We fail to consider the system as a whole. Then, if something goes wrong, we place all of the blame on the other parts and accept none ourselves.*

We practitioners are citizens, and, as with all citizens, we should become practitioners in crime prevention. The effectiveness of the criminal justice system depends upon us all. We must, however, have knowledge and understanding of that system. This book is designed to introduce the citizen, the student citizen in particular, to the criminal justice system and its components. We have attempted to balance the considerations, for all too frequently introductory criminal justice books have been weighted in favor of one or another component of the system—police, corrections, or the courts. There is no attempt to provide a comprehensive coverage of the system and its parts, if in fact there is a system. We do not expect the book to answer all the questions. In fact, it raises more questions than it answers—hopefully the right ones; for to solve problems we must ask the proper questions. To the student we hope that this book will interest you in criminal justice and provide you with an incentive to delve deeper into its specific areas.

We wish to express deep and sincere thanks to our many colleagues for their suggestions of materials for this reader. Unfortunately space does not permit us to include all of the items suggested. Special thanks to the secretaries who have typed and retyped manuscript materials, to the research assistants who have spent many hours going over the materials, and especially to the several classes of students that have served as the guinea pigs for testing the validity and relevance of the materials herein presented. Lastly we thank our own families for their patience.

Readings in criminal justice

Part one

Crime, the public, and the criminal justice system

W e speak of a criminal justice system in the United States, but is there a system? Do we need a comprehensive criminal justice system? What is the public's attitude toward crime? How do communities respond to crime? Do crime rates reflect breaches of the law? These are a few of the issues examined in Part One.

The Criminal Justice Non-system suggests that the idea of a single criminal justice system in the United States is a fallacy. The so-called system is composed of separate components—law enforcement, corrections, and the courts—each doing their own thing with relatively little communication or cooperation among them. Students of criminal justice must begin to think in terms of a single system rather than the component parts. If criminal justice in the United States is to substantially improve, we must move rapidly toward acceptance of a single system.

The Flow of the Criminal Case examines the path an accused follows through the criminal justice system. It begins with arrest, the most likely first formal contact of an accused with the system; goes through the pre-trial procedures, the formal trial, and the appellate processes; and ends with the final disposition of the case.

Insights into the attitudes of the public toward crime are provided in Gauging Public Opinion About the Crime Problem. Perceptions of what is considered to be a crime may differ according to neighborhoods. The feelings of safety, security, and the trustfulness of others has a direct relation to how persons perceive crime and the dimensions of public response to the crime problem. Matters such as personal fear of crime, attitudes toward due process, punitive measures, and the seriousness of crime in a community, establish a base for understanding what reactions can be expected from the public toward crime.

Social Change and Criminal Law *stresses the impact that urbanization and the social sciences have had on law. As social change occurs so does the law. With change and the failure of past approaches, especially in reference to punishment as a deterrent, comes the necessity for designing new concepts that will eventually provide an adequate model for crime control.*

Production of Crime Rates *points out some of the reasons why official crime rates underrepresent crime. Whether a crime is put into the official reports depends on a number of factors including: proportionally more recognition of serious crimes than of minor ones; the complainant's preference for police action; the closer the relation between the complainant and the suspect the less likelihood of official recognition; and the more deferential the complainant toward the police the greater the likelihood of official recognition of the complainant. Surprisingly, no substantial evidence is found of racial discrimination in crime reporting. However, there is some evidence of discrimination in favor of white collar complainants. This article furnishes an excellent view of the actual practice of official reporting of crimes.*

Richter H. Moore, Jr.

The criminal justice non-system

Collectively the agencies in the United States responsible for the administration of justice have in recent years been referred to as the criminal justice system. This is a delusion. What we call a criminal justice system is merely a group of components which do not function together as a comprehensive or comprehensible whole. The report of the President's Commission on Law Enforcement and the Administration of Justice in 1967 found the system a pervasive fragmentation of police, court, and correctional agencies.

A Task Force of the National Commission on the Causes and Prevention of Violence in its report *Law and Order Reconsidered* examined in detail the absence of a single criminal justice system. It found,

Our society has commissioned its police to patrol the streets, to prevent crime, arrest suspected criminals, "enforce the law." It has established courts to conduct trials of accused offenders, sentence those who are found guilty and 'do justice.' It has created a correctional process consisting of prisons to punish convicted persons and a program to rehabilitate and supervise them so they might become useful citizens.

It is commonly assumed that these three components—law enforcement (police, sheriffs, marshals), the judicial process (judges, prosecutors, defense lawyers), and corrections (prison officials, probation and parole officers)—add up to a "system" of criminal justice. The system, however, is a myth.[1]

The concept of a system carries with it the idea of a unity of purpose, and organized inter-relationships among the component parts. In the United States today instead of recognized connections the criminal justice "system," be it local, state, or federal, is composed of a well defined group of separate agency responsibili-

5

ties. In other words, it is a continuum through which each accused may pass: from the police, to the courts, to the prison and back to the streets.

The end result is that what we call the criminal justice system does not deter crime, does not detect crime, does not convict, and does not correct, so concluded Lloyd Cutler, the director of the 1970 President's Commission on Violence.

A recent survey by the Law Enforcement Assistance Administration (LEAA) supported that assessment. It found that some 16.7 million serious crimes had been committed in the United States during the first half of 1973 but that only 5.3 million had been reported by the victims. Of these, only 3.9 million found their way into the FBI's uniform crime statistics.[2]

Other studies indicate that only about 12 percent of the crimes committed in the United States result in arrest and 6 percent in convictions. The convictions include a large number of bargained pleas. Of those who commit crimes, only about 1.5 percent are ever incarcerated.[3]

Such facts turn people off to the criminal justice system according to LEAA administrator Richard Velde. Their cynicism is reflected in the low faith they have that the police will solve the crimes, their frustration at the delays in the courts, and their feeling that those convicted are prematurely released from prison.

The public has not been alone in its dissatisfaction with such poor performance. Members and officials of the agencies that participate in the criminal justice process become frustrated by the apparent inefficiencies and unfairness of the system they perceive as perpetrated by the other components of it. Every group is the critic and target of criticism of every other group.

The effectiveness of the system or the mission and priorities of the system are going to be viewed differently by the policeman, the trial judge, the prosecutor, the defense attorney, the corrections administrator, the appellate tribunal, the slum dweller and the residents of the suburbs. Isolated and antagonistic within their traditional responsibilities, each component analyzes its problems from its own point of view and each vies with the others for public funds. Each is jealous of its authority and each proceeds according to a different set of priorities. This attitude reflects a lack of guidance oriented toward a single criminal justice system.

All of the Presidential Commissions and advisory commissions have found not only a lack of overall direction in the criminal justice field, but have found even within the parts almost no attempt to approach tasks from the point of view of the system. One of the primary causes for these deficiencies according to the Commission on Violence is a weakness in leadership, poor management practices and a lack of information. The task force report says, "A recognized profession of criminal justice system administrators does not exist today." [4]

They found few court administrators, and the idea of court management by trained professionals taking hold very slowly. They found effective police administration to be rare. The great majority of police agencies were headed by chiefs who had started as patrolmen and had risen through the ranks without benefit of higher education and with no training in modern management, finance, personnel, communications, or community relations. Tradition and antiquated civil service concepts barred lateral entry and thereby inhibited the recruitment of police administrators from other departments or from sources outside government. The Commission found no structure for formulating cohesive crime budgets, only individual agency requests. They found no central collection and analysis of criminal justice information. Crime received high attention only as a short-term reaction to crisis.

The crime crisis of the past few years has resulted in an upsurge of support for the police by the so-called silent majority, even civil libertarian politicians have become champions of law and order. Riots, assassinations, muggings, and rapes have created major political pressures from the public, demanding a solution to the crime problem—but there seems to be no consensus as to the nature of the problem.

A part of the responsibility for the crisis lies in the nature of society today. Among the problems and conditions contributing to it are the alarming increase in narcotics, drug abuse, urban overcrowding, inability of urban government to meet the needs of citizens, the gap between affluence and poverty, overpopulation, economic recession, discrimination and an increase of revolutionary activities. Transient populations have lost their concern for community. Assimilation has become internal and intramural rather than international. Attempts to adjust to a standardized environment through racial integration have led to conflicts. The ideal of family unity has seriously declined. The responsibility for child training is frequently delegated to schools, organizations or other parent surrogates, sometimes even to movie houses and often to television sets. New attitudes toward the young have resulted in their greater freedom to participate in adult activities, without at the same time being required to assume responsibility for their actions. Alliances between criminals and ostensibly law-abiding citizens and complacency toward organized crime involving corruption, bribery, extortion and murder all contribute to crime crisis.

In an attempt to face the changing crime challenge a type of fear reactive solution has been employed. Money has been poured into impressive new equipment for local police forces. New agencies have been created to fight crime, often without proper guidelines or guidance, and without consideration of the effect they will have on the system as a whole. The public persists in the unfortunate ranking in terms of superiority-inferiority of those in the criminal justice field with the judiciary in the superior position, the police following and the prison officials at the bottom of the efficacy ladder.

This muddle has been exploited by a radical minority who attempt to discredit the criminal justice system, especially the police. At the same time, another vocal minority cries for a "super" police force that will eliminate crime, the opponents of law and order, and probably freedom as well. For their part, the police confront the problem of overcoming public opposition to their authority even while the public demands increased protection from crime.

The violence of the decade of the 60's, and the report of the 1967 President's Commission, brought a recognition that the criminal justice system was in a state of dynamic change. It said:

The police must adapt themselves to the rapid changes and patterns of behavior that are taking place in America. This is a time when traditional ideas and institutions are being challenged with increasing insistence. The poor want an equal opportunity to earn a share of America's wealth. Minority groups want a final end put to the discrimination they have been subjected to for centuries. Young people, the fastest growing segment of the population have more freedom than they ever have had. The police must be willing and able to deal understandingly and constructively with these often unsettling, even threatening changes.[5]

Acknowledging these social and political sources of lawlessness and unrest police administrator O. W. Wilson observed:

Police service today extends beyond mere routine investigation and disposition of complaints; it also has as an objective the welfare of the individual and of society. If society is to be effectively safeguarded against crime, the police must actively seek out and destroy delinquency inducing influences in the community and assist in providing suitable treatment for the maladjusted.[6]

The Commission found a compelling need for a new vision among all the agencies that make up the criminal justice system. This new vision requires new concepts to meet the needs of a changing crime environment. It demands recognition that the tasks of the criminal justice system have changed and that attitudes toward it, its personnel and its role in modern society must change.

Until recently few Americans perceived a need for an educated policeman or prison guard. Such jobs were considered to require only a hard head, plenty of muscle, a sadistic character and the favor of a local politician. To consider the law enforcement officer, corrections official or court clerk as a professional was unheard of. When the demand for professionalism in these roles began to be heard, it applied only to practitioners within the separate parts of the system, not for a criminal justice professional equally at home in its several parts.

If the pervasive fragmentation of the criminal justice system into police, court and correctional agencies is to be eliminated, these parts must be recognized as components of a whole. To achieve this, those concerned with criminal justice must look to systems management, systems analysis and systems creation for aid in integrating the parts which make up the direct delivery apparatus into one criminal justice system. To accomplish this goal a task force of the President's Commission on Violence envisioned a new office or agency to serve as a catalyst for bringing together the fragmented efforts in the criminal justice field.

The obvious instrumentality to provide the unifying force is an educational experience at the college level. This will enable criminal justice practitioners to understand the concept of a system and their role as a part of it. To fulfill this need and aid in developing a single system concept, O. W. Wilson wrote:

Related to the need to consider the system of justice as an entity, is the urgency for a recognized discipline or field of study which encompasses the law enforcement and criminal justice systems as a whole. Until very recently no college or university in the United States offered a degree in the administration of criminal justice—that is, a generalized degree covering expertise in police, courts and corrections.[7]

The report of the 1967 President's Commission, *The Challenge of Crime in a Free Society* gave impetus for the establishment of criminal justice programs at the college level:

Individual citizens, social service agencies, universities, religious institutions, civic and business groups and all types of governmental agencies at all levels must become involved in planning and executing changes in the criminal justice system.[8]

The report stressed the need for universities to provide the professional education essential to the development of effective personnel for the criminal justice system:

The problem of personnel is at the root of most of the criminal justice systems problems. The system cannot operate fairly unless its personnel are fair. The system cannot operate swiftly and certainly unless its personnel are efficient and well informed. The system cannot make wise decisions unless its personnel are thoughtful. In many places, many police departments, congested urban lower courts, the understaffed county jails, the entire prison, probation and parole apparatus, more manpower is needed . . . everywhere more skilled, better trained, more imaginative manpower is needed.[9]

The Commission concluded that the system of criminal justice must attract more and better people—police, prosecutors, judges, defense attorneys, probation and parole officers and correction officials—with more knowledge, expertise, initiative, and integrity. Criminal justice education can help provide these better people.

Disturbances growing out of ethnic or racial tensions can be dealt with more effectively if the persons responsible for handling them have some understanding of ethnic relations, racial politics, civil rights, and racial history. University level study of such issues may not guarantee solutions, but it can contribute to more rational reactions. A college education diminishes prejudice and reveals the falsity of racial and ethnic stereotypes. It will enable the law enforcement officer, the correctional custodian, the juvenile staffer, or the court clerk to bring greater resources to bear on their work and to react in a more rational and a more detached manner. The educated law enforcement officer may recognize a mental or physical abnormality where another might see only a drunk or disturber of the peace. An educated correctional custodian may observe danger signals and move to prevent prison riots where another would enflame the situation by treating prisoners as caged animals. A knowledgeable juvenile staffer can discriminate between criminal intent and emotional disturbance and deal with the problem accordingly.

Criminal justice students must be provided with an education that will enable them to weigh alternative courses of action when they become practitioners. They must gain insight into the effects of their actions on the persons with whom they deal and on the image of the system their performance conveys to the public. Their education must not be limited to a single area within the system but, as O. W. Wilson urges, must encompass the criminal justice system as a whole. They must be equipped to become competent systems managers and professional administrators with a broad understanding of the system and of the entire structure of government of which they are an integral part.

Such a broad education will not be possible without intensive new research into the needs and relationships of criminal justice agencies. Lack of such knowledge has slowed the development of a comprehensive approach to the criminal justice system. Partly from lack of research, the system has moved without any sense of direction, without testing its assumptions or establishing priorities. Tradition, convenience, or fashion have too often been substituted for analysis. Since less than one percent of the monies in criminal justice are spent on research, it is not surprising that relatively little work has been done to learn how best to deter crime and how to detect, apprehend, and rehabilitate criminals.[10] Even less investigation has been done on the problems faced in creating an atmosphere conducive to breaking down the separate agency syndrome and establishing recognition of a single criminal justice system.

The 1967 President's Commission's call for research into all fields of criminal justice has brought about some limited responses. The blue curtain of secrecy screening police departments from any sort of study by outsiders has parted slightly to allow researchers entree into the life and world of the police. In his book *Behind the Shield*, Arthur Niederhoffer suggested that police forces have resisted outside study for fear of learning too much about themselves,[11] but such probing is necessary for evaluation and program development.

Research has encountered suspicion at even higher levels. Findings of promising studies and successful pilot projects have been rejected out of hand, as when then President Nixon dismissed some of the recommendations offered by the National Commission on Criminal Justice Standards and Goals. Research organizations producing positive results have been discouraged by bureaucratic ineptness, sometimes exhibited even by the LEAA and its state counterparts. One very promising crime prevention project nationally acclaimed by operating agencies and professional groups ran afoul of an examiner in the state planning agency at the end of its first year. He responded to its continuation request with four pages of questions that showed he had not read the results and had no understanding of the study's potential. The university conducting the research observed that it would take nearly as much time to prepare the new proposal required by his action as to carry out the remaining work, and it withdrew from the project. Thus valuable insights have been lost, at least temporarily.

Inadequate, incompetent and insufficient planning share the responsibility for the lack of research and the mediocre strides which have been made toward the development of a homogenous criminal justice system. For only in the last eight years has any thought been given to comprehensive criminal justice planning. Even so planning has not been comprehensive and frequently has been unrealistic. Planning agencies established to develop comprehensive criminal justice plans have bowed to agency pressures and allowed planning to be done unilaterally by persons representing parts of the system without considering how the plans for that one part will affect the other parts. This has occurred partly because of a lack of personnel educated to look at the criminal justice system as a whole.

When LEAA began to pour monies into the states for planning, state authorities drew personnel largely from existing agencies, most often law enforcement. Frequently these people brought with them parochial attitudes and agency prejudices and biases, not a systems outlook. The upshot was that law enforcement agencies which at the local level are the most active and visible have tended to dominate the planning perspective. In some states, the planning agencies have even been called law enforcement planning agencies.

The outcome of such unwise planning practices can be dramatically demonstrated in the consequences of attempting to strengthen part of the system unilaterally without considering the impact on the whole structure. In concentrating on law enforcement, by giving the police more manpower and equipment, the desired result will be more arrests. More arrests increase prosecutions. Cases become stalled for months and even years in the courts. To lessen the impact on the courts pleas are bargained. Serious charges are reduced to lesser ones, often to misdemeanors. Criminals are released on bond to commit other offenses before they are tried for the first. Seeing their efforts go for nothing, many police develop a negative and uncooperative attitude toward the courts. If the courts produce increased convictions the prison system, already under-manned and overcrowded, becomes even more so. The probation and parole system is innundated and case workers have far more people than they can supervise. The whole system is weakened when planning does not consider the effect of action on an agency in light of the system as a whole. It is obvious that if all the branches of the system are not strengthened, growth in one will overwhelm the others.[12]

The single agency syndrome with its historical tradition of minimum communication and virtually no cooperation among the parts of this "non-system" must be overcome. The elements can no longer pursue their own objectives exclusively and relentlessly without regard for the rest of the system. Lines of communication must be developed between police, courts, corrections, juvenile authorities, and other agencies within the criminal justice system. Research and education in the colleges and universities must be urgently pursued to establish a basis for new cooperative relationships between formerly compartmentalized and jealous agencies.

Planners and administrators must be educated to consider the agencies merely as elements of a total system. The problems and special viewpoints of each part must be taken into account, of course, but any solutions will only further the present chaos if they are not related to the needs of a single comprehensive criminal justice system.

Notes

1   James S. Campbell, Joseph R. Sahid, David P. Stang, Task Force on the Law and Law Enforcement of National Commission on the Causes and Prevention of Violence, *Law and Order Reconsidered.* New York: Bantam Books, 1970, p. 264.

2   "Much Crime Is Unreported," *The Washington Post*, Nov. 28, 1974, p. A-3.

3   T. M. Thompson, "The Criminal Justice System: A View from the Outside," *Crime and Delinquency*, January 1972, p. 23–29.

4   Ibid., p. 267.

5   Report of the President's Commission on Law Enforcement and Administration of Justice. *The Challenge of Crime in a Free Society.* Washington: U.S. Government Printing Office, 1967, p. 100.

6   Wilson, O. W. and McLaren, Roy C., *Police Administration* (3d Edition) New York: McGraw-Hill, 1972, p. 6.

7   Ibid., p. 11.

8   Commission on Law Enforcement and Administration of Justice, p. IX.

9   Ibid., p. 12.

10   Thompson, p. 24.

11   Garden City, N.Y.: Doubleday Anchor, 1969.

12   Thompson, p. 25.

National Advisory Commission on Criminal Justice Standards and Goals

The flow of the criminal case

Introduction

The role of courts in the criminal justice system and in the fight against crime is related to their formal function in the processing of a fully litigated criminal prosecution. But any examination of potential changes or improvements in the role of the courts requires a basic understanding of the formal procedural framework in which the courts participate in the criminal justice system.

ARREST

The first formal contact of an accused with the criminal justice system is likely to be an arrest by a police officer. In most cases, the arrest will be made upon the police officer's own evaluation that there is sufficient basis for believing that a crime has been committed by the accused. However, the arrest may be made pursuant to a warrant; in this case, the police officer or some other person will have submitted the evidence against the accused to a judicial officer, who determines whether the evidence is sufficient to justify an arrest. In some situations, the accused may have no formal contact with the law until he has been indicted by a grand jury. Following such an indictment, a court order may be issued authorizing police officers to take the accused into custody. But these are exceptional situations. Ordinarily, the arrest is made without any court order and the court's contact with the accused comes only after the arrest.

Even if there has been no court involvement in the initial decision to arrest the defendant, courts may have been involved in the case at an earlier stage. The requirement of the fourth amendment to the

Reprinted from *Courts*, Washington, D.C.: U.S. Government Printing Office, 1973, pp. 11–15.

U.S. Constitution that all searches be reasonable has been interpreted to mean that a warrant be obtained from a judicial officer before all searches unless there are specific reasons for not obtaining a warrant. Thus investigations that precede arrest sometimes involve searches made pursuant to a search warrant issued by a court. The court role in criminal investigation is broadening in other areas, and procedures are being developed whereby suspects may be compelled to submit to photographing, fingerprinting, and similar processes by court order. The potential for court involvement in the criminal justice system, then, extends to early parts of the police investigatory stage.

INITIAL JUDICIAL APPEARANCE

In all jurisdictions, a police officer or other person making an arrest must bring the arrested person before a judge within a short period of time. It is at this initial appearance that most accused have their first contact with the courts. This initial appearance is usually before a lower court—a justice of the peace or a magistrate. Thus in prosecutions for serious cases the initial appearance (and some further processes) occur in courts that do not have jurisdiction to determine the guilt or innocence of the accused. Often by the time of the initial appearance, the prosecution will have prepared a formal document called a complaint, which charges the defendant with a specific crime.

At the initial appearance, several things may occur. First, the defendant will be informed of the charges against him, usually by means of the complaint. Second, he will be informed of his rights, including his constitutional privilege against self-incrimination. Third, if the case is one in which the accused will be provided with an attorney at State expense, the mechanical process of assigning the attorney at least may begin at this stage. Fourth, unless the defendant is convicted of an offense at this point, arrangements may be made concerning the release of the defendant before further proceedings. This may take the traditional form of setting bail, that is, establishment of an amount of security the defendant himself or a professional bondsman whom he may hire must deposit with the court (or assume the obligation to pay) to assure that the defendant does appear for later proceedings. Pretrial release, in some jurisdictions, also may take the form of being released on one's own recognizance, that is, release simply upon the defendant's promise to appear at a later time. Other forms of encouraging a released defendant's later appearance sometimes are used.

In addition to these matters collateral to the issue of guilt, it is at the initial appearance that judicial inquiry into the merits of the case begins. If the charge is one the lower court has authority to try, the defendant may be asked how he pleads. If he pleads guilty, he may be convicted at this point. If he pleads not guilty, a trial date may be set and trial held later in this court.

However, if the charge is more serious, the court must give the defendant the opportunity for a judicial evaluation to determine whether there is enough evidence to justify putting him to trial in the higher court. In this type of case, the judge at the initial appearance ordinarily will ask the defendant whether he wants a preliminary hearing. If the defendant does, the matter generally is continued, or postponed to give both the prosecution and the defense time to prepare their cases.

The matter will be taken up again later in the lower court at the preliminary hearing. At this proceeding, the prosecutor introduces evidence to try to prove the defendant's guilt. He need not convince the court of the defendant's guilt beyond a reasonable doubt, but need only establish that there is enough evidence from which an average person (juror) could conclude that the defendant was guilty of the crime charged. If this evidence is produced, the court may find that the prosecution has established probable cause to believe the defendant guilty.

At this preliminary hearing the defendant may cross-examine witnesses produced by the prosecution and present evidence himself. If the court finds at the end of the preliminary hearing that probable cause does not exist, it dismisses the complaint. This does not ordinarily prevent the prosecution from bringing another charge, however. If the court finds that probable cause does exist, it orders that the defendant be bound over to the next step in the prosecution. As a practical matter, the preliminary hearing also serves the function of giving the defendant and his attorney a look at the case the prosecution will produce at trial. It gives a defense attorney the opportunity to cross-examine witnesses he later will have to confront. This informal previewing function may be more valuable to defendants than the theoretical function of the preliminary hearing.

FILING OF FORMAL CRIMINAL CHARGE

Generally, it is following the decision of the lower court to bind over a defendant that the formal criminal charge is made in the court that would try the case if it goes to formal trial. If no grand jury action is to be taken, this is a simple step consisting of the prosecutor's filing a document called an information. But in many jurisdictions the involvement of the grand jury makes the process more complex. There, the decision at the preliminary hearing simply is to bind the defendant over for consideration by the grand jury. In these areas, the prosecutor then must go before the grand jury and again present his evidence. Only if the grand jury determines that there is probable cause does it act. Its action—consisting of issuing a document called an indictment—constitutes the formal charging of the defendant. If it does not find probable cause, it takes no action and the prosecution is dismissed.

In some jurisdictions, it is not necessary to have both a grand jury inquiry and a preliminary hearing. In most Federal jurisdictions, for example, if a defendant has been indicted by a grand jury he no longer has a right to a preliminary hearing, on the theory that he is entitled to only one determination as to whether probable cause exists.

Although the defendant is entitled to participate in the preliminary hearing, he has no right to take part in a grand jury inquiry. Traditionally, he has not been able to ascertain what went on in front of the grand jury, although increasingly the law has given him the right, after the fact, to know.

Following the formal charge—whether it has been by indictment or information—any of a variety of matters that require resolution may arise. The defendant's competency to stand trial may be in issue. This requires the court to resolve the question of whether the defendant is too ill mentally or otherwise impaired to participate meaningfully in his trial. If he is sufficiently impaired, trial must be postponed until he regains his competency.

The defendant also may challenge the validity of the indictment or information or the means by which they were issued. For example, he may assert that those acts with which he is charged do not constitute a crime under the laws of the jurisdiction. Or, if he was indicted by a grand jury, he may assert that the grand jury was selected in a manner not consistent with State or Federal law and, therefore, that the indictment is invalid.

A defendant also may—and in some jurisdictions must—raise, before trial, challenges to the admissibility of certain evidence, especially evidence seized by police officers in a search or statements obtained from him by interrogation. In view of the rapid growth of legal doctrine governing the admissibility of statements of defendants and evidence obtained by police search and seizure, resolution of the issues raised by defendants' challenges to the admissibility of such evidence may be more complex and time-consuming than anything involved in determining guilt or innocence.

The criminal law also is increasingly abandoning the traditional approach that neither side is entitled to know what evidence the other side is going to produce until the other side actually presents it at trial. In the main, this has taken the form of granting defendants greater access to such things as physical evidence (e.g., fingerprints) that will be used against them. Access to witness' statements sometimes is required, and some jurisdictions are compelling the defendant to grant limited disclosure to the prosecution.

ARRAIGNMENT

In view of the potential complexity of pretrial matters, much of the significant activity in a criminal prosecution already may have occurred at the time the defendant makes his first formal appearance before the court that is to try him. This first appearance—the arraignment—is the point at which he is asked to plead to the charge. He need not plead, in which case a plea of not guilty automatically is entered for him. If he pleads guilty, the law requires that certain precautions be taken to assure that this plea is made validly. Generally, the trial judge accepting the plea first must inquire of the defendant whether he understands the charge against him and the penalties that may be imposed. The judge also must assure himself that there is some reasonable basis in the facts of the case for the plea. This may involve requiring the prosecution to present some of its evidence to assure the court that there is evidence tending to establish guilt.

TRIAL

Unless the defendant enters a guilty plea, the full adversary process is put into motion. The prosecution now must establish to a jury or a judge the guilt of the defendant beyond a reasonable doubt. If the defendant elects to have the case tried by a jury, much effort is expended on the selection of a jury. Prospective jurors are questioned to ascertain whether they might be biased and what their views on numerous matters might be. Both sides have the right to have a potential juror rejected on the ground that he may be biased. In addition, both have the right to reject a limited number of potential jurors without having to state any reason. When the jury has been selected and convened, both sides may make opening statements explaining what they intend to prove or disprove.

The prosecution presents its evidence first, and the defendant has the option of making no case and relying upon the prosecution's inability to establish guilt beyond a reasonable doubt. He also has the option of presenting evidence tending to disprove the prosecution's case or tending to prove additional facts constituting a defense under applicable law. Throughout, however, the burden remains upon the prosecution. Procedurally, this is effectuated by defense motions to dismiss, which often are made after the prosecution's case has been presented and after all of the evidence is in. These motions in effect assert that the prosecution's case is so weak that no reasonable jury could conclude beyond a reasonable doubt that the defendant was guilty. If the judge grants the motion, he is in effect determining that no jury could reasonably return a verdict of guilty. This not only results in a dismissal of the prosecution but also prevents the prosecution from bringing another charge for the same crime.

After the evidence is in and defense motions are disposed of, the jury is instructed on the applicable law. Often both defense and prosecution lawyers submit instructions which they ask the court to read to the jury, and the court chooses from those and others it composes itself. It is in the formulation of these instructions that many issues regarding the definition of the applicable law arise and must be resolved. After—or sometimes before—the instructions are read, both sides present formal arguments to the jury. The jury then retires for its deliberations.

Generally, the jury may return only one of two verdicts: guilty or not guilty. A verdict of not guilty may be misleading; it may mean not that the jury believed that the defendant was not guilty but rather that the jury determined that the prosecution had not established guilt by the criterion—beyond a reasonable doubt—the law imposes. If the insanity defense has been raised, the jury may be told it should specify if insanity is the reason for acquittal; otherwise, there is no need for explanation. If a guilty verdict is returned, the court formally enters a judgment of conviction unless there is a legally sufficient reason for not doing so.

The defendant may attack his conviction, usually by making a motion to set aside the verdict and order a new trial. In his attack, he may argue that evidence was improperly admitted during the trial, that the evidence was so weak that no reasonable jury could have found that it established guilt beyond a reasonable doubt, or that there is newly discovered evidence which, had it been available at the time of trial, would have changed the result. If the court grants a motion raising one of these arguments, the effect generally is not to acquit the defendant but merely to require the holding of a new trial.

SENTENCING

Sentencing then follows. (If the court has accepted a plea of guilty, this step follows acceptance of the plea.) In an increasing number of jurisdictions, an investigation called the presentence report is conducted by professional probation officers. This involves investigation of the offense, the offender and his background, and any other matters of potential value to the sentencing judge. Following submission of the report to the court, the defendant is given the opportunity to comment upon the appropriateness of sentencing. In some jurisdictions, this has developed into a more extensive court hearing on sentencing issues, with the defendant given the opportunity to present evidence as well as argument for leniency. Sentencing itself generally is the responsibility of the judge, although in some jurisdictions juries retain that authority.

APPEAL

Following the conclusion of the proceeding in the trial court, the matter shifts to the appellate courts. In some jurisdictions, a defendant who is convicted of a minor offense in a lower court has the right to a new trial (trial de novo) in a higher court. But in most situations—and in all cases involving serious offenses—the right to appeal is limited to the right to have an appellate court examine the record of the trial proceedings for error. If error is found, the appellate court either may take definitive action—such as ordering that the prosecution be dismissed—or it may set aside the conviction and remand the case for a new trial. The latter gives the prosecution the opportunity to obtain a valid conviction. Generally, a time limit is placed upon the period during which an appeal may be taken.

COLLATERAL ATTACK

Even if no appeal is taken or the conviction is upheld, the courts' participation in the criminal justice process is not necessarily ended. To some extent, a convicted defendant who has either exhausted his appeal rights or declined to exercise them within the appropriate time limits can seek further relief by means of collateral attack upon the conviction. This method involves a procedure collateral to the standard process of conviction and appeal.

Traditionally this relief was sought by applying for a writ of habeas corpus on the ground that the conviction under which the applicant was held was invalid. Many jurisdictions have found this vehicle too cumbersome for modern problems and have developed special procedures for collateral attacks. Despite variations in terminology and procedural technicalities, however, opportunities remain for an accused convicted in Federal court to seek such collateral relief from his conviction in Federal courts and for those convicted in State courts to seek similar relief in State and, to a somewhat more limited extent, in Federal courts.

The matter has become an increasingly significant point of State-Federal friction as issues of Federal constitutional law have become more important parts of criminal litigation. Defendants convicted in State courts apparently have thought that Federal courts offered a more sympathetic forum for assertions that Federal constitutional rights were violated during a State criminal prosecution. State judges and prosecutors have indicated resentment with the actions of Federal courts in reversing State convictions for reasons State courts either considered of no legal merit or refused to consider for what they felt were valid reasons.

In any case, because collateral attack upon a conviction remains available until (and even after) the defendant has gone through the correctional process, the courts' role in the criminal justice process extends from the earliest points of criminal investigation to the final portions of the correctional process.

DISPOSITION OF CASES

Although the role of courts in the criminal justice system clearly is related to the formal procedures invoked in the litigated case, it is erroneous to assume that the major role of courts is the processing of cases through the steps described above.

According to figures developed by the President's Crime Commission, the criminal justice system processed the 467,000 adults apprehended in 1965 as suspects in index crimes as follows: formal charges were brought against only 177,000; 38,000 went to trial, with the result that 30,000 were convicted and 8,000 acquitted. This means that 290,000 accused either had no complaint filed against them or were charged with a less serious crime. Even after formal charging, 9,000 of 47,000 cases were dismissed. (President's Commission on Law Enforcement and Administration of Justice, *The Challenge of Crime in a Free Society*, 262–63 (1967).) In sum, only about 8 percent of those apprehended as suspects in index crimes were processed fully through the formal steps of a criminal prosecution.

There is inadequate knowledge as to what happened to the other 92 percent. But it is clear that few cases involved a simple decision to abandon any effort to deal with the suspect as a danger to society. In a number of cases, the defendant was convicted of a less serious offense. In others, the defendant was permitted to participate without criminal conviction—in a program that seemed to hold some hope of making him a useful and law-abiding member of the community. In the vast majority of cases—130,000—the accused simply agreed to criminal conviction by pleading guilty, often in return for some corresponding action that he regarded as beneficial.

The point is that the traditional model of the litigated criminal prosecution in which the formal procedures are used corresponds to only a small fraction of the cases processed. In the remainder of the cases the processing is essentially administrative in the sense that flow is accomplished by negotiation and agreement rather than by adversary presentations to an independent decisionmaker. "Much of the criminal process," the President's Crime Commission concluded, "is administrative rather than judicial." (President's Commission on Law Enforcement and Administration of Justice, *The Challenge of Crime in a Free Society*, 130 (1967).)

The need to provide for efficient and fair administration of the litigated case must not be ignored. But a realistic evaluation of the courts' role in the processing of criminal cases requires that emphasis also be placed on the role of the court—including the judge and other court functionaries such as prosecutors and defense counsel—in the administrative disposition of the majority of cases.

Despite the fact that the administrative model of criminal-case processing is inconsistent with the "Perry Mason" stereotype, it is not a cause for alarm. As the President's Commission explained:

There are good reasons for [much of the criminal process being administrative rather than judicial]. The most readily apparent is the enormous number of cases that come into the process, especially in the Nation's metropolitan areas. If substantial percentages of them were not dropped or carried to negotiated conclusions administratively, justice would not be merely slowed down; it would be stopped. A second reason is that the facts in most cases are not in dispute. The suspect either clearly did or clearly did not do what he is accused of having done. In these cases a trial, which is a careful and expensive procedure for determining disputed facts, should not be needed. (President's Commission on Law Enforcement and Administration of Justice, *The Challenge of Crime in a Free Society*, 130 (1967).)

Nor is the fact that administrative disposition of criminal cases often results in the imposition of less than the maximum penalty the law permits necessarily a defect in the process:

[M]any, if not most, defendants are not dangerous or threatening enough to warrant the "full treatment" of conviction for the crime probably committed. Tempering the harshness and severity of the criminal law by settlement, not unlike the compromise in civil actions, is both a necessary and desirable aspect of criminal law administration. (McIntyre and Lippman, *Prosecutors and Early Disposition of Felony Cases*, 56 A.B.A.J. 1154 (1970).)

Most criminal statutes have been drafted so that the maximum penalty provided would be appropriate for the worst conceivable criminal offense. Since most offenses fall short of this status, an administrative process that often results in imposition of less than the most severe disposition is an effective and efficient method of implementing legislative intent.

Finally, the fact that the administrative nature of the criminal process results in important decisions being made by nonjudicial personnel should not be considered a defect. Experienced prosecutors, upon whom much of the responsibility falls, are especially appropriate individuals to have this authority because of their experience and specialization in dealing with antisocial individuals as well as their experience in dealing with formally litigated cases that permits them to predict what disposition would be likely should an administrative route not be taken in a particular case.

Don C. Gibbons
Joseph F. Jones
Peter G. Garabedian

Gauging public opinion about the crime problem

Because punitive and correctional actions against law-breakers are often undertaken in the name of the public, it is frequently said that the citizenry demands that some specific penalty be visited upon offenders. Only in recent years, however, as pollsters and social scientists began to take soundings on citizen opinions regarding the crime problem and the handling of lawbreakers, have we come to learn anything about public sentiments on these matters.

Previous studies

One study of citizen attitudes by Rose and Prell asked a number of persons to indicate the most serious offenses from a list of thirteen minor felonies.[1] Examination of the sentences actually handed out to offenders indicated that many of the crimes regarded as *least* serious by citizens were the ones which received the heaviest penalties in the courts.

Newman examined food, drug, and cosmetic violations by asking a sample of adults to indicate the punishment they considered appropriate for cases of these offenses taken from federal files.[2] Most of the respondents thought that these activities should be more heavily punished than they actually had been.

A third study, by Gibbons, dealt with citizen knowledge of criminality and correction.[3] Few of the laymen had any detailed understanding of the workings of the correctional system. Similar results

Reprinted from *Crime and Delinquency*, April 1972, pp. 134–146, with the permission of the National Council on Crime and Delinquency.

were obtained in a survey commissioned by the California state legislature, which found that few citizens had any detailed knowledge of the correctional machinery, and the majority thought that penalties for most crimes were less severe than they actually are.[4]

Another study by Rooney and Gibbons questioned citizens regarding abortion, homosexuality, and drug addiction.[5] The respondents held that abortion laws should be liberalized, but they were not so tolerant of homosexuality, and they were particularly strident in their demands for severe penalties for drug addicts.

Gibbons also conducted an inquiry in which California citizens were asked about the degree of punishment they considered appropriate for twenty different crimes.[6] The most visible and coercive offenses received the most severe penalty choices, often exceeding in harshness the dispositions actually pronounced for similar offenses in the state.

McIntyre has summarized the studies of public attitudes undertaken for the President's Commission on Law Enforcement and Administration of Justice.[7] These indicated that most people throughout the nation see crime as a growing problem in their own communities, although they do not feel unsafe near their own homes, even when they live in high crime areas. The majority of them asserted that such things as the "breakdown of moral standards" rather than deleterious social conditions are responsible for increased crime. Many of them recommended repressive rather than ameliorative steps to curb crime, and many claimed that the courts are too lenient with offenders. Large numbers of citizens favored "get tough" policies of the police, but many were simultaneously ambivalent about increasing other powers of the police in law enforcement.

A nation-wide survey of citizen views of the correctional system authorized by the Joint Commission on Correctional Manpower and Training showed that only about a quarter of the respondents held that the law enforcement system is efficient in deterring crime, while half thought that the courts are too lenient, and half believed that the national prison system is doing an inadequate job.[8]

Some related observations were obtained in a survey of the readers of *Psychology Today*.[9] These relatively young and well-educated citizens were of the opinion that crime rates are currently higher than in the past. Most of them held that some kind of treatment rather than punishment should be given to drug addicts, alcoholics, prostitutes, and homosexuals. Many of them said that white-collar criminals are dealt with too leniently, most of them opposed the death penalty, and most asserted that penalties for juveniles should be different from and less harsh than those for adults. Liberal respondents voiced approval of Supreme Court decisions concerning due process, while conservatives opposed these rulings. Most of the respondents held that responsibility for crime rests on the individual, not on adverse societal conditions.

One indication of historical changes in public attitudes is found in a study by Pattison, Bishop, and Linsky which examined perceptions of drug addiction in a sample of popular magazines.[10] Their data indicated that, in contrast to opinions expressed in 1900, contemporary views regard drug addicts as less responsible for their behavior, give greater attention to the social milieu, and stress rehabilitation rather than a strictly punitive approach.

In addition to these studies, which have focused on adults, some reports are available concerning public perceptions of the juvenile justice system. In one of these, Lentz surveyed a sample of Wisconsin adults concerning attitudes toward juvenile control.[11] Most of the citizens favored swift and impartial justice, punishment that fits the crime, and probation in place of institutional commitment. Over half advocated publishing the names of juvenile offenders, and many asserted that juvenile offenders are "ill" and in need of expert treatment.

A study made by Parker dealt with citizen views of the juvenile court in four Washington state communities.[12] Many of the respondents asserted that the juvenile court was not tough enough in its dealings with offenders. But when these same laymen were asked how they would punish offenders, the penalties they chose were similar to or less severe than the ones actually handed out by the juvenile courts!

The study reported here is a continuation of the line of research reviewed above. In it, citizens in San Francisco, Calif., and Portland, Oreg., were surveyed regarding their attitudes on the crime problem, personal fear of crime, due process for adults and juveniles, and punitive measures.

Study design and procedures

This investigation employed a relatively short, self-administered questionnaire[13] dealing with (1) opinions on the seriousness of the crime problem; (2) perceptions of personal safety from crime; (3) attitudes toward due process for adult offenders; (4) attitudes toward due process for juvenile offenders; (5) attitudes toward punitive measures; and (6) related attitudes and information, including questions on the socio-demographic characteristics of the respondents. The questionnaire was pretested and then administered by a group of trained interviewers. These workers, advanced sociology students at San Francisco State College and Portland State University, sought out respondents and remained present while the questionnaire was completed so as to be available to deal with queries concerning the questions. The questionnaires were administered during the spring of 1970.

A total of 466 persons in San Francisco and 353 in Portland completed questionnaires.[14] No formalized sampling procedure such as stratified random sampling was employed; instead, interviewers were sent to widely separated areas and neighborhoods in Portland and San Francisco, including adjacent suburbs. The intent was to obtain a broad cross section of citizens within the two communities, although areas of very low income were avoided. The social characteristics of the two samples are shown in Table 1.

Table 1 indicates that the two samples were similar in age, educational status, and residential stability; however, the Portland group had greater numbers of older individuals and persons with high incomes. In both areas, the higher levels of education are overrepresented.

This study differs from those cited previously in several ways. For one, it involves responses of a rather large number of persons in two cities of different size and character in states that are adjacent but unlike in a number of important ways; thus, the data allow an opportunity for comparative analysis. Second, the questionnaire utilized here was multidimensional, so that opinions concerning a number of facets of the crime problem, law enforcement, correction, and related matters were tapped. Third, the study involved some questions regarding citizen preferences for due process standards for juveniles, which is a matter that has not been probed in other investigations.

The general working hypotheses of this study were that California respondents would view the crime problem as more serious and would exhibit greater personal fear of crime than would citizens in Oregon. It was anticipated that persons in both samples would show considerable willingness to suspend due process standards in the interest of repressing crime and would show relative insensitivity to the rights of juveniles. Finally, we expected to find that many citizens would opt for punitive responses to lawbreakers rather than for ameliorative ones.

Table 1 Background characteristics of samples

Characteristics	Per cent	
	San Francisco (N = 466)	Portland (N = 353)
Sex		
Male	50.0	49.0
Female	50.0	50.1
No response	0	.9
Age		
45 and over	20.6	35.1
35–44	17.2	15.6
25–34	30.9	26.6
Under 25	30.0	21.8
No response	1.3	.9
Education		
College graduate	24.0	25.8
Some college	42.3	36.5
High school graduate	23.4	27.5
Some high school	7.7	7.4
Grade school	1.7	2.0
No response	.9	.9
Income		
$15,000 and over	13.5	22.9
$10,000–$14,999	27.3	30.3
$6,000–$9,999	33.9	30.6
Under $6,000	21.2	13.3
No response	4.1	2.8
Residence		
10 years or more in state	68.2	76.8
5–10 years in state	16.3	8.5
1–5 years in state	10.9	10.2
Under 1 year in state	3.6	3.1
No response	.9	1.4

Results

PERCEPTIONS OF THE CRIME PROBLEM

The distribution of responses to the items tapping public conceptions of the current crime problem are shown in Table 2.[15] Although most citizens in both cities considered the crime problem in their state to be worse than in 1950, marked differences showed up on other items. The San Francisco residents held that the crime problem was worse in their state than in Oregon or Washington, and many of them also perceived crime to be as marked in California as in the East. The Portland respondents asserted that their state was less ridden with crime than California or the East. We would argue that the Portland citizens were probably fairly accurate in their view that they live in a less crime-filled city than San Francisco residents.

Another indication of public perceptions of the crime problem can be found in Table 3. These results were obtained by asking persons to rank the eight social problems listed in that table.[16] More than two-thirds of the respondents in both cities asserted that crime was a leading social problem, a result in accord with the findings of other investigations cited in this paper. A slightly greater percentage of Portland respondents considered juvenile delinquency a major social problem. Poverty was identified as a major social problem by a larger share of San Francisco respondents. Somewhat surprisingly, student protests were identified as a major problem by more Portlanders even though their city has experienced few major student demonstrations.

PERCEPTIONS OF PERSONAL SAFETY

Three items on the questionnaire dealt with feelings of personal safety from crime, the results of which are shown in Table 4. Responses to all three questions showed Portland citizens as somewhat less fearful of being robbed or burglarized in their neighborhoods or of being the victim of a crime somewhere in the wider community. In both cities, respondents said they were less apprehensive for their safety in their own neighborhoods than they were in the rest of the city. These findings are also in accord with results of previous investigations. We would contend that here again the respondents were accurately reflecting the realities of crime, so that it probably was the case that people were generally safer in Portland than in San Francisco.

Table 2 Perceptions of the crime problem

Questions	Per cent	
	San Francisco (N = 466)	Portland (N = 353)
1 Crime problem in California [Oregon] compared with 1950		
Somewhat or much worse now than in 1950	89.1	85.6
About the same or better than in 1950	9.0	12.2
No response	1.9	2.3
2 Crime problem in California [Oregon] compared with Oregon [California]		
Worse in home state	79.0	3.1
Same in both states	16.3	20.1
Worse in other state	1.9	75.6
No response	2.8	1.1
3 Crime problem in California [Oregon] compared with the East		
Worse in home state	11.8	1.1
Same in both areas	53.0	15.0
Worse in the East	33.5	83.0
No response	1.7	.8
4 Crime problem in California [Oregon] compared with Washington State		
Worse in home state	63.5	6.2
Same in both states	25.2	81.0
Worse in other state	8.2	12.0
No response	2.8	.8
5 Seriousness of crime problem in California [Oregon] these days		
Not very serious	6.7	14.4
Quite serious	62.9	73.9
Most serious problem in state	28.3	10.8
No response	2.1	.8

Table 3 **Rank order of eight social problems**

Social problems	Per cent	
	San Francisco (N = 466)	Portland (N = 353)
Crime		
Ranked in top three	69.5	67.6
Ranked in lower five	25.1	28.3
No response	5.4	4.0
Poverty		
Ranked in top three	60.3	41.3
Ranked in lower five	35.6	54.7
No response	4.1	4.0
Drug Use		
Ranked in top three	54.5	62.6
Ranked in lower five	41.2	35.0
No response	4.3	2.3
Air Pollution		
Ranked in top three	40.3	50.1
Ranked in lower five	55.0	47.2
No response	4.7	2.5
Juvenile Delinquency		
Ranked in top three	26.8	39.4
Ranked in lower five	68.2	56.7
No response	4.9	4.0
High Taxes		
Ranked in top three	26.0	17.3
Ranked in lower five	69.7	78.6
No response	4.3	4.0
Student Protests		
Ranked in top three	7.7	10.7
Ranked in lower five	86.3	84.5
No response	6.0	4.8
Traffic Congestion		
Ranked in top three	6.4	8.2
Ranked in lower five	88.2	87.8
No response	5.4	4.0

Table 4   Perceptions of personal safety

	Per cent	
Questions	San Francisco (N = 466)	Portland (N = 353)
1 How safe in your neighborhood from being beaten up or robbed?		
Quite safe or reasonably safe	69.2	87.6
Somewhat or very fearful	30.7	12.5
No response	.1	0
2 How safe from being burglarized?		
Quite safe or reasonably safe	53.2	68.5
Somewhat or very fearful	46.4	30.9
No response	.4	.6
3 How safe in general San Francisco [Portland] area from being beaten up or robbed?		
Quite safe or reasonably safe	41.8	67.4
Somewhat or very fearful	57.8	31.8
No response	.4	.8

ATTITUDES TOWARD DUE PROCESS FOR ADULTS

Table 5 presents the findings on eight items dealing with due process for adult offenders. These data indicated that more than half of the respondents from each city agreed that the Supreme Court has hindered the police through such decisions as *Mapp* and *Miranda*. But only about a quarter of the citizens believed that the police should be allowed to conduct periodic searches of the houses of known criminals, and most of the respondents agreed that the police should warn suspects of their right to remain silent. From one viewpoint, it might optimistically be reported that only a few persons disagreed with the Court regarding admonitions about citizen rights and that, similarly, only a few persons were willing to allow the police to "rough up" suspects. However, a civil libertarian might find these same figures alarming; he would be appalled that *any* citizens sanctioned the use of police tactics identified in these questions. Nearly half of the respondents held that when a person is apprehended for a crime, the police should be allowed to conduct general searches of him, his property, etc., for evidence of other

Table 5 Attitudes toward due process for adults

	Per cent	
Questions	San Francisco (N = 466)	Portland (N = 353)
1 Supreme Court decisions have hindered the police in efforts to fight crime		
Agree or strongly agree	54.3	67.7
Disagree or strongly disagree	44.4	30.1
No response	1.3	2.3
2 Police should periodically search houses of known criminals		
Agree or strongly agree	26.8	26.3
Disagree or strongly disagree	72.1	73.4
No response	1.1	.3
3 Police should not question suspects without advising them of right to be silent		
Agree or strongly agree	82.7	77.7
Disagree or strongly disagree	16.4	21.8
No response	1.1	.6
4 When police catch a person for a crime, should search him, his car, etc., for evidence of other crimes		
Agree or strongly agree	43.4	54.1
Disagree or strongly disagree	55.6	44.7
No response	1.1	1.1
5 Police should use any necessary technique to catch criminals who commit robberies, etc.		
Agree or strongly agree	54.9	55.5
Disagree or strongly disagree	43.0	43.0
No response	2.1	1.4
6 Police should be allowed to "rough up" rape suspect to get confession from him		
Agree or strongly agree	13.1	10.4
Disagree or strongly disagree	85.6	88.7
No response	1.3	.8
7 State should provide lawyer to person arrested for *serious* crime		
Agree or strongly agree	87.5	87.5
Disagree or strongly disagree	10.9	11.6
No response	1.5	.8
8 State should provide lawyer to person arrested for *minor* crime		
Agree or strongly agree	77.1	69.7
Disagree or strongly disagree	21.6	29.4
No response	1.3	.8

crimes. Over half agreed that the police ought to use whatever technique is expedient in catching criminals. Due process considerations appear to have had only a tenuous hold on the allegiance of many persons. Our own view of these results is pessimistic, particularly when we consider the relatively high educational level of these respondents, who might, therefore, be expected to be the most liberal. As can be seen from Table 5, respondents in the two communities did not differ markedly in their opinions on these issues.

ATTITUDES TOWARD DUE PROCESS FOR JUVENILES

The *Kent* and *Gault* decisions of the Supreme Court in 1966 and '67 laid down substantial rights of due process for juveniles, holding that accused offenders must be notified of charges, allowed lawyers, given the right of appeal, and so on, while the 1970 *Winship* decision requires juvenile courts to observe the "beyond a reasonable doubt" standard of evidence in court proceedings. In addition, several states in recent years have initiated reforms in juvenile court practice to ensure due process and legal safeguards for juveniles. Finally, many social scientists have begun to voice skepticism about the rehabilitative potential of the juvenile court and have begun to agitate against such relaxed procedures as informal probation. In all of this, there is a growing suspicion that even though the juvenile court operates out of good intentions, its effects may often be less than beneficial. If this is so, the reasoning goes, juvenile courts ought to become more legalistic in operation than they have been in the past.

Table 6 shows the distribution of responses to questions dealing with matters of due process in juvenile proceedings. As can be seen in the first item, more than two-thirds of the respondents favored policies of "informal probation," in which the court retains control over children who have not been given a hearing or been adjudicated. Along the same line, nearly all the respondents asserted that the courts should continue to handle offenders who fall within the omnibus part of delinquency laws—that is, ungovernability, waywardness, immorality, and the like. Clearly, citizen views have not yet been influenced by criticisms that have pointed out the hazards of utilizing the crude machinery of the court for children who fall under these rubrics.

But citizen approval apparently does not extend to informal procedures of the sort that have characterized juvenile courts in the past. Less than a quarter of the respondents agreed that judges should remand delinquents to criminal court without holding hearings. Therefore, the majority were in accord with the principle

Table 6   Attitudes toward due process for juveniles

Questions	Per cent	
	San Francisco (N = 466)	Portland (N = 353)
1 Juvenile court should not hold formal hearing for petty delinquent but should give him treatment		
Agree or strongly agree	66.5	70.8
Disagree or strongly disagree	31.9	27.5
No response	1.5	1.7
2 Juvenile court should work with ungovernable, wayward, or immoral conduct cases		
Agree or strongly agree	78.3	89.3
Disagree or strongly disagree	19.7	10.5
No response	1.9	.3
3 Judge should remand "tough guy" delinquent to criminal court, without holding a hearing		
Agree or strongly agree	19.9	22.9
Disagree or strongly disagree	78.3	76.5
No response	1.7	.6
4 Juveniles should not have jury trials in juvenile court		
Agree or strongly agree	38.6	47.0
Disagree or strongly disagree	58.6	51.8
No response	2.8	1.1
5 Juveniles should have lawyers in juvenile court		
Agree or strongly agree	74.5	66.6
Disagree or strongly disagree	23.9	30.8
No response	1.7	2.5

enunciated in *Kent*. While more than a third of the citizens thought that juveniles should not have jury trials, over half of them contended that they should. Finally, two-thirds or more of the respondents agreed that lawyers should be provided for juveniles in court hearings. On all of these items, the differences between San Francisco and Portland respondents did not appear to be marked.

ATTITUDES TOWARD PUNITIVE MEASURES

The questions that probed the punitive orientations of the citizens are shown in Table 7. Over half of the respondents in both samples

Table 7 Attitudes toward punitive measures

Questions	Per cent	
	San Francisco (N = 466)	*Portland* (N = 353)
1 How much time should prisoners serve, on the average?		
1½ years or less	29.6	24.9
3 years	25.3	29.5
5 years	21.9	20.4
10 years	6.0	7.1
No response	17.2	18.1
2 Circumstances under which crime is least likely		
Likely to be caught, mild penalty	49.6	49.6
Severe penalty, unlikely to be caught	46.1	45.6
No response	4.3	4.8
3 Opinion on proportion of offenders sent to prison		
Not enough get prison terms	24.5	51.0
About right number get prison	23.4	28.0
Too many are put in prison	47.9	16.7
No response	4.3	4.2
4 Criminals should not be executed		
Agree or strongly agree	56.0	51.0
Disagree or strongly disagree	41.4	42.4
No response	2.6	6.6
5 Which programs would help most to reduce the crime problem in California [Oregon]?		
Better education or employment opportunities, social and psychiatric help, more study of crime causes	70.4	64.9
Emphasis on moral standards, pass more laws, stiffer penalties, put religion back into schools	20.1	31.5
No response	9.5	3.6

asserted that offenders should serve three years or less in prison; at the same time, a considerable number refrained from offering any estimate of the appropriate time to be served. It should be noted that prisoners in these two states spend markedly different periods of time in prison: terms in California run about three years on the average; those in Oregon, about a year and a half.[17]

Table 7 shows the samples equally divided on the question of whether certainty or severity of punishment is the more effective deterrent. Also, about equal proportions in both samples opposed the death penalty.[18]

More Portland residents held that not enough offenders get prison sentences. This is a curious finding, given the earlier observation that San Franciscans were more concerned than Portlanders about the crime problem. Actually, a larger proportion of the offender population was placed on probation in California than in Oregon. Several conjectures can be offered to account for this finding. One is that Oregon residents are generally more conservative than Californians and for this reason adopt a harsher posture toward offenders. It is also possible that the hearings of the Assembly Committee on Criminal Procedure in California had directed the public's attention to parole policies and the high costs of operating prisons in that state.

The respondents were also asked to identify from a list of seven possibilities the procedure which they thought would make the most impact upon crime control. These are enumerated in the final question in Table 7. About two-thirds of the respondents chose some type of ameliorative or therapeutic approach, while only a third or less took refuge in a popular belief such as "Religion should be put back into the schools."

ADDITIONAL QUESTIONS ON CRIME

The questionnaire used in this study included a number of items related to crime and correction which do not fit into the previous categories. These items are shown in Table 8.

About one-third of the respondents in both groups thought that prison inmates served less than two years in prison, while nearly half of the Portland citizens thought that prisoners serve three-year terms. As we have already noted, California inmates do spend three years on the average in institutions, while the average term in Oregon is about eighteen months. Thus, most of the Portland residents were incorrect in naming three years or more as the average prison term, while a fair number of San Francisco respondents thought prison terms were shorter than they actually are.

More than half of the Portland residents asserted that juvenile correctional workers were doing a good job of rehabilitating

Table 8 Additional questions on crime

Questions	Per cent	
	San Francisco (N = 466)	Portland (N = 353)
1 How much time do prisoners serve in state prisons, on the average?		
1½ years or less	35.9	31.7
3 years	38.0	45.3
5 years	19.3	16.1
10 years	1.9	2.0
No response	4.9	4.8
2 How well are state juvenile correctional workers doing their job?		
Very well or reasonably well	33.5	53.3
Somewhat poorly or very poorly	65.2	44.7
No response	1.3	2.0
3 How well are state adult correctional workers doing their job?		
Very well or reasonably well	31.9	44.2
Somewhat poorly or very poorly	66.9	53.2
No response	1.1	2.5
4 Opinion on "plea copping"		
Approve or strongly approve	28.4	20.9
Disapprove or strongly disapprove	70.1	77.1
No response	1.5	2.0
5 Opinion on halfway house in own neighborhood		
Support or strongly support	66.7	62.3
Oppose or strongly oppose	31.7	36.2
No response	1.5	1.4
6 Police should not arrest skid row drunks solely for drunkenness		
Agree or strongly agree	65.6	60.6
Disagree or strongly disagree	33.1	38.8
No response	1.5	1.1

Table 8 (cont'd)

Questions	Per cent	
	San Francisco (N = 466)	Portland (N = 353)
7 Police and courts are almost always fair with accused persons		
Agree or strongly agree	41.6	56.4
Disagree or strongly disagree	57.3	42.5
No response	1.1	1.1
8 Opinion on release on "own recognizance"		
Approve or strongly approve	63.1	67.2
Disapprove or strongly disapprove	34.7	31.4
No response	2.1	1.4
9 Police know who the people are that make their living committing burglaries, robberies, etc.		
Agree or strongly agree	54.7	62.6
Disagree or strongly disagree	44.2	35.7
No response	1.1	1.7
10 Know anyone who has been arrested for a major crime?		
Yes	42.9	35.7
No	56.0	62.3
No response	1.1	2.0
11 Any close friends been the victim of a major crime?		
Yes	30.7	23.2
No	68.0	73.9
No response	1.3	2.8

offenders, but less than half of them judged that adult correctional agents were performing well. On the other hand, about two-thirds of the San Francisco respondents asserted that neither the adult nor juvenile workers were doing a good job.

Negotiated pleas of guilty as a means of disposing of criminal cases failed to receive the support of very many of the respondents, even though "plea copping" does account for most of the convictions that are obtained in the courts. Two-thirds of the respondents in both communities said that they would support a halfway house located in their neighborhood. Furthermore, about two-thirds of the citizens asserted that the police ought to handle skid row drunks in some other way than arresting them for drunkenness. Two-thirds of them also said that they approved of releasing persons on their own recognizance.

The two samples differed widely on the question of whether the police and courts are fair in their dealings with accused persons. Over half of the Portland residents contended that they were fair, while over half of the San Francisco respondents believed they were not fair.

The final observation from Table 8 is that while a sizable proportion of persons—43 per cent in San Francisco and 36 per cent in Portland—said that they knew someone who had been arrested for a major crime, a markedly smaller percentage—31 per cent in San Francisco and 23 per cent in Portland—asserted that many of their close friends had been the victim of a major crime.

Summary

This study deals with public attitudes and opinions on a number of matters involving the crime problem. Many of the results are consistent with findings reported in previous studies.

In general, Portland citizens appeared to be less concerned about the crime problem and their own personal safety than San Francisco residents. The respondents from the two communities differed little in their attitudes on due process and civil liberties. However, on one or two items, Portland residents appeared to favor more repressive tactics directed at offenders.

Notes

1   Arnold E. Rose and Arthur E. Prell, "Does the Punishment Fit the Crime? A Study in Social Valuation," *American Journal of Sociology*, November 1955, pp. 247–59.

2 Donald J. Newman, "Public Attitudes toward a Form of White-Collar Crime," *Social Problems*, January 1957, pp. 228–32.

3 Don C. Gibbons, "Who Knows What about Correction?" *Crime and Delinquency*, April 1963, pp. 137–44.

4 Assembly Committee on Criminal Procedure, *Deterrent Effects of Criminal Sanctions* (Sacramento: California State Legislature, 1968).

5 Elizabeth A. Rooney and Don C. Gibbons, "Social Reactions to 'Crimes without Victims,'" *Social Problems*, Spring 1966, pp. 400–10.

6 Don C. Gibbons, "Crime and Punishment: A Study in Social Attitudes," *Social Forces*, June 1969, pp. 391–97.

7 Jennie McIntyre, "Public Attitudes toward Crime and Law Enforcement," *Annals of the American Academy of Political and Social Science*, November 1967, pp. 34–46.

8 Joint Commission on Correctional Manpower and Training, *The Public Looks at Crime and Corrections* (Washington, D.C.: Joint Commission on Correctional Manpower and Training, 1968).

9 "Your Thoughts on Crime and Punishment," *Psychology Today*, May 1969, pp. 53–58.

10 E. M. Pattison, L. A. Bishop, and A. S. Linsky, "Changes in Public Attitudes on Narcotic Addiction," *American Journal of Psychiatry*, August 1968, pp. 160–67.

11 William P. Lentz, "Social Status and Attitudes toward Delinquency Control," *Journal of Research in Crime and Delinquency*, July 1966, pp. 147–54.

12 Howard A. Parker, "Juvenile Court Actions and Public Response," *Becoming Delinquent*, P. G. Garabedian and D. C. Gibbons, eds. (Chicago: Aldine, 1970), pp. 252–65.

13 Copies of the questionnaire are available on request from the authors.

14 Actually, more than 466 and 353 individuals completed questionnaires. In the case of married couples, both often filled out questionnaires. One person from each of these married pairs was randomly selected for inclusion in the final sample to eliminate husband-wife bias of responses.

15 These items are shown in an abridged form of the wording in the questionnaire.

16 These items are presented in Table 3 in order of decreasing frequency of being listed as one of the top three major social problems. In the questionnaire, they were presented in the following order: air pollution, traffic congestion, juvenile delinquency, poverty, student protests, drug use, crime, and high taxes.

17 *Supra* note 4, p. 44.

18 The death penalty was abolished by referendum in Oregon in 1964. It might be noted that 60.1 per cent of the voters approved abolition in that election, so that it appears that support for abolition may have declined somewhat in Oregon.

C. Ray Jeffery

Social change and criminal law

Historical developments

The impact of social change on law will be discussed in at least two different ways: (1) The impact of urbanization on criminal law and the extension of law into the area of morality. As a result there exists in a heterogeneous society many behaviors which are labelled "criminal" which are contrary to the value systems of a significant part of the population. (2) The impact of the social sciences on law, with the result that psychiatric and sociological concepts designed to rehabilitate the offender have changed the form and the administration of the law.

THE IMPACT OF SOCIAL CHANGE ON LAW AS SOCIAL CONTROL

Criminal law represents the formal means by which control and order are maintained in today's society. Based on a system of formal sanctions, primarily punitive, criminal law assumes many of the functions that in an earlier society were performed informally by the family, church, school, and neighborhood. The courtroom today handles, in some instances, what in a more rural society was handled in the woodshed.

The direction of social change has been variously characterized by social philosophers as folk to urban, mechanical to organic, Gemeinschaft to Gesselschaft, primary to secondary, or sacred to secular (Becker and Boskoff, 1957: 18–32; Jeffery, 1956b, 1959).

The weakness of criminal law as a means of social control is a reflection of the deterioration of the informal controls and the inability of the criminal law to operate effectively in a complex urban setting. As a result of social change, we are involved in a legal system where the rules of conduct are unenforced and unenforceable, and where the law has been overextended into many areas of conduct not before subject to criminal sanction. Writers speak

Reprinted from *Law and Social Change*, ed. Stuart S. Nagel (1974) SCSSI, No. 3, pp. 45–56, with the permission of Sage Publications, Inc., and C. Ray Jeffery.

about "crimes without victims" (Schur, 1965) and "the overcriminalization of the system" (Kadish, 1967) when referring to the extension of criminal sanctions to alcoholism, drug addiction, abortion, and homosexuality. Not only do we use the criminal law to control personal morality, but to control student unrest and racial protests, thus adding to an already overburdened system.

The process by which behavior is labeled deviant or criminal has come to be of concern to criminologists and sociologists in recent years (Becker, 1963; Jeffery, 1956a, 1959; Quinney, 1969), and more attention needs to be paid to the use of criminal law to enforce morality and social welfare (Allen, 1958). The criminal law developed out of a religious-rural tradition, and the purpose of criminal law within an industrial-urban complex must be reappraised.

FROM PUNISHMENT TO DETERRENCE TO REHABILITATION

As a result of the growth of social science during the twentieth century, the criminal law has shifted from social control via punishment and deterrence to social control via rehabilitation and the study of the traits of individual criminals.

Capital punishment came into widespread use from the twelfth century on as a result of the decline of the blood feud. The harsh and arbitrary use of capital punishment during the Middle Ages led to the use of transportation and imprisonment as alternatives to execution, and the classical school of criminology, as exemplified by the writings of Bentham and Beccaria, advocated deterrence as a main rationale of law based on the theme that the punishment should fit the crime, with strict legal definitions of crime and punishment to safeguard the rights of the accused (Radzinowicz, 1966; Mannheim, 1960; Hall, 1945).

The deterrence theory was challenged in the nineteenth century by the positive school, Lombroso, Garofalo, and Ferri, which, reflecting the new science of behavior movement, advocated rehabilitating criminals by means of individualized treatment while rejecting legal definitions of crime and punishment (Radzinowicz, 1966; Mannheim, 1960; Hall, 1945). The positive school has so dominated American criminology that the study of individual offenders and their rehabilitation has come to be the major concern (Hall, 1945; Jeffery, 1956a; Vold, 1958: 39). As a result of the "rehabilitative ideal," we have sick people in place of criminals and hospitals in place of prisons (Allen, 1959; Wootton, 1959: 336; Szasz, 1965). Mechanisms for carrying out the rehabilitative ideal include probation, parole, juvenile courts, sexual psychopath laws, and community-based programs.

Positive criminology makes the following assumptions which form the theoretical structure for our thinking about criminal behavior:

1. The causes of crime can be found through the study of individual offenders.
2. Individual offenders can be rehabilitated through the use of psychiatric and sociological concepts.
3. Punishment is not a successful means to change human behavior.
4. Criminal behavior can be controlled indirectly through the manipulation of noncriminal behavior, e.g., therapy, job training, and remedial education.
5. Criminals can be changed by giving them services, rather than through basic research into the behavioral foundations of criminality.

The failure of past approaches emphasizing the individual

THE INDIVIDUAL REHABILITATIVE APPROACH

The success of programs to rehabilitate criminals has been negligible. The recidivism rate of men released from prison has been placed at sixty-seventy percent (Sutherland and Cressey, 1966: 665), and though this figure has been challenged by Glaser (1964: 13–35) as being too high, his own study of the federal penal system documented the failure of therapeutic, educational, and job training programs within the prison system. Glaser concluded that postrelease experiences related to family, employment, and friendships are more crucial in the rehabilitation of criminals than are prisons, the same conclusion Conrad (1965: 64–65) reached from his survey of international correctional practices. A study of the California prison system revealed that the longer a man was in prison, the higher the rate of recidivism (Crowther, 1969: 152). A recent issue of *The Annals* (January, 1969) devoted to "The Future of Corrections" advocated alternatives to imprisonment such as community-based programs, though one writer (Moeller, 1969: 86) found little hard evidence that such programs have been successful in reaching the objectives which they have sought.

Psychotherapy and social casework have failed to reform criminals, as seen in the failure of the Judge Baker Clinic (Witmer and Tufts, 1964: 37–39), the Cambridge-Somerville project (Powers and Witmer, 1951), and the Vocational High School project (Meyer et al., 1966). Several behavioral scientists have written about the lack of evidence to support the claims of a therapeutic approach to behavioral disorders (Berelson and Steiner, 1964: 287; Eysenck, 1961: 712–713; McConnell, 1968). The failure of the therapy-case-work model had led some correctional people to turn to group therapy, guided group interaction, and the use of ex-inmates for changing criminals into law-abiding citizens. If criminals learn criminal behavior through contact with criminal attitudes and values, then the way to reform criminals is to use group pressures upholding law-abiding values as a means of changing behavior (Sutherland and Cressey, 1966: 675–680: Joint Commission on Correctional Manpower and Training, 1968). The President's Commission on Law Enforcement and Administration of Justice (1967a: 38–39) found no clear evidence for the success or failure of such programs, and a recent publication by the Joint Commission on Correctional Manpower and Training (1968) was silent on this crucial issue. Since the model is one of treating the individual offender through indirect means, through the manipulation of noncriminal behavior, the prospects for success at a significant level are not great.

A summary of the report on juvenile delinquency by the President's Commission (1967b: 410) concluded that "there are no demonstrable proven methods for reducing the incidence of serious delinquent acts through prevention or rehabilitative procedures." Michael and Adler (1933) concluded that criminology would not be a science until we first developed a science of human behavior. The President's Commission, 37 years later (1967b: 8), concluded that "until the science of human behavior matures far beyond its present confines, an understanding of delinquency is not likely to be forthcoming." The inability of our criminal justice system to rehabilitate offenders is in no small measure due to our lack of scientific knowledge about human behavior.

The courts in recent years have accepted the "rehabilitative ideal." In Durham v. United States (214 F. 2d 862, 1954), Driver v. Hinnant (356 F. 2d 761, 1966), California v. Robinson (370 U.S. 660, 1962), and Easter v. District of Columbia (361 F. 2d 50, 1966), courts have broadened the scope of mental illness and criminal responsibility and have held that alcoholism and drug addiction are mental illnesses to be treated as illness, rather than crimes to be punished. On the other hand, the failure of rehabilitation has resulted in the court stating in Kent v. United States (383 U.S. 556, 1966) that "there may be grounds for concern that the child receives the worst of both worlds: that he get neither the protections accorded to adults nor the solicitous care and regenerative treatment postulated for children." In re Gault (87 S.Ct. 1428, 1966) Justice Fortas wrote that "the high crime rate among juveniles could not lead to the conclusion that . . . the juvenile system is effective to reduce or rehabilitate offenders." In Powell v. Texas (392 U.S. 514, 1968), the Supreme Court rejected the notion that alcoholics are without responsibility, or that placing a sign saying "hospital" where "jail" stood before is to the benefit of either the alcoholic or the public. In Rouse v. Cameron (373 F. 2d 451, 1967) the court held that persons committed to mental hospitals by reasons of insanity under the Durham rule had a right to treatment, and if treatment is not forthcoming the patient must be released from custody.

We thus arrived at a point in legal history where the offender cannot be placed in prison because the law states he should be rehabilitated, and he cannot be retained in a mental hospital because such institutions fail to rehabilitate.

THE PUNITIVE-DETERRENCE APPROACH

The classical school viewed the criminal law as a means of deterring criminal behavior via punishment. Deterrence has failed, and many criminologists regard punishment as barbaric (Ball, 1955). The rejection of punishment as a means of controlling human behavior has been so complete as to lead to statements such as made in a recent book by Karl Menninger (1968) that punishment is our (the punisher's) need for crime, and our need to displace guilt feelings by punishing criminals.

The statements made in criminology about punishment are contradicted by experimental evidence from behavioral psychology. Experiments in the effect of punishment on behavior have shown that punishment is a powerful means to control behavior (Honig, 1966: 380–477). Punishment, to be effective, must be certain and immediate. However, because of the uncertainty of punishment within the criminal justice system, and because of the long delay between the criminal act and the punishment, the criminal law makes the use of punishment ineffective at best. Very few criminal offenses are cleared by arrest, and, of those arrested, even fewer are sentenced or imprisoned. The President's Commission (1967c: 61) published the following figures:

2,780,000	reported crimes
727,000	arrests
177,000	complaints
160,000	sentences
63,000	imprisoned

The police system is geared to order, law enforcement, and services, and less than twenty percent of police activity involves what can be called serious felonies (Packer, 1966; Wilson, 1968a, 1968b). Congestion, plea bargaining, and administrative inefficiencies have made punishment anything but certain and swift as practiced by our courts (Newman, 1966; President's Commission, 1967d). The police and courts operate on the "apprehend, convict, and rehabilitate the individual after the crime" model, which has failed up till now. Current recommendations, such as hire more policemen, give the police better training, hire more judges and prosecutors, and make use of preventive detention will not change the basic structure of the criminal justice system.

The role of deterrence in criminal law has received little attention in the past fifty years, though Norval Morris (1969: 137–146) and his associates at the University of Chicago Law School have undertaken a project on deterrence and criminal law. To be effective, punishment must be certain, not necessarily severe. The deterrent power of criminal law as an instrument for social control depends on certainty of punishment, which at this stage of development is lacking in both our police and our courts. If correctional agencies have failed to rehabilitate, it is not less true that the police and courts have failed to deter criminal activities.

If we cannot deter criminal behavior via police, courts, and prisons, and if we cannot rehabilitate criminals via correctional programs, what then is the proper relationship between criminal law, behavioral science, and law enforcement?

Modern approaches through social manipulation

REHABILITATION THROUGH COMMUNITY ACTION PROGRAMS

The thesis that poverty causes crime has been a popular one in criminology. Vold (1958: 169–172) summarized the studies made of poverty and crime by noting that

from the earlier studies to the present, the conclusion has usually been taken for granted that poverty and unemployment are major factors producing criminality. . . . It would be more logical to conclude that neither poverty nor wealth . . . is a major determining influence in crime and delinquency.

In recent years, poverty and criminality have been reemphasized by the Cloward-Ohlin thesis of differential opportunity structure. The federal government, through the office of Juvenile Delinquency, used the opportunity theory as the basis of its delinquency prevention program (Marris and Rein, 1967). Mobilization for Youth in New York City was based on this theory of delinquent behavior. "A year after the project had entered its action phase, reducing poverty was given first priority in order to prevent and control delinquency" (Brager and Purcell, 1967: 88–89).

Commenting on this theory, the British criminologist Radzinowicz (1966: 98) writes:

When Cloward and Ohlin speak of criminal opportunities they are thinking primarily of the chance to learn criminal attitudes and techniques. It seems to me, however, that in trying to account for crime in an affluent society we cannot ignore criminal opportunities in another sense—the sheer frequency with which situations present themselves which make crime both tempting and easy.

Speaking of the heavy investment the Ford Foundation made in action programs, Radzinowicz (1965: 30–31) stated that "these schemes are primarily concerned with social policy, social welfare, and social services, and it is essential to emphasize that . . . they should not be identified too closely in the public mind with programs of crime prevention." Marshall Clinard (1968: 157–161) also rejects the idea that poverty causes crime, and he questions the validity of the Cloward-Ohlin thesis.

A total community action program undertaken in Boston, involving the community, family, and gangs, had a negligible impact on delinquency. Miller (1962) points out that the model that was a failure in Boston was used for the total community action approach to delinquency undertaken in the United States in the 1960s.

From a comprehensive study of community action projects, Marris and Rein (1967: 89, 132, 195) concluded that "while projects could claim many individual successes, and may well have increased somewhat the range of opportunities, they did so at great cost and without benefit to perhaps two-thirds of those who sought their help." They found that the poverty program was never primarily concerned with delinquency, since the assumption was made that if poverty were reduced, then ipso facto crime and delinquency would be reduced.

Daniel P. Moynihan (1968: 46, 102, 188), presently the Assistant to the President for Urban Affairs, has published a most critical statement of the poverty program, especially the Mobilization for Youth project and the role of social scientists in the poverty program. He argues that social scientists did not have the knowledge to alleviate poverty and delinquency, and they then became advocates of social reform rather than scientific evaluators of results.

The President's Commission (1967b: 41–56) placed great emphasis on job training and remedial education, yet such an approach to crime prevention is based on indirect controls over behavior via education and employment. The assumption is made that education and employment (one class of behaviors) control delinquency and crime (another class of behaviors). There is no psychological reason why the environmental contingencies controlling educational or employment behavior should control delinquent behavior, and the failure of the poverty program can in part be related to the faulty behavioral analysis involved in its formulation.

CRIME CONTROL AND DIRECT ENVIRONMENTAL ENGINEERING

An adequate model of crime control must (a) prevent crime before it occurs, not deal with it after it has occurred; (b) establish direct controls rather than indirect controls over criminal behavior; and (c) change the criminal environment in which crimes occur, rather than dealing with the personality of the individual criminal.

The most recent developments in behavioral science have given rise to such concepts as behaviorism, environmentalism, adaptive behavior, systems analysis, and decision theory. Behaviorism has had its origins in the learning theorists in psychology (Kretch, et al., 1969: 287–484), and now has advocates in sociology, public administration, and political science (Handy and Kurtz, 1964; Charlesworth, 1967). Though a lack of space forbids any detailed discussion of behaviorism, its basic ingredients include, among others, a scientific and experimental analysis of behavior, and a view of behavior as a response or adaptation to given environmental conditions. The organism is viewed as an input-output system, with environmental experiences (stimuli) serving as the input, while the nervous-muscular system serves as the output or response system. The individual responds to and operates upon his environment— thus the phrase "operant behavior." The major focus of behaviorism is the adaptation of the organism to the environment through behavior based upon a system of rewards and punishment.

Systems analysis is likewise interested in organism-environment interaction, the interaction of parts to systems, or one system to another system. Decision theory is concerned with the response of an individual so as to maximize gain and minimize loss.

The crucial role of behavior, environment, reward, and punishment in contemporary behavioral science has vast implications for criminal law and law enforcement. The major lesson relevant to criminal law and corrections is that to change the behavior of the individual criminal, we must change the environment to which he responds. The failure of psychotherapy, group counseling, probation, parole, prisons, job training programs, and remedial education programs is in no small measure due to the fact that such programs operate on the individual offender and do not change the environment in which crimes occur.

Jane Jacobs (1961) has pointed out how unsafe our city streets, parks, and buildings are because of the way we make use of urban planning and design. Alexander (1967: 60–109) notes that urban environments have created isolation, alienation, and social deviance, and he advocates a program of urban design which will create human contact at a primary intimate level. Boggs (1965) has demonstrated how crime rates can be studied as properties of environmental opportunities to commit crimes.

If we view criminal behavior as a response to an environmental opportunity to commit a crime, rather than as a psychological or sociological trait of an individual offender, then law enforcement becomes a matter of environmental engineering. If we use a decision-theory model, criminal behavior becomes a matter of potential gain (reward) versus potential loss (punishment), and as our judicial system now operates, the gain outweighs the loss. By making the commission of a criminal act impossible or at least difficult, we would reduce the potential gain to a minimum while increasing the potential loss. This will require extensive use of science and technology in the prevention of crimes, as well as the use of urban design and planning as an integral part of law enforcement and crime control. Police departments would change from agencies "responding to crime after it has occurred" to agencies "preventing crime before it occurs."

The focus of criminal justice administration would change from deterrence and rehabilitation of individual offenders to prevention and control through environmental engineering. The old concepts and practices of furnishing services to inmates, such as are involved in therapy, probation, imprisonment, and community action programs would be replaced with science, technology, urban planning and design, decision theory, and systems analysis.

Criminal law would thus become part of behaviorism, environmentalism, urban planning, and so forth. It would return to its basic function of deterrence, though in a different form from that in classic criminology. Law would be viewed as a social instrumentality for spelling out the consequences of behavior and for guaranteeing both the consequences and due process in the application of the law. Criminal law would remove itself from the social work-rehabilitative model and assume its historic role as a source of social control, with its emphasis on the external environment, not on the individual offender. Crime as a characteristic of the environment would be researched in place of the rehabilitative emphasis on the individual criminal. The positive school denied the relevance of criminal law either as a means of social control or as a means of guaranteeing due process, and in 1970 we are witnessing the consequences of such a strong commitment to positivistic individualistic criminology.

References

Allen, F. A. (1959) "Criminal justice, legal values and the rehabilitative ideal." J. of Criminal Law, Criminology, and Police Sci. 50 (September–October): 226–232.

——— (1958) "The borderland of the criminal law: problems of socializing criminal justice." Social Service Rev. 32 (June): 107–119.

Alexander, C. (1967) "The city as a mechanism for sustaining human contact," pp. 60–109 in W. Ewald (ed.) Environment for Man. Bloomington: Indiana Univ. Press.

Ball, J. (1955) "The deterrence concept in criminology and law." J. of Criminal Law, Criminology, and Police Sci. 44 (September–October): 347–352.

Becker, H. P. and *A. Boskoff* (1957) Modern Sociological Theory. New York: Dryden.

Becker, H. S. (1963) Outsiders. New York: Free Press.

Berelson, B. and *G. A. Steiner* (1964) Human Behavior. New York: Harcourt, Brace & World.

Boggs, S. (1965) "Urban crime patterns." Amer. Soc. Rev. 30 (December): 899–908.

Brager, C. and *F. P. Purcell* (1967) Community Action Against Poverty. New Haven: College & Univ. Press.

Charlesworth, J. [ed.] (1967) Contemporary Political Analysis. New York: Free Press.

Clinard, M. (1968) Sociology of Deviant Behavior. New York: Holt, Rinehart & Winston.

Conrad, J. (1965) Crime and its Correction. Berkeley: Univ. of California Press.

Crowther, C. (1969) "Crimes, penalties, and legislatures." Annals 381 (January): 147–158.

Eysenck, H. J. (1961) Handbook of Abnormal Psychology. New York: Basic Books.

Glaser, D. (1964) The Effectiveness of a Prison and Parole System. Indianapolis: Bobbs-Merrill.

Hall, J. (1945) "Criminology," pp. 342–365 in G. Gurvitch and W. Moore (eds.) Twentieth Century Sociology. New York: Philosophical Press.

Handy, R. and *P. Kurtz* (1964) A Current Appraisal of the Behavioral Sciences. Great Barrington: Behavioral Research Council.

Honig, W. (1966) Operant Behavior. New York: Appleton-Century-Crofts.

Jacobs, J. (1961) The Death and Life of Great American Cities. New York: Random House.

Jeffery, C. R. (1959) "An integrated theory of crime and criminal behavior." J. of Criminal Law, Criminology, and Police Sci. 49 (March–April): 533–552.

————— (1956a) "The structure of American criminological thinking." J. of Criminal Law, Criminology, and Police Sci. 46 (January–February): 658–672.

————— (1956b) "Crime, law, and social structure." J. of Criminal Law, Criminology, and Police Sci. 47 (November–December): 423–435.

Joint Commission on Correctional Manpower and Training (1968) Offenders as a Correctional Manpower Resource. Washington, D.C.: Government Printing Office.

Kadish, S. H. (1967) "The crisis of overcriminalization." Annals 374 (November): 157–170.

Kretch, D. et al. (1969) Elements of Psychology. New York: Alfred A. Knopf.

Mannheim, H. (1960) Pioneers in Criminology. London: Stevens.

Marris, P. and *M. Rein* (1967) Dilemmas of Social Reform. New York: Atherton.

McConnell, J. V. (1968) "Psychoanalysis must go." Esquire (October): 176.

Menninger, K. (1968) The Crime of Punishment. New York: Viking.

Meyer, H. J. et al. (1966) Girls at Vocational High. New York: Russell Sage.

Michael, J. and *M. J. Adler* (1933) Crime, Law, and Social Science. New York: Harcourt, Brace.

Miller, W. (1962) "The impact of a total community delinquency control project." Social Problems 10 (Fall): 168–190.

Moeller, H. G. (1969) "The continuum of correction." Annals 381 (January): 86.

Morris, N. and *F. Zimring* (1969) "Deterrence and correction." Annals 381 (January): 137–146.

Moynihan, D. P. (1968) Maximum Feasible Misunderstanding. New York: Free Press.

Newman, D. R. (1966) Conviction. Boston: Little, Brown.

Packer, H. L. (1966) "The courts, the police, and the rest of us." J. of Criminal Law, Criminology, and Police Sci. 57 (September): 238–243.

Powers, E. and *H. L. Witmer* (1951) An Experiment in the Prevention of Delinquency. New York: Columbia Univ. Press.

President's Commission on Law Enforcement and Administration of Justice (1967a) Corrections. Washington, D.C.: Government Printing Office.

————— (1967b) Juvenile Delinquency and Youth Crime. Washington, D.C.: Government Printing Office.

————— (1967c) Science and Technology, Washington, D.C.: Government Printing Office.

———— (1967d) The Courts. Washington, D.C.: Government Printing Office.

Quinney, R. (1969) Crime and Justice in Society. Boston: Little, Brown.

Radzinowicz, L. (1966) Ideology and Crime. New York: Columbia Univ. Press.

———— (1965) The Need for Criminology. London: Heinemann.

Schur, E. H. (1965) Crimes Without Victims. Englewood Cliffs, N.J.: Prentice-Hall.

Sutherland, E. H. and D. R. Cressey (1966) Principles of Criminology. Philadelphia: Lippincott.

Szasz, T. (1965) Psychiatric Justice. New York: Macmillan.

Vold, G. (1958) Theoretical Criminology. New York: Oxford Univ. Press.

Wilson, J. Q. (1968a) Varieties of Police Behavior. Cambridge: Harvard Univ. Press.

———— (1968b) "Dilemmas of police administration." Public Administration Rev. (September–October): 407–416.

Witmer, H. L. and E. Tufts (1964) The Effectiveness of Delinquency Prevention Programs. Washington, D.C.: Children's Bureau.

Wootton B. (1959) Social Science and Social Policy. New York: Macmillan.

Donald J. Black

Production of crime rates

This paper makes problematic the situational conditions under which policemen write official crime reports in field encounters with complainants. These reports are the raw materials for official crime rates—"crimes known to the police." They also are a prerequisite of further investigation

The findings in this paper derive from a larger research project under the direction of Professor Albert J. Reiss, Jr., Department of Sociology, University of Michigan. The project was supported by Grant Award 006, Office of Law Enforcement Assistance, U.S. Department of Justice, under the Law Enforcement Assistance Act of 1965. Other grants were awarded by the National Science Foundation and the Russell Sage Foundation. Preparation of this paper was facilitated by the Russell Sage Program in Law and Social Science at Yale Law School. The author is indebted to the following for their constructive suggestions: Maureen Mileski, Albert J. Reiss, Jr., Stanton Wheeler, Abraham S. Goldstein, and Sheldon Olson.

Reprinted from ASR, August 1970, pp. 733–748, with the permission of the American Sociological Association and Donald J. Black.

of the crime by the detective bureau and thus of apprehension of the offender. They constitute official recognition of crimes. The findings derive from a three-city observation study of routine police encounters. Among the conditions that relate to the production of official crime reports are the following: the legal seriousness of the complaint, the complainant's observable preference for police action, the relational distance between the complainant and the suspect, the complainant's degree of deference toward the police, and the complainant's social-class status. However, there is no evidence of racial discrimination in crime-reporting. We interpret these empirical patterns not only from the standpoint of crime rates as such but also from the standpoint of the relation between police work and other aspects of social organization.

Sociological approaches to official crime rates generally fail to make problematic the production of the rates themselves. Theory has not directed inquiry to the principles and mechanisms by which some technically illegal acts are recorded in the official ledger of crime while others are not. Instead crime rates ordinarily are put to use as data in the service of broader investigations of deviance and control. Yet at the same time it has long been taken for granted that official statistics are not an accurate measure of all legally defined crime in the community (e.g., de Beaumont and de Tocqueville, 1964; Morrison, 1897; Sellin, 1931).

The major uses of official crime statistics have taken two forms (see Biderman and Reiss, 1967); each involves a different social epistemology, a different way of structuring knowledge about crime. One employs official statistics as an index of the "actual" or "real" volume and morphology of criminal deviance in the population. Those who follow this approach typically consider the lack of fit between official and actual rates of crime to be a methodological misfortune. Historically, measurement of crime has been the dominant function of crime rates in social science. A second major use of official statistics abandons the search for "actual" deviance. This is managed either by defining deviance with the official reactions themselves—a labeling approach—or by incorporating the official rates not as an index of deviant behavior but as an index of social control operations (e.g., Kitsuse and Cicourel, 1963; Erikson, 1966; Wilson, 1968). In effect this second range of work investigates "actual" social control rather than "actual" deviance. Hence it encounters methodological problems of its own, since, without question, social control agencies do not record all of their official attempts to counteract or contain what they and others regard as deviant conduct.[1] A striking feature of police work, for instance, is the degree to which officers operate with informal tactics, such as harassment and manipulative human-relations techniques, when they confront law-violative behavior (e.g., Skolnick, 1966; LaFave, 1965; Bittner, 1967; Black, 1968; Black and Reiss, 1970). In sum, when official statistics are used as a *means* of measurement and analysis, they usually function imperfectly. This is not to deny that such methods can be highly rewarding in some contexts.

This paper follows an alternative strategy that arises from an alternative conceptual starting point. It makes official records of crime an end rather than a means of study (see Wheeler, 1967; Cicourel, 1968:26–28). It treats the crime rate as itself a social fact, an empirical phenomenon with its own existential integrity. A crime rate is not an epiphenomenon. It is part of the natural world. From this standpoint crime statistics are not evaluated as inaccurate or unreliable. They are an aspect of social organization and cannot, sociologically, be wrong. From the present perspective it nevertheless remains interesting that social control systems process more than they report in official statistics and that there is a good deal more rule-violative behavior than that which is processed. These patterns are themselves analytically relevant aspects of crime rates.

An official crime rate may be understood as a rate of *socially recognized*[2] deviant behavior; deviance rates in this sense are produced by all control systems that respond on a case-by-case basis to sanctionable conduct. This does not say that deviant behavior as a general category is synonymous with socially recognized deviant behavior. As a general category deviance may be defined as any behavior in a *class* for which there is a *probability* of negative sanction subsequent to its detection (Black and Reiss, 1970). Thus, whether or not an agent of control detects or sanctions a particular instance of rule-violative behavior is immaterial to the issue of whether or not it is deviant. Deviance is behavior that is *vulnerable* to social control. This approach generates three empirical types of deviance: (1) undetected deviance, (2) detected, unsanctioned deviance, and (3) sanctioned deviance. It should be apparent that, while every control system may produce a rate of socially recognized deviance, much unrecognized deviance surely resides in every social system.[3] By definition undetected deviance cannot be recognized by a control system, but, as will become apparent in this presentation, even detected deviance may not be recognized as such. The notion of sanctioned deviance, by contrast, presumes that a social recognition process has taken place. The concept of social recognition of deviance is nothing more than a short-hand, more abstract way of stating what we mean by concrete expressions such as invocation of the law, hue and cry, bringing a suit, blowing the whistle, and so forth.

The concept of deviance should be applied with reference to specific systems of social control. For example, deviance that is undetected from the standpoint of a formal, legal control system, such as the police, may be detected or even sanctioned in an informal control context, such as a business organization, neighborhood or friendship group or family. Crime rates then are rates of deviance socially recognized by official agencies of criminal-law enforcement. They are official rates of *detection* ("crimes known to the police") and of *sanctioning* (arrest rates and conviction rates).[4] Enforcement agencies handle many technically illegal acts that they omit from their official records. This paper explores some of the conditions under which the police produce official rates of crime detection in field encounters with citizens.

Social organization of crime detection

Detection of deviance involves (1) the discovery of deviant *acts* or behavior and (2) the linking of *persons* or groups to those acts. Types of deviance vary widely according to the extent to which either or both of these aspects of detection are probable. Some deviant acts are unlikely to be discovered, although discovery generally is equivalent to the detection of the deviant person as well. Examples are homosexual conduct and various other forms of consensual sexual deviance. Acts of burglary and auto theft, by contrast, are readily detected, but the offending persons often are not apprehended. These differential detection probabilities stem in part from the empirical patterns by which various forms of violative behavior occur in time and social space. In part they stem as well from the uneven climate of social control.

The organization of police control lodges the primary responsibility for crime detection in the citizenry rather than in the police. The uniformed patrol division, the major line unit of modern police departments, is geared to respond to citizen calls for help via a centralized radio-communications system. Apart from traffic violations, patrol officers detect comparatively little crime through their own initiative. This is all the more true of legally serious crime.

Thus crime detection may be understood as a largely *reactive* process from the standpoint of the police as a control system. Far less is it a *proactive* process. Proactive operations aimed at the discovery of criminal behavior predominate in the smaller specialized units of the large police department, particularly in the vice or morals division, including the narcotics squad, and in the traffic division. Most crimes, unlike vice offenses, are not susceptible to detection by means of undercover work or the enlistment of quasi-employed informers (see Skolnick, 1966). Unlike traffic offenses, furthermore, most crimes cannot be discovered through the surveillance of public places. Since the typical criminal act occurs at a specifically unpredictable time and place, the police must rely upon citizens to involve them in the average case. The law of privacy is another factor that presses the police toward a reactive detection system (Stinchcombe, 1963). Even without legal limitations on police detective work, however, the unpredictability of crime itself would usually render the police ignorant in the absence of citizens. Most often the citizen who calls the police is a victim of a crime who seeks justice in the role of *complainant*.

Vice control and traffic enforcement generally operate without the assistance of complainants. It appears that most proactive police work arises when there is community pressure for police action but where, routinely, there are no complainants involved as victims in the situations of violative behavior in question. In the average case proactive detection involves a simultaneous detection of the violative act and of the violative person. Proactively produced crime rates, therefore, are nearly always rates of arrest rather than rates of known criminal acts. In effect the proactive clearance rate is 100%. Crime rates that are produced in proactive police operations, such as rates of arrest for prostitution, gambling, homosexual behavior, and narcotics violation, directly correlate with police manpower allocation. Until a point of total detection is reached and holding all else constant, these vice rates increase as the number of policemen assigned to vice control is increased. On the other hand, the more important variable in rates of "crimes known to the police," is the volume of complaints from citizens.

Nevertheless, rates of known crimes do not perfectly reflect the volume of citizen complaints. A complaint must be given official status in a formal written report before it can enter police statistics, and the report by no means automatically follows receipt of the complaint by the police. In the present investigation patrol officers wrote official reports in only 64% of the 554 crime situations where a complainant, but no suspect, was present in the field setting. The decision to give official status to a crime ordinarily is an outcome of face-to-face interaction between the police and the complainant rather than a programmed police response to a bureaucratic or legal formula. The content and contours of this interaction differentially condition the probability that an official report will be written, much as they condition, in situations where a suspect is present, the probability that an arrest will be made (Black, 1968; Black and Reiss, 1970).

Whether or not an official report is written affects not only the profile of official crime rates; it also determines whether subsequent police investigation of the crime will be undertaken at a later date. Subsequent investigation can occur only when an official report is forwarded to the detective division for further processing, which includes the possibility of an arrest of the suspect. Hence the rate of detection and sanctioning of deviant *persons* is in part contingent upon whether the detection of deviant *acts* is made official. In this respect justice demands formality in the processing of crimes. This paper considers the following conditions as they relate to the probability of an official crime report in police-complainant encounters: the legal seriousness of the alleged crime, the preference of the complainant, the relational distance between the complainant and the absentee suspect, the degree of deference the complainant extends to the police, and the race and social-class status of the complainant.

Field method

Systematic observation of police-citizen transactions was conducted in Boston, Chicago, and Washington, D.C., during the summer of 1966. Thirty-six observers—persons with law, social science, and police administration backgrounds—recorded observations of routine encounters between uniformed patrolmen and citizens. Observers accompanied patrolmen on all work-shifts on all days of the week for seven weeks in each city. However, the times when police activity is comparatively high (evening shifts, particularly weekend evenings) were given added weight in the sample.

Police precincts were chosen as observation sites in each city. The precincts were selected so as to maximize observation in lower socioeconomic, high crime rate, racially homogeneous residential areas. This was accomplished through the selection of two precincts in Boston and Chicago and four precincts in Washington, D.C.

The data were recorded in "incident booklets," forms structurally similar to interview schedules. One booklet was used for each incident that the police were requested to handle or that they themselves noticed while on patrol. These booklets were not filled out in the presence of policemen. In fact the officers were told that our research was not concerned with police behavior but only with citizen behavior toward the police and the kinds of problems citizens make for the police. Thus the study partially utilized systematic deception.

A total of 5,713 incidents were observed and recorded. In what follows, however, the statistical base is only 554 cases, roughly one-in-ten of the total sample. These cases comprise nearly all of the police encounters with complainants in crime situations where no suspect was present in the field situation. They are drawn from the cases that originated with a citizen telephone call to the police, 76% of the total. Excluded are, first, encounters initiated by policemen on their own initiative (13%). Police-initiated encounters almost always involve a suspect or offender rather than a complainant; complainants usually must take the initiative to make themselves known to the police. Also excluded are encounters initiated by citizens who walk into a police station to ask for help (6%) or who personally flag down the police on the street (5%). Both of these kinds of police work have peculiar situational features and should be treated separately. The great majority of citizen calls by telephone are likewise inappropriate for the present sample. In almost one-third of the cases no citizen is present when the police arrive to handle the complaint. When a citizen is present, furthermore, the incident at issue pertains to a noncriminal matter in well over one half of the cases. Even when there is a criminal matter a suspect not infrequently is present. When a suspect is present the major official outcome possible is arrest rather than a crime report. Finally, the sample excludes cases in which two or more complainants of mixed race or social-class composition participated. It may appear that, in all, much has been eliminated. Still, perhaps surprisingly, what remains is the *majority of crime situations* that the police handle in response to citizen telephone calls for service. There is no suspect available in 77% of the felonies and in 51% of the misdemeanors that the police handle on account of a complaint by telephone. There is only a complainant. These proportions alone justify a study of police encounters with complainants. In routine police work the handling of crime is in large part the handling of complainants. Policemen see more victims than criminals.

Legal seriousness of the crime

Police encounters with complainants where no suspect is present involve a disproportionately large number of felonies, the legally serious category of crime. This was true of 53% of the cases in the sample of 554. When a suspect is present, with or without a citizen complainant, the great majority of police encounters pertain only to misdemeanors (Black, 1968). In other words, the police arrive at the scene too late to apprehend a suspect more often in serious crime situations than in those of a relatively minor nature.[5] In police language, felonies more often are "cold." A moment's reflection upon the empirical patterns by which various crimes are committed reveals why this is so. Some of the more common felonies, such as burglary and auto theft, generally involve stealth and occur when the victim is absent; by the time the crime is discovered, the offender has departed. Other felonies such as robbery and rape have a hit-and-run character, such that the police rarely can be notified in time to make an arrest at the crime setting. Misdemeanors, by contrast, more often involve some form of "disturbance of the peace," such as disorderly conduct and drunkenness, crimes that are readily audible or visible to potential complainants and that proceed in time with comparative continuity. In short, properties of the social organization of crime make detection of felony offenders relatively difficult and detection of misdemeanor offenders relatively simple, given detection of the act.[6]

When the offender has left the scene in either felony or misdemeanor situations, however, detection and sanctioning of the offender is precluded unless an official report is written by the police. Not surprisingly, the police are more likely to write these reports in felony than in misdemeanor situations.[7] Reports were written in 72% of the 312 felonies, but in only 53% of the 242 misdemeanors. It is clear that official recognition of crimes becomes more likely as the legally defined seriousness of the crime increases. Even so, it remains noteworthy that the police officially disregard one-fourth of the felonies they handle in encounters with complainants. These are not referred to the detective division for investigation; offenders in these cases thus unknowingly receive a pardon of sorts.

Now the reader might protest an analysis that treats as crimes some incidents that the police themselves do not handle as crimes. How can we call an event a law violation when a legal official ignores that very event? This is a definitional problem that plagues a sociology of law as well as a sociology of deviance and social control. How is a violation of the "law on the books" properly classified if "in practice" it is not labeled as such? It is easy enough to argue that either of these criteria, the written law or the law-in-action, should alone define the violative behavior in question. No answer to this dilemma is true or false. It is of course all a matter of the usefulness of one definition or another. Here a major aim is to learn something about the process by which the police select for official attention certain technically illegal acts while they bypass others. If we classify as crimes only those acts the police officially recognize as crimes, then what shall we call the remainder? Surely that remainder should be conceptually distinguished from acts that are technically legal and which carry no sanctions. For that reason, the present analysis operates with two working categories, crimes and officially recognized crimes, along with an implicit residual category of non-crimes. Crime differs from other behavior by dint of a probability, the probability that it will be sanctioned in a particular administrative system if it is detected. The written law usually—though not always—is a good index of whether that probability exists. "Dead letter" illegal acts, i.e., those virtually never sanctioned, are not classified as crimes in this analysis. Crime as a *general category* consists in a probability of sanction; official recognition in the form of a crime report is one factor that escalates that probability for a *specific instance* of crime. It is worthwhile to have a vocabulary that distinguishes *between crimes* on the basis of how the police relate to them. Without a vocabulary of this kind police invocation of the law in the face of a law violation cannot be treated as empirically or theoretically problematic. Rather, invocation of the law would *define* a law violation and would thereby deprive sociology of an intriguing problem for analysis. Indeed, if we define a law violation *with* invocation of the law, we are left with the peculiar analytical premise that enforcement of the law is total or universal. We would definitionally destroy the possibility of police leniency or even of police discretion in law enforcement.

The complainant's preference

Upon arriving at a field setting, the police typically have very little information about what they are going to find. At best they have the crude label assigned to the incident by a dispatcher at the communications center. Over the police radio they hear such descriptions as "a B and E" (breaking and/or entering), "family trouble," "somebody screaming," "a theft report," "a man down" (person lying in a public place, cause unknown), "outside ringer" (burglar-alarm ringing), "the boys" (trouble with juveniles), and suchlike. Not infrequently these labels prove to be inaccurate. In any case policemen find themselves highly dependent upon citizens to assist them in structuring situational reality. Complainants, biased though they may be, serve the police as primary agents of situational intelligence.

What is more, complainants not infrequently go beyond the role of providing information by seeking to influence the direction of police action. When a suspect is present the complainant may pressure the police to make an arrest or to be lenient. When there is no available suspect, it becomes a matter of whether the complainant prefers that the crime be handled as an official matter or whether he wants it handled informally. Of course many complainants are quite passive and remain behaviorally neutral. During the observation period the complainant's preference was unclear in 40% of the encounters involving a "cold" felony or misdemeanor. There were 184 felony situations in which the complainant expressed a clear preference; 78% lobbied for official action. Of the 145 misdemeanor situations where the complainant expressed a clear preference, the proportion favoring official action was 75%, roughly the same proportion as that in felony situations. It seems that complainants are, behaviorally, insensitive to the legal seriousness of crimes when they seek to direct police action.

Police action displays a striking pattern of conformity with the preferences of complainants. Indeed, in not one case did the police write an official crime report when the complainant manifested a preference for informal action. This pattern seen in legal perspective is particularly interesting given that felony complainants prefer informal action nearly as frequently as misdemeanor complainants. Police conformity with those complainants who do prefer official action, however, is not so symmetrical. In felony situations the police comply by writing an official report 84% of the cases, whereas when the complaint involves a misdemeanor their rate of compliance drops to 64%. Thus the police follow the wishes of officially-oriented complainants in the majority of encounters, but the majority is somewhat heavier when the occasion is a legally more serious matter. In the field setting proper the citizen complainant has much to say about the official recognition of crimes, though the law seemingly screens his influence.[8]

Recall that the raw inputs for the official detection rate are generated by the citizenry who call the police. At two levels, then, the operational influence of citizens gives crime rates a peculiarly democratic character. Here the servant role of the police predominates; the guardian role recedes. Since an official report is a prerequisite for further police investigation of the crime, this pattern also implies that complainants are operationally endowed with an adjudicatory power. Their observable preferences can ultimately affect probabilities of arrest and conviction. While the structure of the process is democratic in this sense, it most certainly is not universalistic. The moral standards of complainants vary to some extent across the citizen population, thereby injecting particularism into the production of outcomes. There appears a trade-off between democratic process and universalistic enforcement in police work. This is an organizational dilemma not only of the police but of the legal system at large. When the citizenry has the power to direct the invocation of law, it has the power to discriminate among law-violators. Moral diversity in the citizen population by itself assures that some discrimination of this kind will occur. This is true regardless of the intentions of individual citizens. When a legal system organizes to follow the demands of the citizenry, it must sacrifice uniformity, since the system responds only to those who call upon it while it ignores illegality that citizens choose to ignore. A legal system that strives for universalistic application of the law, by contrast, must refuse to follow the diverse whims of its atomized citizenry. Only a society of citizens homogeneous in their legal behavior could avoid this dilemma.

Relational distance

Like any other kind of behavior, criminal behavior is located within networks of social organization. One aspect of that social organization consists in the relationship existing between the criminal offender and the complainant prior to a criminal event. They may be related by blood, marriage, friendship, neighborhood, membership in the same community, or whatever. In other words, the adversarial relation that is created by a crime may itself be viewed as it is structured within a wider social frame. The findings in this section permit the conclusion that the probability of official recognition of a crime varies with the relational network in which the crime occurs.[9]

The greater the relational distance between citizen adversaries, the greater is the likelihood of official recognition.

Citizen adversaries may be classified according to three levels of relational distance: (1) fellow family members, (2) friends, neighbors, or acquaintances, and (3) strangers. The vast majority of the cases fall into the "stranger" category, though some of these probably would be reclassified into one of the other relational categories if the criminal offender were detected. The complainant's first speculation generally is that a stranger committed the offense in question.

Table 1 shows that when a complainant expresses a preference for official action the police comply most readily when the adversaries are strangers to one another. They are less likely to comply by writing an official crime report when the adversaries are friends, neighbors, or acquaintances, and they are least likely to give official recognition to the crime when the complainant and suspect are members of the same family. The small number of cases in the "fellow family members" category prohibits comparison between felony and misdemeanor situations. In the other relational categories this comparison reveals that the police follow the same pattern in the handling of both felonies and misdemeanors. With the relational distance between the adversaries held constant, however, the probability of an official report is higher for felony than for misdemeanor situations. The highest probability of an official response occurs when the crime is a felony and the adversaries are strangers to one another (91%); the lowest calculable probability is that for misdemeanors when the adversaries are related by friendship, neighborhood, or acquaintanceship (42%). On the other hand, it appears that relational distance can override the legal seriousness of crimes in conditioning police action, since the police are more likely to give official recognition to a misdemeanor involving strangers as adversaries (74%) than to a felony involving friends, neighbors, or acquaintances (62%). Here again, therefore, the law screens but does not direct the impact of an extra-legal element in the production of crime rates.

Beyond the importance of relational distance for an understanding of crime rates as such is another implication of these findings. Because a follow-up investigation of the crime report by the detective division may result in apprehension of the criminal offender, it is apparent that the probability of an official sanction for the offender lessens as the degree of social intimacy with his adversary—usually his victim—increases. When an offender victimizes a social intimate the police are most apt to let the event

Table 1 **Percent of police encounters with complainants according to type of crime and relational tie between citizen adversaries, by situational outcome: complainant prefers official action**

Situational outcome	Family members	Friends, neighbors, acquaintances	Strangers
Felony			
Official report	(4)	62	91
No official report	(5)	38	9
Total percent	. . .	100	100
Total number	(9)	(16)	(92)
Misdemeanor			
Official report	(3)	43	74
No official report	(5)	57	26
Total percent	. . .	100	100
Total number	(8)	(23)	(62)
All crimes			
Official report	41	51	84
No official report	59	49	16
Total percent	100	100	100
Total number	(17)	(39)	(154)

remain a private matter, regardless of the complainant's preference. A more general consequence of this pattern of police behavior is that the criminal law gives priority to the protection of strangers from strangers while it leaves vulnerable intimates to intimates. Indeed, victimizations of strangers by strangers may be comparatively more damaging to social order and hence, from a functional standpoint, require more attention from the forces of control. A victimization between intimates is capsulated by intimacy itself. Furthermore, as social networks are more intimate, it surely is more likely that informal systems of social control operate. Other forms of legal control also may become available in the more intimate social relationships. In contrast there is hardly anyone but the police to oversee relations among strangers. Seemingly the criminal law is most likely to be invoked where it is the only operable control system. The same may be said of legal control in general (see Pound, 1942; Schwartz, 1954; Nader and Metzger, 1963). Legal control melds with other aspects of social organization.

The complainant's deference

Evidence accumulates from studies of police sanctioning that the fate of suspects sometimes hangs upon the degree of deference or respect they extend to policemen in field encounters (Westley, 1953; Piliavin and Briar, 1964; Black, 1968; Black and Reiss, 1970). As a rule, the police are especially likely to sanction suspects who fail to defer to police authority whether legal grounds exist or not. Situational etiquette can weigh heavily on broader processes of social life (see Goffman, 1956 and 1963). This section offers findings showing that the complainant's deference toward the police conditions the official recognition of crime complaints.

The deference of complainants toward the police can be classified into three categories: (1) very deferential or very respectful, (2) civil, and (3) antagonistic or disrespectful. As might be expected, complainants are not often antagonistic toward policemen; it is the suspect who is more likely to be disrespectful (Black and Reiss, 1967:63–65). The number of cases of police encounters with antagonistic complainants is too few for separate analysis of felony and misdemeanor situations. When felonies and misdemeanors are combined into one statistical base, however, it becomes clear that by a large margin the probability of an official crime report is lowest when the complainant is antagonistic in the face-to-face encounter. (See Table 2.) Less than one-third of the disrespectful complainants who prefer official action see their wishes actualized in a crime report. Because of the small number of cases this finding nevertheless should be taken as tentative. The comparison between the very deferential and the civil complainants, which is more firmly grounded, is equally striking. The police are somewhat more likely to comply with very deferential complainants than with those who are merely civil. In sum, then, the less deferential the complainant, the less likely are the police to comply with his manifest preference for official action in the form of an official crime report.[10]

Table 2 also shows that the complainant's degree of deference conditions crime-reporting in both felony and misdemeanor situations. In fact, it seems that the complainant's deference can predict official recognition as well, or even slightly better than the legal seriousness of the crime. The probability of a crime report in misdemeanor situations where the complainant is very deferential (85%) is as high as it is in felony situations where he is only civil toward the police (80%). Still, when we hold constant the complainant's deference, the legal seriousness of the incident looms to

Table 2 **Percent of police encounters with complainants according to type of crime and complainant's degree of deference, by situational outcome: complainant prefers official action**

	Very deferential	Civil	Antagonistic
Felony			
Official report	100	80	(2)
No official report	. . .	20	(1)
Total percent	100	100	. . .
Total number	(15)	(127)	(3)
Misdemeanor			
Official report	85	65	(1)
No official report	15	35	(6)
Total percent	100	100	. . .
Total number	(20)	(79)	(7)
All crimes			
Official report	91	73	30
No official report	9	26	70
Total percent	100	99	100
Total number	(35)	(206)	(10)

importance. In felony situations where the complainant is very respectful, the police satisfy his preference for official action in no less than 100% of the cases.

The findings in this section reveal that the level of citizen respect for the police in field encounters has consequences beyond those known to operate in the sanctioning of suspects. Here we see that the fate of citizens who are nominally served, as well as those who are controlled by the police, rides in part upon their etiquette. The official response to an avowed victimization in part depends upon the situational *style* in which the citizen presents his complaint to the control system. Official crime rates and the justice done through police detection of criminal offenders, therefore, reflect the politeness of victims. That sanctions are sometimes more severe for alleged offenders who are disrespectful toward the police can be understood in many ways as a possible contribution to the control function. Perhaps, for example, disrespectful offenders pose a greater threat to society, since they refuse to extend legitimacy to its legal system. Perhaps deterrence is undermined by leniency toward disrespectful suspects. Perhaps not. The point is that rationales are available for understanding this pattern as it relates to the police control function. It should be apparent that such rationales do not apply as readily to the tendency of the police to underreport the victimizations of disrespectful complainants. Surely this pattern could have only the remotest connection to deterrence of illegal behavior. Etiquette, it would seem, can belittle the criminal law.

The complainant's status

The literature on police work abounds in speculation but provides little observational evidence concerning the relation of social status to police outcomes. The routine policing of Negroes differs somewhat from that of whites, and the policing of blue-collar citizens differs quite massively from that of white-collar citizens. Nevertheless, there is a dearth of evidence that these differences arise from discriminatory behavior by policemen. It appears that more consequential in determining these outcomes are aggregative differences between the races and classes in the kinds of incidents the police handle along with situational factors such as those the present analysis examines (e.g., Skolnick, 1966; Black, 1968; Black and Reiss, 1970). Nevertheless, the research literature remains far too scanty to permit confident generalization on these questions.

Studies in the discretionary aspects of police work focus almost solely upon police encounters with suspects. The present sample provides an opportunity to investigate the relation between a complainant's race and social-class status and the probability that the police will give official recognition to his complaint. The tabulation limits the cases to those where the complainant expresses a preference for official action and to those where he is civil toward the police. This section concludes that the race of complainants does not independently relate to the production of official crime rates, but there is some evidence that the police give preferential treatment to white-collar complainants in felony situations.

For all crimes and social-class statuses taken together, the difference between Negroes and whites in the probability of an official crime report is slight and negligible (see Table 3); it is a bit higher for whites. Table 3 also shows that this probability is the same for blue-collar Negroes and blue-collar whites in felony

Table 3 **Percent of police encounters with complainants according to type of crime and complainant's social-class status and race, by situational outcome: complainant prefers official action and is civil toward police**

Situational outcome	Felony						Misdemeanor						All crimes and classes	
	Blue-collar		White-collar		Class unknown		Blue-collar		White-collar		Class unknown			
	Negro	White	Negro	White	Negro	White	Negro	White	Negro	White	Negro	White	Negro	White
Official report	77	77	(5)	100	(3)	90	69	55	(2)	64	(2)	80	72	76
No official report	23	23	...	...	(5)	10	31	45	...	36	(3)	20	28	24
Total percent	100	100	...	100	...	100	100	100	...	100	...	100	100	100
Total number	(64)	(22)	(5)	(18)	(8)	(10)	(26)	(22)	(2)	(14)	(5)	(10)	(110)	(96)

situations, though it is comparatively higher for blue-collar Negroes in misdemeanor situations. Evidence of racial discrimination thus appears weak and inconsistent. It should nonetheless be noted that if there were consistent evidence of a race differential it is not readily clear to whom a disadvantage could be attributed. Considered from the complainant's standpoint, a higher frequency of police failure to comply with complainants of one race could be viewed as discrimination *against* that race. But police failure to write a crime report also lowers the likelihood that the offender will be subjected to the criminal process. Since we may assume that complainants more commonly are victims of offenses committed by members of their own race than by members of another race (Reiss, 1967), then disproportionate police failure to comply with complainants could be viewed as discrimination *in favor* of that race, considered from the offender's standpoint. Race differentials in arrest rates for crimes where there is an identifiable victim necessarily pose a similar dilemma of interpretation. Definitionally, there always is a conflict of legal interests between offenders and victims. Offender-victim relationships tend to be racially homogeneous. The social organization of crime therefore complicates questions of racial discrimination in law enforcement.[11]

Along social-class lines there is some evidence of discrimination against complainants and offenders. Table 3 shows that in felony situations the police are somewhat more likely to comply with white-collar complainants than with those of blue-collar status. In fact an official crime report resulted from every encounter between the police and a white-collar felony complainant of either race. The probability of official recognition drops to about three-fourths for blue-collar felony complainants. There does not appear to be a clear social-class differential in misdemeanor situations, however.

Only in felony situations, then, does an inference of discrimination offer itself. In these encounters the police seem to discriminate against blue-collar complainants. Moreover, when both white-collar and blue-collar complainants report felonious offenses, we should be able to assume that the offenders characteristically are of blue-collar status. There is every reason to believe, after all, that white-collar citizens rarely commit the common felonies such as burglary, robbery, and aggravated assault. A possible exception is auto theft, a crime in which youths from white-collar families occasionally indulge. Since this study was conducted in predominantly blue-collar residential areas the assumption should be all the more warranted. It would follow that the police discriminate against blue-collar citizens who feloniously offend white-collar citizens by being comparatively lenient in the investigation of felonies committed by one blue-collar citizen against another. In this instance the legal system listens more attentively to the claims of higher status citizens. The pattern is recorded in the crime rate.

Overview

The foregoing analysis yields a number of empirical generalizations about the production of crime rates. For the sake of convenience they may be listed as follows:

I. The police officially recognize proportionately more legally serious crimes than legally minor crimes.
II. The complainant's manifest preference for police action has a significant effect upon official crime-reporting.
III. The greater the relational distance between the complainant and the suspect, the greater is the likelihood of official recognition.
IV. The more deferential the complainant toward the police, the greater is the likelihood of official recognition of the complaint.
V. There is no evidence of racial discrimination in crime-reporting.
VI. There is some evidence that the police discriminate in favor of white-collar complainants, but this is true only in the official recognition of legally serious crime situations.

On the surface these findings have direct methodological relevance for those who would put official statistics to use as empirical data, whether to index actual crime in the population or to index actual police practices. Crime rates, as data, systematically underrepresent much crime and much police work. To learn some of the patterns by which this selection process occurs is to acquire a means of improving the utility of crime rates as data.

It should again be emphasized that these patterns of police behavior have consequences not only for official rates of detection as such; they also result in differential investigation of crimes and hence differential probabilities of arrest and conviction of criminal offenders. Thus the life chances of a criminal violator may depend upon who his victim is and how his victim presents his claim to the police. The complainant's role is appreciable in the criminal process. Surely the complainant has a central place in other legal and nonlegal control contexts as well, though there is as yet little research on the topic. Complainants are the consumers of justice. They are the prime movers of every known legal system, the human mechanisms by which legal services are routed into situations where there is a felt need for law. Complainants are the most invisible and they may be the most important social force binding the law to other aspects of social organization.

Notes

1 An approach that operationally defines criminal deviance as that which the police record as criminal—and nothing else—is immune to these problems. This would be the most radical "labeling" approach. It would exclude from the category of crime, for example, a murder carried out so skillfully that it goes undetected. It would necessarily exclude most "police brutality," since crimes committed by policemen are seldom detected and officially recorded as such.

2 In his definition of law, Hoebel (1954:28) notes that enforcement of law is a "socially recognized" privilege. In the same vein a crime rate may be understood as a socially recognized product of law enforcement work. Malinowski (1962:79–80) stresses the importance of social recognition of deviant acts for the community as well as for the deviant person.

3 The moral and physical organization of social life into public and private places guarantees contemporary society some volume of secret deviance (Schwartz, 1968; Lofland, 1969:62–68). As far as criminal deviance is concerned, other well-known factors are the failure of citizens to report victimizations to the police and the failure of the police to report what is reported to them.

Evidence from victimization surveys suggests that underreporting of crime in official statistics is more a consequence of police discretion than of the failure of citizens to notify the police. Citizens claim that they report far more crimes to the police than the police ultimately report; this margin of unreported crime exceeds that which citizens admit they withhold from the police (Biderman, 1967).

4 The "clearance rate" is a hybrid form of crime rate produced in American police systems. This is the proportion of "crimes known to the police" that have been solved, whether through arrest or some other means (see Skolnick, 1966:164–181).

5 It is interesting to note that in ancient Roman law the offender caught in the act of theft was subject to a more serious punishment than the offender apprehended some time after detection of his theft. In the *Laws of the Twelve Tables* these were called "manifest" and "non-manifest" thefts. The same legal principle is found in the early Anglo-Saxon and other Germanic codes (Maine, 1963:366–367). It could well be that a similar pattern is found in present-day law-in-action. What is formal in one legal system may be informal in another.

6 The heavier penalties that the law provides for felonies may compensate for a loss in deterrence that could result from the relatively low rate at which felons are apprehended. Likewise, the law of arrest seemingly compensates for the social organization of crime that gives felons a head start on the police. In most jurisdictions the police need less evidence in felony than in misdemeanor situations to make a legal arrest without warrant. By a second technique, then, the legal system increases the jeopardy of felony offenders. The power of substantive law increases as procedural restrictions on legal officials are weakened. By both penalty and procedure, the law pursues the felon with a special vengeance.

7   Crime situations were classified as felonies or misdemeanors according to legal criteria. These criteria were applied to the version of the crime that prevailed in the police-citizen transaction. The observation reports required the observer to classify the incident in a detailed list of categories as well as to write a long-hand description of the incident. The felony-misdemeanor breakdown was made during the coding stage of the investigation.

The major shortcoming of this strategy is that the tabulation allows no gradations of legal seriousness within the felony and misdemeanor categories. This shortcoming was accepted in order to facilitate more elaborate statistical analysis with a minimum of attrition in the number of cases.

It should also be noted that the tabulations do not provide information pertaining to the kind of official report the police wrote for a given kind of crime situation. Occasionally, the police officially characterize the crime with a category that seems incorrect to a legally sophisticated observer. Most commonly this involves reducing the legal seriousness of the crime. However, there are cases where the officer, sometimes through sheer ignorance of the law or inattention, increases the legal seriousness of the crime. In one case, for example, a woman complained about two young men in an automobile who had made obscene remarks to her as she walked along the street near her residence. She claimed she was prepared to press charges. After leaving the scene the officer filled out an official report, classifying the incident as an "aggravated assault," the felonious level of assault. Before doing so he asked the observer for his opinion as to the proper category. The observer feigned ignorance.

8   Here two general remarks about analytical strategy seem appropriate. One is that the present approach abdicates the problematics of psychological analysis. The observational study does not provide data on the motives or cognitions of the police or the citizens whose behavior is described. Still, findings on patterns of behavior make prediction of police behavior possible. They also offer opportunities for drawing inferences about the impact or implications of police work for social organization. Much can be learned about man's behavior in a social matrix without knowing how he experiences his behavior. The consequences of behavior, moreover, are indifferent to their mental origins.

Secondly, the strategy pursued in this analysis is not sensitive, except in the broadest terms, to the temporal dimension of police-citizen transactions. Thus, simply because the complainant's preference is treated prior to other variables does not mean that it is temporally prior to other aspects of police-citizen interaction. Like the other variables treated in this investigation, the complainant's preference is prior in time only to the final police response to the encounter.

9   Hall (1952:318) suggests that the relational distance between the victim and offender may influence the probability of *prosecution*. The present investigation, following Hall, seeks to predict social control responses from variations in relational distance. A different strategy is to predict community organization from the relationships between adversaries who enter the legal system, under the assumption that legal disputes bespeak a relative absence of informal control in the relational contexts where they arise (see Nader, 1964).

10   The findings in this section present a problem of interpretation, since no information about the police officer's behavior toward the citizen is provided apart from whether or not he wrote an official report. Therefore, nothing is known from the tabulation about whether the officer behaved in such a way as to *provoke* the citizen into one or another degree of deference. Nothing is known about the subtle exchange

of cues that takes place in any instance of face-to-face interaction. Other studies of the role of deference in police work are subject to the same criticism. Here, again, no inquiry is made into the motivational dimensions of the pattern. It nevertheless should be emphasized that whatever the motivation of the complainant behavior, the motivation was not the failure of the police to write an official report. In the cities studied the complainant ordinarily did not even know whether or not an official report was written, since the police ordinarily wrote the report in the police car or at the police station after leaving the encounter with the complainant. During the encounter they recorded the relevant facts about the incident in a notebook, whether or not they intended to write an official report. As some officers say, they do this "for show" in order to lead the complainant to believe they are "doing something." Thus, in the average case, it can be assumed that the complainant's deference is not a consequence of the situational outcome. Furthermore, the observers were instructed to record only the level of citizen deference that appeared prior to the situational outcome. A separate item was provided in the observation booklet for recording the citizen's manifest level of satisfaction at the close of the encounter. It therefore remains reasonable to hold that the complainant's deference can aid in calculating the probability of an official crime report.

11 It may seem that in criminal matters the costs are slight for the complainant when the police fail to comply with his preference for official action. However, it should be remembered that crimes frequently involve an economic loss for the victim, a loss that can sometimes be recouped if and when the offender is discovered. In other cases, discovery and punishment of the offender may net the victim nothing more than a sense of revenge or security or a sense that justice has been done—concerns that have received little attention in social science. For that matter, social scientists generally examine questions of discriminatory law enforcement *only* from the offender's standpoint. Ordinary citizens in high crime rate areas probably are more interested in questions of discrimination in police allocation of manpower for community protection.

References

Biderman, Albert D.
1967   "Surveys of population samples for estimating crime incidence." The Annals of the American Academy of Political and Social Science 374:16–33.
Biderman, Albert D. and Albert J. Reiss, Jr.
1967   "On exploring the 'dark figure' of crime." The Annals of the American Academy of Political and Social Science 374:1–15.
Bittner, Egon
1967   "The police on skid-row: A study of peace-keeping." American Sociological Review 32:699–715.
Black, Donald J.
1968   Police Encounters and Social Organization: An Observation Study. Unpublished Ph.D. Dissertation, Department of Sociology, University of Michigan.
Black, Donald J. and Albert J. Reiss, Jr.
1967   "Patterns of behavior in police and citizen transactions." Pp. 1–139 in President's Commission on Law Enforcement and Administration of Justice, Studies in Crime and Law Enforcement in Major Metropolitan Areas, Field

Surveys III, Volume 2. Washington, D. C.: U.S. Government Printing Office.
1970   "Police control of juveniles." American Sociological Review 35 (February): 63–77.

Cicourel, Aaron V.
1968   The Social Organization of Juvenile Justice. New York: John Wiley and Sons, Inc.

de Beaumont, Gustave and Alexis de Tocqueville
1964   On the Penitentiary System in the United States and Its Application in France. Carbondale, Ill.: Southern University Press. (orig. pub. 1833)

Erikson, Kai T.
1966   Wayward Puritans: A Study in the Sociology of Deviance. New York: John Wiley and Sons.

Goffman, Erving
1956   "The nature of deference and demeanor." American Anthropologist 58:473–502.
1963   Behavior in Public Places: Notes on the Social Organization of Gatherings. New York: The Free Press.

Hall, Jerome
1952   Theft, Law and Society. Indianapolis, Ind.: The Bobbs-Merrill Company. (2nd Ed.)

Hoebel, E. Adamson
1954   The Law of Primitive Man: A Study in Comparative Legal Dynamics. Cambridge: Harvard University Press.

Kitsuse, John I. and Aaron Cicourel
1963   "A note on the uses of official statistics." Social Problems 11:131–139.

LaFave, Wayne R.
1965   Arrest: The Decision to Take a Suspect into Custody. Boston: Little, Brown and Company.

Lofland, John
1969   Deviance and Identity. Englewood Cliffs, N.J.: Prentice-Hall.

Maine, Henry Sumner
1963   Ancient Law: Its Connection with the Early History of Society and Its Relation to Modern Ideas. Boston: Beacon Press. (orig. pub. 1861)

Malinowski, Bronislaw
1962   Crime and Custom in Savage Society. Paterson, N. J.: Littlefield, Adams and Co. (orig. pub. 1926)

Morrison, William Douglas
1897   "The interpretation of criminal statistics." Journal of the Royal Statistical Society 60:1–24.

Nader, Laura
1964   "An analysis of Zapotec Law cases." Ethnology 3:404–419.

Nader, Laura and Duane Metzger
1963   "Conflict resolution in two Mexican communities." American Anthropologist 65:584–592.

Piliavin, Irving and Scott Briar
1964   "Police encounters with juveniles." American Journal of Sociology 70:206–214.

Pound, Roscoe
1942   Social Control Through Law. New Haven: Yale University Press.

Reiss, Albert J., Jr.
1967   "Measurement of the nature and amount of crime." Pp. 1–183 in President's

Commission on Law Enforcement and Administration of Justice, Studies in Crime and Law Enforcement in Major Metropolitan Areas, Field Surveys III, Volume 1. Washington, D.C: U.S. Government Printing Office.

Schwartz, Barry
1968   "The social psychology of privacy." American Journal of Sociology 73:741–752.

Schwartz, Richard D.
1954   "Social factors in the development of legal control: A case study of two Israeli settlements." Yale Law Journal 63:471–491.

Sellin, Thorsten
1931   "Crime." Pp. 563–569 in Edwin R. A. Seligman (ed.), Encyclopaedia of the Social Sciences, Volume 4. New York: The Macmillan Company.

Skolnick, Jerome H.
1966   Justice Without Trial: Law Enforcement in Democratic Society. New York: John Wiley and Sons.

Stinchcombe, Arthur L.
1963   "Institutions of privacy in the determination of police administrative practice." American Journal of Sociology 69:150–160.

Westley, William A.
1953   "Violence and the police." American Journal of Sociology 59:34–41.

Wheeler, Stanton
1967   "Criminal statistics: A reformulation of the problem." Journal of Criminal Law, Criminology and Police Science 58:317–324.

Wilson, James Q.
1968   Varieties of Police Behavior: The Management of Law and Order in Eight Communities. Cambridge, Mass.: Harvard University Press.

Part two

Police

L aw enforcement is one of the major components of the criminal justice system. Its history, role, personalities, changes, status, and relation to the community it serves are examined in Part Two.

A thumbnail sketch of the history of local and state law enforcement in the United States is presented in Development of Local and State Law Enforcement. *The sheriff-constable-watchman system, which is in the Anglo-Saxon tradition of local community enforcement, was transplanted from England to the American colonies. By the early 1800s it was becoming increasingly evident that the night watch by itself was inadequate. This recognition led to the evolution of law enforcement from the night watch to both day and night watches, to their combination into a police force under a single chief, through the tangle of partisan politics in the developing city police systems, and finally to present-day city and state police forces.*

Too many academics find themselves attempting to teach professionalism in criminal justice without any practical experience. George Kirkham, a professor of criminology, thought it necessary to gain this experience. To do so he became a temporary patrolman. In A Professor's "Street Lesson" *he examines very lucidly his experiences and how they altered his ideas about the police, criminals, and crime victims. This article provides one of the most engaging examples of the necessity for some practical experiences by those teaching criminal justice.*

The Police Role *emphasizes that police are not separate from people and describes how a productive relationship between the people and the police can be established. The ultimate goal of such an association is developing a greater public trust in the police and a consequent reduction of crime through public cooperation.*

The Police Budget's Lot *reveals what law enforcement officials have long contended, that in terms of societal resources law enforcement has not gained as measured by expenditures since 1902. The expenditure changes between 1902 and the present are not due to the real increase in resources available to improve the quality of police efforts, but are due to the joint effect of components which are substantially independent of the changes in crime rates. These components are population, government inflation, urbanization, and motor vehicle increase. If the present-day police are more effective it is not because of greater financial resources but increased administrative and technological efficiency.*

The way in which a policeman looks at himself, either as a professional or merely as a person with a job, has an influence on his view of his responsibilities, his political and social outlook and his outlook toward the use of physical force. Professionalism and the Police *notes that there is no one set of factors but a number of social variables which produce the self-conception and its relation to occupational conception. The way in which situations and crises are handled by those with different occupational conceptions provide some perception into the factors which may have a bearing on the selection and training of police officers.*

Virgil W. Peterson

Development of local and
state law enforcement

The development of local and state law enforcement in
this country has followed a long, slow and tortuous path—a path
that leads back to early English history.

The Saxons brought to England a tribal system of justice which
relied heavily on community organization. People were divided into
groups of families in tens, called "tythings," headed by a "tything
man," and into larger groups, each of ten tythings, under a
"hundred-man" who was responsible to the "shire-reeve" (sheriff)
of the county. Thus each person was accountable to his group for
observing the laws, and the group, in turn, was responsible for the
individual's law-abiding behavior.

Following the Norman conquest in 1066, the Anglo-Saxon shires
and hundreds were continued for the purpose of local administration and for local justice under the sheriffs, who were subject to
removal by the king. The communities were held responsible for
maintaining order, and the sheriff was an essential link between
them and the central government. Eventually, the tithing man
became the parish constable and gradually many of the functions of
the sheriff were transferred to the Knights of the Shire who, in time,
became justices of the peace. The constable, as representative of
the people of the parish, was responsible to the justice of the peace.

In each parish, an unarmed, able-bodied citizen was appointed or
elected to serve as constable without pay for one year. In the towns,
the responsibility for law and order was vested not only in the
constable and the citizens generally, but in the guilds and other
groups who supplied bodies of men known as "The Watch" to
guard the gates and patrol the streets at night.

Reprinted from *Current History*, June 1971, pp. 327–334, with the permission of
Current History, Inc.

Citizens increasingly objected to performing the somewhat onerous and dangerous duties required of a constable. Eventually, the
right to appoint paid deputies to serve in their stead was granted.
The deputy constables developed into a professional class who sold
their services to one citizen after another. Often they worked in
league with the lawless elements. Corruption was prevalent. And
the night watchmen appointed to patrol the streets were frequently
feeble elderly men unfit for other work.

The American colonies

It was the sheriff-constable-watchman system that the colonists
transplanted to American shores following their settlement early in
the seventeenth century. From this base there evolved the 40,000
separate and independent police forces in the United States today.[1]

Forerunners of present day police forces in this country were
parish constables and night watchmen appointed by the colonists to
patrol the streets of towns at night and to cry out the time and give
the state of the weather.

The night watch

In 1636, a night watch was established in Boston and before long
almost every settlement in New England had at least a few
watchmen. Even in the Dutch town of New Amsterdam, later New
York City, an ordinance was passed on April 29, 1654, providing for
the establishment of a "rattle-watch" of from four to six men to
guard the city at night. Because of a lack of response on the part of
the residents, the watch was not placed into actual operation until
October, 1658.[2] After English rule was established, the Dongan
charter of 1686 provided for a high constable, sub-constables and
watchmen. Exercising supervision over the watchmen were the
constables elected from the various wards. In Philadelphia, a night
watchman was appointed by the provincial council in 1700 and a
system was initiated which required all citizens to take turns in
performing watch duties. In Boston, following a petition to the
general court in 1762, an act was passed which gave the selectmen
the right to choose a number of inhabitants, not to exceed 30, to

serve as watchmen. This provision, later reenacted, remained in force until Boston became a city in 1822.[3]

In the early 1800's, it became increasingly apparent that the night watch was inadequate to meet the needs of the time. The ranks of the professional watchmen were comprised largely of men who were employed at other jobs during the day time. Their selection was based on political considerations. The watch was organized by wards and districts, each operating independently of the other. In New York City, the watch service extended from 9 P.M. to sunrise and some watch captains interpreted sunrise at 3 A.M. while others insisted it was 5 A.M.

In Philadelphia, the will of Stephen Girard bequeathed a large sum of money to finance a competent police force for the city. As a result, an ordinance, passed in 1833, provided for a force of 24 policemen to serve in the day as well as 120 watchmen to serve at night. The control of the force was centralized in one officer, a captain, and eliminated the chaos which had stemmed from the district autonomy prevailing up to that time. However, only two years later, this ordinance was repealed and the city returned to the old system of district independence.

In 1838, Boston adopted a plan of forming a day force of six watchmen. Within eight years this force had grown to thirty. There was no connection, however, between the day force and the night watch of 150 men. In 1842, Cincinnati created a day watch of two men selected by the council. Eight years later the council provided for the election by popular vote of six day watchmen for each of the city's wards. In 1844, the day watch in New York City was comprised of 16 officers appointed by the mayor in addition to 108 for Sunday duty. The night watch, consisting of 1,100 watchmen, was completely separate from the day force. A third force in New York City was made up of 100 "mayor's marshals" who, with 34 constables of whom two were elected from each ward, served as general peace officers.[4]

In city after city, friction existed between two independent police forces—one for day and the other for night. It was an impossible arrangement, totally incapable of coping with increasing lawlessness in the cities. In 1844, the New York legislature passed an act which created a unified "day and night" force of 800 men for New York City and abolished the watch system altogether. Supervision of the force was vested in a chief of police, to be appointed by the mayor with the consent of the council. Opposition to the act by local officials resulted in much bickering and confusion for five months but on May 23, 1845, an ordinance was passed by the city fathers making the act effective. This action in New York formed the basis for modern police organization in the United States. Police forces under a single head were created in Chicago in 1851, in New Orleans and Cincinnati in 1852, in Baltimore and Newark in 1857 and in Providence in 1864. In Boston, the night watch which had been in existence over 200 years was consolidated with the day force in 1854 and a department of 250 men was created under the control of a chief of police to be appointed by the mayor.[5]

Partisan politics

The movement to consolidate day and night police forces under a single head, known as a chief or marshal, was a highly significant step in the development of police organization in American cities. But the road ahead to create efficient municipal police departments was long and rocky. And a principal stumbling block was partisan politics.

Under the New York law of 1844, policemen as well as their superior officers were appointed for one year only following nomination to their posts by aldermen and assistant aldermen of the wards to which they belonged. The chief of police was largely a figurehead with little, if any, authority over his force, a situation that has prevailed in many cities until modern times.[6] It was a common practice for political parties in power to use their police forces to control elections.

During the 1850's it was not uncommon for cities to provide for the popular election of the police department chief or marshal. This was true in Philadelphia, San Francisco, Chicago and Cleveland. In Brooklyn, the people not only elected the chief of police but the captains as well.[7]

It is not surprising that the heads of police departments were unable to maintain necessary discipline. Officers commonly defied departmental regulations and occasionally assaulted their superiors. For a long time there was great resistance to wearing uniforms. By 1855, a few communities required regulation hats and caps but no city at that time had a completely uniformed force. And when the New York City police required uniforms in 1856, each ward decided on its own style.[8]

Following the movement to consolidate day and night police forces, the departments of most cities were controlled by city councils for the greater part of a decade. In 1850, the administrative control of the Philadelphia department was vested in a police board consisting of the marshal and the presidents of town boards of communities within the police district. In 1853, New York City created an administrative body called the Board of Police Commissioners comprised of the mayor, recorder and city judge. For the next 48 years, the New York City department was in the hands of some form of police board.

Following the example of Philadelphia and New York City, other municipalities that created administrative boards with control over their police departments were New Orleans, in 1853, Cincinnati and San Francisco, in 1859, Detroit, St. Louis and Kansas City, in 1861, Buffalo and Cleveland, in 1866. In the decade beginning in 1870, almost all important cities experimented with some kind of police board.[9]

Police departments were generally inefficient; often corrupt. Frequently action by state legislatures to create boards to administer police departments was based on political considerations—struggles for power between state administrations controlled by one party and city administrations dominated by the other party.

By an act of the New York legislature on April 15, 1857, New York, Kings, Westchester and Richmond counties were combined into a Metropolitan Police District under the administration of a board of five commissioners appointed by the governor. The mayors of New York City and Brooklyn were ex-officio members of the board but they were subject to removal by the governor. Fernando Wood, mayor of New York City, refused to recognize the authority of the state-appointed police commissioners and on June 16, 1857, there was an open clash at city hall between members of the new Metropolitan force and the existing municipal department. Military forces were called in to quell the battle. Within a short time, the courts upheld the legality of the new Metropolitan Police District and Mayor Wood capitulated. In the interim, however, whenever a member of the Metropolitan force arrested a criminal, an officer of the municipal department would release him. And members of the two rival forces would battle each other with their clubs while the offender proceeded on his way unmolested.[10]

The Illinois state legislature, in February, 1861, enacted a law which established state control over the Chicago Police Department through the creation of a Board of three police commissioners. The board held its first meeting on the night of March 21, 1861. Chicago's mayor, Long John Wentworth, in defiance of the new law, summoned all men on the city force to his office at 2 A.M. and discharged them. Chicago, then overrun with criminals, was left with no police protection at all for a short time.[11]

Ostensibly, the purpose of placing the management of local police departments in state-controlled boards was to eliminate the influence of politics. In general, this goal was not achieved and there was much objection to state control because it violated the principle of local autonomy—home rule. By 1915, 12 of 23 cities having a population in excess of 250,000 had experimented with state-controlled police systems. By 1920, such systems had survived in only four—Baltimore, Boston, Kansas City and St. Louis.[12]

In 1931, the Wickersham Commission concluded that the underlying causes for general police ineffectiveness were the politicians' control of the chief which resulted in his insecurity and short term in office and the political favoritism which prevailed in the selection of patrolmen and other personnel. The commission related instances where underworld elements such as gamblers, through their political alliances, had named the chiefs of police of several large cities. In others, competent chiefs of police had been removed by the same influences. In the city of Detroit there had been four police heads in the preceding year. In Chicago, there were 14 chiefs of police in 30 years and the average tenure of office for police heads in cities of 500,000 population was only a fraction over 2 years.[13] Under such conditions, the development of outstanding leadership from within the ranks and the building of sound police organizations based on careful planning were virtually impossible.

An effective police operation includes not only competent personnel working under sound management policies but an efficient communications system and the equipment necessary to patrol the streets and pursue offenders. The Wickersham Commission reported in 1931 that based on its study, with perhaps two exceptions, not a single police force in cities above 300,000 population had "an adequate communication system and equipment essential . . . to meet the criminal on even equal terms." [14]

During the first two decades of the present century, the central siren, the telephone and call box constituted the sole means of communication between patrolmen on the street and headquarters. Some departments had a bell, a light or a horn installed on top of the call box to summon officers. A further advance in communications was the development of the teletype system. But the most important police communication system involved the radio. With the advent of the radio-equipped police car late in the 1920's there arrived a new era in police communication.

The first practical police radio installation was inaugurated in Detroit in 1928. A national study in 1931 disclosed that of cities in excess of 500,000 population, only one, Detroit, had police radio equipment and of all other cities of over 10,000 people, there were only 3 with such police installations. Of 390 cities studied, only 34 were equipped with teletype reception instruments.[15]

Today, there are few departments in cities of any size, as well as county and rural departments, that do not have police radio equipment. The development of efficient communication systems since 1930 has been phenomenal. For the year 1929, it was considered a remarkable feat that the Detroit department made 22,598 broadcasts which resulted in 1,325 arrests. In 1967, the Federal Bureau of Investigation established a National Crime Information Center in Washington, D.C., which maintains a computerized index of documented police information that is made available to all law enforcement agencies. At the end of the fiscal year 1970, the entries in the master computer totaled 2,032,150. On a single day, 63,246 transactions were handled and, at times, the hourly rate of messages from police departments located in all sections of the country exceeded 3,000.[16]

The development of a systematic plan to transmit criminal information throughout the United States had been a principal subject of discussion when the administrators of police departments held their first general conference in St. Louis in 1871. Other matters of primary concern were identification systems, criminal statistics and the formation of a permanent National Police Association which was reorganized in 1893 as the International Association of Chiefs of Police (I.A.C.P.).

A national clearinghouse

A national clearinghouse for criminal identification records was established by I.A.C.P. in 1896. The records consisted of photographs of known criminals and a system of anthropometric measurements devised by the French criminologist, Alphonse Bertillon, in 1882. Originally, the clearinghouse records were maintained in Chicago. After 1904, the Bertillon system was gradually replaced by fingerprints.

During the early years of the national bureau of criminal identification, it was supported by fees from less than 150 police forces and an occasional congressional appropriation of $500. This represented the first systematic attempt at cooperative activity in United States police work.

The I.A.C.P. entered into negotiations to have the federal government maintain the national identification bureau which was set up in 1924. The records of the national bureau were consolidated with those of federal prisoners maintained at Leavenworth, Kansas, and were transferred to Washington, D.C., under the jurisdiction of the F.B.I., where the fingerprint collection grew into the largest in the world.[17]

Although the compilation of crime statistics was of concern to the National Police Association at its first meeting in 1871, over a half century passed before a successful project was launched. In 1927, the I.A.C.P. organized a Committee on Uniform Crime Records, and a system of uniform crime statistics was developed. The first returns in January, 1930, included 400 police jurisdictions located in 43 states. On July 31, 1930, the entire system of uniform crime reports was transferred by the I.A.C.P. to the F.B.I., which assumed the role as the national clearinghouse and has published regular reports since that time.[18]

Scientific crime detection laboratories were virtually unknown when police administrators first gave attention to the need for adequate crime statistics, communication and identification systems. Crime laboratories had their origin in Europe and the first well-equipped police science laboratory was established on this continent in 1929 by private interests in Chicago working through Northwestern University. After a few years, the Northwestern University laboratory was acquired by the Chicago Police Department and major police departments throughout the country began establishing laboratories with technical staffs. Since 1933, the extensive facilities of the F.B.I. laboratory in Washington, D.C., have been made available to police agencies throughout the nation.[19]

Training programs

The American police were also slow to recognize the need for training programs. It was not until 1920 that training programs became common. In 1931, the Wickersham Commission reported that the establishment of the police school was perhaps the most important change that had taken place in the police world during the preceding 35 years. Yet, at that time in cities with a population under 10,000, nothing was being done which "by any stretch of the imagination could be considered police training." In 1935, the F.B.I. established the National Police Academy. Its extensive courses are attended by officers from all parts of the nation. One of its primary goals is to train instructors attached to local and state police schools. In recent years, police training has made rapid progress. Outstanding police academies have been established in some of the major cities. Inadequate training programs are still problems in many of the smaller municipalities.

The major burden for maintaining law and order in American cities and urban centers rests with our police departments. They have developed their present status largely without plan. Their structures represent a patchwork—the addition of a division here and a service there to meet some pressing need of the time.

In consequence, the quality of police service varies from city to city—some are inept and inefficient; others will compare favorably with the finest in the world. All had their origin in the English sheriff-constable system of colonial days. And as the United States became more and more urbanized, the sheriff as well as the constable deteriorated in significance as a factor in the overall law enforcement picture in this country.

About 40 per cent of the constitutions of our 50 states give recognition to the office of constable. Legally, there are more separate and distinct police units constructed around the office of constable than any other type. Yet the law enforcement activities of the constable have largely lapsed. In some places the citizens do not bother to elect constables because no one will accept the offices. Even in rural counties in some states, such as Illinois and New York, most constables perform no police duties of any kind. In smaller villages, the fee-compensated constable has been displaced by the full-time village policeman. At the present time, the office of constable has virtually no impact insofar as law enforcement is concerned.[20]

Office of sheriff

In county government, the sheriff is the principal law enforcement officer. Once the Anglo-Saxon King's steward, he was deprived of many of his judicial powers by the Magna Carta in 1215. By the beginning of the sixteenth century, the justices of the peace had secured control of local police systems in England and thereafter the law enforcement powers of the sheriff were progressively trimmed until they virtually disappeared.

Sheriffs and politics

The early American sheriff was a landed proprietor and his office was one of honor as well as profit. Since the United States was founded, the sheriff's office has been elective. Thus, the principal law enforcement officer of the county is directly involved in partisan politics.

The golden days of the sheriff occurred as the frontiers of America swept westward. His exploits in engaging in gunplay with outlaws and leading a posse to capture desperadoes were widely heralded and became embedded in the traditions of the Wild West.

Today, in many places the sheriff performs few, if any, law enforcement duties but confines himself to caring for the county jail and serving civil processes. In counties in which cities are located, the sheriff usually engages in law enforcement work only beyond the municipal boundaries or on rare occasions when the city police specifically request his aid.[21]

In 1931, the Wickersham Commission noted that partisan politics dictate the appointment of personnel to the sheriff's office. And with the handful of deputies to aid him, it was impossible for the sheriff to maintain any kind of adequate patrol. The commission concluded that "While there may be isolated examples of competent forces under this plan they are, at present, rare, and can hardly be expected to become the model for an extensive system." [22]

At the present time in the United States, there are 3,050 counties, each with a sheriff's office. These range in size from a one-man force in Putnam County, Georgia, to a 5,515-man force in Los Angeles. Of the 3,050 sheriff's offices, only 200 have a staff of more than 50 officers.[23]

A number of sheriff's offices have developed competent highway patrols with full law enforcement powers. And in some places there have been created county police forces that operate independently of the sheriff's office. This is true of the Nassau County Police Department in New York, which was established in 1925 and is the second largest police force in the state.

At the state level of government, the dominant law enforcement agencies are state police or highway patrols. Such organizations exist in all states except Hawaii.[24]

State-wide agencies

State-wide police agencies were slow to develop in the United States. In some respects, the forerunner of present day state police forces were the Texas Rangers, organized in 1835 by the provisional government of Texas. Originally, three Ranger companies were formed under the direction of the military service to guard the borders, a function that was performed for many years. Eventually, criminal investigation became a principal activity of the Rangers, and in 1935 the Texas Department of Safety took over control of this highly publicized force.

In 1865, Massachusetts appointed a few constables with state-wide powers to suppress vice. Since they were granted general police powers throughout the state, Massachusetts may be credited with having established the first state police force. Following recurrent legislation, the Massachusetts District of Police, a state detective unit, was formed in 1879. In 1903, Connecticut formed a small state force to suppress commercialized vice. Gradually it acquired the characteristics of a state detective force.

The origins of the modern state police

The establishment of the Pennsylvania State Police in 1905 marked the beginning of modern state police organization in this country. Governor Pennypacker, who became the chief executive in 1903, learned that while he had the duty to enforce the state laws, he was without any instrument to carry out his responsibilities. He therefore created the state police to serve as a general executive arm for the state, to cope with disturbed conditions in the coal and iron regions which local law enforcement officers had demonstrated an incapacity to handle, and to provide police protection in the rural districts where the sheriff-constable system had broken down.

The new superintendent of the state police was responsible only to the governor. His force, a mounted and uniformed body, operated out of troop headquarters and substations and adopted a policy of providing continuous patrol throughout the rural areas. It also pioneered in the field of police training. It was the first force in the country to provide a systematic police training program for its recruits.

The Pennsylvania State Police served as a pattern for the creation of state police organizations in several states. This was true of the New York State Police which was formed in 1917. The same year the Michigan State Police was hastily organized as a war measure and it acquired permanent status in 1919. Also formed in 1919 was a state police force in West Virginia.

In 1920, Massachusetts took steps to consolidate into the Department of Public Safety all state agencies, including its detective units, that had any relationship to public safety. At the same time it established a state-wide, uniformed patrol force patterned after the Pennsylvania State Police. State police forces were also formed in New Jersey in 1921 and in Rhode Island in 1925.

In 1927, Connecticut completed a series of changes which brought its state force more nearly into line with Pennsylvania. In 1929, a state force in Maine which had been created specifically to enforce the motor vehicle laws had its powers extended to include the maintenance of general police patrols and to conduct criminal investigations throughout the state.[25]

The creation of state forces with general law enforcement powers met with substantial opposition in many places, particularly from labor unions. Today, there are state police forces in twenty-five states and state highway patrols in twenty-four. The highway patrols are largely restricted to traffic law enforcement and conducting accident prevention programs. At the beginning of 1970, the forty-nine state police and highway patrols had a total personnel of 52,812.

At every level of government, there are special purpose law enforcement agencies that are independent of the traditional local and state police forces. They add to the problems of fragmentation, frequent duplicating and overlapping agencies which characterize the law enforcement structure all over the United States.

Of 40,000 federal, state and local law enforcement agencies in the United States, 39,750 are local. And the full-time personnel of local law enforcement comprises 83 per cent of the total. Obviously, throughout its history, the United States has continued to adhere to the old Anglo-Saxon tradition which relied heavily on local, community organization in law enforcement matters.

Notes

1 Charles Reith, *A Short History of The British Police* (London: Oxford University Press, 1948), pp. 1–9. The parish-constable system was in the process of deterioration in England at the time the colonists were settling America. With the advent of the Industrial Revolution and the social problems it created, the law enforcement machinery in London broke down completely. Lawlessness overwhelmed the populace. A new police system for England originated in 1829 with the passage of Sir Robert Peel's "Bill for Improving the Police in and near the Metropolis." Under the British system, the various police forces have been given unity through the influence of the Home Secretary, although the local governments have never relinquished control over their police forces.

2 A. E. Costello, *Our Police Protectors*, 2nd edition (New York: 1885), p. 10.

3 Raymond B. Fosdick, *American Police Systems* (New York: The Century Co., 1920), pp. 59, 60.

4 Ibid., pp. 62–65.

5 Ibid., pp. 66, 67.

6 See *Night Stick, the Autobiography of Lewis J. Valentine, Former Police Commissioner of New York* (New York: The Dial Press, 1947), p. 287. Valentine, a career policeman, who served with distinction as commissioner of police during the reform Fiorello LaGuardia administration, wrote that the time-honored rule is that the commissioner is "simply a king on sufferance. . . . With the exception of a few commissioners—thanks to a rare few honest city governments—the incumbents have been the playthings of rotten administrations."

7 Raymond B. Fosdick, pp. 74, 75.

8 Ibid., pp. 67–71.

9 Ibid., pp. 76–79.

10 Samuel Augustus Pleasants, *Fernando Wood of New York* (New York: Columbia University Press, 1948), pp. 77–83.

11 Virgil W. Peterson, *Barbarians in Our Midst* (Boston: Little, Brown & Co., 1952), pp. 29, 30.

12 Raymond B. Fosdick, p. 97. Subsequently, the power to appoint the head of the Boston Police Department was taken from the governor and vested in the mayor. Of the major police departments in the U.S. today, only Baltimore, Kansas City and St. Louis retain state-controlled systems. Beginning in 1864, a movement started to appoint bipartisan police boards whenever the board form of control had been adopted. Gradually, the whole plan of administrative control through boards was largely discarded and the bipartisan principle which was an outgrowth of the system shared the same fate. See Raymond B. Fosdick, *op. cit.*, pp. 89, 107.

13 National Commission on Law Observance and Enforcement, *Report on Police*, No. 14 (Washington, D.C.: U.S. Government Printing Office, 1931), pp. 1, 3, 4, 43, 44, 45, 51.

14 Ibid., p. 5.

15 Ibid., p. 88.

16 *Chicago Tribune,* Sunday, October 11, 1970.

17 Bruce Smith, *Police Systems in the United States* (New York: Harper & Bros., 1949), pp. 272–276.

18 Ibid., pp. 292, 293.

19 Ibid., pp. 279–281.

20 Ibid., pp. 90–100.

21 Ibid., pp. 75–84.

22 National Commission on Law Observance & Enforcement, *Report on Police,* No. 14 (Washington, D.C.: U.S. Government Printing Office, 1931), p. 128.

23 The President's Commission on Law Enforcement and Administration of Justice, *Task Force Report: The Police* (Washington, D.C.: U.S. Government Printing Office, 1967), pp. 8, 9.

24 James Cramer, *The World's Police* (London: Cassell & Co., Ltd. 1964), pp. 414, 415. In 1834, King Kamehameha, III, organized the first police force in Hawaii which consisted of a chief and two men. In 1843 a police corps for the Hawaiian islands was organized which consisted of a captain, a sergeant, a corporal and 24 privates. In 1845, the King appointed a marshal of the Hawaiian islands to supervise and control the sheriffs of the several islands appointed by the governors. In the same year, the police were incorporated into a military system of government. In the spring of 1850, all soldiers in the police force were removed and replaced by full-time police officers. The police force eventually became a tool of political parties and in 1932 a special session of the legislature created a police commission.

25 Bruce Smith, pp. 166–172, 296.

George L. Kirkham

A professor's "street lessons"

As policemen have come under increasing criticism by various individuals and groups in our society in recent years, I cannot help but wonder how many times they have clenched their teeth and wished they could expose their critics to only a few of the harsh realities which their job involves.

Persons such as myself, members of the academic community, have traditionally been quick to find fault with the police. From

Reprinted from *FBI Law Enforcement Bulletin,* March 1974, pp. 14–22.

isolated incidents reported in the various news media, we have fashioned for ourselves a stereotyped image of the police officer which conveniently conforms to our notions of what he is. We see the brutal cop, the racist cop, the grafting cop, the discourteous cop. What we do not see, however, is the image of thousands of dedicated men and women struggling against almost impossible odds to preserve our society and everything in it which we cherish.

For some years, first as a student and later as a professor of criminology, I found myself troubled by the fact that most of us who write books and articles on the police have never been policemen ourselves. I began to be bothered increasingly by many of my students who were former policemen. Time and again, they would respond to my frequently critical lectures on the police with the argument that I could not possibly understand what a police officer has to endure in modern society until I had been one myself. Under the weight of this frustration, and my personal conviction that knowledge has an applied as well as a theoretical dimension, I decided to take up this challenge: I would become a policeman myself as a means of establishing once and for all the accuracy of what I and other criminologists had been saying about the police for so long.

From professor to cop

Suffice it to say that my announced intention to become a uni-formed patrolman was at first met with fairly widespread disbelief on the part of family, friends, and colleagues alike. At 31, with a family and an established career as a criminologist, I was surely an unlikely candidate for the position of police recruit. The very idea, it was suggested to me, was outrageous and absurd. I was told that no police administrator in his right mind would allow a representative of the academic world to enter his organization. It had never been done and could not be done.

Fortunately, many of my students, who either had been police-men or were at the time, sounded a far more optimistic and enthusiastic note. Police administrators and officers alike, they said, would welcome the opportunity to expose members of the academic community to the problems of their occupation. If one of us were really willing to see and feel the policeman's world from behind a badge and blue uniform, instead of from the safe and comfortable vantage point of a classroom or university office, police officers themselves would do everything in their power to make the opportunity available. Despite these assurances from my police-men-students, I remained skeptical over my chances of being allowed to do such an unorthodox thing.

This skepticism was, however, soon to be overcome. One of my better criminology students at the time was a young police officer on educational leave from the Jacksonville, Fla., Sheriff's Office. Upon learning of my desire to become a police officer in order to better understand the problems of policemen, he urged me to contact Sheriff Dale Carson and Undersheriff D. K. Brown of his department with my proposal. I had earlier heard other police officers describe the consolidated 800-man force of Jacksonville-Duval County as one of the most progressive departments in the country. I learned that Sheriff Carson and Undersheriff Brown, two former FBI Agents, had won considerable respect in the law enforcement profession as enlightened and innovative administrators.

The size and composition of Jacksonville, as well as its nearness to my university and home, made it appear to be an ideal location for what I wished to do. Numbering just over one-half million residents, Jacksonville impressed me as being the kind of large and rapidly growing American city which inevitably experiences the major social problems of our time: crime and delinquency, racial unrest, poverty, and mental illness. A seaport and industrial center, Jacksonville offered a diversity of urban, suburban, and even rural populations in its vast land area. I took particular note of the fact that it contained a fairly typical inner-city slum section and black ghetto, both of which were in the process of being transformed through a massive program of urban redevelopment. This latter feature was especially important to me insofar as I wanted to personally experience the stresses and strains of today's city policeman. It was, after all, he who had traditionally been the subject of such intense interest and criticism on the part of social scientists such as myself.

Much to my surprise, both Sheriff Carson and Undersheriff Brown were not only supportive but enthusiastic as well over my proposal to become a city patrolman. I made it clear to them at the outset that I did not wish to function as an observer or reserve officer, but rather wanted to become a fully sworn and full-time member of their department for a period of between 4 and 6 months. I further stated that I hoped to spend most of this period working as a uniformed patrolman in those inner city beats most characterized by violence, poverty, social unrest, and high crime rates. They agreed to this, with the understanding that I would first have to meet the same requirements as any other police candidate. I would, for example, have to submit to a thorough character investigation, a physical examination, and would have to meet the same training standards applied to all other Florida police officers. Since I was to be unpaid, I would be exempted from departmental civil service requirements.

Restyling an image

Both Carson and Brown set about overcoming various administrative and insurance problems which had to be dealt with in advance of my becoming a police officer. Suppose, for example, I should be injured or killed in the line of duty, or should injure or kill someone else. What of the department and city's liability? These and other issues were gradually resolved with considerable effort on their part. The only stipulation set forth by both administrators was one with which I strongly agreed: for the sake of morale and confidence in the department, every officer must know in advance exactly who I was and what I was doing. Other than being in the unusual position of a "patrolman-professor," I would be indistinguishable from other officers in every respect, from the standard issue .38 Smith and Wesson revolver I would carry to the badge and uniform I would wear.

The biggest and final obstacle which I faced was the necessity that I comply fully with a 1967 Florida Police Standards law, which requires that every police officer and deputy sheriff in the State complete a minimum of 280 hours of law enforcement training prior to being sworn in and assigned to regular duty. Since I had a full-time university job nearly 200 miles from Jacksonville, this meant that I would be unable to attend the regular sheriff's academy. I would have to attend a certified academy in my own area, something which I arranged to do with Sheriff Carson's sponsorship.

For 4 months, 4 hours each evening and 5 nights a week, I attended the Tallahassee area police academy, along with 35 younger classmates. As a balding intellectual, I at first stood out as an oddity in the class of young men destined to become local law enforcement officers. With the passage of time, however, they came to accept me and I them. We joked, drank coffee, and struggled through various examinations and lessons together. At first known only as "the professor," the men later nicknamed me "Doc" over my good-natured protests.

As the days stretched into weeks and the weeks into months, I took lengthy notes on the interviewing of witnesses at crime scenes, investigated imaginary traffic accidents, and lifted fingerprints. Some nights I went home after hours of physical defense training with my uniformly younger and stronger peers with tired muscles, bruises, and the feeling that I should have my head examined for undertaking such a rugged project.

As someone who had never fired a handgun, I quickly grew accustomed to the noise of 35 revolvers firing at the cardboard silhouettes which our minds transformed into real assailants at the sound of the range whistle. I learned how to properly make car stops, approach a front door or darkened building, question suspects, and a thousand other things that every modern police officer must know. After what seemed an eternity, graduation from the academy finally came, and with it what was to become the most difficult but rewarding educational experience of my life: I became a policeman.

The school of hard knocks

I will never forget standing in front of the Jacksonville police station on that first day. I felt incredibly awkward and conspicuous in the new blue uniform and creaking leather. Whatever confidence in my ability to "do the job" I had gained during the academy seemed to evaporate as I stood there watching other blue figures hurrying in the evening rain toward assembly. After some minutes, I summoned the courage to walk into the station and into my new career as a core city patrolman.

That first day seems long ago now. As I write this, I have completed over 100 tours of duty as a patrolman. Although still a rookie officer, so much has happened in the short space of 6 months that I will never again be either the same man or the same scientist who stood in front of the station on that first day. While it is hard to even begin to describe within a brief article the many changes which have occurred within me during this time, I would like to share with fellow policemen and colleagues in the academic community a few of what I regard as the more important of what I will call my "street lessons."

I had always personally been of the opinion that police officers greatly exaggerate the amount of verbal disrespect and physical abuse to which they are subjected in the line of duty. During my first few hours as a street officer, I lived blissfully in a magic bubble which was soon to burst. As a college professor, I had grown accustomed to being treated with uniform respect and deference by those I encountered. I somehow naively assumed that this same quality of respect would carry over into my new role as a policeman. I was, after all, a representative of the law, identifiable to all by the badge and uniform I wore as someone dedicated to the protection of society. Surely that fact would entitle me to a measure of respect and cooperation—or so I thought. I quickly found that my badge and uniform, rather than serving to shield me from such things as disrespect and violence, only acted as a magnet which drew me toward many individuals who hated what I represented.

I had discounted on my first evening the warning of a veteran sergeant who, after hearing that I was about to begin work as a patrolman, shook his head and cautioned, "You'd better watch yourself out there, Professor! It gets pretty rough sometimes!" I was soon to find out what he meant.

Several hours into my first evening on the streets, my partner and I were dispatched to a bar in the downtown area to handle a disturbance complaint. Inside, we encountered a large and boisterous drunk who was arguing with the bartender and loudly refusing to leave. As someone with considerable experience as a correctional counselor and mental health worker, I hastened to take charge of the situation. "Excuse me, Sir," I smiled pleasantly at the drunk, "but I wonder if I could ask you to step outside and talk with me for just a minute?" The man stared at me through bloodshot eyes in disbelief for a second, raising one hand to scratch the stubble of several days' growth of beard. Then suddenly, without warning, it happened. He swung at me, luckily missing my face and striking me on the right shoulder. I couldn't believe it. What on earth had I done to provoke such a reaction? Before I could recover from my startled condition, he swung again—this time tearing my whistle chain from a shoulder epaulet. After a brief struggle, we had the still shouting, cursing man locked in the back of our cruiser. I stood there, breathing heavily with my hair in my eyes as I surveyed the damage to my new uniform and looked in bewilderment at my partner, who only smiled and clapped me affectionately on the back.

Theory vs. practice

"Something is very wrong," I remember thinking to myself in the front seat as we headed for the jail. I had used the same kind of gentle, rapport-building approach with countless offenders in prison and probation settings. It had always worked so well there. What was so different about being a policeman? In the days and weeks which followed, I was to learn the answer to this question the hard way. As a university professor, I had always sought to convey to students the idea that it is a mistake to exercise authority, to make decisions for other people, or rely upon orders and commands to accomplish something. As a police officer myself, I was forced time and again to do just that. For the first time in my life, I encountered individuals who interpreted kindness as weakness, as an invitation to disrespect or violence. I encountered men, women, and children who, in fear, desperation, or excitement, looked to the person behind my blue uniform and shield for guidance, control, and direction. As someone who had always condemned the exercise of authority, the acceptance of myself as an unavoidable symbol of authority came as a bitter lesson.

I found that there was a world of difference between encountering individuals, as I had, in mental health or correctional settings and facing them as the patrolman must: when they are violent, hysterical, desperate. When I put the uniform of a police officer on, I lost the luxury of sitting in an air-conditioned office with my pipe and books, calmly discussing with a rapist or armed robber the past problems which had led him into trouble with the law. Such offenders had seemed so innocent, so harmless in the sterile setting of prison. The often terrible crimes which they had committed were long since past, reduced like their victims to so many printed words on a page.

Now, as a police officer, I began to encounter the offender for the first time as a very real menace to my personal safety and the security of our society. The felon was no longer a harmless figure sitting in blue denims across my prison desk, a "victim" of society to be treated with compassion and leniency. He became an armed robber fleeing from the scene of a crime, a crazed maniac threatening his family with a gun, someone who might become my killer crouched behind the wheel of a car on a dark street.

Lesson in fear

Like crime itself, fear quickly ceased to be an impersonal and abstract thing. It became something which I regularly experienced. It was a tightness in my stomach as I approached a warehouse where something had tripped a silent alarm. I could taste it as a dryness in my mouth as we raced with blue lights and siren toward the site of a "Signal Zero" (armed and dangerous) call. For the first time in my life, I came to know—as every policeman knows—the true meaning of fear. Through shift after shift it stalked me, making my palms cold and sweaty, and pushing the adrenalin through my veins.

I recall particularly a dramatic lesson in the meaning of fear which took place shortly after I joined the force. My partner and I were on routine patrol one Saturday evening in a deteriorated area of cheap bars and pool halls when we observed a young male double-parked in the middle of the street. I pulled alongside and asked him in a civil manner to either park or drive on, whereupon he began loudly cursing us and shouting that we couldn't make him go anywhere. An angry crowd began to gather as we got out of our patrol car and approached the man, who was by this time shouting that we were harassing him and calling to bystanders for assistance. As a criminology professor, some months earlier I would have urged that the police officer who was now myself simply leave the car double-parked and move on rather than risk an incident. As a policeman, however, I had come to realize that an officer can never back down from his responsibility to enforce the law. Whatever the risk to himself, every police officer understands that his ability to back up the lawful authority which he represents is the only thing which stands between civilization and the jungle of lawlessness.

The man continued to curse us and adamantly refused to move his car. As we placed him under arrest and attempted to move him to our cruiser, an unidentified male and female rushed from the crowd which was steadily enlarging and sought to free him. In the ensuing struggle, a hysterical female unsnapped and tried to grab my service revolver, and the now angry mob began to converge on us. Suddenly, I was no longer an "ivory-tower" scholar watching typical police "overreaction" to a street incident—but I was part of it and fighting to remain alive and uninjured. I remember the sickening sensation of cold terror which filled my insides as I struggled to reach our car radio. I simultaneously put out a distress call and pressed the hidden electric release button on our shotgun rack as my partner sought to maintain his grip on the prisoner and hold the crowd at bay with his revolver.

How harshly I would have judged the officer who now grabbed the shotgun only a few months before. I rounded the rear of our cruiser with the weapon and shouted at the mob to move back. The memory flashed through my mind that I had always argued that policemen should not be allowed to carry shotguns because of their "offensive" character and the potential damage to community relations as a result of their display. How readily as a criminology professor I would have condemned the officer who was now myself, trembling with fear and anxiety and menacing an "unarmed" assembly with an "offensive" weapon. But circumstances had dramatically changed my perspective, for now it was *my* life and safety that were in danger, *my* wife and child who might be mourning. Not "a policeman" or Patrolman Smith—but *me*, George Kirkham! I felt accordingly bitter when I saw the individual who had provoked this near riot back on the streets the next night, laughing as though our charge of "resisting arrest with violence" was a big joke. Like my partner, I found myself feeling angry and frustrated shortly afterward when this same individual was allowed to plead guilty to a reduced charge of "breach of peace."

Loud defendants and silent victims

As someone who had always been greatly concerned about the rights of offenders, I now began to consider for the first time the rights of police officers. As a police officer, I felt that my efforts to protect society and maintain my personal safety were menaced by many of the very court decisions and lenient parole board actions I had always been eager to defend. An educated man, I could not answer the questions of my fellow officers as to why those who kill and maim policemen, men who are involved in no less honorable an activity than holding our society together, should so often be subjected to minor penalties. I grew weary of carefully following difficult legal restrictions, while thugs and hoodlums consistently twisted the law to their own advantage. I remember standing in the street one evening and reading a heroin "pusher" his rights, only to have him convulse with laughter halfway through and finish reciting them, word for word, from memory. He had been given his "rights" under the law, but what about the rights of those who were the victims of people like himself? For the first time, questions such as these began to bother me.

As a corrections worker and someone raised in a comfortable middle class home, I had always been insulated from the kind of human misery and tragedy which become part of the policeman's everyday life. Now, the often terrible sights, sounds, and smells of my job began to haunt me hours after I had taken the blue uniform and badge off. Some nights I would lie in bed unable to sleep, trying desperately to forget the things I had seen during a particular tour of duty: the rat-infested shacks that served as homes to those far less fortunate than I, a teenage boy dying in my arms after being struck by a car, small children clad in rags with stomachs bloated from hunger playing in a urine-spattered hall, the victim of a robbery senselessly beaten and murdered.

In my new role as a police officer, I found that the victims of crime ceased to be impersonal statistics. As a corrections worker and criminology professor, I had never given much thought to those who are victimized by criminals in our society. Now the sight of so many lives ruthlessly damaged and destroyed by the perpetrators of crime left me preoccupied with the question of society's responsibility to protect the men, women, and children who are victimized daily.

For all the tragic victims of crime I have seen during the past 6 months, one case stands out above all. There was an elderly man who lived with his dog in my apartment building downtown. He was a retired bus driver and his wife was long deceased. As time went by, I became friends with the old man and his dog. I could usually count on finding both of them standing at the corner on my way to work. I would engage in casual conversation with the old man, and sometimes he and his dog would walk several blocks toward the station with me. They were both as predictable as a clock: each evening around 7, the old man would walk to the same small restaurant several blocks away, where he would eat his evening meal while the dog waited dutifully outside.

One evening my partner and I received a call to a street shooting near my apartment building. My heart sank as we pulled up and I saw the old man's mutt in a crowd of people gathered on the sidewalk. The old man was lying on his back, in a large pool of blood, half trying to brace himself on an elbow. He clutched a bullet wound in his chest and gasped to me that three young men had stopped him and demanded his money. After taking his wallet and seeing how little he had, they shot him and left him on the street. As a police officer, I was enraged time and again at the cruelty and senselessness of acts such as this, at the arrogance of brazen thugs who prey with impunity on innocent citizens.

A different perspective

The same kinds of daily stresses which affected my fellow officers soon began to take their toll on me. I became sick and tired of being reviled and attacked by criminals who could usually find a most sympathetic audience in judges and jurors eager to understand their side of things and provide them with "another chance." I grew tired of living under the ax of news media and community pressure groups, eager to seize upon the slightest mistake made by myself or a fellow police officer.

As a criminology professor, I had always enjoyed the luxury of having great amounts of time in which to make difficult decisions. As a police officer, however, I found myself forced to make the most critical choices in a time frame of seconds, rather than days: to shoot or not to shoot, to arrest or not to arrest, to give chase or let go—always with the nagging certainty that others, those with great amounts of time in which to analyze and think, stood ready to judge and condemn me for whatever action I might take or fail to take. I found myself not only forced to live a life consisting of seconds and adrenalin, but also forced to deal with human problems which were infinitely more difficult than anything I had ever confronted in a correctional or mental health setting. Family fights, mental illness, potentially explosive crowd situations, dangerous individuals—I found myself progressively awed by the complexity of tasks faced by men whose work I once thought was fairly simple and straight-forward.

Indeed, I would like to take the average clinical psychologist or psychiatrist and invite him to function for just a day in the world of the policeman, to confront people whose problems are both serious and in need of immediate solution. I would invite him to walk, as I have, into a smoke-filled pool room where five or six angry men are swinging cues at one another. I would like the prison counselor and parole officer to see their client Jones—not calm and composed in an office setting, but as the street cop sees him—beating his small child with a heavy belt buckle, or kicking his pregnant wife. I wish that they, and every judge and juror in our country, could see the ravages of crime as the cop on the beat must: innocent people cut, shot, beaten, raped, robbed, and murdered. It would, I feel certain, give them a different perspective on crime and criminals, just as it has me.

Humaneness in uniform

For all the human misery and suffering which police officers must witness in their work, I found myself amazed at the incredible humanity and compassion which seems to characterize most of them. My own stereotypes of the brutal, sadistic cop were time and again shattered by the sight of humanitarian kindness on the part of the thin blue line: a young patrolman giving mouth to mouth resuscitation to a filthy derelict; a grizzled old veteran embarrassed when I discovered the bags of jelly beans which he carried in the trunk of his car for impoverished ghetto kids—to whom he was the closest thing to an Easter Bunny they would ever know; an officer giving money out of his own pocket to a hungry and stranded family he would probably never see again; and another patrolman taking the trouble to drop by on his own time in order to give worried parents information about their problem son or daughter.

As a police officer, I found myself repeatedly surprised at the ability of my fellow patrolmen to withstand the often enormous daily pressures of their work. Long hours, frustration, danger, and anxiety—all seemed to be taken in stride as just part of the reality of being a cop. I went eventually through the humbling discovery that I, like the men in blue with whom I worked, was simply a human being with definite limits to the amount of stress I could endure in a given period of time.

I recall in particular one evening when this point was dramatized to me. It had been a long, hard shift—one which ended with a high-speed chase of a stolen car in which we narrowly escaped serious injury when another vehicle pulled in front of our patrol car. As we checked off duty, I was vaguely aware of feeling tired and tense. My partner and I were headed for a restaurant and a bite of breakfast when we both heard the unmistakable sound of breaking glass coming from a church and spotted two long-haired teenage boys running from the area. We confronted them and I asked one for identification, displaying my own police identification. He sneered at me, cursed, and turned to walk away. The next thing I knew I had grabbed the youth by his shirt and spun him around, shouting, "I'm talking to you, punk!" I felt my partner's arm on my shoulder and heard his reassuring voice behind me, "Take it easy, Doc!" I released my grip on the adolescent and stood silently for several seconds, unable to accept the inescapable reality that I had "lost my cool." My mind flashed back to a lecture during which I had told my students, "Any man who is not able to maintain absolute control of his emotions at all times has no business being a police officer." I was at the time of this incident director of a human relations project designed to teach policemen "emotional control" skills. Now here I was, an "emotional control" expert, being told to calm down by a patrolman!

A complex challenge

As someone who had always regarded policemen as a "paranoid" lot, I discovered in the daily round of violence which became part of my life that chronic suspiciousness is something that a good cop cultivates in the interest of going home to his family each evening. Like so many other officers, my daily exposure to street crime soon had me carrying an off-duty weapon virtually everywhere I went. I began to become watchful of who and what was around me, as things began to acquire a new meaning: an open door, someone loitering on a dark corner, a rear license plate covered with dirt. My personality began to change slowly according to my family, friends, and colleagues as my career as a policeman progressed. Once quick to drop critical barbs about policemen to intellectual friends, I now became extremely sensitive about such remarks—and several times became engaged in heated arguments over them.

As a police officer myself, I found that society demands too much of its policemen: not only are they expected to enforce the law, but to be curbside psychiatrists, marriage counselors, social workers, and even ministers, and doctors. I found that a good street officer combines in his daily work splinters of each of these complex professions and many more. Certainly it is unreasonable for us to ask so much of the men in blue; yet we must, for there is simply no one else to whom we can turn for help in the kind of crises and problems policemen deal with. No one else wants to counsel a family with problems at 3 a.m. on Sunday; no one else wants to enter a darkened building after a burglary; no one else wants to confront a robber or madman with a gun. No one else wants to stare poverty, mental illness, and human tragedy in the face day after day, to pick up the pieces of shattered lives.

As a policeman myself, I have often asked myself the questions: "Why does a man become a cop?" "What makes him stay with it?" Surely it's not the disrespect, the legal restrictions which make the job increasingly rough, the long hours and low pay, or the risk of being killed or injured trying to protect people who often don't seem to care.

The only answer to this question I have been able to arrive at is one based on my own limited experience as a policeman. Night after night, I came home and took off the badge and blue uniform with a sense of satisfaction and contribution to society that I have never known in any other job. Somehow that feeling seemed to make everything—the disrespect, the danger, the boredom—worthwhile.

An invaluable education

For too long now, we in America's colleges and universities have conveyed to young men and women the subtle message that there is somehow something wrong with "being a cop." It's time for that to stop. This point was forcibly brought home to me one evening not long ago. I had just completed a day shift and had to rush back to the university with no chance to change out of uniform for a late afternoon class. As I rushed into my office to pick up my lecture notes, my secretary's jaw dropped at the sight of the uniform. "Why, Dr. Kirkham, you're not going to go to class looking like *that*, are you?" I felt momentarily embarrassed, and then struck by the realization that I would not feel the need to apologize if I appeared before my students with long hair or a beard. Free love advocates and hate-monger revolutionaries do not apologize for their group memberships, so why should someone whose appearance symbolizes a commitment to serve and protect society? "Why not," I replied with a slight smile, "I'm proud to be a cop!" I picked up my notes and went on to class.

Let me conclude this article by saying that I would hope that other educators might take the trouble to observe firsthand some of the policeman's problems before being so quick to condemn and pass judgment on the thin blue line. We are all familiar with the old expression which urges us to refrain from judging the worth of another man's actions until we have walked at least a mile in his shoes. To be sure, I have not walked that mile as a rookie patrolman with barely 6 months' experience. But I have at least tried the shoes on and taken a few difficult steps in them. Those few steps have given me a profoundly new understanding and appreciation of our police, and have left me with the humbling realization that possession of a Ph.D. does not give a man a corner on knowledge, or place him in the lofty position where he cannot take lessons from those less educated than himself.

National Advisory Commission on Criminal Justice Standards and Goals

The police role

The police in the United States are not separate from the people. They draw their authority from the will and consent of the people, and they recruit their officers from them. The police are the instrument of the people to achieve and maintain order; their efforts are founded on principles of public service and ultimate responsibility to the public.

This chapter describes the way a productive relationship between the people and their police can be established. The standards propose broad functional objectives. The ultimate goal toward which all the standards are directed is greater public trust in the police and a resulting reduction in crime through public cooperation.

To a police officer, public service is more than a vague concept. When people need help, it is to a police officer that they are most likely to turn. He responds—immediately—without first ascertaining the status of the person in need. It does not matter if that person is rich or poor; he need not meet complicated criteria to qualify as a recipient of aid or as a potential client.

Reprinted from *Police*, Washington, D.C.: U.S. Govt. Printing Office, 1973, pp. 9–11.

Decisionmaking

Police officers are decisionmakers. A decision—whether to arrest, to make a referral, to seek prosecution, or to use force—has a profound effect on those a police officer serves. Most of these decisions must be made within the span of a few moments and within the physical context of the most aggravated social problems. Yet, the police officer is just as accountable for these decisions as the judge or corrections official is for decisions deliberated for months.

The role the police officer plays in society is a difficult one; he must clearly understand complex social relationships to be effective. He is not only a part of the community he serves, and a part of the government that provides his formal base of authority, he is also a part of the criminal justice system that determines what course society will pursue to deter lawbreakers or rehabilitate offenders in the interest of public order.

Although the police service is a formal element of local government, it is responsible to the people in a more direct way. The specific goals and priorities which the police establish within the limits of their legislatively granted authority are determined to a large extent by community desires. These desires are transmitted to the police through the community and the governing body of the jurisdiction in which the police operate. For example, elements of the community might urge increased patrols around schools, stricter enforcement of parking regulations in congested areas, or reduced enforcement activities against violations of certain crimes. The priorities established by police agencies in such cases are often influenced more by the wishes of those policed than by any other consideration. The police officer is accountable to the people for his decisions and the consequences. The success of his mission depends to a great extent on the support of the people.

Police responsibility

In the exercise of its police power, government enacts laws designed to protect the health, welfare, and morals of its citizens. Under this Nation's form of government, police power is exercised by the States and their political subdivisions in the promulgation of laws and regulations concerning building and safety, zoning, health, noise and disturbance, disorderly conduct, and traffic regulations. Repeated and willful violation of these regulations is generally considered criminal conduct.

Each State has developed a comprehensive criminal code defining crimes and providing punishments. Responsibility for the enforcement of these laws, however, has been largely delegated to local government.

Although local government provides many services the police are its most visible representatives. Because they are the agents of government who are most frequently in contact with the public, and because they are accessible around-the-clock, police are often contacted regarding services provided by other municipal, county, State, and Federal agencies.

Often the public does not differentiate between various elements of local government. An irate citizen is simply concerned that he is not receiving a service to which he feels entitled. If he is bewildered by the profusion of government divisions, he turns to the one most familiar and most recognizable—the police. Because their service to the citizen affects his respect for government in general and the police in particular, police should respond as helpfully as possible, even if the matter is outside their immediate jurisdiction.

Criminal justice process

Through the identification and arrest of a suspected offender, the police initiate the criminal justice process. The individual's guilt or innocence is then determined in the courts. If the individual is found guilty, an attempt is made to rehabilitate him through a corrections process that may include probation, confinement, parole, or any combination of these.

While each of the elements of the criminal justice system is organizationally separate, these elements are functionally interrelated. In most cases, for example, the police act before the other elements of the system. The subsequent release of an otherwise guilty person from custody because a court found the evidence necessary for his conviction to be unlawfully seized, the reluctance of a prosecutor to present a case for court determination, or the failure of corrections to reform a convict prior to his release, have a direct effect upon the manner and conditions in which the police must perform their tasks.

A very high percentage of police work is done in direct response to citizen complaints. This underlines the frequently unrecognized fact that members of the public are an integral part of the criminal justice system; in fact, the success of the system depends more on citizen participation than on any other single factor.

The police are the criminal justice element in closest contact with the public; as a result, they are often blamed for failures in other parts of the system. In like manner, public confidence in the criminal justice system depends to a large extent on the trust that the people have in their police.

The police, the criminal justice system, and government in general could not control crime without the cooperation of a substantial portion of the people. In the absence of public support, there would be little that an army could not do better than the police.

Community relations

Currently, the relationship in most communities between the police and the public is not entirely satisfactory. Members of the public frequently do not notify the police of situations that require enforcement or preventive action. Often, they avoid involvement in averting or interfering with criminal conduct, and many are suspicious of the police, the criminal justice system, and the entire political process.

During the 20 years following World War II, the police became increasingly isolated from their communities. Reasons for this isolation include urbanization, rapidly changing social conditions, greater demands for police services, increased reliance by the police on motorized patrol, police efforts to professionalize, and reduced police contact with noncriminal elements of society. These factors, combined with public apathy, caused many police agencies to attempt to combat rising crime without actively involving their communities in their efforts.

Due in large part to the widespread riots in the sixties, and the report of the President's Commission on Law Enforcement and Administration of Justice, many police agencies reassessed their role and made changes that resulted in greater community involvement in crime control. Police agencies throughout the Nation have significantly improved their ability to deal with crime and disorder. They have also taken great strides in responding to the demands of their communities for greater service involvement and responsiveness. Perhaps more than any other institution, the police have advanced their ability to cope with rapidly changing social conditions.

In less than 10 years, the nature of debate in the police service has changed. The question no longer is, "Should we be involved in nonenforcement programs?" Now the question is, "How should we be involved in them?" As is usual during any time of great change, experimentation has resulted in both success and failure.

In attempting to reduce tension and improve their relationships with the public, the police have experimented with innovative programs. In some communities policemen wear blazers instead of the traditional military-type uniform, operate storefront offices, discuss local problems at neighborhood "coffee klatches," and engage in "rap sessions" with juveniles.

Inside and outside the service, there is little agreement on the role of the police. While one citizen group demands more nonenforcement programs, another demands that police devote all resources to direct protection and vigorous enforcement. Lack of manpower and fiscal resources has caused delay or abandonment of many programs to improve police-community relations, and the police have had to assign priorities to the delivery of direct protection services.

Programs

Attempts to involve the community in programs to prevent crime and improve police-community relations have often been met by both public apathy and resistance within police agencies. Middle managers and police officers, accustomed to taking public support for granted and dealing primarily with law violators, had little faith in nonenforcement programs. Members of the public, accustomed to relying upon the police to deal with crime, were slow to respond to public involvement programs. However, there are many successful programs, and relations between the people and the police have improved.

A program is defined as the planning, development, and implementation of specific solutions to identified problems. These solutions should take the form of organizational goals and objectives rather than specific activities. Where programs are constructed of specific activities rather than goals and objectives, implementation tends to be delegated to a specialized person or group rather than to all employees. Such programs tend to be uncoordinated with other agency efforts and are often, from the outset, destined for failure.

The broad objectives of most nonenforcement programs have been improved police-community relations, reduced tension, and greater mutual understanding between the police and the people. Functional objectives vary, however. Some programs appear to be primarily educational, while others are designed to prevent specific crimes or to improve communications.

The success of a nonenforcement program is often determined by the number of people involved or by the absence of unfavorable incidents. Programs that do not produce results that justify their cost may still be difficult to discontinue. In these cases, administrators may be reluctant to admit failure or they may fear the criticism that the program was merely window dressing. However, programs that were planned on a cost-effective basis with identified functional objectives, built-in methods for measuring effectiveness, and suggested alternatives in case of failure, have produced significant and lasting results.

David J. Bordua
Edward W. Haurek

The police budget's lot:
components of the increase in local police expenditures, 1902–1960

From 1902 to 1960, annual local police expenditures in the United States went from $50,000,000 to $1,612,000,000 (U.S. Bureau of the Census, 1960; 1965). This is a spectacular increase of $1,562,000,000 or 31.24 times the amount spent in 1902. The initial impression from these data is that the increased expenditure for

The authors wish to thank Otis Dudley Duncan, Robert E. Kennedy, Jr., and Gene F. Summers for critical comments on earlier drafts of this paper.

Reprinted here from *American Behavioral Scientist* 13 (May–August 1970), pp. 667–680, with the permission of Sage Publications and David J. Bordua.

local police activities reflects a very large increment in public investment in the traditional police function of criminal law enforcement. Such an impression can lead to the conclusion that the dramatic expenditure increase provides the local police with much greater financial resources that they can translate into more effective law enforcement. A more ominous interpretation of rising police expenditures has been that this increase is the necessary response to a rise in national crime rates. Thus, it has been argued that increasing police expenditures are one of the "costs" of rising crime rates (President's Commission on Law Enforcement, 1967: 53).

Major premises

This paper will attempt to demonstrate that the expenditure change is not due to a real increase in resources available to improve the quality of police efforts in the area of criminal law enforcement, and that it is due to the joint effect of components which are largely independent of changes in crime rates. These components are population growth, inflation, urbanization, and motor vehicle increase. The preceding statement can be considered the major hypothesis of the paper.

A second purpose of the authors is to illustrate that the use of fiscal data and analysis with relatively simple control and standardization techniques is a useful approach to understanding social phenomena of this type (see, for example, Barclay, 1958: 161–162). In a market economy, fiscal expenditures are excellent indicators of the process of societal resource allocation. More importantly, these data often are readily available, and yet they have been largely ignored by sociologists.

It is apparent that if expenditures increased simply to cope with a larger crime problem due to population growth, the *quality* of law enforcement as measured by per capita expenditure would not have increased. A second possible component of the increase in expenditure is inflation. Police expenditures are especially susceptible to the effects of inflation because a very large proportion is for wages and salaries, and it is the rising cost of labor that has mainly contributed to inflation.[1] The third possible component of the expenditures increase is the change since 1902 of the proportion of population residing in urban areas. This component is independent of population growth. The size-of-place distribution of the population is important for analysis of police expenditures because it has been consistent through time that expenditures for police services are a function of size of place.

This may be illustrated with ratios of police employees to population. In 1907, cities with over 300,000 population had 19.4 officers, detectives, and patrolmen per 10,000 inhabitants while cities with 30,000 to 50,000 inhabitants had 10.5 per 10,000 inhabitants (U.S. Bureau of the Census, 1907: 394). In 1960 this differential still exists. Cities over 500,000 population had a median of 24.9 police employees per 10,000 population, and cities with population of 25,000 to 50,000 had 13.8 police employees per 10,000 population (International City Manager's Association, 1961: 396). The increased use of police personnel as city size increases reflects the greater expenditure for law enforcement in urban areas.

The fourth component of expenditure increases studied is the growth of motor vehicle use and the concomitantly higher proportion of police resources devoted to traffic control. Data necessary for computing the effects of this last component are very limited. However, a reasonable approximation can be made for the expected police expenditure in 1960 if per capita motor vehicle registration had not increased since 1902.

Findings

To improve the clarity of presentation of the central argument, details of computations, assumptions, and data sources are presented in the Appendix. Table 1 summarizes the findings. The joint effect of population growth, inflation, urbanization, and motor vehicle increase was determined by calculating the expected expenditures in 1960 if none of the four had occurred since 1902. These expected expenditures are $44 million which is *less* than the $50 million which was actually expended in 1902. The net decrease may be interpreted as signifying that the nominal increases since 1902 in local police expenditures have been explained by the operation of the 4 components studied. Of much greater significance is the interpretation that the local police have not received increases in resources that have kept pace with the increased demands that social changes have placed upon them and the input of resources available for criminal law enforcement into the police

Table 1 **Components of increase in local police expenditures: 1902–1960**

| | | Effect of single components | | |
Item	Amount (millions)	Percentage of increase	Multiple of urbanization
1960 Unadjusted expenditures	$1,612	. . .	. . .
1960 Expected expenditures	44	. . .	. . .
1960 Expenditures due to components jointly	1,568	100	. . .
Due to inflation	718	46	5.52
Due to population growth	453	29	3.48
Due to motor vehicles	267	17	2.05
Due to urbanization	130	8	1.00

function is *less today* than at the turn of the century. Some implications of this finding are discussed in the conclusions.

Subtracting the $44 million expected 1960 expenditure from the unadjusted 1960 total of $1,612 million leaves $1,568 million of nominal increase accounted for by the 4 components jointly. The relative weight of each component in contributing to the increase from 1902 to 1960 when all components are jointly operating is expressed in percentages of the total increase accounted for and in multiples of the least important component—urbanization.

Conclusions

The implications suggested by the analysis are numerous, but the authors will limit themselves to a few. After the four components of increase are taken into account, it appears that local police departments have not made any gains since 1902 in terms of societal resources (as measured by expenditures) available to them. Therefore, any conclusions that local police must be more effective today than at the turn of the century, because of a large increase in financial resources available to them, are unwarranted. This is not to deny the possibility that the police may have become more effective. However, the source of such increased effectiveness would be, not greater financial resources, but increased administrative and technological efficiency. The potential of increased police productivity through investment of a larger proportion of their financial resources in technological development has the seeming limit that policing is fundamentally a labor-intensive activity. Both at the turn of the century and in 1960, the percentage of police expenditures that was consumed by wages and salaries was about ninety percent. This allows only ten percent of expenditures to be invested in capital equipment which is a major source of increased technological productivity. The productivity benefits of patrol cars, two-way radios, computerization, and the like, cannot be denied. However, the potential of productivity increases from technological innovations appears more limited for policing than for other societal activities which are less labor intensive and are continually becoming less so.

LABOR

Two examples, although not entirely comparable, suffice to point out the gross contrast between the greater labor intensity of policing and other societal activities. In 1960, the total expenditure for salaries of the instructional staffs of public elementary and secondary schools was forty-nine percent of the total expenditures in this area of education. National defense provides a more extreme contrast. In 1965, the federal budget expenditure for military personnel was thirty-two percent of the total budget of the Department of Defense. Even more pertinent, the cost category of "research, development, test and evaluation" was fourteen percent of the total defense budget (U.S. Bureau of the Census, 1966: tables 164, 353). The fourteen percent of the total defense budget consumed by this item alone is greater than the ten percent of police expenditures that must cover all nonsalary costs.

The labor-intensive character of police work coupled with a lack of gain in financial resources makes the efforts of the police "professionalizers" more understandable. Technical development and administrative reorganization become the main foci of efforts to increase effective police resources because those changes seem the major sources of increased police labor productivity. One may speculatively suggest that if the police are even as effective today as in 1902, it is only because they have incorporated administrative and technological innovations which have offset the net decrease of financial resources.

The hypothesis of this paper was in part that the increases in police expenditures were largely independent of any rise in crime rates, and, therefore, the increasing police expenditures could not be legitimately considered a "cost" of rising crime rates. Inflation and traffic control are clearly independent of crime rates in the standardization technique utilized. Population growth would not in itself result in an increase in *per capita* crime rates. These three components alone account for more than ninety percent of the increase without reference to changing crime rates, and the hypothesis is considered confirmed at this point.

URBANIZATION

The control for urbanization did eliminate the effects on police expenditures due to rising national crime rates which might result from a larger proportion of the population living in urban areas which are in turn assumed to have higher crime rates. Even if the crime rates specific to size of place remained the same in 1960 as in 1902, the national crime rate would have risen if the 1902 urban crime rates were higher than the rural rates. Therefore, urbanization is not entirely independent of changing national crime rates. However, it should be noted that urbanization accounted for only eight percent of the expenditure increases and was the least important of the four components. Moreover, whether to attribute this proportion entirely to higher urban than rural crime rates is a moot question.

The authors can only state with any certitude that this proportion of explained expenditure increase is due to the traditionally higher per capita police expenditures in urban areas. It is also reasonable to assume that this higher per capita expenditure partially reflects a higher urban crime rate. To maintain that the higher urban expenditure *only* reflects higher urban crime rates is, however, very dubious. Urban life differs from rural life in many more dimensions which could influence police expenditures than just in crime rates, though the analysis does not identify or control the effects of these dimensions upon expenditures. Therefore, only a part of the already small proportion of expenditure increases accounted for by urbanization can be safely attributed to increasing national crime rates, assuming size-of-place specific rates remain constant over the period.

The control for urbanization as operationalized in this paper did *not* eliminate the possible effects that any assumed increases in size-of-place specific crime rates have upon police expenditures. Such effects would therefore be included in the remaining $44 million expended in 1960. Data necessary for the analysis of the effects of possible changes in urban crime rates since 1902 are not available. However, if increases in urban crime rates were added to the four components, such increases could only approach the explanatory power of population growth, inflation and motor vehicles if the expected amount of resources remaining to the police were far less in 1960 than the already low figure of $44 million. Yet, these far fewer remaining resources would still have to cope with law enforcement problems of the same magnitude as 1902, because the model utilized here standardizes upon 1902 conditions.

This additional hypothetical decrease in resources, while coping with the same magnitude problem, at the 1902 level of effectiveness, would have had to be absorbed by a remarkable increase in police efficiency or by some sort of "surplus" available to police. A "surplus" would be available if the police had been able to eliminate some responsibilities which are costly but unrelated to law enforcement. If one assumes that increased efficiency or an available surplus are not adequate to absorb a further reduction in "net" resources, one is tempted to speculate that local policing in 1960 was "underfinanced" by 1902 standards or was less effective than in 1902. The authors forego this temptation and suggest instead that increases in crime rates have been unduly emphasized as a major component of increasing police costs.

Moreover, it seems appropriate to question any scheme of social accounting that allocates the growth in local police expenditures as an increase in the cost of crime. Given the results of our analysis, it is much more sensible to say that as far as local law enforcement costs are concerned, the per capita, deflated "cost" of the average crime may well have decreased since 1902—a result which should redound to the credit of the police professionalization movement.

We may draw out one final implication of the analysis. Faced with the real budgetary limitations documented in this paper, it is not surprising, as we have mentioned, that police reformers have turned to organizational modernization—technological innovation and managerial sophistication—as cost-reducing devices. Such devices have had—in the minds of some observers at least—the consequence of making police work less personal, more withdrawn from parts of the community, and less sensitive to the variety of human situations (Bordua, 1968; Tifft and Bordua, 1969; Wilson, 1968: ch. 9 esp.).

Suggestions for dealing with these consequences of modernization all seem to involve more manpower used less "efficiently" from a cost viewpoint. Clearly, developments in this direction will require substantial changes in the pattern of investment in police service that has prevailed thus far in this century.

Appendix

COMPUTATIONAL PROCEDURES

Controlling for inflation The 1960 expenditures were divided into two parts. Ninety percent of the $1,612 million expenditures in 1960, or $1,451 million, was classified as police salaries and wages and the remaining $161 million as expenditures for all other police purchases of goods and services. This 90% estimate of expenditures for salaries is based upon the total police expenditure of 1,303 cities with over 10,000 population in 1960 of which 90% was for salaries and wages (International City Manager's Association, 1961: 400). This division of 1960 expenditures was made in order that a deflator index geared specifically to police salaries could be applied to this most important component of the expenditures. The 90% estimate for the salary proportion appears to be relatively constant through time. A gross estimate of this proportion for the turn of the century is that in 1907 the average patrolman's salary ($1,052) divided by the 1907 average annual departmental expenditure per police employee equaled .87 or 87% (U.S. Bureau of Census, 1907: 394, 407). These two separate components were simply added together again after each was separately deflated to 1902 dollars by different indexes.

Salary expenditures or 90% of the 1960 expenditures were deflated as follows:

$$1960 \text{ salary expenditures } \frac{1907 \text{ patrolman's annual salary}}{1960 \text{ patrolman's annual salary}} \times$$

$$\frac{1960 \text{ annual policemen working days}}{1913 \text{ annual policemen working days}} \frac{1960 \text{ police hours per day}}{1907 \text{ police hours per day}} \times$$

$$\frac{\text{Value of 1907 dollars in constant dollars}}{\text{Value of 1902 dollars in constant dollars}} = \frac{1960 \text{ salary expenditures in 1902 dollars.}}{}$$

The logic of this formula and its possible shortcomings will be spelled out here because inflation is by far the most important component of expenditure increase. The second factor (annual salary ratio) is a coefficient of reduction which eliminates the effect of salary increases since 1907. The year 1907 was used instead of 1902 because this was the earliest source of usable data. Data for 1960 are more complete, but the 1960 data that could be utilized were limited by the available 1907 data since information had to be comparable for both years. The best available 1907 datum on annual police salaries was the mean salary of patrolmen in cities with more than 30,000 population (U.S. Bureau of the Census, 1907: 394). The 1960 datum used was the mean salary of patrolmen in cities over 25,000 (Fraternal Order of Police, 1961).[2]

Salary increases alone are an inadequate deflator because a concomitant decrease in annual working days has occurred. The third factor (annual working days ratio) deflates for this. The earliest usable source for this datum was from 1913 (Milwaukee Municipal Reference Library, 1913). Thus, any decrease in annual working days from 1907 to 1913 is not included in the deflator, and this contributes to a slight underestimate of the effects of inflation. The 1913 source provided a mean number of annual working days based upon 29 police departments in cities with more than 100,000 population. The computed mean was weighted by the number of patrolmen in each city in 1907. Similarly, the 1960 mean was weighted and was based upon cities over 100,000 population although the sample of cities used was much larger (Fraternal Order of Police, 1961).

The fourth factor (working hours ratio) deflates for the decrease in the working day length. The 1907 datum was a mean based upon 75 cities with over 35,000 population weighted by the number of patrolmen in each city (Fuld, 1909: 122–123). The 1960 datum was based upon a 1956 survey of 122 cities of which 120 had exactly 8-hour working days (American Federation of State, County and Municipal Employees, 1956). The remaining 2 had reduced their weekly hours to 40 and 40.5 by 1960 (Fraternal Order of Police, 1961). Therefore, the figure of 8 hours was utilized for 1960.

Finally, the fifth factor (1902/1907 constant dollar ratio) serves to deflate the product of the other four factors. The product of the first four factors is the 1960 salary expenditure in 1907 dollars. The final factor is the price deflator for the gross national product (U.S. Bureau of the Census, 1960). The gross national product price index was the only deflator available for this period and it converts the current 1902 and 1907 dollars into 1929 dollars.

In addition to the underestimation of inflation effects due to use of 1913 data for annual number of working days, none of the costs of 1960 salary expenditures due to increased fringe benefits such as pensions are included in the formula. Vacations and holidays are included in the working-days factor. However, the amount of underestimation due to using 1913 data and excluding fringe benefits is slight. The final figures used in the salary deflation computation are as follows:

$$\left(\$1{,}451 \text{ million}\right)\left(\frac{\$1{,}052}{\$5{,}681}\right)\left(\frac{243.4}{344.2}\right)\left(\frac{8.0}{9.4}\right)\left(\frac{100/54.5}{100/49.5}\right)$$

$$= \$146.84 \text{ million.}$$

The remaining 10% of the 1960 expenditures ($161 million) was deflated by the utilization of 2 price indices. The 1960 expenditure for goods and services was converted into constant 1929 dollars by using the price index for state and local government purchases of goods and services (U.S. Department of Commerce, 1959: 2–3; 1963: 4, 6). Because this goods and services price index was only available back to 1929, the expenditures expressed in 1929 dollars were then converted into 1902 dollars by the price index for gross national product (U.S. Bureau of the Census, 1960). This resulted in the figure of $29.72 million. The sum of the two deflated components of 1960 expenditures thus was $176.56 million.

Controlling for population growth

"Expected" expenditures in 1960
with 1902 population $\quad = \left(\dfrac{E}{P}\right) \text{ p } = \$706 \text{ million}$

Where E = 1960 Police Expenditure, P = 1960 Population,
p = 1902 Population (U.S. Bureau of the Census, 1965).

Controlling for urbanization

"Expected" expenditures in
1960 with 1902 Urban $\quad = \sum_i (Ai)\,(Bi)\,(C) = \$1{,}353 \text{ million}$
Population Distribution

Where i = size of place: 7 categories in thousands of population; 500+, 250–500, 100–250, 50–100, 25–50, 10–25, below 10.

A = Per Capita Expenditure in 1960 (International City Manager's Association, 1961: 400).

B = Proportion of Population in 1902 (U.S. Bureau of the Census, 1960, 1965).

C = 1960 Population (U.S. Bureau of the Census, 1965).

Controlling for motor vehicle increase In 1902, there were 23,000 motor vehicles registered and per capita motor vehicle registration was .0002905 (U.S. Bureau of the Census, 1960). Multiplying this per capita rate by the 1960 population as follows:

$$180,684,000 \times .0002905 = 52,489$$

provides the number of motor vehicles in 1960 that could be expected if only population growth had contributed to this increase. However, in 1960 there were 73,768,565 motor vehicles registered (U.S. Bureau of the Census, 1965). This is an increase of 73,716,076 (73,768,565 − 52,489) motor vehicles beyond that expected from population growth alone.

It is necessary to have an estimate of the cost per registered motor vehicle of police traffic control. Data of this nature are extremely limited, but one study based upon budget analyses of 9 cities enabled us to make an estimate of $7.23 per vehicle in 1960 (Seburn and Marsh, 1959: 77).

This study was based on the year 1957, and the mean cost weighted by number of vehicles of the 9 cities was $6.52 per vehicle. Because this was the only source the authors found, this estimate was assumed to also hold in 1960, and with a correction for inflation, the figure is $7.23 in 1960 dollars.[3]

The smallest city in this study had a population of 85,000. However, this figure of $7.23 does not appear biased in the direction of a high estimate when used as a national estimate by the general trend of higher general police expenditures in large urban areas because the per vehicle rate increased as size decreased. If a national estimate is extrapolated from these data, the conclusion would be that inclusion of smaller cities in these data would have *increased* the estimate of $7.23 as a national estimate.

This figure may appear too high if only the percentage of police personnel assigned to traffic division is considered. The $7.23 estimate multiplied by the total number of registered vehicles in 1960 provides a total of $533 million as the national cost of local police traffic control. This is $\dfrac{\$533 \text{ million}}{\$1,612 \text{ million}}$ or 33% of the total local police expenditure in 1960. Percentages based upon data from the 1940s indicate that the percentages of police personnel assigned to traffic divisions range from 11 to 23%, depending on city size (Smith, 1946: 32; Smith, 1949: 131).

It should be noted here that proportion of police assigned to traffic divisions in the 1940s appears to increase as city size decreases, which is somewhat consistent with the previous observation that if smaller cities were included in this paper's source of data, the national estimate of $533 million would perhaps be higher. Nevertheless, this percentage range of 11–23% is less than 33%. However, large proportions of the traffic control function are handled also by police not assigned to the traffic division. For example, in 43% of cities in the Wilbur Smith study, street patrol personnel investigated minor accidents and in 38% of the cities, street patrol personnel enforced parking regulations and in the same percentage of cities, handled traffic control at intersections. Thus, the total proportion of police resources utilized in traffic control can be reasonably expected to be appreciably higher than the 11–23% estimate provided by personnel assignment to traffic divisions. Another factor that should be emphasized is the 11–23% estimate occurs with the lower per capita automobile registration of the 1940s. In 1945, per capita motor vehicle registration was .219 while in 1960 it was .408. With the increase in per capita motor vehicle registration since 1945, it may be expected that the proportion of police resources utilized in traffic control would have also increased.

Multiplying the $7.23 per vehicle cost by the 73,716,076 vehicle increase not due to population growth gives the figure of $533 million. Thus, if this $533 million is subtracted from the $1,612 million expenditures in 1960, it provides us with an estimate of the police expenditure that would have occurred in 1960 if per capita motor vehicle registration had not increased since 1902. This estimated expenditure is $1,079 million.

The above calculation assumes a per vehicle national estimate which is a constant over different size-of-place groups. The discussion indicates that this is probably not the case, but adequate size-of-place specific data on costs of traffic control and per capita vehicle registration are not available. Moreover, the only data available for size-of-place specific per capita police expenditures do not report separate traffic and nontraffic expenditures.

Had such data been available, urbanization would be expected to account for more of the increase in nontraffic expenditures than it did of traffic and nontraffic combined expenditures since the ratio of nontraffic to total expenditures presumably increases with size of place. At the same time, expected 1960 traffic expenditures also would be greater if urban population proportions had not changed since 1902 because the smaller size-of-place groupings have higher per vehicle traffic control costs. This latter statement assumes per capita motor vehicle registration is constant across all size-of-place

groupings. The effect of standardizing traffic and nontraffic expenditures separately upon the 1902 urban population distribution
would have further reduced the remaining $44 million, although the
additional reduction is expected to be slight.

Joint effect of all components and their relative contributions Expected
1960 expenditures produced by controlling each component separately are summarized in Table 2 and each expected value given a
symbol for further computation.

Table 2   **Expected 1960 local police expenditures**

Component controlled	Expected amount (millions)	Symbol
Inflation	$ 177	B 1960
Population	706	C 1960
Motor vehicle increase	1,079	D 1960
Urbanization	1,353	E 1960

Because these components are conceptually independent, their
joint effect may be conceived of as analogous to the probability of
joint events occurring. The 1960 expected expenditures when any
one component, such as inflation, is held constant since 1902 are a
proportion of the total unadjusted expenditures (A 1960). Thus, the
proportion for inflation is $\dfrac{\text{B 1960}}{\text{A 1960}}$ or $\dfrac{\$\,177,000,000}{\$1,612,000,000}$. This proportion can provide the expected expenditures in dollars simply by
multiplying it by A 1960 (the total 1960 unadjusted expenditures) as
follows:

$$\left(\frac{\text{B 1960}}{\text{A 1960}}\right) \times \text{A 1960} = \text{B 1960}$$

This formula can be expanded to compute the joint effect of the 4
components by incorporating the expected expenditures when the
components are each controlled separately as below.

$$\left(\frac{\text{B 1960}}{\text{A 1960}}\right)\left(\frac{\text{C 1960}}{\text{A 1960}}\right)\left(\frac{\text{D 1960}}{\text{A 1960}}\right)\left(\frac{\text{E 1960}}{\text{A 1960}}\right)(\text{A 1960}) = \$44 \text{ million.}$$

The figure of $44 million (F 1960) represents the expected expendi-
ture in 1960 if population growth, inflation, urbanization, and motor
vehicle increase taken jointly had not occurred since 1902.

The amount of expenditure increase that each component has

contributed from 1902 to 1960 when all four components operate *jointly* can be derived as follows. The amount that each component contributes to the increases from 1902 to 1960 when computed *separately* provides a measure of the relative importance of each component. This amount is the unadjusted total 1960 expenditures minus the adjusted or "expected" 1960 expenditures for a component. The following formula utilizes these relative increase contributions that each component accounts for when analyzed separately and provides the amount of increase each has contributed when the four components operate jointly.

$$(A\ 1960 - B\ 1960)\ Z + (A\ 1960 - C\ 1960)\ Z + (A\ 1960 - D\ 1960)$$
$$Z + (A\ 1960 - E\ 1960)\ Z + F\ 1960 = A\ 1960$$

Solving for the constant Z (Z = .50047) and multiplying by Z the increase amount that each component accounts for when analyzed separately, provides the amount of increase in 1960 dollars due to each component when all are operating. These amounts and the percentage of the total increase each has contributed are reported in Table 1.

Notes

1   For example, in 1960 among 1,303 cities with populations over ten thousand, ninety percent of police department expenditures were for salaries and wages (International City Manager's Association, 1961: 400).

2   The specific publication date, is March 15, and because of this early 1961 date, this source was considered a better source for 1960 data than the equivalent 1960 publication. The 1961 publication data must have been collected at the end of 1960 or very early in 1961.

3   The $6.52 figure was inflated as follows: The salary proportion ($6.52 × .9 = $5.87) was inflated by an inflation index for police patrolmen (U.S. Bureau of Labor Statistics, 1962: 20). The other proportion was inflated by a price index for local government purchases of goods and services (U.S. Department of Commerce, 1963: 4, 6).

References

American Federation of State, County and Municipal Employees (1956) Employment Conditions for Police Officers. October 18 (mimeo).

Barclay, G. W. (1958) Techniques of Population Analysis. New York: John Wiley.

Bordua, D. J. (1968) "Comments on police-community relations," pp. 204–221 in S. I. Cohn (ed.) Law Enforcement Science and Technology II. Chicago: ITT Research Center.

Fraternal Order of Police (1961) A Survey of 1961 Salaries and Working Conditions of the Police Departments in the United States (March 15).

Fuld, L. F. (1909) Police Administration. New York: G. P. Putnam's Sons.

International City Manager's Association (1961) The Municipal Year Book. Chicago.

Milwaukee Municipal Reference Library (1913) Schedule of Salaries, Hours, Vacations, and Costs of Uniforms of Patrolmen in Various Cities.

President's Commission on Law Enforcement and Administration of Justice (1967) Task Force Report: Crime and Its Impact—An Assessment. Washington, D.C.: U.S. Government Printing Office.

Seburn, T. J. and *B. L. Marsh* (1959) Urban Transportation Administration. New Haven: Yale University.

Smith, B. (1949) Police Systems in the United States. New York: Harper & Brothers.

Smith, W. S. (1946) The Organization of Official Traffic Agencies in Cities and States. New York: Eno Foundation for Highway Traffic Control.

Tifft, L. L. and *D. J. Bordua* (1969) "Police organization and future research." J. of Research on Crime & Delinquency.

U.S. Bureau of Labor Statistics (1962) Salary Trends; Firemen and Policemen, 1924–1961, Report 233. Washington, D.C.: U.S. Government Printing Office.

U.S. Bureau of the Census (1966) Statistical Abstract of the United States. Washington, D.C.: U.S. Government Printing Office.

——(1965) Historical Statistics of the United States from Colonial Times to 1957: Continuation to 1962 and Revisions. Washington, D.C.: U.S. Government Printing Office.

——(1960) Historical Statistics of the United States from Colonial Times to 1957. Washington, D.C.: U.S. Government Printing Office.

——(1907) Statistics of Cities Having Population of Over 30,000: Special Reports. Washington, D.C.: U.S. Government Printing Office.

U.S. Department of Commerce (1963) Business Statistics. Washington, D.C.: U.S. Government Printing Office.

——(1959) Business Statistics. Washington, D.C.: U.S. Government Printing Office.

Wilson, J. Q. (1968) Varieties of Police Behavior. Cambridge: Harvard Univ. Press.

James Leo Walsh

Professionalism and the police: the cop as medical student

The role of the police in modern life has attracted considerable attention in recent years.[1] Both social scientific research and ideological pronouncements have sought to explain police behavior in terms of such variables as ethnicity, social class, religion, role conflicts, age, rank, and organizational differences in police departments.[2] Others have examined the police from a more psychological vantage point stressing factors such as authoritarianism, childhood socialization experiences, and the personality syndromes of violently inclined police officers.[3]

The occupational setting

More recently, however, students of police behavior have begun to examine the occupational settings within which police officers work. These research efforts have sought to explain the attitudes and behavior of policemen in terms of the theoretical framework of the sociology of the professions. With one modification, the research reported here fits into this latter approach.

Specifically, concepts and propositions advanced by Hughes (1958, 1959, 1963), Hall (1961), Wilson (1963) and others[4] concerning the impact of professionalism on members of an occupational grouping form the theoretical base of this study. On the basis of other research in the professions, sociologists can argue that variations in professional stature and position lead to variations in

This is a revised version of a paper, "The Professional Cop," presented September 4, 1969 at the meetings of the American Sociological Association, San Francisco, California.

Reprinted here from *American Behavioral Scientist* 13 (May–August 1970), pp. 705–725, with the permission of Sage Publications, Inc. and James Leo Walsh.

attitudes and behavior.[5] Those who view their work as being highly professional should, therefore, express different attitudes toward it and behave differently in fulfilling occupational roles than those in the same occupation whose conception of the work is that it is located further down the occupational prestige ladder.

Policemen do differ considerably in their conceptions of the social position of their work. Some view themselves as professionals, highly trained to provide service in meeting and solving problems the community cannot itself handle (Hughes, 1958: 139–144). On the other hand, many policemen consider their work simply a job involving relatively little more commitment than putting in the time demanded by any other eight-hour factory shift. The initial emphasis of this paper is focused on attitudinal and behavioral differences between the highly professional police officers and those classified as low-professionals. But, to deal adequately with an examination of professionalism and the police requires an expansion of the theoretical perspective of the sociology of the professions to include the process of professional striving.

A rich body of theory and research exists to lend credence to the argument that police officers who are professional strivers differ significantly in their attitudes and behavior from those policemen who place less value on the quest for higher professional stature.[6] Indeed, in many ways, the professionally striving policeman is not unlike a jazz musician or a medical student and the sociological factors explaining their attitudes and behavior also hold promise for explaining attitudinal and behavioral variations among policemen.[7]

In his analysis of the factors leading jazz musicians to harbor less-than-favorable attitudes toward the music-consuming public, Becker described the turmoil created when the artist-musician faced the dilemma of "going commercial" and playing what the fans want in return for status and financial reward, or of sticking by their artistic principles and contenting themselves with status among other musicians only (Becker 1951, 1953). When forced to make such a choice, the jazz musician felt embittered toward society. His occupational self-image as an artist and a creator did not coincide with the public view of him solely as an entertainer.

A similar process has been reported in studies of medical students. Hughes has listed the student criteria for desirable patients as including, among other things, the effect of the patient on the physician's career, income, reputation, and development of further skills (Hughes, 1958: 124–125). Becker and Geer have extended this to point out that student ideas and expectations of patients include in great measure attitudes drawn from the medical culture in which the concept of medical responsibility "pictures a world in which patients may be in danger of losing their lives and identifies the true work of the physician as saving those endangered lives" (Becker and Geer, 1958: 70–71). To lack this sense of medical responsibility is to lack the essence of physicianhood, and medical students come to value those patients who can be cured over those who cannot. Those who are not organically ill in the first place—the hypochondriacs of "crocks"—are the worst of all. Becker and Geer go on to point out that the student physician worries a great deal about managing his interaction with his patients so that they will be pleasant and cooperative. The most difficult scenes come about when patients have no respect for the doctor's authority. Physicians resent this immensely.[8]

So it is with the police officer and the professionally striving police officer in particular. He is involved in the quest for occupational identity (Fisher, 1969) and part of that quest is the management of his relationships with his "clients," the citizens with whom he comes into contact.[9] Managing this relationship is a difficult task for the police for, unlike the continuous excitement and successful arrest records of heroic television policemen, boredom and lack of tangible results are a part of police work (Reiss and Bordua, 1967: 35–37). Similar to the physician, the essence of the police vocation is seen as crime prevention and detection, but the demands placed on the police frequently run counter to this view. The professionally striving officer is the one most likely to feel this and to value experiences in which he "really did some police work." [10]

Further, as was the case with the aspirant professionals in the medical schools, the professionally striving police officers were those who most resented attempts by their clientele to question their authority or balk at their demands (see Freidson, 1968: 33). Fully seventy percent of the striving police officers listed their most unpleasant experience as a policeman as having been a situation in which their authority had been challenged.[11] One of the results of such resentment has been pointed out by Fisher. She argued that one reaction open to an "agent group" (in this case the police) encountering challenge from its clientele may be to depart from efforts to enlighten and woo and, instead, either to discredit clients' motives and knowledge or to use direct coercion. (Fisher, 1969: 430).[12]

Hypotheses

Examining the police from the perspective of the sociology of the professions led to the formulation and testing of five hypotheses in this research. These include:

Section I:
1. Police officers classified as low-professional are more likely to support political candidates of the right and to have voted for George Wallace more frequently than those police officers who were classified as highly professional.

2. Highly professional police officers differ significantly from low-professional policemen as to when they think it appropriate "to rough a man up."

3. Highly professional police officers differ significantly from low-professional policemen in attitudes toward racial and economic minorities.

4. Highly professional police officers differ significantly from low-professional policemen as to the types of people with whom physical force is used differently.

Section II:
5. High professional striving levels among policemen lead to significantly different attitudes toward the use of physical force with certain types of citizens than do lower levels of professional striving.

Method

The data for this study were gathered in personal, largely open-ended interviews conducted by the author in four police departments in small and medium-sized cities in the Middle West during the winter and spring of 1969. The police departments were located in communities ranging from suburban bedrooms for nearby cities to ethnically-diverse mill towns.

A total of seventy-nine police officers were interviewed while on duty. Analysis was limited to uniformed police officers. Interviews were conducted on all three turns or shifts and observational data on the routine of the police stations and the behavior of the police officers while on duty were recorded. Prior to the actual interviewing, several months were spent visiting, calling, and writing the police departments studied so as to explain the purposes of the research and answer questions in advance. Cooperation was excellent and only three policemen refused to be interviewed. One of these later changed his mind.[13]

Seemingly endless arguments often result when efforts are made to define precisely the meaning of the term "profession" (Carr-Saunders, 1937: 491–492; Faunce and Clelland, 1967; Wilensky, 1964). Becker (1962: 33) has offered perhaps the most helpful solution to the problem of definition, arguing that any work group that succeeds in getting itself called such is a profession. Extending Becker's argument somewhat, it can be argued with Vollmer and Mills (1966: vii–viii) that the concept "profession" be used to refer to an abstract model of occupational organization. Professionalism, on the other hand, refers to a dynamic process, an ideology, used by members of an occupational group whose members aspire to professional status. There is clear evidence that many policemen are seeking this recognition and whether they are "real" professionals or not does not affect the fact that policemen vary on both subjective and objective measures of "professionalism." Though sidestepping the difficult definitional problems involved with the concept "profession," suffice it to say that police officers do respond readily, if differently, to questions concerning the professional stature of their work and that variations in attitude related to such variations in professional level provide useful sociological insights. In sum, whether they have "made it" or not, or even whether they ever will achieve the coveted status of a profession, does not seem to affect the efforts of the police to garner this elusive goal, and it is this quest and not so much the success or possibilities of success which is of interest in the formulation of the research reported here.

The respondents to this study were classified into categories based on their responses to seven items from the interview schedule.[14] These items had all proven useful in other research (Walsh and Elling, 1968; Walsh, 1969). This seven-item "professionalism score" facilitated categorizing the respondents into highly professional, medium-professional, and low-professional categories.

Following the collection of the data, social class, rank, age, organizational differences between the departments, ethnicity and, finally, authoritarianism were utilized as independent variables insofar as all have been used in other studies of the police. Neither significant differences nor consistent trends appeared in this analysis and emphasis was placed on testing the importance of level of professionalism and professional striving in differentiating and explaining police attitudes and behavior. Chi-square tests of significance were utilized in testing these relationships. The results of these tests are reported below.

Findings: professional stature and police attitudes

VOTING BEHAVIOR

Voting behavior of police officers has been considered in several studies and generally the argument has been that they tend to vote conservatively (Lipset, 1969; Skolnick, 1966; Niederhoffer, 1969; Vega, 1968). However, measures of voting behavior in this research indicate that police officers vary in their voting practices and that the professional stature of a policeman is helpful in explaining that variation. Specifically, the low-professional police officer was the policeman most likely to have voted for George Wallace in the past presidential election while Hubert Humphrey and Richard Nixon were supported more frequently by the more professional police officers.

Considering the data presented in Table 1, further insight into the voting behavior of the policemen interviewed comes into view. Two questions were asked dealing with voting behavior in this study. The first asked if the respondent generally voted as a Republican, a Democrat, or an Independent. Later, the respondent was asked which of the three presidential candidates he had voted for in 1968. As the data indicate, the low-professional policemen were those most likely to bolt from traditional Democratic voting practices and to vote for George Wallace. One-half of the low-professional policemen voted for Wallace in 1968 whereas forty-five percent of these low-professional officers said they usually voted for Democrats. Only fifteen percent of the low-professional policemen voted for Hubert Humphrey.

Moving up the professional stature index, the data in Table 1 indicate that the more professional police officers also frequently altered their usual practices but that most of them voted for Richard Nixon, not George Wallace. Indeed, in the case of the highly professional policemen, the Democrats remained Democrats in all cases while twenty-six percent of those highly professional policemen who were usually independents voted for Nixon, not for Wallace.

If voting for George Wallace for President in 1968 is a good

Table 1 **Comparison of usual voting practices with actual voting behavior in 1968 presidential election by professional level of policemen (in percentages)**

a Usual voting practice b How actually voted in 1968	Low professional			Medium			High			All levels		
	a	b	Change from a to b	a	b	Change from a to b	a	b	Change from a to b	a	b	Change from a to b
Democratic Hubert Humphrey	45	15	−30	43	33	−10	28	29	+1[a]	38	21	−17
Republican Richard Nixon	15	35	+20	10	37	+27	14	39	+25	13	37	+24
Independent George Wallace	40	50	+10	47	30	−17	58	32	−26	49	36	−13
Total	100	100		100	100		100	100		100	100	
	n=20	n=20		n=30	n=30		n=29	n=28[a]		n=79	n=78[a]	

[a] One policeman did not vote.

operational definition of right-wing political behavior on the part of the police, then it is clear that most policemen are not reactionary politically and that the professional stature of a policeman helps to predict voting behavior. While in general the Democrats lost seventeen percent of their traditional supporters among the police in the 1968 presidential election, the highly professional Democratic policemen remained in the fold. At the other end of the continuum, however, thirty percent of the low-professional policemen deserted the Democrats. And, only among the low-professional policemen did the defections go to George Wallace more readily than to Richard Nixon. Thus, the first hypothesis tested in this study seems to be supported by the data.

ATTITUDES TOWARD ETHNIC AND ECONOMIC MINORITIES

A second finding of this research relates to an observation made in a recent work by Bayley and Mendelsohn (1969: 148) who observed, "Very little credence is given by policemen to charges that policemen treat minority people unfairly or improperly." To test this notion and to examine further the dynamics of police-minority interactions, respondents to this research were asked a series of nine questions concerning the position and treatment of ethnic and minority groups in the society. On the basis of the responses to these nine items, an "orientation score" was calculated on which respondents were compared by level of professionalism.[15] Table 2 reports these data where orientations toward minorities are classified either as negative, mixed or positive.

Table 2   Orientation score by professional level

Orientation toward ethnic and economic minorities	Low level		Medium		High		All levels	
	n	%	n	%	n	%	n	%
Positive	1	5	10	33	11	38	22	28
Mixed	7	35	14	47	12	41	33	42
Negative	12	60	6	20	6	21	24	30
Total	20	100	30	100	29	100	79	100

NOTE: $X^2 = 13.261$, 4 degrees of freedom, significant at. 02.

The efficacy of utilizing this multi-item measure was suggested in other research wherein it was argued that if racial or economic characteristics were of no importance to professionals in dealings with a variety of citizens, most respondents would list problems germane to the nature of the professional-client interaction, not concentrate on social class or ethnic factors in describing problems with clients (Walsh and Elling, 1968). But the police, like other professionals, did list ethnic and social class factors as being important considerations in their dealings with some persons. Again, the professional stature of a police officer appears as a critical variable in explaining which policemen are most likely to approach ethnic and economic minorities negatively and which are positive in their orientations.

The differences between the three groupings of police officers on the orientation score are statistically significant as predicted. The low-professional policemen were most likely (sixty percent) to harbor negative attitudes toward minority groups. For example, one such policeman argued, "A Negro in the community has more opportunities to get something for nothing than I do. It's their fault if they don't get good treatment. Hell, everyone has the same opportunity" (interview 36).

The professional policemen, on the other hand, appeared much more empathetic toward minority groups and scored positively on the orientation score. These police officers frequently argued that no small proportion of the difficulties between the police and the minority groups developed because of inadequate training or insight on the part of policemen working with such groups. The need for training for the police, not repression of the minorities, was stressed by the professionals. The second hypothesis of this research, then, seems to be verified.

THE POLICE AND PHYSICAL FORCE—I

Data concerning the role of professionalism in explaining attitudes toward the use of physical force provided the impetus to introduce a modification of the more traditional theoretical statements of the sociology of the professions. At first glance it would appear, as the data in Table 3 indicate, that the more professional a police officer is, the less likely he is to condone the use of physical force in situations other than defending himself or making an arrest. But, as Table 4 will indicate, a more complicated explanation for the differential use of force by the police is needed.

In Table 3 the evidence is clear that low-professional police officers differ significantly from their professional counterparts in their responses to a question asking, "When do you think a policeman is justified in roughing a man up?" (Westley, 1953: 38).

Table 3 **When do policemen think a police officer is justified in roughing a man up?**

	Low professional level		Medium		High		All levels	
	n	%	n	%	n	%	n	%
To make an arrest	5	25	10	33	15	52	30	38
To defend myself	6	30	14	47	12	41	32	41
When they look or talk tough	9	45	6	20	2	7	17	21
Total	20	100	30	100	29	100	79	100

NOTE: $X^2 = 11.370$, 4 degrees of freedom, significant at .05.

On this question, it is interesting to note, none of the low-professional police officers questioned the use of the term "roughing up" or asked if it meant using sufficient force to make an arrest. The professionals, on the other hand, frequently objected to the term "roughing up" and asked that the wording be changed to mean using sufficient force to defend myself or make an arrest.

Almost one half (forty-five percent) of the low-professional police officers interviewed argued that a policeman was justified in roughing a man up if he "looked rough" or "talked tough." [16] One low-professional policeman explained that he thought a man should be roughed up in order to defend himself and, he added, "I'm defending myself when someone calls me a son-of-a-bitch and means it" (interview 38).

The data in Table 3, then, seem to indicate again that professional policemen differ significantly from their low-professional counterparts and that the third hypothesis tested in this study is borne out. The professional police officer is far less likely to condone the use of force in dealing with citizens. This finding, however, is confounded somewhat when the data presented in Table 4 are considered.

THE POLICE AND PHYSICAL FORCE—II

When asked, "From your experience does it seem that physical force is something a policeman finds he uses differently with different kinds of people?" both low-professional and professional police officers responded affirmatively. But the kinds of people they labelled as the likely recipients of such differential uses of force

Table 4 **Is physical force used differently by the police with different kinds of people?**

Force is used differently by . . .	Low professional level		Medium		High		All levels	
	n	%	n	%	n	%	n	%
Race and class	11	55	8	31	5	21	24	34
With animals	9	45	18	69	19	79	46	66
Total	20	100	26	100	24	100	70[a]	100

NOTE: X^2 = 6.497, 2 degrees of freedom, significant at .05.
[a] Seven did not answer this question and two gave "unclassifiable" responses.

varied! Racial and social class differences were cited by the low-professional policemen much more frequently than by the professionals. But, a novel category of citizens, "animals," appear as those with whom the professionals use force more frequently.

To explain this difference between professional and low-professional policemen, several propositions from studies of professional-client interaction in nonpolice settings provide insight into the findings reported in Table 4. This explanation follows.

Findings: professional striving and police attitudes

Considering the policeman as a jazz musician or a medical student proved to be a fruitful perspective in analyzing the data for the second section of this paper. A nine-item professional striving score was utilized in this research to separate the respondents into "low," "medium," and "high" striving categories.[17]

Effective statistical controls are difficult to impose in studies involving small numbers of cases but several were attempted in the analysis of these data. Of specific interest is the finding that the data in Table 4, when professional striving was used as a control variable, indicate that the highly striving segments of the low, medium, and highly professional categories were those who specified "animals" as citizens with whom force was used differently.

Classifying the respondents in terms of their professional-striving levels led to the finding that the professionally striving police officer expressed attitudes considerably different from those of his less-actively striving counterparts. These differences appear to result from similarities in the role of the police officer and those of the jazz musician and medical students as outlined earlier.

CITIZENS AS "ANIMALS"

Police officers have their own term for those whom Becker's medical students would have labeled "crocks." The police have their "crocks" also but call them "animals." An understanding of their perceptions of such citizens sheds further light on the use of physical force by the police.

To the police officer the concept "animal" covers a variety of sins; but generally animals are those persons with whom very little likelihood of a positive outcome faces the officer as he sets out to handle a family dispute, to face a mentally disturbed citizen,[18] a belligerent drunk, a neighborhood quarrel in which the police must play the role of middlemen, or the known cop fighter.

The "animal" is frequently known to the police officer and often when interviews were interrupted and respondents were called to take care of citizens they characterized as animals, the officer stated before leaving that the chances were very high that a physical encounter would take place with the person in question. The police dislike such citizens intensely and for reasons similar to the medical students' dislike of the crock or the noninteresting patient.[19]

The animal is seen as putting the police officer in a "damned if he does, damned if he doesn't" position. If, for example, a police officer battles a citizen, he faces criticism for the use of force and frequently enhances the standing of the animal in the eyes of the latter's peers. If he doesn't, he must subject himself to the insults of the animal and lose respect both with the animal and his friends and with his fellow police officers (Whyte, 1943: 138; Bordua, 1967: 65–68).

It is interesting, in continuing this analogy between policemen and medical students, that those police officers who most actively seek higher professional stature are also those who are most likely to view the animal as problematic to police work. In fact, as the data in Table 5 indicate, the animal is set apart as the type of citizen with whom physical force is most likely to be utilized by eighty percent of the highly striving police officers interviewed. The willingness to use force against animals by professionally striving policemen resulted from, I think, many of the same reasons the medical student resents the hypochondriac.

Table 5   **With what kinds of persons do you find that a police officer must use force differently?**

Force is used differently by . . .	Low professional level		Medium		High		All levels	
	n	%	n	%	n	%	n	%
Race and social class	12	57	10	33.3	4	20	26	37
With animals	9	43	20	66.6	16	80	45	63
Total	21	100	30	99.9	20	100	71[a]	100

NOTE: $X^2 = 6.285$, 2 degrees of freedom, significant at .05.
[a] Seven policemen did not answer this question and one response was unclassifiable.

To the professionally striving police officers, engaging in barroom brawls or street fights is seen as being detrimental to the stature of the police in the eyes of the general public (Sutherland and Cressey, 1966). Such behavior is seen by the striving policeman as opening the way to charges of police brutality, and it is seen as engaging in dangerous duty for little, if any, reward. The animal is expected to be back on the streets after a brief time and the police officer must face him again and again. Parenthetically, the police-animal relationship is perhaps one of the chief causes of police resentment of the public and the courts (Sutherland and Cressey, 1966). And, as Reiss and Bordua (1967: 33–37) have spelled out, may in fact lead to further use of force against animals. It is frustrating to the police officer to face the same animals time and again when they see the courts dispensing what they view to be lenient treatment. They interpret this as a sign that their efforts have not been appreciated and that justice has not been served (Reiss and Bordua, 1967: 33–37).

Comparing the policeman's animal with the medical student's crock, does seem to shed some light on the use of violence by the police. The analogy begins to break down when pushed further, however. The reason for this breakdown suggests that police perceptions of animals may be of even greater importance to their interaction than the crock's impact on the medical student's relations with his patients.

One of the textbook steps in the process of professionalizing has been to shed "dirty-work," and many professionalizing occupational groups have included shedding or altering relationships with those clients seen as being akin to dirty work (Walsh and Elling,

1968; Walsh, 1969). Such a step, however, is far more difficult for the police. They, too, view dealing with animals as dirty work, and the professional strivers in particular resent their inability to shed such duties to persons lower on the professional prestige ladder. Wrestling with drunks and dealing with animals remain firmly entrenched in the occupational duties of policemen, and, instead of being able to shed dirty work, the police are convinced that such tasks will continue as a major part of their responsibility. Cynicism toward the public is one result.[20] Increased willingness to use excessive force with some citizens is another.

Discussion

Utilizing the theoretical perspective of the sociology of the professions, then, has utility in efforts to understand better the dynamics of the role of the police. Verification of the five hypotheses tested in this study indicates that the impact of professionalism does play a major role in explaining variations in police attitudes and behavior.

In this research, variables such as social class, ethnicity, age, rank, authoritarianism, and the like did not explain the variations noted in this paper. For example, the interesting work of Niederhoffer (1969), Lipset (1969), and Bayley and Mendelsohn (1969) emphasizing the role of police authoritarianism as a variable affecting police attitudes, was not substantiated in this research.[21] Nor did any consistent or significant differences in attitudes and behavior appear to result from the other, more traditional variables.

This is not to say that these are not important factors to consider in studies of the police; rather, these variables appear to play a significant role in determining which police officers come to consider themselves as high versus low professionals and also which policemen become professional strivers.[22]

While occupational conceptions do appear to separate professional police officers from their nonprofessional colleagues, such occupational prestige differences did not seem to divide the police forces studied into hostile or even separate camps. Indeed, the data seem to indicate that some highly striving police officers come to hold attitudes analogous to those of the nonprofessional policemen.[23]

The attitudes and behavior of policemen, therefore, are not the result of any one set of factors. Several social variables combine to produce occupational self-conceptions and levels of professional striving. And, in turn, those police officers who strive with confidence are, it seems, different from those who also strive but do so with awareness of Wilson's glum prediction that the police probably face more severe obstacles in their quest for recognition than do most other occupational groups (J. Wilson, 1963). Frustration, discontent, cynicism, and a continuation of the feeling that the police are set apart from other work groups (Lipset, 1969; Niederhoffer, 1969) and asked to play incompatible roles as stern defenders of the law in some cases and, somehow, also be able to use professional discretion and insight in handling still other situations with widely variant meanings to diverse sets of persons, are likely to continue.

The feeling for policemen and police work gained through this study suggests that a better understanding of the impact of the policeman's professional stature and of the results of professional striving on police attitudes will provide a useful inroad for better theoretical understanding of the sociology of the professions in general, and the police in particular.

Three final comments need to be made. The first is to emphasize that the findings reported in this paper are based on measures of the attitudes of policemen, not their behavior.[24] Numerous social scientists have cautioned against making the leap from studies of attitudes to predictions of behavior by those expressing such attitudes (see Deutscher, 1966; deFleur and Westie, 1958; Ehrlich, 1969; Tittle and Hill, 1967; and LaPiere, 1934).

Deutscher (1969) has raised this issue once again in a recent discussion. He (1969: 40) concludes, "Validity poses a serious problem when we use instruments designed to provide estimates of hypothetical behavior. If, instead, our data consist of direct behavioral observations, the problem of validity becomes negligible."

Clearly the data presented here tapped hypothetical behavior and must be interpreted as such. But, far from being as valueless as Deutscher would have us believe attitudinal data to be, such findings seem to me to be of value in paving the theoretical ground for future behavioral studies of the police—or other professions for that matter.

Secondly, the "last gospel" of many sociological reports needs to be emphasized strongly here. The findings reported in this article were based on a limited number of interviews and can claim to be representative only of the policemen interviewed. To generalize these conclusions further without first testing the theoretical perspective of this study on a more ambitious level would be inappropriate.

Finally and despite these cautions, it does seem apparent that the results of research such as this have bearing upon the selection and training of police officers. It also has implications for those with the task of administering police departments and consulting with policemen. If the social scientists have only recently embarked upon serious efforts to trace the impact of social variables upon police behavior, consider the need for policemen themselves to comprehend the subtle social factors affecting themselves, their work, and their "clientele."

Notes

1   See for example Banton (1965), Chevigny (1969), Cray (1967), Fox (1966), Grimshaw (1963), Hopkins (1931), Jacobs (1966), Lane (1967), Piliavin and Briar (1964), Atlantic (1969), Issues in Criminology (1968), Stoddard (1968), Turner (1968), Van Allen (1968), Wiener (1950), and O. Wilson (1964).

2   See for example Bordua (1967), Ehrlich (1959), Goldstein (1960), Koenig (1960), Levy (1968), Niederhoffer (1969), Skolnick (1966), Stinchcombe (1963), and J. Wilson (1964).

3   See for example Knupfer (1947), Lipset (1969), Rankin (1959), Toch (1969), and Zimbardo (1968).

4   See for example Becker (1962), Goode (1961), New (1965), Niederhoffer (1969), Wilensky (1964), Zola and Croog (1968), Walsh (1969).

5   See for example Becker (1952), Davis (1968), Fanshel (1959), Gold (1952), and Hughes (1958).

6   See for example Eaton (1962), Bucher (1962), Bucher and A. Strauss (1961), Elling (1967), Goode (1960), G. Strauss (1964), Walsh and Elling (1968).

7   Comparisons of medical students and policemen are not novel to this paper. The only difference here lies in the interpretation of the data based on that analogy. For a different approach see McNamara (1967: 221–222).

8   The police resent attacks upon their authority in a manner analogous to the medical community. See Reiss and Bordua (1967: 48). Also, see Becker (1951–1952: 459), and Westley (1951: 30).

9   Reiss and Bordua (1967: 30) argue that the police are essentially a service without clients. In a different light, J. Wilson (1963: 201) has pointed out a major difference in the efforts of the police to professionalize when he wrote "professionalism among policemen will differ from professionalism in other occupations in that the primary function of the professional code will be to protect the practitioner from the client rather than the client from the practitioners."

10   The professionally striving police officers interviewed in this study were those who consistently named their most pleasant experiences as police officers as having actually solved crimes or done "something to help." Fifty-six percent of the

professional strivers responded this way while only 30.6% of the low-striving policemen saw their most pleasant experience as having been a crime-solving or "professional" police task.

11 These data were drawn from an unstructured question, "What would you say your most unpleasant experience as a police officer has been?" Unlike the striving officer, only thirty-six percent of their low-striving counterparts described such an experience as having been a situation in which their authority had been challenged.

12 See also Cumming et al. (1965). Jacobs (1966) has argued that the police often view the public as the enemy.

13 In light of intervening events in two departments in terms of local-level political furor involving the police, it was thought that such factors could effect the results of the study and the remaining policemen were not interviewed. An additional twelve officers would have been added to the sample.

14 The professionalism score was based on the following items: (1) rank, (2) membership in professional police organizations, (3) reading of professional police publications, (4) the number and frequency of journals read, (5) "cosmopolitan" versus "local" role identity, (6) self-adjudged professional status, and (7) academic training in police work. Code categories were numbered low to high on each item and the professionalism score was obtained by adding the codes of the seven items.

15 The orientation score consisted of nine items, the responses to which were coded so that the highest code categories indicated the most negative orientation toward minorities and the lowest codes the least negative. The nine items included perceptions of public hostility from minority groups toward the police, specifying minority groups as the "greatest problem" facing the police, specifying minority group members as those with whom it is most difficult to work, arguing that physical force is a necessity in minority areas, anticipating trouble from minority group members, blaming lazy minority group members for any discrimination in existence today, and specifying past dealings with minority group members as having been among a policeman's most unpleasant experiences as an officer. These items and codes can be obtained from the author.

16 McNamara (1967: 222) has reported similar findings and argued that experience in the field lead to such attitudes. Field experience, however, did not seem to be a major factor in this research while the professional level of the police interviewed did. All of the respondents were involved in similar field experiences.

17 This professional striving score was developed in earlier research (Walsh and Elling, 1968: 21) and includes measures of the following characteristics: (1) delegating or shedding menial or unpleasant tasks to less highly trained persons; (2) attempting to assume more responsibilities on a higher level, such as seeking more voice in setting policy or undertaking new and novel activities; (3) seeking to become better known among professional colleagues in order to advance or gain professional respect; (4) developing or expressing willingness to join professional associations whose purpose is to advance the professional status of the police.

18 "Mentals" was another concept used frequently by the police to categorize persons with mental instabilities. They disliked mentals for they were thought to be unpredictable and often violent. Mentals are, however, a subgroup of animal.

19 One important difference between the medical students' "crocks" and those of the police did appear in this research. While the medical students resented uninteresting, nonenriching cases and sought to avoid them, the police officer often reacts to calls to provide assistance or solve problems not necessarily within the realm of law enforcement as at least enhancing the status of the police in the community and, therefore, does not seek to debunk or avoid them. It could be hypothesized that the police officers viewing their work as a job would be more likely to view such calls as coming from "crocks" than would the professional strivers and therefore be more likely to become involved in unsavory confrontations with citizens than would be the strivers. No such data were gathered in this study but findings indicating the utility of such a hypothesis were obtained from a question asking the police if they thought it appropriate for the police to become involved in health and welfare activities. The professional strivers overwhelmingly thought they should, the nonstrivers said no.

20 A recent excellent discussion of police cynicism can be found in Niederhoffer (1969: 95–108). Another perspective that seems to have application to the police is Levitin (1964).

21 In the pretest of this research an effort was made to utilize measures of authoritarianism employed in other studies. Bayley and Mendelsohn (1969) used the five-item F scale developed by Leo Srole (1956). Koenig (1960) used a similar measure, as did Niederhoffer (1969: 129).

The questions did not work, however, partially because some of the police involved in the pretest had had college training and recognized the items immediately and partially because, as one officer said, "Those questions are dumb." I think he was arguing, as most of the respondents would, that the police are exceptionally sensitive to criticism these days and that these questions were threatening.

An alternative measure of authoritarianism based on Milton Rokeach's work was utilized in this study. This consisted of a ten-item rigidity-flexibility score. Thus, the claim that authoritarianism is not a major factor in police attitudes may be a function of the measures employed.

22 These data are presented in an unpublished paper available through the author.

23 It is interesting to note, for example, that the highly striving police officers were those who were more likely to vote for George Wallace in the last presidential election. Earlier, data were presented to demonstrate that low-professional policemen were most likely to vote for Wallace. Those data were reported in Table 1 and the similarities between the voting behavior of the highly striving and low-professional police officers indicates the validity of the argument that the two types of policemen do share attitudes if for divergent reasons.

Voting behavior by professional striving level

	Low striving level n	%	Medium n	%	High n	%	All levels n	%
Humphrey	5	20	9	29	7	32	21	27
Nixon	12	48	11	35.4	5	23	28	36
Wallace	8	32	11	35.4	10	45	29	37
Total	25	100	31	99.8	22	100	78	100

24 It could be argued that the voting data are behavioral but insofar as they are based on self-reports, many of the pitfalls of attitudinal data are also involved.

References

Atlantic (1969) "The police and the rest of us." 223 (March): 74–135.

Banton, M. (1965) The Policeman in the Community. New York: Basic Books.

Bayley, D. and *H. Mendelsohn* (1969) Minorities and the Police. New York: Free Press.

Becker, H. (1962) "The Nature of a profession," pp. 27–46 in Sixty-First Year-Book of the National Society for the Study of Education, Part II, Education for the Professions. Chicago: Univ. of Chicago Press.

————(1958) Boys in White. Chicago: Univ. of Chicago Press.

————(1953) "Some contingencies of the professional dance band musician's career." Human Organization 12 (Spring): 22–26.

————(1952) "The career of the Chicago public school teacher." Amer. J. of Sociology 57 (March): 473–477.

————(1951–1952) "Social class variations in the teacher-pupil relationship." J. of Educational Sociology 25: 459.

————(1951) "The professional jazz musician and his audience." Amer. J. of Sociology 57 (September): 136–144.

————and *B. Geer* (1958) "Student culture and medical school." Harvard Educational Rev. 28: 70–71.

Bordua, D. (1967) The Police: Six Sociological Essays. New York: John Wiley.

Bucher, R. (1962) "Pathology: a study of social movements within a profession." Social Problems 10 (Summer): 40–51.

————and *A. Strauss* (1961) "Professions in process." Amer. J. of Sociology 46 (January): 325–334.

Carr-Saunders, A. (1955) "Metropolitan conditions and traditional professional relationships," pp. 279–314 in R. M. Fisher (ed.) The Metropolis in Modern Life. New York: Doubleday.

Chevigny, P. (1969) Police Power. New York: Pantheon Books.

Cray, E. (1967) The Big Blue Line—Police Power vs. Human Rights. New York: Coward-McCann.

Cumming, E., I. Cumming, and *L. Edell* (1965) "Policeman as philosopher, guide and friend." Social Problems 12 (Winter): 276–286.

DeFleur, M. and *F. Westie* (1958) "Verbal attitudes and overt acts: an experiment on the salience of attitudes." Amer. Soc. Rev. 23: 667–673.

Davis, F. (1968) "Professional socialization as subjective experience: the process of doctrinal conversion among student nurses," pp. 235–251 in H. Becker et al. (eds.) Institutions and the Person. Chicago: Aldine.

Deutscher, I. (1969) "Looking backward: case studies on the progress of methodology in sociological research." Amer. Sociologist 4 (February): 35–41.

———(1966) "Words and deeds; social sciences and social policy." Social Problems 13 (Winter): 235–254.

Eaton, J. W. (1962) Stone Walls not a Prison Make. Springfield, Ill.: Charles C. Thomas.

Ehrlich, H. (1969) "Attitudes, behavior and the intervening variables." Amer. Sociologist 4 (February): 29–34.

———(1959) "The analysis of role conflicts in a complex organization: the police." Ph.D. dissertation. Michigan State University.

Elling, R. H. (1967) "Occupational group striving and administration in public health," in M. Arnold, V. Blankenship, and J. Hill (eds.) Public Health Administration. New York: Atherton Press.

Fanshel, D. (1959) "A study of caseworkers' perceptions of their clients." Social Casework 39 (December): 543–551.

Faunce, W. and D. Clelland (1967) "Professionalization and stratification patterns in an industrial community." Amer. J. of Sociology 72 (January): 341–350.

Fisher, B. (1969) "Claims and credibility: a discussion of occupational identity and the agent-client relationship." Social Problems 16 (Spring): 423–433.

Fox, V. (1966) "Sociological and political aspects of police administration." Sociology and Social Research 51 (October): 39–48.

Freidson, E. (1968) "The impurity of professional authority," pp. 25–35 in H. Becker et al. (eds.) Institutions and the Person. Chicago: Aldine.

Gold, R. (1952) "Janitors vs. tenants: a status income dilemma." Amer. J. of Sociology 57 (March): 486–493.

Goldstein, F. (1960) "Police discretion not to invoke the criminal process." Yale Law J. 69 (March): 543–594.

Goode, W. (1961) "The librarian: from occupation to profession?" Library Q. 31 (October): 306–320.

———(1960) "Encroachment, charlatanism and the emerging profession: psychology, sociology and medicine." Amer. Soc. Rev. 25 (December): 902–914.

Grimshaw, A. D. (1963) "Actions of police and the military in American race riots." Phylon 24 (Fall): 271–289.

Hall, O. (1961) "The place of the professions in the urban community," pp. 117–134 in S. D. Clark (ed.) Urbanism and the Changing Canadian Society. Toronto: Univ. of Toronto Press.

Hughes, E. C. (1963) "Professions." Daedalus 92 (Fall): 655–668.

———(1959) "The study of occupation," pp. 442–460 in R. Merton et al. (eds.) Sociology Today. New York: Basic Books.

———(1958) Men and Their Work. Glencoe: Free Press.

Hopkins, E. (1931) Our Lawless Police. New York: Viking Press.

Issues in Criminology (1968) "Race and the Police." 4 (Fall).

Jacobs, P. (1966) Prelude to Riot. New York: Random House.

Knupfer, G. (1947) "Portrait of the underdog." Public Opinion Q. 11: 103–114.

Koenig, M. (1960) "Congruency, satisfaction and attitudes: a study of the police." M.A. thesis. Oberlin College.

Lane, R. (1967) Policing the City. Cambridge: Harvard Univ. Press.

LaPiere, R. (1934) "Attitudes vs. actions." Social Forces 13 (March): 230–237.

Levitin, T. E. (1964) "Role performance and role distance in a low-status occupation: the puller." Soc. Q. 5 (Summer): 251–260.

Levy, B. (1968) "Cops in the ghetto: a problem of the police system." Amer. Behavioral Scientist 2 (March–April): 31–34.

Lipset, S. (1969) "Why cops hate liberals—and vice versa." Atlantic 223 (March): 76–83.

McNamara, J. (1967) "Uncertainties in police work: recruits' backgrounds and training," pp. 221–222 in D. Bordua (ed.) The Police: Six Sociological Essays. New York: John Wiley.

Miller, W. (1958) "Lower class culture as a generating milieu of gang delinquency." J. of Social Issues 14.

New, P. K. (1965) "Communication: problems of interaction between professionals and clients." Community Mental Health J. (Fall): 251–255.

Niederhoffer, A. (1969) Behind the Shield. Garden City: Anchor Books.

Piliavin, I. and S. Briar (1964) "Police encounters with juveniles." Amer. J. of Sociology 70 (September): 209–211.

Rankin, J. (1959) "Psychiatric screening of police recruits." Public Personnel Rev. 20 (July): 191–196.

Reiss, A. and D. Bordua (1967) "Environment and organization: a perspective on the police," in D. Bordua (ed.) The Police: Six Sociological Essays. New York: John Wiley.

Skolnick, J. H. (1966) Justice Without Trial. New York: John Wiley.

Smith, A., B. Locke, and W. Walker (1968) "Authoritarianism in police college students and non-police college students." J. of Criminal Law, Criminology & Police Sci. 59 (December): 624–631.

Stinchcombe, A. L. (1963) "Institutions of privacy in the determination of police administrative practice." Amer. J. of Sociology 69 (September): 150–161.

Stoddard, E. (1968) "The informal 'code' of police deviancy: a group approach to blue-coat crime." J. of Criminal Law, Criminology & Police Sci. 59 (June): 201–213.

Srole, L. (1956) "Social integration and certain corollaries: an explanatory study." Amer. Soc. Rev. 21 (December): 709–716.

Strauss, E. (1964) "Work-flow frictions, interfunctional rivalry and professionalism: a case study of purchasing agents." Human Organization 23 (Summer): 137–149.

Sutherland, E. and *D. Cressey* (1966) Principles of Criminology. Philadelphia: J. B. Lippincott.

Tittle, C. and *R. Hill* (1967) "Attitude measurement and prediction of behavior: an evaluation of conditions and measurement techniques." Sociometry 30: 199–213.

Toch, H. (1969) Violent Men. Chicago: Aldine.

Turner, W. W. (1968) The Police Establishment. New York: Putnam.

Van Allen, E. (1968) Our Handcuffed Police. Mineola, N.Y.: Repertorial Press.

Vega, W. (1968) "The liberal policeman: a contradiction in terms." Issues in Criminology 4 (Fall): 15.

Vollmer, H. and *D. Mills* (1966) Professionalization. Englewood Cliffs, N.J.: Prentice-Hall.

Walsh, J. L. (1969) "Nurses, professional striving and the poor—a case of incompatibility." Social Sci. and Medicine 3 (forthcoming).

————and *R. H. Elling* (1968) "Professionalism and the poor-structural effects and professional behavior." J. of Health and Social Behavior 9 (March): 16–28.

Westley, W. (1953) "Violence and the police." Amer. J. of Sociology 59 (July): 34–41.

————(1951) "The police: a sociological study of law, custom and morality." Ph.D. dissertation. University of Chicago.

Whyte, W. F. (1943) Street Corner Society. Chicago: Univ. of Chicago Press.

Wiener, M. (1950) "The grand privilege: a scholar's appreciation." Saturday Rev. 43 (March 5): 54.

Wilensky, H. L. (1964) "The professionalization of everyone?" Amer. J. of Sociology 70 (September): 137–158.

Wilson, J. Q. (1964) "Generational and ethnic differences among career police officers." Amer. J. of Sociology 69 (March): 522–529.

————(1963) "The police and their problems: a theory." Public Policy 12: 189–216.

Wilson, O. W. (1964) "Police authority in a free society." J. of Criminal Law, Criminology & Police Sci. 54 (June): 175–177.

Zimbardo, P. (1968) "Coercion and compliance: the psychology of police confessions," pp. 550–570 in R. Perrucci and M. Pilesuk (eds.) The Triple Revolution: Social Problems in Depth. Boston: Little, Brown.

Zola, I. and *S. Croog* (1968) "Work perceptions and their implication for professional identity." Social Sci. & Medicine 2 (March): 15–28.

Part three

Law enforcement and the courts

Part Three consists of articles in which edited court opinions together with some commentary are presented. A student interested in criminal justice administration should be familiar with court opinions. Together with the common law, statutes, and court rules of procedure, these opinions are the building blocks of the criminal law.

With the exception of Justice Harlan's concurring opinion in Terry and the dissenting opinion of Chief Justice Burger in Bivens, all the opinions presented here express the view of a majority of the court.* Most of the cases had dissenting opinions which said that the majority was wrong. Many of them also had concurring opinions which agreed with the majority but wished to express either a somewhat different view or additional views. The dissenting and concurring opinions have been deleted.

The editors have selected five areas of law enforcement (as that term is used in its broadest sense) to be treated by edited versions of important court opinions in those areas. This should not be interpreted to mean that these are the only areas of importance—they aren't. Also, the assembled edited court opinions should not be considered, when taken together, as being a complete discourse on the topic of the article. They were selected to give the reader an overview of the problems involved and a familiarity with court opinions.

* *Kirby* and *Atz* do represent slight variations from the usual majority opinion.

Stop and frisk

TERRY v. OHIO
392 U.S. 1 (1968)

Mr. Chief Justice WARREN delivered the opinion of the Court.

This case presents serious questions concerning the role of the Fourth Amendment in the confrontation on the street between the citizen and the policeman investigating suspicious circumstances.

Petitioner Terry was convicted of carrying a concealed weapon and sentenced to the statutorily prescribed term of one to three years in the penitentiary. Following the denial of a pretrial motion to suppress, the prosecution introduced in evidence two revolvers and a number of bullets seized from Terry and a codefendant, Richard Chilton, by Cleveland Police Detective Martin McFadden. At the hearing on the motion to suppress this evidence, Officer McFadden testified that while he was patrolling in plain clothes in downtown Cleveland at approximately 2:30 in the afternoon of October 31, 1963, his attention was attracted by two men, Chilton and Terry, standing on the corner of Huron Road and Euclid Avenue. He had never seen the two men before, and he was unable to say precisely what first drew his eye to them. However, he testified that he had been a policeman for 39 years and a detective for 35 and that he had been assigned to patrol this vicinity of downtown Cleveland for shoplifters and pickpockets for 30 years. He explained that he had developed routine habits of observation over the years and that he would "stand and watch people or walk and watch people at many intervals of the day." He added: "Now, in this case when I looked over they didn't look right to me at the time."

His interest aroused, Officer McFadden took up a post of observation in the entrance to a store 300 to 400 feet away from the two men. "I get more purpose to watch them when I seen their movements," he testified. He saw one of the men leave the other one and walk southwest on Huron Road, past some stores. The man paused for a moment and looked in a store window, then walked on a short distance, turned around and walked back toward the corner, pausing once again to look in the same store window. He rejoined his companion at the corner, and the two conferred briefly. Then the second man went through the same series of motions, strolling down Huron Road, looking in the same window, walking on a short distance, turning back, peering in the store window again, and returning to confer with the first man at the corner. The two men repeated this ritual alternately between five and six times apiece—in all, roughly a dozen trips. At one point, while the two were standing together on the corner, a third man approached them and engaged them briefly in conversation. This man then left the two others and walked west on Euclid Avenue. Chilton and Terry resumed their measured pacing, peering, and conferring. After this had gone on for 10 to 12 minutes, the two men walked off together, heading west on Euclid Avenue, following the path taken earlier by the third man.

By this time, Officer McFadden had become thoroughly suspicious. He testified that after observing their elaborately casual and oft-repeated reconnaissance of the store window on Huron Road, he suspected the two men of "casing a job, a stick-up," and that he considered it his duty as a police officer to investigate further. He added that he feared "they may have a gun." Thus, Officer McFadden followed Chilton and Terry and saw them stop in front of Zucker's store to talk to the same man who had conferred with them earlier on the street corner. Deciding that the situation was ripe for direct action, Officer McFadden approached the three men, identified himself as a police officer and asked for their names. At this point his knowledge was confined to what he had observed. He was not acquainted with any of the three men by name or by sight, and he had received no information concerning them from any other source. When the men "mumbled something" in response to his inquiries, Officer McFadden grabbed petitioner Terry, spun him around so that they were facing the other two, with Terry between McFadden and the others, and patted down the outside of his clothing. In the left breast pocket of Terry's overcoat Officer McFadden felt a pistol. He reached inside the overcoat pocket, but was unable to remove the gun. At this point, keeping Terry between himself and the others, the officer ordered all three men to enter Zucker's store. As they went in, he removed Terry's overcoat completely, retrieved a .38-caliber revolver from the pocket and ordered all three men to face the wall with their hands raised. Officer McFadden proceeded to pat down the outer clothing of Chilton and the third man, Katz. He discovered another revolver in the outer pocket of Chilton's overcoat, but no weapons were found on Katz. The officer testified that he only patted the men down to see whether they had weapons, and that he did not put his hands beneath the outer garments of either Terry or Chilton until he felt their guns. So far as appears from the record, he never placed his hands beneath Katz' outer garments. Officer McFadden seized Chilton's gun, asked the proprietor of the store to call a police wagon, and took all three men to the station, where Chilton and Terry were formally charged with carrying concealed weapons.

On the motion to suppress the guns the prosecution took the position that they had been seized following a search incident to a lawful arrest. The trial court rejected this theory, stating that it "would be stretching the facts beyond reasonable comprehension" to find that Officer McFadden had had probable cause to arrest the men before he patted them down for weapons. However, the court denied the defendants' motion on the ground that Officer McFadden, on the basis of his experience, "had reasonable cause to believe . . . that the defendants were conducting themselves suspiciously, and some interrogation should be made of their action." Purely for his own protection, the court held, the officer had the right to pat down the outer clothing of these men, whom he had reasonable cause to believe might be armed. The court distinguished between an investigatory "stop" and an arrest, and between a "frisk" of the outer clothing for weapons and a full-blown search for evidence of crime. The frisk, it held, was essential to the proper performance of the officer's investigatory duties, for without it "the answer to the police officer may be a bullet, and a loaded pistol discovered during the frisk is admissible."

After the court denied their motion to suppress, Chilton and Terry waived jury trial and pleaded not guilty. The court adjudged them guilty. . . .

. . . .

The Fourth Amendment provides that "the right of the people to be secure in their persons, houses, papers, and effects, against unreasonable searches and seizures, shall not be violated. . . ." This inestimable right of personal security belongs as much to the citizen on the streets of our great cities as to the homeowner closeted in his study to dispose of his secret affairs.

. . . .

The question is whether in all the circumstances of this on-the-street encounter, his [*Terry's*] right to personal security was violated by an unreasonable search and seizure.

We would be less than candid if we did not acknowledge that this question thrusts to the fore difficult and troublesome issues regarding a sensitive area of police activity—issues which have never before been squarely presented to this Court. Reflective of the tensions involved are the practical and constitutional arguments pressed with great vigor on both sides of the public debate over the power of the police to "stop and frisk"—as it is sometimes euphemistically termed—suspicious persons.

On the one hand, it is frequently argued that in dealing with the rapidly unfolding and often dangerous situations on city streets the police are in need of an escalating set of flexible responses, graduated in relation to the amount of information they possess. For this purpose it is urged that distinctions should be made between a "stop" and an "arrest" (or a "seizure" of a person), and between a "frisk" and a "search." Thus, it is argued, the police should be allowed to "stop" a person and detain him briefly for questioning upon suspicion that he may be connected with criminal activity. Upon suspicion that the person may be armed, the police should have the power to "frisk" him for weapons. If the "stop" and the "frisk" give rise to probable cause to believe that the suspect has committed a crime, then the police should be empowered to make a formal "arrest," and a full incident "search" of the person. This scheme is justified in part upon the notion that a "stop" and a "frisk" amount to a mere "minor inconvenience and petty indignity," which can properly be imposed upon the citizen in the interest of effective law enforcement on the basis of a police officer's suspicion.

On the other side the argument is made that the authority of the police must be strictly circumscribed by the law of arrest and search as it has developed to date in the traditional jurisprudence of the Fourth Amendment. It is contended with some force that there is not—and cannot be—a variety of police activity which does not depend solely upon the voluntary cooperation of the citizen and yet which stops short of an arrest based upon probable cause to make such an arrest. The heart of the Fourth Amendment, the argument runs, is a severe requirement of specific justification for any intrusion upon protected personal security, coupled with a highly developed system of judicial controls to enforce upon the agents of the State the commands of the Constitution. Acquiescence by the courts in the compulsion inherent in the field interrogation practices at issue here, it is urged, would constitute an abdication of judicial control over, and indeed an encouragement of, substantial interference with liberty and personal security by police officers whose judgment is necessarily colored by their primary involvement in "the often competitive enterprise of ferreting out crime" *[Case citation omitted].* This, it is argued, can only serve to exacerbate police-community tensions in the crowded centers of our nation's cities.

In this context we approach the issues in this case mindful of the limitations of the judicial function in controlling the myriad daily situations in which policemen and citizens confront each other on the street.

. . . .

Having thus roughly sketched the perimeters of the constitutional debate over the limits on police investigative conduct in general and the background against which this case presents itself, we turn our attention to the quite narrow question posed by the facts before us: whether it is always unreasonable for a policeman to seize a person and subject him to a limited search for weapons unless there is probable cause for an arrest. Given the narrowness of this question, we have no occasion to canvass in detail the constitutional limitations upon the scope of a policeman's power when he confronts a citizen without probable cause to arrest him.

II.

Our first task is to establish at what point in this encounter the Fourth Amendment becomes relevant. That is, we must decide whether and when Officer McFadden "seized" Terry and whether and when he conducted a "search." There is some suggestion in the use of such terms as "stop" and "frisk" that such police conduct is outside the purview of the Fourth Amendment because neither action rises to the level of a "search" or "seizure" within the meaning of the Constitution. We emphatically reject this notion. It is quite plain that the Fourth Amendment governs "seizures" of the person which do not eventuate in a trip to the station house and prosecution for crime—"arrests" in traditional terminology. It must be recognized that whenever a police officer accosts an individual and restrains his freedom to walk away, he has "seized" that person. And it is nothing less than sheer torture of the English language to suggest that a careful exploration of the outer surfaces of a person's clothing all over his or her body in an attempt to find weapons is not a "search." Moreover, it is simply fantastic to urge that such a procedure performed in public by a policeman while the citizen stands helpless, perhaps facing a wall with his hands raised, is a "petty indignity." It is a serious intrusion upon the sanctity of the person, which may inflict great indignity and arouse strong resentment, and it is not to be undertaken lightly.

. . . .

The distinctions of classical "stop-and-frisk" theory thus serve to divert attention from the central inquiry under the Fourth Amendment—the reasonableness in all the circumstances of the particular governmental invasion of a citizen's personal security. "Search" and "seizure" are not talismans. We therefore reject the notions that the Fourth Amendment does not come into play at all as a limitation upon police conduct if the officers stop short of something called a "technical arrest" or a "full-blown search."

In this case there can be no question, then, that Officer McFadden "seized" petitioner and subjected him to a "search" when he took hold of him and patted down the outer surfaces of his clothing. We must decide whether at that point it was reasonable for Officer McFadden to have interfered with petitioner's personal security as he did.[16] And in determining whether the seizure and search were "unreasonable" our inquiry is a dual one—whether the officer's action was justified at its inception, and whether it was reasonably related in scope to the circumstances which justified the interference in the first place.

III.

If this case involved police conduct subject to the Warrant Clause of the Fourth Amendment, we would have to ascertain whether "probable cause" existed to justify the search and seizure which took place. However, that is not the case. We do not retreat from our holdings that the police must, whenever practicable, obtain advance judicial approval of searches and seizures through the warrant procedure [Case citations omitted], or that in most in-

---

[16] We thus decide nothing today concerning the constitutional propriety of an investigative "seizure" upon less than probable cause for purposes of "detention" and/or interrogation. Obviously, not all personal intercourse between policemen and citizens involves "seizures" of persons. Only when the officer, by means of physical force or show of authority, has in some way restrained the liberty of a citizen may we conclude that a "seizure" has occurred. We cannot tell with any certainty upon this record whether any such "seizure" took place here prior to Officer McFadden's initiation of physical contact for purposes of searching Terry for weapons, and we thus may assume that up to that point no intrusion upon constitutionally protected rights had occurred.

stances failure to comply with the warrant requirement can only be excused by exigent circumstances *[Case citations omitted]*. But we deal here with an entire rubric of police conduct—necessarily swift action predicated upon the on-the-spot observations of the officer on the beat—which historically has not been, and as a practical matter could not be, subjected to the warrant procedure. Instead, the conduct involved in this case must be tested by the Fourth Amendment's general proscription against unreasonable searches and seizures.

Nonetheless, the notions which underlie both the warrant procedure and the requirement of probable cause remain fully relevant in this context. In order to assess the reasonableness of Officer McFadden's conduct as a general proposition, it is necessary "first to focus upon the governmental interest which allegedly justifies official intrusion upon the constitutionally protected interests of the private citizen," for there is "no ready test for determining reasonableness other than by balancing the need to search [or seize] against the invasion which the search [or seizure] entails" *[Case citation omitted]*. And in justifying the particular intrusion the police officer must be able to point to specific and articulable facts which, taken together with rational inferences from those facts, reasonably warrant that intrusion. The scheme of the Fourth Amendment becomes meaningful only when it is assured that at some point the conduct of those charged with enforcing the laws can be subjected to the more detached, neutral scrutiny of a judge who must evaluate the reasonableness of a particular search or seizure in light of the particular circumstances. And in making that assessment it is imperative that the facts be judged against an objective standard: would the facts available to the officer at the moment of the seizure or the search "warrant a man of reasonable caution in the belief" that the action taken was appropriate? *[Case citations omitted.]* Anything less would invite intrusions upon constitutionally guaranteed rights based on nothing more substantial than inarticulate hunches, a result this Court has consistently refused to sanction *[Case citations omitted]*. And simple " 'good faith on the part of the arresting officer is not enough.' . . . If subjective good faith alone were the test, the protections of the Fourth Amendment would evaporate, and the people would be 'secure in their persons, houses, papers and effects,' only in the discretion of the police" *[Case citation omitted]*.

Applying these principles to this case, we consider first the nature and extent of the governmental interests involved. One general interest is of course that of effective crime prevention and detection; it is this interest which underlies the recognition that a police officer may in appropriate circumstances and in an appropriate manner approach a person for purposes of investigating possibly criminal behavior even though there is no probable cause to make an arrest. It was this legitimate investigative function Officer McFadden was discharging when he decided to approach [Terry] and his companions. He had observed Terry, Chilton, and Katz go through a series of acts, each of them perhaps innocent in itself, but which taken together warranted further investigation. There is nothing unusual in two men standing together on a street corner, perhaps waiting for someone. Nor is there anything suspicious about people in such circumstances strolling up and down the street, singly or in pairs. Store windows, moreover, are made to be looked in. But the story is quite different where, as here, two men hover about a street corner for an extended period of time, at the end of which it becomes apparent that they are not waiting for anyone or anything; where these men pace alternately along an identical route, pausing to stare in the same store window roughly 24 times; where each completion of this route is followed immediately by a conference between the two men on the corner; where they are joined in one of these conferences by a third man who leaves swiftly; and where the two men finally follow the third and rejoin him a couple of blocks away. It would have been poor police work indeed for an officer of 30 years' experience in the detection of thievery from stores in this same neighborhood to have failed to investigate this behavior further.

The crux of this case, however, is not the propriety of Officer McFadden's taking steps to investigate [Terry's] suspicious behavior, but rather, whether there was justification for McFadden's invasion of Terry's personal security by searching him for weapons in the course of that investigation. We are now concerned with more than the governmental interest in investigating crime; in addition, there is the more immediate interest of the police officer in taking steps to assure himself that the person with whom he is dealing is not armed with a weapon that could unexpectedly and fatally be used against him. Certainly it would be unreasonable to require that police officers take unnecessary risks in the performance of their duties. American criminals have a long tradition of armed violence, and every year in this country many law enforcement officers are killed in the line of duty, and thousands more are wounded. Virtually all of these deaths and a substantial portion of the injuries are inflicted with guns and knives.

In view of these facts, we cannot blind ourselves to the need for law enforcement officers to protect themselves and other prospective victims of violence in situations where they may lack probable cause for an arrest. When an officer is justified in believing that the individual whose suspicious behavior he is investigating at close range is armed and presently dangerous to the officer or to others, it would appear to be clearly unreasonable to deny the officer the power to take necessary measures to determine whether the person is in fact carrying a weapon and to neutralize the threat of physical harm.

We must still consider, however, the nature and quality of the intrusion on individual rights which must be accepted if police officers are to be conceded the right to search for weapons in situations where probable cause to arrest for crime is lacking. Even a limited search of the outer clothing for weapons constitutes a severe, though brief, intrusion upon cherished personal security, and it must surely be an annoying, frightening, and perhaps humiliating experience. *[Terry]* contends that such an intrusion is permissible only incident to a lawful arrest, either for a crime involving the possession of weapons or for a crime the commission of which led the officer to investigate in the first place. However, this argument must be closely examined.

[Terry] does not argue that a police officer should refrain from making any investigation of suspicious circumstances until such time as he has probable cause to make an arrest; nor does he deny that police officers in properly discharging their investigative function may find themselves confronting persons who might well be armed and dangerous. Moreover, he does not say that an officer is always unjustified in searching a suspect to discover weapons. Rather, he says it is unreasonable for the policeman to take that step until such time as the situation evolves to a point where there is probable cause to make an arrest. When that point has been reached, *[Terry]* would concede the officer's right to conduct a search of the suspect for weapons, fruits or instrumentalities of the crime, or "mere" evidence, incident to the arrest.

There are two weaknesses in this line of reasoning, however. First, it fails to take account of traditional limitations upon the scope of searches, and thus recognizes no distinction in purpose, character, and extent between a search incident to an arrest and a limited search for weapons. The former, although justified in part by the acknowledged necessity to protect the arresting officer from assault with a concealed weapon *[Case citation omitted]*, is also justified on other grounds . . . and can therefore involve a relatively extensive exploration of the person. A search for weapons in the absence of probable cause to arrest, however, must, like any other search, be strictly circumscribed by the exigencies which justify its initiation [Case citation omitted]. Thus it must be limited to that which is necessary for the discovery of weapons which might be used to harm the officer or others nearby, and may realistically be characterized as something less than a "full" search, even though it remains a serious intrusion.

A second, and related, objection to [Terry's] argument is that it assumes that the law of arrest has already worked out the balance between the particular interests involved here—the neutralization of danger to the policeman in the investigative circumstance and the sanctity of the individual. But this is not so. An arrest is a wholly different kind of intrusion upon individual freedom from a limited search for weapons, and the interests each is designed to serve are likewise quite different. An arrest is the initial stage of a criminal prosecution. It is intended to vindicate society's interest in having its laws obeyed, and it is inevitably accompanied by future interference with the individual's freedom of movement, whether or not trial or conviction ultimately follows. The protective search for weapons, on the other hand, constitutes a brief, though far from inconsiderable, intrusion upon the sanctity of the person. It does not follow that because an officer may lawfully arrest a person only when he is apprised of facts sufficient to warrant a belief that the person has committed or is committing a crime, the officer is equally unjustified, absent that kind of evidence, in making any intrusions short of an arrest. Moreover, a perfectly reasonable apprehension of danger may arise long before the officer is possessed of adequate information to justify taking a person into custody for the purpose of prosecuting him for a crime. [Terry's] reliance on cases which have worked out standards of reasonableness with regard to "seizures" constituting arrests and searches incident thereto is thus misplaced. It assumes that the interests sought to be vindicated and the invasions of personal security may be equated in the two cases, and thereby ignores a vital aspect of the analysis of the reasonableness of particular types of conduct under the Fourth Amendment [Case citation omitted].

Our evaluation of the proper balance that has to be struck in this type of case leads us to conclude that there must be a narrowly drawn authority to permit a reasonable search for weapons for the protection of the police officer, where he has reason to believe that he is dealing with an armed and dangerous individual, regardless of whether he has probable cause to arrest the individual for a crime. The officer need not be absolutely certain that the individual is armed; the issue is whether a reasonably prudent man in the circumstances would be warranted in the belief that his safety or that of others was in danger *[Case citations omitted].* And in determining whether the officer acted reasonably in such circumstances, due weight must be given, not to his inchoate and unparticularized suspicion or "hunch," but to the specific reasonable inferences which he is entitled to draw from the facts in light of his experience *[Case citation omitted].*

IV.

We must now examine the conduct of Officer McFadden in this case to determine whether his search and seizure of *[Terry]* were reasonable, both at their inception and as conducted. He had observed Terry, together with Chilton and another man, acting in a manner he took to be preface to a "stick-up." We think on the facts and circumstances Officer McFadden detailed before the trial judge a reasonably prudent man would have been warranted in believing *[Terry]* was armed and thus presented a threat to the officer's safety while he was investigating his suspicious behavior. The actions of Terry and Chilton were consistent with McFadden's hypothesis that these men were contemplating a daylight robbery—which, it is reasonable to assume, would be likely to involve the use of weapons—and nothing in their conduct from the time he first noticed them until the time he confronted them and identified himself as a police officer gave him sufficient reason to negate that hypothesis. Although the trio had departed the original scene, there was nothing to indicate abandonment of an intent to commit a robbery at some point. Thus, when Officer McFadden approached the three men gathered before the display window at Zucker's store he had observed enough to make it quite reasonable to fear that they were armed; and nothing in their response to his hailing them, identifying himself as a police officer, and asking their names served to dispel that reasonable belief. We cannot say his decision at that point to seize Terry and pat his clothing for weapons was the product of a volatile or inventive imagination, or was undertaken simply as an act of harassment; the record evidences the tempered act of a policeman who in the course of an investigation had to make a quick decision as to how to protect himself and others from possible danger, and took limited steps to do so.

. . . .

V.

We conclude that the revolver seized from Terry was properly admitted in evidence against him. At the time he seized *[Terry]* and searched him for weapons, Officer McFadden had reasonable grounds to believe that *[Terry]* was armed and dangerous, and it was necessary for the protection of himself and others to take swift measures to discover the true facts and neutralize the threat of harm if it materialized. The policeman carefully restricted his search to what was appropriate to the discovery of the particular items which he sought. Each case of this sort will, of course, have to be decided on its own facts. We merely hold today that where a police officer observes unusual conduct which leads him reasonably to conclude in light of his experience that criminal activity may be afoot and that the persons with whom he is dealing may be armed and presently dangerous, where in the course of investigating this behavior he identifies himself as a policeman and makes reasonable inquiries, and where nothing in the initial stages of the encounter serves to dispel his reasonable fear for his own or others' safety, he is entitled for the protection of himself and others in the area to conduct a carefully limited search of the outer clothing of such persons in an attempt to discover weapons which might be used to assault him. Such a search is a reasonable search under the Fourth Amendment, and any weapons seized may properly be introduced in evidence against the person from whom they were taken.

    Affirmed.

             [All footnotes except 16 are omitted.]

. . . .

    Mr. Justice HARLAN, concurring.

    While I unreservedly agree with the Court's ultimate holding in this case, I am constrained to fill in a few gaps, as I see them, in its opinion. I do this because what is said by this Court today will serve as initial guidelines for law enforcement authorities and courts throughout the land as this important new field of law develops.

    A police officer's right to make an on-the-street "stop" and an accompanying "frisk" for weapons is of course bounded by the protections afforded by the Fourth and Fourteenth Amendments. The Court holds, and I agree, that while the right does not depend upon possession by the officer of a valid warrant, nor upon the existence of probable cause, such activities must be reasonable under the circumstances as the officer credibly relates them in court. Since the question in this and most cases is whether evidence produced by a frisk is admissible, the problem is to determine what makes a frisk reasonable.

If the State of Ohio were to provide that police officers could, on articulable suspicion less than probable cause, forcibly frisk and disarm persons thought to be carrying concealed weapons, I would have little doubt that action taken pursuant to such authority could be constitutionally reasonable. Concealed weapons create an immediate and severe danger to the public, and though that danger might not warrant routine general weapons checks, it could well warrant action on less than a "probability." I mention this line of analysis because I think it vital to point out that it cannot be applied in this case. On the record before us Ohio has not clothed its policemen with routine authority to frisk and disarm on suspicion; in the absence of state authority, policemen have no more right to "pat down" the outer clothing of passers-by, or of persons to whom they address casual questions, than does any other citizen. Consequently, the Ohio courts did not rest the constitutionality of this frisk upon any general authority in Officer McFadden to take reasonable steps to protect the citizenry, including himself, from dangerous weapons.

The state courts held, instead, that when an officer is lawfully confronting a possibly hostile person in the line of duty he has a right, springing only from the necessity of the situation and not from any broader right to disarm, to frisk for his own protection. This holding, with which I agree and with which I think the Court agrees, offers the only satisfactory basis I can think of for affirming this conviction. The holding has, however, two logical corollaries that I do not think the Court has fully expressed.

In the first place, if the frisk is justified in order to protect the officer during an encounter with a citizen, the officer must first have constitutional grounds to insist on an encounter, to make a *forcible* stop. Any person, including a policeman, is at liberty to avoid a person he considers dangerous. If and when a policeman has a right instead to disarm such a person for his own protection, he must first have a right not to avoid him but to be in his presence. That right must be more than the liberty (again, possessed by every citizen) to address questions to other persons, for ordinarily the person addressed has an equal right to ignore his interrogator and walk away; he certainly need not submit to a frisk for the questioner's protection. I would make it perfectly clear that the right to frisk in this case depends upon the reasonableness of a forcible stop to investigate a suspected crime.

Where such a stop is reasonable, however, the right to frisk must be immediate and automatic if the reason for the stop is, as here, an articulable suspicion of a crime of violence. Just as a full search incident to a lawful arrest requires no additional justification, a limited frisk incident to a lawful stop must often be rapid and routine. There is no reason why an officer, rightfully but forcibly confronting a person suspected of a serious crime, should have to ask one question and take the risk that the answer might be a bullet.

The facts of this case are illustrative of a proper stop and an incident frisk. Officer McFadden had no probable cause to arrest Terry for anything, but he had observed circumstances that would reasonably lead an experienced, prudent policeman to suspect that Terry was about to engage in burglary or robbery. His justifiable suspicion afforded a proper constitutional basis for accosting Terry, restraining his liberty of movement briefly, and addressing questions to him, and Officer McFadden did so. When he did, he had no reason whatever to suppose that Terry might be armed, apart from the fact that he suspected him of planning a violent crime. McFadden asked Terry his name, to which Terry "mumbled something." Whereupon McFadden, without asking Terry to speak louder and without giving him any chance to explain his presence or his actions, forcibly frisked him.

I would affirm this conviction for what I believe to be the same reasons the Court relies on. I would, however, make explicit what I think is implicit in affirmance on the present facts. Officer McFadden's right to interrupt Terry's freedom of movement and invade his privacy arose only because circumstances warranted forcing an encounter with Terry in an effort to prevent or investigate a crime. Once that forced encounter was justified, however, the officer's right to take suitable measures for his own safety followed automatically.

Upon the foregoing premises, I join the opinion of the Court.

[*In his opinion in the combined cases of* Sibron v. New York, *and* Peters v. New York, *Mr. Chief Justice Warren contrasted the situation in* Sibron *to that in* Terry v. Ohio.]

SIBRON v. STATE OF NEW YORK
392 U.S. 41 (1968)

The facts . . . may be stated briefly. Sibron . . . was convicted of the unlawful possession of heroin. He moved before trial to suppress the heroin seized from his person by the arresting officer,

Brooklyn Patrolman Anthony Martin. After the trial court denied his motion, Sibron pleaded guilty to the charge, preserving his right to appeal the evidentiary ruling. At the hearing on the motion to suppress, Officer Martin testified that while he was patrolling his beat in uniform on March 9, 1965, he observed Sibron "continually from the hours of 4:00 p.m. to 12:00 midnight . . . in the vicinity of 742 Broadway." He stated that during this period of time he saw Sibron in conversation with six or eight persons whom he (Patrolman Martin) knew from past experience to be narcotics addicts. The officer testified that he did not overhear any of these conversations, and that he did not see anything pass between Sibron and any of the others. Late in the evening Sibron entered a restaurant. Patrolman Martin saw Sibron speak with three more known addicts inside the restaurant. Once again, nothing was overheard and nothing was seen to pass between Sibron and the addicts. Sibron sat down and ordered pie and coffee, and, as he was eating, Patrolman Martin approached him and told him to come outside. Once outside, the officer said to Sibron, "You know what I am after." According to the officer, Sibron "mumbled something and reached into his pocket." Simultaneously, Patrolman Martin thrust his hand into the same pocket, discovering several glassine envelopes, which, it turned out, contained heroin.
. . . .

Although the Court of Appeals of New York wrote no opinion in this case, it seems to have viewed the search here as a self-protective search for weapons and to have affirmed on the basis of § 180-a *[the stop and frisk statute]*, which authorizes such a search when the officer "reasonably suspects that he is in danger of life or limb." The Court of Appeals has, at any rate, justified searches during field interrogation on the ground that "[t]he answer to the question propounded by the policeman may be a bullet; in any case the exposure to danger could be very great" *[Case citation omitted]*. But the application of this reasoning to the facts of this case proves too much. The police officer is not entitled to seize and search every person whom he sees on the street or of whom he makes inquiries. Before he places a hand on the person of a citizen in search of anything, he must have constitutionally adequate, reasonable grounds for doing so. In the case of the self-protective search for weapons, he must be able to point to particular facts from which he reasonably inferred that the individual was armed and dangerous (Terry v. Ohio) . . . . Patrolman Martin's testimony reveals no such facts. The suspect's mere act of talking with a number of known narcotics addicts over an eight-hour period no more gives rise to reasonable fear of life or limb on the part of the police officer than it justifies an arrest for committing a crime. Nor did Patrolman Martin urge that when Sibron put his hand in his pocket, he feared that he was going for a weapon and acted in self-defense. His opening statement to Sibron—"You know what I am after"—made it abundantly clear that he sought narcotics, and his testimony at the hearing left no doubt that he thought there were narcotics in Sibron's pocket.

Even assuming *arguendo* that there were adequate grounds to search Sibron for weapons, the nature and scope of the search conducted by Patrolman Martin were so clearly unrelated to that justification as to render the heroin inadmissible. The search for weapons approved in *Terry* consisted solely of a limited patting of the outer clothing of the suspect for concealed objects which might be used as instruments of assault. Only when he discovered such objects did the officer in *Terry* place his hands in the pockets of the men he searched. In this case, with no attempt at an initial limited exploration for arms, Patrolman Martin thrust his hand into Sibron's pocket and took from him envelopes of heroin. His testimony shows that he was looking for narcotics, and he found them. The search was not reasonably limited in scope to the accomplishment of the only goal which might conceivably have justified its inception—the protection of the officer by disarming a potentially dangerous man. Such a search violates the guarantee of the Fourth Amendment, which protects the sanctity of the person against unreasonable intrusions on the part of all government agents.
. . . .

[The Court went on to reverse Sibron's conviction.]
[Footnotes omitted.]

Search incident to lawful arrest: narrowed scope of permissible search, wide application to arrests, and state response to Robinson and Gustafson

The Constitution of the United States, as a general rule, requires that the police have a search warrant before carrying out any search. There are a number of exceptions to this requirement for a search warrant, one of which is that a police officer needs no warrant to search a person whom he has arrested. There are two principal problem areas dealing with this so-called search incident to lawful arrest. The first of these is, to what extent may the officer search? Must his search be limited merely to the person of the individual he has arrested or may it be broader than that, including the place or a portion of the place in which the individual is arrested? The second problem deals with whether the rule of search incident to lawful arrest may be applied to any arrest or only some types of arrest. The present answer to these questions is to be found in the portions of court opinions which follow.

CHIMEL v. CALIFORNIA
395 U.S. 752 (1969)

Mr. Justice STEWART delivered the opinion of the Court.

This case raises basic questions concerning the permissible scope under the Fourth Amendment of a search incident to a lawful arrest.

The relevant facts are essentially undisputed. Late in the afternoon of September 13, 1965, three police officers arrived at the Santa Ana, California, home of [Chimel] with a warrant authorizing his arrest [they did not have a search warrant] for the burglary of a coin shop. The officers knocked on the door, identified themselves to [Chimel's] wife, and asked if they might come inside. She ushered them into the house, where they waited 10 or 15 minutes until [Chimel] returned home from work. When [Chimel] entered the house, one of the officers handed him the arrest warrant and asked for permission to "look around." *[Chimel]* objected, but was advised that "on the basis of the lawful arrest," the officers would nonetheless conduct a search. No search warrant had been issued.

Accompanied by *[Chimel's]* wife, the officers then looked through the entire three-bedroom house, including the attic, the garage, and a small workshop. In some rooms the search was relatively cursory. In the master bedroom and sewing room, however, the officers directed *[Chimel's]* wife to open drawers and "to physically move contents of the drawers from side to side so that [they] might view any items that would have come from [the] burglary." After completing the search, they seized numerous items—primarily coins, but also several medals, tokens, and a few other objects. The entire search took between 45 minutes and an hour.

At *[Chimel's]* subsequent state trial on two charges of burglary, the items taken from his house were admitted into evidence against him, over his objection that they had been unconstitutionally seized. He was convicted. . . .

· · · ·

Approval of a warrantless search *[that is, no search warrant]* incident to a lawful arrest seems first to have been articulated by the *[Supreme]* Court in *[an earlier case when it was said:]*

What then is the present case? Before answering that inquiry specifically, it may be well by a process of exclusion to state what it is not. It is not an assertion of the right on the part of the Government, always recognized under English and American law, to search the person of the accused when legally arrested to discover and seize the fruits or evidences of crime. *[Case citation omitted.]*

That statement made no reference to any right to search the *place* where an arrest occurs, but was limited to a right to search the "person". Eleven years later the case of *Carroll v. United States [citation omitted]* brought the following embellishment of the *[above]* statement:

When a man is legally arrested for an offense, whatever is found upon his person, *or in his control* which it is unlawful for him to have and which may be used to prove the offense, may be seized and held as evidence in the prosecution (emphasis added). *[Citation omitted.]*

Still, that assertion was too far from a claim that the "place" where one is arrested may be searched so long as the arrest is valid. Without explanation, however, the principle emerged in expanded form a few months later in *[another Supreme Court case].*

· · · ·

[Justice Stewart then went on to mention a number of Supreme Court cases that discussed the extent of a search without a search warrant when the search was incident to a lawful arrest. Many of these cases were inconsistent with each other. After this analysis of earlier cases, Justice Stewart continued:]

When an arrest is made, it is reasonable for the arresting officer to search the person arrested in order to remove any weapons that the latter might seek to use in order to resist arrest or effect his escape. Otherwise, the officer's safety might well be endangered, and the arrest itself frustrated. In addition, it is entirely reasonable for the arresting officer to search for and seize any evidence on the arrestee's person in order to prevent its concealment or destruction. And the area into which an arrestee might reach in order to grab a weapon or evidentiary items must, of course, be governed by a like rule. A gun on a table or in a drawer in front of one who is arrested can be as dangerous to the arresting officer as one concealed in the clothing of the person arrested. There is ample justification, therefore, for a search of the arrestee's person and the area "within his immediate control"—construing that phrase to mean the area from within which he might gain possession of a weapon or destructible evidence.

There is no comparable justification, however, for routinely searching rooms other than that in which an arrest occurs—or, for that matter, for searching through all the desk drawers or other closed or concealed areas in that room itself. Such searches, in the absence of well-recognized exceptions, may be made only under the authority of a search warrant.

. . . .

Application of sound Fourth Amendment principles to the facts of this case produces a clear result. The search here went far beyond *[Chimel's]* person and the area from within which he might have obtained either a weapon or something that could have been used as evidence against him. There was no constitutional justification, in the absence of a search warrant, for extending the search beyond that area. The scope of the search was, therefore, "unreasonable" under the Fourth and Fourteenth Amendments and *[Chimel's]* conviction cannot stand.

Reversed.

[Footnotes omitted.]

UNITED STATES v. ROBINSON
414 U.S. 218 (1973)

Mr. Justice REHNQUIST delivered the opinion of the Court.

Respondent Robinson was convicted in United States District Court for the District of Columbia of the possession and facilitation of concealment of heroin.

. . . .

On April 23, 1968, at approximately 11 o'clock p.m., Officer Richard Jenks, a 15-year veteran of the District of Columbia Metropolitan Police Department, observed *[Robinson]* driving a 1965 Cadillac near the intersection of 8th and C Streets, Southeast, in the District of Columbia. Jenks, as a result of previous investigation following a check of *[Robinson's]* operator's permit four days earlier, determined there was reason to believe that *[Robinson]* was operating a motor vehicle after the revocation of his operator's permit. This is an offense defined by statute in the District of Columbia which carries a mandatory minimum jail term, a mandatory minimum fine, or both *[Citation omitted]*.

Jenks signaled *[Robinson]* to stop the automobile, which *[Robinson]* did, and all three of the occupants emerged from the car. At that point Jenks informed *[Robinson]* that he was under arrest for "operating after revocation and obtaining a permit by misrepresentation." It was assumed by the majority of the Court of Appeals, and is conceded by *[Robinson]* here, that Jenks had probable cause to arrest *[Robinson]*, and that he effected a full custody arrest.

In accordance with procedures prescribed in Police Department instructions, Jenks then began to search *[Robinson]*. He explained at a subsequent hearing that he was "face to face" with *[Robinson]*, and "placed [his] hands on *[Robinson]*, my right hand on his left breast like this (demonstrating) and proceeded to pat him down thus (with the right hand)." During this patdown, Jenks felt an object in the left breast pocket of the heavy coat *[Robinson]* was wearing, but testified that he "couldn't tell what it was" and also that he "couldn't actually tell the size of it." Jenks then reached into the pocket and pulled out the object, which turned out to be a "crumpled up cigarette package." Jenks testified that at this point he still did not know what was in the package:

> As I felt the package I could feel objects in the package but I couldn't tell what they were. . . . I knew they weren't cigarettes.

The officer then opened the cigarette pack and found 14 gelatin capsules of white powder which he thought to be, and which later analysis proved to be, heroin. Jenks then continued his search of *[Robinson]* to completion, feeling around his waist and trouser legs, and examining the remaining pockets. The heroin seized from *[Robinson]* was admitted into evidence at the trial which resulted in his conviction in the District Court.

. . . .

It is well settled that a search incident to a lawful arrest is a traditional exception to the warrant requirement of the Fourth Amendment. This general exception has historically been formulated into two distinct propositions. The first is that a search may be made of the *person* of the arrestee by virtue of the lawful arrest. The second is that a search may be made of the area within the control of the arrestee.

Examination of this Court's decisions in the area show that these two propositions have been treated quite differently. The validity of the search of a person incident to a lawful arrest has been regarded as settled from its first enunciation, and has remained virtually unchallenged until the present case. The validity of the second proposition, while likewise conceded in principle, has been subject to differing interpretations as to the extent of the area which may be searched.

. . . .

In *Chimel*, . . . full recognition was again given to the authority to search the person of the arrestee:

> When an arrest is made, it is reasonable for the arresting officer to search the person arrested in order to remove any weapons that the latter might seek to use in order to resist arrest or effect his escape. Otherwise, the officer's safety might well be endangered, and the arrest itself frustrated. In addition, it is entirely reasonable for the arresting officer to search for and seize any evidence on the arrestee's person in order to prevent its concealment or destruction. *[Citation omitted.]*

Three years after the decision in *Chimel* . . . we upheld the validity of a search in which heroin had been taken from the person of the defendant after his arrest on a weapons charge, in *Adams v. Williams [Citation omitted]*, saying:

> Under the circumstances surrounding Williams' possession of the gun seized by Sgt. Connolly, the arrest on the weapons charge was supported by probable cause, and the search of his person and of the car incident to that arrest was lawful. *[Citation omitted.]*

Last Term in *Cupp v. Murphy [Citation omitted]*, we again reaffirmed the traditional statement of the authority to search incident to a valid arrest.

Thus the broadly stated rule, and the reasons for it, have been repeatedly affirmed in the decisions of this Court. . . . Since the statements in the cases speak not simply in terms of an exception to the warrant requirement, but in terms of an affirmative authority to search, they clearly imply that such searches also meet the Fourth Amendment's requirement of reasonableness.

. . . .

Then Chief Judge Cardozo of the New York Court of Appeals summarized his understanding of the historical basis for the authority to search incident to arrest in these words:

The basic principle is this: Search of the person is unlawful when the seizure of the body is a trespass, and the purpose of the search is to discover grounds as yet unknown for arrest or accusation *[Citation omitted]*. Search of the person becomes lawful when grounds for arrest and accusation have been discovered, and the law is in the act of subjecting the body of the accused to its physical dominion.

The distinction may seem subtle, but in truth it is founded in shrewd appreciation of the necessities of government. We are not to strain an immunity to the point at which human nature rebels against honoring it in conduct. The peace officer empowered to arrest must be empowered to disarm. If he may disarm, he may search, lest a weapon be concealed. The search being lawful, he retains what he finds if connected with the crime. *[Citation omitted.]*

While these earlier authorities are sketchy, they tend to support the broad statement of the authority to search incident to arrest found in the successive decisions of this Court, . . .

. . . .

The justification or reason for the authority to search incident to a lawful arrest rests quite as much on the need to disarm the suspect in order to take him into custody as it does on the need to preserve evidence on his person for later use at trial *[Citation omitted]*.

. . . .

Nor are we inclined, on the basis of what seems to us to be a rather speculative judgment, to qualify the breadth of the general authority to search incident to a lawful custodial arrest on an assumption that persons arrested for the offense of driving while their license has been revoked are less likely to be possessed of dangerous weapons than are those arrested for other crimes. It is scarcely open to doubt that the danger to an officer is far greater in the case of the extended exposure which follows the taking of a suspect into custody and transporting him to the police station than in the case of the relatively fleeting contact resulting from the typical *[stop and frisk type situation. See* Terry v. Ohio *earlier in*

Part 3.]. This is an adequate basis for treating all custodial arrests alike for purposes of search justification.
. . . .

The authority to search the person incident to a lawful custodial arrest, while based upon the need to disarm and to discover evidence, does not depend on what a court may later decide was the probability in a particular arrest situation that weapons or evidence would in fact be found upon the person of the suspect. A custodial arrest of a suspect based on probable cause is a reasonable intrusion under the Fourth Amendment; that intrusion being lawful, a search incident to the arrest requires no additional justification. It is the fact of the lawful arrest which establishes the authority to search, and we hold that in the case of a lawful custodial arrest a full search of the person is not only an exception to the warrant requirement of the Fourth Amendment, but is also a "reasonable" search under that Amendment.
. . . .

Since it is the fact of custodial arrest which gives rise to the authority to search, it is of no moment that Jenks did not indicate any subjective fear of *[Robinson]* or that he did not himself suspect that *[Robinson]* was armed. Having in the course of a lawful search come upon the crumpled package of cigarettes, he was entitled to inspect it; and when his inspection revealed the heroin capsules, he was entitled to seize them as "fruits, instrumentalities, or contraband" probative of criminal conduct. *[Citations omitted.]*
       [Footnotes omitted.]
. . . .

GUSTAFSON v. FLORIDA
414 U.S. 260 (1973)

Mr. Justice REHNQUIST delivered the opinion of the Court.
    Petitioner James Gustafson was convicted in a Florida trial court for unlawful possession of marijuana. At his trial the State introduced into evidence marijuana which had been seized from him during a search incident to his arrest on a charge of driving without an operator's license.
. . . .

At approximately 2 a.m., on January 12, 1969, Lieutenant Paul R. Smith, a uniformed municipal police officer of Eau Gallie, Florida, was on a routine patrol in an unmarked squad car when he observed a 1953 white Cadillac, bearing New York license plates, driving south through the town. Smith observed the automobile weave across the center line and back to the right side of the road "three or four times" Smith testified that he observed the two occupants of the Cadillac look back; after they apparently saw the squad car, the car drove across the highway and behind a grocery store, and then headed south on another city street.

At that point Smith turned on his flashing light and pulled the Cadillac over to the side of the road. After stopping the vehicle, Smith asked [Gustafson], the driver, to produce his operator's license. [Gustafson] informed Smith that he was a student and that he had left his operator's license in his dormitory room in the neighboring city of Melbourne, Florida. [Gustafson] was then placed under arrest for failure to have his vehicle's operator's license in his possession. It was conceded . . . that the officer had probable cause to arrest upon learning that [Gustafson] did not have his license in his possession, and that he took [Gustafson] into custody in order to transport him to the stationhouse for further inquiry.

Smith then proceeded to search [Gustafson's] person. Smith testified that he patted down the clothing of [Gustafson] "outside and inside, I checked the belt, the shirt pockets and all around the belt, completely around the inside." Upon completing his patdown, he testified, he placed his hand into the left front pocket of the coat [Gustafson] was wearing. From that pocket he extracted a "long chain" and a Benson and Hedges cigarette box. Smith testified that he then "opened [the cigarette box] and it appeared there were marijuana cigarettes in the box. I had been shown this in training at the police department and these appeared to be marijuana to me."
. . . .

We have held today in United States v. Robinson that "it is the fact of the lawful arrest which establishes the authority to search, and . . . in the case of a lawful custodial arrest a full search of the person is not only an exception to the warrant requirement of the Fourth Amendment, but is also a 'reasonable' search under that Amendment" [Citation omitted]. Our decision in Robinson indicates that the limitations placed by Terry v. Ohio, . . . on protective searches conducted in an investigatory stop situation based on less than probable cause are not to be carried over to searches made incident to lawful custodial arrests.
. . . .

Though the officer here was not required to take [Gustafson] into custody by police regulations as he was in Robinson, and there did not exist a departmental policy establishing the conditions under

which a full scale body search should be conducted, we do not find
these differences determinative of the constitutional issue *[Citation
omitted]*. It is sufficient that the officer had probable cause to arrest
[Gustafson] and that he lawfully effectuated the arrest, and placed
[Gustafson] in custody. In addition, as our decision in *Robinson*
makes clear, the arguable absence of "evidentiary" purpose for a
search incident to a lawful arrest is not controlling *[Citation
omitted]*. "The authority to search a person incident to a lawful
custodial arrest, while based upon the need to disarm and to
discover evidence, does not depend on what a court may later
decide was the probability in a particular arrest situation that
weapons or evidence would in fact be found upon the person of the
suspect" *[Citation omitted]*.

II.

We hold therefore that upon arresting *[Gustafson]* for the offense
of driving his automobile without a valid operator's license, and
taking him into custody, Smith was entitled to make a full search of
[Gustafson's] person incident to that lawful arrest. Since it is the
fact of custodial arrest which gives rise to the authority to search, it
is of no moment that Smith did not indicate any subjective fear of
[Gustafson], or that he did not himself suspect that *[Gustafson]* was
armed. Having in the course of his lawful search come upon the box
of cigarettes, Smith was entitled to inspect it; and when his
inspection revealed the homemade cigarettes which he believed to
contain an unlawful substance, he was entitled to seize them as
"fruits, instrumentalities or contraband" probative of criminal
conduct *[Case citations omitted]*. The judgment of the Supreme
Court of Florida is therefore affirmed.

[Footnotes omitted.]

PEOPLE v. KELLY
353 N.Y.S. 2d 111 (1974)

*[The defendant was arrested in the State of New York
for trying to drive away in his car after a police officer demanded to
see his driver's license; a demand the officer was, by New York law,
entitled to make. A search of the defendant after his arrest revealed
a forged driver's license and some pills. The defendant, as a result*

of the discovery of the forged driver's license, was charged with driving with a suspended driver's license and forgery. A charge against the defendant of possession of a controlled substance resulted from the discovery of the pills.

The defendant asked the court to refuse to allow the prosecution to use either the forged driver's license or the pills as evidence against him (in legal terminology he "moved to have them suppressed") because he claimed that the police had no right to search him.]

HOWARD E. GOLDFLUSS, Judge.

The issues raised herein place into focus the conflict between the New York State Rule which limits search incidental to a traffic violation arrest *[Citation omitted]*, and the Federal Rule recently decided which permits full scale search under such circumstances. *[Judge Goldfluss here mentions the* Gustafson *and* Robinson *cases already referred to in this article.]*

. . . .

The *[New York]* Court of Appeals, in *[an earlier New York case,* People v. Marsh], decided that where there is an arrest for a traffic offense, the admissibility of the fruits of *the ensuing search must be limited to evidence in connection with the purpose of the arrest.* It cannot be said that the drugs found in the defendant's possession in the stationhouse and not at the scene would fall under this limitation.

. . . .

However, when the Supreme Court of the United States decided Gustafson v. Florida and United States v. Robinson, . . . they created the judicial dilemma we are faced with herein because the Supreme Court held that a valid arrest provides sufficient basis for a thorough, full scale and unlimited search of the defendant, regardless of the grounds of the arrest. In the *Robinson* case, the police officer, after checking the defendant's operator's permit, arrested the defendant for driving while his license was revoked. The court stated that pursuant to this custodial arrest, the officer was authorized to make a full scale search of defendant's person and the heroin discovered on his person was admissible in evidence. In Gustafson, defendant had no driver's license in his possession—was arrested—and a patdown search revealed marijuana cigarettes, which were admitted into evidence.

The principle, as set down by the Supreme Court, is that the custodial arrest justifies a thorough search, not limited or confined by the fact that the arrest was based upon a traffic violation.

Is this court bound to enforce a decision by the Court of Appeals of the State of New York or is it obliged to follow this diametrically opposed ruling? Unquestionably, the decision herein must be based solely upon the Fourth Amendment of the United States Constitution.

. . . .

It appears, therefore, that the *[New York]* Court of Appeals may not narrow Fourth Amendment protections further than the Supreme Court *[of the United States]* dictates, but there is no prohibition against the State . . . extending such protection. For these reasons, it is the opinion of this Court that Marsh is not replaced by Gustafson and Robinson and is still the law in New York. The principle of Marsh is fair, reasonable, and equitable, and was consistent with Federal interpretation of the Fourth Amendment prior to Gustafson and Robinson. These latter cases take issue with Marsh on the theory that the privacy of interest guarded by the Fourth Amendment is subordinate to a "legitimate and overriding governmental concern." Such a phrase has connotations which could erode Fourth Amendment protections . . .

The motion to suppress the dangerous drugs in connection with the *[charge of possession of a controlled substance]* is granted. . . .

[The motion to suppress the forged driver's license was refused since its discovery was "connected with the purpose of the arrest. This case purports to allow a state court to interpret a provision of the United States Constitution differently from the way interpreted by the United States Supreme Court if that interpretation places greater restrictions on police activity. This is incorrect as indicated by the United States Supreme Court in Oregon v. Hass: "[A] State is free as a matter of its own law to impose greater restrictions on police activity than those this Court holds to be necessary upon federal constitutional standards. . . . But, of course, a state may not impose such greater restrictions as a matter of federal constitutional law when this Court specifically refrains from enforcing them."]

In re RULE 6.13, FLORIDA TRAFFIC COURT RULES
Supreme Court of Florida
287 So. 2d 677 (1974)

A Case of original jurisdiction—Florida Traffic Court Rules.
   PER CURIAM.

At the request and suggestion of the Traffic Court Review Committee, Rule 6.13, Florida Traffic Court Rule, is amended by adding thereto the following provisions:

RULE 6.13. PRACTICE AS IN CRIMINAL CASES

Rule 3.191, Rules of Criminal Procedure, shall be applicable to traffic offenses. A person shall be considered "taken into custody" when he is arrested *or when a traffic citation or notice to appear is served upon him.*

This Rule shall be effective and govern the trial dates of all persons taken into custody after 12:01 a.m., Daylight Savings Time, on February 15, 1974.

The trial of all persons taken into custody prior to the effective date of this Rule shall commence on or before May 15, 1974, unless a written demand for speedy trial is made. Upon such demand trial shall commence within sixty days from service of such demand upon the prosecuting attorney.

In all other respects the Florida Traffic Court Rules are ratified and confirmed.

It is so ordered.

CARLTON, C. J., and ROBERTS, ERVIN, ADKINS, BOYD, McCAIN and DEKLE, JJ., concur.

[Emphasis added.]

The Miranda warning, its rise and seeming decline:
a series of cases

In part, the Fifth Amendment to the United States Constitution provides:

No person shall . . . be compelled in any criminal case to be a witness against himself . . .

This is the constitutional provision that protects against compelled self-incrimination.

In Escobedo, *and to a greater extent in* Miranda, *the Supreme Court considered the impact of the pressures of being in police custody on a person's right not to be compelled to incriminate himself.* Orozco *expanded the circumstances in which the protections set out in* Miranda *would apply. After* Orozco, *the Court began to limit the application of the* Miranda *protections, or at least refused to expand them further. The cases are* Harris *and* Tucker.

Escobedo *relied in large part on the right to counsel found in the Sixth Amendment.* Miranda *was based principally on the portion of the Fifth Amendment quoted above, although it seemed to rely to some extent on the right to counsel provision in the Sixth Amendment.*

Kirby, *the last case in this section, discusses the use of the Sixth Amendment right to counsel guarantee as applied in* Escobedo *and what had appeared to be some reliance on it in* Miranda.

ESCOBEDO v. ILLINOIS
378 U.S. 478 (1964)

[The opinion of the Court in Escobedo *was written by Mr. Justice Goldberg and included the following comments:]*

We have learned the lesson of history, ancient and modern, that a system of criminal law enforcement which comes to depend on the "confession" will, in the long run, be less reliable and more subject to abuses than a system which depends on extrinsic evidence independently secured through skillful investigation.

. . . .

This Court also has recognized that "history amply shows that confessions have often been extorted to save law enforcement officials the trouble and effort of obtaining valid and independent evidence . . ." *[Case citation omitted].*

We have also learned the companion lesson of history that no system of criminal justice can, or should, survive if it comes to depend for its continued effectiveness on the citizens' abdication through unawareness of their constitutional rights. No system worth preserving should have to *fear* that if an accused is permitted to consult with a lawyer, he will become aware of, and exercise, these rights. If the exercise of constitutional rights will thwart the effectiveness of a system of law enforcement, then there is something very wrong with that system.

We hold, therefore, that where, as here, the investigation is no longer a general inquiry into an unsolved crime but has begun to focus on a particular suspect, the suspect has been taken into police custody, the police carry out a process of interrogations that lends itself to eliciting incriminating statements, the suspect has requested and been denied an opportunity to consult with his lawyer, and the police have not effectively warned him of his absolute constitutional right to remain silent, the accused has been denied "the Assistance of Counsel" in violation of the Sixth Amendment to the Constitution as "made obligatory upon the States by the Fourteenth Amendment," Gideon v. Wainwright *[Case citation omitted]*, and that no statement elicited by the police during the interrogation may be used against him at a criminal trial.

    [Footnotes omitted.]

. . . .

MIRANDA v. ARIZONA
384 U.S. 436 (1966)

Mr. Chief Justice WARREN delivered the opinion of the Court.

. . . .

Today, then, there can be no doubt that the Fifth Amendment privilege is available outside of criminal court proceedings and serves to protect persons in all settings in which their freedom of action is curtailed in any significant way from being compelled to incriminate themselves. We have concluded that without proper safeguards the process of in-custody interrogation of persons suspected or accused of crime contains inherently compelling pressures which work to undermine the individual's will to resist and to compel him to speak where he would not otherwise do so freely. In order to combat these pressures and to permit a full opportunity to exercise the privilege against self-incrimination, the accused must be adequately and effectively apprised of his rights and the exercise of those rights must be fully honored.

It is impossible for us to foresee the potential alternatives for protecting the privilege which might be devised by Congress or the States in the exercise of their creative rule-making capacities. Therefore we cannot say that the Constitution necessarily requires adherence to any particular solution for the inherent compulsions of the interrogation process as it is presently conducted. Our decision in no way creates a constitutional straitjacket which will handicap sound efforts at reform, nor is it intended to have this effect. We encourage Congress and the States to continue their laudable search for increasingly effective ways of protecting the rights of the individual while promoting efficient enforcement of our criminal laws. However, unless we are shown other procedures which are at least as effective in apprising accused persons of their right of silence and in assuring a continuous opportunity to exercise it, the following safeguards must be observed.

At the outset, if a person in custody is to be subjected to interrogation, he must first be informed in clear and unequivocal terms that he has the right to remain silent. For those unaware of the privilege, the warning is needed simply to make them aware of it—the threshold requirement for an intelligent decision as to its exercise. More important, such a warning is an absolute prerequisite in overcoming the inherent pressures of the interrogation atmosphere. It is not just the subnormal or woefully ignorant who succumb to an interrogator's imprecations, whether implied or expressly stated, that the interrogation will continue until a confession is obtained or that silence in the face of accusation is itself damning and will bode ill when presented to a jury. Further, the warning will show the individual that his interrogators are prepared to recognize his privilege should he choose to exercise it.

The Fifth Amendment privilege is so fundamental to our system of constitutional rule and the expedient of giving an adequate warning as to the availability of the privilege so simple, we will not pause to inquire in individual cases whether the defendant was aware of his rights without a warning being given. Assessments of the knowledge the defendant possessed, based on information as to his age, education, intelligence, or prior contact with authorities, can never be more than speculation; a warning is a clearcut fact. More important, whatever the background of the person interrogated, a warning at the time of the interrogation is indispensable to overcome its pressures and to insure that the individual knows he is free to exercise the privilege at that point in time.

The warning of the right to remain silent must be accompanied by the explanation that anything said can and will be used against the individual in court. This warning is needed in order to make him aware not only of the privilege, but also of the consequences of forgoing it. It is only through an awareness of these consequences that there can be any assurance of real understanding and intelligent exercise of the privilege. Moreover, this warning may serve to make the individual more acutely aware that he is faced with a phase of the adversary system—that he is not in the presence of persons acting solely in his interest.

The circumstances surrounding in-custody interrogation can operate very quickly to overbear the will of one merely made aware of his privilege by his interrogators. Therefore, the right to have counsel present at the interrogation is indispensable to the protection of the Fifth Amendment privilege under the system we delineate today. Our aim is to assure that the individual's right to choose between silence and speech remains unfettered throughout the interrogation process. A once-stated warning, delivered by those who will conduct the interrogation, cannot itself suffice to that end among those who must require knowledge of their rights. A mere warning given by the interrogators is not alone sufficient to accomplish that end. . . . Thus, the need for counsel to protect the Fifth Amendment privilege comprehends not merely a right to consult with counsel prior to questioning, but also to have counsel present during any questioning if the defendant so desires.

The presence of counsel at the interrogation may serve several significant subsidiary functions as well. If the accused decides to talk to his interrogators, the assistance of counsel can mitigate the dangers of untrustworthiness. With a lawyer present the likelihood that the police will practice coercion is reduced, and if coercion is nevertheless exercised, the lawyer can testify to it in court. The presence of a lawyer can also help to guarantee that the accused gives a fully accurate statement to the police and that the statement is rightly reported by the prosecution at trial *[Case citation omitted]*.

An individual need not make a pre-interrogation request for a lawyer. While such request affirmatively secures his right to have one, his failure to ask for a lawyer does not constitute a waiver. No effective waiver of the right to counsel during interrogation can be recognized unless specifically made after the warnings we here delineate have been given. The accused who does not make a request may be the person who most needs counsel.
. . . .

Accordingly, we hold that an individual held for interrogation must be clearly informed that he has the right to consult with a lawyer and to have the lawyer with him during interrogation under the system for protecting the privilege we delineate today. As with the warnings of the right to remain silent and that anything stated can be used in evidence against him, this warning is an absolute prerequisite to interrogation. No amount of circumstantial evidence that the person may have been aware of this right will suffice to stand in its stead. Only through such a warning is there ascertainable assurance that the accused was aware of this right.

If an individual indicates that he wishes the assistance of counsel before any interrogation occurs, the authorities cannot rationally ignore or deny his request on the basis that the individual does not have or cannot afford a retained attorney. The financial ability of the individual has no relationship to the scope of the rights involved here. The privilege against self-incrimination secured by the Constitution applies to all individuals. The need for counsel in order to protect the privilege exists for the indigent as well as the affluent. In fact, were we to limit these constitutional rights to those who can retain an attorney, our decisions today would be of little significance.

. . . .

In order fully to apprise a person interrogated of the extent of his rights under this system then, it is necessary to warn him not only that he has the right to consult with an attorney, but also that if he is indigent, a lawyer will be appointed to represent him. Without this additional warning, the admonition of the right to consult with counsel would often be understood as meaning only that he can consult with a lawyer if he has one or has the funds to obtain one. The warning of a right to counsel would be hollow if not couched in terms that would convey to the indigent—the person most often subjected to interrogation—the knowledge that he too has a right to have counsel present. As with the warnings of the right to remain silent and of the general right to counsel, only by effective and express explanation to the indigent of this right can there be assurance that he was truly in a position to exercise it.

Once warnings have been given, the subsequent procedure is clear. If the individual indicates in any manner, at any time prior to or during questioning, that he wishes to remain silent, the interrogation must cease.[44] At this point he has shown that he intends to exercise his Fifth Amendment privilege; any statement taken after the person invokes his privilege cannot be other than the product of compulsion, subtle or otherwise. Without the right to cut off questioning, the setting of in-custody interrogation operates on the individual to overcome free choice in producing a statement after the privilege has been once invoked. If the individual states that he wants an attorney, the interrogation must cease until an attorney is present. At that time, the individual must have an opportunity to confer with the attorney and to have him present during any

---

[44] If an individual indicates his desire to remain silent, but has an attorney present, there may be some circumstances in which further questioning would be permissible. In the absence of evidence of overbearing, statements then made in the presence of counsel might be free of the compelling influence of the interrogation process and might fairly be construed as a waiver of the privilege for purposes of these statements.

subsequent questioning. If the individual cannot obtain an attorney and he indicates that he wants one before speaking to police, they must respect his decision to remain silent.

[All footnotes except number 44 omitted.]

OROZCO v. TEXAS
394 U.S. 324 (1969)

Mr. Justice BLACK delivered the opinion of the Court.

The petitioner, Reyes Arias Orozco, was convicted in the Criminal District Court of Dallas County, Texas, of murder without malice and was sentenced to serve in the state prison not less than two nor more than 10 years. The Court of Criminal Appeals of Texas affirmed the conviction, rejecting petitioner's contention that a material part of the evidence against him was obtained in violation of the provision of the Fifth Amendment to the United States Constitution, made applicable to the States by the Fourteenth Amendment, that "No person . . . shall be compelled in any criminal case to be a witness against himself."

The evidence introduced at trial showed that petitioner and the deceased had quarreled outside the El Farleto Cafe in Dallas shortly before midnight on the date of the shooting. The deceased had apparently spoken to petitioner's female companion inside the restaurant. In the heat of the quarrel outside, the deceased is said to have *[insulted Orozco and to have]* beaten *[him]* about the face. A shot was fired, killing the deceased. Petitioner left the scene and returned to his boardinghouse to sleep. At about 4 a.m., four police officers arrived at petitioner's boardinghouse, were admitted by an unidentified woman, and were told that petitioner was asleep in the bedroom. All four officers entered the bedroom and began to question petitioner. From the moment he gave his name, according to the testimony of one of the officers, petitioner was not free to go where he pleased but was "under arrest." The officers asked him if he had been to the El Farleto restaurant that night and when he answered "yes", he was asked if he owned a pistol. Petitioner admitted owning one. After being asked a second time where the pistol was located, he admitted that it was in the washing machine in a backroom of the boardinghouse. Ballistics tests indicated that the gun found in the washing machine was the gun that fired the fatal shot. At petitioner's trial . . . the trial court allowed one of the officers, over the objection of petitioner's lawyer, to relate the statements made by petitioner concerning the gun and petitioner's presence at the scene of the shooting. The trial testimony clearly shows that the officers questioned petitioner about incriminating facts without first informing him of his right to remain silent, his right to have the advice of a lawyer before making any statement, and his right to have a lawyer appointed to assist him if he could not afford to hire one. The Texas Court of Criminal Appeals held, with one judge dissenting, that the admission of testimony concerning the statements petitioner had made without the above warnings was not precluded by Miranda. We disagree and hold that the use of these admissions obtained in the absence of the required warnings was a flat violation of the Self-Incrimination Clause of the Fifth Amendment as construed in Miranda.

The State has argued here that since petitioner was interrogated on his own bed, in familiar surroundings, our Miranda holding should not apply. It is true that the Court did say in Miranda that "compulsion to speak in the isolated setting of the police station may well be greater than in courts or other official investigations, where there are often impartial observers to guard against intimidation or trickery" [Citation omitted]. But the opinion iterated and reiterated the absolute necessity for officers interrogating people "in custody" to give the described warnings. [Case citation omitted.] According to the officer's testimony, petitioner was under arrest and not free to leave when he was questioned in his bedroom in the early hours of the morning. The Miranda opinion declared that the warnings were required when the person being interrogated was "in custody at the station *or otherwise deprived of his freedom of action significant in any way*" [Citation omitted]. (Emphasis supplied). The decision of this Court in Miranda was reached after careful consideration and in lengthy opinions were announced by both the majority and dissenting Justices. There is no need to canvass those arguments again. We do not, as the dissent implies, expand or extend to the slightest extent our Miranda decision. We do adhere to our well-considered holding in that case and therefore reverse the conviction below.

Reversed.

[*Footnotes omitted.*]

HARRIS v. NEW YORK
401 U. S. 222 (1971)

Mr. Chief Justice BURGER delivered the opinion of the Court.

We [*agreed to hear*] this case to consider [*Harris's*] claim that a statement made by him to police under circumstances rendering it inadmissible to establish the prosecution's case in chief under Miranda v. Arizona *[Citation omitted]*, may not be used to impeach his credibility.

The State of New York charged *[Harris]* in a two-count indictment with twice selling heroin to an undercover police officer. At a subsequent jury trial the officer was the State's chief witness, and he testified as to details of the two sales. A second officer verified collateral details of the sales, and a third offered testimony about the chemical analysis of the heroin.

[Harris] took the stand in his own defense. He admitted knowing the undercover police officer but denied a sale on January 4, 1966. He admitted making a sale of contents of a glassine bag to the officer on January 6 but claimed it was baking powder and part of a scheme to defraud the purchaser.

On cross-examination *[Harris]* was asked seriatim whether he had made specified statements to the police immediately following his arrest on January 7—statements that partially contradicted *[Harris's]* direct testimony at trial. In response to the cross-examination, *[Harris]* testified that he could not remember virtually any of the questions or answers recited by the prosecutor. At the request of *[Harris's]* counsel the written statement from which the prosecutor had read questions and answers in his impeaching process was placed in the record for possible use on appeal; the statement was not shown to the jury.

The trial judge instructed the jury that the statements attributed to *[Harris]* by the prosecution could be considered only in passing on *[Harris's]* credibility and not as evidence of guilt. In closing summations both counsel argued the substance of the impeaching statements. The jury then found *[Harris]* guilty on the second count of the indictment.

. . . .

At trial the prosecution made no effort in its case in chief to use the statements allegedly made by *[Harris]* conceding that they were inadmissible under Miranda v. Arizona *[Citation omitted]*. The transcript of the interrogation used in the impeachment, but not given to the jury, shows that no warning of a right to appointed counsel was given before questions were put to *[Harris]* when he was taken into custody. *[Harris]* makes no claim that the statements made to the police were coerced or involuntary.

Some comments in the *Miranda* opinion can indeed be read as indicating a bar to use of an uncounseled statement for any purpose, but discussion of that issue was not at all necessary to the

Court's holding and cannot be regarded as controlling. *Miranda* barred the prosecution from making its case with statements of an accused made while in custody prior to having or effectively waiving counsel. It does not follow from *Miranda* that evidence inadmissible against an accused in the prosecution's case in chief is barred for all purposes, provided of course that the trustworthiness of the evidence satisfies legal standards.

. . . .

Every criminal defendant is privileged to testify in his own defense, or to refuse to do so. But that privilege cannot be construed to include the right to commit perjury *[Case citations omitted]*. Having voluntarily taken the stand, *[Harris]* was under an obligation to speak truthfully and accurately, and the prosecution here did no more than utilize the traditional truth-testing devices of the adversary process. Had inconsistent statements been made by the accused to some third person, it could hardly be contended that the conflict could not be laid before the jury by way of cross-examination and impeachment.

The shield provided by *Miranda* cannot be perverted into a license to use perjury by way of a defense, free from the risk of confrontation with prior inconsistent utterances. We hold, therefore, that *[Harris's]* credibility was appropriately impeached by use of his earlier conflicting statements.

. . . .

[Footnotes omitted.]

MICHIGAN v. TUCKER
_____U.S._____94 S. Ct. 2357 (1974)

Mr. Justice REHNQUIST delivered the opinion of the Court.

This case presents the question whether the testimony of a witness in *[Tucker's]* state court trial for rape must be excluded simply because police had learned the identity of the witness by questioning *[Tucker]* at a time when he was in custody as a suspect, but had not been advised that counsel would be appointed for him if he was indigent *[Case citations omitted]*.

. . . .

On the morning of April 19, 1966, a 43-year-old woman in Pontiac, Michigan, was found in her home by a friend and co-worker . . . in serious condition. At the time she was found the woman was tied, gagged, and partially disrobed, and had been both raped and severely beaten. She was unable to tell [the person who found her] anything about her assault at that time and still remains unable to recollect what happened.

While [the person who found her] was attempting to get medical help for [her] and to call for the police, he observed a dog inside the house. This apparently attracted [his] attention for he knew that the woman did not own a dog herself. Later, when talking with police officers, [he] observed the dog a second time, and police followed the dog to [Tucker's] house. Neighbors further connected the dog with [Tucker].

The police then arrested [Tucker] and brought him to the police station for questioning. Prior to the actual interrogation the police asked [Tucker] whether he knew for what crime he had been arrested, whether he wanted an attorney, and whether he understood his constitutional rights. [Tucker] replied that he did understand the crime for which he was arrested, that he did not want an attorney, and that he understood his rights. The police further advised him that any statements he might make could be used against him at a later date in court. The police, however, did not advise [Tucker] that he would be furnished counsel free of charge if he could not pay for such services himself.

The police then questioned [Tucker] about his activities on the night of the rape and assault. [Tucker] replied that during the general time period at issue he had first been with [a friend] and then later at home, alone, asleep. The police sought to confirm this story by contacting [the friend], but [his] story served to discredit rather than to bolster [Tucker's] account. [He] acknowledged that [Tucker] had been with him on the night of the crime but said that he had left at a relatively early time. Furthermore, [he] told police that he saw [Tucker] the following day and asked him at that time about scratches on his face—"asked him if he got hold of a wild one or something." [Tucker] answered, "[S]omething like that." Then, [he] said, he asked [Tucker] "[W]ho it was," and [Tucker] said: "[S]ome woman lived the next block over," adding "She is a widow woman" or words to that effect.

. . . .

Prior to trial [Tucker's] appointed counsel made a motion to exclude [the friend's] expected testimony because [Tucker] had revealed [his] identity without having received full *Miranda* warnings.

. . . .

[The Court of Appeals for the Sixth Circuit held that Henderson's testimony should have been excluded.]

[Tucker's] argument *[relies]* upon the Fifth Amendment right against compulsory self-incrimination and the safeguards designed in *Miranda* to secure that right. In brief, the position urged upon this Court is that proper regard for the privilege against compulsory self-incrimination requires, with limited exceptions not applicable here, that all evidence derived solely from statements made without full *Miranda* warnings be excluded at a subsequent criminal trial. For purposes of analysis in this case we believe that the question thus presented is best examined in two separate parts. We will therefore first consider whether the police conduct complained of directly infringed upon *[Tucker's]* right against compulsory self-incrimination or whether it instead violated only the prophylactic rules developed to protect that right. We will then consider whether the evidence derived from this interrogation must be excluded.

   [The Court here looks at the historical purpose of the Fifth Amendment.]
. . . .

Where there has been genuine compulsion of testimony, the right has been given broad scope. Although the constitutional language in which the privilege is cast might be construed to apply only to situations in which the prosecution seeks to call a defendant to testify against himself at his criminal trial, its application has not been so limited. The right has been held applicable to proceedings before a grand jury *[Case citation omitted]*, to civil proceedings *[Case citation omitted]*, to congressional investigations *[Case citation omitted]*, to juvenile proceedings *[Case citation omitted]*, and to other statutory inquiries *[Case citation omitted]*. The privilege has also been applied against the states by virtue of the Fourteenth Amendment *[Case citation omitted]*.

The natural concern which underlies many of these decisions is that an inability to protect the right at one stage of a proceeding may make its invocation useless at a later stage.
. . . .

A comparison of the facts in this case with the historical circumstances underlying the privilege against compulsory self-incrimination strongly indicates that the police conduct here did not deprive *[Tucker]* of his privilege against compulsory self-incrimination as such, but rather failed to make available to him the full measure of procedural safeguards associated with that right since *Miranda*.
. . . .

Our determination that the interrogation in this case involved no compulsion sufficient to breach the right against compulsory self-incrimination does not mean there was not a disregard, albeit an inadvertent disregard, of the procedural rules later established in *Miranda*. The question for decision is how sweeping the judicially imposed consequences of this disregard shall be. This Court said in *Miranda* that statements taken in violation of the *Miranda* principles must not be used to prove the prosecution's case at trial. That requirement was fully complied with by the state court here: *[Tucker's]* statements, claiming that he was with [the friend] and then asleep during the time period of the crime were not admitted against him at trial.

[The Court then discusses the concept that information derived from an involuntary statement may not be used and concludes that earlier Supreme Court cases do not decide if this rule should be applied when there was no actual compulsion but only a partial departure from the requirements of Miranda.*]*
. . . .

Thus, in deciding whether [the friend's] testimony must be excluded, there is no controlling precedent of this Court to guide us. We must therefore examine the matter as a question of principle.
. . . .

[The Court then discusses arguments in favor of excluding the testimony of the friend which was obtained from the statement made by Tucker without a complete Miranda warning. These were, among others:
1. The exclusion would deter other officers from failure to give a complete warning.
2. The exclusion was required because the testimony was untrustworthy.]

In summary, we do not think that any single reason supporting exclusion of this witness' testimony, nor all of them together, are very persuasive. By contrast, we find the arguments in favor of admitting the testimony quite strong. For, when balancing the interests involved, we must weigh the strong interest under any system of justice of making available to the trier of fact all concededly relevant and trustworthy evidence which either party seeks to adduce. In this particular case we also "must consider society's interest in the effective prosecution of criminals in light of the protection our pre-*Miranda* standards afford criminal defendants" *[Case citation omitted]*. These interests may be outweighed by the need to provide an effective sanction to a constitutional right,

Weeks v. United States *[Citation omitted]*, but they must in any event be valued. Here *[Tucker's]* own statement, which might have helped the prosecution show *[Tucker's]* guilty conscience at trial, had already been excised from the prosecution's case. . . . To extend the excision further under the circumstances of this case and exclude relevant testimony of a third-party witness would require far more persuasive arguments than those advanced by *[Tucker]*.

This Court has already recognized that a failure to give interrogated suspects full *Miranda* warnings does not entitle the suspect to insist that statements made by him be excluded in every conceivable context. In Harris v. New York *[Citation omitted]*, the Court was faced with the question of whether the statements of the defendant himself, taken without informing him of his right of access to appointed counsel, could be used to impeach defendant's direct testimony at trial. The Court concluded that they could, saying:

> Some comments in the *Miranda* opinion can indeed be read as indicating a bar to use of an uncounseled statement for any purpose, but discussion of that issue was not at all necessary to the Court's holding and cannot be regarded as controlling. *Miranda* barred the prosecution from making its case with statements of an accused made while in custody prior to having or effectively waiving counsel. It does not follow from *Miranda* that evidence inadmissible against an accused in the prosecution's case in chief is barred for all purposes, provided of course that the trustworthiness of the evidence satisfies legal standards. *[Citation omitted.]*

We believe that this reasoning is equally applicable here. Although *[an earlier case]* enabled *[Tucker]* to block admission of his own statements, we do not believe that it requires the prosecution to refrain from all use of those statements, and we disagree with the courts below that [the friend's] testimony should have been excluded in this case.

Reversed.

[Footnotes omitted.]

KIRBY v. ILLINOIS
406 U.S. 682 (1972)

Mr. Justice STEWART announced the judgment of the Court in an opinion in which THE CHIEF JUSTICE, Mr. Justice BLACKMUN, and Mr. Justice REHNQUIST join.

. . . .

On February 21, 1968, a man . . . reported to the Chicago police that the previous day two men had robbed him on a Chicago street of a wallet containing, among other things, travellers checks and a Social Security card. On February 22, two police officers stopped [Kirby] and a companion, Ralph Bean, on West Madison Street in Chicago. When asked for identification, [Kirby] produced a wallet that contained three travellers checks and a Social Security card, all bearing the name of [the man who had earlier reported the theft]. Papers with [that] name on them were also found in Bean's possession. When asked to explain his possession of [that] property, [Kirby] first said that the travellers checks were "play money," and then told the officers that he had won them in a crap game. The officers then arrested [Kirby] and Bean and took them to a police station.

Only after arriving at the police station, and checking the records there, did the arresting officers learn of the . . . robbery. A police car was then dispatched to [the robbery victim's] place of employment, where it picked [him] up and brought him to the police station. Immediately upon entering the room in the police station where [Kirby] and Bean were seated at a table, [he] positively identified them as the men who had robbed him two days earlier. No lawyer was present in the room, and neither [Kirby] nor Bean had asked for legal assistance, or been advised of any right to the presence of counsel.
. . . .

We note at the outset that the constitutional privilege against compulsory self-incrimination is in no way implicated here.

[The Court then quotes from an earlier case.]
. . . .

We have no doubt that compelling the accused merely to exhibit his person for observation by a prosecution witness prior to trial involves no compulsion of the accused to give evidence having testimonial significance. It is compulsion of the accused to exhibit his physical characteristics, not compulsion to disclose to any knowledge he might have. . . . *[Case citation omitted.]*

It follows that the doctrine of Miranda v. Arizona *[Citation omitted]*, has no applicability whatever to the issue before us. For the *Miranda* decision was based exclusively upon the Fifth and Fourteenth Amendment privilege against compulsory self-incrimination, upon the theory that custodial *interrogation* is inherently coercive.
. . . .

In a line of constitutional cases in this Court stemming back to the Court's landmark opinion in Powell v. Alabama *[Citation omitted]*, it has been firmly established that a person's Sixth and Fourteenth Amendment right to counsel attaches only at or after the time that adversary judicial proceedings have been initiated against him *[Case citations omitted]*.

This is not to say that a defendant in a criminal case has a constitutional right to counsel only at the trial itself. *[An earlier]* case makes clear that the right attaches at the time of arraignment, and the Court has recently held that it exists also at the time of a preliminary hearing *[Case citation omitted]*. But the point is that, while members of the Court have differed as to the existence of the right to counsel in the contexts of some of the above cases, *all* of those cases have involved points of time at or after the initiation of adversary judicial criminal proceedings—whether by way of formal charge, preliminary hearing, indictment, information, or arraignment.

The only seeming deviation from this long line of constitutional decisions was Escobedo v. Illinois *[Citation omitted]*. But *Escobedo* is not apposite here for two distinct reasons. First, the Court in retrospect perceived that the "prime purpose" of *Escobedo* was not to vindicate the constitutional right to counsel as such, but, like *Miranda*, "to guarantee full effectuation of the privilege against self incrimination. . . ." (Johnson v. New Jersey) *[Citation omitted]*. Secondly, and perhaps even more important for purely practical purposes, the Court has limited the holding of *Escobedo* to its own facts, Johnson v. New Jersey *[Citation omitted]*.

[Footnotes omitted.]

. . . .

The search and seizure exclusionary rule, its rationale and future: the judiciary speaks

Beginning with a 1914 decision of the United States Supreme Court in a case called Weeks v. United States, *there has been in existence in United States Constitutional Law something known as the "Exclusionary Rule." It simply means that if material is seized in violation of the Fourth Amendment's prohibition against unreasonable searches and seizures, the material thus seized cannot be used by the government against the person or persons whose rights were violated. Since 1914, a number of issues about the Exclusionary Rule have arisen. Among these were the following:*

1. Does the rule apply the actions of the states (and their counties and municipalities) since Weeks only decided the issue as to the Federal Government?

2. Can the government make any use of the unconstitutionally seized material even if it cannot use it as evidence in court against the person whose rights were violated?

3. Why should there be an Exclusionary Rule?

4. Does it do more harm than good?

The following six excerpts from court opinions* discuss these problems. Not all of them represent the present view which is that unconstitutionally seized material may not be used in any court against the person whose rights were violated. Nor may such material be used to lead the authorities to other evidence or it too will be excluded from the trial. However, the reason(s) for the Exclusionary Rule have varied from time to time and the rule itself is now under attack. See how much you can learn from what the judiciary has said.

SILVERTHORNE LUMBER COMPANY, INC. v. UNITED STATES
251 U.S. 385 (1920)

[The United States Government seized all the records of the Silverthornes in clear violation of the Fourth Amendment to the United States Constitution. At the Silverthorne's request a federal court ordered the return of the originals of the records, but not the copies of them which the government had made. The government then used the copies to convince a court to issue a subpoena duces tecum (a court order requiring a person to appear in court as a witness and bring documents with him) for the Silverthornes, and the originals of the records they had just gotten back from the government. The Silverthornes refused to obey the subpoena duces tecum and were charged with contempt of court.

---

* Four are cases decided by the United States Supreme Court and one each is from Florida and New York.

(Refusal to obey a court order can be contempt of court.) The case reached the United States Supreme Court.]

Mr. Justice HOLMES delivered the opinion of the Court.

The proposition could not be presented more nakedly. It is that although of course its seizure was an outrage which the Government now regrets, it may study the papers before it returns them, copy them, and then may use the knowledge that it has gained to call upon the owners in a more regular form to produce them; that the protection of the Constitution covers the physical possession but not any advantages that the Government can gain over the object of its pursuit by doing the forbidden act.
. . . .

In our opinion such is not the law. It reduces the Fourth Amendment to a form of words *[Case citations omitted]. The essence of a provision forbidding the acquisition of evidence in a certain way is that not merely evidence so acquired shall not be used before the Court, but that it shall not be used at all. Of course this does not mean that the facts thus obtained become sacred and inaccessible. If knowledge of them is gained from an independent source they may be proved like any others, but the knowledge gained by the Government's own wrong cannot be used by it in the way proposed.*
. . . .

Judgment reversed *[Emphasis added].*

ATZ v. ANDREWS
94 So. 329 (Fla. 1922)

BROWNE, C. J.

George Atz was convicted in the county judge's court of Lake County for unlawfully having alcoholic and intoxicating liquor in his possession.

On appeal to the circuit court of the Seventeenth judicial circuit the judgment was affirmed.

The case is before us for review on certiorari. Several questions are presented that involve constitutional guarantees.
. . . .

There was in this instance, however, no search made, and none attempted, nor was there any demand by the officer that the defendant deliver to him any intoxicating liquor that he had in his possession.

Had there been, the introduction of the illegally acquired evidence would have been reversible error.

. . . .

Whatever other state courts may do, the Supreme Court of Florida will guard and protect the constitutional rights, privileges, and immunities of the people, as sacredly as the federal courts.

Why a court should encourage its officers *illegally to acquire* evidence to be used against a person on trial for having *illegally* acquired some commodity, is a problem in morals that is a bit confusing to one not a zealot or a fanatic.

For one to acquire illegally, or illegally to possess, intoxicating liquors is a crime; but it is a crime that generally affects a few persons in a restricted locality. To permit an officer of the state to *acquire evidence illegally* and in *violation of sacred constitutional* guarantees, and to use the *illegally acquired* evidence in the prosecution of the person who illegally acquired the intoxicants, strikes at the very foundation of the administration of justice, and where such practices prevail, make law enforcement a mockery.

In this era, when earnest-thinking men and women are ardently trying to arouse public sentiment on the subject of strict law enforcement, it would seem most meet and proper for the courts to set the example, and not sanction law-breaking and constitutional violation in order to obtain testimony against another lawbreaker. Better the mob and the Ku-Klux, than the conviction obtained in a temple of justice by testimony illegally acquired by agents of the government and officers of the law. The distinction between illegally acquired testimony and perjured testimony is not in kind, but in degree, and a conviction obtained by the use of either or both of these methods condemns the administration of justice at the same time that it condemns the prisoner. The liberties of the people cannot safely be intrusted to those who believe that violation of prohibition laws is more heinous than violations of the Constitution.

In view of the unlawful acts done in the name of law enforcement, it may be well to recall the Fifty-fifth clause of Magna Charta, which the Barons required King John to sign for the preservation of the liberties of the people:

We will not make any justices, constables, sheriffs or bailiffs, but of such as know the law of the realm, and mean duly to observe it.

[Emphasis in the original.]

. . . .

PEOPLE v. DEFORE
242 N.Y. 13, 150 N.E. 585 (1926)

CARDOZO, J.*

We hold, then, with the defendant that the evidence against him was the outcome of *[an unconstitutional search and seizure]*. The officer *[who carried out the search]* might have been resisted, or sued for damages, or even prosecuted for oppression. *[Citation omitted.]* He was subject to removal or other discipline at the hands of his superiors. These consequences are undisputed. The defendant would add another. We must determine whether evidence of criminality, procured by an *[unconstitutional search and seizure]* is to be rejected *[for use in court because of]* the misconduct of the *[authorities]*.
. . . .

[Judge Cardozo then discussed certain United States Supreme Court cases which, like the Silverthorne *case, held that material seized in violation of the Fourth Amendment to the United States Constitution could not be used in court as evidence against the person from whom it was seized. However, he pointed out that these rulings were binding only on the Federal Government and not the states, a fact that was correct in 1926. This has since changed; see* Mapp v. Ohio, *which appears later in this article.]*
. . . .

There has been no blinking the consequence. The criminal is to go free because the constable has blundered.
. . . .

The pettiest peace officer would have it in his power, through overzeal or indiscretion, to confer immunity upon an offender for crimes the most flagitious. A room is searched against the law, and the body of a murdered man is found. If the place of discovery may not be proved, the other circumstances may be insufficient to connect the defendant with the crime. The privacy of the home has been infringed, and the murderer goes free. Another search, once more against the law, discloses counterfeit money or the implements of forgery. The absence of a warrant means the freedom of the forger. Like instances can be multiplied. We may not subject society to these dangers *[unless the New York legislature acts to require such a course]*.
. . . .

* Judge Cardozo later became a Justice of the United States Supreme Court.

The question is whether protection for the individual would not be gained at a disproportionate loss of protection for society. On the one side is the social need that crime shall be repressed. On the other, the social need that law shall not be flouted by the insolence of office. There are dangers in any choice.
. . . .

[Judge Cardozo then says that New York will follow an earlier New York case which allowed unconstitutionally seized material to be used as evidence in court against the person from whom it was seized.]

MAPP v. OHIO
367 U.S. 643 (1961)

Mr. Justice CLARK delivered the opinion of the Court.

The State says that even if the search were made without authority, or otherwise unreasonably, it is not prevented from using the unconstitutionally seized evidence at trial, citing Wolf v. People of State of Colorado *[Citation omitted]*, in which this Court did indeed hold "that in a prosecution in a State court for a State crime the Fourteenth Amendment does not forbid the admission of evidence obtained by an unreasonable search and seizure." On this appeal . . . it is urged once again that we review that holding.
. . . .

Since the Fourth Amendment's right of privacy has been declared enforceable against the States through the Due Process Clause of the Fourteenth, it is enforceable against them by the same sanction of exclusion as is used against the Federal Government. Were it otherwise, then just as without the *[Exclusionary Rule in Federal courts]* the assurance against unreasonable federal searches and seizures would be "a form of words", valueless and undeserving of mention in a perpetual charter of inestimable human liberties, so too, without that rule the freedom from state invasions of privacy would be so ephemeral and so neatly severed from its conceptual nexus with the freedom from all brutish means of coercing evidence as not to merit this Court's high regard as a freedom "implicit in 'the concept of ordered liberty.' " At the time that the Court held in Wolf that the Amendment was applicable to the States through the Due Process Clause, the cases of this Court, as we have seen, had steadfastly held that as to federal officers the Fourth Amendment

included the exclusion of the evidence seized in violation of its provisions. Even Wolf "stoutly adhered" to that proposition. The right to privacy, when conceded operatively enforceable against the States, was not susceptible of destruction by avulsion of the sanction upon which its protection and enjoyment had always been deemed dependent under the Boyd, Weeks and Silverthorne cases. Therefore, in extending the substantive protections of due process to all constitutionally unreasonable searches—state or federal—it was logically and constitutionally necessary that the exclusion doctrine—an essential part of the right to privacy—be also insisted upon as an essential ingredient of the right newly recognized by the Wolf case. In short, the admission of the new constitutional right by Wolf could not consistently tolerate denial of its most important constitutional privilege, namely, the exclusion of the evidence which an accused had been forced to give by reason of the unlawful seizure. To hold otherwise is to grant the right but in reality to withhold its privilege and enjoyment.
. . . .

There are those who say, as did Justice (then Judge) Cardozo, that under our constitutional exclusionary doctrine "[t]he criminal is to go free because the constable has blundered." People v. Defore *[Citation omitted]*. In some cases, this will undoubtedly be the result. But as *[the United States Supreme Court said in an earlier case]*, "there is another consideration—the imperative of judicial integrity" *[Citation omitted]*. The criminal goes free, if he must, but it is the law that sets him free. Nothing can destroy a government more quickly than its failure to observe its own laws, or worse, its disregard of the charter of its own existence. As Mr. Justice Brandeis *[said in an earlier United States Supreme Court case]*, "Our government is the potent, the omnipresent teacher. For good or for ill, it teaches the whole people by its example. . . . If the government becomes a lawbreaker, it breeds contempt for law; it invites every man to become a law unto himself; it invites anarchy." Nor can it lightly be assumed that, as a practical matter, adoption of the exclusionary rule fetters law enforcement.
. . . .

The ignoble shortcut to conviction left open to the State tends to destroy the entire system of constitutional restraints on which the liberties of the people rest. Having once recognized that the right to privacy embodied in the Fourth Amendment is enforceable against the States, and that the right to be secure against rude invasions of privacy by state officers is, therefore, constitutional in origin, we can no longer permit that right to remain an empty promise.

Because it is enforceable in the same manner and to like effect as other basic rights secured by the Due Process Clause, we can no longer permit it to be revocable at the whim of any police officer who, in the name of law enforcement itself, chooses to suspend its enjoyment. Our decision, founded on reason and truth, gives to the individual no more than that which the Constitution guarantees him, to the police officer no less than that to which honest law enforcement is entitled, and, to the courts, that judicial integrity so necessary in the true administration of justice.

The judgment of the Supreme Court of Ohio is reversed and the cause remanded for further proceedings not inconsistent with this opinion.

Reversed and remanded.

[Footnotes omitted.]

MR. JUSTICE POWELL in
CALANDRA v. UNITED STATES
414 U.S. 338 (1974)

"In sum, the *[exclusionary]* Rule is a judicially-created remedy designed to safeguard Fourth Amendment rights generally through its deterrent effect, rather than a personal constitutional right of the party aggrieved."

[Calandra also decided that unconstitutionally seized evidence could be used in a grand jury proceeding.]

BIVENS v. SIX UNKNOWN
FEDERAL NARCOTICS AGENTS
403 U.S. 388 (1971)

CHIEF JUSTICE BURGER, dissenting.

For more than 55 years this Court has enforced a rule under which evidence of undoubted reliability and probative value has been suppressed and excluded from criminal cases whenever it was obtained in violation of the Fourth Amendment *[Case citations omitted]*. The rule has rested on a theory that suppression of evidence in these circumstances was imperative to deter law enforcement authorities from using improper methods to obtain evidence.

The deterrence theory underlying the Suppression Doctrine, or

Exclusionary Rule, has a certain appeal in spite of the high price society pays for such a drastic remedy. Notwithstanding its plausibility many judges and lawyers and some of our most distinguished legal scholars have never quite been able to escape the force of Cardozo's statement of the doctrine's anomalous result:

"The criminal is to go free because the constable has blundered. . . . A room is searched against the law, and the body of a murdered man is found. . . . The privacy of the home has been infringed, and the murderer goes free." People v. Defore *[Citation omitted]*.

The . . . opinion *[of the United States Supreme Court]* in Irvine v. California *[Citation omitted]*, catalogued the doctrine's defects:

"Rejection of the evidence does nothing to punish the wrong-doing official, while it may, and likely will, release the wrong-doing defendant. It deprives society of its remedy against one lawbreaker because he has been pursued by another. It protects one against whom incriminating evidence is discovered, but does nothing to protect innocent persons who are the victims of illegal but fruitless searches."

From time to time members of the Court, recognizing the validity of these protests, have articulated varying alternative justifications for the suppression of important evidence in a criminal trial. Under one of these alternative theories the rule's foundation is shifted to the "sporting contest" thesis that the government must "play the game fairly" and cannot be allowed to profit from its own illegal acts *[Case citations omitted]*. But the Exclusionary Rule does not ineluctably flow from a desire to ensure that government plays the "game" according to the rules. If an effective alternative remedy is available, concern for official observance of the law does not require adherence to the Exclusionary Rule. Nor is it easy to understand how a court can be thought to endorse a violation of the Fourth Amendment by allowing illegally seized evidence to be introduced against a defendant if an effective remedy is provided against the government.

The Exclusionary Rule has also been justified on the theory that the relationship between the Self-Incrimination Clause of the Fifth Amendment and the Fourth Amendment requires the suppression of evidence seized in violation of the latter *[Case citations omitted]*.

Even ignoring, however, the decisions of this Court which have held that the Fifth Amendment applies only to "testimonial" disclosures *[Case citations omitted]*, it seems clear that the Self-Incrimination Clause does not protect a person from the seizure of evidence that is incriminating. It protects a person only from being the conduit by which the police acquire evidence. Mr. Justice Holmes once put it succinctly, "A party is privileged from producing the evidence but not from its production" *[Case citation omitted]*.

It is clear, however, that neither of these theories undergirds the decided cases in this Court. Rather, the Exclusionary Rule has rested on the deterrent rationale—the hope that law enforcement officials would be deterred from unlawful searches and seizures if the illegally seized, albeit trustworthy, evidence was suppressed often enough and the courts persistently enough deprived them of any benefits they might have gained from their illegal conduct.
. . . .

I do not question the need for some remedy to give meaning and teeth to the constitutional guarantees against unlawful conduct by government officials. Without some effective sanction, these protections would constitute little more than rhetoric. Beyond doubt the conduct of some officials requires sanctions as cases like Irvine indicate. But the hope that this objective could be accomplished by the exclusion of reliable evidence from criminal trials was hardly more than a wistful dream. Although I would hesitate to abandon it until some meaningful substitute is developed, the history of the Suppression Doctrine demonstrates that it is both conceptually sterile and practically ineffective in accomplishing its stated objective.
. . . .

Some clear demonstration of the benefits and effectiveness of the Exclusionary Rule is required to justify it in view of the high price it extracts from society—the release of countless guilty criminals. See Allen, Federalism and the Fourth Amendment: A Requiem for Wolf, 1961 Sup. Ct. Rev. 1, 33 n. 172. But there is no empirical evidence to support the claim that the rule actually deters illegal conduct of law enforcement officials. Oaks, Studying the Exclusionary Rule in Search and Seizure, 37 U. Chi. L. Rev. 665, 667 (1970).

There are several reasons for this failure. The rule does not apply any direct sanction to the individual official whose illegal conduct results in the exclusion of evidence in a criminal trial. With rare exceptions law enforcement agencies do not impose direct sanctions on the individual officer responsible for a particular judicial application of the Suppression Doctrine. Id., at 710. Thus there is virtually nothing done to bring about a change in his practices. The immediate sanction triggered by the application of the rule is visited upon the prosecutor whose case against a criminal is either weakened or destroyed. The doctrine deprives the police in no real sense; except that apprehending wrongdoers is their business, police have no more stake in successful prosecutions than prosecutors or the public.

The Suppression Doctrine vaguely assumes that law enforcement is a monolithic governmental enterprise. For example, the dissenters in Wolf v. Colorado *[Citation omitted]*, argued that:

"Only by exclusion can we impress upon the zealous *prosecutor* that violation of the Constitution will do him no good. And only when that point is driven home can the *prosecutor* be expected to emphasize the importance of observing the constitutional demands in *his instructions to the police*" (Emphasis added). But the prosecutor who loses his case because of police misconduct is not an official in the police department; he can rarely set in motion any corrective action or administrative penalties. Moreover, he does not have control or direction over police procedures or police action that lead to the exclusion of evidence. It is the rare exception when a prosecutor takes part in arrests, searches, or seizures so that he can guide police action.

Whatever educational effect the rule conceivably might have in theory is greatly diminished in fact by the realities of law enforcement work. Policemen do not have the time, inclination, or training to read and grasp the nuances of the appellate opinions that ultimately define the standards of conduct they are to follow. The issues which these decisions resolve often admit of neither easy nor obvious answers, as sharply divided courts on what is or is not "reasonable" amply demonstrate. Nor can judges, in all candor, forget that opinions sometimes lack helpful clarity.

The presumed educational effect of judicial opinions is also reduced by the long time lapse—often several years—between the original police action and its final judicial evaluation. Given a policeman's pressing responsibilities, it would be surprising if he ever becomes aware of the final result after such a delay.

. . . .

Although unfortunately ineffective, the Exclusionary Rule has increasingly been characterized by a single, monolithic, and drastic judicial response to all official violations of legal norms. Inadvertent errors of judgment that do not work any grave injustice will inevitably occur under the pressure of police work. These honest mistakes have been treated in the same way as deliberate and flagrant . . . violations of the Fourth Amendment.

. . . .

In characterizing the Suppression Doctrine as an anomalous and ineffective mechanism with which to regulate law enforcement, I intend no reflection on the motivation of those members of this Court who hoped it would be a means of enforcing the Fourth Amendment. Judges cannot be faulted for being offended by arrests, searches, and seizures that violate the Bill of Rights or statutes intended to regulate public officials. But we can and should be faulted for clinging to an unworkable and irrational concept of law. My criticism is that we have taken so long to find better ways to accomplish these desired objectives. And there are better ways.

Instead of continuing to enforce the Suppression Doctrine, inflexibly, rigidly, and mechanically, we should view it as one of the experimental steps in the great tradition of the Common Law and acknowledge its shortcomings. But in the same spirit we should be prepared to discontinue what the experience of over half a century has shown neither deters errant officers nor affords a remedy to the totally innocent victims of official misconduct.

I do not propose, however, that we abandon the Suppression Doctrine until some meaningful alternative can be developed. In a sense our legal system has become the captive of its own creation. To overrule Weeks and Mapp, even assuming the Court was now prepared to take that step, could raise yet new problems. Obviously, the public interest would be poorly served if law enforcement officials were suddenly to gain the impression, however erroneous, that all constitutional restraints on police had somehow been removed—that an open season on "criminals" had been declared. I am concerned lest some such mistaken impression might be fostered by a flat overruling of the Suppression Doctrine cases. For years we have relied upon it as the exclusive remedy for unlawful official conduct; in a sense we are in a situation akin to the narcotics addict whose dependence on drugs precludes any drastic or immediate withdrawal of the supposed prop, regardless of how futile its continued use may be.

. . . .

I conclude, therefore, that an entirely different remedy is necessary, but it is one that in my view is as much beyond judicial power as the step the Court takes today. Congress should develop an administrative or quasi-judicial remedy against the government itself to afford compensation and restitution for persons whose Fourth Amendment rights have been violated.

. . . .

[Footnotes omitted.]

The right to counsel
in criminal trials

The Sixth Amendment to the United States Constitution provides in part:

In all criminal prosecutions, the accused shall enjoy the right . . . to have the assistance of counsel for his defense.

The principal question concerning this right deals with the constitutional necessity of government providing a lawyer for a person who cannot afford one. In 1938 the Supreme Court held that the United States government was required to provide counsel for indigents in federal criminal trials.

Because of the way the Bill of Rights has been interpreted, it is necessary insofar as requiring the states to provide most of the safeguards in the Bill of Rights (including the right to counsel), to find those safeguards in the due process clause of the Fourteenth Amendment to the United States Constitution which provides:

. . . nor shall any state deprive any person of life, liberty, or property without due process of law. . . .

There are really two questions to be answered:
1. Are the states required to provide counsel for indigents in criminal cases?
2. If the answer to the first question is "yes", then to what types of criminal cases does this right apply?

The current answers to these two questions is found in the portions of the Supreme Court opinions in Gideon *and* Argersinger *found in this article.*

GIDEON v. WAINWRIGHT
372 U.S. 335 (1963)

Mr. Justice BLACK delivered the opinion of the Court.

[Gideon] was charged in a Florida state court with having broken and entered a poolroom with intent to commit a misdemeanor. This offense is a felony under Florida law. Appearing in court without funds and without a lawyer, [Gideon] asked the court to appoint counsel for him, whereupon the following colloquy took place:

"The COURT: Mr. Gideon, I am sorry, but I cannot appoint Counsel to represent you in this case. Under the laws of the State of

Florida, the only time the Court can appoint Counsel to represent a Defendant is when that person is charged with a capital offense. I am sorry, but I will have to deny your request to appoint Counsel to defend you in this case.

"The DEFENDANT: The United States Supreme Court says I am entitled to be represented by Counsel."

Put to trial before a jury, Gideon conducted his defense about as well as could be expected from a layman. He made an opening statement to the jury, cross-examined the State's witnesses, presented witnesses in his own defense, declined to testify himself, and made a short argument "emphasizing his innocence to the charge contained in the Information filed in this case." The jury returned a verdict of guilty, and [Gideon] was sentenced to serve five years in the state prison.

> [The Florida Supreme Court, whom Gideon had requested to review the case, held that Gideon was not entitled to have a lawyer appointed to represent him.]

. . . .

The Sixth Amendment provides, "In all criminal prosecutions, the accused shall enjoy the right . . . to have the Assistance of Counsel for his defense." We have construed this to mean that in federal courts counsel must be provided for defendants unable to employ counsel unless the right is competently and intelligently waived.

> [The Court then discusses earlier cases dealing with the right to counsel in state courts and finds that most of these cases point in the direction of a right to counsel in state courts even though the last case to rule on the subject, Betts v. Brady, said that there was no such requirement. The Court then says that Betts v. Brady is wrong.]

. . . .

Not only these precedents but also reason and reflection require us to recognize that in our adversary system of criminal justice, any person haled into court, who is too poor to hire a lawyer, cannot be assured a fair trial unless counsel is provided for him. This seems to us to be an obvious truth. Governments, both state and federal, quite properly spend vast sums of money to establish machinery to try defendants accused of crime. Lawyers to prosecute are everywhere deemed essential to protect the public's interest in an orderly society. Similarly, there are few defendants charged with crime, few indeed, who fail to hire the best lawyers they can get to prepare and present their defenses. That government hires lawyers to prosecute and defendants who have the money hire lawyers to defend are the strongest indications of the wide-spread belief that lawyers in criminal courts are necessities, not luxuries. The right of one charged with crime to counsel may not be deemed fundamental and essential to fair trials in some countries, but it is in ours. From the very beginning, our state and national constitutions and laws have laid great emphasis on procedural and substantive safeguards designed to assure fair trials before impartial tribunals in which every defendant stands equal before the law. This noble ideal cannot be realized if the poor man charged with crime has to face his accusers without a lawyer to assist him. A defendant's need for a lawyer is nowhere better stated than in the moving words of Mr. Justice Sutherland in Powell v. Alabama:

> The right to be heard would be, in many cases, of little avail if it did not comprehend the right to be heard by counsel. Even the intelligent and educated layman has small and sometimes no skill in the science of law. If charged with crime, he is incapable, generally, of determining for himself whether the indictment is good or bad. He is unfamiliar with the rules of evidence. Left without the aid of counsel he may be put on trial without a proper charge, and convicted upon incompetent evidence, or evidence irrelevant to the issue or otherwise inadmissible. He lacks both the skill and knowledge adequately to prepare his defense, even though he have a perfect one. He requires the guiding hand of counsel at every step in the proceedings against him. Without it, though he be not guilty, he faces the danger of conviction because he does not know how to establish his innocence. *[Citation omitted.]*

> *[The Supreme Court then reversed the decision of the Florida Supreme Court which had held that Gideon was not entitled to counsel.]*

> *[Footnotes omitted.]*

ARGERSINGER v. HAMLIN
407 U.S. 25 (1972)

Mr. Justice DOUGLAS delivered the opinion of the Court.

[Argersinger], an indigent, was charged in Florida with carrying a concealed weapon, an offense punishable by imprisonment up to six months and a $1,000 fine. The trial was to a judge and *[Argersinger]* was unrepresented by counsel. He was sentenced to serve 90 days in jail and brought this habeas corpus action in the Florida Supreme Court, alleging that, being deprived of his right to counsel, he was unable as an indigent layman properly to raise and present to the

trial court good and sufficient defenses to the charges for which he stands convicted. The Florida Supreme Court by a four-to-three decision, in ruling on the right to counsel, followed the line we marked out in Duncan v. Louisiana *[Citation omitted]*, as respects the right to trial by jury and held that the right to court-appointed counsel extends only to trials "for non-petty offenses punishable by more than six months imprisonment" *[Citation omitted]*.
. . . .

The Sixth Amendment . . . provides specified standards for "all criminal prosecutions."

[The Court discusses the historical differences between the guarantee of jury trial and right to counsel.]
. . . .

We reject, therefore, the premise that since prosecutions for crimes punishable by imprisonment for less than six months may be tried without a jury, they may always be tried without a lawyer.

The assistance of counsel is often a requisite to the very existence of a fair trial. The court in Powell v. Alabama *[Citation omitted]*, said:

The right to be heard would be, in many cases, of little avail if it did not comprehend the right to be heard by counsel. Even the intelligent and educated layman has small and sometimes no skill in the science of law. If charged with crime, he is incapable, generally, of determining for himself whether the indictment is good or bad. He is unfamiliar with the rules of evidence. Left without the aid of counsel he may be put on trial without a proper charge, and convicted upon incompetent evidence, or evidence irrelevant to the issue or otherwise inadmissible. He lacks both the skill and knowledge adequately to prepare his defense, even though he have a perfect one. He requires the guiding hand of counsel at every step in the proceedings against him. Without it, though he be not guilty, he faces the danger of conviction because he does not know how to establish his innocence. If that be true of men of intelligence, how much more true is it of the ignorant and illiterate, or those of feeble intellect.

In Gideon v. Wainwright *[Citation omitted]*, we dealt with a felony trial. But we did not so limit the need of the accused for a lawyer. We said:

. . . in our adversary system of criminal justice, any person haled into court, who is too poor to hire a lawyer, cannot be assured a fair trial unless counsel is provided for him. This seems to us to be an obvious truth. Governments, both state and federal, quite properly spend vast sums of money to establish machinery to try defendants accused of crime. Lawyers to prosecute are everywhere deemed essential to protect the public's interest in an orderly society. Similarly, there are few defendants charged with crime, few indeed, who fail to hire the best lawyers they can get to prepare and present their defenses. That government hires lawyers to prosecute and defendants who have the money hire lawyers to defend are the strongest indications of the widespread belief that lawyers in criminal courts are necessities, not luxuries. The right of one charged with crime to counsel may not be deemed fundamental and essential to fair trials in some countries, but it is in ours. From the very beginning, our state and national constitutions and laws have laid great emphasis on procedural and substantive safeguards designed to assure fair trials before impartial tribunals in which every defendant stands equal before the law. This noble ideal cannot be realized if the poor man charged with crime has to face his accusers without a lawyer to assist him. *[Citation omitted.]*

Both *Powell* and *Gideon* involved felonies. But their rationale has relevance to any criminal trial, where an accused is deprived of his liberty.

. . . .

The requirement of counsel may well be necessary for a fair trial even in a petty offense prosecution. We are by no means convinced that legal and constitutional questions involved in a case that actually leads to imprisonment even for a brief period are any less complex than when a person can be sent off for six months or more *[Case citations omitted]*.

[The court then discusses examples of complexities in trials of persons charged with petty offenses.]

. . . .

We must conclude, therefore, that the problems associated with misdemeanor and petty offenses often require the presence of counsel to insure the accused a fair trial. Mr. Justice POWELL suggests that these problems are raised even in situations where there is no prospect of imprisonment. *[This is in a concurring opinion that is omitted.]* We need not consider the requirements of the Sixth Amendment as regards the right to counsel where loss of liberty is not involved, however, for here, *[Argersinger]* was in fact sentenced to jail. And, as we said in Baldwin v. New York *[Citation omitted]*, "[T]he prospect of imprisonment for however short a time will seldom be viewed by the accused as a trivial or 'petty' matter and may well result in quite serious repercussions affecting his career and his reputation."

We hold, therefore, that absent a knowing and intelligent waiver, no person may be imprisoned for any offense, whether classified as petty, misdemeanor, or felony, unless he was represented by counsel at his trial.

. . . .

Under the rule we announce today, every judge will know when the trial of a misdemeanor starts that no imprisonment may be imposed, even though local law permits it, unless the accused is represented by counsel. He will have a measure of the seriousness and gravity of the offense and therefore know when to name a lawyer to represent the accused before the trial starts.

The run of misdemeanors will not be affected by today's ruling. But in those that end up in the actual deprivation of a person's liberty, the accused will receive the benefit of "the guiding hand of counsel" so necessary when one's liberty is in jeopardy.

Reversed.

[Footnotes omitted.]

Part four

Courts

The courts handle a wide range of problems and are the intermediaries that society looks to for the equitable application of law to individuals. They sit in a strategic position to minimize the effects on the community of those criminal activities which grow out of poverty or antisocial actions. After the court's decisions are made their execution must be assured. When the executive branch fails to fill this responsibility it falls to the courts. Consequently, the court has a responsibility in addition to being a decider of being an implementer and counsellor. The roles that the courts play today are very diverse. They encompass far more than serving merely as determiners of guilt or innocence. Courts not only mete out punishment but must be concerned with rehabilitation. These facts are made cogently clear in The Court as a Social Force.

The officers of the court, in particular the prosecuting attorney, are part of the community in which they live. The actions by the prosecutor in determining how to handle a case may be affected and influenced by numerous factors. The prominence of the individuals involved, the role of the police and police attitudes, the congestion of the courts, community pressures and organizational strains, all influence prosecutorial behavior. The Decision to Prosecute presents an excellent discussion of the factors which do influence the prosecutor in his decision to act, and if so how, or his decision not to act.

In American Judges: Their Selection, Tenure, Variety and Quality, the ways in which judges are selected: partisan election,

217

nonpartisan election, merit plan, executive appointment, and legislative appointment are examined. The various provisions for tenure: life, reappointment, election, and nonpartisan tenure election are scanned. And, the wide variety of social, political, and economic backgrounds which are represented on the bench are perused. The article provides a brief but comprehensive view of the American judge.

In Constraints and Conflicts in Court Administration, *the reader is presented with a succinct view of the American legal system and the difficulties which some of its traditions now cause the courts. Problems raised by the adversary theory as practiced, the jury system, the selection and tenure of judges, as well as court organization, call for increased management of the courts by professionals with managerial experience. Traditionalism has placed some constraints on such management and conflicts are bound to occur, but the professionals in the system must be willing to accept those with managerial expertise if what is good in the traditions is to survive. The need for reform is echoed in* The Need for Judicial Reform. *There are seven major problem areas: bail reform, legal counsel for the poor in civil and criminal cases, delay in civil and criminal cases, mass media reporting of pending cases, judicial selection, the jury system, and judicial review which nullifies legislative and administrative acts. These two articles compliment each other and provide an excellent picture of why we need reform in the courts and effective court management.*

Edward C. Gallas

The court as a social force

The law is a primary instrument of social order, social control, and social justice. In all civilized cultures the judiciary is designated to see that the operation of law serves the purposes of society. To achieve this result, courts are expected to apply sanctions where the law has been breached and to resolve equitable matters that are in dispute.

In some countries the courts are in much the same position as the English judicial officers in America at the time of the Revolution. They are expected to carry out parliamentary and executive mandates. In England today, Parliament, rather than the courts, acts to conserve individual rights.[1] This is in contrast to judicial responsibilities in the United States where the courts are obligated to prevent the application of group power against individuals who might not otherwise have the strength or resources to resist abuses of their liberties and rights.[2]

The American tradition

Despite the constitutional obligation of American courts to protect individual rights and liberties, there has—during much of our history and particularly in some places even today—been a denial of these rights, since the judicial branch of the government has elected to maintain a passive posture. Courts did not ordinarily become involved in disputes between individuals unless the matter was brought to them by one of the parties involved. Under the formal practice of law, even an obviously aggrieved party was denied access to the court if there was a technical mistake in identification of the cause of action, the form of the pleading, or the

Reprinted from *Public Administration Review*, March/April 1971, pp. 125–133, with the permission of the American Society for Public Administration and Edward C. Gallas.

forum designated for the type of proceeding. This anachronistic method is now, for the most part, a matter of history. Its hallmark was meeting technical and formal requirements. Equity was secondary. This often could have no other result than a denial of justice to the poor, the young, the minorities, and the mentally disabled, when pitted against rich and influential adversaries.

The background of passivity and formalism so common to judicial operations during the early days of the Republic have not been entirely overcome. In our adversary system, the courts have long been viewed, and have viewed themselves, as a referee.[3] This is a posture ill-fitted to social progress. The discipline and system of legal training, which carries over when the lawyer is appointed to the bench, also caused a reluctance to do more than require that parties before the bench abide by the accepted rules of behavior, regardless of inequitable consequences.

There is reason to believe that the authors of the Constitution intended the courts to play at least as responsible a role in the American governmental system—and in doing so to bring balance to the country's social system—as the legislative and executive branches. Many of the social ills impinging on individual rights in this country have come about because of a resource imbalance among the branches of government. This resulted, in part, from the passive posture of the judiciary which caused it to react rather than act on matters of social concern—a stance that is understandable in an environment dominated by a *stare decisis* syndrome. This stance, plus the failure of legislative and executive branches to act, or to act slowly, on matters of social concern, has resulted in growing uneasiness among minorities and less affluent members of American society.[4]

Some public and other concerned agencies have also maintained that the courts should do no more than react to matters presented to them for adjudication. Again, the traditional role of the court is viewed as passive and that of the legislative and executive branch as the proper forum for correcting social injustice and for inventing innovative approaches to social problems.

Judicial interest in social concerns

Nevertheless, the executive and legislative bodies, although keyed to be responsive to the needs of the people by reason of frequent elections—and are so perceived by the voters—have not fully realized their potential as a significant force in the shaping of our society. Their response has been *laissez-faire* unless there has been a demand for legislative action from the majority, or at least no perceived objection to social reform. Even then, the response is not always effective in matters involving social questions, because these do not depend so much on the passage of laws, but require imaginative implementation for effectiveness. Thus, there has been an apparent unwillingness, or inability, in some legislative and executive bodies to perform responsibly on many matters of social concern because of the political conflicts that arise out of efforts to cope with urban problems. It is no accident, therefore, that the first real progress on the subjects of segregation,[5] equal voting rights,[6] and search and seizure[7] originated within the judicial branch of the government. Other problems of our urban society such as minority voting,[8] pollution, women's rights, capital punishment, etc., are not likely to be resolved until the judiciary precipitates a crisis through decisions that have grave financial or political consequences.

The more active involvement of the judiciary in social problems is, therefore, not revolutionary, but evolutionary. It is a response to the inability or unwillingness of other public bodies to deal politically or practically with the theses of radicals and militants that individual rights and minority rights are not achievable by operation of law; therefore, disorder and violence are to be condoned. This is a problem, to some an insoluble one, because of judicial attitudes and political inertia on the part of those designated to respond to the electorate.

The most promising solution to the dilemma lies in the judicial system which has at the national level and in some states assumed the initiative in stabilizing the situation. Militants disrupt legal processes and claim that the judiciary is the tool of the "establishment" and the protector of the "status quo." At the same time, the courts demonstrate almost daily their responsiveness to the social needs of the community, despite brickbats received from the right side of the political spectrum.

The disruption in the Chicago trial and the murder of a Superior Court judge in Marin County, California, are manifestations of the disdain with which some segments of the society hold judicial institutions.[9] The courts in these circumstances acquire contempt from perceptions that they merely referee contests and refuse to aggressively involve themselves in the resolution of disputes. While the evidence points to progress toward involvement, many courts do not yet see, as Solomon did, that there is not just a winner or a loser in each case, but rather the possibility that everyone loses where justice is passive, slow, or subject to political control.

What has been alluded to thus far relates to the judiciary's passive role as arbitrator and conciliator. Its decisions from the bench at trial and appellate levels have responded to the importunings of those parts of our society that need the protection of the law—and that protection has been extended by gradual and subtle growth in the law through interpretation.

Recent decisions on such subjects as abortions,[10] search and seizure, school desegregation, voting, air pollution, capital punishment demonstrate that despite a reputation for passivity, the courts are in the forefront of progress in meeting the needs of society.[11] The judicial branch of the government, as illustrated by these decisions, is far ahead of the legislative and executive branches and their bureaucracies in promoting social justice in America. Admittedly, in some areas and in some states the record is spotty. In others, however, there has been an unmistakable movement by courts to fill the vacuum created by legislative inertia.

The implementation of judicial decisions in areas of social concern

The decisions on these forays of the court into the social sphere are not enough to ensure their implementation. Just as the laws and the Constitution are ignored in some places, so are court decisions. Where judicial progress has been greatest in social matters, resistance has been most evident. Courageous judges who lead their profession and "make law" often face frustration from the failure of others to provide the financial and human resources needed to implement their decisions. This has led courts in some places to assume direct responsibility for protecting the rights, not only of those accused of crimes—as in search and seizure decisions—and the community in general—as in voting rights and pollution decisions—but the rights of children, the aged, the widowed, the deserted, the handicapped, and the poor, in order to protect them against those who would profit from their weaknesses.

This is not only a question of justice, but survival. Decisions not properly implemented, or failure to bring appropriate matters to the courts for decisions, are a denial of justice unlikely to be countenanced by militant and enraged minorities. These things come into focus by the rebellion of persons not permitted bail or not promptly brought to trial. They are, therefore, deprived of the American concept of a man's innocence until proven guilty. The holding of hostages by prisoners awaiting trial in New York City demonstrated the breakdown in the criminal justice system that impels the courts to an active role. The implications for all branches and levels of government when the courts fail to act in a timely fashion are clear. In that instance, the courts neither brought prisoners to speedy trial nor exerted pressure on legislative bodies to provide the facilities and staff so that this could be done.[12]

An effective judicial system requires that judicial decisions, when made under authorized circumstances, be executed as intended. In most situations this means that court orders be promptly carried out by the responsible bureaucracy or by individual action. An enforcement officer or agency such as the sheriff, marshall, or appropriate department of the government are expected to be staffed to assure that court orders are executed without undue delay.

Decisions unacceptable to the executive branch, to the bureaucracy (and these are not the same thing), to certain states, to certain local governments, or to certain agencies are prone to be ignored or retested in different courts and on different and obscure aspects of the same issue. The net result is a denial of a specific social reform, if not its interminable delay.

Tendencies to inertia persist in some jurisdictions because of the formidable size of the challenge, the lack of staff or understanding of the consequences, or countervailing community pressures. The resultant attitude is for the judge, like Pontius Pilate, to wash his hands of his decisions as soon as he can do so. In this situation, courts assume little responsibility for follow up, since the bureaucracy is expected to do this. The courts have not, therefore, felt a need to "interfere."

The implementing role of the court

More progressive courts, however, take a course seen by some students of management as a more realistic one. This involves creating the capacity within the court itself to assure the enforcement of court orders when the executive branch or the lawyers fail in their responsibility to the court or to the litigants. The court, in addition to being a decider in executing its social obligations to the community, becomes an implementer and a counsellor.

The responsibility of the court in the maintenance of "law and order" is no less than that of the other branches of the government. Failure to become actively involved through deliberate utilization of the processes it controls contributes to, rather than thwarts, community disorder. Speedy trials, realistic practices for the release of persons awaiting trial, proper representation of the accused, employment of investigative staffs to assist in the sentencing of the convicted, and establishment of viable bail or probation systems when detention or incarceration is not in the public interest all add to community efforts to find an orderly system of swift and equitable criminal justice.[13]

A key question is whether direct court involvement is necessary and appropriate when its decisions are self-executing and should, therefore, flow routinely from normal governmental processes, or not require its intervention because it is within the capacity of the individual affected to see that the end desired by the court is reached. Must something more be added to assure that judicial decisions are quickly and aggressively implemented? Is it reasonable for the courts to staff themselves to assure that their decisions are not ignored or altered by administrative abuse or blunder, not only on criminal cases and community concerns, but on divorce, child support, probation, bankruptcy, juvenile crimes and detention, probate, guardianship, or mental illness matters? Many students of court management believe that judicial effectiveness and respect for judicial processes is guaranteed only when the courts are staffed to monitor the operationalizing of judicial decisions that affect individual rights and liberties. The assumption is that identification and resolution of socially undesirable situations—made visible by matters brought before the court that culminate in a judicial decision—are as much a judicial responsibility as an executive, legislative, or bureaucratic one. The courts are uniquely suited to protect society, as well as individuals, against misuse of authority or unwarranted attacks, even when the abuse emanates from official agencies and the bureaucracy shirks its responsibility for seeking remedial action. Grand juries, as an arm of the court, vested with broad responsibility for reporting to the court and to the public on governmental nonfeasance, misfeasance, and malfeasance, are a continuing and readily understood aspect of this judicial responsibility.

Responsiveness to court decisions

When an executive agency fails to function as intended, by law the court may have to institute, direct, and control a program to assure compliance with its orders. Such a program requires support by human resources—persons trained in many of the same disciplines as those available to the executive branch of the government. Failure to meet this need endangers the protection of individual rights entrusted to the courts, since some states continue to deny constitutional rights to minorities and individuals through local laws, but more frequently through the way official agencies are administered. This illustrates why the courts, as a social force, are not in a position to allow federal, state, city, county, and special agencies of the government to maintain the social balance without supervision.[14] All or none of the agencies may opt to assume such responsibility, depending on their view of the law and the pressures upon them to act, or refrain from acting. The proper utilization of judicial power can facilitate the realization of results when supplemented by skilled staff and adequate fiscal resources. The image of the court in many communities as a referee is not helpful when it starts to assume an activist role. This is particularly true when it is staffed to deal with problems of a social nature that threaten the entrenched bureaucracy and the politicians who are unresponsive to the needs of minorities.

An even more important judicial impact comes from family matters and matters where the court stands *in loco parentis*. The question here is not only a desire on the part of the court to be helpful or to fill a void in the system, but a matter of capacity. Developing this capacity requires a court competently staffed with investigators, inspectors, counsellors, and case workers. The propriety of a court so staffing itself is sometimes questioned by fiscal authorities who believe that the judiciary should, without exception, limit itself to basic decisions, with implementation left to the executive branch of the government. Despite these objections, courts are gradually assuming responsibility for inspecting children's detention homes and foster homes, reviewing proposed adoptions, and approving minors' contracts, e.g., child motion picture personalities or young jockeys, in order to protect the resources of juveniles against employers and the dissipation of resources by parents.

The court appointment of investigative staffs in marital matters involving the welfare of the children is also found to be necessary. Follow-up inspections of a home condition are required to assure compliance with the standards that the courts have established.

Experience demonstrates that controls need to be established if court standards for detention facilities, foster homes, conditions of receivership, arrangements for support of dependent children, and conditions for probation are to be maintained at an acceptable level. Failure to do so is symptomatic of judicial impotence or judicial indifference, even in jurisdictions where the bureaucracy is supposed to support and execute court orders.

Where the court is asked to sever a marriage contract, a society that values such contracts seeks to salvage as many marriages as possible and to persuade the couples, particularly when children are involved, to resolve their differences through professional counselling. To treat this and similar societal problems, the question arises as to which of our institutions are best suited to intervene. The advantage of the critical moment rests with the court. As in other human crises, sensitivity to timing is the essence of problem solving and conflict resolution.

The institutions needed to find solutions to underlying social problems are not automatically created by the passing of a law. They result from an evolutionary process in which the courts can, if they wish, play a significant part. Such institutions can be created within the court, as was the conciliation court of Los Angeles with administrative innovations being pioneered by two judges, e.g., the development and use of a "marriage contract" designed to effect reconciliation of estranged couples where reconciliation was possible; and, by rule of court, a system designed to guarantee payments for child support through a court trustee where divorce or separation resulted from court action.[15] The latter is accomplished by providing that the violation of court orders with respect to such payments is punishable as a contempt matter and that certain classes of child support payments be paid through a trustee appointed by the court. The wife is relieved of the obligation to bring the husband to court in the event of nonpayment. The sheriff acts on the wife's behalf when the court trustee so requests upon a default in payment. The district attorney prosecutes the case without the necessity of expenditure by the wife on behalf of the child. The procedure not only assures respect for and enforcement of court orders, but also that hardships do not befall innocent children through nonpayment, nor that children and their mothers are forced on to welfare rolls when the fathers are able to provide for them. The court program operates under court control, court staffing, and dedicated court direction of a system for the collection and disbursement of monies the court directs be paid for support of dependent children.[16]

The building of court operations of this kind is possible not only in matters surrounding marriage and the family, but in support of programs that call for judicial solutions to poverty, crime, race relations, personal injury disputes, and the environment. Despite voluminous laws, these problems remain unresolved or dealt with on an ad hoc and imperfect basis by harassed and overcrowded courts. As long as there is failure to recognize that the passing of laws does not automatically create an appropriate institution for coping with the underlying cause for which legislation was passed, no more than a weak cure can be expected for a virulent social disease. It is like prescribing, by law, that all persons with a fever take aspirin. Crime, poverty, and other social malfunctions, like fever, are only symptomatic. The judicial field, like the medical field, must locate the causes of the maladies that beset them before lack of treatment is fatal.

Time, place, and personnel factors in court involvement

The timing of the court's involvement on serious family matters enhances its ability to be effective. The intelligent exercise of judicial authority on other social problems contributes to their resolution when the courts, to a limited extent, "make law" because they have the final authority to say what the laws mean. The ability of the courts to establish ground rules that minimize the advantages of utilizing judicial processes for personal gain through imposition of requirements that make utilization of court processes disadvantageous to the litigants in some cases is evident.

Some matters of social concern need more court attention—but not necessarily in the courtroom. Rather, the strength of leadership and the ability to apply sanctions for nonperformance provide the basis for court contributions to societal improvement by ameliorating some of its ills. The approach must be multifaceted, ranging from deeper involvement in matters where individual rights are threatened, to staffing itself to aid the young, the old, the depressed, the talented, the handicapped, and the resolution of family problems, to gradually divesting itself of those matters better handled by other institutions.

Court cases more logically resolved outside the court are legend. Hundreds of thousands of disputes between landlords and tenants tried in the state courts each year turn the courts into glorified collection agencies. Each of the thousands of bankruptcies filed annually require economic and social determinations by a federal court.[17] The automobile accident cases clogging every metropolitan court's civil docket turn the judiciary into an "insurance adjuster-referee." Criminal dockets become buried under a morass of litigation more appropriately consigned to a social work agency, a hospital, or a treatment facility, including cases involving victimless offenders such as narcotic addicts, alcoholics, traffic offenders, gamblers, prostitutes, and consenting adult homosexuals. Each represent social and health problems that law enforcement agencies and the courts do little to alleviate. The required processing of such cases by the courts deflects attention from other litigation. The inclusion of atypical behavior as crimes is a contributing factor to police corruption, loss of respect for the law, the undermining of family life, and the forming of associations conducive to more serious crimes.

These are examples of the causes of court congestion and the inability of the justice system to respond effectively to the needs of a complex society. The cliché in this country that every man is entitled to his day in court leads to such over-utilization of judicial process that the courts are ready to collapse under the weight of the system.

The problem is ripe for resolution. Many courts and judges are balking at the premise that since the legislative and executive branches are the activist ends of government, the judiciary should be passive. Where courts reject this dictum as illogical, cases that do not warrant judicial attention are diverted from the courts and case loads thereby restricted.

Other areas exist where judges can both lighten their load and extend judicial involvement in community affairs. The administration of most estate matters can be reduced to a formula easily administered by a clerk or other court functionary. In some courts, probate examiners, who are lawyers, are designated to review such matters before routine approval by the judge. The logic is clear. The lawyer examiners are qualified and deemed competent by the judge. Their recommendations are accepted if there is no objection from the lawyer handling the estate. Even in this kind of situation, the full social advantage is realizable only when legislators are convinced that expensive legal assistance is not a prerequisite to probating a simple will involving a small estate. Judicial resistance to the idea that the role of the courts is to be passive and a referee rather than a principal, an innovator, and an originator of a new way of doing things, acts to expedite litigation. In some cases this requires additional professional and clerical court personnel, but generally it permits greater utilization of judicial staff. Marriage counsellors in the courts are more effective than counsellors in private social agencies or public welfare agencies, since their work commences at the most critical juncture in the proceedings. Arrangements for the payment of child support through court trustees are more effective than payments through a local welfare department or directly to the recipient of the child support. Settlement discussions instead of trials in personal injury cases, bolstered by tight calendar arrangements that prohibit continuances once settlement discussions are held on a schedule determined by the court through its executive staff, enables individual litigants to see things in a more reasonable light than if the option existed to take their time about placing the matter on the court calendar for a hearing. Assuming responsibility for the rights of persons in custody and requiring trials within a reasonable period, or in the alternative, requiring automatic dismissal as a constitutional right of the individual unless so brought to trial, acts to curb unusual delays in bringing persons to trial and to stop persons guilty of crimes from seeking and gaining an advantage through delays. Aggressive and positive control over persons in custody, viewing them solely as the court's responsibility, serves to limit their exposure to interviews about the state of their guilt, and thereby protects rather than prejudices their rights at the time of trial.

These positive court actions plus cooperative legislative actions to remove from the courts minor cases amenable to settlement without government assistance or by a nonjudicial official are the directions that must be taken to maximize judicial effectiveness. The latter category includes most traffic offenses,[18] landlord and tenant disputes, as well as the settling of marital disputes by divorce or separation upon consent of both parties as to property distribution where minor children are not involved or where public policy questions are not at issue. The resolution of such matters without judicial assistance, or with only nominal help, preserves judicial talent for other more deserving work.

Conclusion

The law, as a primary instrument of social justice, assures an orderly functioning of the sovereign power rather than a morass of individual sanctions. The courts are the intermediary that society looks to for the equitable application of law to individuals, regardless of how popular this is with the majority of the community. Only in this way is the application of group power against the individual prevented.

After judicial decisions are made, their execution must be assured, even though this requires the courts to engage in the supervision of community or social affairs. Execution may require action programs bolstered by investigative, inspectional, counselling, and casework staff. Further controls must be established if standards for facilities, foster homes, and prisons, the interrogation of persons in custody, and the distribution and control of estates, are to be met as prescribed by the court.

The range of problems brought to the court for solution include not only contractual and business disputes, but the settlement of disagreements between neighbors, the punishment of persons who refuse to subject themselves to social norms imposed by law, the determination of parenthood, the ascertainment of sanity, the guardianship of the young and the elderly, the change of names, the approval of administration of minors' contracts and trust funds, the pollution of the environment, the safety of the streets and public areas, and so forth. All of these matters bear on whether or not a healthy society is maintained.

The courts sit in a strategic position to minimize the effects of criminal activities on the community, criminal actions that grow out of poverty or antisocial behavior. It is the only agency able to assure that punishment or treatment institutions are adequate to accomplish rehabilitation. If appropriately staffed, courts are in a position to see that any punishment imposed provides a payoff through probationary and rehabilitation programs.

Litigants seeking court assistance in personal injury cases, in disputes involving property or contracts, whether insurance carriers, corporations, or individuals, need their problems expedited. To this extent, the court affects the social life of the community, particularly in those communities where population is increasing and business is growing more complex.

The various roles the court plays are diverse in character. Some are rehabilitation, others arbitration. In family matters the judiciary often finds itself in the social work field. As a determiner of guilt or innocence, the court is also the agency which metes out punishment. This role includes a concern for the rehabilitation growing out of the punishment determined to be applicable.

Where courts reject their role as rehabilitator and protector, the judiciary is not seen as a total system involving social responsibility as well as decision making. As a result, the informational resources at the command of the judiciary that could be applied on behalf of the community are lost.

The legal profession and the courts are becoming increasingly sensitive to using trained social scientists and social workers in resolving matters that might appear to be most appropriate for adjudication. Progressive local governments responsible for financing the courts are beginning to see how social services in selective cases produce results that represent a direct return on investment.

No other institution within or without the government holds a more strategic position for exerting influence on individuals, organizations, and governments to improve the social environment. Not only the court's prestige, but the vast amounts of information uniquely available to it place the court in the forefront for an attack on antisocial behavior.

The involvement of the courts is justifiable solely in terms of a financial advantage to the community. The ability of the court to minimize or to reduce detention of persons in public facilities at costs ranging from $15 to $50 per day, and the ability of the court to minimize the utilization of its judicial process at costs in excess of $100 per hour, are reason enough for public administrators and financing authorities to look to the judiciary for both assistance and leadership.

Notes

1 A hazardous arrangement given the historical tyranny of majorities even in democratic societies.

2 Justice Hugo Black in *Chambers et al. v. the State of Florida*, 60 S. Ct. 472, 477, 478 (1939) stated: "Under our constitutional system courts stand against any winds that blow as havens of refuge for those who might otherwise suffer because they are helpless, weak, outnumbered, or because they are nonconforming victims of prejudice and public excitement."

3 Robert A. Liston, *The Tides of Justice—The Supreme Court and the Constitution in Our Time* (New York: Delacorte Press, 1966), p. 17.

4 The 78th Federalist, "The Judges as Guardians of the Constitution."

5 *Brown v. The Board of Education of Topeka*, 347 U.S. 483 (1954).

6 *Westbury v. Sanders*, 376 U.S. I (1964), II L ed 2nd 481, 84 S. Ct. 526.

7 *Katz v. The United States*, 389 U.S. 347, 88 S. Ct. 507.

8 The voting rights of minorities, especially of the Negro, have been dealt with extensively by the court as witnessed by its decisions eliminating the poll tax (*Harper v. Virginia Board of Elections*, 383 U.S. 663 (1966))), literacy tests (*United States of America v. Arizona*), and white primaries (*Terry v. Adams*, 345 U.S. 461 (1953))).

9 *United States of America v. David Dellinger et al.*, 69 CR 180.

10 *United States of America v. Milan Viutch* and *United States of America v. Shirley A. Boyd* (11/10/69), 305 F. Supp. 1032 (1969).

11 *William Ralph v. Warden, Maryland Penitentiary*—U.S. Court of Appeals for Fourth Circuit. In the case, the United States Court of Appeals for the Fourth Circuit declared the death penalty to be unconstitutional in rape cases, at least where the victim's life was neither taken or endangered. The three-judge panel ruled unanimously that "In such cases a death sentence violates the evolving standards of decency that the Supreme Court has held are implicit in the Eighth Amendment's prohibition of cruel and unusual punishment."

12 The New York City prison riots on Monday, August 17, 1970, involved 800 prisoners who engaged in window smashing, furniture throwing, bedsheet burning, and a general display of frustration brought about by conditions within the prison coupled with apparent indifference of the City to their plight. Five guards were captured and held hostage until the prisoners' grievances had been heard by the authorities. The riots erupted again on October 1, 1970, in the Branch Queens House of Detention for Men, from which it spread to four other city jails, lasting for five days. The total cost of the damages amounted to $1 million. This time the chief demand of the prisoners was a speedier trial. Mayor Lindsay admitted the failings of the penal system that led to the riots with the following statement: "Of the 1968 arrest population, 43% of prisoners held in detention through trial were held for over one year. Half of those detained through trial were found not guilty, or sentenced after conviction to time already served. Compounding the problem of delays in the judicial process is the fact that the 'City's adult detention institutions are at 183% of capacity.' "

13 Chief Justice Burger in his "State of the Federal Judiciary" address before the 1970 American Bar Association meeting stated: "If ever the law is to have a genuine deterrent effect on the criminal conduct giving us immediate concern, we must make some drastic changes. The most simple and most obvious remedy is to give the courts the manpower and the tools—including prosecutors and defense lawyers—to try criminal cases within sixty days after indictment and let us see what happens. I predict it would sharply reduce the crime rate."

14 In September 1963, Governor Wallace of Alabama attempted to block the enrollment of Vivian Malone and James Hood in the University of Alabama, even though the District Court of the Northern District of Alabama had found the two Negroes clearly qualified for admission. In order to enforce the court's decision, the Alabama National Guard was federalized by Executive Order No. 11118, "Providing Assistance for Removal of Unlawful Obstructions of Justice in the State of Alabama," September 11, 1963, 28 F.R. 9863. See also *South Carolina v. Katzenbach*, 383 U.S. 301, 315 (1966).

15 The Los Angeles judges who led the way were Louis H. Burke (now associate justice of the California Supreme Court) and Roger A. Pfaff.

16 Rule 28, Los Angeles Superior Court. Also, more recently Joint Administrative Order #49 of the First and Second Departments of the Appellate Division of the New York State Supreme Court (March 3, 1967), delegated responsibility to the New York City Office of Probation for receiving and disbursing monies paid for child support under orders of the Family Court.

17 Burger, *op. cit.*: "The entire structure of the administration of bankruptcy and receivership matters should be studied to evaluate whether they could be more efficiently administered in some other way."

18 On July 1, 1970, all traffic offenses in which there is no criminal liability were removed from the jurisdiction of the Criminal Court of New York City, in accordance with Chapter 337 of the Laws of New York 1970. These cases were turned over to either the Parking Violations Bureau or the Moving Traffic Infractions Bureau, depending on the nature of the violation. Traffic offenses in 1969 accounted for 84.7 per cent of the 5,065,554 violations, misdemeanors, or felonies that came before the court. While no definitive results of the new arrangement are yet available, it is anticipated that several judges will be freed from the handling of such traffic offenses.

George F. Cole

The decision to prosecute

This paper is based on an exploratory study of the Office of Prosecuting Attorney, King County (Seattle), Washington. The lack of social scientific knowledge about the prosecutor dictated the choice of this approach. An open-ended interview was administered to one-third of the former deputy prosecutors who had worked in the office during the ten year period 1955–1965. In addition, interviews were conducted with court employees, members of the bench, law enforcement officials, and others having reputations for participation in legal decision-making. Over fifty respondents were contacted during this phase. A final portion of the research placed the author in the role of observer in the prosecutor's office. This experience allowed for direct observation of all

Reprinted from *Law and Society Review* 4 (February 1970): 331–343, with the permission of the Law and Society Association.

phases of the decision to prosecute so that the informal processes of the office could be noted. Discussions with the prosecutor's staff, judges, defendant's attorneys, and the police were held so that the interview data could be placed within an organizational context.

The primary goal of this investigation was to examine the role of the prosecuting attorney as an officer of the legal process within the context of the local political system. The analysis is therefore based on two assumptions. First, that the legal process is best understood as a subsystem of the larger political system. Because of this choice, emphasis is placed upon the interaction and goals of the individuals involved in decision-making. Second, and closely related to the first point, it is assumed that broadly conceived political considerations explained to a large extent "who gets or does not get—in what amount—and how, the good (justice) that is hopefully produced by the legal system" (Klonski and Mendelsohn, 1965: 323). By focusing upon the political and social linkages between these systems, it is expected that decision-making in the prosecutor's office will be viewed as a principal ingredient in the authoritative allocation of values.

The prosecutor's office in an exchange system

While observing the interrelated activities of the organizations in the legal process, one might ask, "Why do these agencies cooperate?" If the police refuse to transfer information to the prosecutor concerning the commission of a crime, what are the rewards or sanctions which might be brought against them? Is it possible that organizations maintain a form of "bureaucratic accounting" which, in a sense, keeps track of the resources allocated to an agency and the support returned? How are cues transmitted from one agency to another to influence decision-making? These are some of the questions which must be asked when decisions are viewed as an output of an exchange system.

The major findings of this study are placed within the context of an exchange system (Evan, 1965: 218).[1] This serves the heuristic purpose of focusing attention upon the linkages found between actors in the decision-making process. In place of the traditional assumptions that the agency is supported solely by statutory authority, this view recognizes that an organization has many clients with which it interacts and upon whom it is dependent for certain resources. As interdependent subunits of a system, then, the organization and its clients are engaged in a set of exchanges across their boundaries. These will involve a transfer of resources between the organizations which will affect the mutual achievement of goals.

The legal system may be viewed as a set of interorganizational exchange relationships analogous to what Long (1962: 142) has called a community game. The participants in the legal system (game) share a common territorial field and collaborate for different and particular ends. They interact on a continuing basis as their responsibilities demand contact with other participants in the process. Thus, the need for the cooperation of other participants can have a bearing on the decision to prosecute. A decision not to prosecute a narcotics offender may be a move to pressure the United States' Attorney's Office to cooperate on another case. It is obvious that bargaining occurs not only between the major actors in a case—the prosecutor and the defense attorney—but also between the clientele groups that are influential in structuring the actions of the prosecuting attorney.

Exchanges do not simply "sail" from one system to another, but take place in an institutionalized setting which may be compared to a market. In the market, decisions are made between individuals who occupy boundary-spanning roles, and who set the conditions under which the exchange will occur. In the legal system, this may merely mean that a representative of the parole board agrees to forward a recommendation to the prosecutor, or it could mean that there is extended bargaining between a deputy prosecutor and a defense attorney. In the study of the King County Prosecutor's Office, it was found that most decisions resulted from some type of exchange relationship. The deputies interacted almost constantly with the police and criminal lawyers, while the prosecutor was more closely linked to exchange relations with the courts, community leaders, and the county commissioners.

The prosecutor's clientele

In an exchange system, power is largely dependent upon the ability of an organization to create clientele relationships which will support and enhance the needs of the agency. For, although interdependence is characteristic of the legal system, competition with other public agencies for support also exists. Since organizations operate in an economy of scarcity, the organization must exist in a favorable power position in relation to its clientele. Reciprocal and unique claims are made by the organization and its clients. Thus, rather than being oriented toward only one public, an organization is beholden to several publics, some visible and others seen clearly only from the pinnacle of leadership. As Gore (1964: 23) notes, when these claims are "firmly anchored inside the organization and the lines drawn taut, the tensions between conflicting claims form a net serving as the institutional base for the organization."

Figure 1   **Disposition of felony cases—King County, 1964**

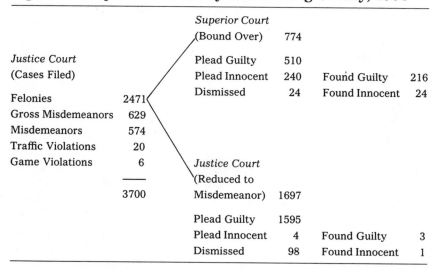

		Superior Court (Bound Over)	774		
Justice Court		Plead Guilty	510		
(Cases Filed)		Plead Innocent	240	Found Guilty	216
		Dismissed	24	Found Innocent	24
Felonies	2471				
Gross Misdemeanors	629				
Misdemeanors	574				
Traffic Violations	20				
Game Violations	6	*Justice Court*			
——		(Reduced to			
3700		Misdemeanor)	1697		
		Plead Guilty	1595		
		Plead Innocent	4	Found Guilty	3
		Dismissed	98	Found Innocent	1

An indication of the stresses within the judicial system may be obtained by analyzing its outputs. It has been suggested that the administration of justice is a selective process in which only those cases which do not create strains in the organization will ultimately reach the courtroom (Chambliss, 1969: 84). As noted in Figure 1, the system operates so that only a small number of cases arrive for trial, the rest being disposed of through reduced charges, *nolle pros.*, and guilty pleas.[2] Not indicated are those cases removed by the police and prosecutor prior to the filing of charges. As the focal organization in an exchange system, the office of prosecuting attorney makes decisions which reflect the influence of its clientele. Because of the scarcity of resources, marketlike relationships, and the organizational needs of the system, prosecutorial decision-making emphasizes the accommodations which are made to the needs of praticipants in the process.

POLICE

Although the prosecuting attorney has discretionary power to determine the disposition of cases, this power is limited by the fact that usually he is dependent upon the police for inputs to the system of cases and evidence. The prosecutor does not have the investigative resources necessary to exercise the kind of affirmitive control over the types of cases that are brought to him. In this relationship, the prosecutor is not without countervailing power. His main check on the police is his ability to return cases to them for further investigation and to refuse to approve arrest warrants. By maintaining cordial relations with the press, a prosecutor is often able to focus attention on the police when the public becomes aroused by incidents of crime. As the King County prosecutor emphasized, "That [investigation] is the job for the sheriff and police. It's their job to bring me the charges." As noted by many respondents, the police, in turn, are dependent upon the prosecutor to accept the output of their system; rejection of too many cases can have serious repercussions affecting the morale, discipline, and workload of the force.

A request for prosecution may be rejected for a number of reasons relating to questions of evidence. Not only must the prosecutor believe that the evidence will secure a conviction, but he must also be aware of community norms relating to the type of acts that should be prosecuted. King County deputy prosecutors noted that charges were never filed when a case involved attempted suicide or fornication. In other actions, the heinous nature of the crime, together with the expected public reaction, may force both the police and prosecutor to press for conviction when evidence is less than satisfactory. As one deputy noted, "In that case [murder and molestation of a six-year-old girl] there was nothing that we could do. As you know the press was on our back and every parent was concerned. Politically, the prosecutor had to seek an information."

Factors other than those relating to evidence may require that the prosecutor refuse to accept a case from the police. First, the prosecuting attorney serves as a regulator of case loads not only for his own office, but for the rest of the legal system. Constitutional and statutory time limits prevent him and the courts from building a backlog of untried cases. In King County, when the system reached the "overload point," there was a tendency to be more selective in choosing the cases to be accepted. A second reason for rejecting prosecution requests may stem from the fact that the prosecutor is thinking of his public exposure in the courtroom. He does not want to take forward cases which will place him in an embarrassing position. Finally, the prosecutor may return cases to check the quality of police work. As a former chief criminal deputy said, "You have to keep them on their toes, otherwise they get lazy. If they aren't doing their job, send the case back and then leak the situation to the newspapers." Rather than spend the resources necessary to find additional evidence, the police may dispose of a case by sending it back to the prosecutor on a lesser charge, implement the "copping out" machinery leading to a guilty plea, drop the case, or in some instances send it to the city prosecutor for action in municipal court.

In most instances, a deputy prosecutor and the police officer assigned to the case occupy the boundary-spanning roles in this exchange relationship. Prosecutors reported that after repeated contacts they got to know the policemen whom they could trust. As one female deputy commented, "There are some you can trust, others you have to watch because they are trying to get rid of cases on you." Deputies may be influenced by the police officer's attitude on a case. One officer noted to a prosecutor that he knew he had a weak case, but mumbled, "I didn't want to bring it up here, but that's what they [his superiors] wanted." As might be expected, the deputy turned down prosecution.

Sometimes the police perform the ritual of "shopping around," seeking to find a deputy prosecutor who, on the basis of past experience, is liable to be sympathetic to their view on a case. At one time, deputies were given complete authority to make the crucial decisions without coordinating their activities with other staff members. In this way the arresting officer would search the prosecutor's office to find a deputy he thought would be sympathetic to the police attitude. As a former deputy noted, "This meant that there were no departmental policies concerning the treatment to be accorded various types of cases. It pretty much depended upon the police and their luck in finding the deputy they wanted." Prosecutors are now instructed to ascertain from the police officer if he has seen another deputy on the case. Even under this more centralized system, it is still possible for the police to request a specific deputy or delay presentation of the case until the "correct" prosecutor is available. Often a prosecutor will gain a reputation for specializing in one type of case. This may mean that the police will assume he will get the case anyway, so they skirt the formal procedure and bring it to him directly.

An exchange relationship between a deputy prosecutor and a police officer may be influenced by the type of crime committed by the defendant. The prototype of a criminal is one who violates person and property. However, a large number of cases involve "crimes without victims" (Schur, 1965). This term refers to those crimes generally involving violations of moral codes, where the general public is theoretically the complainant. In violations of laws against bookmaking, prostitution, and narcotics, neither actor in the transaction is interested in having an arrest made. Hence, vice control men must drum up their own business. Without a civilian complainant, victimless crimes give the police and prosecutor greater leeway in determining the charges to be filed.

One area of exchange involving a victimless crime is that of narcotics control. As Skolnick (1966: 120) notes, "The major organizational requirement of narcotics policing is the presence of an informational system." Without a network of informers, it is impossible to capture addicts and peddlers with evidence that can bring about convictions. One source of informers is among those arrested for narcotics violations. Through promises to reduce charges or even to *nolle pros.*, arrangements can be made so that the accused will return to the narcotics community and gather information for the police. Bargaining observed between the head of the narcotics squad of the Seattle Police and the deputy prosecutor who specialized in drug cases involved the question of charges, promises, and the release of an arrested narcotics pusher.

In the course of postarrest questioning by the police, a well-known drug peddler intimated that he could provide evidence against a pharmacist suspected by the police of illegally selling narcotics. Not only did the police representative want to transfer the case to the friendlier hands of this deputy, but he also wanted to arrange for a reduction of charges and bail. The police officer believed that it was important that the accused be let out in such a way that the narcotics community would not realize that he had become an informer. He also wanted to be sure that the reduced charges would be processed so that the informer could be kept on the string, thus allowing the narcotics squad to maintain control over him. The deputy prosecutor, on the other hand, said that he wanted to make sure that procedures were followed so that the action would not bring discredit on his office. He also suggested that the narcotics squad "work a little harder" on a pending case as a means of returning the favor.

COURTS

The ways used by the court to dispose of cases is a vital influence in the system. The court's actions effect pressures upon the prison, the conviction rate of the prosecutor, and the work of probation agencies. The judge's decisions act as clues to other parts of the system, indicating the type of action likely to be taken in future cases. As noted by a King County judge, "When the number of prisoners gets to the 'riot point,' the warden puts pressure on us to slow down the flow. This often means that men are let out on parole and the number of people given probation and suspended sentences increases." Under such conditions, it would be expected that the prosecutor would respond to the judge's actions by reducing the inputs to the court either by not preferring charges or by increasing the pressure for guilty pleas through bargaining. The adjustments of other parts of the system could be expected to follow. For instance, the police might sense the lack of interest of the prosecutor in accepting charges, hence they will send only airtight cases to him for indictment.

The influence of the court on the decision to prosecute is very real. The sentencing history of each judge gives the prosecutor, as well as other law enforcement officials, an indication of the treatment a case may receive in the courtroom. The prosecutor's expectation as to whether the court will convict may limit his discretion over the decisions on whether to prosecute. "There is great concern as to whose court a case will be assigned. After Judge _____ threw out three cases in a row in which entrapment was involved, the police did not want us to take any cases to him." Since the prosecutor depends upon the plea-bargaining machinery to maintain the flow of cases from his office, the sentencing actions of judges must be predictable. If the defendant and his lawyer are to be influenced to accept a lesser charge or the promise of a lighter sentence in exchange for a plea of guilty, there must be some basis for belief that the judge will fulfill his part of the arrangement. Because judges are unable formally to announce their agreement with the details of the bargain, their past performance acts as a guide.

Within the limits imposed by law and the demands of the system, the prosecutor is able to regulate the flow of cases to the court. He may control the length of time between accusation and trial; hence he may hold cases until he has the evidence which will convict. Alternatively, he may seek repeated adjournment and continuances until the public's interest dies; problems such as witnesses becoming unavailable and similar difficulties make his request for dis-

missal of prosecution more justifiable. Further, he may determine
the type of court to receive the case and the judge who will hear it.
Many misdemeanors covered by state law are also violations of a
city ordinance. It is a common practice for the prosecutor to send a
misdemeanor case to the city prosecutor for processing in the
municipal court when it is believed that a conviction may not be
secured in justice court. As a deputy said, "If there is no case—send
it over to the city court. Things are speedier, less formal, over
there."

In the state of Washington, a person arrested on a felony charge
must be given a preliminary hearing in a justice court within ten
days. For the prosecutor, the preliminary hearing is an opportunity
to evaluate the testimony of witnesses, assess the strength of the
evidence, and try to predict the outcome of the case if it is sent to
trial. On the basis of this evaluation, the prosecutor has several
options: he may bind over the case for trial in Superior Court; he
may reduce the charges to those of a misdemeanor for trial in
Justice Court; or he may conclude that he has no case and drop the
charges. The President Judge of the Justice Courts of King County
estimated that about seventy percent of the felonies are reduced to
misdemeanors after the preliminary hearing.

Besides having some leeway in determining the type of court in
which to file a case, the prosecutor also has some flexibility in
selecting the judge to receive the case. Until recently the prosecutor
could file a case with a specific judge. "The trouble was that Judge
_____ was erratic and independent, [so] no one would file with
him. The other judges objected that they were handling the entire
workload, so a central filing system was devised." Under this
procedure cases are assigned to the judges in rotation. However, as
the chief criminal deputy noted, "the prosecutor can hold a case
until the 'correct' judge came up."

DEFENSE ATTORNEYS

With the increased specialization and institutionalization of the bar,
it would seem that those individuals engaged in the practice of
criminal law have been relegated, both by their profession and by
the community, to a low status. The urban bar appears to be divided
into three parts. First, there is an inner circle which handles the
work of banks, utilities, and commercial concerns; second, another
circle includes plaintiff's lawyers representing interests opposed to
those of the inner circle; and finally, an outer group scrapes out an
existence by "haunting the courts in hope of picking up crumbs

from the judicial table" (Ladinsky, 1963: 128). With the exception of a few highly proficient lawyers who have made a reputation by winning acquittal for their clients in difficult, highly publicized cases, most of the lawyers dealing with the King County Prosecutor's Office belong to this outer ring.

In this study, respondents were asked to identify those attorneys considered to be specialists in criminal law. Of the nearly 1,600 lawyers practicing in King County only eight can be placed in this category. Of this group, six were reported to enjoy the respect of the legal community, while the others were accused by many respondents of being involved in shady deals. A larger group of King County attorneys will accept criminal cases, but these lawyers do not consider themselves specialists. Several respondents noted that many lawyers, because of inexperience or age, were required to hang around the courthouse searching for clients. One Seattle attorney described the quality of legal talent available for criminal cases as "a few good criminal lawyers and a lot of young kids and old men. The good lawyers I can count on my fingers."

In a legal system where bargaining is a primary method of decision-making, it is not surprising that criminal lawyers find it essential to maintain close personal ties with the prosecutor and his staff. Respondents were quite open in revealing their dependence upon this close relationship to successfully pursue their careers. The nature of the criminal lawyer's work is such that his saleable product or service appears to be influence rather than technical proficiency in the law. Respondents hold the belief that clients are attracted partially on the basis of the attorney's reputation as a fixer, or as a shrewd bargainer.

There is a tendency for ex-deputy prosecutors in King County to enter the practice of criminal law. Because of his inside knowledge of the prosecutor's office and friendships made with court officials, the former deputy feels that he has an advantage over other criminal law practitioners. All of the former deputies interviewed said that they took criminal cases. Of the eight criminal law specialists, seven previously served as deputy prosecutors in King County, while the other was once prosecuting attorney in a rural county.

Because of the financial problems of the criminal lawyer's practice, it is necessary that he handle cases on an assembly-line basis, hoping to make a living from a large number of small fees. Referring to a fellow lawyer, one attorney said, "You should see _____. He goes up there to Carroll's office with a whole fist full of cases. He trades on some, bargains on others and never goes to court. It's amazing but it's the way he makes his living." There are incentives, therefore, to bargain with the prosecutor and other decision-makers. The primary aim of the attorney in such circumstances is to reach an accommodation so that the time-consuming formal proceedings need not be implemented. As a Seattle attorney noted, "I can't make any money if I spend my time in a courtroom. I make mine on the telephone or in the prosecutor's office." One of the disturbing results of this arrangement is that instances were reported in which a bargain was reached between the attorney and deputy prosecutor on a "package deal." In this situation, an attorney's clients are treated as a group; the outcome of the bargaining is often an agreement whereby reduced charges will be achieved for some, in exchange for the unspoken assent by the lawyer that the prosecutor may proceed as he desires with the other cases. One member of the King County Bar has developed this practice to such a fine art that a deputy prosecutor said, "When you saw him coming into the office, you knew that he would be pleading guilty." At one time this situation was so widespread that the "prisoners up in the jail had a rating list which graded the attorneys as either 'good guys' or 'sell outs.' "

The exchange relationship between the defense attorney and the prosecutor is based on their need for cooperation in the discharge of their responsibilities. Most criminal lawyers are interested primarily in the speedy solution of cases because of their precarious financial situation. Since they must protect their professional reputations with their colleagues, judicial personnel, and potential clientele, however, they are not completely free to bargain solely with this objective. As one attorney noted, "You can't afford to let it get out that you are selling out your cases."

The prosecutor is also interested in the speedy processing of cases. This can only be achieved if the formal processes are not implemented. Not only does the pressure of his caseload influence bargaining, but also the legal process with its potential for delay and appeal, creates a degree of uncertainty which is not present in an exchange relationship with an attorney with whom you have dealt for a number of years. As the Presiding Judge of the Seattle District Court said, "Lawyers are helpful to the system. They are able to pull things together, work out a deal, keep the system moving."

COMMUNITY INFLUENTIALS

As part of the political system, the judicial process responds to the community environment. The King County study indicated that there are differential levels of influence within the community and that some people had a greater interest in the politics of prosecution than others. First, the general public is able to have its values translated into policies followed by law enforcement officers. The public's influence is particularly acute in those gray areas of the law where full enforcement is not expected. Statutes may be enacted by legislatures defining the outer limits of criminal conduct, but they do not necessarily mean that laws are to be fully enforced to these limits. There are some laws defining behavior which the community no longer considers criminal. It can be expected that a prosecutor's charging policies will reflect this attitude. He may not prosecute violations of laws regulating some forms of gambling, certain sexual practices, or violations of Sunday Blue Laws.

Because the general public is a potential threat to the prosecutor, staff members take measures to protect him from criticism. Respondents agreed that decision-making occurs with the public in mind—"will a course of action arouse antipathy towards the prosecutor rather than the accused?" Several deputies mentioned what they called the "aggravation level" of a crime. This is a recognition that the commission of certain crimes, within a specific context, will bring about a vocal public reaction. "If a little girl, walking home from the grocery store, is pulled into the bushes and indecent liberties taken, this is more disturbing to the public's conscience than a case where the father of the girl takes indecent liberties with her at home." The office of King County Prosecuting Attorney has a policy requiring that deputies file all cases involving sexual molestation in which the police believe the girl's story is credible. The office also prefers charges in all negligent homicide cases where there is the least possibility of guilt. In such types of cases the public may respond to the emotional context of the case and demand prosecution. To cover the prosecutor from criticism, it is believed that the safest measure is to prosecute.

The bail system is also used to protect the prosecutor from criticism. Thus it is the policy to set bail at a high level with the expectation that the court will reduce the amount. "This looks good for Prosecutor Carroll. Takes the heat off of him, especially in morals cases. If the accused doesn't appear in court the prosecutor can't be blamed. The public gets upset when they know these types are out free." This is an example of exchange where one actor is shifting the responsibility and potential onus onto another. In turn, the court is under pressure from county jail officials to keep the prison population down.

A second community group having contact with the prosecutor is composed of those leaders who have a continuing or potential interest in the politics of prosecution. This group, analogous to the players in one of Long's community games, are linked to the prosecutor because his actions affect their success in playing another game. Hence community boosters want either a crackdown or a hands-off policy towards gambling, political leaders want the prosecutor to remember the interests of the party, and business leaders want policies which will not interfere with their own game.

Community leaders may receive special treatment by the prosecutor if they run afoul of the law. A policy of the King County Office requires that cases involving prominent members of the community be referred immediately to the chief criminal deputy and the prosecutor for their disposition. As one deputy noted, "These cases can be pretty touchy. It's important that the boss knows immediately about this type of case so that he is not caught 'flat footed' when asked about it by the press."

Pressure by an interest group was evidenced during a strike by drug store employees in 1964. The striking unions urged Prosecutor Carroll to invoke a state law which requires the presence of a licensed pharmacist if the drug store is open. Not only did union representatives meet with Carroll, but picket lines were set up outside the courthouse protesting his refusal to act. The prosecutor resisted the union's pressure tactics.

In recent years, the prosecutor's tolerance policy toward minor forms of gambling led to a number of conflicts with Seattle's mayor, the sheriff, and church organizations. After a decision was made to prohibit all forms of public gaming, the prosecutor was criticized by groups representing the tourist industry and such affected groups as the bartenders' union which thought the decision would have an adverse economic effect. As Prosecutor Carroll said, "I am always getting pressures from different interests—business, the Chamber of Commerce, and labor. I have to try and maintain a balance between them." In exchange for these considerations, the prosecutor may gain prestige, political support, and admission into the leadership groups of the community.

Summary

By viewing the King County Office of Prosecuting Attorney as the focal organization in an exchange system, data from this exploratory study suggests the market-like relationships which exist between actors in the system. Since prosecution operates in an environment of scarce resources and since the decisions have potential political ramifications, a variety of officials influence the allocation of justice. The decision to prosecute is not made at one point, but rather the prosecuting attorney has a number of options which he may employ during various stages of the proceedings. But the prosecutor is able to exercise his discretionary powers only within the network of exchange relationships. The police, court congestion, organizational strains, and community pressures are among the factors which influence prosecutorial behavior.

Notes

1 See also Levine and White (1961: 583) and Blau (1955).

2 The lack of reliable criminal statistics is well known. These data were gathered from a number of sources, including King County (1964).

References

Blau, P. M. (1955) The Dynamics of Bureaucracy. Chicago: Univ. of Chicago Press.

Chambliss, W. J. (1969) Crime and the Legal Process. New York: McGraw-Hill.

Evan, W. M. (1965) "Towards a theory of inter-organizational relations." Management Sci. 11 (August): 218–230.

Gore, W. J. (1964) Administrative Decision Making. New York: John Wiley.

King County (1964) Annual Report of the Prosecuting Attorney. Seattle: State of Washington.

Klonski, J. R. and *R. I. Mendelsohn* (1965) "The allocation of justice: a political analysis." J. of Public Law 14 (May): 323–342.

Ladinsky, J. (1963) "The impact of social backgrounds of lawyers on law practice and the law." J. of Legal Education 16, 2: 128–144.

Levine, S. and *P. E. White* (1961) "Exchange as a conceptual framework for the study of inter-organizational relationships." Administrative Sci. Q. 5 (March): 583–601.

Long, N. (1962) The Polity. Chicago: Rand McNally.

Schur, E. M. (1965) Crimes Without Victims. Englewood Cliffs, N.J.: Prentice-Hall.

Skolnick, J. E. (1966) Justice Without Trial. New York: John Wiley.

Sheldon Goldman

American judges: their selection, tenure, variety and quality

There are over 5,500 American judges serving on both federal and state trial and appellate courts.[1] They serve in a wide variety of court systems because each state and the federal government has its own set of courts. As can be expected, the rules as well as the politics governing judicial selection and tenure vary widely, and furthermore it is believed that there are diverse groups of judges on the bench both in terms of their political and sociological characteristics and their "quality."

Judicial Selection: There are essentially five methods for selecting judges currently in the United States. They are: partisan election, non-partisan election, merit plan selection, executive appointment and legislative appointment. The *partisan election* method, with its roots in the age of Jacksonian democracy,[2] is still the method most used by the states. Today, fourteen states are committed to it for the selection of most or all their judges. This means that candidates for judicial office run with a party designation (determined by the party primary or convention) and (typically) are legally allowed to conduct a fully partisan campaign. The *non-partisan election* method, which dates back to the progressive movement at the turn of the century,[3] is also prominent. Thirteen states now use non-partisan elections to select most or all their judges. Under this scheme, judges run for office without a party designation and are usually restricted as to the nature of their campaigning. In sum, then, some form of election process, partisan or non-partisan, is found in over half the states.

Merit plan selection (also known as the "Missouri Plan" because it was first adopted there in 1940) is the method most favored by the organized bar and has been the subject of extensive lobbying efforts in recent decades. By 1971, eleven states had legally adopted the

Reprinted from *Current History*, July 1971, pp. 1–8, with the permission of Current History, Inc.

plan (eight since 1962) to select most or all judges. In several other states and localities a merit type procedure has been informally utilized by mayors and governors sensitive to the wishes of bar and reform groups.[4] Under merit selection, a nominating commission (usually consisting of lawyers elected by the bar, lay gubernatorial appointees and members of the judiciary) submits to the Governor a panel of judicial nominees (usually three) for a particular judicial post. The Governor must make his appointment from the panel of names presented to him.

The method which relies largely on *executive appointment* is currently in use by eight states and the federal government. As specified in the United States Constitution, the President appoints federal judges with the consent of the Senate. Similarly, in Delaware, Hawaii and New Jersey, the Governor appoints with the consent of the State Senate. In Maine, Massachusetts and New Hampshire, however, the Executive Council must approve gubernatorial appointees, while in California the Commission on Judicial Appointments must give its consent. Only in Maryland does the Governor have an exclusive appointment power; however, his appointees must subsequently run for election.

Judicial *selection by the full legislature* is an anachronism that stems back to the early colonial experience. Only four states place major reliance on this method and in one state, Connecticut, the Governor formally submits nominations.

Table One presents the principal methods of judicial selection and where they are predominantly used. It should be noted that a majority of the states do not select all their judges by any one method. For example, in the state of Iowa, judges of the Supreme and District courts are selected under the merit plan. But municipal court judges are selected in non-partisan elections and justices of the peace run for office in partisan elections. Police court judges are appointed either by the city council or elected by the voters.

Judicial selection in practice

To understand judicial selection it is necessary to know not only the formal requirements for selection but also what actually occurs in practice. This requires the investigation of the politics of selection and the determination of the actual process by which those who are judges obtained their jobs. Of course, to understand why one individual and not another seemingly similar person receives a

Table 1 Principal methods of judicial selection in the United States

Partisan election	Non-partisan election	Legislative election	Executive appointment	Merit plan
Alabama[a]	Arizona[a]	Connecticut[a]	California[b]	Alaska
Arkansas	Kentucky[a]	Rhode Island[b]	Delaware	Colorado[a]
Florida	Michigan	South Carolina[c]	Hawaii[b]	Idaho
Georgia[a]	Minnesota	Virginia[a]	Maine[a]	Indiana[b]
Illinois[a]	Montana[a]		Maryland[a]	Iowa[a]
Louisiana	Nevada		Massachusetts	Kansas[b]
Mississippi[a]	North Dakota		New Hampshire	Missouri[a]
New Mexico	Ohio		New Jersey[a]	Nebraska[a]
New York[a,c]	Oregon[a]		United States[a]	Oklahoma[a,c]
North Carolina	South Dakota[a]			Utah[a]
Pennsylvania	Washington[a]			Vermont[a,c]
Tennessee	Wisconsin			
Texas	Wyoming[a]			
West Virginia				

[a] Minor court judges chosen by other methods.
[b] Appellate judges only. Other judges selected by different methods.
[c] Most but not all major judicial positions selected this way.

judicial appointment it is necessary to discover the intimate details of all the various transactions that propelled the ultimately successful judicial candidacy. However, on the basis of several studies, it is possible with some degree of confidence to make some broad observations about judicial selection in practice and what appear to be the relevant variables.

Perhaps the most important point worthy of emphasis is that all selection methods involve politics. The partisan and typically the non-partisan election devices concern political party politics often focused at the local party level.[5] The electoral voting patterns of such elections suggest that they are generally consistent with overall partisan trends in the states.[6] In many states which use non-partisan elections, such partisan influences as partisan endorsement of judges and even campaigning with partisan overtones are prominent.[7] However, judicial elections tend to be much less competitive than other elections.

Legislative and gubernatorial appointments involve state-wide party politics and gubernatorial politics. Gubernatorial selection of judges often involves many participants (including state legislators, judges, bar association leaders, party leaders, interest group spokesmen) and considerations (legal, political, strategic, policy). It is of interest to note that gubernatorial politics is present in elective systems because a substantial number of judges in elective systems receive gubernatorial interim appointments to fill vacancies created by resignation, retirement, or death.

Merit selection not only has gubernatorial politics built into the system by the provision for gubernatorial appointment, but it also institutionalizes bar association politics by the creation of nomination commissions staffed in part by lawyers elected by the bar. In an extensive study of the merit plan in Missouri, it was discovered that rival bar associations reflecting different socio-economic interests had long contested the elections to the nominating commissions.[8] It was further found that the commissions themselves engaged in extensive internal negotiations and that the panels of names presented to the Governor were often "stacked" to favor a particular nominee. In some instances, the Governor was found to have exerted influence on the selection of names to the panels.[9]

The evidence suggests that all selection methods involve a negotiations process with a variety of participants and interests (although the participants and the importance given to different interests vary with the method). There are a variety of criteria that are used to narrow considerably the population from which the appointee will be chosen. Partisan considerations may considerably reduce that population (note that for the most part judicial positions are filled by those with a background of partisan activism). Bar association activism also appears to be important, particularly in those systems in which the organized bar has established a formal or informal role in the selection process. The legal qualifications of potential candidates may be important especially for the higher and more visible judicial offices (newspaper editors frequently focus on this aspect, often in concert with bar association leaders). The policy or ideological perspectives of the candidates may at times be relevant for selection. Finally, having friends in high places (on the bench, on nominating commissions, in bar associations, in the media, in party organizations, in public office) may be instrumental in securing a judgeship.

Federal judicial selection

Federal judicial selection is similar in many instances to judicial selection in the states. The negotiations process (particularly for lower federal court positions) is centered in the office of the Deputy Attorney General and includes United States senators and other important party leaders of the President's party from the state "receiving" the appointment and from the American Bar Association's Standing Committee on Federal Judiciary. When the senator from the President's party pushes a candidate not preferred by the Justice Department officials or when the state has two senators of the President's party and they cannot agree on a candidate or candidates or if they and other important party leaders from the state are in wide disagreement, negotiations may continue over many months and possibly beyond a year.[10] Negotiations with the A.B.A. Committee are more subtle. The Committee receives the names of the principal candidates for a position and then investigates and rates them ("Exceptionally Well Qualified," "Well Qualified," "Qualified," or "Not Qualified"). Occasionally, the committee will vigorously promote a candidacy.[11] In the past, it has fought nominations for those rated "Not Qualified." The Nixon administration, however, agreed not to nominate such candidates; thus the A.B.A. Committee now has a veto power in federal judicial selection.

The considerations that appear to be important for all administrations in deciding whom to nominate include: (1) the legal competence of the candidates; (2) partisan considerations (note that at least 90 per cent of judicial appointments go to members of the President's party); (3) approval of the senator(s) of the President's party from the state of the prospective nominee (without such approval a concerned senator may invoke senatorial courtesy whereby the Senate will ordinarily refuse to confirm); and (4) the ideological or policy positions of the candidates (Democratic administrations have tended to place more political liberals on the bench than political conservatives while Republican administrations have done the reverse).[12] In general, however, political considerations take precedence over the ideological or policy views of the candidates while the latter tend to be more important than the appointment of brilliant legal scholars, or, indeed, those given the highest rating by the A.B.A.

Supreme Court appointments have traditionally been considered the exclusive domain of the President and have been based on a variety of political, personal or ideological/policy considerations. However, during the nineteenth century and more recently, the Senate has declined to rubber-stamp the President's nominees. After President Richard Nixon's nominations of Clement Haynsworth and Harrold Carswell met defeat, the administration agreed to give the A.B.A. Committee the same opportunity it now has with regard to lower court positions to rate the leading candidates for a Supreme Court nomination and to exercise a virtual veto power. However, it is doubtful that a strong A.B.A. endorsement will result in less senatorial scrutiny of the nominee (note that both Haynsworth and Carswell had received favorable ratings from the A.B.A.).

Judicial tenure

There are six principal provisions for tenure on the bench in the United States. Four states and the federal government appoint most or all their judges for life tenure.[13] In three states, tenure for most or all judges depends upon reappointment by the Governor with the consent of another body (either the Senate or Executive Council) for terms of office varying from four to twelve years. In twelve states, periodic partisan elections are held with the terms of office varying from two to fourteen years. In fifteen states, non-partisan elections are held with the term of office varying widely by office and state. In four states, the legislature is responsible for reappointment and in twelve states the tenure provisions of the merit plan are in effect.

Under merit plan tenure provisions, judges, at periodic intervals, run unopposed in non-partisan retention elections. Nine of the original eleven states which utilize the selection provisions of the merit plan also use the plan's tenure scheme.[14] Illinois and Pennsylvania use partisan elections for selection purposes but use the merit plan for tenure. California (which uses gubernatorial appointment with commission approval for selection purposes) also uses the merit plan's tenure provisions.

In practice, most judges once on the bench stay there at their pleasure regardless of the formal tenure provisions. Most judicial incumbents running for reelection do not face opposition.[15] Generally, those who do are seldom defeated[16] (although there are occasional notable exceptions, for example, in Missouri in the over two decades before the merit plan was adopted, incumbents were beaten at the polls in seven out of twelve partisan elections held for Supreme Court Justice). In states using the merit plan's tenure provisions it is almost (but not quite) a certainty that a judge will win the retention election (in Missouri, for example, in over two decades subsequent to the adoption of the plan only one judge failed in the bid for retention).

It has been extraordinarily difficult to remove judges from office for their unwillingness or inability to perform their duties satisfactorily. This is true not only for judges with life tenure but also for judges with set terms of office. Although the latter, if their offenses are grave enough and public enough, may fail to win reappointment or reelection (or lose a recall election), they and their brethren with life tenure have in the past been disciplined only by the tortuous processes of impeachment and conviction. Only the most serious offenses have triggered such extreme action, and consequently it has occurred infrequently.[17]

In recent years, there has been increasing attention given to the judicial discipline problem and to methods for coping with it. Particularly since the early 1960's, judicial removal commissions have been instituted in many states. By early 1971, at least half the states had some machinery (usually in the form of a commission) with disciplinary and removal powers. The recent District of Columbia crime bill created the first federal judicial removal commission with jurisdiction over the "local" judges (with fixed terms of office) in the District of Columbia. There has also been some movement in the federal judicial circuits to use the circuit councils for disciplinary purposes, and this was given some encouragement when the United States Supreme Court refused to reverse the severe disciplinary steps taken by the Judicial Council of the Tenth Circuit against a federal district judge.[18] However, it is probably too early to assess the impact of all these developments.

Variety of judges

There are a wide variety of social, political, and economic backgrounds represented on the bench, due largely to the multiple levels of judicial office, the varying judicial systems, and the different party systems in the states. Over one-third of all states still have justices of the peace and most of these positions are low-paying (most rely on a fee basis) and require little or no legal training. Other state positions at the trial level and in local courts of limited jurisdiction are relatively low-paying but can only be filled by lawyers. The lawyers attracted to these positions tend to be from the lower (but far from the lowest) end of the socio-economic continuum.[19] The pool of candidates for the higher-paying and more prestigious state appellate court positions and particularly the handsomely paid lifetime tenured federal judgeships is undoubtedly distinctly different. These judges, especially at the highest state court level and the federal level, tend to come from the middle class or above, tend to have had a good undergraduate and legal education, and tend to have achieved some distinction in their main occupation before ascending the bench (law practice, elective or appointed public office or, in some cases, a lower court judgeship). Like the large majority of judges at all levels, they also tend to have a background of partisan activism.

Over the years, the party balance on the bench has not diverged radically from the partisan make-up of the states, although there are sometimes pronounced short-term discrepancies caused by the relatively lengthy terms of judicial office, notably at the highest levels. At the federal level, most new administrations in recent decades have had the opportunity to fill large numbers of federal judgeships, because of the continued expansion of the number of judicial positions in the federal system.

There is little doubt that black Americans and women are severely underrepresented at all levels of the judiciary. At the higher levels, particularly the federal level, those of minority religious and white ethnic affiliation and those from a lower status socio-economic background are underrepresented in terms of their make-up in the population as a whole. However, at least on the federal level, there is evidence that there are some differences in the backgrounds of judicial appointees of Democratic administrations as compared to Republican administrations. Democratic (in contrast to Republican) administrations tend to appoint proportionately more black Americans as well as those of other minority ethnic and religious affiliation, those of lower status religious affiliation, those from lower socio-economic backgrounds and those from the smaller law firms.

On the state level, there appear to be some differences in the social and political backgrounds of those selected according to the type of selection process utilized.[20] For example, there is a marked pattern of localism in the attribute profiles of judges selected by partisan elections as compared to judges selected by other methods. However, there is little evidence that any one selection system rather than another will necessarily result in the selection of predominantly one social class.[21]

Quality

The Chairman of the Oklahoma Judicial Nominating Commission wrote in a recent article: "[O]ur biggest problem has been . . . a lack of qualified candidates. Too many of the men interested in being appointed a judge are either too young and inexperienced, too old, or have not been successful in their own law practice." [22] A distinguished law professor, Philip B. Kurland, lamented about the scarcity of judges with real talent and he asserted: "[t]here is a crisis of confidence in American law and the American judiciary. . . ." He suggested that "[i]f we do not provide the necessary quality of judicial officials" society will come apart, and he added, "It may already be too late." [23] A committee of the North American Judge's Association recently observed, "It is evident the qualities of decision, composure and compassion which make good judges are not easily found nor easily recognized in advance" [24]—a conclusion reached some years earlier by the noted Chief Justice of the New Jersey Supreme Court after extensively reviewing in the abstract the attributes of a good judge (he noted "the difficulties of measuring judicial attributes objectively").[25]

These statements about the quality of American judges represent the type of arguments that have continued over many years. It is a rare participant in the debate who will not assert the importance of having good judges on the bench. The problems, of course, are how one defines and measures "goodness" and furthermore the discovery (if that is possible) of objective attributes that will enable the selection of persons who will be "good" judges. Complicating matters is that people often have honest differences in their appraisals of others as well as in their personal value hierarchies. Nominating commissions (and bar associations as well) believe that there are criteria associated with being qualified for a judgeship (for example, the Oklahoma commission chairman cited earlier suggested that sex, age, experience and success in law practice are such criteria). Surveys of lawyers and judges as to what they regard as the qualities of superior judges indicate such attributes as common sense, knowledge of the law, courtesy, open-mindedness, and hard work.[26] Furthermore, some surveys of lawyers reveal a preference for merit plan selection on the ground that better quality judges are then chosen.[27] But the connection between the qualities of superior judges and the criteria that are currently used by nominating commissions and bar groups as well as the connection with the selection system used are simply not clear-cut. One is led to the conclusion reached some years ago by a student of the subject, Rodney Mott, who noted: "We may not be able to measure the goodness of a judge, but it is very possible to measure the extent he is thought to be good." [28]

If this, then, is our point of departure for investigating the quality of American judges, we must decide whose opinion to examine. If it is the organized bar's views we investigate (assuming we can find a predominance of bar opinion) we are likely to find a paradox. Members of the bar individually and collectively may decry in general the scarcity of high quality judges on the bench and even attribute this to the partisan aspects of selection, but when it comes down to specifics, they endorse and give good ratings to these very same judges. By the professed standards of the A.B.A. Standing Committee on Federal Judiciary, the federal judiciary is almost entirely dominated by judges who have received "qualified" or better ratings. On the state level, it is rare for a bar association to oppose the reelection or retention of an incumbent judge. The latter, however, may simply reflect the reluctance of lawyers to challenge the judges before whom they practice.

Public opinion surveys have tended to focus on public views of court decisions. For example, in a recent poll, close to three out of four surveyed thought the courts too lenient towards criminal defendants.[29] Such a finding could be interpreted to reflect negative public attitudes concerning the quality of American judges. But it is more plausible to argue that such polls really tap attitudes towards the *quality of justice.* Perhaps it is more fruitful, then, to divert attention from the effort to assess the quality of judges to the related but distinct consideration of the quality of justice they dispense. Admittedly there are ambiguities and subjectivity in this sort of enterprise, but surely it is more directly related to the central concerns of understanding, evaluating, and reforming a judicial system.

Notes

1 For state judges see *The Book of the States 1970–1971,* Vol. 18 (Lexington, Kentucky: Council of State Governments, 1970), p. 121. For federal judges see *United States Government Organizational Manual—1970/71* (Washington, D.C.: Office of the Federal Register, 1970), pp. 44–52.

2 Arthur T. Vanderbilt, *Judges and Jurors: Their Functions, Qualifications and Selection* (Boston: Boston University Press, 1956), p. 36.

3 Richard A. Watson and Rondal G. Downing, *The Politics of the Bench and the Bar: Judicial Selection Under the Missouri Nonpartisan Court Plan* (New York: Wiley, 1969), p. 3n.

4 Ibid., pp. 12–13.

5 See, for example, Wallace W. Sayre and Herbert Kaufman, *Governing New York City: Politics in the Metropolis* (New York: Norton, 1965), pp. 522–557.

6 Kenneth N. Vines, "Courts as Political and Governmental Agencies," in Herbert Jacob and Kenneth N. Vines (eds.), *Politics in the American States* (Boston: Little, Brown, 1965), pp. 266–267.

7 Ibid., p. 267. Also see S. Sidney Ulmer, "The Political Party Variable in the Michigan Supreme Court," in Glendon Schubert (ed.), *Judicial Behavior* (Chicago: Rand McNally, 1964), pp. 279–281; David W. Adamany, "The Party Variable in Judges' Voting," *American Political Science Review*, 63 (1969), 62–63, 69–72.

8 Watson and Downing, pp. 20–43.

9 Ibid., pp. 101–120, 187–194.

10 Sheldon Goldman, "Judicial Appointments to the United States Courts of Appeals," *Wisconsin Law Review* (1967), 191–192, 199–200.

11 Ibid., 193–196.

12 Sheldon Goldman and Thomas P. Jahnige, *The Federal Courts as a Political System* (New York: Harper & Row, 1971), pp. 58–59, 60–61.

13 New Hampshire judges are appointed to age 70; New Jersey superior and appellate court judges are appointed for an initial seven-year term and are eligible for reappointment for life.

14 The other two are accounted for as follows: Vermont uses a legislative vote to determine retention; Utah uses non-partisan elections for retention purposes in which opposing candidates may enter.

15 Vines, pp. 265–266; Sayre and Kaufman, p. 534.

16 Vines, ibid.; Watson and Downing, pp. 229–230.

17 See Joseph Borkin, *The Corrupt Judge* (Cleveland: World Publishing, 1966); Raoul Berger, "Impeachment of Judges and 'Good Behavior' Tenure," *Yale Law Journal*, 79 (1970), 1475–1531; Frank Thompson, Jr. and Daniel H. Pollitt, "Impeachment of Federal Judges: An Historical Overview," *North Carolina Law Review*, 49 (1970), 87–121; Charles D. Harris, "The Impeachment Trial of Samuel Chase," *American Bar Association Journal*, 57 (1971), 53–57.

18 *Chandler v. Judicial Council of the Tenth Circuit*, 398 U.S. 74 (1970).

19 See, for example, Watson and Downing, p. 73.

20 Vines, pp. 261–262; Herbert Jacob, "The Effect of Institutional Differences in the Recruitment Process: The Case of State Judges," *Journal of Public Law*, 13 (1964), 104–119.

21 Watson and Downing, pp. 343–344.

22 Lowe Runkle, "The Judicial Nominating Commission," *Judicature*, 54 (1970), 117.

23 Philip B. Kurland, "The Judicial Process," *The New York Times*, December 12, 1970, p. 31.

24 As reported in *Judicature*, 54 (1971), 348.

25 Vanderbilt, p. 32.

26 Watson and Downing, pp. 296–297.

27 Ibid., p. 345. Also see Charles H. Sheldon, "The Degree of Satisfaction with State Judicial Selection Systems: Lawyers vs. Judges," *Judicature*, 54 (1971), 331–334. Note that the recent National Conference on the Judiciary in which numerous judges, lawyers, and bar association leaders participated recommended that "all state court judges should be appointed to long terms by a non-partisan commission rather than elected." *The New York Times*, March 15, 1971, p. 27.

28 As quoted in Watson and Downing, p. 273n.

29 *Newsweek*, March 8, 1971, p. 39.

Ernest C. Friesen

Constraints and conflicts in court administration

The recognition of courts as unique and complex institutions in our society is forcing all who are concerned with the administration of justice to reassess their conclusions about the way they can be administered. New Jersey, the first of the centrally administered systems, has not succeeded in solving all problems of court administration. In all fairness to New Jersey, the demands on the courts have far outstripped the capacity of the courts to expand, but the inability of the system to deal flexibly with the problem suggests that a deeper look be taken at the courts and their potential for administration. It may well be that, as some have suggested, the courts are not manageable. More hopefully, they are

Reprinted from *Public Administration Review*, March/April 1971, pp. 120–124, with the permission of the American Society for Public Administration and Ernest C. Friesen.

not manageable without new concepts and clearer recognition of the underlying problems.

An examination of the uniqueness of the courts and the constraints and conflicts which their unusual role creates may help in the search for a better model or at least a helpful analog.

Resource dependency

The courts, as presently organized are almost totally dependent on political processes for their resources. Though dependent upon both legislative and executive activity they must regularly judge such action. They act as the arbiter of disputes between individuals and the executive branch of government which may actually provide or at least have veto power over necessary court resources.

The courts in almost all states derive their routine support from many political sources. The sheriff, the county clerk, and the county commissioners, each separately elected, provide essential services to the courts. The salaries of judges are usually dependent upon the largess of legislatures, which in times of rising costs can punish the judges by inaction. County supplements to judicial salaries often leave the judges doubly at the mercy of separated political authority.

Responsibility for broad social problems is often placed on the courts with no resources for their effective resolution. The responsibility for sentencing convicted felons is invariably fixed on courts, with control of or support for presentence investigations placed in a county or state executive agency. The problems of child custody are regularly dumped on the courts, with no resources with which to evaluate critical decisions about custody. Mental health, juvenile neglect, alcoholism are all loaded onto the courts in differing ways, with no support provided to carry out the complex duties imposed.

The courts, perhaps the most critical institution in a government of laws, are complex beyond present rational comprehension, yet they have received almost no attention from students of administration. Long the private domain of the legally trained and licensed, the courts are today for the first time being examined from the viewpoint of effective administration. The principal result of this examination is to recognize the constraints in the court environment on traditional concepts of management.

The adversary theory

American courts, built on the English tradition, are lawyer dependent. Justice in the Anglo-American system of law is based upon the assumption that both the proper interpretation of law and the approximation of the truth will best be accomplished when opponents present their positions to an impartial decider. Whether or not the assumption has validity, there is little likelihood that the system will be changed. Courts will continue to be dependent in their administration of justice upon the performance, the availabilities, the quality, and the attitudes of the American lawyer.

This dependency carries with it several corollary constraints. The resolution of disputes will depend upon the availability of groups of people at a given time and place. At the very least two lawyers must get together to settle a case. To perform the elaborate ritual of a jury trial there must be a judge, at least two lawyers, witnesses, court reporter, clerks, bailiffs, jurors, and the parties. In a criminal case the complexity is substantially increased by the large portion of indigent defendants requiring court-appointed counsel and the usual understaffing of the prosecutor's office.

Traditional adversary theory requires the judge to play a passive role. The lawyers move cases as they are available (or delay them as they believe it will be to their or their client's best interest). Under this traditional view, the lawyers are to be left alone and allowed to delay the justice process for reasons sufficient to themselves.

A developing judicial attitude recognizes that the justice process cannot be left to the convenience or special interest of the lawyers involved. Recognizing that the adversary, witness-oriented process diminishes in effectiveness with the loss of memory and the disappearance of witnesses, many judges today resist the traditional deference to lawyers in moving their cases to conclusion.

Lawyers and judges as soloists

From the commencement of an attorney's career in the law he is trained as a soloist. His law school emphasizes individual work to the almost complete exclusion of any team or organization work. The practice of law whether in a prosecutor's office or with a private law firm is highly individual. While this tends to develop persons who are individually very thorough, it does not prepare them for membership in an organization. As judges they value their independence, recognize its importance to impartiality in decision making, but have no awareness of their duty to the judicial organization. In defending their own independence they tend to protect the individual freedom of all judges in the system, even when such freedom is destructive of necessary administrative action.

Judges, of course, come from the legal profession and, for the most part, come from an extensive practice of law. They bring with them the general antipathy toward administration of the soloist legal profession.

The professional independence manifests itself in court organizations by preventing strong administration. Almost invariably judges left to their own devices will rotate the office of "chief" judge or give the position to the senior judge. Though there are rare instances where the judges have elected a strong administrative judge to manage their affairs, these instances are sufficiently rare to be noted as exceptions.

The jury system

Though closely related to the adversary process, the jury system provides a special constraint on court management. Deeply rooted in tradition, the jury trial and the grand jury indictment will be essential elements of American justice for the foreseeable future.

The existence of a right to a trial by jury results in the necessity of having a basically continuous hearing in a given case and the administration of a program aimed at finding impartial jurors.

The difficulty involved in trying a case with a cohesive team of jurors over any protracted period of time is obvious to any observer of contemporary American justice. Sickness, death in the family, jobs, and many other factors interfere with the continuity of any team of 12 persons. Many judges routinely swear 14 jurors in cases that will last as little as five days. Juror fees are uniformly less than poverty-level pay. Trial must, therefore, be before jurors who can afford the time or who must sacrifice income to perform this civic duty.

The problems involved in getting impartial jurors in sufficient numbers are even greater than keeping a jury in a protracted trial. To get a hundred jurors to the court house, literally hundreds must be summoned, examined, given an opportunity to be excused, and processed to a trial room for screening by the lawyers. Jurors selected from too narrow or broad an area may be challenged as unrepresentative of the community. Inability to read and write may disqualify some. Excessive excuses of certain economic groups may defeat the requirements of a fair cross section of the community.

To maintain an adequate supply of jurors for the cases that must be tried usually involves the maintenance of a pool where hundreds may wait for days without being utilized. The human waste and social cost of a poorly run system has only recently been exposed. The alternative to the pooling of jurors is to waste judicial manpower which in many cities is so short as to be the critical element in court congestion.

Jurors are not employees of the court. Their incentives for performance are different from those of employees generally. If the jury system is to produce justice it must be managed in its own context as a unique feature of an unusual institution.

Selection and tenure of judges

The principal actors in the court system are the judges. Their willingness to take responsibility, their motivation to work, their understanding of their organizational role all contribute to the way the courts are run. Needless to note, the way judges are selected and the security of their office affects the performance of the judicial establishment.

Most judges are selected politically. The degree to which partisan politics is involved varies widely from partisan nomination in the federal courts (never less than 90 per cent of the judges named from the President's party) to nonpartisan ballots where the party of the candidate is often unknown. The Missouri plan of nonpartisan selection has gained in the Midwest in recent years, but even under such a plan of blue ribbon commission nomination the judge must stand for retention after a term of years. Whether politically appointed or politically elected, the political source of the appointment often expects to help select personnel for the court or causes the judge to apply the bureaucratic principle that if you do nothing the electorate will have nothing against you.

There is some evidence that in administrative matters tenure of office is substantially more important than the method of selection. Administration of the courts has been weakest in states where the electorate regularly turns out incumbent judges, and has been strongest where judges have either traditional or constitutional life tenure. There is some indication that Missouri plan-type judges, dependent as they feel they are on the good will of lawyers, may be less effective in managing their cases than judges dependent on the election process for retention in office. Where lawyers are the basic court congesting problem, the influence of the bar on retention clearly affects the operation of the court calendars.

Long tenure in office without any effective removal procedure causes managerial side effects which may counterbalance in part the contribution of long tenure to judicial independence. In any group of human beings, no matter how carefully selected, a certain number of inadequate persons will emerge. A certain number of alcoholics appear in the judicial population as do other psychological and physical disabilities. In some instances very good lawyers are inadequate judges for the very reason they were good lawyers, i.e., their conscientious and thorough attention to detail. In a judge this may manifest itself as indecision.

Most human systems are able to absorb these inadequate people without large dysfunctional effects. In the judiciary, however, an inadequate judge in a small court is disastrous and in a large court leads to administrative structuring that often impedes effective administration. The small court will have to absorb far too much work in a few judges. In the large court the judges often organize to permit the lawyers to avoid the inadequate judge by judge shopping techniques which consume great amounts of judge time and effort. Since the alternative is to expose the inadequate member of their society, the administrative cost is accepted as an unarticulated necessity.

Statutory division of labor

There is no rational explanation for the division of labor among the various levels of courts. The labels on courts such as Circuit Court, Court of Common Pleas, Orphans Court, Superior Court, Supreme Court are more indicative of their historical antecedents than they are of the work which is allocated to them.

There are at least 56 court systems within the United States. Each state has a system, the several territories have different systems, the District of Columbia has a system, and the federal system operates independently though interrelated to all. The term "District Court" is used to label the lowest courts in some systems;

the court of general jurisdiction in other systems, and the intermediate court of appeal in another system. "Circuit Courts" are appellate courts in some and general jurisdiction in other systems. "Superior Courts" are usually courts of general jurisdiction but may be the lowest or have limited appellate jurisdiction. The only valid generality about the distribution of jurisdiction among the courts is that it was accomplished without a rational view to the management of a court system.

Though there are clearly areas of the law and of justice which require more or less skill on the part of judges, the distribution of labor along traditional lines has not taken this into account. The critical legal problems of today are probably in the area of the relation of a tenant to his landlord, consumer credit, or juvenile behavior. The jurisdiction over these matters has traditionally been allocated to courts with lower-paid and lower-status judges. They are often staffed with excellent judges but they are seldom staffed or financed to perform the tasks assigned to them. Because their jurisdiction has been allocated to them by statute or even by constitutional provisions, there is little capacity in these courts to deal effectively with these critical areas of legal development. From an administrative point of view, the barriers to flexible administration are virtually unsurmountable.

Attempts have been made in recent years to develop a model court structure with tiers of judges who could be transferred freely from one area to another. The culture, however, is resistant. There is a strong feeling among judges that the redistribution of jurisdiction may somehow reduce the importance of the court on which they sit.

The status system in the judiciary is very real and should be tampered with only after considerable analysis and experimentation. Most judges become judges because they want the status this affords them in the legal profession. They leave higher paying jobs to take on heavy responsibility. Any reduction in the perceived status of the position might well reduce the number of persons willing to take on the difficult burdens of judging.

The Illinois reforms seem to have accomplished the increase in administrative flexibility without reducing the status of individual judges. There the lowest court, the magistrates, were made subject to the control of the court of general jurisdiction with authority in the general court to assign all the original "jurisdiction of the court as appropriate." If the traditional allocation of work can be broken down in the operation of the trial court, there is now no statutory impediment to the change.

Court organization

The distribution of jurisdiction among courts has been purposeless. The organization of the courts for management purposes is, with notable exceptions, nonexistent.

The federal courts have a central administrative office with basic control functions over the expenditure of funds and the supervision of a judicial salary plan. The authority to administer is in 11 circuit councils which have no staff for the performance of even routine ministerial tasks.

State court administration varies widely, but generally there is no central authority for the administration of the courts. Many states pretend to have central administration where judges can be assigned away from their home district, but in fact exercise this authority without adequate information and, therefore, without design.

New Jersey was the first state to have central administration of the courts, and has developed it to its highest form. Colorado and Connecticut have recently provided for central controls and administration, but most court systems operate without any plan or organization, relying upon appellate processes for the small amount of coordination achieved.

Court organization at the local or county level exists only in Illinois and New Jersey. In Illinois all of the trial courts are unified into a single Circuit Court with an administrative judge in charge. In New Jersey an assignment judge appointed by the state chief justice has supervisory authority over his entire district, including all levels of trial courts. With these principal exceptions, the courts handling interrelated matters on a routine basis are totally fragmented, with neither authority nor staff for integration of efforts.

Change possibilities

The constraints on management and the conflicts inherent in the system present a discouraging picture. The courts are institutions in search of a managerial model. The existence of the American justice, adversary, jury, judicially independent system will depend upon the ability of those seeking the model to find it.

The problem is like the one which faced hospitals a half a century ago and like the one that faces university administration today. The professionals who dominate the system must be respected and their role defined, but organization and management must be brought to the courts or they will continue to lose ground in their effort to provide individual justice in individual cases.

Efforts are now being made to draw in persons from many disciplines to find the answers and to preside over their introduction into the courts. As Arthur Vanderbilt noted, "reform of the administration of justice is not sport for the short winded." Only now by joining the efforts of lawyers with public administration is progress beginning.

Stuart S. Nagel

The need for judicial reform

There are seven judicial reform problems which tend to be felt in criminal and civil cases: (1) bail reform, (2) legal counsel for the poor in criminal and civil cases, (3) delay in civil and criminal cases, (4) mass media reporting on pending cases, (5) judicial selection, (6) the jury system, and (7) judicial nullification of legislative and administrative acts.

Pretrial release

One of the first stages in criminal proceedings which seems to call for judicial reform is the stage at which a decision is made about an arrested suspect prior to his trial. The basic alternatives involve releasing or not releasing him prior to trial depending on (1) whether he can offer a sufficient money deposit to serve as a guarantee or incentive that he will return for trial, or (2) whether his characteristics are such that he is likely to return for his trial rather than risk being prosecuted as a trial jumper. The first alternative is referred to as the traditional bail bond system, and the second

Reprinted from *Current History*, August 1971, pp 65–70, with the permission of Current History, Inc.

alternative as release on one's own recognizance or the ROR system.

In past years, the bail system was by far the dominant method. This was so partly because of the belief that individuals were economically motivated and partly because the system favored middle class people whose interests tended to dominate legal rule-making. The reform trend is increasingly toward a more objective and scientific ROR system for a number of reasons.

Studies by the Vera Institute in New York City have shown that by carefully screening arrested suspects into good risks and bad risks (largely on the basis of their roots in the community and the seriousness of their crimes), one can obtain at least as low a percentage of trial jumpers as one does with the traditional money-deposit system.[1] Trial-day mail or phone reminders also help reduce trial jumping. These studies have further shown that, with the screening and notification system, a far higher percentage of arrested suspects can be released from jail pending their trial than under the money-deposit system. Such release means these good risks can (1) continue their jobs, (2) better prepare their cases to establish their innocence, (3) save the taxpayer money by not occupying jail space, and (4) be less bitter than if they spent time in jail and were then acquitted. The money-deposit system so inherently discriminates against the poor that the United States Supreme Court may someday declare it to be in violation of the equal protection clause of the Constitution.[2]

One objection to the ROR system is that it might result in releasing a number of arrested suspects who will commit crimes while awaiting trial. One response to this objection is that truly dangerous persons should be kept in jail pending a speedy trial regardless of how able they are to offer a large money deposit. Another response is to point out that pretrial crimes are more often due to long delays prior to trial than to poor screening or the lack of a bail bond requirement. The delay problem, however, is a separate area of judicial reform.[3]

Legal counsel for the poor

In the 1962 case of *Gideon v. Wainwright*, the Supreme Court declared that criminal defendants who could not afford to hire an attorney to represent them should be provided with a free attorney by the prosecuting government at least for crimes involving more than a possible six-month jail sentence.[4] Prior to 1962, some states already provided counsel to indigent defendants before the Supreme Court required it, although many states felt that free counsel to the poor was too expensive, or socialistic, or unnecessary.

The big problem now is how, not whether, to provide counsel. The basic alternatives are either (1) relying on unpaid or paid volunteer attorneys, (2) having the courts assign attorneys to represent indigent defendants, or (3) using full-time public defenders who receive a salary from the government to which they are attached.

The unpaid volunteer system has the disadvantage that it too often attracts young attorneys who are seeking experience at the possible expense of a client whose liberty might be jeopardized. The paid volunteer system, however, works well at the federal level, where only well qualified attorneys are allowed to volunteer, and where they are fully compensated for their services. In smaller communities, where assigned counsel is often used, clients are frequently represented by reluctant attorneys or by attorneys who have had little or no criminal case experience.

The full-time public defender system is being increasingly used, although many public defender offices are under-financed and under-staffed and thus cannot investigate and defend their cases as vigorously as they otherwise should. To make the public defender applicable to smaller communities, states like Minnesota are beginning to experiment with regional public defenders who cover a number of rural counties.

Although the Supreme Court has not yet required free counsel for the poor in housing eviction, auto repossession, or other civil cases, the federal Office of Economic Opportunity and most local communities have sought to provide some form of civil legal aid. Their efforts are justified on the grounds that legal aid can promote respect for the law, protect the innocent, encourage orderly law reform, and educate the poor to their legal rights and obligations.

The basic alternatives for civil legal aid are similar to those for criminal legal aid. The traditional system has involved volunteer attorneys whose availability is generally limited and little known. In recent years, the O.E.O. has provided many cities with full-time civil legal services programs similar to public defender offices. Some attorneys have proposed the judicare system for civil legal aid whereby poor clients go to the attorney of their choice, and the government pays the attorney's fee as in medicare. The judicare system has been criticized as lacking visibility, specialists in poverty law, preventative education, and law reform; it is also criticized for an excess of bookkeeping, potential federal regulation and expensiveness.

To provide legal service to middle class people, proposals have been made for various kinds of legal insurance and various plans whereby attorneys for unions or other organizations can represent individual members. Such plans have, however, been opposed by bar associations who fear that organization attorneys will lack a close attorney-client relationship and who also fear the economic competition which such a system would represent to traditional law practice. Certain organizational schemes, however, have been declared by the Supreme Court to be protected by the freedom of assembly clause of the Constitution, and will probably increasingly be established.[5]

Delay in the court

Increased industrialization and urbanization have indirectly produced undesirable delays in both civil and criminal cases. Automobile accidents mainly explain the long delays in civil cases, often extending to five years in the larger cities. Urbanization and the accompanying increased crime rates have significantly added to criminal court congestion.

In a delayed personal injury case, the injured party may be unable to collect what he is entitled to because of the forgetfulness and loss of witnesses and the pressure to settle for quicker, although reduced, damage payments. Although the delays are shorter in criminal cases, they can be especially harmful if the arrested suspect must wait in jail pending his trial and then receives an acquittal or a sentence shorter than the time he has already waited in jail. Criminal case delays are also harmful if the arrested suspect is released pending trial and commits further crimes during the long waiting period.

To reduce delay in civil cases, various reforms have been attempted or proposed. Some reforms are designed to encourage out-of-court settlements by providing for impartial medical experts, pretrial settlement conferences, interest charges beginning with the day of the accident, and pretrial proceedings to enable the parties to know where they stand with regard to each other's evidence. Other reforms are designed to remove personal injury cases from the courts by shifting them to administrative agencies, or by providing that injuried parties automatically collect from their own insurance company regardless of their negligence as with fire insurance.

The time consumed by the jury trial stage can be reduced by having high jury fees, providing earlier trial for non-jury cases, randomly picking 12 jurors without lengthy selection, and by separating the liability and damage issues (so there is no need to discuss damages if the defendant is found non-liable, and so settlement can be facilitated if liability is established). Reformers have also recommended that delay be reduced by having more judges, making them work more days per year and more hours per day, shifting judges from low to high congestion courts, and decreasing wasted judge-time due to poor scheduling of the same attorney in two different courts.

Reforms designed to reduce delay in criminal cases are similar to those in civil cases. There can be better screening of complaints, more encouragement of guilty pleas where merited, more criminal court personnel, less use of grand jury indictment, more pretrial proceedings to narrow the issues, random jury selection, and release of the defendant within a specified period of time if he is not tried. The Supreme Court has recently made speedy trial in criminal cases a constitutional right at both the state and federal levels.[6]

Reporting on pending cases

How to handle the problem of mass media reporting on criminal cases involves an interesting conflict between two civil liberties. On the one side is freedom of speech and freedom of the press which includes the right to report on pending cases. On the other side is the constitutional right to a fair trial which should not be prejudiced by distorted reporting or by reporting evidence that is not admissible in court.

The United States Supreme Court has been more sensitive to the fair trial interest than to the free press interest in cases where the two have conflicted. This was especially so in the 1966 Sam Sheppard case where the Cleveland newspapers published front page editorials demanding Sheppard's conviction, created near chaos outside the courtroom with their numerous photographers, and published unsubstantiated damaging statements by Walter Winchell and the Cleveland police chief that were never testified to at the trial.[7] The Supreme Court declared that in future sensational cases the trial should be held away from the community where the crime was committed; attorneys should be reprimanded for gossiping to reporters; jurors and sometimes witnesses should be kept from seeing newspapers; reporters should be held in contempt for printing gossip while a trial is still in process; and the number of reporters in the courtroom should be severely limited. After many years in prison, Sam Sheppard was eventually retried without prejudicial press publicity, and in that trial he was acquitted.

Since the Sam Sheppard case, many newspapers and newspaper associations have established various rules providing for voluntary press restraints. The American Bar Association has likewise established a set of rules restraining attorneys in criminal cases from communicating prejudicial information to the press. Because these restraints have not been sufficiently effective, some reformers have proposed more use of the British system whereby newspapers are readily held in contempt of court for publishing almost anything other than the barest facts about criminal trials until the trial is completed.[8]

Judicial selection

How should judges be chosen? Basically, they are either (1) appointed by the President, governor, or mayor with or without the approval of a bipartisan nominating commission or legislature, or (2) elected by the general public with partisan or non-partisan election procedures. Originally nearly all United States judges were appointed, but during the period of Jacksonian democracy a shift toward electing state and local judges began. Federal judges have always been appointed as specified in the Constitution. In the last few decades, there has been a shift back to gubernatorial appointment of state and local judges.

Those who argue in favor of elected judges point out that judicial decision-making frequently involves subjective value judgments. In a democracy, these values should probably reflect general public opinion. The electoral advocates also point out that elected judges will come closer in their backgrounds to the general public than appointed judges, especially if the nominating commission tends to be dominated by the state bar association. These and other differences in the attitudes and backgrounds of elected and appointed judges can be tested [9] by comparing elected judges with judges who have been appointed on appointed courts or on elected courts as interim judges to complete the unexpired terms of dead, retired or resigned judges.

Those who argue in favor of appointed judges seek to establish that appointed judges are less partisan in their judicial voting behavior. This may, however, be due more to the bipartisan approval that is needed for appointment, to appointment across party lines by some governors, and to the differences in how appointed judges view their roles, rather than directly to the selection process. The advocates of appointment also argue that appointed judges are technically more competent because they tend to come from the better law schools and colleges than elected judges, but the empirical evidence does not support this point.

Closely related to the method of judicial selection is the length of judicial tenure, since judicial reform movements usually advocate both appointive selection and longer judicial terms. Longer terms give a judge more independence from political party pressures. Such terms, however, are likely to make judges less responsive to public opinion although possibly more sensitive to minority rights.

Because of the somewhat evenly divided controversy over elected versus appointed judges, various compromises have developed. Illinois, for instance, has provided for regular elections for vacant judgeships (with provision for opposition candidates) to be followed periodically by retention elections (whereby each sitting judge runs against his record with the voters being able to vote only yes or no on his retention). Such compromises will probably become increasingly prevalent.[10]

The jury system

Jurors in medieval England were originally persons from the community who were witnesses to the facts in dispute. Eventually the jury evolved into a group of community representatives who resolved factual disputes in cases, while the judge determined the applicable law. Traditionally the jury has consisted of 12 people chosen by both sides from a list of voters, and they have determined guilt in criminal cases and liability civil cases by unanimous decision. In recent years, the idea of having juries to supplement the work of judges has come under attack.

It is argued that jury trials consume too much time or that juries back competence. It is also charged that juries sometimes ignore the legal instructions given them, such as when they are told that plaintiffs in auto accident cases should not collect anything if the plaintiff has been partially negligent regardless of how negligent the defendant may have been. One can counter this criticism by saying that if an old law is unjust, as this rule of contributory negligence may be, the jury system often softens its harsh effects by applying a more contemporary community sense of justice.

The defenders of the jury system point out that a jury trial is more likely to free the innocent than a bench trial because all approximately 12 jury members must agree to convict and because jurors tend to be more like defendants than judges are. Judges and juries agree approximately 83 per cent of the time in criminal cases, but when they disagree the jury is nearly always pro-defendant and the judge pro-prosecutor. This and other findings about jury behavior have been developed as part of the research of the University of Chicago Jury Project.

Defenders also argue that the jury system by providing public participation encourages respect for the law. It has, for instance, been found in before-and-after tests that being a juror does improve one's attitude toward the legal system. This public participation also enables ambiguities in the facts or law to be resolved in the direction of general public opinion.

As a compromise between the attackers and the defenders of the jury system, the trend seems to be in the direction of juries smaller than twelve men deciding by less than unanimous vote. This trend has been especially present in civil cases, and the Supreme Court has recently held it to be constitutional for criminal cases.[11]

Judicial review

After pretrial release, appointment of counsel, possible delay, newspaper reporting, picking of a judge and the jury's decision, there comes the stage of a possible appeal to a higher court. The most controversial aspect of appellate-court decision-making, although it can also occur at the trial court level, is the potential nullification by the court of a state or federal statute or administrative regulation. This process of judicial review is peculiar to countries whose constitutions are embodied in a single written document (unlike Great Britain) and is partly attributable to the personality of John Marshall as manifested in his *Marbury v. Madison* decision.[12]

Many arguments favor giving the courts the power of judicial review rather than leaving it to Congress and the people to determine the constitutionality of legislative acts. It is argued that Congress cannot be trusted to police itself since it has a vested interest in its own legislation. Another strong point is that unpopular minority viewpoints need the courts to protect them. It is also said that constitutional interpretation requires technical legal training which the courts have, and that the courts have less political bias than legislatures do.

Arguments against judicial review emphasize that Congress is more responsive to public opinion, although in the long run the courts are also somewhat responsive, at least via personnel changes. Attacks in the past on judicial review have also stressed the conservatism of the courts, particularly with regard to economic regulation. It is further noted that the lack of preciseness in the Constitution makes it more a political than a legal document, and that there have often been substantial differences between Democratic and Republican judges in constitutional interpretation.

Between the positions of complete judicial review over all types of statutes and no judicial review at all, there are many intermediate positions. It could be made more difficult for the courts to exercise judicial review by (1) requiring more than a simple majority of judicial votes or (2) allowing for congressional overruling, as with presidential vetoes. Other intermediate positions seek to make the Supreme Court more responsive by having it (1) composed of representatives from all three branches of government as in some West European systems, (2) an elected or shorter-term court, or (3) composed of representatives from all 50 states (a suggestion proposed in a constitutional amendment which many states have passed).

Further intermediate positions involve judicial review only over legislation relating to (1) the judiciary where the court has a special protective interest, (2) state legislation, in order to preserve American federalism, or (3) civil liberties matters where ideological, ethnic, or other minority interests need protection. The trend is decidedly toward the latter position of a civil liberties oriented judicial review. Big business, which received so many of the benefits of judicial review in the past, can more adequately protect itself in the legislative process today.[13]

There are other fields of reform in the American system of justice. For example, prior to the bail stage there is considerable controversy over how to make the police more efficient in apprehending criminals while at the same time complying with constitutional requirements relating to searches and interrogation.[14] Likewise subsequent to the appeal and judicial review stage, there is considerable controversy over how to make prisons more rehabilitative while at the same time providing a negative deterrence to criminality.[15]

A changing environment

The fact that reform is needed does not necessarily indicate that the American system of justice has been inefficient or discriminatory as measured by past standards. It does indicate that the American environment is changing with regard to urbanization which affects efficiency, and that middle class Americans are becoming more sensitive to discriminatory injustices that were formerly tolerated. It is certainly encouraging to note that in recent years the courts and other policy-making bodies have instituted numerous innovations to attempt to resolve the problems raised by pretrial release, legal aid, court delay, pretrial reporting, judicial selection, the jury system and judicial review, although more still remains to be done.[16]

Notes

1 C. Ares, A. Rankin, and H. Sturz, "The Manhattan Bail Project: An Interim Report on the Use of Pre-Trial Parole," 38 *N.Y.U. Law Review* 67–95 (1963).

2 *Bandy v. United States*, 364 U.S. 477 (1960).

3 For further detail on bail reform, see Daniel Freed and Patricia Wald, *Bail in the United States* (Washington, D.C.: Govt. Printing Office, 1964) and Ronald Goldfarb, *Ransom: A Critique of the American Bail System* (New York: Harper & Row, 1965). See also the article by Richard Pious in the July, 1971, *Current History.*

4 *Gideon v. Wainwright*, 372 U.S. 335 (1963).

5 For further detail on legal aid programs, see Patricia Wald, *Law & Poverty* (Washington, D.C.: Govt. Printing Office, 1965) and Lee Silverstein, *Defense of the Poor* (Boston: Little Brown, 1966).

6 *Klopfer v. North Carolina*, 386 U.S. 213 (1967). For further detail on court delay, see Hans Zeisel, Harry Kalven, and Bernard Buchholz, *Delay in the Court* (Boston: Little Brown, 1959); Harry Jones, *The Courts, the Public, and the Law Explosion* (Englewood Cliffs, N.J.: Prentice Hall, 1965); and other articles in this symposium.

7 *Sheppard v. Maxwell*, 384 U.S. 333 (1966). For the text see pages 106ff of this issue.

8 For further detail on pretrial publicity, see Alfred Friendly and Ronald Goldfarb, *Crime and Publicity* (New York: Twentieth Century Fund, 1967); Donald M. Gillmor, *Free Press and Fair Trial* (Washington, D.C.: Public Affairs Press, 1966); and other articles in this symposium.

9 Herbert Jacob, "The Effect of Institutional Differences in the Recruitment Process: The Case of State Judges," 13 *Journal of Public Law* 104–119 (1964) and Stuart Nagel, *The Legal Process from a Behavioral Perspective* (Homewood, Ill.: Dorsey Press, 1969), pp. 173–197.

10 For further detail on judicial election, see Richard Watson and Rondal Downing, *The Politics of the Bench and the Bar: Judicial Selection under the Missouri Nonpartisan Court Plan* (New York: John Wiley, 1969) and Evans Haynes, *The Selection and Tenure of Judges* (New York: National Conference of Judicial Councils, 1944).

11 *Williams v. Florida*, 399 U.S. 78 (1970). For further details on the jury system, see Harry Kalven and Hans Zeisel, *The American Jury* (Boston: Little Brown, 1966); Charles Joiner, *Civil Justice and the Jury* (Englewood Cliffs, N.J.: Prentice-Hall, 1962); and other articles in this symposium.

12 *Marbury v. Madison*, 1 *Cranch* 137 (1803).

13 For further detail on judicial review, see Howard Dean, *Judicial Review and Democracy* (New York: Random House, 1966) and Robert Carr, *The Supreme Court and Judicial Review* (New York: Rinehart, 1942).

14 For further detail on police efficiency, see O. W. Wilson, *Police Administration* (New York: McGraw-Hill, 1963); Jerome Skolnick, *Justice without Trial: Law Enforcement in a Democratic Society* (New York: John Wiley, 1967); and other articles in this symposium.

15 For further detail on prison reform, see Daniel Glaser, *The Effectiveness of a Prison and Parole System* (Indianapolis: Bobbs-Merrill, 1964); Paul Tappan, *Crime, Justice, and Correction* (New York: McGraw-Hill, 1960); and other articles in this symposium.

16 For further detail on judicial or justice reform in general, see Howard James, *Crisis in the Courts* (New York: McKay, 1968); Arthur Vanderbilt, *Minimum Standards of Judicial Administration* (New York: National Conference of Judicial Councils, 1949); American Bar Association, *Minimum Standards for Criminal Justice* (Inst. of Judicial Administration, a series of booklets published from 1967 on); and other articles in this symposium.

Part five

Corrections

U*nless we correct our correctional system, the unnecessary problems with criminal offenders will continue to increase. Mr. Chief Justice Warren Burger in* No Man Is An Island *notes that our system of criminal justice has placed a heavy emphasis on criminal trials. We are too much at home with litigation and have neglected to give any substantial attention to the correctional system. Two-thirds of the inmates in federal and state prisons are alumni of our non-correcting correctional system. This rate of recidivism can be described as a national scandal. The Chief Justice sets out a shopping list of the characteristics of the typical American prison and he does not paint a pleasant picture. He insists that the correctional process is as much a part of the administration of criminal justice as adjudication, and he challenges the American legal profession to face the problem and lead the way toward its solution.*

The crime control industry has spent millions of dollars with relatively meager results, especially in the area of corrections. There Is More to Crime Control Than the "Get Tough" Approach *questions the effectiveness of this approach, which has brought about increased apprehension and conviction rates and more severe, longer sentences and imprisonment. Further, there is a question as to whether the nation has the capacity and resources to achieve tougher crime control. The tough punitive approach is and has been one of high cost and low yield, and there is no evidence that this will change. It does not provide the potential that the softer approach of training, education, job placement, counseling, and community acceptance do. We have tried the "get tough" approach without real success. Now more emphasis should be placed on rehabilitation rather than punishment.*

American Prisons: Self-Defeating Concrete *echoes the need for different approaches to corrections. This article provides a bird's-eye view of the development of the American prison system and some of the problems present in it. Some of the new scientific approaches to corrections are described. The need for correctional reform is underscored, particularly the deinstitutionalizing of the correctional system.*

Measuring the Cost of Correctional Services *discusses the criminal offender as a consumer of public resources most of which are tax supported. Because of the deficiencies in the correctional system the public is not getting its money's worth. There has been no real goal setting in corrections and its objectives are uncertain. The article sets forth a series of functions which are starting points in assessing the needs, defining the purposes, and establishing the goals and objectives in corrections. The need for evaluation of programs and the importance of resource management is stressed.*

In Corrections and the Criminal Justice System *the National Commission on Criminal Justice Standards and Goals highlights some of the problems that exist in the criminal justice system and the necessity for establishing standards and goals in corrections. A close working relationship is vital between the correctional portion of the criminal justice system and the other two segments, the courts and the police. Progress can be made only in the context of a criminal justice system operating as an integrated and coordinated response to crime. From the correctional perspective—but in the broader sense—the obstacles to reforms, such as fragmentation in corrections, the lack of effective financial support, community opposition to change, and the lack of a knowledge base for planning, must be overcome if the system is to function effectively.*

Warren E. Burger

"No man is an island"

As we proceeded with the American Bar Association's Criminal Justice Project, of which I had the honor to succeed Judge J. Edward Lumbard as chairman, it became more and more clear that all the improvements in the traditional area of criminal justice would mean little if we did not recognize that a system of criminal justice must be seen as more than litigation within the framework of the adversary system.

Many people tend to think of the administration of justice in terms of the criminal trial alone, because this is the part of the process that occurs in the local community. But, more than that, it is charged with the human element; it is exciting, colorful and dramatic. This is why the movies and TV have given so much time to criminal trials.

But the actual trial is not the whole of the administration of criminal justice. We ought to view it as a system—a total process that begins with an arrest, proceeds through a trial and is followed by a judgment and a sentence to a term of confinement in a prison or other institution. The administration of criminal justice in any civilized country must embrace the idea of rehabilitation and training of the guilty person as well as the protection of society. In recent years, we have been trying to change our thinking in order to de-emphasize punishment and emphasize education and correction.

Our system of trials to determine guilt is the most complicated, the most refined and perhaps the most expensive in the world. We now supply a lawyer for any person who is without means, and it is the lawyer's duty to exercise all of his skill to make use of the many protective devices available to the defendant.

But at best this is not working very well, and at worst it tends to become a spectator sport. In some of these multiple trial and

Reprinted from *American Bar Association Journal*, April 1970, pp. 325–328, with the permission of the American Bar Association.

multiple appeal cases, the accused continues his warfare with society for eight, nine, ten years and more. In one case more than seventy jurors and alternates were involved in five trials; a dozen trial judges heard an array of motions and presided over these trials; more than thirty different lawyers participated either as court-appointed counsel or prosecutors; in all, more than fifty appellate judges reviewed the case on appeals. Once I tried to calculate the cost of all this for one criminal act and ultimate conviction. The best estimates could not be very accurate, but they added up to a quarter of a million dollars. The tragic aspect was the waste and futility, since every lawyer, judge and juror was fully convinced of the defendant's guilt from the beginning to the end.

No one should challenge any expense to afford a defendant full due process and his full measure of days in court. But reasonable people must be excused if they question a spectacle that extends ten years, costs a literal fortune and produces so little to help the accused or the public—the more so when after all this extended procedure we turn away and forget the person convicted.

What we must weigh in the balance is the rationality of a system that is all contest and conflict and offers virtually no treatment of what lies at the heart of the problem—a disorganized and inadequate human being who cannot cope with life. Our system is too much sail and too light an anchor.

I do not disparage the improvements that have been made in the traditional administration of criminal justice over the past twenty or thirty years. In a modest way I have a part in some of them. The almost endless parade of committees and commissions from the 1930s to the 1970s brought many of our standards of criminal justice to a level appropriate for a civilized society. The improvements cover better training of police, better representation for defendants, better training of prosecutors and better training for judges. This represents one of the bright chapters in the history of the organized Bar.

Today it is a rare law office of any size whose younger men—and some not so young—fail to involve themselves in legal aid and public defender activities. This attitude is reflected in virtually every bar association in the country, and especially in the American Bar Association, which has worked in these fields diligently.

Too much at home with litigation

We must concede, however, that our renewed concern has centered almost exclusively on the litigation aspect of criminal justice. This is natural. Litigation is our craft. It is here that we feel at home, but it is also true that it is here that we find lawyers and judges becoming so engrossed with procedures and techniques that they tend to lose sight of the purposes of a system of justice.

I see two basic purposes—the first to protect society; the second to correct the wrongdoer. If this is correct, we should stop thinking of criminal justice as something that begins with an arrest and ends with a final judgment of guilt. We must see it as embracing the entire spectrum, including that crucial period which begins when the litigation is over and the sentence is being carried out. It is here that the success or failure of our society will make itself known.

If, as John Donne told us, "No man is an Island" and every man's death takes something from each of us, how much more is this true of the tragic failure we witness when the judgment of society is pronounced on one man and we decree that he must be placed behind walls? The bell that tolls for one man's death is not a consequence of our collective judgment—except in those rare cases in which society still enforces the death penalty. But when a sheriff or a marshal takes a man from a courthouse in a prison van and transports him to confinement for two or three or ten years, this is our act. We have tolled the bell for him. And whether we like it or not, we have made him our collective responsibility. We are free to do something about him; he is not.

The second purpose of a system of justice is less clear, and it is one on which we are truly ambivalent. Even when we profess rehabilitation and correction as objectives, we probably know that to all of us some of the time and some of us all of the time punishment and retribution are factors. According to some theologians and psychiatrists, this is not necessarily bad. It is only when anger and revenge dominate the process of discipline and correction that we are on a self-defeating course. A distinguished psychiatrist, the late Philip Roche, pointed out that the punishment of a criminal serves an important therapeutic purpose. He said that when a community experiences a horrible crime or a sustained crime wave, there occurs a mass trauma that must have some outlet or build up into irrational expression or explosion. The conviction and imprisonment of a wrongdoer affords a collective release to the pent-up fears and anger of the community.

It is important to remember this so that we do not fall into the easy error of becoming so filled with righteous piety that we accept the cliché that all punishment is somehow an evil thing. Perhaps the real evil underlying our penal system is not its concepts, whether rehabilitation or vengeance or something else, but the lack of any agreed concept, the absence of plan and purpose, and worst of all—the indifference that underlies the neglect.

It may be that, in part at least, the roots of our collective failure to develop effective systems of correction in this country are the same American traits that account for the amazing progress and development we have experienced in the past one hundred years, the very span of life of the American Bar Association. We have in those one hundred years, grown from a divided, war-shattered and very junior nation into one of the two great world powers. We have succeeded because we have demanded instant success, and now the psychologists tell us that instant gratification can be a dangerous thing because it cannot always be achieved.

Prisons can't give us instant gratification

This national background may explain our attitude toward prisoners and prisons, an attitude of indifference on the one hand and impatience on the other. We seem to expect the prisoner to return to society corrected and reasonably ready to earn an honest way in life simply because we have locked him up.

This indifference and impatience with the slow and painful process of changing human beings have developed systems of corrections that do not correct. The harsh reality is reflected in painful figures: two thirds of all of the 200,000 inmates of federal and state prisons in this country are "alumni" of our noncorrecting correctional systems. The President's Commission on Law Enforcement and Administration of Justice estimated that in the next five years this total will increase by 7 per cent, which would bring the total prison population to nearly 240,000 by 1975. The cost of crime, therefore, can be reckoned in billions, on which there are no records or statistics. Our enormous and unparalleled success in doing so many things so well and so swiftly has not conditioned us with the right kind of attitudes for the slow, painful and, as to some offenders, impossible task of changing the human beings who are sent to prisons.

Criminal offenders who go to prison are at least as varied as the human beings who are law-abiding, church-going taxpayers. We know, moreover, that a large proportion of them are seriously maladjusted. Those who are not when they enter prison are likely to be so when they go out.

To have any hope of correcting, reforming, rehabilitating or changing these people calls for a wide variety of programs, including diagnosis, counseling, education, vocational training and often intensive psychiatric therapy. The infinite variety of needs cannot be met in single, large institutions, although with 200,000 prisoners we must use some large institutions. There must be one kind of institution for first offenders, another for the very young— and this is an enormous proportion—and still other institutions for other categories. All of them must be staffed by trained personnel.

We cannot do all this efficiently with fifty state systems and a federal system unless there is some degree of co-ordination among the states and between states and the federal system. President Nixon recently proposed a co-ordinated federal-state program, and this is a significant step in the right direction. It makes little sense in the twentieth century to have each state suffer the waste and inefficiency that accompany the maintenance of a complete range of facilities. Only the large states can afford this.

The training programs in most state institutions are limited to a few skills, and there is almost no effort to correlate the programs with the demand for particular skills. It is no help to prisoners to learn to be pants pressers if pants pressers are a glut in the labor market, or bricklayers or plumbers if they will not be admitted into a union. I suggest these two simple illustrations to indicate the desperate need for comprehensive and co-ordinated planning and research at local and national levels. This requires a monumental effort with the best leadership and brains of labor unions, industry, the Departments of Justice, of Labor, and of Health, Education, and Welfare. To be successful, these programs need local community support that must involve churches, Y.M.C.A.s, chambers of commerce, labor unions and bar associations. Some of the leaders of organized labor have seen this need, and the A.F.L.-C.I.O. has set aside a million dollars for labor's part in corrections work.

If we want prisoners to change, public attitudes toward prisoners and former prisoners must change. We have some community effort along these lines in this country, but with few exceptions it is thin, scattered and not well-led or organized. Few of the participants are well trained.

The contrast between our indifference and the programs in some countries of Europe—Holland and the Scandinavian countries in particular—is not a happy one for us. There they have long engaged in research on lawbreakers and prisoners and on antisocial conduct generally; they use a wide range of institutional treatment and extensively employ work release and open prison techniques. Their use of psychological testing and psychiatric counseling and therapy is far in advance of ours.

Their community involvement in prisoner-aid organizations is far greater than ours. Some of the "after-care" societies, as they are called in those countries, have existed for several hundred years. They are made up of laymen working through churches and related organizations but supported in part by public funds. The volunteers are directed by trained professionals. A common practice is for the part-time volunteer, semiprofessional "parole officer" to be assigned to the prisoner as soon as he is sentenced, so that a relationship is established at an early stage and becomes a basis for counseling and help when the prisoner returns to freedom. Here is an area we must explore so as to make use of the enlarging leisure time available to more and more educated Americans. We have the basic tradition of doing great work through volunteers. We must channel and harness this kind of manpower and give it direction.

It is a paradox to find the world's richest nation being outspent and outperformed, as we are, by these old but less affluent North European societies. Some credit for their lower crime rates must go to their correction systems.

The legal profession can be the most powerful force for good—the most powerful lobby, if you will—that this country knows. Lawyers are perceptive and analytical, and they have the advocate's skills to persuade others. Where do you begin? The same way you prepare a case. By getting all the facts, visiting the scene, if necessary, and then organizing the evidence. In this area most of the facts are available at the prisons and from prison authorities. A visit to most prisons will make one a zealot for prison reform. A fact-finding party of one judge and two or three lawyers will soon discover that 75 to 80 per cent of all prisoners are in substandard institutions.

When you see a prison built a hundred years ago for 600 inmates and find it crowded with 1,500 men with almost no recreational facilities, obsolete vocational training, little or no counseling and two men living—or existing—in a cell 6 by 8 feet, I think you will understand the paradox of why so many of them come back. Prison officials will welcome you, but they will want you to share their sense of frustration and futility. You will find them the most severe critics of their own institutions and sometimes more frustrated than the prisoners.

The range of these needs is staggering. They are expensive, complex and difficult. They rival, if they do not exceed, those of our great cities. But we are suffering and must pay the high price of accumulated and deferred maintenance. And the cost is not in some distant future period: It is here and now, and it is no farther away than the nearest dark street.

Prison administrators are frustrated because over the years they see the same faces returning. Each time the person has been released unprepared and untrained for a useful life. No one can visit prisons and talk with these men without a depressing sense of melancholy for wasted lives, which damage and destroy other lives.

Let me try to state the characteristics of a typical American prison, even at the risk of generalization:

1. It is likely to be old. Buildings erected fifty, a hundred and even 150 years ago are not uncommon. A few are even older.

2. Industrial operations used for training purposes are likely to be old, and the skills taught are limited and often obsolete. A large proportion of prisons are institutions of enforced and devastating idleness.

3. Psychological and psychiatric services are limited or nonexistent. The 200,000 persons in American prisons have barely fifty psychiatrists and psychologists, contrasted with small countries like Denmark, where in some prisons the ratio is approximately one psychiatrist for one hundred prisoners.

4. Recreational facilities for weekend or evening use are limited or nonexistent. Libraries are nonexistent or inadequate.

5. Education and vocational training are generally limited, nonexistent or obsolete.

6. Work release for long-term prisoners is just coming into use, and only in a few places.

7. Transition facilities, such as halfway houses to condition the prisoner for freedom and responsibility, are just coming into use, and only in a few places.

8. On the administrative side, there is little or no research, medical service, screening or training of attendants, and little or no follow-up on former inmates.

9. The pay scales of prison attendants are generally so low that they cannot attract personnel with adequate background to absorb on-job training when it is provided. Prison personnel must be selected with great care, under rigid standards in terms of psycho-

logical adaptation, if we are to have any hope of changing the inmates.

Do you know or can you conceive of an industrial enterprise with 200,000 employees, which turns out a critical product and would use fifty to 150-year-old plants, equipment and techniques, no research, low pay and little or no training for its production workers, no long-range planning, no concern for its output or quality control? This question answers itself.

Yet, with notable exceptions in a few of the states and the federal system, this is a description of the process we use to deal with these 200,000 prisoners. Is it any wonder that we find a grim and distressing "recall" of 65 per cent of the human output of these prisons "back to the factory"? This is a true pollution of society, and it manifests itself in the highest crime rate in our 200 years of existence, with most crimes being committed by "graduates" from these penal institutions.

Winning every prosecution won't win the war

It is in this second phase of justice that society's success or failure becomes known. Prosecutors could win every prosecution, convict every defendant and imprison every guilty person; yet society would still fail. We would fail because there must be two purposes, and the second purpose is not served by a perfect record on the first. Unless we succeed in both, we fail. I am encouraged by the American Bar Association's recently announced program that the Association accepts the concept that criminal justice embraces the correctional process. The Association now has embarked on a program to identify workable standards and implement them with action at the state and federal levels. With such a program we can change the thinking of the country.

To put a man behind walls to protect society and then not try to change him is to win a battle and lose a war. Let us turn to the business of winning the war. I know of only one way: We must bring to bear on it the uniquely American combination of energy, brains, ingenuity, research and innovation that has made us the world's greatest industrial power. And all of this must be backed by those special American assets—idealism and enthusiasm.

When the French writer Jean Paul Sartre writes that free men are captives of their own freedom, I elect to read him as stating something of a modern version of the "obligations of nobility." We take on a burden when we put a man behind walls, and that burden is to give him a chance to change. If we deny him that, we deny his status as a human being, and to deny that is to diminish our own humanity and plant the seeds of future anguish for ourselves.

Daniel L. Skoler

There's more to crime control than the "get tough" approach

Abstract: In addressing today's difficult crime control problems, the focus should not be on a set of "tough" or "soft" prescriptions but rather on crime control that works. Indeed, serious question exists about the nation's capacity and resources, even if we so desired, to achieve "tough crime control" in significant degree—that is, to substantially increase apprehension and conviction rates and intensify the severity and length of sentences and imprisonment. It appears also that the most critical leverage point for crime reduction may lie in the correction of offenders and redirection of repeaters away from criminal behavior. Here, the "tough" or punitive approach is a high-cost, low-yield alternative. It offers much less potential than the "softer" regime of training, education, job placement, counseling, and community reacceptance, designed to equip offenders for a productive, law-observing role in the society to which virtually all will return.

Ever since crime control became focused as a national issue in the mid-sixties[1] and the country stepped back to examine its criminal justice institutions with a new intensity, an undercurrent of divergent philosophy has permeated thinking, writing, and

Reprinted from *The Annals of the American Academy of Political and Social Science*, September 1971, pp. 28–39, with the kind permission of *The Annals* and Daniel L. Skoler.

action in the field.[2] Its parameters have been somewhat hazy and often implicit. Because of this elusiveness, and for want of a better set of labels, the issue is perhaps best identified in terms of its street characterization, that is, "tough" crime control versus "soft" crime control.

These are unfortunate terms because the labels have helped to obscure clear thinking and permitted, on both sides of the fence, a kind of name-calling meant to denigrate—with, indeed, some measure of success—programs, techniques, and new approaches that promised more efficient, more economical, more result-oriented law enforcement, regardless of degree of inherent "softness" or "hardness." Indeed, any effective, cost-achievable measure for actually reducing crime, increasing the public security, and turning lawbreakers into responsible citizens should be viewed as "hard-headed," "tough" law enforcement—whether this involved extended psychotherapy for felons or convicting them within a twenty-four-hour stretch following apprehension.

Notwithstanding, this article will follow the "tough/soft" dichotomy in exploring its implications and the critical need to go beyond usual conceptions of the "get tough" approach in order to produce efficient crime control and better achieve its concomitant, a safer public environment.

By way of definition, the common connotations of the two terms will be used. "Tough" crime control normally denotes more emphasis on police resources, faster apprehension of criminals, quick trials, and more severe sentences for guilty offenders. "Soft" crime control denotes, on the other hand, more emphasis on the rehabilitation side of law enforcement, greater focus on police/community relations, more diversionary programs and informal adjustments in the prosecutive phase, less severe sentences in the courts and, in correction of offenders, less confinement and more community supervision and rehabilitative services. Neither of the foregoing characterizations is meant to be negative and it is believed that elements of both, well administered and directed at proper targets, are essential ingredients to effective law enforcement. Moreover, the definitions are vague, simply because the underlying concepts suffer this infirmity and, thus, should satisfy no one who considers himself primarily in one camp or the other. Nevertheless, it is believed that they convey the respective thrusts of the two approaches in the public mind and will be adequate for analysis.[3]

The plan of development for this article is to provide, first of all, a short profile of the nation's crime control apparatus and its crime problem. This is the inevitable backdrop against which all approaches must be measured. The profile will be followed by (1) an analysis of the outer limits of the law enforcement system's capacity to adopt a "tough approach," (2) some discussion of the cost implications of tough/soft approaches, with particular emphasis on corrections, and (3) a brief for the so-called "soft approach" as a critical ingredient in hard-headed, efficient law enforcement.

It will be the author's strategy (and bias) in this endeavor to make the point that the goal is not "tough" or "soft" crime control as such, but crime control that works. In so doing, the question will be raised as to whether, even if we wanted it, tough crime control is really achievable in significant degree; whether the hard approach, particularly in corrections, is doing much of a job; and, finally, whether the toughest approach to the recidivist who accounts for most of the nation's serious crime is not actually the more humane, educative, rehabilitative, helping, indeed "soft" approach of modern community-based corrections.

The crime control industry

Today, public crime control expenditures aggregate approximately $7.3 billion annually, divided among the major functions into about 60 percent for police services, 25 percent for corrections, and 15 percent for courts (the latter including prosecution and defense).[4] Most of these, nearly 90 percent, are state and local outlays; and the largest cost component, more than 85 percent, is personnel.[5]

More than 650,000 governmental employes are involved in operation of our law enforcement apparatus—about 450,000 in police service, 130,000 in corrections and something less than 75,000 in court, prosecution, and defense activity.[6] They deal with more than nine million reported crimes annually—about five million within the FBI's seven major crime categories[7]—over seven million police arrests, 1.3 million offenders in institutions or under supervision, and 4.5 to 6 million criminal and juvenile court cases.[8] The evidence suggests that total crime, reported and unreported, should be two or three times larger than the known offense figure of nine million,[9] and that, beyond public expenditures, crime costs the nation in personal injury, stolen or damaged property, and concomitant economic loss more than $20 billion annually.[10] Organized crime revenues alone have been estimated at that yearly figure.[11]

Reported major crime in the United States rose some 140 percent during the decade of the 1960's: from 1,200 per 100,000 population to 2,900 per 100,000 population. Of the five million index crimes reported in 1969, about 655,000, or 13 percent, were violent crimes (murder, aggravated assault, rape, and robbery) and 4.3 million were crimes of property (burglary, auto theft, larceny of $50 or more).[12] Crime continues to have an urban emphasis (a rate of more than 6,000 per 100,000 population for cities in excess of one-half million population, compared with the national average of 2,900 and a rural rate of less than 1,000 per 100,000 population) and a big-city emphasis (30 cities account for 35 percent of all major crimes and 50 percent of violent crimes, with 9 cities producing nearly half the robberies in the United States in 1969).[13]

Finally, despite the high volume of total arrests, the actual rate of uniform crime index offenses cleared by arrest of an offender, whether or not ultimately convicted, is less than 25 percent (20 percent in 1969) with somewhat better experience on the violent crimes (46.6 percent).[14]

OUTER LIMITS OF THE GET-TOUGH APPROACH

It may be—indeed, it seems to be—a myth that a "get-tough" approach, even with the addition of significant new resources, can be achieved within our current criminal justice systems. As indicated in the profile, this nation is running at the level of some five million reported serious (index) crimes per year. This is the verified "top of the iceberg" quantum of major crime. We know that a good deal more exists but we are not sure of our estimates. Yet, even on reported crimes, the five-million figure of 1969 resulted in less than a 20 percent clearance rate. That is, not more than 1,000,000 of these crimes were cleared by arrest and probably less than 10 percent were ultimately disposed of by a finding of guilty after being charged.[15] This suggests that less than 2 out 10 offenders is ever brought to justice for serious crime in this nation, and that 9 out of 10, despite the efforts of police, get the "softest" kind of crime control possible—none at all. They are never convicted and in most cases never even apprehended. Well, this isn't quite true. We know that a great many of those five million index crimes in 1969 were committed by the same people. Let us assume, then, that each person found guilty after being charged with an index crime had committed two other major crimes in the same year. The fact would still remain that less than one-third of the index offenders had been identified through arrest or conviction.

Clearance rates fluctuate somewhat but, in the last decade, have always remained at or below the 30 percent level. It is difficult to see how, even with massive manpower supplementation, these could be raised significantly above, say, the 40 percent level. The point is that when a tough approach cannot, under reasonably foreseeable circumstances, hope to identify even half the perpetrators of serious reported crime, other techniques must be utilized—especially those calculated to snare (or influence away from criminal behavior) not only the identified offender, but the large unseen majority who avoid the system completely.[16]

THE FEW WHO GET THE FULL MEASURE

Turning from the large body of offenders who are never called to account for their serious crimes, it may be instructive to move to the few who are subjected to the fullest measure of tough crime control—that small portion of convicted offenders (estimated at less than one-third of those felons sentenced annually) who, after arrest and conviction, are confined in prisons or other correctional institutions.[17] The record does little to confirm that this most stringent degree of offender punishment does much to prevent or control crime. Recidivism studies show that from 40 percent to 70 percent of all offenders released from prisons commit new crimes after release.[18]

The record of those exposed to the "softer" regimes of probation or other community supervision are more encouraging, with lower recidivist rates,[19] but this group is, concededly, a lower-risk population than the incarcerated offender. The important point is that confinement does little to help the process of rehabilitation, however necessary it may be in individual cases for protection of the public—this despite the fact that nearly 80 out of every 100 correctional dollars go for maintenance of the 33 percent of sentenced offenders confined in institutions.[20]

Some cost implications of tough/soft approaches

There are many areas where the cost implications of going beyond the "get-tough" orientation are difficult to quantify. How, for example, can an increased police department investment in community relations programs be traced to cost savings through less reported crime or through citizen help in identification and apprehension of offenders? In corrections, however, the alternatives are more clear and make a persuasive case for the less severe, community-based approach as opposed to imprisonment.

It has been observed that "tough" correction, that is, the locking-up of prisoners, is not very effective as a crime control technique.[21] It is also true that institutionalization is the most expensive form of correctional program. Six years ago, the average costs of institutionalizing juveniles were $3,600 (a figure which is believed to have nearly doubled, since) as opposed to less than $500 for supervision of a juvenile on probation (about 15 percent of the institutional maintenance figure). Even assuming an upgrading of probation services to the point where they become only one-third as costly as incarceration, the dollar implications of an increased emphasis here in lieu of institutionalization are profound. With current corrections expenditures at 1.4 billion annually and, say, 75 percent of system costs going to institutional operation and services (exclusive of new plant),[22] a reduction of institutional populations by 50 percent would free sufficient funds to double the amounts currently spent for probation, parole, and other community supervision programs. Even with a significant increase in services, this could provide for three times as many community-supervised offenders as the released institutional force. Note how this could expand the system's capacity, with no crushing new financial burdens, to handle a greater portion of the unarrested felony offenders who account for the 75 percent to 80 percent of uncleared major crimes each year—a goal of the "tough" as well as "soft" law-enforcement advocate.

This confluence of tough/soft goals in operational techniques is one of the several opportunities so often obscured by debate and feelings surrounding the polarized issue itself. Take another: the enforcement value of prompt adjudication of offenders. To the "tough" enforcer, this promises swift accountability, sure punishment, and safer streets. To the "soft" enforcer, prompt adjudication would promote more equal justice (less detention for the poor), placement of accused offenders into productive corrections programs (jails cannot provide prisoners awaiting trial with viable rehabilitation programs), and eradication of the disgrace of extended pretrial jail confinement (where the accused, before adjudication of guilt, is exposed for lengthy periods to the toughest kind of maximum security without a vestige of the kind of programs and activities that convicted felons would receive even in the worst prisons).[23] For both the "tough" and "soft" enforcer, prompt adjudication could mean millions of dollars saved in new plant and skyrocketing operational costs by virtue of the lower number of detention man-days per jailed inmate awaiting trial. For example, with delays between arrest and trial averaging over 5 months in New York and Philadelphia, over 6 months in Ohio, and 6 to 9 months in Chicago,[24] a major city jail with an average population of 500 pretrial inmates could save some $1 million in costs annually (or make these resources available for enriched programs to others serving sentences) by cutting detention periods in half (that is, by 90 days, on the average, at today's $10 to $15 per diem costs for inmate maintenance)—and at the same time produce surer, quicker, more effective accountability for criminal acts.[25]

Similarly, the kind of restitution for victim loss from criminal acts that the "tough" enforcer views as a salutory form of punishment and accountability is really only feasible within the context of "soft" work release programs. Here, confined or supervised felons can hold jobs while "doing time" in the free community at wages permitting them to make restitution, support families, pay taxes, and bear some of the costs of offender housing and subsistence.[26]

Finally, a word should be offered about the incredible costs of correctional construction. Any general "get-tough" approach that envisioned a significant increase in institutional populations (or over-all length of confinement) would have to confront the critical need for new prison capacity at $25,000 to $30,000 per inmate to accommodate the new emphasis. A planned increase of 100,000 inmates in the current 400,000 to 450,000 offenders confined in adult and juvenile institutions and jails would entail some $3 billion in construction costs. This would be without reference and in addition to the critical need to replace the old, outmoded, inadequate facilities in which current populations are incarcerated.[27]

The rehabilitative approach as hard-headed enforcement

Discussion up to this point has been largely on the negative side. That is, the assertion has been made that tough law enforcement is in reality a "myth" and hardly achievable with respect to most perpetrators of serious crime; those offenders actually exposed to it seem to fare poorly in controlling their future criminal behavior; and the costs of a punitive, secure custody approach are enormous and probably beyond our resources in coping with rising crime rates and increasing pressure points at all levels of criminal administration.

Attention now will be directed to the positive aspects of the "soft" or rehabilitative approach. The poor prognosis for tough crime control, at least in correction of offenders, may be because it focuses too heavily on motivation toward lawful behavior and not enough on capacity for lawful behavior. That is, one might agree that prompt and severe detection, prosecution, and punishment create in the defender either a desire not to commit crime or some apprehension about undertaking further criminal behavior.[28] The problem, however, may be less one of will than sheer capacity to "make it," and here is where the so-called "soft" approach suggests itself as the "hard-headed" one.

The fact is that most serious offenders remain in our communities and in our midst, either on probation or parole (or perhaps as part of the large, indeterminate mass of unidentified offenders). Nearly 70 percent of those convicted (juvenile lawbreakers and adult felons) are either on probation or parole at any one time.[29] It is true also that our most serious offenders, those imprisoned, will return to the community in short periods of time—breathtakingly short. The median number of months served for felony convictions has been decreasing steadily, for a variety of reasons, since the 1930's. The most recent comprehensive survey showed the national median to be nineteen months in state institutions.[30]

While the total prison population at any point in time remains at roughly 250,000, it is significant that nineteen out of twenty offenders are eventually released and that most individuals will serve less than two years. The critical problem, then, must be to prepare or restore in the offender the capacity for lawful, productive behavior in the community—a goal in which punishment alone, in our complex, fast-moving society, is clearly an inadequate prescription for success. The offender needs, rather, to feel more human and strengthen his self-respect; achieve the educational skills necessary to function in the modern community; sharpen the job skills required to handle a productive work role and earn a fair wage; and develop the social skills requisite to operate comfortably in the free community—in short, he must learn better how to handle his freedom. Our emerging knowledge, although still skimpy, confirms the validity of this approach, which largely lays aside punishment and focuses on the special care and attention our nation has been wont to extend to any handicapped group (the sick, the mentally disturbed, the uneducated, the poor). Our work with offenders in manpower programs, for example, shows that (1) prisoners can be trained and placed in employment, regardless of previous education or the nature of their crime; (2) when prisoners are employed in jobs in demand in the marketplace, their rate of recidivism is two to three times less than that of prisoners who are not trained and helped to get jobs; (3) ex-offenders with better-paying jobs are much less likely to repeat than those with no jobs, part-time jobs or lower-paying jobs; (4) independent of work experience in prison, if a prisoner gets a remunerative job on release and is able to keep it for at least six months, the probability of recidivism markedly declines.[31]

An added value of sharpening our techniques and knowledge in these restorative areas is the promise of influence, not only over the identified or convicted offender but over the "uncleared" felon who has as yet escaped the system entirely. Unlike punishment, which is largely personal to the offender,[32] services of this nature can be generalized to the disadvantaged population, thus offering the possibility of catching the early or incipient offender within the rehabilitative net. These individuals must remain as important a target as the apprehended offender, if we are talking about really "hard-headed" crime control.

It is suggested, then, that a "tough-minded softness" toward the offender may hold greater potential for public safety than other available correctional approaches. This means that, to the greatest extent possible, we should keep the offender on the street and seek to overtrain, overcounsel, and oversocialize him.[33]

Soft enforcement in other criminal justice areas

Prior discussion has emphasized, intentionally, the inadequacies of tough crime control in the correctional mission. This was not meant to imply that departures from the "tough" approach have no role to play in the police, court, and prosecution mission. Here too, traditionally "soft" techniques can advance goals of cost-effective, aggressive, and efficient crime control. Three examples will be presented to illustrate the point and to emphasize the thesis that "tough" and "soft" approaches can be complementary. Each requires something more than "getting tough," although exponents of that approach may have little difficulty in recognizing, at least in part, their potential. The three areas are police/community relations, prosecutor discretion, and non-criminal handling of victimless offenses.

No experienced police commander will deny the tangible value and help to his mission offered by an understanding, coöperative community. Moreover, few today hesitate to invest significant training and manpower resources in fostering the community relations and public education programs necessary to achieve that end. This is a good deal more than "getting tough" but it makes for good law enforcement, particularly where community stress, generated by today's difficult social and urban problems, tends to complicate the police function.

It is nearly impossible to measure the value of good police/community rapport in dollars saved. It is believed, however, that most commanders handling hostile inner-city communities would find it a cheap tradeoff to exchange, say, 10 to 20 percent of existing patrol manpower for an ideal community support environment. The insurance provided against urban riots alone would be worth the tradeoff. Benefits derived from taking time to communicate the police role, offer some "helping" services, show an awareness of community mores and attitudes, and educate citizens for a direct prevention or law enforcement contribution can be considerable, ranging from increased line officer safety through valuable investigative assistance and the level of departmental morale that makes the difference between "so-so" and superior police performance. Need it be pointed out also that the stability so provided can free the police to "get tough" in cases that really require this kind of community protection without exhausting resources in constant skirmishes of police/community abrasion?

It has been frequently observed, of both prosecution and courts, that inflexible policies of total prosecution for law violation (a total "get-tough" policy) would soon bring judicial apparatus to a hopeless logjam. Prosecutor discretion (and police street adjustments as well), subject to reasonable and fairly administered standards, offers a dual potential for more efficient crime control. First, it can be a sufficient and perhaps the most effective disposition for the early or non-serious offender, particularly where diversion to appropriate community resources is available to assure treatment of the conditions that threaten continued criminality. Second (and note again the soft/tough congruence), pre-prosecution adjustments of minor or early offenders can free overburdened prosecutive offices to aggressively pursue the dangerous but "hard case to make" offenders. Techniques in this area are developing quickly and most experienced prosecutors recognize their value to an effective enforcement program.[34]

In similar vein, the "soft" approach of foregoing criminal prosecution for victimless offenses is receiving increasing recognition as the best way to handle such problems and to free staff for proper attention to serious crimes against property and person. Recognizing that crime control, as with response to most public needs, is so often a matter of tradeoff, President Nixon recently made the point this way:

We have to find ways to clear the courts of the endless stream of "victimless crimes" that get in the way of serious consideration of serious crimes. There are more important matters for highly skilled judges and prosecutors than minor traffic offenses, loitering, and drunkenness.[35]

Finally, we have only begun to probe the crime control potential of the technology-oriented "target hardening" approach—where success is attended by huge savings on activation of criminal justice machinery itself. Here, crime is prevented or reduced by making it physically difficult to commit—theft-proof autos, unbreakable locks, street lighting, alarm systems. Complete reliance on these preventive "soft" techniques will probably never be possible but where they have a contribution to make, the advantages are obvious.[36]

A role for tough crime control

While effective crime control involves a good deal more than "getting tough," a role for tough, aggressive criminal administration will probably always exist. We should be "tough" in investigation of offenses and prompt identification of offenders, in prompt prosecution and secure custody for those serious offenders who present a danger to the physical safety of citizens (which most corrections authorities estimate to include not more than 20 to 40 percent of current institutional populations)[37] and in obtaining special custody for offenders not at the point of amenability to ordinary rehabilitative services (personality disorders, addicts, and the like).

Maintenance of this capability will require extensive and needed resources such as up-to-date and sophisticated police equipment or a new correctional plant, but the investment is justified so long as there is no delusion that these techniques are the key to all enforcement and correctional problems.

In one respect, the author parts company with "soft" doctrine emphasizing the avoidance of "labeling" early offenders, particularly juveniles. The reasoning is that official identification of youths as delinquents tends to "push the misbehaving juveniles toward further delinquent conduct and . . . make it more difficult for them to reënter the conventional world." [38] It seems essential to the rehabilitative approach that an accurate data base be maintained for intelligent diversion, discretionary adjustment, and treatment programming. While this could, and wherever possible should, stop short of formal charging, trial, or adjudication, it would appear important that at least initial identification of offenders be pursued as an enforcement goal, both as a condition for decision-making on intelligent "soft" techniques and for equal-justice considerations. It is believed that the stigmatic effect of such labeling, valid perhaps for the fifties and sixties, is being rapidly diluted by a new generation that seems less concerned with a prior arrest or conviction record and more inclined to judge peers on merit.[39] Moreover, in an age of automated record-keeping and expanding intelligence files, it is believed that reliance on avoidance of records of unlawful conduct rather than on positive social attitudes and formalized equal-opportunity policies for delinquents or ex-offenders could be a futile and misplaced priority.

Conclusion

It seems hardly necessary to have to establish that effective crime control calls for more than "getting tough." The American people have always been realists and the growing support of their leaders for correctional reform—heartland for the so-called "soft" ap-proach—offers recognition that the lesson has taken hold.[40] Per-haps this article will add to that trend by displaying the futility of "hard/soft" semantics as a key to analysis, understanding, or action on our crime control problems.

Notes

1 See the three Johnson crime messages of the mid-sixties, the first special messages on this subject by any president of the United States. *Crime, Its Prevalence and Measures of Prevention* (March 1965), *Crime and Law Enforcement in the United States* (March 9, 1966), and *Crime in America* (February 6, 1967). It was probably the Johnson/Goldwater campaign of 1964 that first introduced the crime

problem as a national political concern, principally at the initiative of the losing candidate.

2 The principal re-examination effort was that of the President's Commission on Law Enforcement and the Administration of Justice (hereafter cited as the Crime Commission), established by President Johnson in the summer of 1965. Attorney General Nicholas deB. Katzenbach was chairman; findings were reported in *The Challenge of Crime in a Free Society* (Government Printing Office, 1967) plus nine task force report volumes, four field surveys, and several dozen consultant studies and papers. In addition, three other presidential commissions have had occasion to focus substantially, if not solely, on problems of crime and criminal administration: the President's Commission on Crime in the District of Columbia (1965–1966); the National Advisory Commission on Civil Disorders (1967–1968); and the President's Commission on Violence (1968–1969).

3 For further discussion of the tough/soft dichotomy in the area of police services, see "Tough vs. Moderate Cops," *Business Week*, December 12, 1970, pp. 42–44. Polarity is focused here on two leading police administrator personalities, Commissioner Frank Rizzo of Philadelphia ("Fear of punishment is a part of every man's life") and Commissioner Patrick V. Murphy of New York City ("You don't make anyone fear you for twenty years without being afraid yourself").

4 Law Enforcement Assistance Administration, U.S. Department of Justice, *Expenditure and Employment Data for the Criminal Justice System, 1968–69*, p. 11, Table 1 (1970), reporting total expenditures for all government units (federal, state, and local) after exclusion of duplicative transactions, of $7.34 billion ($6.55 billion for state and local government alone). Current 1970–1971 expenditures probably well exceed the quoted $7.3 billion figure, even allowing for the overstatement of court expenditures at $1 billion, since no proration is made in these statistics for civil litigation as opposed to criminal cases handled.

5 International City Manager's Association, *The Municipal Yearbook—1968*, pp. 354–355 (1969).

6 Crime Commission, *The Challenge of Crime in a Free Society*, p. 91 (police personnel), p. 162 (correctional personnel) and *Task Force Report: The Courts*, pp. 55–57, 73 (estimate includes part-time prosecutors and defense counsel, and judges and court personnel whose duties encompass noncriminal as well as criminal proceedings).

7 Federal Bureau of Investigation, *Uniform Crime Reports—1969*, p. 56, Table 1, citing 4.989 million serious crimes reported during 1969, a 12 percent rise over 1968. The seven FBI serious or "index" crime classifications are murder (that is, all criminal homicide), forcible rape, robbery, aggravated assault, burglary, auto theft, and larceny of $50 or over in value.

8 Ibid., p. 113, Table 27 (arrest estimate—projecting from data shown for 71 percent of population @ 5.86 million arrests); Crime Commission, *Task Force Report: Corrections*, p. 192 (offender estimate) and *Task Force Report: The Courts*, pp. 55, 154 (court caseload estimate); and U.S. Children's Bureau, *Juvenile Court Statistics —1966* (juvenile court caseloads).

9 Crime Commission, *Task Force Report: Crime and Its Impact—An Assessment* (1967), pp. 17–18; *Uniform Crime Reports—1969*, p. 116, Table 29 (interpolation of misdemeanor component of total offenses.

10 Presidential Message to the Congress, *Crime and Law Enforcement in the United States*, March 9, 1966 (introductory text estimating cost of crime at $27 billion annually).

11 Crime Commission, *Task Force Report: Organized Crime* (1967), p. 3 and fn. 28 (validates figure for organized crime gambling revenues alone).

12 *Uniform Crime Reports—1969*, p. 57, Table 2.

13 Ibid., p. 94, Table 9.

14 Ibid., pp. 28–31.

15 Ibid., Tables 12 and 17, pp. 98–99 and 103 (assumes, conservatively, that all juvenile referrals resulted in a "guilty" adjudication).

16 This emphasizes the importance of general crime prevention through educational, manpower, and other programs for the disadvantaged, thereby inevitably reaching some portion of the pre-delinquent, pre-criminal, and unidentified-offender population.

17 Crime Commission, *Task Force Report: Corrections*, p. 1 (indicating, on basis of 1965 survey figures, that one-third of all offenders were in institutions and the remaining two-thirds under supervision in the community).

18 See conclusion of the Crime Commission, after review of a number of recidivism studies, that at least a third of the offenders released from prison will be reimprisoned, usually for committing new offenses, within a five-year period (*Challenge of Crime in a Free Society*, p. 45). For example, a 1950 California study showed a reimprisonment rate within three to five years after release of 43 percent, and a Uniform Crime Reports follow-up of federal releases showed a two-year rearrest rate of 48 percent. The most recent UCR "Careers in Crime" tabulation shows, of a 240,000 offender sample, a ten-year reimprisonment rate of 46 percent and reconviction rate of 73 percent (*Uniform Crime Reports—1969*, p. 35).

19 See Crime Commission, *Task Force Report: Corrections* at p. 28, citing probation success outcomes of 60 percent to 90 percent (integrating eleven separate studies), 75 percent (study of New York, Massachusetts, and a variety of foreign countries) and 72 percent (seven-year follow-up of 11,600 adult probationers in California).

20 *Correction in the United States*, 13 Crime and Delinquency 1, at p. 230, Tables 1 and 2 (1967—Survey for the Crime Commission). As regards the enormous segment of addiction-related street crime in our major cities, punishment would have an even lesser effect on the underlying medical and personality problems impelling such behavior. See Crime Commission, *Task Force Report: Narcotics and Drug Abuse* (1967), pp. 55–57 (Blum paper).

21 For a critical assessment of the over-all effectiveness of "tough" corrections and the various needs and trends for reform, see the symposium, *Outside Looking In*, Law Enforcement Assistance Administration (April, 1970) and its component monographs: Norval Morris, *The Snail's Pace of Penal Reform*; Robert Kutak, *Grim Fairy Tales for Prison Administrators;* and A. Leon Higgenbotham, Jr., *Is Yesterday's Racism Relevant to Today's Corrections?*

22 LEAA, *Expenditure and Employment Data for the Criminal Justice System, 1968–69*, p. 36, Table 14 (December, 1970) shows, for example, total state government outlays of $914 million for corrections, $694 million or 76 percent of which were for institutions. This is exclusive of $104 million of capital outlay which undoubtedly would be allocable primarily (at least 80 percent) to institutional programs. Federal and local expenditures for corrections would follow similar patterns.

23 Pre-trial jail confinement usually involves more maximum security, greater idle time, and less program (education, work training, physical exercise) than the most security-oriented prisons, which invariably offer some regular activities in these areas. For discussion of this and the alarming plight generally of the nation's jails, see Richard A. McGee, *Our Sick Jails*, Federal Probation (March, 1971), pp 3–8.

24 See Richard Nixon, *Address to the National Conference on the Judiciary*, Williamsburg, Virginia, March 11, 1971.

25 New York City is about to lead the nation in pursuit of the shorter jail detention period by adoption of a mandatory court rule, the first of its kind, requiring no more than 90 days pre-trial detention and no more than six months for trial of offenders. (See Court Rules 29.1 and 29.2, adopted by the Administrative Board of the Judicial Conference of the State of New York, effective May 1, 1972.) For comparable pending federal legislation, see the proposed Speedy Trial Act of 1971, S.895, 92d Cong., 1st Sess. (60-day limit from arrest or indictment to trial, with exceptions for defendant-initiated delay and dismissal if deadline is not met on virtually all classes of felony and misdemeanor offenses).

26 See Correctional Research Associates, *Community Work—An Alternative to Imprisonment*, U.S. Bureau of Prisons (1967), pp. 1–8; D. L. Skoler, *Future Trends in Adult and Community-Based Corrections*, 21 Juvenile Court Journal (1971), pp. 99–101; American Correctional Association, *Manual of Correctional Standards*, p. 17 (1965 revision).

27 It has been noted that some eighty-five major prisons, for example, are pre-Civil War or immediate post-Civil War facilities, Richard Velde, *Remarks Before Southern States Correctional Association*, Atlanta, Georgia, May 15, 1970; and that replacement of the nation's obsolete prisons and jails would cost over $12 billion dollars. Jerome Rosow, Statement before Subcommittee on National Penitentiaries, U.S. Senate, May 19, 1971.

28 The positive motivational effect of offender punishment is conceded here for purposes of exposition and not presented as ultimate doctrine in this complex area. For impressive skepticism about the psychiatric validity of a punitive approach, see Karl Menninger, *The Crime of Punishment* (New York: Viking Press, 1966), ch. 10 and, for interesting observations about the motivational dynamics of advocates of this approach, ch. 8.

29 *Corrections in the United States*, 13 Crime and Delinquency, pp. 230–231 (1967). An even higher percentage of adjudicated juveniles (82 percent) remains in the community.

30 *Task Force Report: Corrections*, p. 179, Table 1 (1967).

31 George A. Pownell, *Employment Problems of Released Offenders*, 13 Manpower, pp. 27–31 (January, 1971). Compare, generally, Jerome W. Rosow and Richard W. Velde, Testimony before National Penitentiaries Subcommittee, Senate Judiciary Committee (May 19, 1971).

32 There is a claimed deterrent effect for punitive handling of the minority of offenses cleared and this undoubtedly has validity, although not measurable with

304 Corrections

precision. The effect, however, may be overrated with respect to all except a few offenses where deterrence has particular impact (certain forms of white-collar crime, drunken driving offenses, and the like) and particularly with the low clearance and even lower conviction levels previously cited, which make it quite safe for the offender to assume a low risk of apprehension. See Menninger, pp. 206–210; Nigel Walker, *Sentencing in a Rational Society* (London: Penguin Press, 1969), ch. 4 on "General Deterrence," pp. 56–73

33 The reference to "tough-minded softness" was meant to emphasize that programs must be effective and realistic if the approach is to optimize success. Too many training, counseling, and educational programs in the past have been inferior and inadequate to the task. A prime example has been past prison vocational programs focusing on obsolete trades or using obsolete or inadequate equipment to prepare offenders for competitive employment. See Interview with James V. Bennett, *Special Issue on Making Prison Training Work*, 13 Manpower 42–44 (January 1971) and Richard A. McGee, *Idle Hands in the Devil's Workshop*, 3 Manpower 32–37.

34 See New York Criminal Justice Coördinating Council, *The Manhattan Court Employment Project*, 12 pp. (1970); also Manpower Administration, *Final Report on Project Crossroads* (1971), 41 pp. plus appendices (first offender diversionary program in District of Columbia emphasizing manpower services).

35 Nixon. The desired extent of remission for victimless crimes is a matter of disagreement, with consenting sexual offenses, removal of sanctions on certain drug possession, and gambling constituting the most sensitive areas of debate. See Crime Commission, *Task Force Report: The Courts* (1967), ch. 8.

36 Crime Commission, *Task Force Report: Science and Technology* (1967), pp. 48–51.

37 See American Justice Institute, *The Non-Prison* (St. Paul, Minn.: Bruce Publishing, 1970), p. 2 (estimating that 80 percent of young adult offenders committed to California institutions "could be dealt with more effectively or with equal or greater safety in newly conceived community-based programs").

38 Crime Commission, *Task Force Report: Juvenile Delinquency*, pp. 417–419 (Wheeler, Cottrell, and Ramasco paper).

39 Today, a campus or demonstration arrest not involving serious affront to person or property is probably more of a badge of courage or distinction among peers than a key for social ostracism; nor does the serious felon who has seen the light, has suffered his punishment, and is now trying to "make it" seem to be any less an attractive figure to his peer generation.

40 See, for instance, Richard Nixon, *Statement on Corrections*, November 13, 1969, and Address to Conference on the Judiciary:

The time has come to repudiate once and for all the idea that prisons are warehouses for human rubbish; our correctional systems must be changed to make them places that correct and educate.

None of our vocational education programs, our work release efforts, our halfway houses or our probation and parole systems will succeed if the community to which offender returns is unwilling to extend a new opportunity.

See also Warren Burger, *No Man Is an Island*, Address to American Bar Foundation, Atlanta, Georgia, February 21, 1970:

We seem to expect the prisoner to return to society corrected and reasonably ready to earn an honest way in life simply because we have locked him up. . . . To have any hope of correcting, reforming, rehabilitating or changing these people calls for a wide variety of programs including diagnosis, counselling, education and vocational training, and often intensive psychotherapy. . . . If we want prisoners to change, public attitudes toward prisoners and ex-prisoners must change.

Ronald L. Goldfarb

American prisons:
self-defeating concrete

Our prison system does not work. We waste over a billion dollars a year to continue a system that has not undergone fundamental reevaluation in 200 years. As a result, inmates, taxpayers, and victims of crime all lose out. This is no news, of course. Liberals and conservatives alike criticize our correctional system. No one on either side of prison bars seriously doubts the overall negativism of the incarceration process. For one thing, recidivism is very high. The best speculation suggests that between half and four fifths of the convicts now in prison will return.

Presently in the U.S. there are about 5,000 city and county jails, 400 state and Federal prisons, plus innumerable local lockups, work houses, camps, farms, ranches, and detention centers. On an average day we confine about 1.3 million offenders in these places. Over the course of a year, about 2.5 million offenders see the inside of prison. And all these prisoners in all these prisons only breed more crime. If the city slum is the high school of crime, prison is the university and a colossally expensive one, at that.

As Tom Wicker of *The New York Times* has pointed out, "Precisely at the point where the first offender has been apprehended, tried and placed in the custody of society, that crucial point at which—if it is ever to be possible—he ought to be treated, trained, redirected, and sent back to a useful place in society, he is instead cast into squalid and terrifying confinement among hardened criminals, homosexual brutes, and the dregs of society, trained (if at all) in the most menial or useless kind of work, in many cases treated little better than an animal, and effectively separated from any glimpse of decency or beauty or hope in life." In prison a man can learn anything, from safe-cracking to check-forging to murder, and from the nation's leading experts in each field.

Self-defeating concrete

The design of our prisons, oppressive and life-hating, dictates what goes on inside them. Because our institutions are physically what they are, about 80 percent of the more than 50,000 prison workers and 90 percent of the budget go for security and housekeeping, not reform and correction. While two thirds of the correctional system theoretically operates outside prison (probation and parole, for instance), these programs get short rations on money and manpower. Since our prisons are built to last, they cast in concrete self-defeating correctional policies for decades to come.

Ultimately, our prison system is absurd. It accomplishes the opposite of what it is designed to, increasing crime instead of decreasing it. No wonder, then, that the pressure for reform grows more intense. Few citizens want the status quo; the time seems right for change. The key question today is what direction reform is going to take.

Getting tougher

The first possibility is more of the same, only in firmer and more potent doses: longer sentences, less probation and parole, less use of community-based programs like furloughs and halfway houses, no clemency, and renewal of capital punishment. Despite all the evidence that these techniques have failed in the past, this approach, the advocates of which are led by President Nixon, would call for more reliance on old ways, in the guise of toughness.

This approach has simplistic appeal; if someone does something bad, lock him up and throw away the key. But the price we pay in money and public safety for our present correctional system is already high. Revving up this system will only increase the costs. As penologist Hans Mattick has put it, ". . . if men had deliberately set out to design institutions to maladjust their inmates, they would have planned the prisons and jails with which our penal administrators have to work."

Reform could take the opposite direction. We could scrap the old correctional system and tear down most of the prison walls. We could condemn a system predicated on institutionalization. This would mean diverting offenders into varied and versatile community-based programs, and decriminalizing parts of the law relating to vice and victimless crimes. We could use other social welfare and health models to deal with such groups as alcoholics, addicts, young offenders, and sick people.

We could compensate the victims of crimes, and employ offenders and former offenders in the correctional process, and rely as much as possible on contracts with private groups to carry out many correctional functions. Institutions would be few, reserved for the relative minority of hopeless and dangerous cases. Most correctional experts say that only 10 to 20 percent of all prison inmates need to be locked up to protect society from personal harm. And the prisons we did not tear down could be redesigned, restaffed and reprogramed according to more civilized standards. This approach lacks political appeal, has few advocates, and may be considered radical. But it is the approach that I believe might significantly reduce crime in America, and would make much more sense.

"Sweet joints"

A third direction for reform, less radical and more centrist than the first two possibilities, would call for keeping but improving the present system, making what the convicts call "sweet joints." Advocates of this approach want to improve the system but not change it. They would send guards to college, build new "model" prisons, and attempt to alter the custodial atmosphere of institutions to a more social services cast.

This is the rehabilitative model. It would replace simple imprisonment with treatment techniques based on such theories as behavior modification. This approach impresses many reform-minded correctional officials, and demonstration projects are underway. The Government has loosened its purse strings to psychologists expressing an interest in penology.

In my opinion, the rehabilitative model might well lead to disaster. It could lead to a second, well-intentioned but fundamental and centuries-long error in correctional policy.

Consider our history

In colonial America we had corporal and capital punishment, banishment, public ostracism, flogging, stocks and branding. The crudeness and violence of these methods shocked sensitive citizens like the Quakers in Philadelphia. The Quakers sought a more humane, civilized form of punishment, one that would punish but at the same time reform offenders.

At a gathering in the home of Benjamin Franklin on March 9, 1787, Benjamin Rush first suggested the notion of imprisoning offenders. His suggestion led to the founding of the Pennsylvania Prison Society, the construction of the Walnut Street Jail, housing the first prison cells in America, and eventually to the first organized prisons in Philadelphia and Pittsburgh. These penal institutions led to our present penitentiary system, and it spread around the world.

Solitary penitence

The Quakers' idea was to replace punishment with rehabilitative treatment in the form of prolonged solitary confinement. Gradually, prison officials came to believe that confinement combined with labor would lead to rehabilitation. We followed that route with little fundamental reform for almost two centuries.

In the mid-20th century, a few corrections officials began to experiment with new medical and psychiatric techniques. They tried to adapt the techniques developed at nonpenal therapeutic institutions, such as mental asylums, to the prison setting. In theory, their experiments made sense. In practice, the results have been imperfect and disturbing. For example, reformers pushed for indeterminate sentences so that punishment would fit the criminal as well as the crime. The idea was that if a man reformed, he should get out of prison earlier than the hardened criminal. In practice, because it was politically safer to keep everyone locked up for the maximum time to assure against mistakes, sentences got longer and longer. The ideal did not fit reality.

I have visited numerous new treatment-oriented institutions in the United States and abroad. I found these places disquieting and, if notably less violent than traditional prisons, little less futile. They present paradoxes of theory that leave treatment-oriented reformers in a classic correctional quandary.

Franklin Roosevelt once pinpointed this dilemma in asking Sanford Bates, the first director of the Federal Bureau of Prisons, whether the goal of the prison system should be to reform the men incarcerated or to deter the general public from committing crimes. Bates answered, "Why not both?" It is this mentality that has plagued prison reform for two centuries, and is at the heart of the problem of treatment-oriented prisons. A prison cannot punish and reform at the same time.

Clockwork orange

Take the controversial Patuxent Institution in Maryland, created by special statute in 1951 to deal with persons considered emotionally or intellectually deficient, who have a history of antisocial behavior and have been convicted of serious crimes. A psychiatrist runs the place. The staff has an unusually high percentage of psychologists, psychiatrists (about one fifth of all the psychiatrists in the U.S. in full-time correctional work are at Patuxent) and social workers. Patuxent exemplifies the treatment-oriented prison.

After an examination and special hearing, the court sends inmates to the maximum-security enclave of buildings at Patuxent for indeterminate sentences. The inmates must be "cured" to be released, and the keepers decide when the cure has been accomplished. The administrators' power is what makes Patuxent special: it is what upsets me the most, and causes critics to paint the institution Clockwork Orange.

The prison administrators' decisions are subject to judicial review, but who will question an expert? The courts have shown great reluctance to second-guess penal psychologists. And who can say whether the inmates at Patuxent are conning their keepers? For that matter, the system encourages fabrication. If you were locked away in a prison and the only way out was to convince the staff that you were cured, what would you do? The alternative is to fight treatment, and stay incarcerated forever.

On paper, Patuxent's program is impressive. Inmates earn their way up from one tier of cells to another by achieving set goals. They are rewarded for improved behavior with improved living conditions. Vocational training, for example, comes only after a man gets to the third tier. Families of fourth-tier men may visit and picnic on the lawn with the inmates. Individual and group therapy is available. After getting out of Patuxent, ex-cons can get follow-up therapy, a rare and critical part of the correctional process. For all the paper planning, however, Patuxent is besieged with riots and lawsuits.

The constitutionality of Patuxent's program has become snarled up in the courts. Two years ago a state court challenged Patuxent's administrators on pragmatic grounds. In *McCray v. Maryland* (November 1971), a two-judge state court ruled in favor of inmates with grievances against Patuxent's administrators. The inmates claimed that what happened to prisoners who refused to cooperate with the staff was illegal. They argued that recalcitrant prisoners' insulation from the outside world in the name of treatment was illegal.

Cruel and unusual

The court found that authorities at Patuxent placed inmates in solitary confinement as "negative reinforcement" for up to 30 days without adequate light, ventilation, exercise or sanitation, a punishment as bad or worse than what happened to troublemakers in many old-fashioned prisons. Such practices, the court held, are "contrary to the rehabilitation of the inmates, and serve no therapeutic value of any kind." In fact, they are contrary to the Eighth Amendment's ban on cruel and unusual punishment.

The court went beyond the issues raised by the inmates, and dealt with some of Patuxent's basic claims as a "total-treatment facility." It concluded that "the maintenance of prisoners in cells in a prisonlike setting with the offering of group therapy and limited rehabilitative vocational training is not a total rehabilitative effort." The case was later reversed on jurisdictional grounds, as well as on grounds of the courts' reluctance to intervene in administrative affairs.

In another case *(McNeil v. Director, Patuxent Institution)*, decided in June 1972, a Patuxent inmate challenged his continued confinement beyond the five-year sentence levied against him for his crime, assault. The administrators had not released him because he refused to submit to psychiatric examinations designed to assess the appropriateness of his release.

A unanimous Supreme Court ruled that such confinement was an unconstitutional denial of the inmate's 14th Amendment right to due process of law. In an opinion by Justice Thurgood Marshall, the court found that the practical effect of the Patuxent procedure was to make confinement indefinite, possibly perpetual. Since the inmate was ordered into that status without a hearing, the detention to the extent that it exceeded his sentence, was illegal. Justice William Douglas added a concurring opinion stating that Patuxent's procedures also violated the inmate's Fifth Amendment right to remain silent.

At Highfields, New Jersey, in contrast to Patuxent, there is an institution that has successfully applied treatment techniques to one class of criminal. Here young, male, repeat offenders are given one last chance. They live in an old country estate not unlike the English borstals that really are reform schools. They work all day at a nearby hospital. They run their own affairs under the guidance of a social scientist and his wife who live on the premises.

The group itself handles nightly therapy sessions. The group thrashes out each others' day-to-day problems, and evaluates each others' development. And the group, not the administrators, decides when each boy is ready to return to freedom.

Highfields is a therapeutic institution. But for all the behavior modification and group therapy, it works because it does not deprive the individual of his sense of worth and power. Highfields allows its inmates to participate in their own rehabilitation.

Science replaces religion

The danger is that frequently, in moving from old-fashioned prisons to treatment-oriented prisons, all we really do is change our emphasis from physical punishment to enforced personality modification. The Quakers wanted to force prisoners to change through revelatory religious experiences. Today psychologists want the same thing, but they work with the criminals' heads instead of their hearts.

In correction, as in much of our lives, we have substituted the auspices of science for the auspices of religion. The problem is that science, like religion, has proven inexact and frequently unpersuasive in the correction business. And the scientists in correction, like the religionists, have not hesitated to lace their rehabilitative techniques with heavy doses of imprisonment and deprivation. The Quaker called it "penitence"; the psychologists call it "negative reinforcement." My concern is that we will give the scientists more power than the religionists ever had and more than their theories warrant.

The criminal pays the victim

The theories of both these well-intended groups are fundamentally akin. Both make a man his own prison. The intention is to help the offender become happy and whole again, but in practice these theories put too much power over inmates in the hands of fallible prison administrators. I believe the only power society should have in forcing an individual to change his behavior is to require each criminal to pay for what he has done wrong. That is why I favor a program that would require a thief to pay back what he steals; to force a mugger to make adequate restitution to the person he assaults. In many cases this can be done outside prison; in most cases it cannot be done inside prison. Thus, prisons really are useful only for the small minority who need to be sequestered from society. Even treatment-oriented prisons create more behavior problems than they cure.

A few years ago, when I visited the sprawling new Federal institution for young offenders in Morgantown, West Virginia, I was impressed by the physical layout, the program and the staff. The institution's country setting adds to its air of informality and openness. The behavior-modification programs seemed sensible. There was lots of rapping, and some attempt to promote contacts with the local community. But I wondered what would happen when the inmates returned to the ghettos they came from, where a man often gets positive reinforcement for committing crimes.

At dinner after my tour, I talked about this problem with Douglas Skelton, a psychiatrist there. I asked whether he thought psychiatrists made a big difference in prisons. He said, "No. We spend 99 percent of our time dealing with institution-induced anxieties, and never get to the problems that got the guy into prison in the first place." That is why I favor tearing down most prison walls.

When I visited prisons in Finland, I met with criminologists who had recently completed a survey comparing recidivism rates of men in prisons with those of men in open labor camps. The rates were about the same for both groups. I asked the Finns if they felt their survey was a blow to the idea of camps instead of prisons, since they could not show that the open camps were more effective in reforming offenders. The Finns said they thought their results were proof that the camps should be used. "If the results are not worse," they argued, "and costs are less, and the technique is more humane, the camps must be better."

Reform is passé

We should consider open prison camps, or their urban counterparts, the halfway houses. To the general public, however, the idea of tearing down prison walls is scary. It looses images of murderers and rapists wreaking havoc across the land. But those images often are irrational. And, in fact, these alternatives to prison are safe and economical.

"The long history of 'prison reform' is over," writes penologist Robert Martinson. "On the whole, the prisons have played out their allotted role. They cannot be reformed and must gradually be torn down. But let us give up the comforting myth that the remaining facilities (and they will be prisons) can be changed into hospitals.

"Prisons will be small and humane; anything else is treason to the human spirit. We shall be cleansed of the foreign element of forced treatment with its totalitarian overtones. Officials will no longer be asked to do what they cannot do, and they will be relieved of the temptation to do what should not be done.

"Crime arises from social causes and can be controlled and reduced (but not eliminated) through social action. The myth of correctional treatment is now the main obstacle to progress: it has become the last line of defense of the prison system; it prevents the sound use of resources to balance public protection and inmate rights; and it diverts energy away from defending democracy through widening opportunity. It is time to awake from the dream."

Now, when the public seems ready for correctional reform, it is especially important to move carefully. Neither the get-tough approach nor the treatment-in-prison approach will make our correctional system work. For all the fear that it generates, for all the difficulties that it presents, I still believe we should seriously consider tearing down most prison walls, and deinstitutionalizing our whole correctional system.

National Advisory Commission on Criminal Justice Standards and Goals

Corrections and the criminal justice system

The pressures for change in the American correctional system today are building so fast that even the most complacent are finding them impossible to ignore. The pressures come not only from prisoners but also from the press, the courts, the rest of the criminal justice system, and even practicing correctional personnel.

During the past decade, conditions in several prison systems have been found by the courts to constitute cruel and unusual punishment in violation of the Constitution. In its 1971–72 term, the U.S. Supreme Court decided eight cases directly affecting offenders, and in each of them the offender's contention prevailed.

The riots and other disturbances that continue to occur in the Nation's prisons and jails confirm the feeling of thoughtful citizens that such institutions contribute little to the national effort to reduce crime. Some maintain that time spent in prisons is in fact counterproductive.

It is clear that a dramatic realignment of correctional methods is called for. It is essential to abate use of institutions. Meanwhile much can be done to eliminate the worst effects of the institution— its crippling idleness, anonymous brutality, and destructive impact. Insofar as the institution has to be relied on, it must be small enough, so located, and so operated that it can relate to the problems offenders pose for themselves and the community.

These changes must not be made out of sympathy for the criminal or disregard of the threat of crime to society. They must be made precisely because that threat is too serious to be countered by ineffective methods.

Reprinted from *Corrections*, Washington, D.C.: U.S. Govt. Printing Office, 1973, pp. 1–14.

Many arguments for correctional programs that deal with offenders in the community—probation, parole, and others—meet the test of common sense on their own merits. Such arguments are greatly strengthened by the failing record of prisons, reformatories, and the like. The mega-institution, holding more than a thousand adult inmates, has been built in larger number and variety in this country than anywhere else in the world. Large institutions for young offenders have also proliferated here. In such surroundings, inmates become faceless people living out routine and meaningless lives. And where institutions are racially skewed and filled with a disproportionate number of ill-educated and vocationally inept persons, they magnify tensions already existing in our society.

The failure of major institutions to reduce crime is incontestable. Recidivism rates are notoriously high. Institutions do succeed in punishing, but they do not deter. They protect the community, but that protection is only temporary. They relieve the community of responsibility by removing the offender, but they make successful reintegration into the community unlikely. They change the committed offender, but the change is more likely to be negative than positive.

It is no surprise that institutions have not been successful in reducing crime. The mystery is that they have not contributed even more to increasing crime. Correctional history has demonstrated clearly that tinkering with the system by changing specific program areas without attention to the larger problems can achieve only incidental and haphazard improvement.

Today's practitioners are forced to use the means of an older time. And dissatisfaction with correctional programs is related to the permanence of yesterday's institutions. We are saddled with the physical remains of last century's prisons and with an ideological legacy that has implicitly accepted the objectives of isolation, control, and punishment, as evidenced by correctional operations, policies, and programs.

Corrections must seek ways to become more attuned to its role of reducing criminal behavior. Changing corrections' role from one of merely housing society's rejects to one of sharing responsibility for their reintegration requires a major commitment on the part of correctional personnel and the rest of the criminal justice system.

Behind these clear imperatives lies the achievable principle of a much greater selectivity and sophistication in the use of crime control and correctional methods. These great powers should be reserved for controlling persons who seriously threaten others. They should not be applied to the nuisances, the troublesome, and the rejected who now clutter our prisons and reformatories and fill our jails and youth detention facilities.

The criminal justice system should become the agency of last resort for social problems. The institution should be the last resort for correctional problems.

Of primary importance as the pressures for change gain force are definition of corrections' goals and objectives, articulation of standards to measure achievement, and establishment of benchmarks to judge progress. That is the purpose of this report on corrections.

Definition and purposes
of corrections

Technical terms can be defined as they arise later in this report, but to begin with a definition of corrections is needed. Corrections is defined here as the community's official reactions to the convicted offender, whether adult or juvenile.

This is a broad definition and it suffers, as most definitions do, from several shortcomings. The implications of the definition for the management of juveniles and for pretrial detention require further discussion. So does the fact that it states no purpose for corrections.

JUVENILE CORRECTIONS

Use of the term "convicted offender" in a definition of corrections would seem to exclude all juveniles who pass through the juvenile court process, since that process is noncriminal and no conviction may result from it. Juvenile court operations are based on the parens patriae concept in which the state assumes responsibility for a juvenile only to protect "the child's best interests." There is no charge or conviction; rather there is a hearing and a finding as to what action is in the child's interests. Only when the juvenile is tried as an adult on a criminal charge can he be termed a "convicted offender."

But the definition is worded with full understanding of the problem it creates. Juveniles who have not committed acts considered criminal for adults should not be subject to the coercive treatment that vague labels such as "juvenile delinquency" now allow. This is most obvious in the case of such categories as "minors in need of supervision," "dependent and neglected" children, or youths "lapsing into moral danger." The distinction is less clear for the groupings of "delinquent," "beyond parental control," or "habitually unruly." The point here, however, is that if we are concerned with helping the child rather than with the child's noncriminal act, then such help is not a proper function of the criminal justice system.

To define away corrections' role in the treatment of juveniles, however, is not automatically to change the current situation in which correctional systems are deeply enmeshed in juvenile programs, both in the community and in institutions. Regardless of propriety, corrections has accepted the role of "treating" and "helping" juveniles. By so doing, corrections has assumed a responsibility it cannot now evade, responsibility for reforming the manner and processes of treating juveniles. Such an assumption implies that reform must be approached realistically, recognizing current practice and the systems supporting it.

This report, therefore, will discuss the diversion of juveniles from the criminal justice system, juvenile intake and detention, juvenile institutions, and community programs for youth. As a long-range objective, juveniles not tried as adults for criminal acts should be removed from the purview of corrections. However, the current investment in juvenile corrections and the attitudes acquired by correctional staff over the years indicate that the ultimate goal is not immediately feasible.

JAILS AND PRETRIAL DETENTION

The second major difficulty raised by the definition used here is that it would seem to include the jailing of convicted misdemeanants but would not cover pretrial detention. Again, the wording is intentional. This report does discuss the elimination of jails in their present form and the development of community correctional centers. These centers would serve some functions traditionally performed by jails and some new ones, with most functions being "correctional." Jails have not traditionally been part of the correctional system but rather have been run by law enforcement agencies. Still, as long as convicted offenders require services, provision of those services should be the responsibility of the correctional system, regardless of the type of conviction or sentencing disposition.

In addition, what happens to the offender through every step of the criminal justice process has an effect on corrections. If he has been detained before conviction, the nature and quality of that detention may affect his attitude toward the system and his participation in correctional programs. Corrections, therefore, has a very real interest in how pretrial detention is conducted and should make its concerns known.

Detention before trial should be used only in extreme circumstances and then only under careful judicial control. The function of detention prior to trial is not correctional. However, as long as pretrial detention is used at all, it should be carried out in the recommended community correctional centers because of the resources that will be available there. Thus, by implication, corrections is assuming responsibility for the pretrial detainee, even though this is not properly its function as defined here.

VARYING PURPOSES OF CORRECTIONS

The definition of corrections as the community's official reactions to convicted adult and juvenile offenders neither states nor implies what corrections should try to achieve. This is essential if realism is to replace rhetoric in the field. In particular, corrections is not defined here as being directed exclusively toward the rehabilitation (or habilitation, which is more often the case) of the convicted offender.

If correctional processes were, or could be, truly rehabilitative, it is hard to see why they should be restricted to the convicted. Corrections is limited to the convicted because there are other justifications for coercively intervening in their lives in addition to helping them. Clearly, the penal sanctions imposed on convicted offenders serve a multiplicity of purposes, of which rehabilitation is only one.

Even when correctional purposes are both benevolent and rehabilitative, there is no reason to assume they are so viewed and experienced by the convicted offender. He may believe our intent is to punish, to deter others from crime, or merely to shut him up while he grows older and the fires of violence or criminality die down. Furthermore, insofar as the word "rehabilitation" suggests compulsory cure or coercive retraining, there is an impressive and growing body of opinion that such a purpose is a mistaken sidetrack that corrections has too long pretended to follow.

In the new view, crime and delinquency are symptoms of failure and disorganization in the community as well as in the offender himself. He has had too little contact with the positive forces that develop law-abiding conduct—among them good schools, gainful employment, adequate housing, and rewarding leisure-time activities. So a fundamental objective of corrections must be to secure for the offender contacts, experiences, and opportunities that provide a means and a stimulus for pursuing a lawful style of living in the community. Thus, both the offender and the community become the focus of correctional activity. With this thrust, reintegration of the offender into the community comes to the fore as a major purpose of corrections.

Corrections clearly has many purposes. It is important to recognize that correctional purposes can differ for various types of offenders. In sentencing the convicted murderer we usually are serving punitive and deterrent rather than rehabilitative purposes. Precisely the contrary is true with respect to the deprived, ill-educated, vocationally incompetent youth who is adjudged delinquent; with him, rehabilitative and reintegrative purposes predominate.

There is no doubt that corrections can contribute more than it does to the reduction and control of crime, and this is clearly one of its purposes. What is done in corrections may reduce recidivism. To the extent that recidivist crime is a substantial proportion of all crime, corrections should be able to reduce crime. A swift and effective criminal justice system, respectful of due process and containing a firm and humane corrections component, may provide useful deterrents to crime. Through these mechanisms corrections can contribute to the overall objective of crime reduction. This is an entirely worthy objective if it can be achieved without sacrificing other important human values to which this society is dedicated.

There are other limits to the overarching purpose of reducing crime and the extent to which it can be accomplished. The report of the President's Task Force on Prisoner Rehabilitation (April 1970) was surely correct when it stressed that:

> . . . some of the toughest roots of crime lie buried in the social conditions, especially poverty and racial discrimination, that prevail in the nation's inner cities. These conditions not only make it difficult for millions of Americans to share in America's well-being, but make them doubt society's good faith toward them, leaving them disposed to flout society. America's benefits must be made accessible to all Americans. How successfully America reduces and controls crime depends, in the end, upon what it does about employment and education, housing and health, areas far outside our present mandate or, for that matter, our particular competence. This is not to say that improvements in the correctional system are beside the point. . . . Our point is that improvements in the correctional system are necessarily tactical maneuvers that can lead to no more than small and short-term victories unless they are executed as part of a grand strategy of improving all the nation's systems and institutions.[1]

It is a mistake to expect massive social advance to flow either from corrections or from the criminal justice system as a whole. That system can be fair; it can be humane; it can be efficient and expeditious. To an appreciable extent it can reduce crime. Alone, it cannot substantially improve the quality and opportunity of life. It cannot save men from themselves. It can be a hallmark of a harmonious and decent community life, not a means of achieving it.

There is another limitation on corrections' potential to reduce and control crime. Corrections is only a small part of a social control system applied to define, inhibit, reduce, and treat crime and criminals. It is but a subsystem of the criminal justice system. And it is the inheritor of problems created by the many defects in the other subsystems.

Corrections alone cannot solve the diverse problems of crime and delinquency confronting America, but it can make a much more significant contribution to that task. Correctional planning and programs must be closely related to the planning and programs of police and courts. Corrections' goals must be defined realistically and pursued with determination by application of achievable and measurable standards.

Standards and goals in corrections

It may be objected: Here is still another list of uplifting aspirations for corrections. Will they never learn that rhetoric is not self-fulfilling? It will be argued: More emphatic reaffirmations of the obvious are not needed; the need is for implementation of what we already know. The argument has force, but it misses the distinction between general principles that abound in corrections and specific standards that have been dismally scarce. Precise definition of goals, and of standards marking steps toward their achievement, is no waste of energy. Operating without them invites, if it does not guarantee, failure.

STANDARDS VS. PRINCIPLES

A comprehensive and soundly based body of guiding principles to direct correctional reform has existed ever since the American Prison Association's "Declaration of Principles" in 1870. The principles, revised in 1930 and reformulated in more modern language in 1960 and 1970, still remain a contemporary document. We have yet to achieve the aspirations of 1870. And there have been many subsequent attempts in this country to guide those who would improve corrections.

Both the Wickersham Commission's report in 1931 and the report in 1967 of the President's Commission on Law Enforcement and Administration of Justice (often referred to as the Crime Commission) contain a wealth of recommendations. Many of them continue to attract substantial support but have yet to be implemented. With such a treasury of past recommendations, why should there be further effort to articulate standards and goals for corrections? Quite apart from the need to be clearer in purpose and direction in a time of rapid change, there is a compelling practical reason for the present definition of standards and goals.

The reason is this: Principles and recommendations are neither self-fulfilling nor self-interpreting. Standards and goals may be much more precise, while retaining sufficient flexibility to allow agencies some freedom. When clearly formulated and precisely stated in measurable terms, they can serve as the basis for objective evaluation of programs as well as development of statutes and regulations relating to correctional services.

Standards and goals set forth in this report may lack automatic enforcing machinery, but it has been the Commission's intention to minimize vagueness in definition. Correctional administrators can readily discern whether or not standards have been achieved. All concerned with running or observing an institution, agency, or program will know whether the standard has been applied or the goal achieved. That was not true of the 1870 Declaration of Principles or of the several series of Commission recommendations that followed. The range for individual interpretation has been too great in view of endemic political and social problems confronting correctional administrators.

The standard has another important practical advantage over the principle and the recommendation. It supports more strongly and authoritatively the passage of legislation, promulgation of regulations, and development of other quality control mechanisms that provide an element of enforcement. It encourages public opinion to focus on and press for correctional reform. It prevents all of us from concluding that what we have is right simply because we have it. It reduces room for rationalization.

ACHIEVING STANDARDS

As a State moves from accepting these standards and goals to achieving them, new legislation may be required. More often, merely administrative and regulatory expression will be needed. The recent promulgation by the State of Illinois of an extensive system of administrative regulations for adult correctional institutions is a step of great significance toward the introduction of an enforceable rule of law into a penal system. The regulations were discussed with the staff before adoption and made readily available to the prisoners when instituted. They contain what are in effect self-enforcement mechanisms. For example, they include well-defined provisions concerning disciplinary offenses and hearings and a grievance procedure available to all prisoners. Indeed, one of the most effective methods of attaining standards and achieving goals is to add to them mechanisms for their enforcement.

Standards and goals must be realistic and achievable, but that certainly does not mean that they need to be modest. The American culture has not only a bursting energy but also a remarkable capacity for adapting to change. What was unthinkable yesterday may be accepted as common practice today. In the criminal justice system, such changes have been observable in recent years with respect to the treatment of narcotics addiction and in the law's attitude toward a range of victimless crimes. They have been seen in the remarkable sweep of the movement toward procedural due process in all judicial and quasi-judicial hearings within the criminal justice system. When the courts abandoned the "hands-off" doctrine that led them to avoid inquiry into prison conditions, this was another aspect of change.

In recent years the Federal Government and many of the States have begun to demonstrate in budgets their seriousness of purpose in correctional reform. For whatever reason, more money is now being allocated to this task. The low priority traditionally assigned to budgetary support for the penal system and to prisoners generally is being changed. It is being supplanted by realization that the quality of life depends in part on creation of a humane, just, and efficient criminal justice system. Coupled with this realization is the knowledge that achievement of such a system must entail substantial correctional reform.

On the other hand, it must be recognized that the road to correctional reform is littered with discarded panaceas. Politically, there has been no great incentive to invest in correctional reform. Until quite recently, there was scant public recognition of the importance of the criminal justice system to community life, and so fiscal support for corrections was little more than a pittance grudgingly doled out. These attitudes have not disappeared completely. Simple solutions are still offered with the promise of dramatic consequences. Correctional reform has lacked both a constituency and a sound political base. Such support as it is now attracting flows in part from the increasing recognition that, if there is to be an effective criminal justice system, an integral part of it must be an effective, humane correctional system.

Formulation and specification of standards and goals can be a step of permanent significance in moving from admirable rhetoric toward a working blueprint for correctional reform with built-in quantitative and qualitative yardsticks of progress.

Corrections in the criminal justice system

A substantial obstacle to development of effective corrections lies in its relationship to police and courts, the other subsystems of the criminal justice system. Corrections inherits any inefficiency, inequity, and improper discrimination that may have occurred in any earlier step of the criminal justice process. Its clients come to it from the other subsystems; it is the consistent heir to their defects.

The contemporary view is to consider society's institutionalized response to crime as the criminal justice system and its activities as the criminal justice process. This model envisions interdependent and interrelated agencies and programs that will provide a coordinated and consistent response to crime. The model, however, remains a model—it does not exist in fact. Although cooperation between the various components has improved noticeably in some localities, it cannot be said that a criminal justice "system" really exists.

Even under the model, each element of the system would have a specialized function to perform. The modern systems concept recognizes, however, that none of the elements can perform its tasks without directly affecting the efforts of the others. Thus, while each component must continue to concentrate on improving the performance of its specialized function, it also must be aware of its interrelationships with the other components. Likewise, when functions overlap, each component must be willing to appreciate and utilize the expertise of the others.

The interrelationships of the various elements must be understood in the context of the purposes for which the system is designed. It is generally agreed that the major goal of criminal law administration is to reduce crime through use of procedures consistent with protection of individual liberty. There is less agreement on the specific means of achieving that goal and the relative priority when one set of means conflicts with another.

For example, the criminal justice system must act in relation to two sets of individuals—those who commit crimes and those who do not. Sanctions thought to deter potential lawbreakers may be destructive to offenders actually convicted. Long sentences of confinement in maximum security penitentiaries once were thought to deter other individuals from committing criminal offenses. It is now recognized that long periods of imprisonment not only breed hostility and resentment but also make it more difficult for the offender to avoid further law violations. Long sentences likewise fuel the tension within prisons and make constructive programs there more difficult. Thus, whatever weight may be given to the deterrent effect of a long prison sentence, the benefits are outweighed by the suffering and alienation of committed offenders beyond any hope of rehabilitation or reintegration.

Offenders, perhaps long before the reformers, viewed the criminal justice apparatus as a system. The "they-versus-us" attitude is symptomatic of their feeling that police, courts, and corrections all represent society. Thus it is critically important that all elements of the system follow procedures which insure that offenders are, and believe themselves to be, treated fairly, if corrections is to release individuals who will not return to crime.

CORRECTIONS AND THE POLICE

The police and corrections are the two elements of the criminal justice system that are farthest apart, both in the sequence of their operations and, very often, in their attitudes toward crime and criminal offenders. Yet police and corrections serve critical functions in society's response to crime. And cooperation between police and correctional personnel is essential if the criminal justice system is to operate effectively.

Police because of their law enforcement and order maintenance role often take the view that shutting up an offender is an excellent, if temporary, answer to a "police problem." The police view the community at large as their responsibility, and removal of known offenders from it shifts the problem to someone else's shoulders.

Police are more intimately involved than correctional staff are with a specific criminal offense. They often spend more time with the victim than with the offender. They are subjected to and influenced by the emotional reactions of the community. It is thus understandable that police may reflect, and be more receptive to, concepts of retribution and incapacitation rather than rehabilitation and reintegration as objectives of corrections.

Correctional personnel more often take a longer view. They seldom are confronted with the victim and the emotions surrounding him. While the police can hope for, and often achieve, a short-range objective—the arrest of a criminal—the correctional staff can only hope for success in the long run. Corrections seeks to assure that an offender will not commit crimes in the future.

Corrections with its long-range perspective is required, if not always willing, to take short-run risks. The release of an offender into the community always contains some risks, whether it is at the end of his sentence or at some time before. These risks, although worth taking from the long-range perspective, are sometimes unacceptable to the police in the short run.

For the most part the released offenders whom police encounter are those who have turned out to be bad risks. As a result the police acquire an imprecise and inaccurate view of the risks correctional officials take. With correctional failures—the parole or probation violator, the individual who fails to return from a furlough—adding a burden to already overtaxed police resources, misunderstanding increases between police and corrections.

If many of the standards proposed in this report are adopted, the police will perhaps take an even dimmer view of correctional adequacy. If local jails and other misdemeanant institutions are brought within the correctional system and removed from police jurisdiction, corrections will bear the responsibility for a substantially larger number of problems that would otherwise fall to the police. Likewise, as additional techniques are implemented that divert more apparently salvageable offenders out of the criminal justice system at an early stage, those offenders who remain within the system will be the most dangerous and the poorest risks. Obviously, a higher percentage of these offenders are likely to fail in their readjustment to society.

The impact of police practices on corrections, while not so dramatic and tangible as the effects of correctional risk-taking on the police, nonetheless is important and often critical to the correctional system's ability to perform its functions properly. The policeman is the first point of contact with the law for most offenders. He is the initiator of the relationship between the offender and the criminal justice system. He is likewise the ambassador and representative of the society that system serves. To the extent that the offender's attitude toward society and its institutions will affect his willingness to respect society's laws, the police in their initial and continued contact with an offender may have substantial influence on his future behavior.

It is recognized widely that the police make a number of policy decisions. Obviously, they do not arrest everyone found violating the criminal law. Police exercise broad discretion in the decision to arrest, and the exercise of that discretion determines to a large extent the clientele of the correctional system. In fact, police arrest decisions may have a greater impact on the nature of the correctional clientele than do the legislative decisions delineating what kinds of conduct are criminal.

Police decisions to concentrate on particular types of offenses will directly affect correctional programming. A large number of arrests for offenses that do not involve a significant danger to the community may result in misallocation and improper distribution of scarce correctional resources. The correctional system may be ill-prepared to cope with a larger than normal influx of certain types of offenders.

The existence of broad, all-encompassing criminal statutes including dangerous, nondangerous, and merely annoying offenders assures broad police arrest discretion. Real or imagined discrimination against racial minorities, youth, or other groups breeds hostility and resentment against the police, which inevitably is reflected when these individuals enter the correctional system.

Carefully developed, written criteria for the use of police discretion in making arrests of criminal offenders would relieve the present uncertainties and misunderstandings between police and correctional personnel. If the goals and purposes of the police in making these decisions are publicized, correctional staff should be able to work more effectively with police departments in arriving at meaningful standards and policies.

Similarly, community-based correctional programs cannot hope to be successful without police understanding and cooperation. Offenders in these programs are likely to come in contact with the police. The nature of the contact and the police response may directly affect an offender's adjustment.

Police understandably keep close surveillance on released felons, since they are a more easily identifiable risk than the average citizen. Where police make a practice of checking ex-offenders first whenever a crime is committed, the ex-offenders may begin to feel that the presumption of innocence has been altered to a presumption of guilt.

When a felon returning to a community is required to register with the police and his name and address are published in police journals, his difficulties in readjusting to community life are compounded. Mass roundups of ex-offenders or continued street surveillance have limited or questionable advantages for the police and significant disadvantages for correctional programs.

Where evidence suggests that an ex-offender is involved in criminal activity, the police obviously must take action. However, the police should recognize that the nature of their contact with ex-offenders, as with citizens in general, is critically important in developing respect for law and legal institutions. To conduct contacts with the least possible notoriety and embarrassment is good police practice and a help to corrections as well.

It should also be noted that the police can make affirmative contributions to the success of community-based programs. The police officer knows his community; he knows where resources useful for the offender are available; he knows the pitfalls that may tempt the offender. The police officer is himself a valuable community resource that should be available for correctional programs. This of course requires the police to take a view of their function as one of preventing future crime as well as enforcing the law and maintaining public order.

Bringing about a better working relationship between the police and corrections will not be an easy task. Progress can be made only if both recognize that they are performing mutually supportive, rather than conflicting, functions. Corrections has been lax in explaining the purposes of its programs to the police. Today corrections is beginning to realize that much of its isolation in the criminal justice system has been self-imposed. Closer working relationships are developed through mutual understanding, and both police and corrections should immediately increase their efforts in this regard. Recruit and inservice training programs for each group should contain discussions of the other's programs. Police should designate certain officers to maintain liaison between correctional agencies and law enforcement and thus help to assure better police-corrections coordination. The problems and recommendations discussed in this section are addressed in the Commission's report on the police. Standards set out in that report's chapter on criminal justice relations, if fully implemented, would materially enhance the working relationships between police and corrections.

CORRECTIONS AND THE COURTS

The court has a dual role in the criminal justice system: it is both a participant in the criminal justice process and the supervisor of its practices. As participant, the court and its officers determine guilt or innocence and impose sanctions. In many jurisdictions, the court also serves as a correctional agency by administering the probation system.

In addition to being a participant, the court plays another important role. When practices of the criminal justice system conflict with other values in society, the courts must determine which takes precedence over the other.

In recent years the courts have increasingly found that values reflected in the Constitution take precedence over efficient administration of correctional programs. Some difficulties presently encountered in the relationship between corrections and the courts result primarily from the dual role that courts must play.

The relationship between courts and corrections is clearly understood by both parties when the court is viewed as a participant in the administration of the criminal law. Correctional officers and sentencing judges recognize each other's viewpoints, although they may not always agree. Those practices of the courts that affect corrections adversely are recognized by the courts themselves as areas needing reform.

Both recognize that sentencing decisions by the courts affect the discretion of correctional administrators in applying correctional programs. Sentencing courts generally have accepted the concept of the indeterminate sentence, which grants correctional administrators broad discretion in individualizing programs for particular offenders.

There is growing recognition that disparity in sentencing limits corrections' ability to develop sound attitudes in offenders. The man who is serving a 10-year sentence for the same act for which a fellow prisoner is serving 3 years is not likely to be receptive to correctional programs. He is in fact unlikely to respect any of society's institutions. Some courts have attempted to solve the problem of disparity in sentencing through the use of sentencing councils and other devices. Appellate review of sentencing would further diminish the possibility of disparity.

The appropriateness of the sentence imposed by the court will determine in large measure the effectiveness of the correctional program. This report recognizes that prison confinement is an inappropriate sanction for the vast majority of criminal offenders.

Use of probation and other community-based programs will continue to grow. The essential ingredient in the integration of courts and corrections into a compatible system of criminal justice is the free flow of information regarding sentencing and its effect on individual offenders.

The traditional attitude of the sentencing judge was that his responsibility ended with the imposition of sentence. Many criminal court judges, often with great personal uneasiness, sentenced offenders to confinement without fully recognizing what would occur after sentence was imposed. In recent years, primarily because of the growing number of lawsuits by prisoners, courts have become increasingly aware of the conditions of prison confinement. Continuing judicial supervision of correctional practices to assure that the program applied is consistent with the court's sentence should result in increased interaction between courts and corrections.

Correctional personnel must recognize that they are to some extent officers of the court. They are carrying out a court order and, like other court officers, are subject to the court's continuing supervision. Corrections has little to lose by this development and may gain a powerful new force for correctional reform.

LEGAL RIGHTS, THE COURTS, AND CORRECTIONS

The United States has a strong and abiding attachment to the rule of law, with a rich inheritance of a government of law rather than men. This high regard for the rule of law has been applied extensively in the criminal justice system up to the point of conviction. But beyond conviction, until recently, largely unsupervised and arbitrary discretion held sway. This was true of sentencing, for which criteria were absent and from which appeals were both rare and difficult. It was true of the discretion exercised by the institutional administrator concerning prison conditions and disciplinary sanctions. It applied to the exercise by the parole board of discretion to release and revoke.

Within the last decade, however, the movement to bring the law, judges, and lawyers into relationships with the correctional system has grown apace. The Commission welcomes this development, and many of the standards and goals prescribed in this report rely heavily on increasing substantive and procedural due process in the authoritative exercise of correctional discretion. Since this is a contentious issue, introductory comments may be appropriate.

The American Law Institute took legal initiative in the criminal justice field in drafting the Model Penal Code, which has stimulated widespread recodifications of substantive criminal law at the Federal and State levels. An important subsequent step was extension of legal aid to the indigent accused, a development achieved by a series of Supreme Court decisions and by the Criminal Justice Act of 1964 and similar State legislation. This move brought more lawyers of skill and sensitivity into contact with the criminal justice system. Then the remarkable project on Minimum Standards for Criminal Justice, pursued over many years to completion by the American Bar Association, began to have a similar widespread influence.

But for the correctional system, historically and repeatedly wracked by riot and rebellion, the most dramatic impact has been made by the courts' abandonment of their hands-off doctrine in relation to the exercise of discretion by correctional administrators and parole boards.

It was inevitable that the correctional immunity from constitutional requirements should end. The Constitution does not exempt prisoners from its protections. As courts began to examine many social institutions from schools to welfare agencies, prisons and other correctional programs naturally were considered. Once the courts agreed to review correctional decisions, it was predictable that an increasing number of offenders would ask the court for relief. The courts' willingness to become involved in prison administration resulted from intolerable conditions within the prisons.

Over the past decade in particular, a new and politically important professional group, the lawyers, has in effect been added to corrections, and it is not likely to go away. The Supreme Court of the United States has manifested its powerful concern that correctional processes avoid the infliction of needless suffering and achieve standards of decency and efficiency of which the community need not be ashamed and by which it will be better protected. Stimulated by the initiative of Chief Justice Burger, the American Bar Association has embarked on an ambitious series of programs to involve lawyers in correctional processes, both in institutions and in the community.

Federal and State legislatures have concerned themselves increasingly with correctional codes and other correctional legislation. The National Council on Crime and Delinquency in 1972 drafted its Model Act for the Protection of Rights of Prisoners. But more important than all these, lawyers and prisoners are bringing—and courts are hearing and determining—constitutional and civil rights actions alleging unequal protection of the law, imposition of cruel and unusual punishments, and abuse of administrative discretion.

A series of cases has begun to hold correctional administrators accountable for their decisionmaking, especially where such decisions affect first amendment rights (religion, speech, communication), the means of enforcing other rights (access to counsel or legal advice, access to legal materials), cruel and unusual punishments, denial of civil rights, and equal protection of the law. The emerging view, steadily gaining support since it was enunciated in 1944 in *Coffin* v. *Reichard*,[2] is that the convicted offender retains all rights that citizens in general have, except those that must be limited or forfeited in order to make it possible to administer a correctional institution or agency—and no generous sweep will be given to pleas of administrative inconvenience. The pace and range of such litigation recently has increased sharply. The hands-off doctrine that used to insulate the correctional administrator from juridical accountability is fast disappearing.

Correctional administrators have been slow to accept this role of the courts and many of the specific decisions. It is understandably difficult to give up years of unquestioned authority. Yet the courts, in intervening, required correctional administrators to reevaluate past policies and practices that had proved unsuccessful. Without the courts' intervention and the resulting public awareness of prison conditions, it is unlikely that the present public concern for the treatment of criminal offenders would have developed. Thus, the courts' intervention has provided corrections with public attention and concern. In the long run, these cases bring new and influential allies to correctional reform.

Increasingly, these new allies of corrections are fitting themselves better for this collaboration. The law schools begin to provide training in correctional law. The American Bar Association provides energetic leadership. The Law Enforcement Assistance Administration supports these initiatives. The Federal Judicial Center develops creative judicial training programs, and judicial administration finally is acknowledged as an important organizational problem. Federal and State judges in increasing number attend sentencing institutes. Bridges are being built between the lawyers and corrections.

What it comes to is this: Convicted offenders remain within the constitutional and legislative protection of the legal system. The illogic of attempting to train lawbreakers to obey the law in a system unresponsive to law should have been recognized long ago. Forcing an offender to live in a situation in which all decisions are made for him is no training for life in a free society. Thus the two sets of alternatives before the judiciary in most cases involving correctional practices are the choice between constitutional principle and correctional expediency, and the choice between an institution that runs smoothly and one that really helps the offender. In exercising their proper function as supervisors of the criminal justice system, the courts have upset practices that have stifled any real correctional progress.

The courts will and should continue to monitor correctional decisions and practices. The Constitution requires it. The nature of the judicial process dictates that this supervision will be done case by case. A period of uneven and abrupt change and uncertainty will inevitably result. Some court rulings will indeed make administration of correctional programs more difficult. To hold hearings before making decisions that seriously affect an offender is a time-consuming task. Allowing free correspondence and access to the press by offenders creates the risk of unjustified criticism and negative publicity. Eliminating inmate guards (trusties) requires the expenditure of additional funds for staff. Correctional administrators could ease the transition by adopting on their own initiative new comprehensive procedures and practices that reflect constitutional requirements and progressive correctional policy.

THE NEED FOR COOPERATION IN THE SYSTEM

It is unrealistic to believe that the tensions and misunderstandings among the components of the criminal justice system will quickly disappear. There are—and will continue to be—unavoidable conflicts of view. The police officer who must subdue an offender by force will never see him in the same light as the correctional officer who must win him with reason. The courts, which must retain their independence in order to oversee the practices of both police and corrections, are unlikely to be seen by either as a totally sympathetic partner.

On the other hand, the governmental institutions designed to control and prevent crime are closely and irrevocably interrelated, whether they function cooperatively or at cross-purposes. The success of each component in its specific function depends on the actions of the other two. Most areas of disagreement are the result of inadequate understanding both of the need for cooperation and of the existing interrelationships. The extent to which this misunderstanding can be minimized will determine in large measure the future course of our efforts against crime.

The Commission recognizes that correctional progress will be made only in the context of a criminal justice system operating as an integrated and coordinated response to crime. Thus corrections must cooperate fully with the other components in developing a system that uses its resources more effectively. If there are persons who have committed legally proscribed acts but who can be better served outside the criminal justice system at lower cost and little or no increased risk, then police, courts, corrections, legislators, and the public must work together to establish effective diversion programs for such persons. If persons are being detained unnecessarily or for too long awaiting trial, the elements of the system must work together to remedy that situation. If sentencing practices are counterproductive to their intended purposes, a comprehensive restructuring of sentencing procedures and alternatives must be undertaken.

This perspective is in large measure responsible for the broad scope of this report on corrections. The time is ripe for corrections to provide the benefits of its knowledge and experience to the other components of the system. Such issues as diversion, pretrial release and detention, jails, juvenile intake, and sentencing, traditionally have not been considered within the scope of correctional concern. But corrections can no longer afford to remain silent on issues that so vitally affect it. Thus this report on corrections addresses these and other issues that have previously been considered problems of other components of the criminal justice system. It could be said that they are addressed from a correctional perspective, but in a broader sense they are presented from a criminal justice system point of view.

Obstacles to correctional reform

FRAGMENTATION OF CORRECTIONS

One of the leading obstacles to reforming the criminal justice system is the range and variety of governmental authorities—Federal, State, and local—that are responsible for it. This balkanization complicates police planning, impedes development of expeditious court processes, and divides responsibility for convicted offenders among a multiplicity of overlapping but barely intercommunicating agencies. The organizational structure of the criminal justice system was well-suited to the frontier society in which it was implanted. It has survived in a complex, mobile, urban society for which it is grossly unsuited. Accordingly, this report seriously addresses large-scale organizational and administrative restructuring of corrections.

One set of solutions is to accept the present balkanization of corrections, recognizing its strong political support in systems of local patronage, and to prescribe defined standards, buttressed by statewide inspection systems to attain those standards. Local jails provide a good example. At the very least, if they are to be retained for the unconvicted, they must be subject to State-controlled inspection processes, to insure the attainment of minimum standards of decency and efficiency. A further control and support that might be added is State subsidy to facilitate attainment of defined standards and goals by the local jails, the carrot of subsidy being added to the stick of threatened condemnation and closure. However, these measures are but compromises.

The contrasting mode of organizational restructuring of corrections is an integrated State correctional system. There is much support for movement in that direction. For example, it is recommended in this report that supervision of offenders under probation should be separated from the courts' administrative control and integrated with the State correctional system.

If prisons, probation, parole, and other community programs for adult and juvenile offenders are brought under one departmental structure, there is no doubt of that department's improved bargaining position in competition for resources in cabinet and legislature. Other flexibilities are opened up; career lines for promising staff are expanded, to say nothing of interdepartmental inservice training possibilities. Above all, such a structure matches the developing realities of correctional processes.

An increasing interdependence between institutional and community-based programs arises as their processes increasingly overlap; as furlough and work-release programs are expanded; as institutional release procedures grow more sophisticated and graduated; and as more intensive supervisory arrangements are added to probation and parole supervision. Institutional placement, probation, and parole or aftercare grow closer together and structurally intertwine. This is true for both adult and juvenile offenders.

Development of further alternatives to the traditional institution, and diversion of offenders from it, will increase this pressure toward an integrated statewide correctional system, regionalized to match the demography and distribution of offenders in the State. Administrative regionalization of such structurally integrated statewide correctional systems may be necessary in the more populous or larger States to link each regional system with the needs, opportunities, and social milieu of the particular offender group. Regionalization greatly facilitates maintaining closer ties between the offender and his family (as by visits, furloughs, and work release) than is possible otherwise.

In sum, the task of achieving an effective functional balance between State and local correctional authorities is complex and uncertain, yet it offers opportunity. It will require political statesmanship that transcends partisan, parochial, and patronage interests. But whatever the interagency relationships may be, the enunciation of precisely defined standards and goals for those agencies will aid in attainment of effective and humane correctional processes.

OVERUSE OF CORRECTIONS

The correctional administrator (and for the present purposes, the sentencing judge too) is the servant of a criminal justice system quite remarkable in its lack of restraint. Historically, the criminal law has been used not only in an effort to protect citizens but also to coerce men to private virtue. Criminal law overreaches itself in a host of "victimless" crimes; that is, crimes without an effective complainant other than the authorities. This application of the law is a major obstacle to development of a rational and effective correctional system.

When criminal law invades the sphere of private morality and social welfare, it often proves ineffective and criminogenic. What is worse, the law then diverts corrections from its clear, socially protective function. The result is unwise legislation that extends the law's reach beyond its competence. Manifestations are seen in relation to gambling, the use of drugs, public drunkenness, vagrancy, disorderly conduct, and the noncriminal aspects of troublesome juvenile behavior. This overreach of criminal law has made hypocrites of us all and has confused the mission of corrections. It has overloaded the entire criminal justice system with inappropriate cases and saddled corrections with tasks it is unsuited to perform.

The unmaking of law is more difficult than the making; to express moral outrage at objectionable conduct and to urge legislative proscription is politically popular. On the other hand, to urge the repeal of sanctions against any objectionable conduct is politically risky since it can be equated in the popular mind with approval of that conduct. But corrections, like the rest of the criminal justice system, must reduce its load to what it has some chance of carrying. Too often we are fighting the wrong war, on the wrong front, at the wrong time, so that our ability to protect the community and serve the needs of the convicted offender is attenuated. It is for this reason that a major emphasis in this report is placed on developing diversions from and alternatives to the correctional system.

It is particularly urgent to evict from corrections many of the alcoholics and drug addicts who now clutter that system. They should be brought under the aegis of more appropriate and less punitive mechanisms of social control. The same is true of truants and other juveniles who are in need of care and protection and have not committed criminal offenses. They should be removed from the delinquency jurisdiction of the courts as well as corrections.

At the same time, the rapid expansion of those diverse community-based supervisory programs called probation and parole is needed. Most States still lack probation and parole programs that are more than gestures toward effective supervision and assistance for convicted offenders. Standards and goals for correctional reform depend largely on the swift, substantial improvement of probation and parole practices.

OVEREMPHASIS ON CUSTODY

The pervasive overemphasis on custody that remains in corrections creates more problems than it solves. Our institutions are so large that their operational needs take precedence over the needs of the people they hold. The very scale of these institutions dehumanizes, denies privacy, encourages violence, and defies decent control. A moratorium should be placed on the construction of any large correctional institution. We already have too many prisons. If there is any need at all for more institutions, it is for small, community-related facilities in or near the communities they serve.

There is also urgent need for reducing the population of jails and juvenile detention facilities. By using group homes, foster care arrangements, day residence facilities, and similar community-based resources, it should be possible to eliminate entirely the need for institutions to hold young persons prior to court disposition of their cases. Likewise, by other methods discussed in this report, it will be practicable to greatly reduce the use of jails for the adult accused. By placing limitations on detention time and by freely allowing community resources, agencies, and individuals to percolate the walls of the jail, it will be possible to minimize the social isolation of those who must be jailed.

Nevertheless, it must be recognized that at our present level of knowledge (certainly of adult offenders) we lack the ability to empty prisons and jails entirely. There are confirmed and dangerous offenders who require protracted confinement because we lack alternative and more effective methods of controlling or modifying their behavior. At least for the period of incarceration, they are capable of no injury to the community.

Even so, far too many offenders are classified as dangerous. We have not developed a means of dealing with them except in the closed institution. Too often we have perceived them as the stereotype of "prisoner" and applied to all offenders the institutional conditions essential only for relatively few. Hence, this report stresses the need for development of a broader range of alternatives to the institution, and for the input of greater resources of manpower, money, and materials to that end.

Community-based programs are not merely a substitute for the institution. Often they will divert offenders from entering the institution. But they also have important functions as part of the correctional process. They facilitate a continuum of services from the institution through graduated release procedures—such as furloughs and work release—to community-based programs.

Large institutions for adult and juvenile offenders have become places of endemic violence. Overcrowding and the admixture of diverse ethnic groups, thrown together in idleness and boredom, is the basic condition. Race relations tend to be hostile and ferocious in the racially skewed prisons and jails.

Increasing political activism complicates inmate-staff relations. Knives and other weapons proliferate and are used. Diversion of the less violent and more stable from institutions will leave in the prisons and jails a larger proportion of hardened, dangerous, and explosive prisoners. The correctional administrator thus confronts a stark reality. While making needed changes to benefit the great majority of inmates, he must cope with a volatile concentration of the most difficult offenders, whose hostility is directed against the staff.

For these reasons and others, continuing attention must be paid to conditions within the remaining institutions. Although the institution must be used only as a last resort, its programs must not be neglected. Such attention is essential if the institution is to serve as the beginning place for reintegration and not as the end of the line for the offender.

The principle of community-based corrections also extends to prisons and jails. We must make those institutions smaller, for only then can they cease to hold the anonymous. We must make them more open and responsive to community influences, for only thus can we make it possible for prisoners and staff alike to see what the community expects of them.

LACK OF FINANCIAL SUPPORT

The reforms envisioned in this report will not be achieved without substantially increased government funds being allocated to the criminal justice system and without a larger portion of the total being allocated to corrections. There is little sense in the police arresting more offenders if the courts lack the resources to bring them to trial and corrections lacks the resources to deal with them efficiently and fairly. Happily, the Federal Government, followed by many States, already is providing important leadership here.

Budgetary recognition is being given to the significance of crime and the fear it produces in the social fabric. For example, statutory provisions now require that at least 20 percent of the Federal funds disbursed by the Law Enforcement Assistance Administration to the States to aid crime control be allocated to corrections. It is clearly a proper role for the Federal Government to assist States by funds and direct services to increase the momentum of the movement toward community-based corrections and to remedy existing organizational inefficiencies.

Two other obstacles to reform merit mention in this litany of adversity and the means of overcoming it. Like the other impediments to change, these obstacles are not intractable, but, like the rest, they must be recognized as genuine problems to be reckoned with if they are not to frustrate progress. They are, first, the community's ambivalence, and second, the lack of knowledge on which planning for the criminal justice system can be firmly based.

AMBIVALENCE OF THE COMMUNITY

If asked, a clear majority of the community would probably support halfway houses for those offenders who are not a serious criminal threat but still require some residential control. But repeated experience has shown that a proposal to establish such a facility in the neighborhood is likely to rouse profound opposition. The criminal offender, adult or juvenile, is accorded a low level of community tolerance when he no longer is an abstract idea but a real person. Planning must be done, and goals and standards drafted, in recognition of this fact.

Responsible community relations must be built into all correctional plans. The antidote to intolerance of convicted offenders is the active involvement of wide segments of the community in support of correctional processes. With imagination and a willingness to take some risks, members of minority groups, ex-offenders, and other highly motivated citizens can play an effective supporting role in correctional programs.

Part of this process of opening up the institution to outside influences is the creation of a wider base for staff selection. Obviously, recruitment of members of minority groups is vitally important and must be energetically pursued. Of parallel importance, women must be employed in community-based programs and at every level of the institution (for men and women, for adults and youths) from top administration to line guard. Corrections must become a full equal opportunity employer.

Correctional administrators have tended to isolate corrections from the general public—by high walls and locked doors. In light of the community's ambivalence toward corrections, lack of effort at collaboration with community groups and individual citizens is particularly unfortunate. In almost every community there are individuals and social groups with exceptional concern for problems of social welfare whose energies must be called upon. A lobby for corrections lies at hand, to be mobilized not merely by public information and persuasion, but also by encouraging the active participation of the public in correctional work.

There are yet other advantages in such a determined community involvement in corrections. Obstacles to the employment of ex-offenders will be lowered. Probation and parole caseloads could be reduced if paraprofessionals and volunteers, including ex-offenders, assist. And the "nine-to-five on weekdays" syndrome of some probation and parole services can be cured, so that supervision and support can be available when most needed.

LACK OF KNOWLEDGE BASE FOR PLANNING

In this catalog of problems in corrections to be solved, the need for a knowledge base must be seriously considered. Research is the indispensable tool by which future needs are measured and met. Chapter 15 surveys present correctional knowledge and prescribes means to determine which of our correctional practices are effective and with which categories of offenders.

Lack of adequate data about crime and delinquency, the consequences of sentencing practices, and the outcome of correctional programs is a major obstacle to planning for better community protection. It is a sad commentary on our social priorities that every conceivable statistic concerning sports is collected and available to all who are interested. One can readily find out how many lefthanders hit triples in the 1927 World Series. Yet if we wish to know how many one-to-life sentences were handed out to the 1927 crop of burglars—or the 1972 crop for that matter—the facts are nowhere to be found.

Baseline data and outcome data are not self-generating; no computer is self-activating. Research is of central significance to every correctional agency. It is not, as it so often is regarded, merely a public relations gimmick to be manipulated for political and budgetary purposes. It is an indispensable tool for intelligent decisionmaking and deployment of resources.

It is time we stopped giving mere lip service to research and to the critical evaluation of correctional practices. To fail to propound and to achieve ambitious research and data-gathering goals is to condemn corrections to the perpetual continuance of its present ineptitude.

Notes

1   President's Task Force on Prisoner Rehabilitation, *The Criminal Offender—What Should Be Done?* (Washington: Government Printing Office, 1970), p. 7.

2   143 F. 2d 443 (6th Cir. 1944). Cert. denied 325 U.S. 887 (1945).

Mark S. Richmond

Measuring the cost of correctional services

The purpose of this paper is to identify and examine major issues related to the concept of the offender as a consumer of resources. These perspectives should contribute to increased effectiveness of correctional planning and program management.

The immediate problem is two-fold: the costs of dealing with the offender are enormous and increasing and there are virtually no indications that present correctional methods are effective interventions in criminal careers. A complicating set of additional problems arises from the failure to define and synthesize the goals of criminal justice and correction. This paper proposes a number of goal-setting assumptions and illustrates cost-effectiveness approaches to program design. Important related questions of resource management are raised. The paper's thesis is that resource consumption must become goal-oriented rather than process-oriented.

From the moment of his arrest, if not before, the offender becomes a consumer of public resources, most of which are tax supported. The cost of his apprehension and booking are the first expenses on the list. Unless he is released immediately on bail or personal recognizance, the taxpayers pay for his confinement in jail until his trial. Add the costs of prosecution (and defense, if he cannot afford to hire counsel) and the expense of trial and related court services. In the event of his conviction, probation or imprisonment and parole will be paid for with tax money. Expenditures for correctional programs and services will include the use of health and welfare services, education and training programs, legal services, and any other resources that may be employed until the offender is discharged from the system.

Twelve years ago the estimated cost of operating criminal and juvenile courts and correction (probation, institutions, and parole)

Reprinted from *Crime and Delinquency*, July 1972, pp. 243–252, with the permission of the National Council on Crime and Delinquency.

in one state (Massachusetts) was more than $30-million a year. This amounted to about $6.30 for each man, woman, and child who lived in the state. These figures did not include estimates of loss or damage resulting from the commission of offenses; the costs of law enforcement, arrest, or prosecution; capital investments in and maintenance of buildings, facilities, and equipment other than correctional institutions; and any extra-agency costs associated with trial, conviction, and imprisonment. The President's Commission on Law Enforcement and Administration of Justice estimated that national expenditures for police, prosecution and defense, the courts, and correction exceeded $4-billion for the fiscal year that ended June 30, 1965. These costs are borne primarily by taxpayers at the state and local levels.

But how much does *correction* cost? NCCD conducted a survey for the President's Crime Commission and estimated that the cost of operating state and local correctional services in 1965 was almost $1-billion. About 80 per cent of the total operating cost was allocated for institutions, and more than half of that allocation went to support state adult correctional institutions. It was estimated that the average daily cost per case ranged from $11.15 for juvenile detention to $.38 for adult probation. The daily cost of a juvenile in an institution was ten times that of juvenile probation or aftercare. For adults, state institutional cost was about six times that of parole and about fourteen times that of probation. Construction being planned in 1965 for completion by 1975 in state and local institution systems could increase bed capacity by 24 per cent at a cost of over $1-billion (based on a very conservative estimate of $10,000 per bed).

Another way of looking at the cost of correction is to consider the cost of a criminal career, but this is as difficult as estimating the total cost of crime and delinquency. Records are often incomplete; data relating to one component or jurisdiction may be incompatible with data from another; it is often a matter of personal judgment as to what costs to include; and many costs are frankly unknown.

A partial view of career costs can be gained from applying estimated daily average costs per case to a hypothetical, yet fairly typical, offender. Cost rates in the following illustration are estimated national averages reported to the President's Crime Commission in 1965.[1] This hypothetical offender made his first appearance in juvenile court at the age of sixteen. For twenty-five years he has been in and out of trouble. Now, at age forty-one, he is in prison. When he is released again, the statistical probability is that he will not return to prison, but he will probably continue to consume public resources in other ways.

1. Arrested at age sixteen and placed in a juvenile detention facility. Released on probation. Committed to a state training school for a new offense and violation of probation. Paroled.

14 days juvenile detention @ $11.15 per day	$ 156
6 months on probation @ $.92 per day	166
14 months in training school @ $10.66 per day	4,530
5 months on parole @ $.84 per day	126

2. Violated parole by committing a new offense. Sentenced to jail instead of being returned as a parole violator. Over the next three years he was in and out of jails awaiting trial on subsequent offenses or serving short sentences.

14 months in local jails @ $2.86 per day	$1,215

3. Committed a felony offense and placed in jail to await trial. Placed on probation. Violated by committing a new offense and sentenced to a state reformatory. Paroled; violated.

6 months in jail awaiting trial and sentence @ $2.86 per day	$ 515
4 months probation @ $.38 per day	46
18 months in state reformatory @ $5.24 per day	3,256
2 months on parole @ $.88 per day	53
12 months in reformatory @ $5.24 per day	1,913

4. Arrested a few months after release for a felony offense. Committed to jail to await trial and sentence. Charges reduced to a misdemeanor; sentenced to jail.

4 months in local jail @ $2.86 per day	$ 343
5 months served on jail sentence @ $2.86 per day	429

5. Committed a more serious felony offense. Detained in jail awaiting trial and disposition. Sentenced to state prison. Paroled; violated, and returned to serve remainder of sentence.

8 months in local jail @ $2.86 per day	$ 684
3 years in state prison @ $5.24 per day	5,737
4 months on parole @ $.88 per day	106
2 years in prison @ $5.24 per day	3,301

6. The commission of a subsequent offense resulted in the same sequence of events. He is still serving his sentence.

5 months in jail awaiting trial, etc., @ $2.86 per day		$ 429
6 years in prison @ $5.24 per day		11,476
	Total	$34,481

If this illustration can be accepted as at least remotely representing the cost of a typical criminal career that can be multiplied by

tens of thousands, it has many implications relating to the consumption of resources. The most salient question is, What has been
accomplished by the expenditure of these funds? But there are other
questions. Is it possible that a greater commitment of resources at
the onset of a criminal career like this could have produced better
results? Do the astonishingly low daily costs of probation and
parole suggest that these are starvation rates which cannot buy
actual services and controls? Is it significant that the offender spent
a total of 3½ years in local jails in which there were no correctional
programs?

Goals and assumptions

The foregoing measures of resource consumption are process-
oriented rather than goal-oriented. The customary approach to all
correction has tended to be process-oriented; the preoccupation
with operating procedures and the sequences in which they occur
has been almost ritualistic. Decision points in the process have
offered little more than the exercise of either-or choices: whether or
not to arrest, whether or not to prosecute, whether to place on
probation or sentence to imprisonment, whether or not to grant
parole.

This situation must no longer be tolerated. Rising costs will
eventually outstrip the availability of funds for meeting them. The
ineffectiveness of the system is now seen as a major contributor to
the alarming increase in the crime rate. Waste and inefficiency
cannot be condoned in the competition for tax funds. Programs
whose results are unknown and to which evaluations of outcome
have not been systematically applied will not be given continuing
support. Therefore, since the offender will remain a consumer of
resources, ways of insuring better returns on resource investment
must be found.

A goal-oriented approach provides the most practical solutions to
this problem because it is the only approach in which outcomes
carry more weight than processes and programs in the allocation of
resources. Goal-setting is a painstaking and difficult process in
itself. It begins with defining and formulating broad aims and
objectives and obtaining consensus about them. These are supported by specific, measurable goals, whose feasibility and practi-
cality can be considered only in terms of required strategies and
possible alternatives. The strategies that are selected are imple-

mented by a series of action steps and checkpoints at which progress can be assessed and subsequent courses of action can be modified as circumstances dictate. Objectives and goals are related to purpose and needs.

What are the objectives of criminal justice and correction? Correction today displays evidence of a number of ideas and practices, some of which are in conflict, each seeking to cope with the difficult problems of punishing, deterring, restraining, and rehabilitating offenders. None has resolved these problems, and change from one to another probably has been more the result of humanitarian concern than the product of rational or scientific process.

Notions of punishment still underlie much of correctional practice today, particularly in popular views of what ought to be done with those who commit criminal acts. These notions satisfy primitive needs for retribution, but the focus is exclusively on the offender, and punishment is measured according to the type and seriousness of offense. As the focus broadens to include concerns for society, punishment is seen as a deterrent to the future behavior of the offender and as an inner control for those who might otherwise be tempted to commit a criminal act. The idea of restraint as a necessary ingredient of correction is associated primarily with the objective of public protection, but this is a relatively temporary means of achieving it. The rationale for rehabilitation is related to humanitarian concerns for the offender and to the ultimate objective of public protection.

Thus the problems of goal-setting in correction are compounded at the outset by uncertain objectives and limited knowledge of the direct causes of criminal behavior. In addition to many unresolved basic issues, other concerns have been growing—questions of due process, equitable treatment of offenders, the efficiency of the criminal justice system, and the cost-effectiveness of correctional efforts. Yet certain assumptions can be made on the basis of facts that are known. In the absence of a better starting point, the following assumptions can be used to assess needs, define purpose, and establish objectives and goals:

1. "The general underlying premise for the new directions in corrections is that crime and delinquency are symptoms of failures and disorganization of the community as well as of individual offenders. . . . The task of corrections therefore includes building or rebuilding solid ties between offender and community, integrating or reintegrating the offender into community life. . . . This requires not only efforts directed toward changing the individual offender, which has been almost the exclusive focus of rehabilitation, but also

mobilization and change of the community and its institutions." [2]

2. The task of correction is to intervene in delinquent and criminal careers, through management and control of crises and through programs designed to overcome handicapping deficiencies.

3. The more an offender is plunged into correctional processes and the longer he is locked up, the greater the cost and the improbability of his successful reintegration in the community.

4. An offender's need for control or help should be considered and treated individually, whatever his status in the criminal justice system.

To assess the feasibility of change, one must consider some alternative strategies: improved operations within correctional systems and agencies, mobilization of resources outside correctional systems for the prevention of crime, and increased fairness in the administration of correctional systems.

The first of these may include more efficient procedures to promote a faster flow of people through the system, methods of upgrading personnel, reorganization, and new information systems and management methods. There may be many obstacles to change in these areas, and changes of this kind are unlikely to be achieved unless they are treated as part of a broader approach toward organizational development and renewal.

The second and third alternatives call for new involvement of schools, medical services, welfare agencies, business and industry, labor organizations, civic groups, and legal services. But many of these resources are already inadequate to the tasks they are expected to perform. Action strategies that would funnel offenders into outside resources must confront the capabilities and interests of the agencies involved. Effective collaboration with other agencies requires them to perceive offenders as legitimate recipients of their services and to give the criminal justice system a visibility and a place of central importance which, for the most part, it now lacks.

The cost-effectiveness approach

While some people have difficulty understanding or accepting theories of criminal behavior, are confused over correctional goals and objectives, or question the purposes of specific correctional programs and procedures, few have trouble understanding the meaning of dollars. Dollar values have a universal appeal to taxpayers when they are expressed as ways of spending less money or getting more for the money spent. Applying the cost-effective-ness approach to goal-setting does not simplify the tasks involved; it merely uses terms and concepts that have instant meaning to everyone.

The obvious starting point is an analysis of existing costs. It has already been said that this can be a major undertaking because of incomplete and incompatible records, unresolved questions of what costs to include, and unknown costs. However, there are ways of making approximations that will suffice for planning purposes. One was illustrated above in spreading the correctional costs of a "criminal career." Take an "average" offender's history and tally known or estimated unit costs for the various programs, services, and procedures in which he has been involved. This computation can be manipulated and projected according to the number of offenders known to have been involved in different programs and procedures. Often the actual costs of programs, services, and procedures are not known, but these too can be estimated closely enough for planning purposes. Fairly accurate figures are available for costs of materials and supplies. The costs of procedures such as supervision, instruction, or counseling can be expressed in man-hours or man-days at estimated rates. Supportive costs, such as utilities, depreciation of equipment or facilities, and transportation can be prorated from known categories of expense. Known or estimated equivalent costs can be applied when necessary.

IDENTIFICATION AND APPLICATION OF RESOURCES

Goal-setting cannot proceed far without much thought being given to the resources that will be needed. These generally consist of money, manpower, materials, and facilities. The resources to deliver the programs and services in question do not have to be provided all at once to all offenders, or even by the agency directly responsible for the activities. The feasibility of programs and goals must be considered in terms of the kinds and amounts of support that may be available from all sources. This will enable priority choices; for example: Shall the greater emphasis be placed on diagnostic work or on expansion of social casework services? The distribution, sequence, timing, and amounts of funding must also be considered.

PROCESS IN RELATION TO OUTCOME

Traditional line budgeting has virtually dictated that costs must be presented on a per capita basis, as summary amounts of money per offender per day, week, month, or year. There are many accounting difficulties and possible questions of policy in computing *all* costs in these summary amounts, but the major limitations of this budgeting procedure for planning purposes are that (1) the figures have no meaning without reference to total time (man-days served) and (2) there is no reference to outcome. For example, the average per-capita operating cost of one community residential facility (halfway house) amounts to $15 a day if it operates at full capacity all of the time. If the average length of stay is ninety days, the total investment per resident amounts to an average of $1,350. The daily per capita cost of another such facility is about $12. At this facility the average length of stay is eighty-five days. Thus, at full capacity, the total average investment per resident is $1,020. The central question is whether the outcome of one is better than that of the other.

The concept of total process cost in relation to outcome is particularly useful to planners and program managers alike. It not only suggests alternative ways to stretch the budgeted dollar without sacrificing program quality, but also constantly focuses attention on benefits to the offender and society in terms of the total investments made. Thus, correctional goals and objectives assume prime importance. For example, it can be shown in dollars that simple safekeeping or minimal domiciliary care at low per capita rates can be more costly over extended periods of time than intensive treatment at high per capita rates for shorter periods when results of the latter demonstrate a reduced or delayed rate of failure in the attainment of preset goals.

This concept introduces a new dimension of cost analysis in which correctional agencies and programs can be seen as vehicles for the delivery of certain services. A number of related issues must be considered. Foremost among them are offender selection, program evaluation, and management.

OFFENDER SELECTION

Not all offenders need the same controls and correctional treatment. Failure of the system or of decision-makers to take this into account can be highly wasteful of resources, and it risks more long-range harm than good to offenders who become saddled with processes they do not need. One of the persistent criticisms of the traditional jail, designed for maximum security, is that commitment to such a facility has not been based on differences in need for control and correctional treatment. The result has been that the most expensive kind of facility is used for all offenders when only a small percentage of the persons committed need this degree of control.

Obviously, selection must be based on careful estimates of danger and risk to the community and on offender problems and needs in relation to certain correctional objectives. Ideally, a correctional system should match types of offenders with types of programs geared to meet specific needs. The choices would range from nonsupervisory measures in structured community programs to total incarceration. Greatest flexibility should attend these choices, but we are far from this ideal, both philosophically and practically; diagnostic procedures, when they occur at all, take place *after* many important decisions have been made and sentences have been imposed.

PROGRAM EVALUATION

The development of a more effective correctional system will require new knowledge and better research. More discriminating criteria are needed for classifying offenders. Whatever the availability of correctional resources, individuals must be differentiated according to the degree of treatment and control they require (intensive, selective, or minimal). There is a continuing need for knowledge for training staff in correctional processes and training offenders in the specific behaviors that are required for successful community adjustment. Research on community-based programs, for example, would contribute much to this knowledge and, at the same time, would enable more sophisticated development of the programs themselves. More must be learned about those types of offenders who can make the most and those who can make the least effective use of various correctional experiences. Questions must be raised about the character of correctional experiences for the offenders involved in them. There is evidence, too, of a need to study the appropriate "dosage" of correction for different types of offenders.

Collaborative management

It is clear from the preceding discussion that neither the criminal justice system itself nor its individual correctional agencies can realistically aspire to have all of the resources needed to conduct a broad range of preventive and corrective programs and services. It should be equally clear by now that such an attempt should be avoided.

The programs and services required for the prevention, treatment, and control of crime and delinquency can be viewed as providing for a spectrum of needs. They include preventive measures that can be applied before an offense is committed, alternatives to court procedures and disposition, correctional treatment of convicted offenders, and aftercare services designed to help and control the processes involved in the offender's reintegration for successful community life.

Correctional agencies in any jurisdiction need far more resources than have been available to them until now. But it is no longer necessary or wise for correction to try to be autonomous. Many of the needed resources can be found increasingly outside of the criminal justice system. Specific services for offenders may be purchased from other agencies and organizations, both public and private; they may become available as extensions of an agency's own programs when offenders are added to the target group; or, as in the case of private industry, they may help meet the needs of the organization offering the services. The vast potentials of volunteer services are just now being explored. But the problem is a much larger one than gaining access to resources.

REDESIGN OF VEHICLES DELIVERING SERVICES

The national profile of correction consists of a number of organizational components: juvenile detention, juvenile probation, juvenile institutions, juvenile aftercare, misdemeanant probation, felony probation, local adult institutions and jails, state and federal adult institutions, and parole. Alaska is the only state in which all nine correctional services are organized into a single department. In most jurisdictions the agencies providing these services function autonomously and their relationships to other correctional programs, if not entirely remote, lack the integration that would enable total coordinated correctional effort.

The primary organizational models are local, regional, and statewide, as well as various kinds of collaborative administration. The precedents for these models are deeply imbedded in patterns of governmental organization and traditional ways of doing things. Program managers and planning groups cannot do much about the political and jurisdictional limits imposed on correctional programs. However, from a painstaking examination of the issues involved and from an understanding of the capabilities and mechanisms needed for the eventual delivery of comprehensive, coordinated correctional services, a design can emerge for the eventual attainment of long-range goals.

Who determines priorities? The planning process itself requires choices among alternatives and the identification of priorities with which feasible action steps can be taken. But there is a management aspect of this as well. In these days when correctional program managers are finding a growing abundance of local resources for services to offenders, the problem is the relatively simple one of obtaining commitment, making necessary arrangements, and adjusting operating schedules. The correctional program manager, however, is not the only agency representative laying claim to these services. As more agencies increase their claims, the time will come when the risks of demand exceeding supply will be foreseen by the organizations possessing the services or resources. The competition that ensues will probably have to be resolved in nontraditional ways. There may be a need for local, regional, and state planning and coordinating groups who will be authorized to cut across customary organizational lines to achieve an equitable distribution of available resources among multiple service needs on a priority basis. This will be an increasingly complex task that will have meaning only if consensus is reached on long-range goals and as responsible agency representatives participate in the choice of program and service alternatives.

What are the management implications of decisions within the criminal justice system? Comprehensive planning is really concerned with future effectiveness. While the initial focus may be on programs and services, planners recognize that the difficulties of planning and implementing change may be tactical and strategic as well as substantive. Clearly, an attempt to cope with existing problems on a massive scale risks outrunning available resources and the level of understanding that can be brought to bear on them. If a strategy is adopted that is consistent with limited resources and understanding, the effort may appear inadequate in relation to the magnitude of the problem. The choice of a starting point should reflect an effort that is part of a larger and more significant undertaking.

The very limited traditional view of correction has not yet been abandoned. In this view, one thinks of imprisonment and what happens after guilt has been established as comprising the universe of correction. This paper has taken a broader view. From the point of first contact between an alleged offender and police there can and should be an increasing range of decision points and alternative courses of action, each of which influences and is influenced by the others. A great deal more must be learned about key decision points—what the choices are and who chooses among them—and there is a need for more information that can be used to evaluate the effects of the decisions that are made. Any significant change, whether planned or unplanned, will decidedly alter the existing system. Changes should be planned with full awareness that they will have impact and that their ultimate effectiveness will be measured as contributions to the value of the system in which they occur.

There is no question that the offender is a consumer of resources, nor is there any doubt that the costs he incurs will increase as new and expanded correctional programs and services are developed for his benefit and society's. The central question now becomes, How can greater returns be produced by the resources that are consumed?

The preceding pages have briefly examined some of the difficult issues related to this question. A common approach may be impossible because of the profusion of special circumstances that surround each situation. It is also evident that the question is of such magnitude that there is no single answer; many solutions must be sought.

Notes

1 Note that these estimates are for one year only and have been extrapolated for a hypothetical 25-year history. This introduces a bias by failing to account for actual cost fluctuations over that span of time. For more detailed applications of this kind of cost analysis, see Barbara Cantor and Stuart Adams, *The Cost of Correcting Youthful Offenders* (Washington, D.C.: Department of Corrections, 1968); and Stuart Adams and Calvin C. Hopkinson, *Interim Evaluation of the Intensive Supervision Caseload Project* (Los Angeles: Los Angeles County Probation Department, 1964).

2 President's Commission on Law Enforcement and Administration of Justice, *Task Force Report: Corrections* (Washington, D.C.: U.S. Government Printing Office, 1967), p. 7.

Part six

Juveniles

C oncern for juveniles is frequently neglected in introductory texts in criminal justice. This neglect permeates the whole criminal justice community. It has led to summary justice for juveniles and has allowed juvenile correction facilities to become breeding grounds for adult criminals. We cannot ignore the importance of juvenile offenders. Without successful rehabilitation they become inputs into the system of adult offenders and increase the burden on an already overburdened criminal justice system.

The article Justice for Juveniles in America: The Neglected Problem asserts that juveniles only recently have been given some protections by the courts including the right to an attorney. But, there has been little real reform. There is still no real differentiation between offenders who have committed criminal acts and children merely in the need of supervision. When children who merely need supervision are placed in a correctional system with so-called hard-core offenders they become targets of criminal recruitment. There is a need for changes in the system, such as community-based preventive and rehabilitative programs and a modification of the system to reduce the numbers of youths classified as delinquents.

The Utopian World of Juvenile Courts provides a brief sketch of the development of juvenile law in the United States. A look at the juvenile court system from its beginnings reveals that the court ideally was supposed to be a social agency to help children in trouble rather than a punitive agency. This conception of the court seems to have remained largely an ideal and an idea. The way in which the juvenile courts have been operated frequently has led to infringement on the rights of juveniles rather than their protection. Only after action by the United States Supreme Court in the Gault Case have juveniles had any assurance that there will be some reasonable protections of their rights. The inadequacies of the juvenile court may no longer be rationalized but must be corrected.

The types of unconscionable activities in the juvenile system are emphasized in Juvenile Delinquency: the Sexualization of Female Crime. The juvenile court system discriminates against the female juvenile delinquent. Different standards of conduct are expected of girls and boys, and these become a basis for a difference in treatment of male and female juvenile offenders. The courts seem to think that all of the crimes of female delinquents are sexual in nature. Consequently, vaginal smears are taken regardless of the offense. The length of sentences for the girls are longer than those for boys, and females are more likely to end up in institutions than their male counterparts. Parents who are unable or unwilling to control their daughters' behavior are more likely to go to the courts than those who are unable to control the behavior of their sons. There is a need for a balance of justice between male and female juvenile offenders.

Justice for Children—for Now and for the Future reinforces what has already been said. It urges the courts and official agencies to distinguish between juvenile delinquents and uncontrolled children. Rehabilitative treatment that has failed must be examined to determine why it failed. Oftentimes treatment does not provide the juvenile with the ability to cope with the type of problems they face on a day to day basis. More emphasis needs to be placed on both the safeguarding of juvenile liberties and providing adequate rehabilitative services.

Police Control of Juveniles defines the deviance which is likely to result in arrest or encounter with the police. Most of the contacts between juveniles and the police are not initiated by the police but by citizens. In most instances the arrest rate is very low for all offenses but increases with the legal seriousness of an alleged offense. Race as a basis for arrest is examined, as well as the effect of the attitudes of juveniles toward police.

Jeanne D. Dreifus

Justice for juveniles in America: the neglected problem

The year 1974 will mark the seventy-fifth anniversary of the Juvenile Court system in the United States. Much has been written describing the purpose, the duties and the ideals of a court which was designed to meet the special needs of its youthful clientele.

Much more research into its future role is desirable and the next few years of the century will be marked by further progress in the developing field of child advocacy.

In 1870 an Illinois Supreme Court judge ruled that commitments of boys aged 6 to 16 to the Chicago Reform School was unconstitutional because the child in question had been placed in an "infant penitentiary" without benefit of trial. Justice Thornton said:

. . . the sovereign power of the State as *parens patriae* has determined the imprisonment beyond recall. Such a restraint upon natural liberty is tyranny and oppression. If, without crime . . . the children of the State are thus to be confined for the "good of Society" then Society had better be reduced to its original elements and free government declared a failure.

The welfare and rights of the child are also to be considered . . . Even Criminals cannot be convicted and imprisoned without due process of law.[1]

This view was opposed vigorously by the reformers who believed in child-saving "by means of institutions which would be places of refuge for juveniles, who would be treated therein with 'tender pity'."

Because the outstanding features of jails in the 1880's were

Reprinted from *Public Affairs Forum*, March 1974 with the kind permission of the Institute of Governmental Studies and Research (Memphis State University) and Jeanne Dreifus.

over-crowding, filth, vermin and brutality, reformers demanded change.

Frederick Wines, an authority on penal institutions and secretary of the Illinois Board of Commissioners of Public Charities, viewed reformatories as a way to rescue children from the contaminating effects of the jails. Detention homes were needed before trials, and reform schools afterwards. The child-saving movement gained momentum upon the election of John P. Altgeld as Governor in 1893. He, too, was a student of penal reform, and, unlike the women's clubs, religious groups and other more sentimental child-savers, Governor Altgeld recognized the economic inequalities which made the criminal justice system and its administration often crushing to the poor. He supported the establishment of reformatories, and probationary parole, as well as indeterminate sentences for youthful offenders.

The concern for separate facilities for children was a central theme in the juvenile court movement. Another concern of the reformers was the fate of dependent and neglected children who were growing up in ignorance and vice, and of particular importance were those who were *liable* to "become the progenitor of generations of criminals."

The Board of Public Charities called for a massive effort to "rescue every child in the State exposed to destruction through neglect or abuse." [2]

The passage of the Illinois Juvenile Court Act of 1899 was brought about through an effective political coalition of the Illinois Bar Association, State Penitentiary Wardens, children's aid societies, and influential philanthropists. The bill passed, culminating thirty years of reform efforts. Most importantly for future generations, the Act nearly eliminated all aspects of criminal procedure from the juvenile court, and substituted instead of indictment and arrest, the informal procedures for custody and hearing. The delinquent child, who was defined as "any child who violates any law of this state, or any city or village ordinance," was to be given separate detention, hearing, and disposition, not as a criminal, but as one who is in need of guidance and correction.

The original Juvenile Court Statute defined what is considered juvenile crime, which was identical to the jurisdiction of criminal courts over the accused adult. In 1907, the Act was amended to include other categories which covered not only criminal aspects, but social and moral implications as well.

The jurisdiction included "incorrigibles," those who left home without consent, those who frequented unsavory places such as houses of ill-repute, public poolrooms, and the like. Also, children found to be "growing up in crime or idleness," using obscene or vulgar language or guilty of any "indecent or lascivious conduct."

The inclusion of such a broad range of human errors expanded the *"parens patriae"* concept even further, seeking wise and humane answers to the problems of children, as would a thoughtful parent. This led inevitably to the concept of the court as a sort of social agency. The child-savers had affirmed the values of home and family, and set such high standards that almost any parent could be found wanting. These standards were applied largely to the lower classes, and were essentially conservative and authoritarian, according to Platt.

The role of the court was exemplified in a statement by Judge Julian W. Mack:

The problem for determination by the judge is *not* has this boy or girl committed a specific wrong, but what is he, how has he become what he is, and what had best be done in his interest and in the interest of the state to save him from a downward career.[3]

This protective and proprietary attitude enunciated the concept that the juvenile court setting should not be an adversary one, but should be a benevolent and constructive experience. The therapeutic overtones were translated into the court, which was to be arranged informally, like a clinic, stressing examination and treatment for the child. The judge was to be "counselor-doctor rather than lawyer."

This expanded concept of the juvenile court is the model which was followed by other states when legislatures began adopting special juvenile courts. The ambiguity of defining delinquency and the difficulties inherent in the therapeutic approach were to be the seeds for criticism in years to come.

The original rationale for the juvenile court's establishment was the recognition and control of youthful deviance.

The idea was evidently one whose time had come, for within five years of the passage of the Illinois Act, ten other states had established juvenile courts, and by 1925 all but two states had done so. By 1945 Wyoming, the last to conform, completed the list.

The intervening years after the founding of the juvenile court were looked upon as an era of noble advancement of social justice. Many agencies designed to assist the rehabilitative concepts of the courts were established, such as detention centers, probationary services, diagnostic facilities and correctional institutions for juveniles. Organizations began to come into existence to provide guidelines for the court, such as the Children's Bureau in 1912; the White House Conference on Children and Youth, held every ten years; and in 1907, the National Probation and Parole Association, now known as the National Council on Crime and Delinquency. The National Council of Juvenile Court Judges was founded in 1937, and began research on how to train juvenile court judges and on such issues as the role of the lawyer as advocate for the child.

In doing away with much of the trappings of that "most hidebound of all human institutions, the court of law," to quote Herbert Lou, an early supporter of the movement, there began to be inevitable questions about the efficacy of what had been put in its place. Early studies by the Children's Bureau[4] revealed that the protective and treatment-oriented services were sadly lacking. Only 16% of the juvenile courts of the country in 1920 were able to measure up to the standards set by law. However, when challenges to the constitutionality of the juvenile court emerged, the courts usually supported the humanitarian goals of the juvenile court, repelling all assaults as not applicable to a non-criminal court. For example, in Pennsylvania, in 1905, a lawyer challenged the law on the grounds that it denied due process in the manner of taking his client into custody, and that the child was denied his right to a jury trial for a felony. The Court held that due process simply was not an issue, and since a delinquency hearing was not a criminal trial, the right to a jury trial did not apply either.[5]

The Supreme Court denied certiorari in a later case, *People v. Lewis*,[6] and for five decades the juvenile courts were allowed to develop, with varying degrees of jurisdiction and judicial support, until the period of the 1950's and 60's.

A turning point in views of the juvenile court occurred in 1949 with the publication of a book by Paul Tappan, a legal sociologist, entitled, *Juvenile Delinquency* which, along with another work, *Delinquent Girls in Court*, questioned the ability of the court to function in the dual role of rehabilitator and legal authority. Tappan refers to the perversion of purposes in which the court is forced to confront conflicts between traditional law and applied sociology.

There is a real lack of justification under our political system for subjecting any person to actually punitive processes without a fair trial or an objectively defined standard of conduct . . . yet as vested inertia in the established methods, sustained in part by an occupational philosophy, has developed in the court . . . which prevents change to develop without a response that one is trying to destroy the court. . . .[7]

Tappan asserts that we are not in an either/or situation and that constructive criticism is in order. The first organized body of critical material, studies of the juvenile court, its laws and its practical problems began to be revealed, leading to the notion that the dream of its founders was yet unfulfilled.

The higher courts of many of the states had been considering constitutional objections to the juvenile court procedure. Many of the cases in state and Federal courts dealt with the right to retain counsel at a delinquency hearing.

The first case which was relied upon in later decisions of the Supreme Court regarding juvenile procedural rights did not actually arise in a juvenile court, but dealt with the trial in adult court of a 15-year-old boy who had confessed to first degree murder.

Haley v. Ohio,[8] provided the Court with the opportunity to express opinion on the admissibility of a confession taken from a minor. The Court held that the due process clause of the Fourteenth Amendment was violated in the method of taking the confession. The facts revealed that the boy was grilled for 12 hours with no counsel. The court held his admission of guilt was obtained under conditions which flouted constitutional requirements. Justice Douglas, in the majority opinion wrote, "Neither man nor child can be allowed to stand condemned by (such) methods. . . . But we are told the boy was advised of his constitutional rights before he signed the confession, and that knowing them, he nevertheless confessed . . . (W)e cannot give weight to recitals which merely formalize constitutional requirements. Formulas of respect for constitutional safeguards cannot prevail over the facts of life which contradict them."

During the 1960's, when civil rights and the aggressive employment of legal means to secure and protect the rights of citizens were rising issues, a trend was set which ultimately influenced the juvenile court. There were a large number of landmark cases in which the procedural rights of the accused were spelled out: *Mapp v. Ohio,*[9] in which the Supreme Court held that evidence illegally obtained could not be used in a criminal trial against the accused.

Gideon v. Wainwright,[10] held that an indigent had a fundamental right to the assistance of counsel.

The "Miranda warnings" which followed, included the right of the accused to remain silent, the right to counsel, and to have such counsel appointed if the accused were indigent, and that anything said by the accused could be used against him in court.

The opinion in *Miranda v. Arizona,*[11] delivered by Chief Justice Warren, held that statements obtained from an individual subjected to custodial police interrogation, "unless it demonstrates the use of procedural safeguards effective to secure the privilege against self-incrimination" are not admissible.

Kent v. United States,[12] another case of importance to the juvenile court, came before the Supreme Court. Kent was a 16-year-old boy charged with housebreaking, robbery and rape. At issue was the propriety of the District of Columbia Juvenile Court's waiver of jurisdiction "after full investigation," as permitted by statute. It was emphasized that the latitude possessed by the court in determining whether it should retain or waive jurisdiction must assume "procedural regularity sufficient in the particular circumstances to satisfy the basic requirements of due process and fairness as well as compliance with the statutory requirement of a 'full investigation'." [13] Justice Fortas remarked, "It is inconceivable that a court of justice dealing with adults would proceed in this manner. It would be extraordinary if society's special concern for children, as reflected in the District of Columbia's Juvenile Court Act, permitted this procedure.[14]

Kent was the first case in which the Supreme Court examined the procedures of the juvenile court. The fact that Justice Fortas drew a comparison with the adult court did not mean that juvenile courts had to become identical to them, but there was a strong indication that the Court did not like what it observed. Justice Fortas indicated that evidence existed that the worst of all possible worlds was emerging for the juvenile; neither the protective and kindly framework of the special court for youth, nor the well-regulated and legalistic safeguards of the criminal court were found in the juvenile system. This opinion led directly to the most far-reaching of the juvenile court cases, that of Gerald Gault.

In re Gault[15] came to the Supreme Court, challenging the constitutionality of the Arizona Juvenile code and the procedures of its Juvenile Court. Gerald Gault, age 15, was taken into custody by a probation officer, on the charge by a neighbor that Gerald and a friend had made some lewd phone calls. Gerald's parents were not informed of his whereabouts, and they were told to appear for a hearing with no notice of the charges, and with no adequate written notice of the hearing. At the hearing, no mention was made of the right to counsel, or that one would be appointed for them. The judge ruled that Gerald was a delinquent, because of a former minor offense on his record, and without hearing any evidence about the indecent phone calls. For this offense, "using vulgar or obscene language," an adult could be fined an amount from $5.00 to $50.00

and given a two-month maximum jail sentence for a misdemeanor. Gerald was committed to the Arizona State Industrial School until his majority, a possible six-year sentence, and he adjudicated "delinquent." No appeal is permitted by Arizona law in juvenile cases, and thus a petition for habeas corpus was filed with the Superior Court. The hearing revealed that there were no written proceedings, the juvenile court judge could not tell under what section of the Arizona Code Gerald's guilt had been adjudged, and that there were no witnesses other than the probation officer to testify. The Superior Court dismissed the writ, and later, so did the Supreme Court of Arizona. The case came to the Supreme Court of the United States on writ of habeas corpus, and asked that the Juvenile Code of Arizona be held invalid on its face and as applied. Because of the unlimited discretion of the Juvenile Court, the petitioners asked that it be ruled a denial of basic rights under the Fourteenth Amendment.

In this case, the Supreme Court scrutinized the promises and practices of the juvenile court system. The issue was stated thus: "The problem is to ascertain the precise impact of the due process requirement upon such proceedings, i.e. proceedings in which a determination is made as to whether a juvenile is a 'delinquent' as a result of alleged misconduct on his part, and with the consequence that he may be committed to a state institution." [16]

Justice Fortas, in the majority opinion, recalled that rights granted to adults are not observed by juvenile courts, i.e., bail, public trial, jury trial, rights of arrest and interrogation. The informality of the court often leads to admission of hearsay evidence, but it is *assumed* that the judge will only give such evidence the proper weight. However, the Court emphasized that the juvenile court judge must be persuaded by *clear* evidence that the child has committed the alleged act, and that the correct burden of proof lies with the judge. The opinion further states that while the procedure is "civil" rather than "criminal" there is only slightly less stigma in the term "delinquent" than there is in the term "criminal," and incarceration is surely "jail" even though it may be called by such titles as "training school," or "industrial school." Furthermore, the Court held that secrecy in proceedings which is supposed to protect the identity of the child, is more rhetoric than reality, and was interpreted by the Arizona Supreme Court as grounds for not giving more complete and specific notice of charges to the parents when ordering them to the initial hearing.

The importance of the *Gault* decision lies in its holdings on several issues. The right to confrontation with the right to cross-examine witnesses, the right against self-incrimination, and the right to appellate review were all denied Gerald Gault and his parents. The Supreme Court ruled in all the issues, that when an accused juvenile is in danger of having his freedom deprived by the court, then he is entitled to all the constitutional guarantees of the Fifth and Fourteenth Amendments. Further, the right to counsel is central to the other holdings. Relying on *Haley v. Ohio* and *Kent,* the Court ruled that a child cannot make incriminating statements against himself without being warned that he did not have to so testify. This constitutional right is extended to hardened criminals, but not to children. Justice Fortas found that the most serious breaches of the Constitution are found in the Juvenile Courts.

In summary, the *Gault* findings guarantee juveniles a specific written petition, reasonable time of notification, and where loss of liberty is possible, both child and parent must be notified of right to counsel, and to court-appointed counsel if they cannot afford one. The Court also held that the constitutional privilege against self-incrimination applies in juvenile court proceedings, and that confrontation of, and sworn testimony from witnesses and accusers were prerequisite to the finding of delinquency.

The opinion was not unanimous, and the Justices' opinions are as follows: Justice Black concurred, agreeing that the rights of the Fifth and Sixth Amendments are denied juveniles. He would not restrict the Fourteenth Amendment only to those constitutional rights deemed "necessary and imperative" to comport with the Court's notion of fundamental fairness. Justice White concurred, except to note that "compulsion" is essential to violation of the Fifth Amendment by a witness against himself, and this he could not find in the *Gault* case, and warned the Court against unsound applications of the Fifth Amendment, as in *Miranda v. Arizona.* Justice Harlan dissented in part, by saying that it was not the constitutionality of the Juvenile Court that was in question, but the *method* by which procedural requirements of due process should be measured. He preferred to require fundamental fairness rather than rigid restriction, and feared that the Court ruling might inhibit further study into the needs of the juvenile court.

Justice Stewart provided the longest dissent, and the one which most supported the original *parens patriae* concept of the juvenile process and emphasized that this procedure is *not* a criminal adversary trial, and that it is unsound policy to try to make the juvenile court into one.

Use of counsel after *Gault*

In the relatively short period of time since the *Task Force Report on Juvenile Delinquency* was published and the *Gault* decision was reported, both in 1967, comment by professional personnel on the use of counsel in the juvenile court has been extensive. Speculation on the changes which *Gault* would bring, and also actual surveys of what the decision has meant, are still in the making.

The *Task Force Report* was extremely critical of prior practices of the court, particularly when due process was denied. Now it was recognized that introduction of counsel to the adjudicative stage was most likely to be achieved.

Robert D. Vinter says that counsel is crucial at the intake and dispositional procedures, because in all cases the fact-finding is done at these levels, and because of the frequency of pre-judicial determinations of juvenile cases. This is especially true with respect to the consent decree, which is a form of plea bargaining in the juvenile court, and waives the juvenile's right to appear before the judge, if he will plead guilty to some form of the charge, and accept probation.

The state of California recognized the right to counsel by law in 1961, and after six years, the increase had been only from 3% of all cases to 15% in the increased use of counsel. Even in those cases, the attitudes of the judges and probations personnel about advising the juvenile of his rights governed its use. The existence of a public defender was found to affect the use of counsel favorably, and the findings of Vinter on this subject revealed that the attorneys benefit their clients somewhat. Largely, they are effective in reducing the severity of the dispositions, not in disproving the allegations of the petitions. He says that attorneys successfully challenged the precision of allegations, causing them to be reduced in number and seriousness, and they also proposed alternatives to commitment, often swaying an uncertain judge. They protected the parents by persuading them to accept probation instead of more severe treatment by the court, and often convinced probation officers to make modified recommendations.[17] All this presupposes attorneys familiar with the specific routine and procedure of the juvenile court, which has been inaccessible to many and, therefore, will take some time to accomplish.

The adversary function of the attorney, according to Vinter, may be marginal, but he may become a negotiator and interpreter of court decisions to child and parent, and psychological support to a client who will find in the juvenile court, a greater social distance between himself and the probation officer.

Another commentator, Anthony Platt, has studied attorneys in juvenile court in Chicago, and he argues that because of a variety of occupational hazards, the lawyer is at an enormous disadvantage in dealing with juveniles. For example, juvenile clients usually bring modest fees; accessibility to court personnel or priority over defendants without lawyers is usually denied; the lawyer may have a conflict of interest between a client and his parents, who have retained counsel; trial is usually not sought; and lastly, vagueness of delinquency laws, unpredictability of juveniles as witnesses and the difficulty of refuting the word of the adult officers of the court make victory a minor possibility. Platt also asserts that advocacy and formal procedures will play only a minor role in the juvenile court, and that to date, the small-fee type lawyers who have been affiliated with it have not enhanced the bargaining power of their young clients. They have, in fact, been co-opted by the system, fearful of freeing future criminals, and generally helping to confirm the dependent status of their youthful clients.[18]

Abraham Blumberg, a veteran lawyer and commentator on criminal justice, states that the same administrative bureaucratic and clinical methods are prevalent in the criminal courts, as in juvenile courts, and that traditional areas of due process are being virtually ignored. He points out that the Supreme Court, in many of the decisions cited here, is operating on the ideological assumption of a criminal case as an adversary proceeding, with the counsel for the defense "assiduously mustering his admittedly limited resources to defend the accused." [19] He finds a movement toward plea bargain justice in the criminal courts, and the slight trend toward more formalism in the juvenile court, but with a strong dose of the traditional sociological and therapeutic practices still present.

These contrasting views indicate some of the problems faced by children in the courts. It is of importance to consider what the young person who is the center of the turmoil thinks of the process. There is evidence to show that juveniles are very sensitive to court proceedings and are disconcerted by informal proceedings. The impact is precisely the opposite of that intended, and is a further obstacle to treatment. The all-powerful judge, the authority of the officers of the court, the lack of firm standards and the lack of role definition, are perceived by juveniles not as just, but as whimsical, personal and hypocritical.[20]

The precise role of the lawyer in juvenile court is yet to be determined because of many factors. Some juvenile courts have not had money to spend for the appointment of counsel for the indigent, and even the use of the public defender for that purpose has been curtailed in many places for this reason. The administrative and economic effectiveness of the juvenile court system was noted in this comment, "While advocates of *'parens patriae'* do not expressly offer administrative convenience as a justification for depriving juveniles of due process, it would be naive to fail to recognize that this is one of the realities which the court must consider." [21]

Longer proceedings, the higher costs of providing free counsel to the poor, and the risk of some guilty youths escaping adjudication are present, but for children are considered normal. Decisions like *Gault* and *Kent* have "infused procedural regularity into juvenile proceedings, and are in effect, recognitions of reality." [22]

Memphis-Shelby County juvenile court

In a recent survey of 41 major cities conducted by the Memphis and Shelby County Youth Guidance Commission, it was found that Memphis had the lowest percentage of juvenile officers in a specialized Juvenile Bureau of all the 38 cities which have such divisions. It had four officers, and one secretary, representing 4% of the officers of the Police Department, but was disbanded in 1973, under a reorganization within the Department.

Of 9085 juvenile complaints filed in the 1972 calendar year, 7542 were detained and 369 children were committed to correctional institutions. In all, 1151 children are under commitment to the Department of Correction, either institutionalized or in community placements.

Of the children who were seen by the court, 7737 were "unruly and delinquent." According to the Tennessee Code Annotated [23], these terms are defined as:

Those under 18 years of age means a child . . . "Delinquent act" means an act designated as a crime under the law, including local ordinances of this state, or of another state if the act occurred in that state, or under federal law . . . and the crime is not a traffic offense as defined in the traffic code of the state other than drunken driving and negligent homicide.

"Delinquent youth" means a youth who has committed a delinquent act and is in need of treatment and rehabilitation.

"Unruly youth" means a youth who has committed an offense applicable only to a youth and is not mentally retarded or otherwise mentally incapacitated or in need of treatment or rehabilitation.

The category of neglected and dependent children is the third area of jurisdiction of the Juvenile Court and accounts for about 15 percent of the case load. These cases are handled in different procedural manner from those mentioned above.

The offenses most often committed by children are burglary, automobile theft and larceny, according to the Memphis and Shelby County Juvenile Court Annual Report of 1972.[24] These are offenses which are also applicable to adults. The status offenses, or those only attributable to children, include runaways, truants and those who are of "ungovernable behavior," which this year accounted for 1309 offenders. This category is the fastest-growing and of most concern to the Court, according to officials, and accounts for one-third of the cases. (2888 status offenses reported, as compared to 5746 delinquent offenses.)[25] This indicates an almost 15 percent increase in the past five years, although the Court statistics show an overall increase of juvenile complaints of only 2 percent.

The types of cases which come before the judge of the juvenile court for adjudication cover all of those mentioned, and also include all cases of adoption, legitimation, permission to marry, work or enlist in the armed services, if under-age, and all cases which commit children to the Tennessee Department of Correction.[26] Other areas of jurisdiction cover parental neglect and failure to support wives and children.

The Tennessee Code section of Juveniles was revised in 1970 and 1971 and now is considered to be one of the model laws in the nation. The section of the Code on the use of Counsel is explicit in its language:[27]

In delinquency hearings a party is entitled to representation by legal counsel at all stages of any proceedings under this chapter and if . . . he is unable to employ counsel, to have the court provide counsel for him. If a party appears without counsel, the court shall ascertain whether he knows of his right thereto and his right to be provided with counsel by the court if he is a needy person.

All of the provisions of the *Gault* decision are now written into the Tennessee Code, under Section 37–227, on basic rights, confessions and sufficiency of proof.

In light of these facts about the laws of the Juvenile Court in Tennessee, the views from the bench are significant.

A handbook prepared by Memphis Juvenile Court Judge Kenneth

A. Turner as a guide to the judges with juvenile court duties in the state of Tennessee includes the contemporary philosophy of the National Council of Juvenile Court Judges, as of June 1967.

In this guidebook, Judge Turner mentions the right to counsel: "As soon as possible prior to a court hearing, the family and child should be informed of their right to counsel. If legal counsel is waived, such waiver should be in writing and made a part of the legal record of the case . . . In the absence of a public defender, there are no funds authorized for the payment of counsel appointed to represent indigents in such cases . . . An attorney in the juvenile court should at all times be guided by what is best for the welfare of the juvenile. In delinquency proceedings, attorneys who advise guilty children to remain silent and demand that the child's guilt be proven 'beyond a reasonable doubt and to a moral certainty' may be doing their clients a disservice. The opposite may be true, of course, in the case of a juvenile subject to trial in the criminal court upon a waiver from the juvenile court." [28]

When questioned about the effect of the *Gault* decision on the Memphis Juvenile Court, Judge Turner said there had been little effect, because 95 percent of the cases waived their rights to counsel. When asked why this was true, the judge replied, "They have confidence in the Court." Judge Turner noted that the *Gault* decision was, in his opinion, a most highly over-rated decision of the Supreme Court. He illustrated his opinion by quoting the entire dissent of Justice Stewart in his handbook, and stating, "Justice Fortas delivered the opinion of the Court, which was rather lengthy, and dealt with issues not raised in the case at hand."

Judge Turner also expressed doubt of the validity of the *Miranda* decision. He feels that children in the court are sufficiently warned of their rights at all times, and that their due process rights are always protected by the public defender, who is present in court at all delinquency hearings.

Judge Turner believes that introducing a prosecutor would be unwise, and the informality of the Court would be destroyed. His major concern is with more alternatives in disposition of cases, and in the channeling of cases out of Court. An example would be that of truancy, which should be rightfully handled by the school system, in the Judge's opinion. In this past year, the Court has successfully handled nearly two-thirds of its unruly and delinquent cases in a non-judicial manner, referring them out of court, and into community agencies for assistance.[29]

Judge Kenneth Turner, in the foreword to the Annual Report of the Memphis and Shelby County Juvenile Court of 1972, notes with optimism that a decrease of as much as 25 percent in placement in Tennessee Department of Corrections institutions has occurred in the past five years. He attributes this to an increase in the use of foster care and states, "This Court is of the opinion that no child who can live in and be part of the community life, who will not be a menace to the community or likely to be harmed himself, whether the child is classified as dependent and neglected, unruly or delinquent, should ever be placed in an institution, even the best institution." But he goes on to add, that there is a need for group homes, cottage-type dwellings where children with family problems and other needs can be attended in a close-knit setting.[30]

Recommendations for research and action

Recently, in 1973, the National Advisory Committee on Criminal Justice Standards and Goals, suggested that only those youths who have committed acts that would be criminal if committed by adults should be subject to the delinquency jurisdiction of the courts. The White House Conference on Children and Youth of 1970 recommended that such offenses should not be processed through the court system but should be diverted to other community resources. These important suggestions are not new. Even in 1967, the year of *Gault*, the President's Commission on Law Enforcement stated: "Serious consideration should be given to complete elimination from the court's jurisdiction of conduct illegal only for a child . . . we must bluntly ask what our present power achieves and must acknowledge in answer that, at the most, we really do not know, and in at least some cases we suspect it may do as much harm as good."

One of the most controversial areas of decriminalizing "children's crimes" includes removal from the statutes all offenses relating only to children, such as playing ball in the streets, pinball, loitering and a raft of minor offenses added to state law. This also includes "incorrigibility," a vague term which permits parents to petition the court to supervise their children, instead of seeking aid in repairing damaged family relations. This further serves to alienate the child, and essentially allows the parent the right to vent his hostility and expose his own inadequacy at the level of the court.

Delinquents to age 18 should have the full attention of the court and distinction between those offenders and children who are in need of supervision, another term for status offenders, should be clearly maintained until such time as the latter are no longer in the jurisdiction of the correctional system.

The provision of counsel at present for these children who are in need of supervision is especially important. Children and parents often have conflicts of interests before the court and it is of utmost importance that every child faced with coercive action, or the increase of restraints, be provided with counsel, without having to ask for such representation.

At this point in the continuum of court and community life, it becomes necessary to seek adequate services and programs to permit diversion of children from the juvenile justice system.

Extensive research is now being undertaken by a variety of national organizations to provide appropriate answers to this problem.

As the anniversary of the Court appears, so too will studies from the American Bar Association's Institute of Judicial Administration. Entitled *Juvenile Justice Standards Project*, its goal is to improve society's treatment of children in trouble.

A national assessment of juvenile corrections is being conducted by the University of Michigan, through the Law Enforcement Administration Agency. On the local level, a Comprehensive Plan for the establishment of a Youth Services System was conducted in the MATCOG area from 1970 to 1972, and has resulted in a Federal grant to establish such a service whose major purpose is to divert youth away from the juvenile justice system, and into community-based preventive and rehabilitative programs. Its ultimate goal is to "modify methods of existing agencies and institutions on those ways which will provide and assist all young people in assuming socially acceptable, responsible and personally gratifying roles." [31] This will inevitably reduce the number of youths classified as delinquents. The revelation by Judge Turner that only approximately 25 percent of those children in state institutions really need secure and isolated treatment points out the essential need for more and better treatment and rehabilitation of minor offenders.

Much research so far reveals that building larger institutions or detention centers is, or should be, a thing of the past. What is needed is to try different dispositions for children within the community.

While reformation in administration of criminal justice on the adult level has merited increased community attention, protecting the rights of children in court, protecting them from severity of punishment, and providing resources to aid troubled children and their families are mandates to which the community must give its attention in the future.

Notes

1 Charles W. Tenney, *The Utopian World of the Juvenile Court*, Annals of the American Academy of Political and Social Science. May, 1969, pp. 102–118. A legal history of the Juvenile Court System.

2 Anthony M. Platt, *The Child Savers/the Invention of Delinquency*, University of Chicago Press, Chicago and London, 1969. A Study of the movement surrounding the founding of the Juvenile Court.

3 Julian W. Mack, 23 Harvard Law Review 104, 119–20 (1909). Quoted in *Juvenile Delinquency and Youth Crimes*. Task Force Report of the President's Commission on Law Enforcement and Administration of Justice. Washington, D.C., 1967 (Hereinafter referred to as *Task Force Report*).

4 *Task Force Report.*

5 Commonwealth v. Fisher, 213 Pa. 48 (1905).

6 People v. Lewis, 289 U.S. 209 (1933) cert. denied.

7 Paul W. Tappan, *Delinquent Girls in Court, A Study of the Minor Court of New York.* Patterson Smith Reprint Series in Criminology, Law Enforcement and Social Problems, Publication No. 67. Montclair, New Jersey, 1969. (Originally pub. 1949) p. 160.

8 332 U.S. 596 (1948).

9 367 U.S. 643 (1961).

10 372 U.S. 335 (1963).

11 384 U.S. 436 (1966).

12 383 U.S. 541 (1966).

13 383 U.S. at 553.

14 383 U.S. at 543.

15 387 U.S. 1–81 (1967).

16 at 13–14.

17 Robert D. Vinter, "The Juvenile Court as an Institution," *Task Force Report*, pp. 102–103.

18 Anthony Platt and Ruth Friedman, "The Limits of Advocacy," *University of Pennsylvania Law Review*, Vol. 116–1156 (1968).

19 Abraham Blumberg, "The Practice of Law as a Confidence Game; Organizational Cooptation of a Profession", in *Criminal Justice*, edited by George F. Cole, Duxbury Press, North Scituate, Mass., and Belmont, Cal., 1972, pp. 214–215. See also Blumberg's *Crime and Justice* for a discussion of the due process vs. administrative efficiency idea in courts.

20   See *Comment*, "Procedural Rights in the Juvenile Court," *Northwestern Law Review*, 64: at 87 and 100. Also, *Task Force Report*, p. 31. Also testimony before U.S. Senate Sub-committee on Juvenile Delinquency, May 3–18, 1971, pp. 433–36, by Dr. Esther Rothman and Morton P. Cohen, Attorney.

21   Monrad Paulsen, "The Legacy of '67", *The Juvenile Offender and the Law: A Symposium*, Leonard W. Levy, ed., Da Capo Press, New York, 1971 (unabridged publication of 43 Indiana Law Journal, 1968), p. 17.

22   Thomas F. Schornhurst, "The Waiver of Kent, Revisited," *Symposium*, p. 64.

23   Vol. 6, Sec. 37–202.

24   An updated report will be issued by the court in the Spring, 1974.

25   Annual Report of the Juvenile Court of Memphis and Shelby County, 1972, pp. 13, 15, 18.

26   T.C.A. 37–231.

27   37–226, Right to Counsel.

28   Kenneth A. Turner, *Juvenile Justice, A Handbook*. The Michie Co., Law Publishers, Charlottesville, Va., 1969. pp. 3–4.

29   Private interview with Judge Turner, at Juvenile Court, November 1, 1972.

30   Annual Report of Juvenile Court, pp. 2–3.

31   See *Comprehensive Plan* of Youth Guidance Commission, statement of purpose.

Charles W. Tenney, Jr.

The utopian world of juvenile courts

Abstract: Born in a period of great social reform, the juvenile courts of the United States promised a new deal for children caught up in the processes of criminal justice. For nearly fifty years, the courts were permitted to grow, and to develop, virtually without interruption, practices and facilities to

Reprinted from the *Annals of the American Academy of Political and Social Science*, May 1969, pp. 101–118, with the kind permission of the Academy and Charles W. Tenney, Jr.

comport with the philosophy of the court as a "social agency," designed not to punish but to help children in trouble. Examinations of the actual nature of the court and its procedures have, however, revealed that as a "social agency" the court remains largely an idea and an ideal. Its traditionally informal procedures, designed to reflect its noncriminal nature, have been criticized in recent Supreme Court cases. The resulting return to a more legalized approach may signal, therefore, a retrenchment in the work of the juvenile courts.

Martin Duberman, in a recent *Atlantic Monthly* article dealing with student rebels, suggested that American adults really do not like their children. "The young, it is becoming clear," he wrote, "are regarded with considerable hatred in our country." According to Duberman, it is not so much what young people do or do not do that causes their elders' hostility; it is "the very fact of their youth that makes them the target for so much murderous abuse." [1] This view contrasts sharply with the generally stated love and deference for youth displayed in American society.

Duberman's view is an interesting one and one against which we may measure our concern for youth, a concern which is not novel and which has, throughout history, manifested itself in a variety of contexts. One such context, and an important one, is that of the law, and in particular the law's treatment of young people in trouble, the subject of our discussion here. Our legal institution generically referred to as the "juvenile court" is the vehicle through which our concern for young people in trouble is reflected and practiced. Throughout this discussion of juvenile law and the juvenile courts, the reader is asked to contemplate the nature of the law's concern for our youth, whether it is indeed a display of our love or of our hatred for them, or, perhaps, an ambivalent admixture of both.

Early developments in juvenile law

The roots of our laws, particularly those applicable to children and young people, run deep in English legal history. One such root is the criminal law. Blackstone reports that children under the age of ten-and-a-half were not punishable for any crime; between ten-and-a-half and fourteen years, they were punishable if found to be "capable of mischief"; and beyond the age of fourteen, the child was subject to criminal conviction and punishment as an adult.[2] In the United States, the generally accepted common-law rules for criminal prosecution of juveniles rendered them exempt if below the age of seven, presumptively exempt (because of the child's presumed incapability of forming a *mens rea,* or intent to commit a crime) if between seven and fourteen years; and presumptively capable of forming a criminal intent beyond the age of fourteen.[3] Despite these ameliorations, young children were often convicted and sometimes executed. Blackstone reported the execution, for example, of a boy of ten found to be of a "mischievous discretion" in murdering his bedfellow.[4] Herbert Lou, an early historian and apologist of the juvenile courts, reported a case in New Jersey as late as 1828 of a boy of thirteen hanged for an offense committed when he was twelve.[5]

It seems indisputable that the common-law criminal rules of responsibility were one of the foundation stones of the juvenile courts. More debatable is the court's linkages to the precedent of the chancery (equity) courts. Partially in response to the need for some relief from the strictures of a rigid common-law system of pleading and available relief, these courts developed in England in the thirteenth and fourteenth centuries. Through them, the crown exercised jurisdiction over the estates of minors on the assumption that children were wards of the state. In time, this jurisdiction was enlarged to include matters affecting the welfare of young persons more broadly. But while much is often made of the chancery "origins" of the juvenile court, its chief contribution to the modern institution appears to lie in its philosophy of protection of young persons as "wards of the state." [6]

Throughout the nineteenth century in the United States, a variety of techniques were developed for softening the effects of criminal conviction on young persons.[7] Legislation enacted in the 1800's provided for the separation of juveniles from adult offenders, first in the penal institutions following conviction, then later in the pretrial and trial phases of the criminal process. As early as 1825, a House of Refuge was opened in New York City, privately maintained, but supported in part with public funds. The first state-supported separate institution for housing juvenile convicts was opened in Massachusetts in 1847. Michigan in 1873 created a state agency to care for juvenile offenders, and New York in 1884 gave the courts discretion to place, with any institution or person suitable and willing to receive him, a juvenile who had been convicted of crime.

Through the good offices of John Augustus, a Boston boot-maker and philanthropist, probation (release on stated conditions following conviction) as an alternative to confinement was developed as early as 1841, first for adult convicts, later for juveniles.

Probation as a sentencing alternative was formalized in Massachusetts in 1878 for Suffolk County and was extended statewide two years later. Earlier, in 1869, the Massachusetts General Court had provided for the appointment of a "juvenile protection agent" to be attached to the State Board of Charities.

Paralleling the states' developing concern for the care and housing of the juvenile offender following conviction was an increasing sensitivity to the adverse effects which the young person might suffer through contacts with the older, more seasoned law-violator during pretrial detention and at the trial itself. Recognizing the potential for harm in such commingling of children and adults, the city of Chicago in 1861 authorized its mayor to appoint a commissioner to conduct hearings on minor charges against boys between the ages of six and seventeen. Nine years later, Massachusetts enacted a law which required separate trials for juveniles in the courts of Suffolk County; in 1872 this requirement was extended to all of the minor courts of the Commonwealth. New York in 1892 and Rhode Island in 1898 provided for the segregation of children under sixteen years of age, before and during trial.

This thumbnail summary of developments in the treatment of children under the law prior to 1900 indicates that, long prior to the advent of the juvenile court, there had developed an awareness of the inequities of a system of retributive criminal justice. It also illustrates the isolated and sporadic development of improved conditions, confined to the more populous, more urbanized states. There seems little doubt, however, that, in time, a specialized system of judicial treatment of children would have spread gradually throughout the nation. But there are periods when (as we are well aware today) a nation's social conscience outruns its institutions. At such times, new institutions must be created and new strategies developed if debilitating frustration and despair are to be avoided. As the United States approached the end of the nineteenth century, the need for a better method of treatment for children, dimly perceived and erratically met in an earlier day, became manifest.

The synthesis of social justice

Progress in the care and treatment of young persons in the criminal courts and institutions of the country was not, of course, the sole manifestation of a developing social conscience in nineteenth-century America. Particularly in the latter half of the century, conditions generated by the Industrial Revolution and the resulting trend to urbanism grew, as the 1900's came to a close, to intolerable proportions. Particularly in the rapidly growing cities of America, a system which produced great wealth, for some, produced onerous working conditions, poverty, vice, and crime as well. A system which had first helped to build a nation and had aided in holding it together had been accompanied by "monstrous perversions in the employment of women and children." [8] To contest and correct these conditions became the task of a long list of politicians, academics, muckraking journalists, and social reformers. Lincoln Steffens, Jacob Riis, Edward Bellamy, and Jane Addams were particularly notable in calling attention to the oppressive conditions of children under the law. For notwithstanding the developments noted above, children at the close of the nineteenth century were still prosecuted criminally for their misdeeds. What this implied (and still does imply) was the imposition of punishment for one's criminal guilt, a philosophy of retribution whose only amelioration was in the rise of the reformatory and penitentiary systems through which the convict might contemplate his social sins and thereby expiate them. Even where progressive legislation did exist, a child might be jailed separately prior to trial, but he was still *jailed;* he might be tried separately from the adult, but he was nevertheless *tried;* and if convicted he might be sent to a separate juvenile institution, but he was sent to be punished for his crimes. What remained lacking in both theory and practice in 1899 was a completely noncriminal system of treatment of the juvenile in the courts and correctional institutions. It was to cure this lack that the first juvenile-court act was enacted in Illinois in 1899.[9] Its passage represented the culmination of almost a decade of efforts by a number of civic-minded organizations in the state, including the Chicago Bar Association, the Chicago Women's Club, and the Illinois Children's Home and Aid Society. The creation of the juvenile court has often been called the greatest single event in Anglo-American jurisprudence since Magna Charta.[10] Considering the fact that this takes in a period of about seven hundred years and includes other events of undebatable importance such as the development of courts of chancery and the adoption of both the English and American Bills of Rights, the case may have been somewhat overstated. Certainly, however, it was an event of major significance not only for children but for the whole legal system as well. For this reason, the original Illinois act merits some further examination.

The act created no new courts. For counties of over 500,000

population, the judges of the circuit court were to designate one of their number to serve as the juvenile-court judge; elsewhere, the county-court judge was given this additional responsibility.

Another important feature of the law was the synthesis of jurisdictions in the juvenile court, not only over the "delinquent child" but also over "dependent" and "neglected" children. The delinquent child was defined simply as "any child under the age of sixteen years who violates any law of this state or any city or village ordinance." The neglected or dependent child, on the other hand, included all those who were destitute, homeless, abandoned, lacking in "proper" parental care, habitual beggars, or living in "unfit" homes.

A third, and perhaps most important, aspect of the Illinois statute was, however, its virtual elimination of all features of the criminal trial, including arrest and indictment, and the substitution, instead, of informal procedures for custody and hearing. The standard to be applied in formulating a disposition was that it should "approximate as nearly as may be that which should be given by its parents." Broad use was to be made of probation officers (for whom public compensation was prohibited, however) in investigating cases before hearing, as well as in placing and supervising a child following hearing. Children could be sentenced only to institutions created for their care, or to an adult institution, provided they were there completely segregated from adult inmates.

In short, the Illinois Act of 1899 wove into an integrated procedure provision for separate detention and hearing for juveniles, probation supervision, and disposition within a (theoretically, at least) broad range of alternatives—all to the end that the child be treated, not as a criminal to be punished, but as a "delinquent" to be guided and corrected.

Seldom in legal history has aspiration so quickly led to inspiration and the law put to such noble purpose. Novelty alone has its allure. Novelty allied with nobility may create a movement. It is not, therefore, surprising to note the speed with which the juvenile-court movement spread across the land.

The era of good feeling: 1900–1950

Within five years following the passage of the Illinois act, ten states had established some form of juvenile court. By the end of the first decade, another ten states and the District of Columbia had enacted juvenile-court legislation, and by 1925, all but two states, Maine and Wyoming, had joined the ranks. In 1945 Wyoming at last capitulated, and the roster was complete.

In 1907, Illinois expanded its original definition of "delinquent child," to include not only one who violated any state law or local ordinance, but also one who was "incorrigible," or who left home without consent, or who "knowingly frequented" any number of unsavory establishments such as a house of ill-repute, a "policy shop," "bucket shop," "public poolroom," and the like. A child might also be found delinquent if he was "growing up in idleness or crime"; or if he used "vile, obscene, vulgar, profane or indecent language in any public place or about any schoolhouse"; or if he was guilty of "indecent or lascivious conduct." [11]

These amendments reflected a shift in the orientation of the juvenile court, from one in which the procedures of the law were recast while leaving the substance intact, to a court with considerably broadened substantive jurisdiction as well.

Under the original act, the jurisdiction of the juvenile court over an alleged delinquent child was identical to that of the criminal courts over the adult accused. Under the 1907 amendments, however, not only was a child considered delinquent if he trespassed the criminal norms; he could also be adjudged delinquent for violating what, for adults, might only be the social norms or mores. Under the original act, the judge was adjured to treat the offending child as a "wise parent" would—with kindness, sympathy, and understanding. But the wise parent does not stand idly by and permit his children to mature without guidance and control. It seemed no more than logical, therefore, that the juvenile court should assume such positive control and guidance of the children of society. What this implied was the remolding of the court into a kind of social agency, with positive therapeutic responsibilities well beyond simply the gentle treatment of youthful violators of the criminal law. This expanded concept of delinquency was an important one. Not only was it the model for the legislation which followed in other states; it was also, with its implied therapeutic approach and ambiguous definitions, the cause of most of the criticism and reaction which eventually arose concerning the juvenile court.

Criticism of the juvenile court in its formative years was, however, no more than sporadic; sustained attack lay in the distant future. The first half-century of the court's development was applauded as a noble advancement in "social justice" and was attended by the development of both supporting facilities for the courts and agencies and organizations designed to encourage their creation where they did not yet exist—and to strengthen and improve them where they did exist.

Detention homes, designed to take children out of the local jails, were established in a number of states, either as separate agencies or within the framework of the juvenile court itself. Probation departments, again, either separately or as a part of the court, were established and expanded. Diagnostic facilities employing psychologists and psychiatrists were inaugurated. Correctional facilities were built to house juvenile offenders.

It was also during this first half-century that several organizations and agencies came into being. The Children's Bureau of the Department of Labor (located today in the Department of Health, Education, and Welfare) was established in 1912 to draw attention at the national level to the needs of children. It continues today, one of the few agencies in the nation which conducts sustained research and publicity on matters affecting juveniles. In 1922 the Bureau issued its first set of standards for juvenile courts, a document which has been revised twice since that time,[12] and which has served as an important model for juvenile-court legislation.

The Children's Bureau developed as a result of recommendations of the first of the White House Conferences on Children and Youth. These conferences, held decennially, have themselves provided an important forum for the exchange of opinion on all matters affecting children, and have stimulated the creation of state conferences to foster interest and initiate programs at the local level.

In 1907 the National Probation and Parole Association (now the National Council on Crime and Delinquency) was organized as both a membership and a national service agency. Noteworthy among its contributions to the development of the juvenile courts have been its *Standard Juvenile Court Act*, first published in 1925 and revised periodically since that time; *Guides for Juvenile Court Judges*, issued in 1957 and prepared by the organization's Advisory Council of Judges; and *Procedure and Evidence in the Juvenile Court*, published in 1962 and also prepared by the Advisory Council of Judges.

The National Council of Juvenile Court Judges, an organization whose membership consists exclusively of juvenile- and family-court judges throughout the United States, was established in 1937. In recent years it has undertaken a nationwide training program for juvenile-court judges and has initiated research projects on previously little studied matters such as communication in the court, and the role of the lawyer as advocate for the child.

By the 1950's the development of the juvenile court as a recognized legal institution was complete. Legislation had been enacted in every state and in many foreign countries as well, commencing with Great Britain in 1908. State statutes characteristically included a broad Illinois-type definition of delinquency; wide discretion for the judge in formulating a disposition; jurisdiction over dependent and neglected children, and over some adult offenses against children, for example, "contributing" to their delinquency; and provision in the law for supporting facilities for detention, investigation, diagnosis, and probation. To match the nonpunitive, rehabilitative philosophy of the court, a whole new vocabulary was developed: trials became "hearings"; sentences, "dispositions"; punishment, "treatment"; and reformatories, "training schools." Hearings were denominated as "informal" and "nonadversary," and the guiding principle for the court, both in its findings and in its dispositions, was "the best interests of the child." No better nor more lyric summary of the high hopes and aspirations of the Chicago reformers and those who followed them can be found than that of Herbert Lou, writing in 1927:

In place of judicial tribunals, restrained by antiquated procedure, saturated in an atmosphere of hostility, trying cases for determining guilt and inflicting punishment according to inflexible rules of law, we have now juvenile courts, in which the relations of the child to his parents or other adults and to the state or society are defined and adjusted summarily according to the scientific findings about the child and his environments. In place of magistrates, limited by the outgrown custom and compelled to walk in the paths fixed by the law of the realm, we have now socially-minded judges, who hear and adjust cases according not to rigid rules of law but to what the interests of society and the interests of the child or good conscience demand. In place of juries, prosecutors, and lawyers, learned in the old conception of law and staging dramatically, but often amusingly, legal battles, as the necessary paraphernalia of a criminal court, we have now probation officers, physicians, psychologists, and psychiatrists, who search for the social, physiological, psychological, and mental backgrounds of the child in order to arrive at reasonable and just solutions of individual cases. In other words, in this new court we tear down primitive prejudice, hatred, and hostility toward the lawbreaker in that most hide-bound of all human institutions, the court of law, and we attempt, as far as possible, to administer justice in the name of truth, love, and understanding.[13]

What delinquent child ever existed who would not benefit from this fairyland of benevolence? What parent ever existed who would not rest secure in the knowledge that here, in this court of hope, his children, if they ever erred, and all erring children would be treated wisely and with love, as he in his wisdom and love would treat them had he the time and tools. And yet—and yet—was it really possible to alter so dramatically "that most hide-bound of all human institutions?" Was it possible, after all, after centuries of painfully slow progress in the law and the courts, that a new and better path of justice had been blazed, paved with "love and understanding?" Surely, there must be more to change than its announcement. Surely, shadows must exist between the ideal and the reality.[14]

Reaction and reform: 1950–1968

Almost from the time of their inception, there were indications that matters were not always as well as they were said to be in the juvenile courts of America. As early as 1920, Evelina Belden, in a survey of the courts, conducted under the auspices of the then recently created Children's Bureau, reported that there was indeed a shadow falling between the ideal and the reality, "between the emotion and the response." Her study included the more than two thousand courts for hearing children's cases which existed at that time. For evaluating them, she used as criteria three commonly accepted features of a juvenile court: separate hearings, probation services, and the recording of social information. While most of the courts in the larger cities were able to meet these minimum standards, the study revealed that, over-all, only 16 percent of the juvenile courts in the country could measure up, and for other services and facilities, the picture was even more bleak. Less than 10 percent of the courts had services available to them for conducting mental examinations; only thirteen courts reported such facilities as part of their machinery. Many courts reported that separate hearings for juveniles were not held, that children continued to be detained in jails unsegregated from adult prisoners, and that although legislation existed to provide them, probation services were not available.[15]

Nor was critical reaction to the juvenile courts limited to their lack of services and facilities. Despite the contributions to and promotion of the original Illinois act by the Chicago Bar Association, despite the array of stellar judicial talent which graced the bench of many juvenile courts in their early years, and despite the support for the court provided by such leading legal commentators as Roscoe Pound, the principles and practices of the court were not universally acceded to by the bar. Some lawyers, "hide-bound" perhaps, insisted, for example, on applying the "duck test" to the juvenile courts.[16] They did not question what was said about the court, and certainly not its laudable aims and ambitions; they did question what *in fact* happened to children in the courts and beyond, and whether this comported, not so much with "love and understanding" as with deeply rooted concepts of fairness and justice in a democratic system of law, whether, in other words, children were being afforded the "due process of law" to which they were clearly entitled.

The question was considered, for the first time, in 1905 by the Supreme Court of Pennsylvania. Frank Fisher was adjudged a delinquent in the juvenile court in Philadelphia. On appeal, his lawyer challenged the constitutionality of the legislation establishing the court, urging in particular that Fisher was denied due process in the manner in which he was taken into custody and that he was denied his constitutional right to a jury trial for felony. The Pennsylvania Supreme Court upheld the lower court's action. The court found that due process, or lack of it, simply was not an issue, since its guaranty applied only to *criminal* cases. The state could, on the other hand, place a child within its protections without any process at all if it saw fit to do so.

To save a child from becoming a criminal, or from continuing in a career of crime, to end in maturer years in public punishment and disgrace, the Legislature surely may provide for the salvation of such a child, if its parents or guardian be unable or unwilling to do so, by bringing it into the courts of the state without any process at all, for the purpose of subjecting it to the state's guardianship and protection. The natural parent needs no process to temporarily deprive his child of its liberty by confining it in his own home, to save it and to shield it from the consequences of persistence in a career of waywardness; nor is the state, when compelled as *parens patriae,* to take the place of the father for the same purpose, required to adopt any process as a means of placing its hands upon a child to lead it into one of its courts.[17]

Similarly, the court argued, since the right to a jury trial extended to criminal cases and since a delinquency hearing was not a criminal trial, the right did not apply. A jury trial could hardly be necessary to determine whether a child deserved to be saved.

Decisions in the courts of other states where juvenile-court legislation was challenged were of a similarly supportive nature.[18] One might speculate that they were grounded in a genuinely humanitarian desire to permit the juvenile courts to achieve their goals of "salvation" unimpeded by the finely technical requirements of the Constitution. Attacks on the juvenile courts' jurisdiction and

procedures were repelled, almost without exception; the courts'
inadequacies, exemplified in Evelina Belden's report, were acknowledged as no more than the usual shortcomings which one might
expect in any novel and untried enterprise, and which faith, time,
and money surely would cure.[19] For five decades, therefore, the
juvenile courts were permitted to develop and mature, nurtured by
judicial support and large doses of faith, if not of money.

Before continuing, it is worth-while to note briefly several characteristic features of the typical juvenile-court law. We have already
noted that the phrase "juvenile court" is something of a misnomer.
Only in isolated cases were there established *separate* courts for
juveniles, mostly in the larger cities. Boston had a specialized court
for handling juvenile matters, but its jurisdiction was less than
city-wide. A few states (Connecticut, Rhode Island, and Utah) had
separate juvenile-court systems. Elsewhere throughout the country,
juvenile-court jurisdiction resided (and continues today to reside) in
a variety of courts: municipal, county, district, superior, or probate.
Some of these were multijudge courts; others were served by only
one judge.[20]

In the early years of the Cook County Juvenile Court in Chicago, a
number of outstanding jurists graced its bench. To serve in this
court was considered an honor and a high responsibility. Julian
Mack, second judge of the Cook County Juvenile Court, went on to
serve on the United States Court of Appeals. Merritt Pickney,
chosen by his colleagues as presiding judge of the circuit court in
Cook County, elected instead to serve in the juvenile court.[21] Judges
Ben Lindsey in Denver, Gustav Schramm and Paul Alexander in
Toledo, and Harvey Baker in Boston were among the other notable
men who served in the formative years of the juvenile court. They
were notable in large measure, however, because of their exceptional ability compared with most of their counterparts. They
devoted large portions of their lives to the work of the court, on and
off the bench, while the average juvenile-court judge devoted little
more to it than an hour or two each week. In the early years, the
juvenile-court judge might be honored among his peers; by mid-
century, he risked a better-than-even chance of being known as a
member of what one midwestern judge once described as "the
diaper squad."

Not only was there wide disparity in the kind of court which was
a juvenile court; there were also broad differences in their jurisdictions. The upper age of adolescents over whom the courts had
jurisdiction ranged from sixteen to twenty-one years. Moreover, not

all offenses committed by young persons were within the jurisdiction of the juvenile court,[22] and for those which were, there existed no firm assurances that the case would be heard there. For the judge was given discretion to waive his jurisdiction in the matter and to transfer the case for trial in criminal court. A similar authority is vested in the superintendents of some juvenile correctional institutions to transfer custody of a child committed to it, sometimes quite summarily, to an adult penal institution.[23]

The "image" of the juvenile courts and their judges certainly was not aided by the fact that lawyers seldom appeared there. Their absence from the juvenile courts was by no means surprising. "Official" philosophy eschewed any need for them, and, in any event, few clients could afford their services. Law schools devoted little time in their already crowded curricula to either juvenile delinquency or the juvenile courts, relegating the subject to passing mention in the courses in criminal or family law.[24] As a result, all but a handful of the bar knew next to nothing of the work of the court, a misfortune compounded by the fact that proceedings in juvenile courts were, by law, "confidential," that is, secret.

By the 1950's, however, critical sentiment concerning the operations of the nation's juvenile courts had commenced to coalesce. In 1949, Paul Tappan, a lawyer-sociologist, published a volume on juvenile delinquency,[25] in which he drew together and raised, for the first time, a number of problems inhering in the work of the court: the persistence in some courts of punitive practice in contrast to rehabilitative theory; the abandonment altogether by others of all semblance of regularized legal procedures, of "due process of law"; and the jurisdictional accretions by the court in the context of a "preventive" rationale. In Tappan's view, there had been little progress in the development of the court since its inception a half-century earlier, and he expressed strong and sometimes bitter objections to the misfortunes which the "realities" of the juvenile court not infrequently wrought on the child brought before it:

The presumption is commonly adopted that since the state has determined to protect and save its wards, it will do no injury to them through its diverse officials, so that these children need no due process protections against injury. Several exposures to court; a jail remand of days, weeks, or even months; and a long period in a correctional school with young thieves, muggers, and murderers—these can do no conceivable harm if the state's purpose be beneficent and the procedure be "chancery"! Children are adjudicated in this way every day without visible manifestations of due process. They are incarcerated. They become adult criminals, too, in thankless disregard of the state's good intentions as *parens patriae*.[26]

The publication of *Juvenile Delinquency* serves to mark a turning point, not in the work of the juvenile courts as such, but certainly in the extent of sound, informed, and sustained criticism of it. In the decades following its publication, the juvenile courts became a matter of increasing interest to commentators, particularly law-review writers; and as the volume of literature grew, juvenile delinquency and the juvenile courts began to receive greater recognition in the curricula of the law schools. Sheldon Glueck, noted for his research (in concert with his wife) on delinquency-causation, published in 1959 a collection of materials on delinquency, including a number devoted to the court.[27] In 1962, *Justice for the Child*,[28] a volume of essays on the philosophy and practice of the juvenile court, was published under the aegis of the University of Chicago's School of Social Service Administration. Particularly notable in the collection is Judge Orman Ketcham's article on "The Unfulfilled Promise of the Juvenile Court." In it, the judge developed a "compact" theory of the juvenile court: that in return for the relinquishment by the child of certain traditional legal rights, the state had undertaken to provide him with care and rehabilitation, a kind of *quid pro quo* arrangement which, as the essay's title suggests, has remained "unfulfilled."

As a result of these developments, more young lawyers graduated with an interest in and an awareness of the problems of the court. Schools of social work, traditional strongholds of the *parens patriae* doctrine of the court, and a primary source of supply of the probation officers, court administrators, and institutional workers who worked with juvenile delinquents, also began to devote more attention to the legal aspects of the court. Questions commenced to be asked, on the one hand, whether an adequate "helping" relationship with a child could be developed in the authoritarian environment of a court, and, on the other hand, whether enhancing the legal procedures in the court might not promote a feeling of "justice," and thereby improve the prognosis for rehabilitation. These and other issues continue to be debated today.

Throughout the decade of the 1950's and continuing into the next, both the state and federal courts evinced a growing concern over legal rights and due process in the juvenile courts. Often this concern was manifested in the vindication of the child's or his parents' right to have the assistance of retained counsel at a delinquency hearing. The New Hampshire Supreme Court, for example, interpreted that state's juvenile-court statute authorizing the presence at a delinquency hearing of persons "necessary in the interest of justice" as entitling the minor or his parents to have counsel present.[29] Other courts adopted similar approaches, holding that while the child might not be explicitly entitled to the assistance of a lawyer, "fundamental fairness" and the particular circumstances of the case might warrant, at least, notice of the right and permission for counsel to participate in the hearing process.

The development of a more "legalistic" attitude toward the court was not, however, without its interruptions. In 1955, for example, the Pennsylvania Supreme Court again considered a number of constitutional objections to juvenile-court procedures.[30] The court rejected the claim of privilege against self-incrimination, the objection to the use of hearsay evidence, and (most importantly) the objection to the commitment of the delinquent to an institution housing criminal convicts as well as juvenile delinquents. Responding to the first two claims, the court reiterated what it had said fifty years earlier in the *Fisher* case: "The proceedings in such a court are not in the nature of a criminal trial but constitute merely a civil inquiry or action looking to treatment, information and rehabilitation of the minor child." [31] As to the commitment to an institution also housing criminal convicts, the court pointed out that these convicts were only those young men between the ages of fifteen and twenty-one who were not known to have been previously sentenced to a state penitentiary. And nothing in the law prohibits extending to them the "benefits of reformatory treatment." The writer visited this institution in 1964. It is a prison.

Of no inconsiderable significance in catalyzing the courts in this "revisionist" approach to due process in the juvenile court were developments in the United States Supreme Court which expanded the rights of the accused in criminal cases. This expansion is highlighted by several cases decided by the Court, commencing in 1961. In *Mapp v. Ohio*,[32] the Court held that evidence illegally obtained by police could not be used in a criminal trial against its owner, a reversal of its earlier position that evidence otherwise relevant could be so used however it was obtained. In *Gideon v. Wainwright*,[33] the Court decided that an indigent accused had a fundamental right to the assistance of counsel, thus overruling its holding of twenty years earlier that a right to counsel in state prosecutions was not "a fundamental right, essential to fair trial." Most recently, the Supreme Court in *Miranda v. Arizona*[34] has held, on the question of the use of an extra-judicial confession made by an accused, that before it may be introduced into evidence, it must be demonstrated that (prior to making it) he had first been advised that he had an absolute right to remain silent, that anything he said might be used against him in court, that he had a right to consult with a lawyer and to have one present during any interrogation, and that if he could not afford a lawyer, one would be appointed for him—the so-called *Miranda* warnings.

When one views together these two developments of recent years—the crystallizing criticism of lax legal procedures in the juvenile courts and the growth of procedural rights in the criminal courts—it is not difficult to predict that they would eventually become laced together. The significance for the juvenile court of the thinking reflected in *Gideon* seems obvious: the critical importance, at every significant step in the proceedings, of expert legal counsel when one's liberty is at stake. And one's liberty may, of course, be at stake in other than criminal proceedings. Less obvious, perhaps, but similarly portentous for the juvenile courts were *Mapp* and *Miranda*. For they reflect an attitude on the part of the Supreme Court that demands fairness and regularity at every stage of the guilt-determining process. Thus, it is not sufficient that the evidence illegally seized by the police was, in and of itself, enough to convict Dollerie Mapp of the crime of possessing "pornographic" material, and it is not sufficient that the statements made to police by Ernesto Miranda in the interrogation room to which he was taken were, in fact, true. For if justice is to be meaningful in a democratic society, it can only be such through the procedures by which it is sought. "The history of liberty," wrote Justice Felix Frankfurter, "has largely been the history of observance of procedural safeguards." [35]

It requires no great effort of the imagination to perceive the parallels between the problems posed in these cases and the irregularities in juvenile-court procedures publicized by Tappan and other commentators. Where police might "sweat" out a confession from a suspect, the probation officer or juvenile-court judge could "persuade" a child to tell the whole story—to make a clean breast of it. Constitutional proprieties might prevent imposing on the states a requirement to provide counsel for indigent defendants; children in juvenile court not only had no right to a lawyer (because it is not a criminal court); neither had they any *need* for one. And whereas it made no difference how evidence might be obtained, similarly it would make no difference how regular or irregular was the procedure whereby a child might be brought before the juvenile court. And if such similarities did exist, surely the principles applied in criminal prosecutions would eventually be transported to the juvenile courts as well.

A harbinger of the application to the juvenile courts of these recently articulated constitutional principles appeared first in 1966 in *Kent v. United States.*[36] The issue which the Supreme Court faced in *Kent* was the regularity of the procedure by which a juvenile-court judge in the District of Columbia had waived his jurisdiction to the criminal court of the District without holding a hearing (although Kent's lawyer had requested one) to determine whether he should so waive. Following Kent's conviction in criminal court, the Supreme Court accepted his request to review the case, and, in an opinion written by Justice Fortas, reversed. The Court held that while the juvenile-court statute might accord the judge considerable latitude in a waiver proceeding, sufficient procedural regularity was nevertheless needed to satisfy the basic requirements of fairness and due process:

[T]here is no place in our system of law for reaching a result of such tremendous consequences without ceremony—without hearing, without effective assistance of counsel, without a statement of reasons. *It is inconceivable that a court of justice dealing with adults* . . . would proceed in this manner. It would be extraordinary if society's special concern for children, as reflected in the District of Columbia's Juvenile Court Act, permitted this procedure. We hold that it does not [emphasis added].[37]

Although the decision in *Kent* was not explicitly grounded in constitutional principle, there were, in that opinion, indications that the specific problems arising in the case itself, and in others noted in the literature, could pose constitutional issues. The Court noted, for example, that the result was required by the juvenile court statute, but *"read in the context of constitutional principles relating to due process and the assistance of counsel."* [38] Important to note also is the court's reference to procedures in a "court of justice dealing with adults" as, apparently, a standard of the minima required in a juvenile court. Such courts might be better; they certainly should be no worse.

Kent was the first case in which the Supreme Court chose to examine the procedures of the juvenile court. And it was apparent that it was not satisfied with what it saw. It was predictable, therefore, that a further and more detailed examination would not be long in forthcoming.

In 1964, Gerald Gault was committed by Arizona's Gila County Juvenile Court to the State Industrial School, following a "hearing" based on a general petition which specified no particular acts of delinquency and at which neither the complainant nor his lawyer was present. Since Arizona law provides for no appeal from juvenile-court adjudications, Gault's parents petitioned for a writ of habeas corpus, complaining that neither they nor their son had been notified of particular charges against him; that they had been denied the right to confront and cross-examine witnesses and accusers;

and that Gerald had been denied his privilege against self-incrimination and his right to appellate review of the case. The petition for the writ was denied, the Arizona Supreme Court affirmed,[39] and the United States Supreme Court reversed.[40]

Speaking again for the majority of the Court, Justice Fortas undertook to outline in his opinion the dimensions of applicability of the due process clause of the federal Constitution to juvenile-court proceedings. A delinquency petition must, he said, specify the particular charges against the minor. Reasonable time must be given the accused in which to prepare a defense, and where the proceeding may result in the child's loss of liberty, both the child and his parents must be advised of their right to a lawyer and to court-appointed counsel if they cannot afford their own. The Court also held that the constitutional privilege against self-incrimination applies in juvenile-court proceedings and that confrontation of, and sworn testimony from, witnesses and accusers were prerequisite to a finding of delinquency. The Court could, of course, decide only those issues presented to it in the case itself: specificity of charge, right of confrontation, privilege against self-incrimination, and right to counsel. But the promise made in *Kent*, that juvenile courts be at least as good procedurally as adult courts, was well on its way to fulfillment in *Gault*.

What next?

It is still too early to predict the extent of the impact of *Gault* on the work of the juvenile courts throughout the United States.[41] It goes without saying that one's rights (legal or otherwise) are only meaningful if there are advocates to protect and promote them, and advocacy in the juvenile court, despite the seminal work of the Juvenile Court Judges Lawyer Project, Legal Services Programs, and the National Legal Aid and Defender Association, remains today very much in its infancy. Without a lawyer to vindicate them, the rights secured in *Kent* and *Gault* will remain hollow indeed.

There is a more important problem, however, which remains in the wake of these cases, a problem which is, in fact, created by them. For the dilemma of the juvenile court is one which is grounded not only in its questionable "informalities"; it also arises out of the philosophy of the court as a social agency with positive therapeutic capabilities. There is no doubt that *Kent* and *Gault* represent an achievement for the court which was long overdue.

Yet, lost in the celebration of this achievement is the nagging question of whether, legal rights or no, the juvenile courts can ever achieve the goals which we have set for them, of whether the instruments of the law and the courts are ever adequate to accomplish what have been established as the goals of our juvenile courts. The process of effecting individual and social change is, at best, a difficult and exasperating one. Such difficulties are exacerbated in the juvenile courts by the limitations of the legal structure itself, of the court's personnel, and of the public financial support of it.

At the Mad Hatter's tea party, Alice asked why there were so many dishes spread over the table. The Hatter told her that it was because it was always teatime and there was no opportunity, therefore, to wash the dishes. The guests simply moved around the table. When asked what happened when they came back to the beginning, the March Hare said, "Suppose we change the subject." [42] Perhaps now it is time to change the subject. Yet, this essay on the juvenile courts should not conclude without some discussion of the appropriateness of the juvenile court as an instrument for the control of deviant juvenile behavior.

Block and Flynn in their volume on delinquency point out that, since 1900, "things have changed a great deal, but not in the juvenile courts." [43] Following the *Gault* decision, one might conclude that things have now changed a great deal, and will continue to do so in future. It is worth remembering, however, that earlier critics of the juvenile court were concerned with more than its irregular, or sometimes nonexistent, legal procedures. They were concerned also with the lack of adjunctive facilities to support the work of the court, with the paucity of trained probation and judicial staff, with the disreputable condition of many of the institutions to which juveniles were committed, both before and after adjudication, and with the punitive approach (thinly veneered with rehabilitative platitudes) of some judges.

In a 1966 survey of correction in the United States,[44] conducted by the National Council on Crime and Delinquency, it was reported that "93 per cent of the country's juvenile court jurisdictions . . . have no place of detention other than a county jail or police lockup"; that six states had less than complete juvenile-probation coverage and four states had none at all; and that the programs (where they could be called such) of juvenile-training institutions are impeded by diverse populations resulting from contrasting judicial philosophies as to who should be committed. In 1963, the National Council of Juvenile Court Judges surveyed [45] the nation's juvenile-court judges and found that almost one-fifth of them had no college education, and that 25 percent were without any *legal* education. One-third of the judges surveyed reported that they had no probation officers or social workers attached to their court. In an informal analysis of commitments to juvenile institutions in 1963, as reported in the statistical summary of the Children's Bureau,[46] this writer found a high positive correlation between the seriousness of the act of delinquency and the probabilities of commitment to an institution. Offenses against the person caused the greatest likelihood of commitment (over 30 percent) followed by property offenses (15–25 percent), and, finally, minor acts of delinquency (5–20 percent).

These problems remain untouched by the decisions of the Supreme Court or of any other court, and they raise serious questions as to whether, despite the "legalization" of their procedures, the juvenile courts can ever accomplish the tasks set for them. Certainly, it seems fair to say that they have not done so thus far, and the prognosis is poor, for at least two reasons. First is that our commitment to helping children in trouble is erratic, isolated, marginal, and ambivalent. The very fact that communities may, from time to time, mount "all-out attacks" on juvenile delinquency, or campaigns to improve juvenile courts, is fair evidence of the fact that the public interest in these problems is somewhat less than an abiding one. Moreover, such campaigns are usually aimed at only one or a few points on the spectrum of problems. We try to improve the juvenile court's detention facilities, for example, but devote little thought to who should be detained there. We enact legislation broadening the jurisdiction of the juvenile court, but fail to provide funds for the necessary personnel and facilities to handle the increase in cases. It has been suggested, on the one hand, that the public's attitude toward delinquency is predominantly negative and retaliatory, and, on the other hand, that the public is titillated by tales of juvenile sex orgies, LSD "trips," and the like.[47] In either case, the public does not seem especially interested in solving or controlling the problem of delinquency.

But, even assuming such a public interest, it is open to serious debate whether improvements in personnel and facilities would effect measurable changes in the delinquency picture. For eventually we must ask and answer the question whether the courts and the rest of the judicial process are adequate to the task posed. And it appears not unlikely that, whatever the state of their health, they are not adequate. For the problem of delinquency is a most complex one. Numerous theories have been developed to explain it. Is the

child's behavior the result of "anomie," or "differential association," or is he the product of a "delinquent subculture," or perhaps
of "culture conflict?" Ranged against this battery of possible
explanations of the problem is the sole solution—the juvenile court.
But courts do not solve problems; they resolve issues. And as long as
it remains a court, the juvenile court must be limited to this role. A
civil court considering an action for damages arising out of an
automobile accident may determine who will pay for the damage
and how much will be paid. It can resolve the issue of financial
liability, but it cannot solve the problem of dangerous or defective
operators or equipment on the highways. Similarly, the juvenile
court can resolve the issue of "delinquent liability," but it cannot
solve—even for the one child before it—the social or personal
problems which gave rise to that child's delinquency. To characterize the juvenile courts, therefore, as "social agencies," implying that
they do possess some kind of problem-solving capability, is to
create unrealistic expectations which, when they are not fulfilled,
leave the public, the professionals, and the children alike frustrated
and discouraged, and make the public increasingly antagonistic
toward both children and the courts.

What, then, is the answer? Should the juvenile court be abandoned altogether? The thought is an enticing one, and not without
its proponents.[48] Barring this unlikely occurrence, however, there
do seem to be several strategies which hold some promise of im-
planting more realism in the court. One such strategy, that of
recognizing the court as a court, is already underway as a result of
the Supreme Court's mandate in *Gault.* But since it is recognized as
such, it also would seem worth-while to consider reserving the
court for consideration of only those more serious depredations
which threaten life and property in the community. This, in turn,
implies that the myriad of minor delinquencies which are now
processed through the court should be attended to by other than
judicial agencies. It is not difficult to perceive that, once the
meaning of "juvenile delinquency" was expanded to encompass not
only acts which would be criminal if committed by adults but other
"problems" such as truancy, "incorrigibility," and the like, these
cases commenced to proliferate in the courts. As a result, these
minor offenders become labeled as delinquents, and many are
institutionalized. Whatever else we know or do not know about the
etiology of delinquency, we do know that this labeling process tends
to promote a recurrence of the same or of more serious misbehav-
ior.[49] To excise such cases from the dockets of the juvenile courts
may have the effect, therefore, of reducing the incidence of delin-

quency, not only statistically but in reality as well. These behavior problems need not go completely unattended; other agencies exist, or may be created, to handle them.[50]

We have long since passed the point at which we could rationalize and accept the inadequacies of the juvenile court as those inherent in any novel program of reform. As a society of rapidly increasing numbers and complexity, we can no longer tolerate mechanisms of social control which do not return good coin on their investment. Perhaps it is a tribute to our ultimate love for our young that we permit the survival, after nearly seventy years, of an institution from which we have received so little in return, which has indeed perhaps wrought as much mischief as it sought to overthrow. But no sadder commentary can be made on any human institution than that it was well meant. To mean well is no longer sufficient; we must do well. Tocquevilie once commented that it is "the great privilege of Americans to make retrievable mistakes." [51] Despite the difficulties posed in retrieving the mistakes of the juvenile court, we must undertake to do so. A society which genuinely loves its children can do no less.

Notes

1 Duberman, "On Misunderstanding Student Rebels," *Atlantic Monthly*, Nov. 1968, p. 63.

2 Blackstone, *Commentaries on the Laws of England*, Bk. 4, Ch. 2, at 21 (12th ed., 1793).

3 See, *e.g.*, Miller, *Criminal Law* (1934); U.S. President's Commission on Law Enforcement and Administration of Justice [hereinafter cited as National Crime Commission], *Task Force Report: Juvenile Delinquency and Youth Crime* (1967).

4 Blackstone.

5 Lou, *Juvenile Courts in the United States* (1927).

6 See, *e.g.*, The Wellesley Case, 2 Russell Chancery Reports 1 (1827); Tappan, *Juvenile Delinquency* 169 (1949).

7 For discussions of these precursors of modern juvenile-court legislation, see Lou, *Juvenile Courts*; Tappan, *Juvenile Delinquency*; Tappan, *Crime, Justice, and Correction* (1960); Block & Flynn, *Delinquency: The Juvenile Offender in America Today* (1956); U.S. National Crime Commission, *supra* note 3, at 9.

8 Morrison & Commager, *The Growth of the American Republic* 355 (3d ed., 1942).

9 *Ill. Laws* (1899).

10 The encomium is attributed to Roscoe Pound. However, a rather thorough search has failed to locate its source.

11 *Ill. Laws* 70 (1907).

12 U.S. Children's Bureau, *Standards for Specialized Courts Dealing with Children* (1954) and *Standards for Juvenile and Family Courts* (1966).

13 Lou, *supra* note 5, at 2.

14 With apologies to T. S. Eliot, "The Hollow Men" (1925).

15 Belden, *Courts in the United States Hearing Children's Cases* (U.S. Children's Bureau Pub. No. 65, 1920).

16 *I.e.;* If it looks like a duck and walks like a duck, swims like a duck and squawks like a duck—it must be a duck.

17 Commonwealth v. Fisher, 213 Pa. 48, 62 Atl. 198, 5 Ann. Cas. 92 (1905).

18 See, *e.g.*, People v. Lewis, 260 N.Y. 171, 183 N.E. 353 (1932), *cert. denied*, 289 U.S. 709, 53 S. Ct. 786, 77 L. Ed. 1464 (1933), Dendy v. Wilson 142 Tex. 460, 179 S.W. 2d 269 (1944).

19 For an example of such faith, see Lou, *supra* note 5, at 30, 31.

20 For a roster of the variety of state "systems" of juvenile courts, see *National Council of Juvenile Court Judges, Directory and Manual* (1965).

21 Block & Flynn, *supra* note 7, at 314.

22 Delaware and West Virginia, for example, exclude murder and rape; Mississippi excludes capital offenses (murder, rape, and criminal robbery).

23 See Sheridan, *Delinquent Children in Penal Institutions* (1966).

24 The first (and only) case-book on juvenile law and procedure was published in 1966. Ketcham & Paulson, *Cases and Materials on Juvenile Courts* (1966).

25 Tappan, *supra* note 6.

26 Id. at 205.

27 *The Problem of Delinquency* (Glueck ed. 1959).

28 *Justice for the Child* (Rosenheim ed. 1962).

29 *In re* Poulin, 100 N.H. 458, 129 A 2d 672 (1957).

30 *In re* Holmes, 379 Pa. 599, 109 A 2d 523 (1955). Many of the leading cases on the legal aspects of the juvenile court are collected in *The Problem of Delinquency, supra* note 27.

31 *Id.* at 60.

32 Mapp v. Ohio, 367 U.S. 643, 81 S. Ct. 1684, 6 L. Ed. 2d 1081 (1961).

33 372 U.S. 335, 83 S. Ct. 792, 9 L. Ed. 799 (1963).

34 384 U.S. 436, 86 S. Ct. 1602, 16 L. Ed. 2d 694 (1966).

35 McNabb v. United States, 318 U.S. 332, 63 S. Ct. 608, 87 L. Ed. 819 (1943).

36 383 U.S. 541, 86 S. Ct. 1045, 16 L. Ed. 2d 84 (1966).

37 *Id.* at 543. Two years earlier, in an address to the National Council of Juvenile Court Judges, Chief Justice Warren had articulated a similar standard. The juvenile court, he said, "must function within the framework of law . . . in the attainment of its objectives it cannot act with unbridled caprice." Warren, "Equal Justice for Juveniles," *Juvenile Court Judges J.* 14 (Fall 1964).

38 *Id.* at 557 (Emphasis added).

39 99 Ariz. 181, 407 P 2d 760 (1965).

40 *In re* Gault, 387 U.S. 1, 87 S. Ct. 1428, 18 L. Ed. 2d 527 (1967).

41 Since *Gault*, state courts have considered, with differing results, whether, under the doctrine announced there, a juvenile is entitled to a jury trial: Estes v. Superior Court, 73 Wash 2d 272, 4 38 P 2d 205 (1968), *no;* to proof of the allegations of delinquency "beyond a reasonable doubt" *In re* Urbasek, 38 Ill. 2d 535, 232, NE 2d 716, (1968), *yes;* to the "Miranda warnings" *In re* Creek, 7 2d D.C. Ct. App. (1968), *yes;* and to assignment of counsel in every case Boykin v. State, 32 Ill. 2d 617, 237 NE 2d 460 (1968), *yes.*

42 Carroll, *Alice in Wonderland* (Mod. Lib. Ed., n.d.).

43 Block & Flynn, *supra* note 7, at 317.

44 National Council on Crime and Delinquency, *Correction in the United States,* 13 NCCDJ. (1967).

45 McCune & Skoler, *Juvenile Court Judges in the United States: A National Profile,* 11 NCCDJ. 121 (1965).

46 U.S. Children's Bureau, *Juvenile Court Statistics* (1963).

47 Kvaraceus, "Why Don't We Make More Progress in the Prevention and Control of Delinquency?" in NCJCJ, *Current Problems in the Juvenile Court* 55 (1965).

48 See, *e.g.*, Gardner, "Confessions of a Juvenile-Court Judge," *The Rotarian,* Oct. 1963, p. 21.

49 See Tenney, *The New Dilemma in the Juvenile Court,* 47 Neb. L. Rev. 67 (1967).

50 *Id.* at 79.

51 De Tocqueville, *Democracy in America* 214 (Mayer & Lerner ed. 1966).

Meda Chesney-Lind

Juvenile delinquency: the sexualization of female crime

In 1970, a quarter of a million girls under 18 were arrested in the United States. They became the pawns of an antiquated juvenile justice system that possesses unbridled license to intervene in their lives and to enforce 19th-century American values and morality.

According to Anthony Platt, a University of California criminologist and author of *The Child Savers*, if you were to assume that the juvenile justice system was established to protect youngsters from the horrors and excesses of the adult courts, you would be wrong. The real purpose of the founders of the juvenile court, charges Platt, was to insure the normative behavior of youth; to oversee their attitudes to authority, their family relationships, and their personal morality. Adults assumed as Holy Writ both the natural dependence of children and the sanctity of parental authority. They created a special court to prevent "premature" independence and to monitor and enforce traditional sex roles. The system has adhered to its mandate for over 50 years.

Both boys and girls have suffered arrest, detention and institutionalization under vague juvenile-delinquency laws that allow judges to impose traditional morality on juvenile delinquents. And it is easy to attach that label to children. In Alaska, for instance, they used to define a juvenile delinquent as:

> any child under the age of 18 years . . . who is in danger of becoming or remaining a person who leads an idle, dissolute, lewd or immoral life . . . or who is guilty of or takes part in or submits to any immoral act or conduct . . .

Paternalism for "good" girls

This interest in morality and obedience to parental authority clearly poses a greater threat to the rights of girls than boys. The traditional American family exerts close control over its daughters to protect their virginity. A "good" girl is never sexual, although she must be sexually appealing, while a healthy boy must prove his masculinity by experimenting sexually. The courts, therefore, often operate under two sets of juvenile-delinquency laws, one for boys and one for girls. They reserve their harshest and most paternalistic treatment for girls.

Many statutes which apply to boys allow incarceration only for offenses that are also adult crimes. Girls, however, are often committed for offenses that have no adult counterpart. In Connecticut, for instance, up until 1972, girls came under the jurisdiction of this morals statute:

Any unmarried female between the ages of 16 and 21 . . . who is in manifest danger of falling into habits of vice, or who is leading a vicious life, or who has committed any crime . . . may be committed to . . . an institution.

Eight years ago, in *Connecticut vs. Mattiello*, a state circuit court ruled that the statute was not penal because it was concerned with the "care" and "protection" of the female juvenile, and, therefore, not subject to the Constitutional guarantees associated with penal statutes.

In 1967, the President's Commission on Law Enforcement and the Administration of Justice reported that "more than one half of the girls referred to the juvenile courts in 1965 were referred for conduct that would not be criminal if committed by adults." Their offenses consisted of running away from home, incorrigibility, waywardness, truancy, sexual delinquency, ungovernability, or being a "person in need of supervision." Only one fifth of the boys were referred for such conduct. Primarily, boys were charged with larceny, burglary, car theft, or other adult offenses.

People in the criminology business trot out sexual stereotypes to explain this apparent difference in male and female delinquency. They say it is not girls' nature to deviate from prescribed social behavior, but when they do, they do it in a typically feminine way, i.e., sexually. On the other hand, boys, who are naturally more aggressive, break the law. One prominent sociologist summed up this widely held view of female delinquency: "boys collect stamps, girls collect boys."

But this theory fails to explain what studies of undetected and unreported delinquency find. Researchers in three different parts of the country asked children to report their own delinquent behavior. The findings of these studies indicate that official court statistics probably underestimate the volume of female delinquency while overestimating its sexual character. Martin Gold's work in Flint, Michigan, reveals that running away, incorrigibility and fornication account for only eight percent of the delinquency reported by girls. Apparently, if juvenile courts sampled juvenile delinquency randomly, they would continue to find fewer delinquent girls than boys, but the girls would be charged with roughly the same kinds of offenses.

Chivalry is alive

Obviously, the system selects for punishment girls who have transgressed sexually or defied parental authority. In this manner, it defines a narrow range of acceptable behavior for girls, and the courts interpret even minor deviance as a substantial challenge to family authority. As we look at the responses of police and courts to female delinquency, it becomes apparent that girls who have committed noncriminal offenses are overrepresented in court populations and that they tend to receive harsher treatment than boys who have actually broken laws.

In one respect, however, the system discriminates against boys. Attached to the view that women are inferior to men is the traditional male attitude of chivalry. And chivalry is not dead; it has been incorporated into the juvenile-justice system. When police confront a young female suspect, they can either arrest her or let her go. A study by sociologist Thomas P. Monahan in Philadelphia shows that officers tend to release a larger proportion of girls apprehended for law violations than boys. This research, coupled with self-report studies that girls admit to committing the same crimes as boys, suggests that police indeed have the paternalistic mindset which says that girls should be treated chivalrously and released unless they need "protection." That girls thereby escape punishment for adult offenses is patently unfair, but it does not justify the harsh treatment they receive for minor offenses.

The best way to understand how judicial paternalism operates is to follow girls through the juvenile justice system from their initial contact with police to the final disposition of their cases.

When a girl runs away from home or when her parents cannot control her behavior, they often report her to the police. This practice is one reason why girls are charged so often with noncriminal offenses. Since parents have different standards of obedience for girls and boys, they seldom ask police to find and punish a son who doesn't come home after a date.

Middle-income mortification

The parental role in the initiation of complaints is also a major reason why so many girls from lower-income families find themselves in court populations. Middle-income families are mortified at the thought of involving social-control agencies in "family problems"; they seek help from private or professional agencies. Poor families, on the other hand, have few resources to help them solve disciplinary problems. They view the police as a necessary and appropriate mechanism for enforcing authority or saving their daughters' reputations.

Once the police are called in on a complaint, they either arrest the suspect or release her. In Philadelphia, Monahan found that police are more likely to arrest a girl than a boy for a sexual offense. In my study two years ago in Honolulu, I found that 34 percent of the girls and only 22 percent of the boys who had been arrested for juvenile offenses for the first time were referred to courts. I also found that police are more likely to refer to court girls accused of their first juvenile offense than girls charged with a first criminal offense. In fact, almost 70 percent of all girls and only 31 percent of all boys referred to the Honolulu courts in 1972 were charged with juvenile offenses. When I looked at the court statistics over the years, this pattern was consistent. Girls were referred to court primarily for juvenile or sex offenses and boys for adult offenses.

After police have made an arrest, they can either place a juvenile in pretrial detention or release him until his court appearance. A study of the Honolulu Detention Home in 1971 showed that 43 percent of the residents were girls while only 30 percent of the juveniles arrested during that period were girls. And 46 percent of the detention-home population had been arrested for either running away or being incorrigible; most were girls.

An American Association of University Women study in Pennsylvania showed that 45 percent of the girls charged with juvenile or sex-role violations were detained prior to trial, compared to only 24 percent of those charged with misdemeanors and 35 percent of those charged with felonies.

Vaginal smears

There is also evidence from a number of jurisdictions that girls held in detention homes are forced to undergo pelvic examinations. Historically these examinations were employed by officialdom to determine whether girls had had sexual intercourse. While the sexual revolution may have muted this overt concern somewhat, the practice continues under the guise of medical necessity. Jean Strouse, author of *Up Against the Law*, reports that girls, brought before the family court in New York, receive vaginal smears to test for venereal disease, including those charged with nonsexual offenses. This is clearly an invasion of privacy, and it is degrading, unnerving and probably a frightening experience for many young girls. Albert Reiss, a long-time student of the legal enforcement of sexual mores, says girls are much more likely than boys to be given physical exams, because of the stereotypic view that girls are more likely than boys to be "carriers" of venereal disease. More important, the suspicion of venereal disease shows that the court equates female delinquency with sexuality. It assumes that girls who get in trouble for any reason are promiscuous.

A few years ago, court officials in Honolulu routinely questioned girls about their sexual activities; they rarely asked boys. After the girls told the officers about their sexual experiences, the officials often used the information to charge the girls with additional offenses. However, since 1967, the Gault decision (which in part protects the juvenile's right to refuse to answer self-incriminating questions) has forced the court to use vague charges of incorrigibility or ungovernable behavior as substitute charges for suspected sexuality.

No place to go

Once girls are detained, they stay in custody longer than boys. A study in 1971 by Paul Lerman in New York indicates that adolescents charged with juvenile offenses are twice as likely to be detained for over 30 days than other delinquents. And we know that girls make up the bulk of juveniles charged with these offenses. My Honolulu data are older, but more specific. In 1964, girls averaged 19.3 days in pretrial detention while boys averaged only 8.9 days. And in interviews with girls who have recently been detained in Honolulu, I learned that it was normal for them to spend two weeks in detention on a runaway charge while boys charged with adult crimes were usually released in a few days.

The court's rationale for lengthy pretrial detention is that girls have no place else to go. In fact, court officials demand that girls choose between some sort of court-arranged or approved living situation or continued incarceration. They assume that since a girl often comes before the court because her family cannot discipline her properly, the court must provide some other form of control. Only rarely does the juvenile court worry about where boys are going to stay.

When we look at recent statistics on the disposition of juvenile-delinquency cases in court, it appears as if boys receive harsher treatment than girls. In Hawaii, for example, while 30 percent of the juveniles arrested in 1970 through 1971 were girls, only 13.8 percent of the juveniles committed to state institutions during the same period were females. In California, six boys were institutionalized for every girl during the same year. But we must remember that boys are arrested four times more often than girls. And these figures do not reflect the fact that a girl is often sent to a training school for far fewer offenses than her male counterpart, and that most of her offenses are not even criminal ones.

Janice Johnston, an attorney and Ph.D. candidate, recently studied the activities of the Honolulu Family Court. Her data reveal that girls are six times more likely than boys to appear before a juvenile-court judge on their first offense. They are also more likely than boys (5.8 percent to 1.3 percent) to receive probation or be placed under supervision after only one offense. And this pattern does not change much for the second offense.

Sociologist Robert Terry studied a juvenile court in the Midwest and found that while more girls than boys are allowed some form of probation or supervision, if a girl does appear before a judge, she is more likely to be institutionalized. Yona Cohn, in her study of the Bronx Children's Court, found that probation officers are far more likely to recommend incarceration for girls than boys. While girls make up only one sixth of the court population, they constitute one half of those recommended for institutionalization. Finally, national data compiled by Paul Lerman in 1965 show that boys and girls convicted of juvenile offenses are more likely than those convicted of criminal behavior to be incarcerated; girls are the vast majority of these cases.

Longer sentences

In the final analysis, it is clear that the system continues to mete out harsh punishment to girls who are charged with juvenile and sexual offenses. They are more likely than boys who commit adult or juvenile offenses to end up in institutions. Nearly 70 percent of the girls in the state training school in Hawaii from 1970 to 1971 were there for juvenile offenses, compared to 12.9 percent of the boys. In Pennsylvania, 83 percent of the imprisoned girls were there for juvenile or sexual offenses, and similar statistics have been found in New Jersey and Connecticut.

The final step in punishing the wayward girl comes in the length of her sentence. Once in a training school, girls stay there longer than boys. In 1965, the U.S. Children's Bureau reported that the average commitment for boys was 8.2 months, while it was 10.7 months for girls. Again the courts defend this harsher treatment in the name of protection. They are concerned that if they release a girl she may again become involved in promiscuous behavior and become pregnant.

If parents are unwilling or unable to control their daughters' behavior, our society believes, the court can and should. As a consequence, the labels of "incorrigible," "ungovernable" and "runaway" permit the same abuses that characterize the labels of "sick" or "insane." That is, saving or protecting girls often justifies treating them more severely than boys who break the law. Thus the court's commitment to the sexual double standard and the subordinate status of women results in a clear violation of the civil rights of young women. Punishment in the name of protection is much like bombing a village to save it from the enemy.

Nanette Dembitz

Justice for children—
for now and for the future

Advocates of equality for youth have won many victories in the legislatures and the courts across the country during the past decade. Now the important issue in litigation in New York and other states centers on the youth under sixteen who is not charged with a crime but who is brought to court because he is beyond control and discipline by his parents, schools, or any other adults.

William, a thirteen-year-old who is before the family court in New York City, is typical of the "uncontrollable" or "beyond-lawful-authority" child in urban cases.[1] He has been absent from school for practically all of the past year and has been leaving home for days and nights at a time with his whereabouts unknown. He will not reveal where he has been living or the sources of his livelihood while out of the home. William's regime does not promise a lawful occupation for him; indeed, he may now be engaging in undetected crimes when he is on the streets—particularly if he in fact is using heroin.

William's case is not unusual. Often a mother may realize that her on-the-street son is on heroin but cannot prove it with competent evidence. Frequently the child has refused to return, after perhaps one visit, to community agencies where the parent has sought counseling and aid. In New York State nine thousand new cases of uncontrollable children were handled by the family courts in 1972. Almost half of these occurred in New York City, according to the 1973 report of the Judicial Conference of the State of New York.

Juvenile courts were established in Chicago in 1899, primarily to remove from the criminal courts the crimes of children under sixteen and to treat these children as juvenile delinquents to be helped rather than criminals to be punished. (The Family Court in New York State and in a few other states has absorbed the

Reprinted from *American Bar Association Journal*, May 1974, pp. 588–591, with the permission of the American Bar Association.

traditional juvenile court jurisdiction.) Juvenile courts have also always had authority over uncontrollable children on the theory that they were headed for criminality—that they were "predelinquents."

The argument against the court's authority over uncontrollable children is that no court can prevent future crimes or determine for a juvenile what he needs for a healthy life; and, in fact, neither living on the streets nor truancy are crimes for adults (*Fenster* v. *Leary*, 282 N.Y.S. 2d 739). Advocates for equality for youth argue that it is unreasonable discrimination, relative to adults, and a violation of the constitutional guarantee of equal protection for the courts to exert authority over "uncontrollable" conduct merely because the person is under the age of sixteen (in some states, eighteen).

Not only is youth suffering a special restriction relative to adults, but it is also almost always the sons and daughters of the poor who are brought to court. The slum child's environment is discouraging to discipline and motivation. Overt rebellion by middle-class children against parental and school authority tends to begin after the customary juvenile court age of sixteen, and the middle-class parent has resources other than the courts and social agencies for coping with this behavior—sending the child to boarding school, for example.

What are the limits of youth rights?

The United States Supreme Court's decision in the case of fifteen-year-old Gerald Gault, *In re Gault*, 383 U.S. 541 (1966), was a stimulating victory in the crusade for justice for juveniles, extending to juvenile court proceedings many of the protections accorded adult criminals. While the impetus of the 1960s toward equal rights for black and white, poor and rich, and women and men continues to stir judicial currents, the advocates of equality for youth are scoring fewer successes in moving from reform of court procedure to challenging restrictions based on age. The Pennsylvania law penalizing the drinking of alcoholic beverages by anyone under twenty-one years old was held constitutional in *Republican College Council of Pennsylvania* v. *Winner*, 357 F. Supp. 739 (E.D. Pa. 1973). And not long ago the highest court of Utah upheld the authority of birth control clinics to refuse services to unmarried girls younger than eighteen unless they have parental consent (*Doe* v. *Planned Parenthood Association*, 510 P. 2d 75 (1973)). In

Maryland a federal court upheld the discharge of a homosexual junior high school teacher, stating that society has an interest in protecting immature youths. *Acanfora* v. *Board of Education of Montgomery County*, 359 F.Supp. 843 (D. Md. 1973). And the decisions on obscenity continue to speak of special restrictions for "impressionable youth"—for example, *Kaplan* v. *California*, 413 U.S. 115 (1973), and *Ginsberg* v. *New York*, 390 U.S. 629 (1968). In the uncontrollable or beyond-lawful-authority child cases, the same basic question is posed: How should the courts treat the plasticity of children and their incapacity for self-direction as compared to adults? Differentiations between them rest on physiological and psychological fact, rather than cultural bias, as in the case of race or sex.[2]

Juvenile and family courts are limited

A recent decision by the Court of Appeals of New York, *In Re Ellery C.*, 32 N.Y. 2d 588 (1973), was the first by a state court of last resort to limit the power of the juvenile and family courts to control youths under age sixteen who are beyond lawful authority. The court did not go so far as to uphold completely full equality for youth, but it did rule that a youth who had not been proved guilty of a crime could not be confined together with youths who had. The court in effect extended to noncriminal juveniles a phase of the "right to treatment" that the courts have been developing during the past decade in cases of the mentally ill and other individuals who complained that they had been committed to institutions allegedly for treatment but in fact were not receiving treatment. While it is too soon to see the consequences of the *Ellery C.* decision, it is hoped that it will produce a sharper focus on how to help deteriorating boys.

The question of whether all government control over beyond-law-ful-authority juveniles should be abolished, as their attorneys have been urging, will probably be decided by the United States Supreme Court within the next year. The highest court is likely to follow the path of the New York Court of Appeals in preference to abandoning entirely the traditional *in loco parentis* principle.

That principle is premised on the parents' legal duty to support and guide and their legal authority to discipline the child reasonably. Indeed, state laws on assault make an exception for reasonable corporal punishment by a parent.[3] When a parent is unable to persuade or force a child below age sixteen to conform to a healthy and normal program that will equip him for self-support as an adult, can the juvenile and family courts continue to exercise authority in place of the parent, for the sake of the parent, the child, and the community? The Supreme Court will probably answer "yes," as long as the juvenile and family court orders are couched in nonpunitive terms, even though similar orders would be unconstitutional for an adult.

Are the courts helping the uncontrollable child?

With the legal situation of the uncontrollable child on the way to clarification, the major gaps lie not only in treatment but also in our knowledge of social influences. Despite the general upsurge in social science research during the past twenty or thirty years, there are no systematic data or reliable follow-up as to whether and when state intervention proves beneficial in the lives of beyond-lawful-authority youths. A judge unfortunately must rely on personal impression. To a judge who has seen many on-the-street boys of thirteen and fourteen years of age during the course of a year or so while they refuse remedial classes, counseling, planned recreation, and other community services, it often seems that the boy is doomed to failure if left on the streets and that his placement in an institution, where he will be scheduled into remedial programs, offers more hope. Indeed, in the case of fourteen-year-old George, who had for two years been an on-the-street heroin addict, running away from open rehabilitation residences as well as his home, and obtaining heroin in undiscoverable ways, a secured closed treatment facility seemed essential.

On the other hand, to apply truly the constitutional principle that the state can restrict an uncontrollable juvenile's liberty only for the purpose of aiding his development, a court cannot assume authority over a child when his rehabilitation is mere verbiage. It seemed too late, for example, for a renascence through any known treatment methods for fourteen-year-old Margarita, the daughter of a prostitute, herself a prostitute for several years, and the mother of two illegitimate children. The Margaritas of New York can be found and rescued at an early age through schools, hospital clinics, and public assistance workers if these agencies get the resources and responsibility for children before their lives are irretrievably misshapen.

Only by such a search-and-rescue program will the rights of youth be truly fulfilled.

For delinquents, the issue is rehabilitation

With the new turn in the courts as to the handling of the uncontrollable child there is a danger of inattention to the other large class of children brought to the juvenile and family courts—the juvenile delinquents. For these children under sixteen years of age (in some states, eighteen) who have committed crimes, the legal question of their rights in court was largely settled by the *Gault* decision in 1966 and by *McKeiver* v. *Pennsylvania*, 403 U.S. 528 (1971). As a result, practically all the current legal controversies in juvenile delinquency proceedings are the same as those in criminal cases. For juvenile delinquents and for society the issue now is the social one—rehabilitation.

Delinquency is linked to adult crime

Certainly society's stake in both the affirmative and negative potential of these children is tremendous. While we have no statistics on how many of the children brought to court as uncontrollable are thereafter proved guilty of juvenile delinquencies or of adult crimes, statistics do establish the tie between juvenile delinquency and adult crime. Practically all adults apprehended for robberies, rapes, assaults, and the other street crimes that most alarm the public (that is, crimes other than white collar or political) were juvenile delinquents who generally committed less serious crimes as juveniles than as adults. Crimes of personal violence, such as robberies at knife-point or rapes, are still only a small proportion of juvenile delinquencies, although it is true that the proportion is increasing among twelve-to-sixteen-year-old boys. For girls younger than sixteen years of age, crimes more serious than shoplifting are still rare.

In juvenile delinquency cases, if New York City is typical, after a youth's arrest for crime the first step is consideration by social workers of whether the charge should be "adjusted" outside the courtroom. If it is not, and the youth is found guilty, he is generally put on probation, staying in his own home. Generally he is institutionalized in a state school for delinquents only if he disobeys directions to go to a school in the community, or remedial classes (most delinquents are long-time truants), or a mental health clinic, or other rehabilitative programs and commits another crime. Indeed, he may have a record of three or four crimes against property—driving a stolen car, for example—before he is sent away to a state school. While some delinquents are mentally retarded or disturbed, and there is desperate need for special facilities for them, many of the boys in the state schools have no discernibly greater or different psychic maladjustments than law-abiding children. But they have reacted to parental and societal-slum influences with antisocial values and behavior.

Describing a typical state school for delinquents at Warwick, New York, the *New York Times* recently reported that the children live in unlocked, unbarred cottages on an open, rural campus. At the time of the reporter's visit twenty-eight of the one hundred boys placed there by the court had walked off, absent without leave. Despite the freedom from bars, locks, or even fences in many state schools, due process is of course required in any proceeding to institutionalize a youth. Yet any supposition that schools for delinquents and prisons are factually the same because they are treated the same in constitutional principle is erroneous. A true picture of the schools is necessary in order to answer the persistent and insistent question: Why, despite modern facilities and upgraded remediation at these schools (small classes, new remedial reading techniques, better vocational training, more group therapy, off-campus expeditions, ombudsmen), do they have a substantial rate of failure, with a progression of their dischargees to adult crime?

Should the boys be kept in the community?

A popular answer is that removal of a slum boy to a rural school cannot fit him for city life, and supervised urban residences, which fortunately have multiplied through state and federal funding, have given some boys a constructive leg-up onto the main track. But while keeping a boy in his community certainly avoids re-entry shock, by the same token he can be sucked back into the whirlpool of delinquency. The backward pull was too strong, for instance, for fifteen-year-old Joe, for whom we had great hope. He was drug free, a good reader despite school truancy, responsive to an encouraging counselor in an urban-group home, eager to show that he could succeed in school; and he had special motivation because an older youth in his neighborhood delinquent group had tried to kill him. But after doing well for three months, he ran away to his old neighborhood. When he returned to the residence, he cut classes, to his chagrin failed in school, and a short time later was arrested for purse snatching.

Despite the talk of abolishing rural state institutions for delinquent youths, the fact is that a boy who, like Joe, is tried and fails in an urban residence, or a boy who the residence directors fear will be "unmotivated" or disruptive in the residence or dangerous in the community, is rejected for urban residence.

The necessity of enforced removal from the community for many delinquents cannot be wished away. But because of the unpopularity of this painful truth, because of a sense of guilt for society's failure to provide slum children with an upbringing preventive of delinquency, an ineffective ambivalence afflicts the juvenile justice system. On the one hand, no government or court can simply ignore the fact that a youth repeatedly commits crimes despite remedial efforts, nor can all protection be denied to his victims and potential victims—albeit that he may take their possessions without injuring them physically. (It is the residents of the youth's own community, the less affluent, who suffer most from crimes against property.) So the court must eventually institutionalize a crime-committing boy in a state school.

Brief stays can't ensure rehabilitation

But most of the state schools are open, like Warwick, and even for boys who stay until parole, the average period of residence has been eight months.[4] Certainly the youth cannot take the administration of justice seriously if he finds, after proof beyond a reasonable doubt of a serious charge (robbery at knife-point, for example) and protracted hearings on his need for a state school, that he can walk out of the facility and disappear into the streets. Nor in a stay at the school of brief duration can the boy possibly acquire new perceptions and motivations through the counseling, group therapy, or noncriminal role models offered by the schools (which have stressed employment of blacks in recent years), nor can he secure sufficient remedial education or vocational training to have a sense of accomplishment and of equipment for a noncriminal life.

Fifteen-year-old Edward, for example, with a juvenile delinquency record of both attempted and actual purse-snatches, paroled from a state school after ten months, was convicted at the age of sixteen in the adult criminal court on a charge of robbery. As another example, fourteen-year-old Charles, with a record of involvement in car thefts, escaped from a state school and was criminally convicted of assault and burglary soon after he passed his sixteenth birthday. And here is a history of a case before me concerning fifteen-year-old Terence:

Terence (N.Y.C. Family Court, Docket Nos. D 350/72, D 3358/72, D 3070/73, D 3162/73, among others), was placed in a state school in February, 1973, following findings of assaults and purse snatches, and paroled by the school to return home to his mother in August, 1973. In September and October, 1973, he committed a new series of delinquencies. Besides purse snatches, one finding (D 2885/73) was that he was driving a stolen car with license plates stolen from a different car, in the back seat of which was a loaded operable sawed off rifle and sixty-five bullets. According to a reliable informant, he and his two passengers were on the way to hold up a store. The school representative stated Terence had been paroled because he had been doing well at the school. For years before his placement, his mother had been unable to control his complete refusal to attend school and his roaming the streets; a psychiatrist and social worker reported that his major manifestation was annoyance and anger at his detention for the new delinquencies, that he had no feelings of guilt, anxiety, or depression, that psychotherapy was not recommended, and that he needed a "structured setting."

How can we better help delinquents?

Time and again a boy is progressing in a state school for delinquents—reading and other skills being the most objective measurement—only to be returned home after eight months to resume school truancy, street living, and with frequency, crime. One listening to fifteen-year-old boys en route to a state school observes that they know from their friends that their stay will be short. Viewing the school as a place to "do time" for a few months. they have little idea that their delinquencies and the injuries they have inflicted on others are taken seriously or that the school has a serious intention of helping them to change.

Considering that the lauded "therapeutic communities" regard two years as the minimum period in which any stable psychological and characterological change can be accomplished, we are disserving delinquent youths and society by returning them to their delinquent subculture after only a brief removal. As to the difficulty of a boy's re-entry into his home environment after a lengthy transplant out of it, a boy who has shown his antisocial tendency by a series of grave crimes should not be returned at all during his adolescence to the slum soil that produced his criminality. When there is real assurance that the youth will continue on a constructive path, he should be released from the state school to a supervised residence. Indeed, at that point of progress, and at no greater expense to the state, some boys could be transferred to private residential preparatory schools (although proposals for initial use for delinquents of Exeter, Groton, and such are fanciful and foolhardy).

We cannot expect a high success rate from the boys at the state schools, considering that they are places of last resort and that generally boys are sent there, if the situation in New York City is typical, only when they have already failed in rehabilitation programs in their communities. But we can save some of the boys who are growing into adult criminals after the ritual of a brief and inevitably unsuccessful stint at the school. Unless we are ready to give up on thirteen-, fourteen-, and fifteen-year-old delinquent boys and accept the progression of many of them into adult crime, we must aid them over a prolonged period with our best techniques for constructive development, in an atmosphere of growth and respect for individual liberty—except for the liberty to resume delinquency. To grant delinquent boys the right to deteriorate is a misplaced permissiveness, an unconstructive expiation of society's original sin of standing by during their distorted childhood. The hard-to-reach delinquent youth, born in a slum and deprived even before his birth, is the one who needs our most intensive services if we are seriously committed to the triumph of his affirmative potential over his negative potential for crime.

Notes

1 See New York Family Court Act (McKinney's Consol. Laws, Bk. 29A) §§ 712(b), 732; *In the Matter of Mario,* 317 N.Y.S. 2d 659 (Fam. Ct., N.Y. Cnty., N.Y. 1971).

2 Other issues arising in these cases, apart from basic validity, are the applicability of the procedural rights guaranteed by *Gault* in juvenile delinquency proceedings

(see *In the Matter of Walker*, 191 S.E. 2d (1972), and whether the statutory provisions are unconstitutionally vague—see *Commonwealth* v. *Brasher*, 270 N.E. 2d 389 (Mass. 1971)). The courts have been criticized for using the uncontrollable child provisions to attempt to restrict the sexual activity of teenage girls.

3   See, for example, New York Penal Law (McKinney's Consol. Laws, Bk. 39) §35.10.

4   While the New York Family Court Act provides both for placement in a state school for eighteen months, reviewable thereafter yearly to the age of eighteen, and for a commitment of three years, parole is in the discretion of the school.

Donald J. Black
Albert J. Reiss, Jr.

Police control of juveniles

This paper begins by defining deviance as behavior in a class for which there is a *probability* of sanction subsequent to its detection—a control approach. It proceeds to an analysis of detection and sanctioning differentials in the policing of juveniles. Thus, it explores situational properties besides rule-violative behavior that generate a social control response. The data derive from a three-city observation study of uniformed patrolmen in the field. Findings from the study permit propositions to the following effect: Most police-juvenile contacts are initiated by citizens; the great majority pertain to minor legal matters; the probability of arrest is very low; it increases with the legal seriousness of alleged offenses; police sanctioning reflects the manifest preferences

The research reported in this paper was supported by Grant Award 006, Office of Law Enforcement Assistance, United States Department of Justice, under the Law Enforcement Assistance Act of 1965, as well as by grants from the National Science Foundation and the Russell Sage Foundation. Maureen Mileski, Stanton Wheeler and Abraham S. Goldstein made helpful comments on earlier drafts of the paper.

Reprinted here from *American Sociological Review*, February 1970, pp. 63–77, with the permission of the American Sociological Association, Donald Black, and Albert J. Reiss, Jr.

of citizen complainants; Negro juveniles have a comparatively high arrest rate, but evidence is lacking that the police are racially oriented; situational evidence is an important factor in police sanctioning practices; and the sanction probabilities are higher for unusually respectful and disrespectful juveniles. Some implications of these propositions are ventured.

Current theory on deviant behavior and social control inquires very little into either the organized processes by which deviance is detected or the patterns by which deviance is sanctioned, countenanced, or ignored once it is found out. Despite a ground swell of concern with *social reactions* to deviant behavior—the core of the labeling approach to deviance—the sociology of social control remains a conceptually retarded body of knowledge. One way of drawing detection and sanctioning differentials into the analytical bounds of theory is to define deviance in terms of the probability of a control response. Thus, *individual or group behavior is deviant if it falls within a class of behavior for which there is a probability of negative sanctions subsequent to its detection.*[1] For any form of behavior to be classified as deviant, the probability of negative sanctions must be above zero when the behavior is detected. The greater the probability of sanction, the more appropriate is the classification as deviant.[2] Therefore, whether or not a given form of behavior is deviant and the extent to which it is deviant are empirical questions.

Detection and sanctioning involve separate probabilities. Some forms of deviance, such as those that arise in private places, have extremely low probabilities of detection. Types of deviance that rarely are detected may nonetheless have very high sanction probabilities. In other cases the converse may be true. Furthermore, the particular probabilities of detection and sanctioning may be closely tied to particular types of deviance. In the case of homicide, for example, the probability of detection is high, as is the probability of some form of negative sanction. The probability of official detection of incest surely is low, while the likelihood of sanctioning may be high when incest is detected. Public drunkenness would seem to have a high detection but a low sanctioning probability. Analogous probabilities could be calculated for types of deviance that fall within jurisdictions other than the criminal law.[3]

A control approach, as here propounded, implies three basic types of deviance: (1) undetected deviance, (2) detected, unsanctioned deviance, and (3) sanctioned deviance.[4] These are the three conditions under which empirical instances of deviant behavior appear in relation to control systems. An instance of undetected deviance occurs if an act or a behavior pattern occurs for which there would be a probability of sanction *if it were detected.* Undetected marijuana-smoking is deviant, for example, since there is a probability of negative sanction when an instance of this *class* of behavior is discovered. When a clearly drunken person is encountered on the street by a policeman but is not arrested, an instance of detected, unsanctioned deviance has taken place. The third type, sanctioned deviance, is self-explanatory.

An elaboration of the analytical distinctions necessary in a control approach would exceed the bounds of this discussion. However, two additional elementary distinctions must be noted. A distinction must be made between official, or formal, detection and sanctioning, on the one hand, and informal detection and sanctioning, on the other. Any approach to deviant behavior that does not inquire into the relations between official and informal control systems is incomplete. In other words, the notion of "social control of deviant behavior" should always have an organizational or system reference. Secondly, it is important to distinguish between the detection of deviant acts and the detection of persons who commit these acts. The general conditions under which persons are linked to deviant acts is a problem for investigation. Informal as well as official control systems involve detective work and the pursuit of evidence.

It should not be surmised from the foregoing that a sociology of the deviance-control process consists solely in the analysis of detection and sanctioning processes. Such would be an overly narrow conception of the subject matter, as well as a distorted analytical description of how control systems operate. The foregoing is oriented mainly to the *case-by-case* responses of control systems to deviant behavior. The framework is not geared to the analysis of control responses that by-pass the problems of detection and sanctioning altogether. For instance, it ignores totally symbolic social control responses, such as may sometimes be found in the enactment of rules where there is no attempt to detect or sanction violations of those rules (Arnold, 1935; Gusfield, 1963). It also neglects the preventive aspects of social control. For example, control systems sometimes take measures to limit opportunities for deviant behavior by constraining the actions of all members of a social category, a tactic illustrated by curfew ordinances, occupational licensing laws, food stamp requirements for welfare recipients, and preventive detention of felony suspects. Thus, an emphasis upon detection and sanctioning differentials should not deflect interest from other important properties of social control systems.

This paper presents findings on citizen and police detection of juvenile deviance and on the sanctioning of juveniles through arrest in routine police work. It makes problematic situational conditions that increase the probability of sanction subsequent to the detection of violative behavior. Put another way, it makes problematic conditions (besides rule-violative behavior itself) that give rise to differentials in official sanctioning. It is a study of law-in-action. Since all of the data pertain to police encounters with alleged delinquents, the relationship between undetected and detected delinquency is not treated.

The method

The findings reported here derive from systematic observation of police-citizen transactions conducted during the summer of 1966. Thirty-six observers—persons with law, law enforcement, and social science backgrounds—recorded observations of routine patrol work in Boston, Chicago, and Washington, D.C. The observer training period comprised one week and was identical across the three cities. The daily supervision system also was similar across the cities. The observers rode in scout cars or, less frequently, walked with patrolmen on all shifts on all days of the week for seven weeks in each city. To assure the inclusion of a large number of police-citizen encounters, we gave added weight to the times when police activity is comparatively high (evening watches, particularly weekend evenings).

No attempt was made to survey police-citizen encounters in all localities within the three cities. Instead, police precincts in each city were chosen as observation sites. The precincts were selected so as to maximize observation in lower socio-economic, high crime rate, racially homogeneous residential areas. This was accomplished through the selection of two precincts each in Boston and Chicago and four precincts in Washington, D.C. The findings pertain to the behavior of uniformed patrolmen rather than to that of policemen in specialized divisions such as juvenile bureaus or detective units.[5]

The data were recorded by the observers in "incident booklets," forms much like interview schedules. One booklet was filled out for every incident that the police were requested to handle or that they themselves noticed while on patrol.[6] A total of 5,713 of these incidents were observed and recorded. This paper concerns only those 281 encounters that include one or more juvenile suspects among the participants.

The context

Although large police departments invariably have specialized divisions for handling incidents that involve juveniles, the great majority of juvenile encounters with policemen occur with general duty, uniformed patrolmen, rather than with "youth officers." Youth officers receive most of their cases on a referral basis from members of the uniformed patrol division.[7] Usually these referrals enter the police system as arrests of juveniles by uniformed patrolmen. It will be seen, however, that uniformed patrolmen arrest only a small fraction of the legally liable juvenile suspects with whom they have encounters in the field. Youth bureau officers, then, determine what proportion of those arrested will be referred to juvenile court. The outputs of the patrol division thus become the inputs for the youth bureau, which in turn forwards its outputs as inputs to the court.[8] By the time a juvenile is institutionalized, therefore, he has been judged a delinquent at several stages. Correspondingly, sanctions are levied at several stages; institutionalization is the final stage of a sanctioning *process,* rather than *the* sanction for juvenile deviance.

After the commission of a deviant act by a juvenile, the first stage in the elaborate process by which official rates of delinquency are produced is detection. For the police, as for most well-differentiated systems of social control, detection is largely a matter of organizational mobilization, and mobilization is the process by which incidents come to the initial attention of agents of the police organization. There are two basic types of mobilization of the police: *citizen-initiated,* or "reactive" mobilization, and *police-initiated,* or "proactive" mobilization, depending upon who makes the original decision that police action is appropriate. An example of a citizen-initiated mobilization occurs when a citizen phones the police to report an event and the radio dispatcher sends a patrol car to handle the call. A typical police-initiated mobilization takes place when a policeman observes and acts upon what he regards as a law violation or, as in the case of a "stop-and-frisk," a "suspicious" person or situation.

Popular and even sociological conceptions of the police err

through an over-reliance on proactive imagery to characterize police operations. Although some specialized divisions of municipal police departments, such as traffic bureaus and vice units, do depend primarily upon proactive mobilization for their input of cases, in routine patrol work the great majority of incidents come to police attention through the citizen-initiated form of mobilization. The crime detection function is lodged mainly in the citizenry rather than in the police. Moreover, most police work with juveniles also arises through the initiative of citizen complainants. In this sense, the citizen population in good part draws the boundaries of its own official rate of juvenile delinquency.[9]

Detection of juvenile deviance

Observation of police encounters with citizens netted 281 encounters with suspects under 18 years of age, here treated as juveniles.[10] The great majority of the juveniles were from blue-collar families.[11] Of the 281 police-juvenile encounters, 72% were citizen-initiated (by phone) and 28% were initiated by policemen on patrol. Excluding traffic violations, these proportions become 78% and 22%, respectively. The mobilization of police control of juveniles is then overwhelmingly a reactive rather than a proactive process. Hence it would seem that the moral standards of the citizenry have more to do with the definition of juvenile deviance than do the standards of policemen on patrol.[12]

Moreover, the incidents the police handle in citizen-initiated encounters differ somewhat from those in encounters they bring into being on their own initiative. (See Table 1.) This does not mean, however, that the standards of citizens and policemen necessarily differ; the differences between incidents in reactive and proactive police work seem to result in large part from differences in detection opportunities, since the police are limited to the surveillance of public places (Stinchcombe, 1963). For example, non-criminal disputes are more likely to occur in private than in public places; they account for 10% of the police-juvenile contacts in citizen-initiated work but for only 3% of the proactive encounters. On the other hand, the "suspicious person" is nearly always a police-initiated encounter. Traffic violations, too, are almost totally in the police-initiated category; it is simply not effective or feasible for a citizen to call the police about a "moving" traffic violation (and nearly all of these cases were "moving" rather than "standing" violations). In

Table 1 Percent of police encounters with juvenile suspects according to type of mobilization and race of suspect, by type of incident

	Citizen-initiated mobilization		Police-initiated mobilization		All citizen-initiated	All police-initiated	All encounters
	Negro	White	Negro	White			
Felony	10	...	10	...	5	5	5
Misdemeanor: Except Rowdiness	18	11	5	14	15	9	13
Misdemeanor: Rowdiness	62	77	40	33	69	37	60
Traffic Violation	1	...	26	28	*	27	8
Suspicious Person	...	1	17	22	*	19	6
Non-Criminal Dispute	8	12	2	3	10	3	8
Total Percent	99	101	100	100	99	100	100
Total Number	(109)	(94)	(42)	(36)	(203)	(78)	(281)

* .5% or less.

short, there are a number of contingencies that affect the detection of juvenile deviance in routine policing.

A broader pattern in the occasions for police-juvenile transactions is the overwhelming predominance of incidents of minor legal significance. Only 5% of the police encounters with juveniles involve alleged felonies; the remainder are less serious from a legal standpoint. Sixty per cent involve nothing more serious than juvenile rowdiness or mischievous behavior, the juvenile counterpart of "disorderly conduct" or "breach of the peace" by adults. This does not mean that the social significance of juvenile deviance is minor for the citizens who call the police or for the police themselves. It should be noted, moreover, that these incidents do not necessarily represent the larger universe of juvenile deviance, since (1) in many cases the juvenile offender is not apprehended by the police, and (2) an unknown number of delinquent acts go undetected. Nonetheless, these incidents represent the inputs from which uniformed patrolmen produce juvenile arrests and thus are the relevant base for analyzing the conditions under which juveniles are sanctioned in police encounters.

Another pattern lies in the differences between Negro and white encounters with policemen. In the aggregate, police encounters with Negro juveniles pertain to legally more serious incidents, owing primarily to the differential in felony encounters (see Table 1). None of the encounters with white juveniles involved the allegation of a felony, though this was true of 10% of the transactions with Negro juveniles in both citizen- and police-initiated encounters. Apart from this difference between the races, however, the occasions for encounters with Negro and white juveniles have many similarities.

It might be noted that the data on the occasions for police-juvenile encounters do not in themselves provide evidence of racial discrimination in the selection of juveniles for police attention. Of course, the citizen-initiated encounters cannot speak to the issue of discriminatory *police* selection. On the other hand, if the police tend to stop a disproportionate number of Negroes on the street in minor incident situations, we might infer the presence of discrimination. But the findings in Table 1 do not provide such evidence. Likewise, we might infer police discrimination if a higher proportion of the total Negro encounters is police-initiated than that of the total white encounters. Again the evidence is lacking: police-initiated encounters account for 28% of the total for both Negro and white juveniles. More data would be needed to assess adequately the issue of police selectivity by race.

Incidents and arrest

Of the encounters patrol officers have with juvenile suspects, only 15% result in arrest.[13] Hence it is apparent that by a large margin most police-juvenile contacts are concluded in the field settings where they arise.[14] These field contacts, 85% of the total, generally are not included in official police statistics on reported cases of juvenile delinquency, and thus they represent the major invisible portion of the delinquency control process. In other words, if these sample data are reasonably representative, the probability is less than one-in-seven that a policeman confronting a juvenile suspect will exercise his discretion to produce an official case of juvenile delinquency. A high level of selectivity enters into the arrest of juveniles. This and subsequent sections of the paper seek to identify some of the conditions which contribute to that selection process.

A differential in police dispositions that appears at the outset of the analysis is that between Negroes and whites. The overall arrest rate for police-Negro encounters is 21%, while the rate for police-white encounters is only 8%. This difference immediately raises the question of whether or not racial discrimination determines the disposition of juvenile suspects. Moreover, Table 2 shows that the arrest rate for Negroes is also higher within specific incident categories where comparisons are possible. The race difference, therefore, is not merely a consequence of the larger number of legally serious incidents that occasion police-Negro contacts.

Apart from the race difference, Table 2 reveals that patrol officers make proportionately more arrests when the incident is relatively serious from a legal standpoint. The arrest rate for Negro encounters is twice as high for felonies as it is for the more serious misdemeanors, and for encounters with both races the arrest rate for serious misdemeanors doubles the rate for juvenile rowdiness. On the other hand, policemen rarely make arrests of either race for traffic violations or for suspicious person situations. Arrest appears even less likely when the incident is a noncriminal dispute. The disposition pattern for juvenile suspects clearly follows the hierarchy of offenses found in the criminal law, the law for adults.

It is quite possible that the legal seriousness of incidents is more important in encounters between *patrol* officers and juveniles than in those between *youth* officers and juveniles. As a rule, the patrol officer's major sanction is arrest, arrest being the major formal product of patrol work. By contrast, the young officer has the power to refer cases to juvenile court, a prosecutorial discretion with

Table 2 Percent of police encounters with juvenile suspects according to type of incident and race of suspect, by field disposition

	Felony		Mis-demeanor: except rowdiness		Mis-demeanor: rowdiness		Traffic violation		Suspicious person		Non-criminal dispute		All		All en-counters
	Negro	White	Negro	White	Negro	White	Negro	White	Negro	White	Negro	White	Negro	White	
Arrest	73	...	36	20	13	8	8	...	...	(1)	...	...	21	8	15
Release-in-field	27	...	64	80	87	92	92	100	(7)	(8)	100	100	80	92	85
Total percent	100	...	100	100	100	100	100	100	...	...	100	100	101	100	100
Total number	(15)	...	(22)	(15)	(85)	(84)	(12)	(10)	(7)	(9)	(10)	(12)	(151)	(130)	(281)

respect to juveniles that patrolmen in large departments usually do not have. Whether he is in the field or in his office, the juvenile officer plays a role different from that of the patrolman in the system of juvenile justice. For this reason alone, the factors relating to the disposition of juveniles may differ between the two. The youth officer may, for example, be more concerned with the juvenile's past record,[15] a kind of information that usually is not accessible to the patrolman in the field setting. Furthermore, past records may have little relevance to a patrol officer who is seeking primarily to order a field situation with as little trouble as possible. His organizational responsibility ends there. For his purposes, the age status of a suspect may even be irrelevant in the field. Conversely, the youth officer may find that the juvenile court or his supervisor expects him to pay more attention to the juvenile's record than to the legal status of a particular incident. In short, the contingencies that affect the sanctioning of juveniles may vary with the organizational sources of the discretion of sanction.

Situational organization and arrest

Apart from the substance of police encounters—the kinds of incidents they involve—these encounters have a social structure. One element in this structure is the distribution of situational roles played by the participants in the encounter. Major situational roles that arise in police encounters are those of suspect or offender, complainant, victim, informant, and bystander.[16] None of these roles necessarily occurs in every police encounter.

In police encounters with suspects, which account for only about 50% of all police-citizen contacts,[17] particularly important is the matter of whether or not a citizen complainant participates in the situational action. A complainant in search of justice can make direct demands on a policeman with which he must comply. Likewise a complainant is a witness of the police officer's behavior; thus he has the ability to contest the officer's version of an encounter or even to bring an official complaint against the officer himself. In these respects as well as others, the complainant injects constraints into police-suspect confrontations. This is not to deny that the complainant often may be an asset to a policeman who enters a preexisting conflict situation in the field. The complainant can provide what may be otherwise unavailable information to a situationally ignorant patrolman. The patrol officer is a major intelligence arm of modern police systems, but he, like other policemen, must live with a continual dependence upon citizens for the information that it is his allotted responsibility to gather. Furthermore, when a suspect is present in the field situation, the information provided by a complainant, along with his willingness to stand on his word by signing a formal complaint, may be critical to an arrest in the absence of a police witness.

The relationship between arrest and the presence of a complainant in police-juvenile encounters is shown in Table 3. It is apparent that this relation between situational organization and disposition differs according to the suspect's race. Particularly interesting is the finding that when there is no citizen complainant in the encounter the race difference in arrest rates narrows to the point of being negligible—14% versus 10% for encounters with Negro and white juveniles respectively. By contrast, when a complainant participates, this difference widens considerably to 21% versus 8%. This latter difference is all the more striking since felony situations and traffic and noncriminal dispute situations, which may be regarded as confounding factors, are excluded from the tabulation.

It also should be noted that as far as the major citizen participants are concerned, each of these encounters is racially homogeneous. The comparatively rare, mixed race encounters are excluded from these computations. Thus the citizen complainants who oversee the relatively severe dispositions of Negro juveniles are themselves Negro. The great majority of the police officers are white in the police precincts investigated, yet they seem somewhat more lenient when they confront Negro juveniles alone than when a Negro complainant is involved. Likewise, it will be recalled (Table 3) that the arrest difference between Negro and white juveniles all but disappears when no complainant is involved. These patterns complicate the question of racial discrimination in the production of juvenile arrests, given that a hypothesis of discrimination would predict opposite patterns. Indeed, during the observation period a strong majority of the policemen expressed anti-Negro attitudes in the presence of observers (Black and Reiss, 1967:132–139). It might be expected that if the police were expressing their racial prejudices in discriminatory arrest practices, this would be more noticeable in police-initiated encounters than in those initiated by citizens. But the opposite is the case. All of the encounters involving a citizen complainant in this sample were citizen-initiated typically by the complainants themselves. Proactive police operations rarely involve complainants. To recapitulate: the police are particularly likely to arrest a Negro juvenile when a citizen enjoins them to handle the incident and participates as a complainant in the situational action, but this is not characteristic of police encounters with white juveniles. Finally, it is noteworthy that Negro juveniles find themselves in encounters that involve a complainant proportionately more than do white juveniles. Hence, the pattern discussed above has all the more impact on the overall arrest rate for Negro juveniles. Accordingly, the next section examines the role of the complainant in more detail.

The complainant's preference and arrest

If the presence of a citizen complainant increases the production of Negro arrests, then the question arises as to whether this pattern occurs as a function of the complainant's mere presence, his situational behavior, or something else. In part, this issue can be broached by inquiring into the relationship between the complainant's behavioral preference for police action in a particular field situation and the kind of disposition the police in fact make.[18]

Before examining this relationship, however, it should be noted that a rather large proportion of complainants do not express clear preferences for police action such that a field observer can make an accurate classification. Moreover, there is a race differential in this respect. Considering only the misdemeanor situations, the Negro complainant's preference for action is unclear in 48% of the police encounters with Negro juveniles, whereas the comparable proportion drops to 27% for the encounters with white complainants and juveniles. Nevertheless, a slightly larger proportion of the Negro complainants express a preference for arrest of their juvenile adversaries—21%, versus 15% for whites. Finally, the complainant prefers an informal disposition in 31% of the Negro cases and in 58% of the white cases. Thus white complainants more readily express a preference for police leniency toward juvenile suspects than do Negro complainants.

Table 4 suggests that white juveniles benefit from this greater leniency, since the police show a quite dramatic pattern of compliance with the expressed preferences of complainants. This pattern seems clear even though the number of cases necessitates caution in interpretation. In not one instance did the police arrest a juvenile when the complainant lobbied for leniency. When a complainant explicitly expresses a preference for an arrest, however, the tend-

Table 3 **Percent of police encounters with juvenile suspects according to situational organization and race of suspect, by field disposition. (Table excludes felonies, traffic violations, and non-criminal disputes.)**

	Suspect only		Complainant and suspect		All suspect only	All complainant and suspect	All encounters
	Negro	White	Negro	White			
Arrest	14	10	21	8	11	16	13
Release-in-field	86	90	79	92	89	84	87
Total percent	100	100	100	100	100	100	100
Total number	(66)	(93)	(48)	(26)	(159)	(74)	(233)

Table 4 **Percent of police encounters with juvenile suspects that involve a citizen complainant according to race of suspect and complainant's preference, by field disposition. (Table excludes felonies, traffic violations, and non-criminal disputes.)**

	Negro			White			All negro encounters	All white encounters	All encounters
	Prefers arrest	Prefers informal disposition	Preference unclear	Prefers arrest	Prefers informal disposition	Preference unclear			
Arrest	60	...	17	(1)	...	(1)	21	8	16
Release-in-field	40	100	83	(3)	100	(6)	79	92	84
Total percent	100	100	100	...	100	...	100	100	100
Total number	(10)	(15)	(23)	(4)	(15)	(7)	(48)	(26)	(74)

ency of the police to comply is also quite strong. Table 4 includes only the two types of misdemeanor, yet the Negro arrest rate when the complainant's preference is arrest (60%) climbs toward the rate of arrest for felonies (73%, Table 2). In no other tabulation does the arrest rate for misdemeanors rise so high. Lastly, it is notable that when the complainant's preference is unclear, the arrest rate falls between the rate for complainants who prefer arrest and those who prefer an informal disposition.

These patterns have several implications. First, it is evident that the higher arrest rate for Negro juveniles in encounters with complainants and suspects is largely a consequence of the tendency of the police to comply with the preferences of complainants. This tendency is costly for Negro juveniles, since Negro complainants are relatively severe in their expressed preferences when they are compared to white complainants vis-à-vis white juveniles. Furthermore, it will be remembered that it is in encounters with this situational organization rather than in those with suspects alone that the race differential is most apparent. Given the prominent role of the Negro complainant in the race differential, then, it may be inappropriate to consider this pattern an instance of discrimination on the part of policemen. While police behavior follows the same *patterns* for Negro and white juveniles, differential *outcomes* arise from differences in *citizen* behavior (cf. Werthman and Piliavin, 1967).

Another implication of these findings is more general, namely, that the citizen complainant frequently performs an adjudicatory function in police encounters with juveniles. In an important sense the patrol officer abdicates his discretionary power to the complainant. At least this seems true of the encounters that include an expressive or relatively aggressive complainant among the participants. To say that the complainant often can play the role of judge in police encounters is tantamount to saying that the moral standards of citizens often can affect the fate of juvenile suspects. Assuming that the moral standards of citizens vary across social space, i.e., that there are moral subcultures, then it follows that police dispositions of juvenile suspects in part reflect that moral diversity. To this degree policemen become the unwitting custodians of those moral subcultures and thereby perpetuate moral diversity in the larger community. Assuming the persistence of this pattern of police compliance, then it would seem that police behavior is geared, again unwittingly, to moral change. As the moral interests of the citizenry change, so will the pattern of police control. Earlier it was noted that most police encounters with juveniles come into being at the beckoning of citizens. Now it is seen that even the handling of those encounters often directly serves the moral interests of citizens.[19]

Situational evidence and arrest

Another variable that might be expected to affect the probability of arrest is the nature of the evidence that links a juvenile suspect to an incident. In patrol work there are two major means by which suspects are initially connected with the commission of crimes: the observation of the act itself by a policeman and the testimony by a citizen against a suspect. The primary evidence can take other forms, such as a bloodstain on a suspect's clothing or some other kind of physical "clue," but this is very unusual in routine patrol work. In fact, the legally minor incidents that typically occasion police-juvenile contacts seldom provide even the possibility of non-testimonial evidence. If there is neither a policeman who witnesses the incident nor a citizen who gives testimony concerning it, then ordinarily there is no evidence whatever in the field setting. Lastly, it should be emphasized that the concept of evidence as used here refers to "situational evidence" rather than to "legal evidence." Thus it refers to the kind of information that appears relevant to an observer in a field setting rather than to what might be acceptable as evidence in a court of law.

In about 50% of the situations a police officer observes the juvenile offense, excluding felonies and traffic violations. Hence, even though citizens initially detect most juvenile deviance, the police often respond in time to witness the behavior in question. In roughly 25% of the situations the policeman arrives too late to see the offense committed but a citizen gives testimonial evidence. The remaining cases, composed primarily of non-criminal disputes and suspicious person situations, bear no evidence of criminal conduct. In a heavy majority of routine police-juvenile encounters, the juvenile suspect finds himself with incriminating evidence of some sort. The low arrest rate should be understood in this context.

On the other hand, it should not be forgotten that these proportions pertain to misdemeanor situations and that the arrests are all arrests without a formal warrant. The law of criminal procedure requires that the officer witness the offense before he may make a misdemeanor arrest without warrant. If the officer does not observe the offense, he must have a signed complaint from a citizen. Such is the procedural law for adults. The law for juveniles, however, is in flux as far as questions of procedure are concerned.[20] It is not at all clear that an appellate court would decide on a juvenile's behalf if he were to appeal his case on the grounds that he was arrested for a misdemeanor even though the arresting officer neither witnessed the act nor acquired a formal complaint from a citizen. Even so, it might be expected that the rate of arrest would be higher in encounters where the act is witnessed by a policeman, if only because these would seem to be the situations where the juvenile suspect is maximally and unambiguously liable. But this expectation is not supported by the observation data (see Table 5).

In Table 5 it is shown that in "police witness" situations the arrest rate is no higher but is even slightly, though insignificantly, lower than the rate in "citizen testimony" situations. It is possible that some or all of these arrests where the major situational evidence lies with the testimony of a citizen would be viewed as "false" arrests if they involved adult suspects, though this legal judgment cannot be made with certainty. It is conceivable, for example, that some citizen complainants signed formal complaints at the police station subsequent to the field encounters.

The low arrest rate in "police witness" situations is striking in itself. It documents the enormous extent to which patrolmen use their discretion to release juvenile deviants without official sanction and without making an official report of the incident. Official statistics on juvenile delinquency vastly underestimate even the delinquent acts that policemen witness while on patrol. In this sense the police keep down the official delinquency rate.[21] One other implication of the low arrest rate should be noted. Because the vast majority of police-juvenile contacts are concluded in field settings, judicial control of police conduct through the exclusion of evidence in juvenile courts is potentially emasculated. Police control of juveniles—like that of adults (Reiss and Black, 1967)—may be less prosecution-oriented than the law assumes. In other words, much about the policing of juveniles follows an informal-processing or harassment model rather than a formal-processing model of control.[22] From a behavioral standpoint, law enforcement generally is not a legal duty of policemen.

On the other hand, the importance of situational evidence should not be analytically underestimated. Table 5 also shows that the police very rarely arrest juveniles when there is no evidence. In only one case was a juvenile arrested when there was no situational evidence in the observer's judgment; this was a suspicious person situation. In sum, then, even when the police have very persuasive

Table 5 Percent of police encounters with juvenile suspects according to major situational evidence and race of suspect, by field disposition. (Table excludes felonies and traffic violations.)

	Police witness		Citizen testimony		No evidence		Not ascertained		All negro encounters	All white encounters	All encounters
	Negro	White	Negro	White	Negro	White	Negro	White			
Arrest	16	10	22	14	...	4	(2)	...	15	9	12
Release-in-field	84	90	78	86	100	96	(7)	(2)	85	91	88
Total percent	100	100	100	100	100	100	...	...	100	100	100
Total number	(57)	(69)	(36)	(21)	(22)	(28)	(9)	(2)	(124)	(120)	(244)

Table 6 Percent of police encounters with juvenile suspects according to the suspect's race and degree of deference toward the police, by field disposition. (Table excludes felonies.)

	Negro				White				All encounters
	Very deferential	Civil	Antagonistic	Not ascertained	Very deferential	Civil	Antagonistic	Not ascertained	
Arrest	20	15	24	...	10	9	13	12	12
Release-in-field	80	85	76	100	90	91	87	100	88
Total percent	100	100	100	100	100	100	100	100	100
Total number	(20)	(72)	(21)	(23)	(10)	(76)	(23)	(21)	(266)

situational evidence, they generally release juveniles in the field; but, when they do arrest juveniles, they almost always have evidence of some kind. When there is strong evidence against a suspect, formal enforcement becomes a privilege of the police officer. This privilege provides an opportunity for discriminatory practices (Davis, 1969:169–176).

The suspect's deference and arrest

A final factor that can be considered in its relation to the situational production of juvenile arrests is the suspect's degree of deference toward the police. Earlier research on police work suggests a strong association between situational outcomes and the degree of respect extended to policemen by suspects, namely, the less respectful the suspect, the harsher the sanction (Piliavin and Briar, 1964; Westley, 1955). In this section it is shown that the observation data on police-juvenile contacts draw a somewhat more complex profile of this relationship than might have been anticipated.

Before the findings on this relationship are examined, however, it should be noted that the potential impact of the suspect's deference on juvenile dispositions in the aggregate is necessarily limited. Only a small minority of juveniles behave at the extremes of a continuum going from very deferential or very respectful at one end to antagonistic or disrespectful at the other. In most encounters with patrolmen the outward behavior of juvenile suspects falls between these two extremes: the typical juvenile is civil toward police officers, neither strikingly respectful nor disrespectful. The juvenile suspect is civil toward the police in 57% of the encounters, a rather high proportion in view of the fact that the degree of deference was not ascertained in 16% of the 281 cases. The juvenile is very deferential in 11% and antagonistic in 16% of the encounters. Thus if disrespectful juveniles are processed with stronger sanctions, the sub-population affected is fairly small. The majority of juvenile arrests occur when the suspect is civil toward the police. It remains to be seen, however, how great the differences are in the probability of arrest among juveniles who display varying degrees of deference.

The relationship between a juvenile suspect's deference and his liability to arrest is relatively weak and does not appear to be unidirectional. Considering all of the cases, the arrest rate for encounters where the suspect is civil is 16%. When the suspect behaves antagonistically toward the police, the rate is higher—

22%. Although this difference is not wide, it is in the expected direction. What was not anticipated, however, is that the arrest rate for encounters involving very deferential suspects is also 22%, the same as that for the antagonistic group. At the two extremes, then, the arrest rate is somewhat higher.

Table 6 shows the arrest rates of suspects, excluding felony situations, according to their race and degree of deference toward police. The bi-polar pattern appears in the encounters with Negro juveniles, though in the encounters with white juveniles it does not. In fact, the number of cases where a white juvenile is extreme at one end or the other, particularly where he is very deferential, is so small as to render the differences insignificant. Likewise there is a case problem with the Negro encounters, but there the differences are a little wider, especially between the encounters where the suspect is civil as against those where the suspect is antagonistic. Overall, again, the differences are not dramatic for either race.

Because of the paucity of cases in the "very deferential" and "antagonistic" categories, the various offenses, with one exception, cannot be held constant. It is possible to examine only the juvenile rowdiness cases separately. In those encounters the arrest rates follow the bipolar pattern: 16% for very deferential juveniles, 11% for civil juveniles, and 17% for the encounters where a juvenile suspect is antagonistic or disrespectful. When felony, serious misdemeanor, and rowdiness cases are combined into one statistical base, the pattern is again bipolar: 26%, 18%, and 29% for the very deferential, civil, and antagonistic cases respectively.

Nothing more than speculation can be offered to account for the unexpectedly high arrest rate for juveniles who make an unusually great effort to behave respectfully toward policemen. First, it might be suggested that this finding does not necessarily conflict with that of Piliavin and Briar (1964), owing to an important difference between the coding systems employed. Piliavin and Briar use only two categories, "cooperative" and "uncooperative," so the "very deferential" and "civil" cases presumably fall into the same category. If this coding system were employed in the present investigation, the bipolar distribution would disappear, since the small number of "very deferential" cases would be absorbed by the larger number of "civil" cases and the combined rate would remain below the rate for the "antagonistic" cases. This, then, is one methodological explanation of the discrepancy in findings between the two investigations.

One substantive interpretation of the pattern itself is that juveniles who are and who know themselves to be particularly liable to arrest may be especially deferential toward the police as a tactic of situational self-defense. After all, the notion that one is well-advised to be polite to policemen if one is in trouble is quite widespread in the community. It is a folk belief. These findings might suggest that this tactic is by no means fool-proof. In any event the data do not provide for a test of this interpretation. It would seem that a good deal more research is needed pertaining to the relations between situational etiquette and sanctioning.

Overview

This paper examines findings on the official detection and sanctioning of juvenile deviance. It begins with a conception of deviance that emphasizes sanctioning *probabilities,* thereby linking the empirical operation of social control systems to the analytical definition of deviant behavior itself. In the present investigation, the central concern is to specify situational conditions that affect the probability of sanction by arrest subsequent to the mobilization of policemen in field settings. It is a control approach to juvenile deviance. Simultaneously it is a study of interaction between representatives of the legal system and juveniles—a study of law-in-action.

Several major patterns appear in the finding from the observation research. It would seem wise to conclude with a statement of these patterns in propositional form. Observation of police work in natural settings, after all, is hardly beyond an exploratory phase.

I. Most police encounters with juveniles arise in direct response to citizens who take the initiative to mobilize the police to action.

II. The great bulk of police encounters with juveniles pertain to matters of minor legal significance.

III. The probability of sanction by arrest is very low for juveniles who have encounters with the police.

IV. The probability of arrest increases with the legal seriousness of alleged juvenile offenses, as that legal seriousness is defined in the criminal law for adults.

V. Police sanctioning of juveniles strongly reflects the manifest preferences of citizen complainants in field encounters.

VI. The arrest rate for Negro juveniles is higher than that for white juveniles, but evidence that the police behaviorally orient themselves to race as such is absent.

VII. The presence of situational evidence linking a juvenile to a deviant act is an important factor in the probability of arrest.

VIII. The probability of arrest is higher for juveniles who are unusually respectful toward the police and for those who are unusually disrespectful.

Collectively the eight propositions, along with the corollary implications suggested in the body of the analysis, provide the beginning of an empirical portrait of the policing of juveniles. At some point, however, a descriptive portrait of this kind informs theory. This paper proceeds from a definition of deviance as any class of behavior for which there is a probability of negative sanction subsequent to its detection. From there it inquires into factors that differentially relate to the detection and particularly the official sanctioning of juveniles. Hence it inquires into properties that generate a control response. This strategy assumes that sanctioning probabilities are contingent upon properties of social situations besides rule-violative behavior. Since deviance is defined here in terms of the probability of sanction, it should now be apparent that the referent of the concept of deviance may include whatever else, besides rule-violative behavior, generates sanctioning. The present analysis suggests that sanctioning is usually contingent upon a configuration of situational properties. Perhaps, then, deviance itself should be treated theoretically as a configuration of properties rather than as a unidimensional behavioral event. A critical aspect of the sociology of deviance and control consists in the discovery of these configurations. More broadly, the aim is to discover the social organization of deviance and control.

The topic at hand embraces a good deal more than police encounters with juveniles. There is a need for information about other contexts of social control, studies of other detection and sanctioning processes. There is a need for comparative analysis. What is the role of the complainant upon comparable occasions? Is a complainant before a policeman analogous to an interest group before a legislature? Little is known about the differences and similarities between legal and nonlegal systems of social control. What is the effect of evidence in non-legal contexts? How is a policeman before a suspect like a psychiatrist before a patient or a pimp before a whore? Are there varieties of procedural control over the sanctioning process in non-legal contexts? To what extent are other legal processes responsive to moral diversity in the citizen population? The intricacies of social control generally are slighted in sociology. Correspondingly the state of the general theory of deviance and control is primitive.

Notes

1 This conceptualization consciously bears the imprint of Max Weber's work. For example, he defines "power" as "the probability that one actor within a social relationship will be in a position to carry out his own will despite resistance, regardless of the basis on which this probability rests" (Parsons, 1964:152). Weber defines "law" as follows: ". . . An order will be called *law* when conformity with it is upheld by the probability that deviant action will be met by physical or psychic sanctions aimed to compel conformity or to punish disobedience, and applied by a group of men especially empowered to carry out this function" (Parsons, 1964:127). Cf. the translation of this definition in Max Rheinstein (1966:5).

2 This does not, of course, preclude a probability of positive sanctions for the behavior. Some forms of deviant behavior are encouraged by subcultures that bestow positive sanctions for behavior which is handled as deviant in the wider community. One interesting but untouched problem in deviant behavior theory is that of the relative effects of joint probabilities of positive and negative sanctions in producing behavior of a given class.

3 One consequence of following this approach is that a control system can be examined from the standpoint of the deviant who is concerned with calculating his *risks* in the system. Oliver Wendell Holmes (1897) proposed this perspective as an approach to the legal system: "If you want to know the law and nothing else, you must look at it as a bad man, who cares only for the material consequences which such knowledge enables him to predict, not as a good one, who finds his reasons for conduct, whether inside the law or outside of it, in the vaguer sanctions of conscience."

4 The definition of deviance presented above excludes what may appear to be the fourth logical possibility, i.e., undetected, sanctioned deviance.

5 Very little research on the police has dealt with the routine work of the uniformed patrol division. For a review of investigations on the police see Bordua and Reiss (1967). A recent exception is James Q. Wilson (1968); his study, however, relies primarily upon official statistics.

6 These booklets were not filled out in the presence of the policemen. In fact, the officers were told that our research was not concerned with police behavior but, rather, that we were concerned *only* with citizen behavior toward the police and the kinds of problems citizens make for the police. In this sense the study involved systematic deception.

7 In two of the cities investigated, however, aggressive youth patrols ("gang dicks") are employed in the policing of juveniles. Most youth officers spend much of their time behind their desks dealing with referrals and work relatively little "on the street."

8 Most research on the control of juveniles begins at stages beyond the police field encounter. (Examples are Goldman, 1963; Terry, 1967; McEachern and Bauzer, 1967; Cicourel, 1968; Wheeler, 1968.)

9 Even in proactive police work, police initiative may be in response to citizen initiative. Proactive police units often are highly dependent upon citizen intelligence, though the dependence usually is once removed from the field situation (see

Skolnick, 1966). For example, citizens occasionally provide the police with intelligence about *patterned* juvenile behavior, such as complaints provided by businessmen about recurrent vandalism on their block or recurrent rowdiness on their corner. These may lead the police to increase surveillance in an attempt to "clean up" the area.

10 The relatively rare police encounters with suspects of mixed age status—adults and juveniles together—are excluded from this analysis. Further, it should be emphasized that the unit of analysis here is the encounter rather than the individual juvenile. Many encounters include more than one suspect.

11 It sometimes is difficult for a field observer to categorize a citizen according to social class status. During the observation period two broad categories were used, blue-collar and white-collar, but observers occasionally were unable to make the judgment. The precincts sampled were mainly populated by lower status citizens; so, not surprisingly, the vast majority of the citizen participants were labeled blue-collar by the observers. This majority was even larger for the suspects involved. Consequently, there are not enough white-collar suspect cases for separate analysis. However, the small number of juveniles of ambiguous social class status are combined with the blue-collar cases in this analysis.

12 Some police-citizen conflict may be generated when citizens view the police as reluctant to respond to their definitions of deviance. Citizens regard this as "police laxity" or "underenforcement." This complaint has lately been aired by some segments of the Negro community.

13 The concept of arrest used here refers only to transportation of a suspect to a police station, not to the formal booking or charging of a suspect with a crime. This usage follows Wayne R. LaFave (1965).

14 The arrest rate for adult suspects is somewhat higher than that for juvenile suspects. For findings on the policing of adults see Donald J. Black (1968: 170–262). The present analysis is similar to that followed in Black's study.

15 In a study of youth bureau records, it was found that past record was an important factor in the referral of juveniles to the probation department and to the juvenile court (Terry, 1967). Past record was also found to be an important factor in the sanctioning decisions of youth officers in the field (Piliavin and Briar, 1964).

16 For a discussion of the pivotal roles of lay persons in the control of mentally ill persons, see Erving Goffman's discussion of the complainant's role in the hospitalization of the offender (1961:133–146).

17 Less than 50% of the citizen-initiated encounters involve a suspect. Police-initiated encounters, by contrast, typically do result in police-suspect interaction. However, almost nine-in-ten encounters patrol officers have with citizens are initiated by citizens. In the modal police encounter, the major citizen participant is a complainant (Black, 1968:45, 92, and 156).

18 Jerome Hall (1952:317–319) suggests several propositions concerning the probability of criminal prosecution. One of Hall's propositions is particularly relevant in the present context: "The rate of prosecution varies directly in proportion to the advantage to be gained from it by the complainant or, the rate is in inverse proportion to the disadvantages that will be sustained by him."

19 Paul Bohannan (1967) notes that a core function of legal institutions is to reinstitutionalize the normative standards of nonlegal institutions. In other words, the legal process represents an *auxiliary* control resource for *other* normative systems. (Also see Bohannan, 1968.)

The patterned compliance of the police with citizens may be understood partly as an instance of the reinstitutionalization function of the legal process. Police control of juveniles, for example, is partly a matter of reinforcement of the broader institution of authority based upon age status. The police support adult authority; in parent-child conflicts the police tend to support parental authority.

20   This has been all the more the case since the U.S. Supreme Court decision in 1967, *In re Gault*, 387 U.S. 1. The *Gault* decision is a move toward applying the same formal controls over the processing of juvenile suspects as are applied in the adult criminal process. For an observation study of juvenile court encounters see Norman Lefstein, *et al.* (1969). This study includes a discussion of constitutional issues relating to the processing of juveniles.

It might be added that from a social control standpoint, neither police deviance from procedural law, in the handling of juveniles or adults, nor the low rate of detection and sanctioning of this deviance should be surprising. Rarely can a law of any kind be found without deviance, and equally rare is the detection rate or sanctioning rate for any form of legal deviance near the 100% level. Curiously, however, social scientists seem to take for granted low enforcement of substantive law, while they take low control of deviance by the agents of law, such as policemen, to be an empirical peculiarity. Much might be gained from an approach that would seek to understand both forms of legal deviance and control with the same analytical framework. Moreover, substantive control and procedural control can be profitably analyzed in terms of their inter-relations (cf. Llewellyn, 1962:22). Procedural control of the police—for example, limitations on their power to stop-and-frisk—can decrease detection and sanctioning probabilities for certain forms of substantive deviance, such as "possession of narcotics."

21   Citizens do not necessarily perceive the "delinquency problem" as a function of official delinquency rates and are probably more concerned with what they know about patterns of *victimization* in their communities or neighborhoods. Many citizens may be inclined more to a folk version of the control approach than a labeling approach to delinquency. Their very concern about "the problem" may be partly a dissatisfaction with the existing detection and sanctioning probabilities they divine about juvenile deviance.

22   Michael Banton (1964:6–7) makes a distinction between "law officers," whose contacts with citizens tend to be of a punitive or inquisitory character, and "peace officers," who operate within the moral consensus of the community and are less concerned with law enforcement for its own sake. He suggests that patrol officers principally are peace officers, whereas detectives and traffic officers, for example, are more involved in law enforcement as such. Banton's distinction has been elaborated by Bittner (1967) and Wilson (1968). Except when patrolmen handle felony situations involving juveniles, the policing of juveniles is mainly a matter of maintaining peace.

References

Arnold, Thurman N.
1935 The Symbols of Government. New Haven, Connecticut: Yale University Press.
Banton, Michael.
1964 The Policeman in the Community. London: Tavistock Publications Limited.
Bittner, Egon.
1967 "The police on skid-row: A study of peace-keeping." American Sociological Review 32:699–715.
Black, Donald J.
1968 Police Encounters and Social Organization: An Observation Study. Unpublished Ph.D. Dissertation, Department of Sociology, University of Michigan.
Black, Donald J. and *Albert J. Reiss, Jr.*
1967 "Patterns of behavior in police and citizen transactions." Pp. 1–139 in President's Commission on Law Enforcement and Administration of Justice, Studies in Crime and Law Enforcement in Major Metropolitan Areas, Field Surveys III, Volume 2. Washington, D.C.: U.S. Government Printing Office.
Bohannan, Paul.
1967 "The differing realms of the law." Pp. 43–56 in P. Bohannan (ed.), Law and Warfare: Studies in the Anthropology of Conflict. Garden City, New York: The Natural History Press.
1968 "Law and legal institutions." Pp. 73–78 in David L. Sills (ed.), International Encyclopedia of the Social Sciences, Volume 9. New York: The Macmillan Company and the Free Press.
Bordua, David J. and *Albert J. Reiss, Jr.*
1967 "Law enforcement." Pp. 275–303 in Paul Lazarsfeld, William Sewell, and Harold Wilensky (eds.), The Uses of Sociology. New York: Basic Books.
Cicourel, Aaron V.
1968 The Social Organization of Juvenile Justice. New York: John Wiley and Sons, Inc.
Davis, Kenneth Culp.
1969 Discretionary Justice: A Preliminary Inquiry. Baton Rouge, Louisiana: Louisiana State University Press.
Goffman, Erving.
1961 Asylums: Essays on the Social Situation of Mental Patients and Other Inmates. Garden City, New York: Anchor Books.
Goldman, Nathan.
1963 The Differential Selection of Juvenile Offenders for Court Appearance. New York: National Council on Crime and Delinquency.
Gusfield, Joseph R.
1963 Symbolic Crusade: Status Politics and the American Temperance Movement. Urbana, Illinois: University of Illinois Press.
Hall, Jerome.
1952 Theft, Law and Society. Indianapolis, Indiana: The Bobbs-Merrill Company. (Second Edition.)
Holmes, Oliver Wendell.
1897 "The path of the law." Harvard Law Review 10:457–478.
LaFave, Wayne R.
1965 Arrest: The Decision to Take a Suspect into Custody. Boston, Massachusetts: Little, Brown and Company.

Lefstein, Norman, Vaughan Stapleton, and Lee Teitelbaum.
1969   "In search of juvenile justice: Gault and its implementation." Law and Society Review 3:491–562.
Llewellyn, Karl N.
1962   Jurisprudence: Realism in Theory and Practice. Chicago, Illinois: University of Chicago Press.
McEachern, A. W. and Riva Bauzer.
1967   "Factors related to disposition in juvenile police contacts." Pp. 148–160 in Malcolm W. Klein (ed.), Juvenile Gangs in Context. Englewood Cliffs, New Jersey: Prentice-Hall, Inc.
Parsons, Talcott (ed.).
1964   Max Weber: The Theory of Social and Economic Organization. New York: The Free Press.
Piliavin, Irving and Scott Briar.
1964   "Police encounters with juveniles." American Journal of Sociology 70:206–214.
Reiss, Albert J., Jr. and Donald J. Black.
1967   "Interrogation and the criminal process." The Annals of the American Academy of Political and Social Science 374:47–57.
Rheinstein, Max (ed.).
1966   Max Weber on Law in Economy and Society. Cambridge, Massachusetts: Harvard University Press.
Skolnick, Jerome H.
1966   Justice Without Trial: Law Enforcement in Democratic Society. New York: John Wiley and Sons, Inc.
Stinchcombe, Arthur L.
1963   "Institutions of privacy in the determination of police administrative practice." American Journal of Sociology 69:150–160.
Terry, Robert M.
1967   "The screening of juvenile offenders." Journal of Criminal Law, Criminology and Police Science 58:173–181.
Werthman, Carl and Irving Piliavin.
1967   "Gang members and the police." Pp. 56–98 in David J. Bordua (ed.), The Police: Six Sociological Essays. New York: John Wiley and Sons, Inc.
Westley, William A.
1955   "Violence and the police." American Journal of Sociology 59:34–41.
Wheeler, Stanton (ed.).
1968   Controlling Delinquents. New York: John Wiley and Sons, Inc.
Wilson, James Q.
1968   Varieties of Police Behavior: The Management of Law and Order in Eight Communities. Cambridge, Massachusetts: Harvard University Press.

Part seven

Approaches to solutions

T o meet the challenge of crime in the last quarter of the twentieth century, we cannot continue to think in terms of the separate components of the criminal justice system, but must learn to think of the system as a whole. We can no longer operate from day to day or week to week by the seat of our pants. We must plan for the future. The planning must be done for the system to develop innovative and enlightened means of responding to crime. All the elements of the system must be taken into consideration in any plan that is made. For example, a plan for law enforcement agencies may not omit consideration of the courts and the correctional agencies, for all of the parts of the system are affected by what happens in the others.

Towards a Theory of Criminal Justice Administration: A General Systems Perspective discusses the theoretical models for a systems approach for criminal justice. The various systems theories and how they can fit into the needs of criminal justice are examined.

In Planning for Crime Reduction the report of the National Commission on Criminal Justice Standards and Goals surveys the developments of the last decade which have led to serious planning for crime reduction. The development of state criminal justice planning agencies and the role of the Law Enforcement Assistance Administration in providing grant funds for states is surveyed. The requirements of state plans and the changes that have developed such as a move towards program budgeting are reviewed. Evaluation of performance measures becomes essential to assure that plans are effective and successful. One of the great needs to *plan effectively is information. The development of needed information systems and data bases has been developed with the aid of LEAA. There are, however, barriers to effective criminal justice planning and these too must be considered.*

Criminal Justice Planning: Objectives For the Future forecasts what must be done if the criminal justice system is to be improved. Criminal justice planning is a new specialty so we must find what we have learned, see what the constraints are on criminal justice planning, determine whether there is a direct relationship between improvements to the parts of the system and crime reduction. We must recognize the weaknesses of our present criminal justice planning efforts and improve for the future.

Up to this point we have been primarily concerned with enforcement rather than prevention. Crime prevention must become a major focus for the future. In Community Crime Prevention and the Local Official *three views are presented, one from the focus of the police department and its role in community crime prevention; the second the citizen's perspective on developing an entire community-wide approach on attacking crime; and a third examining the futuristic developments in criminal justice.*

The two concluding articles Crime and Justice at the Turn of the Century *and* Horizons in the Criminal Justice System *provide a look to the future. The first article is a bit pessimistic about what the future may hold. It suggests that present-day values expressed in terms of immediate relevance may pave the way toward disaster. If we want a better future for criminal justice, we must invent it now. However, there is no indication that we are ready to consider the necessary issues. The second article observes that change is a constant in the criminal justice system and we must look to what lies ahead. Prevention of crime has attracted considerable attention and makes sense. More consideration must be given to issues such as shortening the pretrial detention period and removing victimless crimes from the criminal statutes. We must move beyond the current horizons, from those practices that were daring and creative yesterday, to challenges which may boggle the mind of some of those now in the system and which to others may appear to be science fiction, but which are possibilities for the future in criminal justice.*

Jim L. Munro

Towards a theory of criminal justice administration:
a general systems perspective

The need for an integrative framework for the analysis of inquiries into criminal justice problems is made evident by even a casual examination of the periodical literature in the area.[1] A variety of methodologies and problems are presented by current field research reports, but while individually frequently quite insightful and illuminating and certainly rich in variety, the overall effect is depressing. Depressing because the research effort is primarily oriented, in spite of the many brave words about a criminal justice system,[2] towards specific agency and/or topical concerns.[3] There are several consequences of this orientation: First the trans-agency nature of the criminal justice process tends to be obscured; second, the current orientation provides an intellectual rationalization for the maintenance of current role/occupational identifications in the criminal justice system; and third, the preoccupation with functional agencies impedes the creation of the kind of interdisciplinary research which has proven so essential to the development of other problem-oriented professional fields; i.e., medicine, business administration, social welfare, etc.

This essay proposes the use of general systems analysis as a research framework. (To make the distinction between closed managerial systems and general systems, the term open systems will be used hereafter.) It is *not* proposed that open systems

Reprinted from *Public Administration Review*, November/December 1971, with the permission of the American Society for Public Administration and Jim L. Munro.

analysis is a theory of crime causation or of social action, although it has implications for the development of theory in those areas; nor is it held that open systems analysis excludes specific methodologies currently employed in the social sciences. What this essay does maintain is that open systems analysis provides a basis for interdisciplinary studies which will serve to stimulate research and teaching that will view the various problems of the administration of criminal justice in an interrelated and interdependent fashion.

Since systems analysis is occasionally used in criminal justice administrative research and is often the cause of the damning of open systems analysis by academicians and practitioners alike, this essay first presents a discussion of administrative systems analysis before proceeding to a consideration of open systems theory and its application to the criminal justice area.

Administrative systems analysis

As a technique for the analysis of management problems, systems analysis grew out of World War II experience with operations research. Using quantitative methods, operations research explored ways of cost cutting in the purchase and use of military equipment. Although systems analysis still leans heavily on mathematical models and the use of quantification, it bears little resemblance to contemporary operations research.[4] In spite of almost a decade of elaboration and the establishment of large consulting organizations dedicated to the use of systems analysis, there is no accepted definiton of the term or agreement on which methods fall under the general rubric of systems analysis. The editor of the Rand Corporation's lectures on systems analysis, E. S. Quade, states that "it is still a form of art"[5] and that "no universally accepted set of ideas existed"[6] among the many studies he examined in an attempt to discover universals used in systems analysis. In lieu of a definition, Wildavsky's description of what systems analysis does is useful:

> Systems analysis builds models that abstract from reality but represent the crucial relationships. The systems analyst first decides what questions are relevant to his inquiry, selects certain quantifiable factors, cuts down the list of factors to be dealt with by aggregation and by eliminating the (hopefully) less important ones, and then gives them quantitative relationships with one another within the system he has chosen for analysis.[7]

The systems analyses advocated for the criminal justice system fall within the above description. Thus the President's Commission on Law Enforcement and Administration of Justice recommended that "systems analysis studies should include development of mathematical models of the criminal justice system and appropriate parts and collection of the data needed to apply these models to improving operations." [8]

Implicit in most administrative systems analyses is what Thompson has aptly called "closed system strategy." [9] This is an approach to organizations which assumes a determinate system that is best characterized as rational, functional, predictable, and striving towards stated goals with maximum efficiency. The limitations of such an approach are most serious and are discussed below, but the utility of viewing organizations as closed systems is substantial and deserves some comment.

First, it is impossible to consider all aspects of a system and its relationships to other systems simultaneously. For certain problems the focus of concern may exclude variables external to the system under study. Obviously such exclusions introduce error into the analysis, but the amount of error may be judged negligible or tolerable for the specific problem being considered.

One problem which is frequently appropriate for closed system analysis is procedures analysis. In a police department standardized procedures for managerial use may be analyzed without reference to external environmental requirements. Even here, however, care must be exercised, for while internal auditing procedures may assume a closed system, an annual audit most likely must assume an open system, for the requirements of the audit are established by agencies external to the department and the audit must be addressed to an audience outside of the organization. If the external factors are stable and known, as is the case with a financial audit, those factors may be taken as givens, and the analysis proceeds by a basically closed system strategy.

Some limited aspects of planning may also reasonably assume a closed system. Much short-range operations planning falls into this category. Personnel scheduling (as opposed to manpower requirement planning which should assume an open system) and some types of facilities utilization planning are examples. Again as noted above, if the external factors are relatively stable and known, many other aspects of planning may proceed using systems analysis. Examples would be developing specifications for future buildings and other capital expenditures and developing tactical operations plans for certain police activities such as the distribution of a mobil patrol force.

A third area which lends itself to conventional systems analysis is cost analysis and much of the other analytical work which is part of a planning-programming-budgeting system.[10] However, here too the utility of closed system strategy is dependent on the amount of error tolerable, the time span, and the specific subject matter of the analysis; in particular the planning activities of PPBS are subject to the same limitations as noted in the preceding paragraph.

As noted above, closed systems analysis may be used only under a limited number of circumstances without running the risk of introducing sizeable error into the analysis. Errors arise from not considering inputs from the environment and from the assumptions of closed system strategy. Error, however, may be reduced by increasing the sophistication of the systems-analysis methodology. Systems analysts already include formally designated environmental inputs in their analyses such as legal requirements of programs, appropriations, contractually mandated obligations, and other organizational parameters.

A source of error much more serious than those mentioned arises from the general orientation of administrators, legislators, and analysts who operate according to the assumptions of closed system strategy. This orientation has certain basic limitations, several of which are discussed below.

Limitations of closed system analysis

What operating administrators have long known by insight and intuition (although they have rarely allowed their practice to be influenced by their knowledge!) formal organization and management theory has been slow to recognize; namely, that organizations are dependent on their environments and are in constant commerce with other organizations in that environment. Modern organizations are not buildings with one door marked receiving and another marked shipping, but rather are patterns of action surrounded by a semipermeable membrane facilitating transactions (in the sociological sense of the term) with their surroundings.

One consequence of *not* taking an open systems view of organizations is that analysts and administrators often view non-system-originated inputs as deviant, dysfunctional, and frequently evil. Much of the administrators inability to cope with conflict between the police and activist racial groups in the U.S. can be understood as an administrative response to perceived threats to organizational integrity coming about because of activist-originated interaction with police (the politics of confrontation is an example). The police endorse human and community relations training programs and projects precisely because such programs allow interaction to be initiated, given substance, and be controlled by the police organization. These projects fail to accomplish the stated objective of reducing police-community conflict for the same reasons. Much agency opposition to community control and participation is understandable in the same terms; a fear of nonorganization-originated transactions with the larger social system. Using open systems analysis may not remove all of the perceptions of threat which the criminal justice agency administrator experiences, but it will allow him to view transactions with his environment as normal and inevitable, rather than as deviant and evil. Presumably this view will better equip the administrator to cope with extra-organizationally originated inputs in a more problem-solving manner than is presently the case.

A second limitation of closed-system analysis is the orientation towards existing institutional arrangements. This orientation is the almost inevitable consequence of viewing organizations as entities. The development plan for the state of New York's Identification and Intelligence System, which is a quite sophisticated use of administrative systems analysis, is an example.[11] The plan draws a distinction between system (the agencies of criminal justice) and process (the decision-making network of criminal justice)[12] and notes that the process is an entity[13] and that the system "is composed of a variety of institutions and agencies that are established by law. . . ."[14] Similarly the President's Commission on Law Enforcement, although describing the criminal justice system as "an enormous complex of operations,"[15] discusses criminal justice in conventional agency terms (police, courts, etc.) and even neatly divides a flow chart of cases into police, prosecution, courts, and corrections segments.[16]

This focusing on present institutional arrangements may well reflect the political realities of reform, but it fails to ask the difficult questions concerning social values, power distribution, and system objectives which might lead to structural reform, rather than just administrative reorganization. A willingness to contemplate structural reform would subject whole traditional criminal justice professions to searching reconsideration; thus the safety-welfare generalist might replace the policeman, corrections worker, and welfare officer.[17] As it will be seen below, open systems analysis avoids the institutional orientation by focusing on system-environment as the unit of analysis.

Other limitations of administrative systems analysis may be noted, but they are basically an elaboration of the two major limitations noted above. A preoccupation with control functions and resistance to change are examples of such subsidiary limitations. Agencies which view nonorganizationally originated transactions as deviant are very likely to elaborate their internal control structures to reduce the possibility of unofficial contacts with the world outside the agency and to buffer agency personnel from nonorganizational inputs. The internal security forces of police departments demonstrate this tendency. Similarly, a focus on present institutional arrangements may well mean a great resistance to change on the part of administrators if only because of their trained incapacity which is promoted by posing all questions within the context of present institutions.

In summary: administrative systems analysis with its assumptions of a closed, rational, and predictable system has many uses for the administrator and analyst alike, but its limitations make it comparatively useless as a framework for social analysis and frequently misleading even for managerial purposes.

Open systems theory

The following discussion is an attempt to present, in barest skeletal form, some of the main elements of open systems theory and its implications for the study of the criminal justice system. A thorough appreciation of the import of open systems theory for the social sciences can only come about through study of the works cited below.

Although the origins of open systems analysis extend back to the 1920's and '30's, it has only been recently that social theorists have seen its utility as a frame of reference for social investigations. Even today the names prominent in open systems analysis are few; from general systems theory there is Ludwig von Bertalanffy;[18] in sociology, Talcott Parsons;[19] and in social psychology, James G. Miller.[20] Pioneering this approach in the study of organizations were Daniel Katz and Robert Kahn.[21] Their work furnishes, to date, the most successful attempt to analyze bureaucracies from an open systems perspective.

A generally agreed-upon definition of systems and systems theory is the following by Miller:

Systems are bounded regions in space-time, involving energy interchange among their parts, which are associated in functional relationships, and with their environments. General systems theory is a series of related definitions, assumptions, and postulates about all levels of systems from atomic particles through atoms, molecules, crystals, viruses, cells, organs, individuals, small groups, societies, planets, solar systems and galaxies. General behavior systems theory is a subcategory of such theory, dealing with living systems, extending roughly from viruses through societies. Perhaps the most significant fact about living things is that they are open systems. . . .[22]

All open systems share certain common characteristics. A number of those characteristics of particular importance to the study of human organizations are discussed below.[23]

Social systems are interrelated and interdependent cycles of events. Unlike a mechanical system, a social system is dynamic and relatively fluid. The extent and activity of a social system may be observed by witnessing the events which characterize that system. These events are interrelated and interdependent, so that a change in one part of the system produces a change of greater or lesser magnitude in all other parts of the system. Thus by considering corrections as a subsystem within the criminal justice system (which would embrace such other functional subsystems as police, the judiciary, probation, and parole), it is easier to judge the role of corrections in the total system and the implications for corrections of changes in other segments of the system.

A second characteristic of open systems is the importation of energy and the acquisition of negative entropy.[24] Open systems do not run down, but rather bring in new energy from the environment to sustain further operation. Indeed, by importing more energy than its uses for the creation of output, the organization gains negative entropy. This ability to improve their survival position has interesting research possibilities for the social scientist. The operating margin or "organizational fat" has been the focal point of much managerial folklore, but of little empirical research.

The through put is another major characteristic of open systems. This is to say that the energy which is imported into the system is altered and used within that system. The appropriation, which is a form of energy input, is transformed by the corrections agency into guards, food, buildings, and electricity.

Output is a further characteristic of an open system. In the case of a corrections agency the output is in terms of services (ignoring prison industries for the moment), some of which are obvious and quantifiable—the number of inmates housed, the number of therapeutic interviews held; other services are much more nebulous in character although perhaps of considerable social significance—protection of society and rehabilitation of inmates are examples.

Open systems, through a process of coding information inputs and negative feedback mechanisms tend to maintain a dynamic homeostasis.[25] This means that the organization tends to keep a steady state through processing environmental information and so changing organizational response (through negative feedback) that its behavior may be adaptive.

Differentiation is a characteristic of open systems which describes the typical growth and maturation patterns of organizations. Task specializations develop and patterns of activity (the organization chart) are elaborated as the organization grows. One aspect of this differentiation is what von Bertalanffy calls progressive mechanization.

. . . the *primary* regulations in organic systems . . . are of such nature of dynamic interaction. They are based upon the fact that the living organism is an open system, maintaining itself in, or approaching a steady state. Superimposed are those regulations which we may call *secondary*, and which are controlled by fixed arrangements, especially of the feedback type. This state of affairs is a consequence of a general principle of organization which may be called progressive mechanization. At first, systems—biological, neurological, psychological or social—are governed by dynamic interaction of their components; later on, fixed arrangements and conditions of constraint are established which render the system and its parts more efficient, but also gradually diminish and eventually abolish its equipotentiality. . . .[26]

These regulatory mechanisms, as Katz and Kahn refer to secondary regulations,[27] may also reduce the amount of equifinality in the open system. This ability of a system to "reach the same final state from differing initial conditions and by a variety of paths"[28] has obvious implications for the survival ability of organizations.

Thus it is seen that open systems possess a number of characteristics. These characteristics are, in reality, scientific propositions: some of which have been well substantiated by empirical observation, others have been investigated and substantiated only for certain types and levels of organizations, and still others, especially in the area of complex organizations, have not been put to an empirical test at all. A central question arises: Through what means can these propositions be operationalized so that (1) the propositions themselves may be tested and (2) the insightful and integrative aspects of open systems analysis may be translated into field research? Even though no totally satisfactory answer is currently

available, in the field of complex organizations a satisfactory
approach to open systems research is provided by role analysis.

Role analysis

The great utility of role analysis, from a behavioral scientist's point
of view, is its ability to allow the researcher to move with
theoretical sure-footedness between the social system-organization
level and that of the individual.[29] Following is a discussion of three
elements of role theory which are especially useful in spanning
levels of analysis: role set, role episode, and a model of factors
relative to the taking of organizational roles.[30]

A role set is composed of all roles which are directly tied together.
Figure 1 illustrates the role set of a corrections officer in a routine

Figure I   Routine organization set for corrections officer

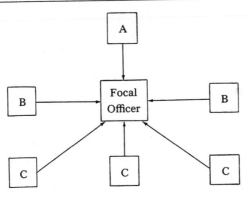

A: Focal role's superior
B: Focal role's peer
C: Focal role's subordinate

organization situation. Since it is the role of the corrections officer
which is of interest in this case, it is identified as the focal role. By
retaining the officer's role as the focal one, but shifting to a new
situation, the role set undergoes changes, as depicted in Figure II.

The role set is of great importance because its members communicate their conceptions of what constitutes "proper" role behavior

Figure II   Field organization set for corrections officer

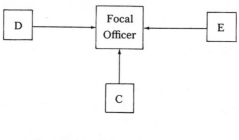

D: Focal role's peers
E: Focal role's inmate clients
C: Focal role's subordinates

to the focal person. Figure III is a representation of a generalized role set for a corrections officer-supervisor. Included in the role set are both extra-organizational and intra-organizational members; thus a variety of people are role senders for the officer. Any particular constellation of roles occurs because of the work flow, the authority-managerial system and/or the dictates of technology.[31] New insights into the processes of authority, work flow, and technology may be gained by examining specific role sets.

The elements of expecting, sending, receiving, and behaving with a feedback loop constitute a role episode. Not only are all of the people in a particular situational role set senders in a role episode, but since each office holder has his own conceptions of correct role behavior, the focal person acts as a self-sender in the episode. A model of the role episode, as developed by Katz and Kahn, is presented in Figure IV.[32] It is suggestive of the complexity and interrelatedness of role sending-receiving activity.

Placing the role episode in its organizational context, Katz and Kahn have proposed a model of factors, Figure V[33], which could well serve as an outline for field research. Basically the model illustrates three factors which influence the sent role. The first of these factors is the organizational input which consists of position description, organization size, patterning activity, and a variety of other factors, perhaps varying widely from one organization to another. The various attributes of the person (the focal role) is the second modifying factor. These attributes include psychological defense mechanisms, behavioral preferences, tendencies to react to specific stimuli in characteristic ways, and the other variables typically ascribed to the concept of personality. A third factor which influences the sent role is that of interpersonal relations. This is primarily the quality, content, and frequency of relationships among the roles of a specific situational role set. All three of these factors influence the sent and received role of the focal person and consequently influence his behavior.[34]

Utilizing role theory, and specifically the model of organizational roles presented above, it is possible to explore a variety of problems in criminal justice within an open systems context. Following is a suggestion for a field study exploring system boundaries with respect to the corrections subsystem.

Figure III Generalized organization set for corrections officer-supervisor

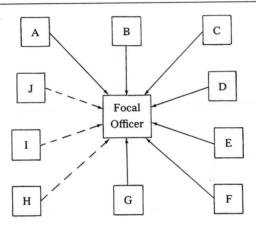

A: Captain from inspection division
B: Immediate supervisor
C: Director of training
D: Director of personnel
E: Supervisory peer group
F: Psychotherapist
G: Immediate subordinates
H: Family service case worker
I: Attorney for inmate
J: Union business agent

..... extra-organization members
_____ intra-organization members

Figure IV **A model of the role episode after Katz and Kahn**

Role Senders
Expectations
Sent Role
Perception of focal person's behavior
Information attempts at influence
Focal Person
Received Role
Role Behavior
Perception of role and perception of role sending
Compliance resistance; side effects
FEEDBACK LOOP

Figure V **A model of factors relative to the taking of organizational roles—after Katz and Kahn**

Attributes of the person
Organiza-tional factors
Role Senders
Role expecta-tions
Sent role
Focal Person
Received role
Role behavior
FEEDBACK LOOP
Inter-personal factors

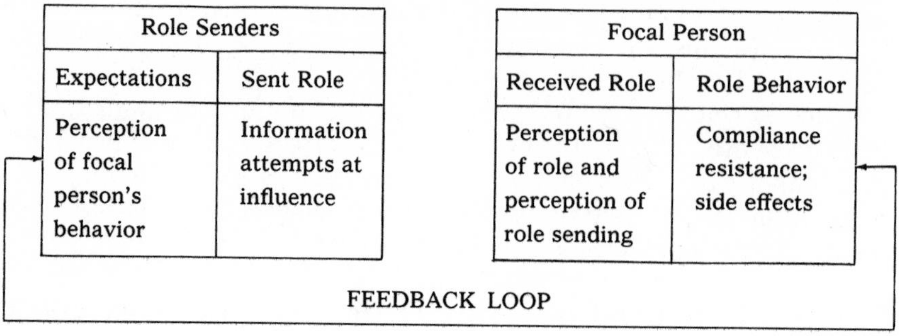

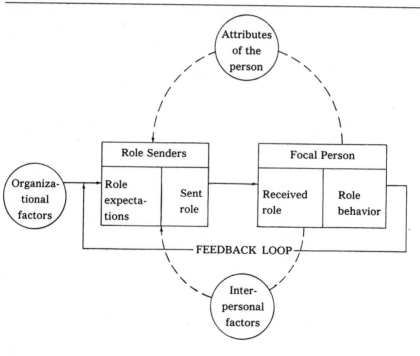

An illustrative application

Frequently management analysts and administrators alike describe positions in their organizations in terms of the core activities of the roles. The further assumption is often made that the important aspects of the role are the core ones and that if core role prescriptions are adequately carried out, the peripheral activities of the role are bound to be satisfactory or at least to have largely inconsequential effects for the agency. This is a simplistic view of agency role patterning that should be subjected to field investigation in corrections, for in the general area of organization theory one of the most challenging problems is the structuring of activities for specific roles at the boundaries of organizations.

In the business world this problem is clearly illustrated by the changing role of the salesman. Technologically innovative companies first tried to cope with the demands of selling sophisticated hardware by retraining sales personnel and through the use of films and other sales aids. Later these companies developed technical assistance departments which could field technically trained personnel at the request of the salesman. Other firms hired engineers and trained them in sales, while still other corporations fielded sales teams composed of both sales and technical members. Irrespective of the particular techniques used, the point remains the same: Changing technology and organization-environmental relationships dictate some kind of change in the role requirements for the office holder at the organization's boundary. The test of the marketplace makes this obvious in business—it seems to be not quite so self-evident in criminal justice agencies.

For purposes of analysis, a family on welfare with a troublesome son confined to an appropriate correctional facility is presented as an illustrative case. The client is viewed as the son from the perspective of the correctional facility, while the family is seen as the client by the welfare agency. Although liable to empirical verification, it is reasonable to assume that welfare agencies and correctional facilities frequently come into contact with the same families.

Figure VI illustrates the conventional way in which correctional and welfare agencies view their boundaries of interaction. Each agency tends to see the client-agency relationship as an exclusive one. Correctional officers and welfare workers have their roles defined in such a way that they see each agency as serving different functions, striving for different goals, and using antipathetic means.

Figure VI   Conventional view of corrections and welfare relationships as a matter of exclusive interaction

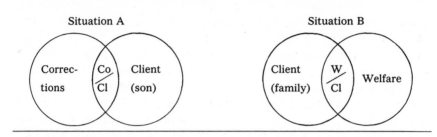

Situation A   Situation B

Correc- Co   Client   Client   W   Welfare
tions   Cl   (son)   (family) Cl

Interagency contact in such a situation would be unlikely and program interface accidental.

When new social programs (half-way houses, released time, etc.) force correction and welfare agencies to take cognizance of one another when they are serving the same client, the view is almost always that depicted in Figure VII. The agencies are forced to recognize the fact that they share a common client, but the overlapping jurisdiction may well produce competition for dominance or, and this is the case more frequently, maneuvering to see who may rid themselves fastest of the burden of responsibility for the client. In any case, interagency relationships tend to be fraught with difficulty, and the interests of the client are frequently sacrificed to the interests and convenience of the agencies.

Utilizing an open systems framework, the problem which the legally inclined administrator would define as one of jurisdictions,

Figure VII   Legalistic view of corrections and welfare relationships to the same client as a matter of overlapping jurisdictions

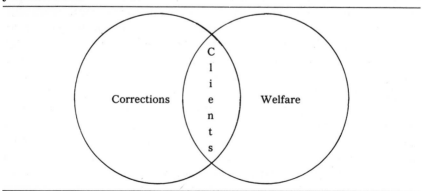

Corrections   Clients   Welfare

the social systems analyst would see as a problem in boundary/permeability. Figure VIII notes the various subsystems in a hypothetical case involving welfare recipients. Existing within the supersystem are three distinct systems: the clients (family and son), the correctional agency, and the welfare agency. An examination of action patterns further reveals four subsystems: client-corrections-welfare, client-welfare, client-corrections, and corrections-welfare.

Each subsystem possesses a distinct role set. Thus the welfare-client role set might consist of members of the client's family in interaction with a case worker while hearing about the degree of disruption that is anticipated in the family once the son is released from custody and about the need for additional money to pay the costs of the son's maintenance. In a similar fashion, the client-correctional role set would be composed of the relevant corrections personnel, the client's inmate peers, and his family members if he is in contact with them (actually, all of these role set illustrations are vastly oversimplified in this sketch). A likely topic for consultation within the role set would be the client's imminent release from the institution. The third role set involved in this action pattern is the correctional facility-welfare agency set. Interaction in such a set might well be a consultation among supervisors of the two agencies for the purpose of setting up a joint case review session between the corrections and welfare people concerned with the client. The final role set would represent the client-corrections facility-welfare subsystem. The set could consist of the son and his mother meeting in the corrections facility with a welfare case worker assigned to the family and the corrections psychologist—who has been the son's counselor—in a joint conference to work out the details of the son's release, the family's desire for additional assistance payments from the welfare agency, and the psychologist's recommendation for further psychotherapy for the son after release.

If the above case followed the pattern typical of many such cases, the family-agency and interagency encounters would have been replete with manipulation of the family; conflicting and contradictory acts by the two agencies, with each pursuing quite different goals; and a compromise problem solution which would have satisfied agency needs—regardless of the needs of the client family.[35] Either a researcher or an administrator, working within the conscious framework of open systems analysis, would more likely be able to focus on meaningful aspects of the problem than would an analyst with a closed system orientation.

In this particular case a role set analysis for each participant might lead to a different definition of functional roles than presently

Figure VIII   **Open systems view of corrections and welfare relationships to same client as an exercise in boundary permeability**

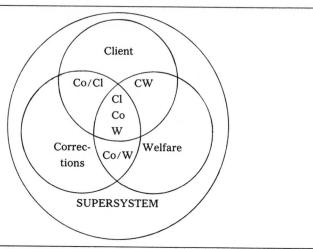

exists. If organizational roles were defined by functional relationships among activities, rather than by organizational fiat, new roles with quite different occupational definitions might emerge. Oslund suggests such a possibility when she states that:

> . . . the needs of a mass or bureaucratic society will necessitate a recasting of the roles, not only of the police, but of all other agencies and individuals concerned with the problems of the socially inadequate. If one takes a systems view of this problem, this type of solution is probably inescapable.[36]

She then suggests a "safety-welfare generalist" or perhaps a "task force approach to the socially ill."[37]

The safety-welfare generalist is a particularly useful concept, for it provides the rationale for developing an entirely new occupational role. Cutting across agency lines, the new safety-welfare generalist would have an education emphasizing the systemic nature of the criminal justice system. The occupational mobility this would give him should aid greatly in developing professionals for employment in the system.

The open systems perspective also suggests a new definition of client. Grosser, in 1960, implicitly recognized the necessity of a redefinition of client in his attack on then (and largely still) existent practice.

. . . an atomistic view of the prisoner is false for two reasons. The prisoner maintains relations with the community—or, better, his subculture—even if direct communication is interrupted; and he maintains relations with others in the inmate culture." [38]

It is apparent that it is useful (for the preservation of conventionally conceived civil liberties, if nothing else) to maintain the social fiction of individual guilt and responsibility, but once the adjudicative process has been completed, the logic of open systems analysis demands that the client be seen as a subsystem of social action, rather than as an individual. Such a conception of the client, combined with the safety-welfare generalist role definition, would open the way for therapeutic societal intervention into the family, work, peer structures, etc., of the individual found guilty by the courts. With treatment of the entire subsystem of social action, presumably more effective change could be realized.

However much the substantive content of an open systems analysis might vary from situation to situation, the important point is that open systems analysis fosters a research and managerial process which is more problem centered, more amenable to the contemplation of social change, and more likely to ask the difficult, but relevant, question than is the case with present closed system-oriented administrators and analysts.

Conclusion

The philosopher B. Hood, in discussing theory-practice relationships in a professional field has said:

Theory must help practice become conscious of itself, must sort out the influences and trends at work, must identify conflicts and incompatibilities and seek their resolution *in practice*. No problem of practice is ever solved merely by thinking about it. Action has to be taken. A task for theory is to diagnose problems of practice and provide plans for resolving them.[39]

Open systems analysis is well suited for this task. Utilizing such an approach, both administrators and social scientists should be able to increase their knowledge of criminal justice processes and to improve the practice of the profession.

Notes

1   This article is a revision of an earlier one published in the *Australian and New Zealand Journal of Criminology*, Vol. 3, No. 3 (September 1970), pp. 142–155.

2 System is defined as an interrelated and interdependent patterning of acts. In the U.S.A. there are various schools and colleges of criminal justice; the President's Commission on Law Enforcement frequently used the term; and one may find it generally in the professional literature.

3 This orientation can best be noted by scanning the contents of *The Journal of Criminal Law, Criminology and Police Science,* or *Excerpta Criminologica.*

4 An excellent example of a text in this area is Norbert Lloyd Enrick, *Management Operations Research* (New York: Holt, Rinehart and Winston, 1965).

5 E. S. Quade, *Analysis for Military Decisions* (Chicago, 1964), p. 153, cited in Aaron Wildavsky, "The Political Economy of Efficiency: Cost-Benefit Analysis, Systems Analysis, and Program Budgeting," PUBLIC ADMINISTRATION REVIEW, Vol. XXVI (December 1966), p. 298.

6 Quade, p. 149.

7 Wildavsky, p. 299.

8 President's Commission on Law Enforcement and Administration of Justice, *The Challenge of Crime in a Free Society* (Washington, D.C.: U. S. Government Printing Office, 1967), p. 270.

9 James D. Thompson, *Organizations in Action* (New York: McGraw-Hill Co., 1967), p. 10.

10 For a brief survey of PPBS which will clarify this point for anyone not already familiar with planning-programming-budgeting systems, see S. Mushkin and M. Willcox, *An Operative PPB System: A Collaborative Undertaking in the States* (Washington, D.C.: George Washington University, State-Local Finances Project, n.d.).

11 The New York State Identification and Intelligence System, *NYSIIS: System Development Plan* (Albany, N.Y.: Georgian Press, 1967).

12 Ibid., p. 13.

13 Ibid., p. 14.

14 Ibid., p. 16.

15 President's Commission, p. 261.

16 Ibid., pp. 8 and 9.

17 John M. Pfiffner, *The Function of the Police in a Democratic Society*, Series 7 (Los Angeles: Center for Training and Career Development, University of Southern California, 1967), p. 50.

18 Ludwig von Bertalanffy, *General Systems Theory* (New York: George Braziller, Inc., 1969).

19 Talcott Parsons, *The Social System* (New York: The Free Press, 1951).

20 James G. Miller, "Toward A General Theory for the Behavioral Sciences," *American Psychologist,* Vol. 10, pp. 513–531.

21 Daniel Katz and Robert L. Kahn, *The Social Psychology of Organizations* (New York: John Wiley and Sons, Inc., 1966).

22 Miller, p. 514.

23 Katz and Kahn; the following discussion is based very largely on pp. 14–29.

24 Ibid., p. 19, defines entropy as follows: "a system moves toward equilibrium; it tends to run down, that is, its differentiated structures tend to move toward dissolution as the elements composing them become arranged in random disorder."

25 Miller gives the following definition of coding: "Coding is a linkage within subsystems whereby process A_1 is coupled with process A_2 so that either will elicit the other in the future. Coding involves conditioning, learning, or pairing of two processes in a system and the memory of retention of this union over a period of time."

26 Ludwig von Bertalanffy, "General Systems Theory," General Systems Yearbook of the Society for the Advancement of General System Theory, Vol. I (1956), p. 6.

27 Katz and Kahn, p. 26.

28 Ibid., pp. 25 and 26.

29 Of course, open systems analysis presents several other research strategies. One which has great potential is the exploration of generic types of subsystems as noted by Katz and Kahn, ibid., pp. 39–47. The subsystems which they name are the production, supportive, maintenance, reward, sanctioning, adaptive, and managerial.

30 The terms role and office are fairly standard in the literature on role theory; however, for those not acquainted with such theory, the Katz and Kahn definitions follow: "Office is essentially a relational concept, defining each position in terms of its relationship to others and to the system as a whole. Associated with each office is a set of activities or expected behaviors. These activities constitute the role to be performed, at least approximately, by any person who occupies that office." Ibid., p. 173.

31 Obviously, affective relationships are also a factor, but one which is considerably more difficult to subject to analysis. See R. K. Merton, *Social Theory and Social Structure*, revised edition (New York: Free Press, 1957).

32 Katz and Kahn, p. 182.

33 Ibid., p. 187.

34 Ibid., pp. 187–197, for a full discussion of these factors and the dynamics of the model.

35 Pfiffner, quoting Oslund, p. 50.

36 Ibid., pp. 50 and 51.

37 Ibid.

38 "External Setting and Internal Relations of the Prison," in George H. Grosser, *Theoretical Studies in Social Organization of the Prison*, (New York: Social Science Research Council), pp. 141–143.

39 Bruce L. Hood, "An Introduction to the Philosophy of Education" (Storrs, Conn.: unpublished manuscript, 1969), p. 2.

National Advisory Commission
on Criminal Justice Standards
and Goals

Planning for crime
reduction

Introduction

Americans have long been skeptical of planning. Yet in a complex
society it is increasingly necessary.

With 50 State criminal justice planning agencies and over 400
regional and local criminal justice planning councils established as
a result of the Omnibus Crime Control and Safe Streets Act of 1968,
a new and important set of structures has emerged. It is clear that
these agencies are evolving institutions. In 1968, State and substate
planning agencies and councils began as little more than conduits
for Federal funds, but they now are becoming planning agencies for
the total criminal justice system in States and localities. The
standards and recommendations in this chapter are intended to
encourage this process. The aim of the National Advisory Commission on Criminal Justice Standards and Goals is the development of
a planning capability below the Federal level that will bind together
a highly fragmented criminal justice system and its environment.

An analysis of the internal management, funding, auditing, and
grant administration roles of State and substate planning agencies
and councils is not an objective of this report. Such matters are
covered only for the purpose of explaining the current responsibilities of such agencies under the Safe Streets Act. Except in the most
general fashion, the activities of the Federal Government are not
addressed. This is in keeping with the mandate given the Commission to confine itself to State and local criminal justice operations.

Reprinted from *Criminal Justice System*, Washington, D.C., U.S. Government
Printing Office, 1973, pp. 5–16.

THE EMERGENCE OF CRIMINAL JUSTICE PLANNING

A decade ago, phases such as "criminal justice planning" or "crime-oriented" planning did not exist in the vocabulary of public officials. Few police, courts, and corrections agencies articulated what was desirable for their own agency, let alone what should be worked for in conjunction with other agencies. Rising crime rates in the sixties, however, focused increasing attention on planning—not only for police, courts, and corrections but for community agencies and citizen action as well.

In 1967, the President's Commission on Law Enforcement and Administration of Justice recommended:

"In every State and every city, an agency or one or more officials should be specifically responsible for planning improvements in crime prevention and control and encouraging their implementation." [1]

The 1967 President's Crime Commission was only a temporary organization and could not spell out, except in the most general fashion, what criminal justice planning would involve. Nevertheless, certain core activities are obvious.

In its broadest sense, planning is the design of desired futures and the selection of ways to achieve them. Planning can occur at any level. Individuals plan; so do program directors and agency-administrators. The focus of planning can be short-range (weeks and months) or long-range (years and decades). Costs can be projected rigorously or all but ignored.

All organizations plan in that they try to shape desirable futures. Differences, however, occur in: (1) the degree of continuity of the planning effort; (2) the duration of the planned-for period; (3) the degree to which feedback from successful and unsuccessful decisions modifies original goals; and (4) the detail in which anticipated costs and benefits are defined.

The recommendations of the President's Crime Commission reflected a concern for systemwide planning. This meant at the very least ad hoc coordination among police, courts, and corrections agencies so that policies implemented in one part of the system would not have an adverse effect on other components. An increase in police officers in a jurisdiction, for example, would require planning for increased workloads in courts and corrections operations to insure smooth processing of an increased number of arrestees.

Planning is becoming more than a concern over processing efficiency. It is becoming impact-oriented. Reductions in the costs, fear, and harm caused by crime are being planned for directly. A more sophisticated, long-range type of planning is slowly being fashioned.

The National Advisory Commission on Criminal Justice Standards and Goals encourages the development of criminal justice planning efforts, and of allied governmental efforts that contribute to the planning process such as program budgeting, intergovernmental emphasis on evaluation, measurement of government performance, and construction of integrated criminal justice information systems.

The creation of State and local criminal justice planning agencies under the Safe Streets Act has given criminal justice planning a systemwide focus. In many States, these planning agencies are becoming active instruments of change. In addition, planning efforts are coinciding with the spread of program budgeting (budgeting by objective), which like planning is future-oriented. Finally, recent Federal and State funding of integrated information systems appears likely to give planners the data base they lack at present. Increased emphasis on performance measurement will be the probable result of the more abundant flow of information. Planners will be engaged heavily in the design and the use of evaluation efforts.

None of the developments described above is advancing evenly in State and local systems. Yet these are national trends that cannot be ignored. In the next sections they are discussed in detail.

The safe streets act and criminal justice planning

The Safe Streets Act established the Law Enforcement Assistance Administration (LEAA) within the Department of Justice. To be eligible for Federal funds, the act required each State to create a State criminal justice planning agency (SPA) and to develop an annual comprehensive plan. Upon approval of the comprehensive plan by LEAA, a block action grant is awarded. The grants are called block action because they are awarded as a lump sum rather than on a categorical program-by-program basis, and because they are for direct law enforcement purposes. Smaller "block planning" grants also are awarded to support the planning and grant administration efforts of the SPA's and whatever regional planning councils the SPA's establish.

(The authorization for the Law Enforcement Assistance Administration contained in the Omnibus Crime Control and Safe Streets Act of 1968 expires on June 30, 1973. The President on March 14, 1973 submitted to Congress the Law Enforcement Special Revenue Sharing Act of 1973. This bill would extend the LEAA program and call for many changes in the structure of the LEAA operation. The bill would require States to prepare comprehensive plans covering a three year period and file these plans with LEAA. Yearly review and comment by LEAA would be required. As written the Special Revenue Sharing bill does not call for States to establish a specific law enforcement planning agency as a precondition to receiving LEAA funds, but it does require a planning process. It is anticipated that all States will continue to maintain a State planning agency or its equivalent in a general purpose State planning operation. The discussion that follows and the recommendations of the Commission that apply to SPA's would still apply to the States in carrying out their programs if the Special Revenue Sharing act is enacted into law.)

Since the passage of the Safe Streets Act, all 50 States, American Samoa, Guam, the District of Columbia, Puerto Rico, and the Virgin Islands have established SPA's. Overseeing the policymaking of the SPA's are supervisory boards whose members represent State and local criminal justice offices, citizen groups, and non-criminal-justice public agencies. (See Figure 1 for statistical data on the membership of SPA supervisory boards). Although an SPA director is administratively responsible to his Governor, the comprehensive plan that he and his staff have designed must usually be approved by the SPA supervisory board. In most cases the Governor formally appoints members of the SPA supervisory board and the boards of any regional planning councils the State might establish.

In developing the Safe Streets Act, a good deal of controversy occurred concerning the role of the State in developing a comprehensive plan. Opponents of the act feared that the State plan would not be responsive to the needs of local government. Administrative devices had to be discovered that would enable units of local government to be involved in planning. As a result, several paths were taken.

First, the act required SPA's to be representative of local government. This, in effect, meant local members on State supervisory boards.[2] Second, the act required that 40 percent of all planning moneys allocated to the States be made available "to units of general local governments or combinations of such units."[3]

In spite of these provisions, large urban areas had difficulty obtaining planning money. Cities and counties experiencing the greatest crime problems sometimes were made part of multicounty regional planning councils containing suburban and rural areas.

Like the SPA's, regional planning councils include supervisory boards made up of State and local officials usually appointed by the Governor. Some councils, especially in metropolitan areas, have full-time staffs and have been delegated substantial powers to plan for Safe Streets Act funds coming from the State. Other councils are merely advisory bodies composed of local officials who meet infrequently.

Figure 1 **Composition of the average SPA supervisory board by functional background 1971**

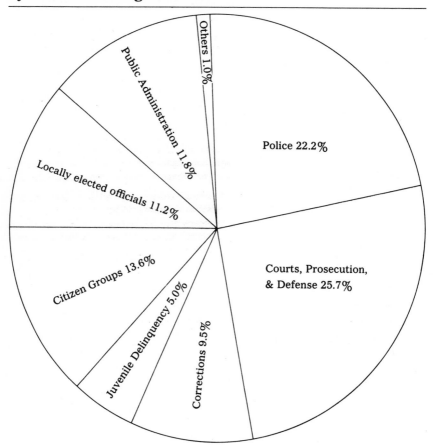

Source: Analysis of Fiscal Year 1971 SPA Statistics (Washington: Law Enforcement Assistance Administration, 1971).

Much of the 40 percent of planning money earmarked for local government went to the regional planning councils as opposed to cities and counties in the initial years of the Safe Streets Act program. As a result, in FY 1970, 17 of the 30 largest cities received no money whatsoever for criminal justice planning.[4] Staff on the regional planning councils often found themselves working in isolation from local governments and overwhelmed by the diversity of planning programs in their jurisdictions.

The problem was addressed in amendments to the Safe Streets Act. In 1971, the revised act required SPA's to "assure that major cities and counties . . . receive planning funds to develop comprehensive plans and coordinate functions at the local level."[5] The 1971 amendments also authorized the use of action funds to establish criminal justice coordinating councils (CJCC's) for "any unit of general local government or any combination of such units . . . having a population of two hundred and fifty thousand or more."[6]

As a result of the amendments and an increased focus on the crime problems of urban areas, the early concerns of the cities have been relieved somewhat. By the end of 1971, at least 17 States had one or more regions composed of a city and its metropolitan area.[7]

Instead of diffusing planning efforts by dividing Safe Streets planning funds among many small regional planning districts, many States in the 1970's began to consolidate previously established districts to use planning and action funds more effectively in high-crime urban areas. The State of Ohio provides a useful model for consolidation efforts. In 1970, it had 15 regional planning districts generally drawn without regard for urban, suburban, and rural differences. In 1971, Ohio consolidated its regional planning structure into six districts, each covering major metropolitan areas in the State. Planning for other parts of Ohio is now done by a central staff based in Columbus.[8]

Cities and counties in most States are now receiving direct planning money either from the State or from regional planning councils. A movement toward local criminal justice coordination councils (CJCC's) has taken place in large metropolitan areas. A main objective of these CJCC's is to plan and coordinate local criminal justice activities. Many CJCC's receive Safe Streets assistance. At the end of 1971, 33 of 50 of the Nation's largest cities had CJCC's.

CJCC's are creations of local government. They may derive formal authority from a resolution or ordinance adopted by the city council and/or county board of supervisors, or from an executive order by the Mayor and/or the county chief executive. On the other hand, CJCC's may operate informally at the request of the Mayor and/or the county chief executive and by the agreement of the various participating agencies.[9]

Usually headed by local chief executives, CJCC's are more than mere conduits of Federal funds. With broad-based representation of various elements of the criminal justice system and competent staffs, they can suggest and plan for programs that have nothing to do with Federal funding.

The oldest and one of the most successful CJCC's is that of New York, N.Y. Planning is accomplished through a 74-member council and a 16-member executive committee headed by the mayor. A staff of 20 professionals supports the council's activities. The NYCJCC has been designated by the State as the regional planning council for New York City, and administers State and Federal subgrants and grants. It also submits proposed legislation to the State Legislature. It engages in program development with every agency in the city that bears directly upon criminal justice and the levels of crime. Acting as an occasional mediator in interagency conflicts, it permits police, prosecutors, and correctional officials to plan for the effects of one part of the system upon another.[10]

Table I provides information on the staffs and budgets of selected CJCC's throughout the country.

State, regional, and local planning agencies have been receiving planning and action grants and subgrants in increasing amounts. Only $43.65 million was made available to the States in 1969. In 1972, the States received $497.44 million in planning and action grants. In 1969, California, as an example, received $1,387,900 in planning funds and $1,936,621 in action funds; in 1972, this state received $2,957,000 in planning funds and $44,781,000 in action funds.[11] (See Table 2 for the appropriations history of Federal block grants.)

Even with the latest appropriations, the Federal block grant contribution appropriated is far less than 10 percent of the combined State and local criminal justice expenditures, which in 1971 totaled $9,302.23 million.[12] Criminal justice is still an activity funded primarily by non-Federal sources.

The most important contribution of Safe Streets assistance may be its encouragement of communication among system components—an obvious prerequisite to integrated planning. State and regional supervisory boards help link police, courts, and corrections. For the first time in many States there are collective discussions among sheriffs, judges, correctional administrators, and police chiefs concerning common problems.

Table 1   Staff and funding of selected CJCC's as of June 1971*

City	Population	Number of professional staff	Total budget
Los Angeles, Calif.	2,782,400	5	$500,000
San Diego, Calif.	675,788	3	190,000
San Francisco, Calif.	704,209	5	150,000
Washington, D.C.	764,000	15	540,000
Chicago, Ill.	3,325,263	13	284,340
Indianapolis, Ind.	742,613	6	48,000
New Orleans, La.	585,787	5	57,972
Boston, Mass.	628,215	14	400,000
Detroit, Mich.	1,492,419	5	289,000
St. Paul, Minn.	308,686	3	34,000
St. Louis, Mo.	607,718	4	90,000
Buffalo, N.Y.	457,814	6	88,200
New York, N.Y.	7,771,730	20	500,000
Memphis, Tenn.	620,873	3	57,000
Dallas, Tex.	836,121	2	75,000

* Adapted from National League of Cities and United States Conference of Mayors, *Criminal Justice Coordinating Councils*, Washington, NLCUSCM, 1971, p. 10.

Table 2   LEAA block grant appropriations history* (in thousands of dollars)

	Fiscal Years			
	1969	1970	1971	1972
Block Planning Grants	$19,000	$ 21,000	$ 26,000	$ 35,000
Part C Block Grants	24,650	182,750	340,000	413,695
Part E Block Action Grants	. . .	. . .	25,000	48,750

*Source: Budget Branch, Law Enforcement Assistance Administration. Part C block grants may be used for general law enforcement and criminal justice purposes. Part E action grants may be used only for aid to correctional institutions and programs. In fiscal years 1971 and 1972, 50 percent of the funds appropriated by Congress under Part E were distributed to the States as "block" grants in accordance with the population formula used to distribute Part C block action funds. The remaining 50 percent were distributed by LEAA on a categorical grant basis.

Because projects funded in State plans are so diverse, elected officials at all levels have become aware of the range of crime control alternatives open to them. Today fighting crime means more than adding more police or building new jails; it means establishing drug treatment and education programs, installing high intensity street lighting, and initiating pretrial diversion projects.

Although in some States many legislators are unaware of the existence of the SPA,[13] in other States they have developed good working relationships with SPA's and local councils. In Nebraska, for example, the legislature's Judiciary Committee and the Nebraska Crime Commission (SPA) in 1971 cooperated in the examination of such problems as court reform, law enforcement consolidation, changes in bail practices, and prison and parole reform.[14] In Kentucky, in 1972, the SPA recommended to the General Assembly a 12-point legislative package that included: revision of the criminal laws, State support of police educational and training incentives, authorization of work and educational release for misdemeanants and felons, and establishment of a public defender system.[15] Much of the recommended legislation subsequently has been passed.

SPA's in several States have set minimum standards for criminal justice agencies receiving Safe Streets Act assistance, principally police services. In Maryland, the Police Standards Committee of the SPA in 1972 held hearings throughout the State on the desired quality and quantity of police services and the appropriate roles of city and county agencies. The standards initially established included requirements for 7-day-a-week, 24-hour-a-day services, full-time police executives, compliance with FBI Uniform Crime Reporting procedures, and a minimum of 10 full-time sworn officers per department.[16] The standards will be continually reviewed, added to, and updated. Standards of the type adopted in Maryland can be tied to State as well as Federal funding. Although they do not always suggest what the optimum arrangements for departments may be, they do eliminate the subsidy of administrative and personnel practices that are clearly not in the interest of public safety.

THE LEAA COMPREHENSIVE STATE PLANS

The Nation's criminal justice systems are badly in need of the thorough analyses that only a detailed and continuous planning process can give; i.e., clear statements of specific goals and priorities, consideration of alternative strategies for reducing crime, and development and evaluation of effective programs. At this writing, the primary source for measuring achievement in these activities is the State comprehensive plan, which must be approved by LEAA to receive Safe Streets Act assistance.

To date, four annual plans have been developed by each SPA based upon guidelines issued by LEAA. LEAA, in accordance with the provisions of the Safe Streets Act, has indicated that the major sections of the plan are to be:

1. Existing law enforcement systems and available resources;
2. A multiyear plan;
3. An annual action program;
4. Related plans, programs, and systems; and
5. Progress report.

Within these guidelines, States generally have produced weighty and lengthy volumes that sometimes have questionable informational value for the executive, legislator, administrator, technician, or concerned citizen.

Comprehensive plans were intended to be more than mechanisms for conveying funds from the Federal Government to units of State and local government; they were expected to deal with the total criminal justice system. The greatest deficiency of the plans produced to date by the SPA's is that they generally attempt only to specify what use will be made of the funds available from LEAA and other Federal sources. In its 1972 planning grant application to LEAA, the Wisconsin Council on Criminal Justice succinctly states the problem:

> A reality that the Safe Streets planning concept does not take into account . . . is that Safe Streets funds represent only a small fraction of local government moneys available for law/enforcement improvement. Regional plans [and state plans] cannot be realistic until the improvement strategy takes into account revenue for law/enforcement improvement from all sources inclusive of local and state moneys. However, . . . planning on such a scope is beyond the current fiscal means of the Safe Streets Act.[17]

If criminal justice planning is to have full impact upon the system, the scope of planning needs to be broadened to include the entire budgetary picture for criminal justice at the State and local levels.

A second major deficiency of the plans to date is their inability to address the question of goals and direction. States have just begun to define their crime problems and make decisions about the patterns of criminal activity in their jurisdictions. A Commission staff survey of the 1972 plans revealed:

1. Four States did not cite any crime statistics in their plans.

2. Only eight State plans had any substantial information on white collar crime—embezzlement, fraud, forgery, and bribery. The statistics in these cases were from traditional sources (crimes reported to the police and police arrests).

3. Only 14 State plans contained statistics on the number of drug-related arrests or cited estimates of the number of addicts within their State.

4. Only 19 States cited in their plans data on the nature and extent of juvenile delinquency. This data usually was based on either police arrests or referrals to juvenile court.

5. Many States did not cite criminal justice performance statistics that relate to crime control; e.g., apprehension rates, recidivism rates, and court processing rates.

The absence of basic crime-oriented statistics in formal planning documents raises questions as to whether many SPA's see themselves as planners or simply grant administrators. A quantitative assessment of State crime problems and criminal justice system response is an obvious first step in even the most basic planning process.

Program funding decisions may change drastically depending on whether the crime problem given top priority is white collar crime, burglary, or various types of violent crime. Critics of the block grant approach have noted that funds frequently are dispersed among many recipients, thus diluting the impact of Federal money. This situation often accompanies a lack of consensus on crime reduction goals, priorities, and action strategies. The criminal justice system has such a widespread need for resources that it is hard to find an undeserving project.

Another deficiency in the planning efforts of SPA's has been lack of evaluation. Although States have attempted to include evaluation in their funding activities at the project and program levels, the evaluation undertaken is relatively primitive. It is difficult to find evidence in many State plans that evaluation of past projects and programs has had any effect on planning. Few activities are evaluated in terms of their direct impact upon crime, primarily because of the extreme difficulty in measuring impact.

If all projects and programs were evaluated with methodological rigor, a great deal more time and money would have to be invested than at present. Programs and projects that clearly represent important advances in criminal justice have to be singled out for detailed evaluations. While SPA's continue to seek the proper balance in this area, it is nevertheless clear that too little evaluation has been undertaken in the past.

Inadequate attention to State and local funding patterns, failure to articulate goals and crime control strategies, and inadequate evaluation have been critical defects in the Safe Streets planning process. These problems are not surprising considering the obstacles and pressures with which the SPA's have had to contend.

For instance, SPA's encounter difficulties because they must perform both planning and funding functions. In their haste to provide operating agencies with the resources to deal with crime, many SPA's become preoccupied with funding. Due to a variety of intergovernmental problems, in the first 3 years of the Safe Streets Act program, SPA's experienced great difficulty in disbursing their action grants. Data released in 1972 indicate that for significant percentages of block action dollars, there is more than a year between Congressional appropriation and SPA disbursement of funds. At the end of fiscal year 1972, for example, 10.2 percent and 47.9 percent of the block action funds appropriated during fiscal years 1970 and 1971 respectively still had not been disbursed.[18]

SPA's were attacked by critics of the Safe Streets Act program for disbursing funds too slowly. They also were criticized for not establishing adequate fiscal controls for the awarding of subgrants. Specific instances of mismanagement of funds by SPA's led to Congressional charges of inefficiency and waste.[19] In more than one SPA, fiscal control people replaced planners, as executive directors acted to insure the financial integrity of their programs.

The initial problems of funding, role definition, and grant administration slowly are being ameliorated. The National Conference on State Criminal Justice Planning Administrators (NCSCJPA) in 1972 adopted standards for audit, monitoring, evaluation, grants management information systems, grant administration, fund flow, organizational structure of SPA's, technical assistance, training, staff development, and planning. The NCSCJPA's action is quite atypical for an association of government officials, and indicates the attention given to self-regulation by the SPA's.

With the setting of standards and the maturation of SPA's as institutions, the early pressures of grant administration should ease. In their brief existence, Safe Streets Act planning agencies and councils have performed many functions, including funding, system coordination, and legislative policy formulation. Their development into true long-range planning agencies for criminal justice, however, appears to be gradual and incremental.

The move toward program budgeting

Implementation of a plan is not part of the planning process, but few would claim that planning without implementation is a salutary exercise. Implementation is considered to begin when concrete steps are taken to translate ideas into action.

Between planning and implementation, however, there is a key step that often is singled out for particular concern because of its attendant complexities. Planning leads to a definition of what is desirable, and the process of allocating resources toward desirable ends is known as budgeting. There should be a symbiotic relationship between planning and budgeting. In practice, however, the two functions have not always been related either at the Federal or State level. Planning has been either sporadic or nonexistent, especially in the criminal justice area. Budgeting traditionally has followed a line item approach focusing on categories of expenditure such as equipment, salaries, and supplies. The overriding purpose of the line item budget is fiscal control—the determination of whether funds are spent by authorized persons for authorized purposes. Although useful for administrative purposes, line item budgeting was not designed to relate to planning. Line budget issues commonly involve comparisons between past and present item requests. Multiyear concerns beyond the annual budget cycle (except in capital budgets) are absent.

In the 1960's, fresh attempts were made to bring about a rapprochement between planning and budgeting. The Federal Government, States, and localities began to orient their budgetary processes toward the goals of government. These systems assumed various labels; e.g., planning-programing-budgeting, integrated planning and budgeting, programing and budgeting, and program budgeting. For the purpose of clarity, program budgeting will be the term used in this report to refer to all of these. In program budgeting, resources are allocated toward reaching objectives through development of needed programs.

Several core activities are associated with program budgeting systems:[20]

1. Goal-setting. The formal establishment of intermediate and long-range goals and objectives is basic to program budgeting. Typically, goals are formulated as statements of some ideal social condition that is to be approached through reaching specific objectives. Goal-setting is more meaningful when statements are associated with quantitative objectives, such as to reduce the

criminal homicide rate to X per 100,000 persons. The purposes of goal-setting can be tied to the principle of accountability—that of agency heads to chief executives and that of chief executives to the public.

2. Program Definition. With the articulation of objectives, the kinds of activities designed to reach goals are considered and in turn broken into smaller parts in a hierarchical structure—programs, categories, subcategories and elements:[21]

  a. Program: Protection of persons and property (one of seven programs);
  b. Category: Control and reduction of crime (one of 10 categories);
  c. Subcategory: Reintegration of offenders (one of three subcategories); and
  d. Element: Maintenance of inmates' physical and mental health (one of 10 elements).

Programs, categories, subcategories, and elements tend to be confined for the sake of convenience within agency lines, but often can involve more than one agency. (The reader should realize that the terms "programs," "categories," "subcategories" and "elements" listed above are unique to program budgeting literature and are merely descriptors for particular levels on a hierarchy of criminal justice goals and objectives.

3. Multiyear Forecasting. Programs must be planned for several years in advance. This requires multiyear forecasts based upon anticipated governmental action and societal needs. It necessarily involves an anticipation of probable social, economic, and governmental trends.

4. Performance Measurement and Evaluation. The establishment of evaluation criteria is necessary to assess the achievements of various programs. This is a critical area and one of extreme difficulty (see following section on Evaluation and Performance Measures).

5. Program Analysis. The identification of program alternatives and projection of costs and benefits of various program alternatives are key elements of program budgeting systems. These, too, are difficult tasks to accomplish. Both costs and benefits often are hard to define. Such analysis naturally is dependent upon the construction of adequate information systems and valid performance measures.

Although not all States and localities have established a formal program budgeting system, many have begun to adopt elements of one. A 1969 survey found that the majority of States were involved to some degree in one or more of the five aforementioned activities, although not necessarily for criminal justice activities.[22] It should be noted that the sponsorship of program budgeting activities is not confined necessarily to central budget offices. Program budgets sometimes are endorsed separately by central planning units and line agencies. Wherever program budgeting activities are performed, however, staff should be trained adequately in their application and the chief executive should give his full support.

Although data are not available for a conclusive statement, it appears that the criminal justice system does not endorse program budgeting techniques as fully as it might. The reasons for this are not clear. One consideration may be that criminal justice is an area of strong emotions and well-entrenched beliefs. Thus any innovation must proceed slowly. A second reason may be that program budgeting is difficult to perform. Its relationship to long-range planning often is misunderstood.

Program budgeting, moreover, is no cure-all. It is one way of projecting, forming, and ordering information to facilitate the consideration of problems and policy alternatives. To date, it has been used as a supplement—not a substitute—for existing budgeting systems. Because of its cost and complexity, program budgeting must be studied carefully before complete or even partial adoption.

One of the major difficulties in establishing program budgeting is that so often it is imposed on operating agencies for the convenience of the Governor, the executive budget agency, or the legislature, who typically require far less detailed information than do operating agencies. In effect, the agencies operate on a line item basis, summarizing into a very small number of elements or subcategories the entire work of each component at budget time. They add to this summation process a variety of gross numbers and estimates and promptly ignore the program budget for the remainder of the year.

In order to develop a program budget that is useful to operating agencies, much more exhaustive analysis must be made and the basic program budgeting hierarchy of program, category, subcategory, and element altered considerably. For example, Michigan developed a gubernatorial program budgeting system (Program Budget Evaluation System—PBES) in which State-level criminal justice agencies cooperated, but the system did not supply the kind of detail they needed for operations.

In mid-1972, the Michigan Office of Criminal Justice Programs (SPA) developed a project team to work with the State agencies in developing a more detailed and hence more useful analytic structure within the original PBES framework. It was the intent of the SPA to develop a plan within the PBES structure that (1) would budget for all State-level criminal justice expenditures, (2) would include local expenditures wherever they could be identified, and (3) would allocate LEAA funds as well. Use of the PBES structure would bring the evaluative strengths of that system to bear on the entire criminal justice system in the State.

The main concepts of the planning and program budgeting system movement appear to be generally accepted. Few practitioners would deny that activities such as goal-setting and program analysis, when properly applied, are vital to the criminal justice planning process. The program budgeting movement should be a sustaining force to the criminal justice planner.

Evaluation and performance measures

One of the most striking characteristics of present criminal justice operations is how little is known about what works and what does not work. The Commission at the outset of its effort undertook a survey of innovative criminal justice projects throughout the country—federally and non-federally funded. The survey utilized news clippings, articles in professional journals, and Federal grant applications, which described potentially successful projects. Commission staff members queried more than 400 agencies for information.

The agency responses, although often enthusiastic, were nonetheless not particularly useful. The outcomes of some projects were described in letters and not formally set forth in documents suitable for public dissemination. Many evaluation reports contained ill-defined objectives providing no specific standards by which to judge the project. Claims of success were generally couched in subjective and intuitive statements of accomplishments. Even when quantitative measures were used, they frequently were not accompanied by analysis and by adequate explanation.

The disappointing results from the Commission's survey (and its review of State criminal justice plans previously discussed) suggest that evaluation has not been considered important by many public officials in either operating or planning agencies.

Evaluation is, or should be, an integral part of the planning and resource allocation process. Evaluation provides feedback on the results of previous planning efforts, prevents planning from occurring in a vacuum, and provides a corrective device to enable modification of previous planning efforts that were unsuccessful.

Evaulation can and should take place at various levels. A statewide program to reduce burglary, for example, can be evaluated in terms of specified reductions in the incidence and cost of burglary. At a different level, the relative effectiveness of various program strategies for reducing burglary can be assessed; e.g., comparisons can be made concerning the relative worth of offender reintegration, reduction of target vulnerability, and increased risk of apprehension strategies. A third type of evaluation can occur at the level of the individual project. In this instance, a tenant patrol in a housing development might be evaluated to determine whether it actually did reduce the incidence of burglary. Finally, several tenant patrol projects might be compared to assess their relative success in reducing burglary.[23]

Because evaluation can occur at many levels, participants often feel that it is someone else's business. Clearly it is not. In the burglary illustration discussed above, program evaluations would be useful to policymakers (legislators, the Governor, and SPA director) who must make funding choices. Program and project evaluation also would be useful to agency heads and project supervisors for the purpose of correcting nonproductive policies and procedures.

Students of evaluation have identified at least three key functions that must be performed: (1) definition of program objectives and impact/output measures of performance; (2) development of evaluation plans and design of evaluation studies; and (3) dissemination and use of evaluation findings.[24] General criminal justice planning merges with functions one and three. Of particular interest is the design of impact/output measures of performance, since this function may be the most difficult to accomplish and certainly the most controversial. Impact measures are indicators used to describe the effect governmental activities have on major societal problems. Indicators that assess the fear, costs, and incidence of crime are impact measures.

Traditionally, crimes known to the police, as reflected in the Federal Bureau of Investigation's *Uniform Crime Reports* (UCR), have been used to assess impact. The problems of reporting, recording, and interpreting police crime statistics are well known.[25] Thus supplementary measures such as victimization surveys currently are being explored by Federal and State agencies.

Output measures are indicators that describe the response of government to major societal problems. Sample criminal-justice-related output measures for diversion, deterrence, apprehension, and rehabilitation activities are listed below:

- Number and percent of police contacts referred to non-criminal-justice sources;
- Average numbers of arrests per officer;
- Average time between arrest and final disposition;
- Number and percent of offenders reconvicted by type of release; and
- Number and percent of offenders successfully completing educational/vocational training.[26]

In the future, planners at all levels will have to become more concerned with the construction and interpretation of performance measures in evaluation efforts. Effective evaluation requires the clear definition of objectives, performance measures, and data sources in the initial stages of new programs.

In spite of the paucity of rigorous evaluation in criminal justice, there are encouraging signs that it is being taken more seriously than in the past. At the metropolitan level, for example, planning units of some law enforcement agencies have developed expertise in evaluation.

At the Federal level, LEAA has made evaluation and performance measurement a high priority in its selection of eight major urban cities to receive grants ($20 million per city over 5 years) for crime reduction programs. The aim of this High Impact Anti-Crime Program is to reduce stranger-to-stranger violent crimes and burglary by 20 percent within 5 years. The cities involved have begun to construct evaluation packages that will indicate to what extent the crime reduction goals are reached and how they were reached. Research from the Impact Program should provide valuable insight into the relationship between the response of the criminal justice system as reflected in performance measures and the incidence of crime.

Developing information systems

Possibly the greatest obstacle to intermediate and long-range planning involves the use of information. Sophisticated blueprints in other areas of domestic research, such as transportation, were only possible after planners were well financed and able to obtain large amounts of data that could be analyzed by computers. The same requirements apply to criminal justice.

Exploratory work has been undertaken to develop mathematical models of crime and the criminal justice system.[27] Such models would be invaluable aids in projecting the workload, personnel requirements, and cost of the criminal justice sytem. Properly structured, they could suggest which dispositional alternatives—pretrial diversion, suspended sentences, prison terms, etc.—would have the best results in decreased recidivism by type of offender.

Unfortunately, such models are not practical tools in most jurisdictions today because of inadequate information bases. The conclusion of the New York City Criminal Justice Coordinating Council, in its 1972 Criminal Justice Plan, summarizes the situation:

[I]nformation sources are so bad, the lack of basic research so complete, and the availability of competent researchers so limited that a detailed, integrated analysis of system operations and all its alternatives is simply not possible. Models based upon existing data can be highly misleading and dangerously simple.[28]

The signs are encouraging for the establishment of comprehensive information systems that can be used for planning and analysis. The Commission has endorsed the concept of offender-based transaction statistics (OBTS). OBTS is a statistical system that describes the aggregate experiences of individuals in terms of the types and sequences of criminal justice processes they encounter. The OBTS system is essential in developing the sophisticated dispositional models and workload projections described above.

A number of States have invested block grant money in information systems since the late sixties. LEAA recently has given high priority to encouraging the establishment of criminal justice data collection systems in each State. Funds will be made available for systems that will include OBTS systems as well as the following related components:

1. State criminal justice data centers;
2. Management and administrative statistics systems;
3. Uniform Crime Reporting systems; and
4. State technical assistance capabilities.

If Federal assistance continues and is accepted, it is reasonable to expect that within 10 years planners will have a tremendously expanded information base.

Barriers to effective
criminal justice planning

In the foreseeable future, planners will continue to be hampered by legal, constitutional, and political conditions beyond their control. Locally, systemwide planning frequently stops at the city limits. Police, courts, and corrections planners are limited by their agency's responsibilities. Responsibility for the crime problem in most urban areas remains fragmented. Formerly, local police chiefs and ultimately their mayors took responsibility for peacekeeping in cities. The day has come, however, when the police alone cannot make a decisive impact on crime. More and more police chiefs and mayors are recognizing that what corrections, courts, schools, and social welfare agencies do in relation to their clients affects crime as much as police activity. In most cities, moreover, these agencies are either controlled or significantly influenced by nonlocal policies and funding.

The separation of powers presents another obstacle to coordinated planning. Legislatures often appropriate funds and enact criminal statutes without considering effects on the administration of justice. The courts, whose primary purpose is justice, also sit astride the flow of offenders. Their traditional independence leads them to be very cautious in engaging in planning activities with the executive branch. In several States this has led to friction with criminal justice planning bodies.

Another problem is traceable to the newness of the planning process. Twenty years ago few criminal justice agencies had planners; many agencies do not even today. Most systemwide criminal justice planning agencies were established in States, regions, and counties only after the 1968 Safe Streets Act. It was inevitable that planners would encounter the same skepticism from established interests that early master planners encounter in the zoning/land use field. The latter assumed that their solutions provided the best of all possible worlds, and that mere publishing of the plans would summon the support needed for implementation. Naturally this did not happen.

When a new bureaucracy is created, it must prove itself. The first 5 years of operation usually are spent gaining a sense of the problem. Confidence is won only gradually. In a field as divided as criminal justice, this is especially true.

Perhaps the most serious problem facing planners is the lack of any firm understanding of the control of crime. It is impossible for planners to identify programs that will absolutely guarantee crime impact. Moreover, the probability of immediate breakthrough is unlikely due to the difficulty in using traditional experimental techniques to evaluate crime control programs. Thus knowledge will be accumulated only gradually and in piecemeal fashion.

Notes

1 President's Commission on Law Enforcement and Administration of Justice, *The Challenge of Crime in a Free Society* (Washington: Government Printing Office, 1967), p. 280.

2 Pub. L. 90–351, Title I, § 203, June 19, 1968, 82 Stat. 199.

3 Ibid.

4 National League of Cities and United States Conference of Mayors, *Criminal Justice Coordinating Councils*, Washington: 1971, p. 3.

5 Pub. L. 90–351, Title I, § 203, June 19, 1968, 82 Stat. 199 as amended by Pub. L. 91–644, Title I §3(a)–(c), Jan. 2, 1971, 84 Stat. 1881.

6 Pub. L. 90–351, Title I, § 301, June 19, 1968, 82 Stat. 199 as amended by Pub. L. 91–644, Title I, § 4 (2), Jan. 2, 1971, 84 Stat. 1882.

7 Source: fiscal year 1972 state planning grant applications submitted to LEAA.

8 Administration of Justice Division, Department of Economics and Community Development, *Towards a Safer, More Just Society*, Columbus: 1972, pp. XX–XXII.

9 National League of Cities, *Criminal Justice Coordinating Council*, p. 5.

10 New York City Criminal Justice Coordinating Council, *1972 Criminal Justice Plan*, New York: 1972.

11 Source: Budget Branch, LEAA. Part C and E action funds are included.

12 Source: Bureau of Census and LEAA.

13 The tentative results of an unpublished 1972 survey by the National Society of State Legislators of standing judiciary and related committees of State legislatures revealed that 25 percent of those committee chairmen responding either had never heard of the State planning agency or had no information on it. At the date this information was obtained, 60 of 123 chairmen in forty States had responded.

14 Nebraska Legislative Council, *Committee Report No. 195,* (Lincoln, Nebraska, March 1972).

15 Kentucky Crime Commission, *Kentucky's 1972 Comprehensive Criminal Justice Plan*, Frankfort, Kentucky, Appendix B.

16 Maryland Governor's Commission on Law Enforcement and the Administration of Justice, *Comprehensive Plan 1973*, Cockeysville, Maryland.

17   Wisconsin Council on Criminal Justice, *Application for Fy 1972 Planning Grant,* Madison, Wisconsin, Attachment D.

18   Source: Budget Branch, LEAA. These figures represent Part C Block Action Grants only. They do not include Part E Block Action Funds which are to be used specifically for aid to correctional institutions and programs. Part E Block Action Funds for 1971 totaled $45,000,000. See Table 1 for appropriations history of Part C and Part E funds.

19   Committee on Government Operations, *Block Grant Programs of the Law Enforcement Assistance Administration,* 92d Congress, 2d Session, 12th Report, May 18, 1972.

20   Council of State Governments, *State Progress in Planning and Budgeting Systems.* (Lexington, Kentucky: CSG, 1969).

21   Robert D. Lee (ed.), *Basic Documents of the Planning-Programming and Budgetary System of the Commonwealth of Pennsylvania: The Criminal Justice System.* University Park, Pennsylvania: Pennsylvania State University, 1971, pp. 1–10.

22   Council of State Governments, *State Progress in Planning and Budgeting,* pp. 1–3.

23   See Joseph S. Wholey, *Federal Evaluation Policy.* (Washington: The Urban Institute, 1970), p. 25.

24   Ibid. p. 28.

25   National Institute of Mental Health, *Criminal Statistics,* (Washington: Government Printing Office, 1972) Daniel Glaser, "National Goals and Indicators for the Reduction of Crime and Delinquency" *Annals of the American Academy of Political and Social Science,* Vol. 371 (May, 1967), pp. 104–126.

26   Law Enforcement Assistance Administration, *Performance Management System,* unpublished report, 1971. The Urban Institute and the International City Management Association, *Improving Productivity Measurement and Evaluation in Local Governments* (Prepared for the National Commission on Productivity) (Washington: UI and ICMA, 1972). Richard B. Hoffman, "Performance Measurements in Crime Control," *Journal of Research in Crime and Delinquency,* Vol. 8 (July, 1972, pp. 165–174).

27   See, for example, Alfred Blumstein and Richard Larson, *Models of a Total Criminal Justice System* (Arlington, Virginia: Institute for Defense Analysis, 1970).

28   NYCJCC, *1972 Criminal Justice Plan,* p. 179.

William R. Drake

Criminal justice planning:
objectives for the future

Criminal justice planning, a speciality unknown six years ago, is still groping for a clear sense of direction, priorities, process, and products. Burdened with the traditional complaint about planning—lack of relevance to the real world—criminal justice planning has suffered even more from exceptionally high expectations on the part of Congress, federal administrators, state and local officials, and planners themselves.

More dramatically than in any recent governmental effort, an entirely new professional specialty was created overnight by the recommendations of the President's Crime Commission in 1967 and passage of the Omnibus Crime Control and Safe Streets Act of 1968. And significantly, the control and direction of criminal justice planning from the beginning was placed directly in the hands of elected and appointed officials at the state and local levels. It is well, then, to reflect on the results of this experiment, particularly at the local level where officials are most directly concerned with the critical problems of crime and justice.

What does criminal justice planning mean to the local official and administrator? At its worst, it is just something you have to do in order to obtain federal funds. At its best, it is an exciting new planning speciality that already is producing tangible results and changing the governmental process in many localities. For most cities, the truth probably lies somewhere between these two extremes. But whatever the state of the art in a given locality, in general it can be said that criminal justice planning is now old enough to know better and still young enough to learn.

One observer of public affairs, a Minnesota state senator, has stated that:

No doctrine has been more firmly imbedded in the American intergovernmental system than the necessity of planning. No grant-in-aid program has been discovered that does not require it and few, if any, public administrators will deny its primacy as a prerequisite for the obtaining of state and federal aid; yet no governmental activity bears as little relevance to the actual operation of the system. (David J. Kennedy, "The Law of Appropriateness: An Approach to a General Theory of Intergovernmental Relations."

Criminal justice planning may become the exception to this rule, but only if we are honest about its flaws and realistic about its future directions. Oddly enough, planning for the criminal justice system clearly was never "firmly imbedded in the intergovernmental system." In fact, it was virtually unknown, except as it had developed within a small number of major police departments, a few correctional agencies, and the most sophisticated court systems. Nowhere, before 1968, was there a planning effort that sought to interrelate or coordinate the numerous, disparate components of the criminal justice system.

This fact has given public officials, their staffs, and criminal justice executives an unusual opportunity to start from scratch, make frustrating and often painful mistakes, and gradually begin to create a new process of communication, coordination, and increased cooperation among the elements of what was only first recognized as a "system" in 1967. And what have we learned?

• The criminal justice system is, first and foremost, a complex intergovernmental network, and any attempts to focus on only one level of government or one agency will be inadequate.

• Traditional methodologies for planning, policy formulation, and coordination are either irrelevant or ineffective.

• Federal grant programs cannot change the world and, moreover, they are a pain in the neck and often get in the way of doing significant planning.

• Elected officials have had, and still have, too little influence on criminal justice policies and agency operations.

• Planning, budgeting, and evaluation are indeed closely related, and we had better start tying them together.

• Comprehensive criminal justice planning (although no one knows precisely what that is) must go beyond the police, courts, and correctional systems to include the social, physical, and economic environment, as well as the public and private institutions that deliver services to people.

• "Writing grants" is easier, often better politics, and more immediately rewarding than planning for long-term change, and this is true at all levels of government.

• Planners often receive rewards for producing exciting, "innovative" plans which the objective observer, as well as the self-interested bureaucrat, know cannot be implemented.

• The level of crime in our cities may have little or nothing to do with the operation of the law enforcement and criminal justice system.

It has been quite popular to point out that criminal justice planning and the LEAA program are "experiments in intergovernmental relations," but this has both a positive and negative side. Although new approaches to intergovernmental coordination and cooperation are badly needed, local officials have frequently felt that the LEAA program was designed with local government as the target of the experiment, rather than as a participant. Although it is essentially a bloc grant program, the LEAA bloc grant normally stops at the state level and is then cut into pieces within a categorical "state plan." Local officials, encouraged to plan and establish priorities, often have discovered that their own priorities are unacceptable to the state, a phenomenon which sounds more like the old truisms of city-state relations than a new experiment.

Beyond the seemingly inevitable tensions between local and state governments, there is a more basic and pervasive problem: Just as in communications, where McLuhan's medium is the message, the grant process tends to become the beginning and end of planning.

This, then, has been the major failing of local, state, and federal criminal justice planning. By the nature of the process, most planners have consumed their time concerned with individual grant projects, rather than with the operation of a given component or the criminal justice system as a whole. The public official, in turn, is forced by the grant planning process to spend inordinate amounts of time on specific, narrow grant programs, rather than on the broad policies and strategies needed to produce substantive change.

It is important to emphasize the difficulty in changing bad habits, and the federal grant process does more than its share to encourage bad planning habits. But the stakes are high. The local official who seeks to improve his criminal justice system needs the most sophisticated analysis possible, along with well designed improvement strategies that go beyond grant programs to assess the performance, needs, budgets, and interrelationships among all elements of that system. He has to recognize that LEAA grants at best contribute only 5 per cent of the operating budget for police, court, and correctional services, and that even the most ingenious use of grant projects will not make a dramatic impact. This is not to say that grant projects cannot be highly successful in their own right; but rather to point out that even the best individual projects often fail to have a major impact on the rest of the system around them.

Institutionalization, the popular term for incorporating on an ongoing basis a pilot or experimental project, demands a kind of continuing planning that seldom exists today. No intelligent planner would deny that planning and implementation are two different creatures, but many planners seem to believe the world is just waiting to accept their brainchild and set it in motion ad infinitum.

Yet the reality is that few organizations enthusiastically welcome a new activity or operation, unless it remains separate from the ongoing machinery and doesn't disrupt the carefully constructed organizational and administrative dynamics of the agency. Planning, which has traditionally maintained a distance from implementation and operation, must step closer to the machinery of the criminal justice system and follow its creations through the difficult struggles for existence, acceptance, and incorporation into the system.

In developing a local capacity for criminal justice planning, it is essential to recognize the structural, procedural, methodological, and political constraints that must be confronted before effective planning can become a reality. Although it is now common to refer to the variety of criminal justice agencies as parts of a system with certain common objectives, the fragmentation and diversity is rather awesome. The typical city or municipality has full responsibility only for police services and some type of limited court structure. Yet even these are subject to only partial control by local officials, with police departments traditionally being quite autonomous from control and leadership by elected officials. Municipal courts, in a variety of forms, are commonly part of a statewide judicial system, and are, at any rate, legally separate from the executive and legislative agencies of government.

Responsibility for other elements of the criminal justice system is vested at the county, state, or federal levels of government, but here too policies and operations are to a large degree beyond the control of elected legislative or executive officials. This organizational and operational fragmentation is compounded by the additional complexities of variations in state criminal codes, municipal ordinances, and procedural rules. Finally, the system at all levels draws upon the services of numerous other public and private agencies which are essential to its operation.

As a result of the complex organization of the various components of the criminal justice system, planning for improvement must from the beginning have an intergovernmental and interagency focus. Even the most basic task of any planning effort—data collection—can proceed only with great difficulty due to the lack of systematic procedures for reporting and exchanging information. Along with the traditional reluctance of most organizations to share information freely, the practical problems of identifying, retrieving, and analyzing relevant data are immense.

Data on crime itself is the most difficult to obtain. Planners and public officials have until very recently been forced to rely upon the analysis of crimes reported to the police, because data on the actual volume or rates of crime could not be obtained. Recently, however, the use of victimization studies, which measure through personal surveys the extent to which persons have been the victims of crimes (whether or not they were reported), have demonstrated that as little as one-third to one-half of actual crime is reported to the police. Now, although this new technique is providing a more accurate picture of the actual crime phenomena, it will become increasingly clear that we know very little about the causes and prevention of crime and the impact of the law enforcement and criminal justice system on the level of crime.

It should be evident that these constraints make it difficult to define the goals of criminal justice planning. Although it is generally assumed that improvements to the police, courts, and corrections systems will lead to crime reduction, it is entirely possible that such a direct relationship does not exist. It is just that dilemma that has led to the definition of several planning methodologies, which should be seen as complementary to each other.

System Improvement Planning proceeds from the assumption that improving the efficiency and effectiveness of the criminal justice system will ultimately reduce crime. This approach was implicit in the Crime Control Act of 1968 and has been the basis for most local planning since that time. Planners have sought to analyze crime, the operations of police, court, and correctional agencies, and develop improved operational techniques within the framework of a comprehensive plan.

Crime Specific or Crime-Oriented Planning. With the recognition that general system improvement did not seem to have the direct impact on crime that had been expected, it has been proposed that a focus on the analysis of specific crimes, with careful scrutiny of victim, offender, and environmental characteristics, could be used to design strategies for prevention, control, or treatment in relation to given types of crime. Analyzing the characteristics of muggings or rapes, for instance, can provide greater understanding of the circumstances under which such crimes are committed and lead to definition of special policing, community action, or educational approaches to prevention. Analysis of offender types can then be used to develop more effective court procedures and correctional treatment.

Standards. Because, as we have seen, the criminal justice system operates in a great variety of legal, organizational, and administrative environments, it has been impossible to establish criteria for operation and measures of performance. The local official had until recently been forced to look at his own system more or less in isolation from other systems, because he lacked both comparative data and a frame of reference upon which to establish local goals or standards. As Mayor Lawrence Cohen describes in another article in this special report, recent work by the National Advisory Commission on Criminal Justice Standards and Goals has led to the development of a recommended set of standards and goals which can be used for planning and policy formulation.

Within these general planning approaches, there exist various possible methodologies for analysis. However, these are less important to the local official or executive than the choices as to emphasis on the different basic approaches and decisions on the structure and process for criminal justice planning. Without clear direction and support from the policy level, any approach will tend to prove the thesis that planning has little relevance to the operation of the system. In other words, the planners, policymakers, and implementors must get together from the very beginning and a vehicle for communication, cooperation, and coordination must be created among what have been in the past largely unrelated agencies and institutions.

The recognition of the separation of powers among executive, legislative, and judicial branches of government (as well as among the various autonomous elements of the criminal justice system) has led in many cities to the creation of criminal justice coordinating councils (CJCC's). A CJCC can be a formal or informal mechanism, but the basic objective is to provide a forum for exploration of criminal justice problems and issues among the key decisionmakers in the governmental system. Typically, a committee is established by ordinance, executive order, or informal agreement, with membership by elected and appointed officials, criminal justice officials, and the public at large.

There is no rigid requirement for a CJCC or similar committee. It is the concept that is important. The council discusses and reviews the work of planners and establishes goals, policies, and programs for implementation. The broad-based participation ensures that a reasonable level of cooperation and coordination will develop, and indeed, many localities have found that issues are readily discussed that officials previously had not had the opportunity to explore in any structured manner. Perhaps most important, key officials and executives have an opportunity to relate planning activities to reality and to develop initiatives that can be focused on priority problems.

The CJCC concept is not without its deficiencies, however. Because most councils have been created in response to LEAA funding, their focus has tended to be overwhelmingly oriented to planning for federal grant projects.

Grants, as has been stated earlier, represent only a small portion of the criminal justice operating budget, and the process of grantsmanship can easily skew the orientation of all concerned away from improvements that can be, or should be, implemented through statutory, administrative, organizational, or local budgetary adjustments. Long-term change will require that criminal justice planning increasingly focus less on federal grants and more on building a multi-faceted strategy for crime prevention and improvement to the quality of justice.

The experience of cities during the last six years has made clear the need for substantial improvement in the planning process itself. Recognizing that the newness of criminal justice planning provides one of the greatest opportunities for continuing innovation, it should be possible to enhance both the process and the products through adoption of a well-developed local approach. The following suggestions are designed to respond to the most critical weaknesses of present criminal justice planning efforts:

• Planning must see federal grants as only one mechanism for change.

• Planning for grants must be related to local budgetary planning. Ideally, a CJCC or other planning committee should establish a role in the review of line agency budgets.

• While a central planning capacity, under the chief executive, is essential, planning in line agencies must also be developed so that effective input can be made and adequate attention given to the internal operations of criminal justice agencies.

• Elected executive and legislative officials must establish a dominant voice in the policies and operations of criminal justice agencies, both in terms of grants and ongoing operational improvements.

• Participation in the planning process must extend beyond the criminal justice system and local officials to include all segments of the community.

• Techniques for incorporating successful grant projects into existing organizations must be planned at the beginning of the funding process, and grants for which institutionalization is highly unlikely should be assigned a low priority for funding.

• Improvement efforts, both grant funded and those implemented through other methods, must be monitored and evaluated from the beginning. Although evaluation need not mean the extensive research which is often associated with the term, collection and analysis of key data is essential for policy control and for making choices concerning allocation of the scarce resource of federal or local dollars.

• Planning methodology must focus as much as possible on prevention and control of specific crimes. At the same time, institutional improvements should be sought through the establishment of standards and goals for the criminal justice system.

• Improving the fairness of the law enforcement and criminal justice system must be an implicit goal throughout the planning process.

• Planning must recognize that our understanding of crime is limited, and that improvements to the social, economic, and physical conditions of our cities will undoubtedly have a greater effect on crime than will criminal justice improvements alone.

Criminal justice planning offers to the local official an opportunity to develop effective and just strategies for crime prevention and control. An honest assessment of existing or proposed local planning efforts is an essential step in bringing this planning specialty to maturity.

Patrick Murphy
Oliver Lofton
Joseph Coates

Community crime prevention
and the local official:
three views

Introduction

The National League of Cities' Public Safety Committee's
seminar at last year's annual Congress of Cities was "Community Crime Prevention and the Public Official." The purpose of the meeting was, in the words of the Committee
Chairman, Mayor James J. Eagan of Florissant, Mo., "to
carefully discuss the issues of how the public official should
and can serve as a bridge between expressed community
needs and capacities and the operation of local criminal
justice agencies."

The concept of "community crime prevention" calls for the
mobilization of all community resources toward removing
the desire or need for an individual to commit crime as well
as toward reducing opportunities to commit crime. The local
official can play a very important role as the link that joins
the citizenry, the criminal justice agencies, and other municipal resources in achieving this mobilization. It is the local
official who makes final decisions about allocating criminal
justice resources and to whom the citizen turns for resolution
of the crime problem.

This Special Report was prepared for *Nation's Cities* by the Criminal Justice Project
of the National League of Cities and U.S. Conference of Mayors, under Grant No.
73TA990004 from the Law Enforcement Assistance Administration, U.S. Department of Justice. Harold F. Klubertanz, Project Associate, coordinated activities for
the report.

Excerpts from the remarks of the three speakers at the seminar—Patrick Murphy, Oliver Lofton, and Joseph Coates —are reprinted in this article. Murphy's presentation focused on involving the police department in community crime prevention. Lofton offered the citizen's perspective on developing a community-wide assault on crime. Coates examined futurist developments in criminal justice.

The edited proceeding of the entire seminar are available in a National League of Cities and U.S. Conference of Mayors publication, *Community Crime Prevention and the Local Official*, from the League's and Conference's Criminal Justice Project.

Patrick Murphy, *President,* *Police Foundation*

The police cannot do the job alone. It takes a team, as some of the public relations talk has put it—the citizen and the police working together. Obviously, the police are very dependent upon citizens for reporting crimes, for reporting suspicious activities, for being willing to appear as witnesses in cases, and to just be supportive of the police.

By being supportive I mean: to understand the police and to cooperate with them. I don't mean it necessarily in the sense that the bumper sticker says "Support Your Local Police and Keep Them Independent." In fact, one of the problems with policing in the United States is that in too many places policing is too independent. That means that too many mayors either don't know how, or have not wanted, to completely fulfill their roles as elected officials responsible for policing of their cities. By the same token, there are too many mayors who want to run their police department and don't know how to run them. And there are too many mayors who want to get their cotton-picking political fingers into their cotton-picking police departments; and that's not always good.

But on the whole police departments aren't quite independent in the United States. One of the reasons may be that the administration and the management of a police department is much more complex than we may be inclined to think on the face of it. Unfortunately, too many people—not only mayors, city managers, budget directors, controllers and legislators, but the man or woman on the street—think they understand the problems and the intricacies of policing. Too often, simple solutions are provided and recommended because not enough work or time is spent on learning what the issues in policing are.

My own view is that the routine patrol concept is not valid: it's part of the military concept. The officer doing street work—the officer in uniform or the marked police car—will be much more valuable if a share of his time is spent in interacting with citizens, in introducing himself to the people, in learning the community.

Many of you have read about the team policing programs and experiments that are under way in the country. Most of these team policing programs are based on two ideas. First, that it makes sense to assign police officers to one neighborhood and, as far as possible, keep them in that one neighborhood. Second, to involve the police officers with the citizens as much as possible.

The officers will then receive more information, they will get greater cooperation from the citizens and they will be much more effective in controlling, preventing, and reducing crime and in providing the many, many other services that the police provide for citizens. Incidentally, more than 80 per cent of the time of the police is spent in providing service rather than in enforcing the law. But much of that 80 per cent of the time is devoted to activities that do have an impact on crime prevention.

As these new models of policing and patrolling are experimented with, it is my belief that we will see police work become more effective; we will see the police more acceptable to all citizens; and we will see an increase in citizen participation and cooperation which I think are essential ingredients to good crime control.

Oliver Lofton, *President, Priorities Investment Corp.*

One way to reduce or prevent crime in this country is for the total community to insist that the criminal justice system redefine what is in fact a crime. And the redefinition that I would embrace and offer is, "behavior that is deviant and which has a specific victim or a clearly deleterious effect upon the total society." While there is some imprecision in this definition, I think it is better than the one currently employed. This redefinition would decriminalize such activities as gambling, prostitution, and marijuana use when engaged in by adults. One of the ways to reduce crime, in other words, is to redefine what is in fact crime.

It can be said without fear of much contradiction that in most communities across the country the relationship between the citizens and the police is less than satisfactory. This problem is accentuated, and is most acute, in the urban areas. I think that this negative relationship between the police and the people is one of the most critical factors militating against an effective crime prevention program being inaugurated in those communities. So it doesn't do much good to talk about specific programs or projects to be undertaken to improve citizen participation in crime prevention without first dealing with the attitudes of the average urban citizen toward the police and vice versa.

Community crime prevention depends to a very large extent upon a healthy attitude existing between the people and the police. It depends upon the people having a high level of confidence and trust in their police. As long as the confidence and trust level remains low, the people will frequently not notify the police of situations that require enforcement or prevention. And the public will avoid involvement in, or interfering with, criminal conduct.

Here's an example of what I'm talking about. During a recent trip, I picked up the paper and read about a community crime prevention effort. It involved a team of plain-clothed black police officers working out of a storefront center. The long and the short of the article was an interview with the officers. The center was enjoying minimal success, they said, because the people were apparently hostile and suspicious of the officers. And this hostility, this suspicion, this lack of trust existed even though these officers were black, in plainclothes and functioning in this low-profile and helpful manner.

This example of a minimally successful community crime prevention program is reflective of the results of most such programs. They are really band-aid efforts which deal with the symptoms of crime and potential criminal behavior and not with the root causes. Now this is not to say that such efforts at segmented community crime prevention should be discontinued, but it does suggest that the expectation level for success should be kept realistic. To summarize:

1. Community crime control programs will enjoy minimal success until the root causes of most criminal behavior are removed.

2. There is a direct connection between the socio-economic level of people and their cooperation with the police in any effort at community crime prevention; that is, the lower the socio-economic level, the less cooperation.

3. In order to reduce or prevent the high level of crime we should decriminalize certain acts which are now classified as crimes.

4. The total society must accept the responsibility for crime prevention and not attempt to relegate that responsibility solely to the criminal justice system.

Joseph Coates, *Office of Exploratory Research, National Science Foundation*

Let me list some of the characteristics of the criminal justice system itself which are impediments to effective action and planning for its new future.

First, there is an almost complete present-orientation. I know of only three papers in the criminal justice literature that have "future" in their titles. This is one rough measure of how the system is locked to the present.

The second issue is the social class structure in the criminal justice system. It's an uncongenial subject for Americans to discuss, but the class origins of lawyers, judges, policemen, and corrections officers may be major inhibitors of change in the system. In the police world, one finds a peculiar brotherhood attitude, an attitude of closure, or secretiveness. This works against openness and receptiveness, not just to citizen participation, but to new modes of action.

Another feature of the criminal justice system, and of our society, is bureaucratization. You can't get away from bureaucracy, and the problem is to learn to control it in new ways. Any mature bureaucracy, and they mature in about three years, has a number of characteristics. They do not primarily address the function for which they ostensibly exist: bureaucracies instead exist predominantly to perpetuate themselves, to keep themselves safe, funded, and adequately employed. They reject new information. They have no memory. They have no adequate reward system. And they tend in general to shy away from bad news, or if it is thrust upon them, to go into paralysis or worse.

They also tend to be susceptible to a condition I call "functional lying." That's different from the kind of lying a 10-year-old experiences. The 10-year-old says, "No, I didn't take the cookies." You slap him, and that's the end of that. He learns he'll be punished if he steals a cookie. But the bureaucracies are different. They functionally lie, very often because one end of the system does not know what the other end of the system is doing. Then the system retracts into its shell; it denies that it lied; it ends up saying, "We didn't do it, and we promise never to do it again," rather than facing the issue squarely. Police brutality is an excellent issue in which to explore this phenomenon.

An adequate reward structure is essential to effectively influence bureaucracy. Just take the police department in your community. Do any of you have a police department that could be characterized as having a special, or an unusual, unique, or particularly effective reward system for effective performance? In a room of 100 people, there will be one or two who claim that they do have such a system. Yet, the reward system is the one way in which change can be brought about in a stable bureaucracy.

The way to challenge a bureaucrat on this issue is to ask him the following questions: Do you have a system for rewarding effective performance? If he says, "No," you proceed in one direction. If he says, "Yes," then you lay it to him in the following way: "Name the last five people you have rewarded and tell me precisely what they did." That usually sets him into a trance.

The lack of reward structures is directly related to the general crisis in authority in our society. Nobody should fully trust a public official, because by and large the public experience is that some public officials up and down the bureaucracy are not trustworthy in performing their duties, i.e., their primary focus is not on understanding and doing their jobs. If you doubt this, let me suggest the following experiment—if you have the gall to try it.

Get a relative—a cousin, an uncle, somebody who is not publicly known—and have him register a complaint with the police, have him try to have the garbage picked up, have her report a rape. Make 10 routine challenges on your bureaucratic system, anywhere, the way a citizen would, and see what happens. Try to get information. Try to put yourself in the position of an ordinary citizen and you'll see some of the second-rate aspects of the system your community is undoubtedly functioning under. And that can only be changed through the manipulation of reward systems.

Leslie T. Wilkins

Crime and criminal justice at the turn of the century

ABSTRACT: The probability that the criminal justice system will suffer a complete breakdown before the year 2000 should not be discounted. If law and social control systems are to accommodate change in their environment at the necessary rate, a new philosophy, as well as quite different operating procedures, must be worked out. The present strategy of law enforcement agencies to develop more-of-the-same can only ensure breakdown. Pressures for control will increase, and with each new pressure on criminals, more side-effects of these pressures will have an impact upon all citizens. The best moral standard which can be expected to guide policy in the intervening years is enlightened self-interest; this may suffice to ensure survival. The quality of that survival may be improved by the development of a new class of moral philosophers out of the ranks of scientists and technicians. No great new moral leadership is expected from organized religions. Politics will mix dangerous sentimentality and nostalgia with more than a small modicum of fear. Much of that fear will be focused on the criminal. Millions of dollars will continue to be wasted on research. If we wish for a better kind of future for criminal justice, we must start to invent it now. However, there is no indication that we are ready to consider the necessary issues.

We are focusing our attention today on the turn of the century—the year 2000. Does this seem a long way off? Does 1986 seem to be half way there, or considerably less than half way? In some respects, we can say that 1986 is half way towards the year

A Ford Foundation Grant facilitated the preparation of this paper.

Reprinted here from *The Annals of the American Academy of Political and Social Science*, July 1973, pp. 13–29, with the kind permission of the Academy and Leslie T. Wilkins.

500

2000, because we can do the simple arithmetic involved. But in terms of the character, quality and types of events, we would do well to assume that a difference of any number of years in the more distant future is greater than a similar difference at more proximate dates. The ten years from 1990 to 2000 may be expected to see more significant changes than the ten years from 1980 to 1990. This is the inference which must be drawn from the best data we have, as interpreted by the great majority of experts in all fields.[1]

Non-linear time

What is the significance of this non-linear idea of time upon our concepts of justice, crime, police, the courts and the other services or procedures concerned with social control through law? Clearly, the legal process has tended, and still tends, to be reactive rather than proactive. Situations first arise, and then procedures are worked out or adapted to cope with the changed situations or changed perspectives. We are all familiar with the Blue Laws; with the divergence between the current legal view of the use of certain stimulants and contemporary social philosophy and medical opinion; with the differential difficulties in legalizing acts currently illegal, as distinct from the difficulties in making additional acts illegal. Laws are easier to make than to un-make. Thus, an increasing residue of inappropriate legislation tends to remain on the statute books. New legislation could, perhaps, be made in advance of a problem, but it would be difficult, or impossible, to remove legislation—to legalize acts—before the climate of opinion was past ready.

Legislation, by reason of its very nature, has difficulties in coping with projections and probabilities; future events, no matter how probable, do not provide a strong argument. Legislation must, by this token, and indeed almost by definition, always be out-of-date![2] If the rate of change is itself changing—and there seems to be considerable agreement that this is so—then it follows that we must postulate that legislation will become more and more irrelevant to current situations, as we project the time base for "current" further and further towards 2000. If the disparity between law and the needs of contemporary social control is mismatched, then that degree of mismatching will tend to increase as we move towards the next century.

Can the rule of law survive to 2000?

If this argument is considered to be reasonable, then we might assess some of the probable consequences for law and social control. We may, indeed, ask whether our present concepts of the nature of law and the legal processes can survive much further into the future. If we wish to continue to have a form of social control through law, then considering new forms of legal philosophies at this time might be essential. We may be able, by means of the legal process, to deal with consequences of some events after they have taken place, but can we postulate the feasibility of reconstructing a legal system once it has broken down? Legal controls may be delayed in dealing with external problems; it may be both feasible and reasonable for law to be reactive rather than proactive about matters external to itself; but could law possibly be reactive to its own failure to operate? This latter form of failure is a different kind of breakdown—the breakdown of the machinery, the thing itself, rather than the things or events to which it reacts. The prospects are none too bright.

Can we see any traces of a new philosophy of law and social control which could begin to accommodate change—and change at an ever increasing rate? Guides to the future may usually be found in the present. Much of the future is in the pipeline today; a product must be on the drawing board before it can be on the production line, and on the production line before it can be on the market. What, then, of the changing state of law and social control as it now appears?

CURRENT PROJECTIONS AND PLANNING

In the current trends, I find little upon which to base hopes of the survival of law as a viable social control mechanism. One thing is clear; the majority of the current planning in the criminal justice system, which is not regressive, seeks solutions by means of more-of-the-same.[3] The idea of more-of-the-same makes projections—using mathematical formulations—extremely easy. Demographers could simply forecast the future populations, if it were given that the birth and death rates would remain constant. Indeed, such projections are trivial, even as projections. If we are a little more sophisticated, we can assume that the rate-of-change of the rate-of-change will remain the same—that the sort of changes which are now currently going on indicate the kinds of changes which may be expected in the future. This basis might give a more useful set of projections. If we make such kinds of projections with regard to our criminal justice processes, there is only one outcome, namely, the total breakdown of the system. This breakdown must take place before the year 2000.

Such an outcome is a distinct possibility. It is, in my view, much more than a possibility; it has the appearance of a certainty, if we assume that the idea of more-of-the-same continues to be invoked as the solution of present and projected problems of crime and social control. What may change this perspective? Perhaps the best known way of ensuring that we do not go down an undesirable road is that we become aware of the contingencies of this course of action, or inaction, and divert the existing trends by the conscious planning and developing of appropriate strategies. In a complex society, such planning calls for the use of all the techniques of modern analysis. It may be that our present techniques are not adequate; but as yet we do not know this because we have not attempted to apply them in the area of criminal justice. Research is too expensive; we cannot bother about long term problems; instant solutions are required to today's problems—preferably by using yesterday's methods.

MAKING PROJECTIONS INVALID

These projections may be invalidated if those concerned see the disaster when its first manifestations appear and then change course, in any direction other than ahead. If we are fortunate—and we may have some slight degree of luck—the breakdown will be somewhat localized, not too widespread, in the first instance. From the local breakdowns we may be able to learn of the consequences of the courses of action to which we are committed. The events at Attica, the Tombs and other dramatic incidents illustrate this kind of breakdown.[4] And it is possible to learn from events like Attica. We can adjust to these kinds of events like a blind man steered by trippings. As I see it, the road toward 2000 which the field of criminal justice seems likely to take is of this form. There will be serious, dramatic and violent breakdowns in our attempts to implement the more-of-the-same of current law and order practices. We will be steered by the resulting dramatic events, quite probably, into random responses and diversionary tactics, rather than into the development of a strategy based on projections, planning and attempts to foresee the consequences of probable events before they occur.

Having thus established my position as a prophet of gloom, it is hardly necessary for me to reveal myself as a critic of the present system. Indeed, the basis for gloom about the future is essentially derived from a critical appraisal of the present. We are inventing the future now.

The dynamic concept of crime

I must now state one theoretical position. I cannot discuss crime in the future without saying something about the dynamics of crime— or more particularly, what we mean when we use that word.

Crime, sin and deviation from normal behavior have been the concern of mankind from earliest times. If people are to live together in groups, it is essential that they be able to make predictions of each other's probable behavior. It is easy to think that if everybody obeyed the law, and if the law were of sufficient coverage and specificity, then we would be able to predict behavior and to have an ordered society. But in the social world of man there seems to be little connection between law and order—despite the conjunction of recent times into one word "law'n'order" which means something different from either law or order! Despite centuries of concern regarding individual actions regarded as intolerable, the behaviors which have been prohibited at different times and in different places fail to reveal many common features. Almost any crime has at some time and in some connection been lauded as a virtue.[5] In history, a very considerable number of methods for stating the prohibitions and for mediating the controls can be found: kings, priests, doctors (medicine men!) and, occasionally, some persons rather akin to academics. Some common feature might be found in functional terms, if not in terms of the particular acts or events. It appears that for a society to function as a social organization, there is a need for some of its members to be treated as outcasts, criminals or heretics. The pretext upon which the exclusion is made does not seem to matter; it is the act of exclusion which is significant. As Kai Erikson has suggested, and I agree, this rejection process provides a boundary defining function for society. The proportion of the population rejected has varied over time and varies within extremely wide limits today between jurisdictions. Clearly, the majority of the population is usually included rather than excluded; but there have been exceptions.[6]

The proportion of the population defined by a society as representing its outcasts is dependent upon its machinery of government. This is almost self-evident, since we may, operationally, define law as that which legislators legislate; these laws describe the kinds of persons who may be incarcerated or otherwise separated from society. If there is any moral basis for law, it must be accepted that that morality is mediated through the political system. We are currently seeing a growing awareness of the close interconnectedness between the political system and the legal system; the moral underpinnings for this are in doubt. The more certainly and the more widely the legal system is thought to be associated with the political system, the more legal concepts and procedures will be questioned, especially by those who do not favor the party in power.

Crime, politics and morals

It is difficult to postulate a system of law which is not supported, to a greater or lesser degree, by some ethical premises. It is difficult to consider the probable future states of a criminal justice system without making somewhat detailed assumptions about the likely political structure. The connection—both logical and operational— between law, morals and politics may take different forms, but the tripartite connections are essential. Where can we look for some indication of the probable nature of moral value systems in the future?

It is likely that, even today, the moral climate of a nation or state and the values subscribed to by the majority of the population are more accurately reflected in the political structure, rather than in the religious protestations. For an indication of the prevailing ideas of what may be right or wrong, we would be advised to consider the speeches and actions of politicians, rather than to analyze the homilies of the priests. And politics is, of course, about power, rather than about morals. There is a further complication, or a fourth dimension; namely, that of technology or knowledge—the moral, the political and the epistemological systems interact in the process of law. The prominence of any one of these as compared with the others varies from time to time, and each may have some elements of conflict with the others.

In the area of law, crime and social control, we have, then, the intersections of several dimensions. At the conceptual level—as distinct from the operational level—two major considerations appear in any attempt to project into the future: namely, the technological and the moral future states. Projecting technological developments accurately is generally thought to be simpler; and indeed, there have been some quite remarkable forecasts. Where serious forecasts have been made, with the use of sophisticated methods of analysis, and have subsequently been disproved, the projected date for the technological development has most often been found to be the inaccurate factor. The developments took place before the expected time.[7] On the other hand, projecting likely future moral standards seems to be much more difficult. We cannot quantify moral positions; we cannot use envelope curves or other numerical analyses of trends. In the current symposium, we do not have a presentation dealing with projections with respect either to moral value systems or to political trends.

MORAL VALUES AND CRIME

Although discussing morals is completely outside my particular field of expertise, it is essential that I make some statements in this area. I may be completely wrong about these issues; but in order to make my analysis hold together, I must make some suggestions with regard to the present connection between the fields of criminology and moral philosophy and then set forth some guesses about the future.

There is little doubt that several aspects of crime and illegal behavior in the United States, and in many other countries, are related to the Judaic-Christian ethic and, particularly, to that aspect which has been termed the White Anglo-Saxon Protestant ethic. I would accept Eric Trist's listing of "four corner-stones of our traditional morality: achievement, self-control, independence, and endurance of distress (grin and bear it!)."[8] Of course, some of these values are shared by cultures which are not dominated by the American way of life. However, we must also acknowledge that economic forces, in addition to moral or religious forces, have tended to spread these kinds of values widely in all developed and developing countries. Linked with this package of values is the political doctrine of democracy as practiced at present. I must confess as an amateur in this area, that I am surprised that the commentators take too little account of the impact of Greek and Roman culture on value systems. I wish only to stress one point: namely, that it is impossible to discuss the future of crime, how it is defined and what may be done about it, without paying considerable attention to the probable changes of moral standards and value systems. If there are doubts about this thesis, perhaps one supporting note might be made. Almost all authorities agree that child-rearing practices are related to the probability of criminal behavior later in life; certainly, it must be agreed that concepts of moral values are learned in childhood. Even if modified or unlearned at a later stage, usually a foundation of moral concepts is set in the home.

As already stated, it is difficult to deal with projections in these terms because we lack any reasonable metric. It is a useful strategy when faced with a problem which cannot be solved to see whether it can be made more complex. In operational research circles, it is recognized that a factor which cannot be measured in absolute terms can often be graded in comparative terms. For example, it would be absurd for me to ask, "How happy are you today?" but, to ask, "Are you happier today than yesterday?" would be somewhat more reasonable. Similarly, it is sometimes possible to obtain a crude measure of an interaction between two factors without being able to assess either singly.[9] In order to attempt to use this strategy, I want to demonstrate that our system of knowledge interacts with our system of morals. I shall then consider some of the interactions which I think I observe in relation to value systems and then try to formulate some conjectures regarding moral values for the future.

THE INTERACTION BETWEEN MORALS AND KNOWLEDGE

A fair presentation of the relationship between our system of knowledge, technology and morals would become a rather lengthy discussion of semantics and the relationship between linguistic glossaries, technology, metaphors and values.[10] However, for our present purposes an example may suffice. One may recall the discussion of the moral issues of abortion. The question as to when life begins relates to aspects of knowledge of the gestation processes, and this is turned into a consideration of a moral nature. I am not arguing for the relevance of this approach, but noting its existence. It might appear that a detailed consideration of almost any issue of morals is related in contemporary thought to technology and the assumed state of knowledge. It is unlikely that a connection between moral and knowledge dimensions will cease in the near future. We will, I suspect, continue to relate our beliefs to our knowledge and to discuss moral issues in the light of technology. I would go so far as to predict that a closer association between knowledge systems and moral values will characterize the future.

Future value conflicts

As in other areas, I would expect conflicting approaches to develop. Cults which may be characterized by an anti-scientific set of rituals may also be expected to gain strength. Attempts, by various means and for a variety of probable ends, to separate the consideration of ethical and belief issues from the field of knowledge, may be expected to find many supporters. Those who find the connection between moral values and knowledge inconvenient may try to find support for their moral claims by bizarre beliefs or in counter-knowledge. Odd, long forgotten and often inconsequential phrases culled from once revered texts will be rediscovered and used to serve as the basis for an image for a new faith. Beliefs, practices and moral standards which could not find support in more rational or scientific concepts may, thus, claim antiquity, revelation or insight. It is then possible to separate beliefs from knowledge and yet to furnish an attractive product. The Bible will continue to be popular as a source of materials for those who find it desirable to separate belief systems from knowledge systems. Other ancient books, as well as rites, rituals and taboos will also become attractive sources. We may expect to see a preference for Eastern or African cultures, rather than Western or even Near Eastern. This class of organization will regard the scientific method and changing technology as irrelevant.

Another class of ritual system may also gain considerable support. Rather than regarding the world of technology as irrelevant, these groups will have a distinctive anti-scientific appeal. Some may claim to have knowledge beyond that offered by scientific explanation. The proponents of this class of rituals hope to capitalize upon the prestige of science while attempting to undermine the basic principles of the scientific method. They can do this by discussing with special confidence those areas of knowledge which scientists consider to be characterized by the greatest degree of uncertainty.

A third class of ritual organization, which will probably attract less support than the other two, may be categorized as pseudo-scientific. The most legitimate of these may be little more, or less, than play groups for working scientists. These organizations, although possessing certain of the qualities of the other groups, may lead to scientific speculation and provide a link with artists, poets and musicians to produce art forms and develop the creative imagination of their participants.

A SELLERS MARKET FOR RITUALS

The origins of the new ritual groups will differ. Some may be invented by well-intentioned persons disturbed by the state of affairs or by society's problems as they perceive them. Many will have a good economic basis in their origin; the leaders will be disguised businessmen providing a product for a market. The important point is, of course, not whether there is or is not an economic base for the ritual pedlars, but that a demand will exist for their product. I think we are due for an extensive sellers market for these products. The world—and the United States in particular —is likely to be in such a state and individual persons so emotionally set, that the new cult producers can expect a great boom. One ingredient will be necessary for a new ritual cult to prosper: the cult must be uncoupled from contemporary problems; put another way, the keynote of success will be social irresponsibility. The emphasis will be on experiential and not upon intellectual content. Belief systems which do not impact upon collective behavior, except in terms of rituals, seem strongly favored. For this reason, a falling market will characterize the older religious organizations which have adapted to contemporary society. The rituals of organized religions will be unable to take care of moral issues, for, at a social level, they will be far too complex and difficult. Thus, the majority of these institutions which in the past have led in setting moral values now seem likely to take a policy of inaction, leaving their individual adherents to take up any personal moral position they might desire. Putting this into commercial terms: the packaging of moral concepts and religious-type observances as the same product will be seen to be poor marketing policy. The Church has carried out some very important market surveys already—commissioning a very respectable, but definitely commercial, research organization to do this work.

It appears most probable that the very organizations which in the past have provided moral directions will be superseded by groups which primarily provide a variety of social contexts in which like-minded persons get together. Such groups will offer a "cop out" at the socio-moral level which will usually be both politically and culturally acceptable. There is, certainly, no indication that these groups are likely to develop into bodies where the focus for their appeal would be the consideration of the problematic social control in terms of moral objectives.

THE NEW MORAL PHILOSOPHERS

It is, accordingly, difficult to guess the source of the development o₁ the moral concepts of the twenty-first century. Certainly, we may hope that a small group of painters, poets, novelists, playrights and, perhaps, musicians will have an impact beyond their proportions.[11] We might also hope for the return of the role of the medieval court jester! The majority of the populace will drop out of involvement in moral issues—they will not be around even to chant the "Amen"; they will express their moral values, if at all, only through the ballot box. That is, if the ballot box can survive.

But there will be moral values to guide policy in the next decade or two, derived mainly from the idea that the survival of the human race is an essential good. Values will be preached more by intellectuals, especially scientists, than by theologians. New and different kinds of conflicts will involve the new moralists, whether technologists or non-scientist.

THE DOCTRINE OF SURVIVAL AND SELF-INTEREST

The emphasis upon the essential good—that is, the survival of the human race—will lead to conflict with values which see the advantage in short term and local or national goals. There will be no conflict between science and religions, as in the nineteenth century. Religious and related kinds of groups will, in certain areas, form loose associations with the values expressed by certain of the new moralists. Other religious and ritual groups will tend to ally themselves with political and reactionary forces, hence, with power rather than academic or intellectual leadership. In the main, we can expect only coalitions of convenience between multifarious pressure groups.

The main value of the late twentieth and early twenty-first century, as I see it, is that of enlightened self-interest; this is, I believe, an optimistic viewpoint. If we cannot achieve this as a value, there is little chance for survival. By main value in this sense, I refer to the dominant value which might characterize those in power. There will be other values and more moral positions taken by quite large minorities, and these secondary values will inform the basic idea of enlightened self-interest. At this level of the value system, I would again agree with Trist[12] who defines the values of the future as: "self-actualisation, self-expression, interdependence and a capacity for joy."

Solution or resolution?

In the light of these projections regarding the nature of the value system of the future and the rise of the new moralists, we may now state certain contingencies regarding the nature of crime and what the society of the turn of the century might do about it. There seem to be a number of consequences arising from these projections which will have an impact upon crime, how it is defined and the action taken to deal with it. However, criminology takes a position which lies uneasily between morals and technology, mediated by the concepts of law. The impact of technology on crime will be as significant as the impact of changing values. Value systems emphasize the human actors in the situation, event or act which is defined as criminal; technology tends to emphasize the circumstances surrounding the event and the techniques available to those who commit crimes, as well as to those who attempt to prevent them.

Until most recently society has attempted to deal with those events which were defined as criminal by seeking to deal with the person who committed the act. We even refer to a crime as being "solved" when we have found someone who can be blamed for committing it; this is an odd use of the term "solved." I know of no teacher who would regard a problem as solved when a student was able to point out some situation which could be blamed. Further, the emphasis on the person who is seen as the criminal—the one who can be blamed—has led us to ignore the other concomitants of the crime: the victim particularly, the situation and often many more factors.[13] A change in any one element of a complex set can result in a different outcome; perhaps, an outcome which may be more desirable. We may find greater success in attempting to deal with crime rather than with criminals. Making crime more difficult may not prevent the professional; however, he who becomes a criminal begins his career as a non-professional. If the first crime, committed by any kind of criminal can be delayed—the first crime which a criminal commits taking place at a later age—we shall have reduced the volume of crime and also the probability of a criminal career as the probability of a serious and lengthy criminal career is most highly correlated with the age at first offense. To delay the first criminal act—not prevent it—may be an expected result of making crime more difficult. Making crimes more difficult, although not preventing them, does not address the criminal in any way; it is a matter of technology and management.

There has been little development of technology which makes

crime more difficult; techniques have been concerned with the various aspects of the finding of guilt and the allocating of blame. Fingerprints, voiceprints, lie-detectors and the like help only in pinning the blame the more certainly upon the person who has already been suspected. Even the modus operandi index is used to identify persons who may have committed the crime, rather than for purposes of preventing further crimes of a similar nature. There will be a growing interest in systems for preventing crime or for making crimes more difficult. As a by-product, however, many of these methods will produce rather unpleasant conditions for those who are protected.

LAW'N'ORDER

It is not possible for us to do things about probable crimes without affecting ourselves. The controller is not independent of the controlled. There is a penalty which we must pay in terms of our own freedom for every restriction we can invent to deal with the criminal. It seems likely that the idea of adding more powers of control—the law'n'order syndrome—will continue to grow for some years yet, but before the turn of the century, a reversal will take place. The prisons have claimed that they could reform and rehabilitate offenders; there is no evidence of that despite the large sums society pays for the incarceration of offenders. The judges have claimed that they have dispensed justice; there is no evidence that sentencing practices are equitable, let alone just. All concerned with the criminal justice system have claimed to be able to perform those miracles society orders; not a claim has been supported. More police, we are told, will lead to less crime; we cannot establish the marginal efficiency of one more—or even less—policeman. This game is almost up. Society is beginning to note that prisons cannot save souls and is suggesting—at present somewhat mildly—the possibility of saving some money and—while we may not know exactly what justice is, while we are trying to find out—at least having equity in the disposition of offenders.

The money which is being fed into the criminal justice machinery at the present time by state and national agencies is going to act exactly like a hormone weed-killer: stimulating an unbalanced growth spurt such that the plant dies. The forces of law'n'order are now in the growth spurt stage, the unhealthy growth spurt which is prognostic of disaster. As knowledge increases, it will become even more apparent that the current view of crime control does a disservice to society, by ignoring all but a few elements in the handling of any antisocial event. An increased ability to deal with complex issues will enable the large number of decision processes, situations, personality factors and many more of the elements of any crime to be considered, without the excessive simplification which characterizes our present tactics.

The fear of crime—and indeed many other kinds of fears—is the main trigger for action, while at the same time, an inefficient motivator. There is a necessity to deal with the dramatic event which generates maximum fear—the mass murderer or kidnapper —without reference to the fact that such events are extremely rare. We move as frightened children away from the sound of one big bang and then from another. The development of information systems will enable a more reasoned use of data to inform policy which eventually will seep through to our bureaucratic structure. We have been told that we should do something about social ills, because they give rise to crime. Hopefully, we shall learn that this is a poor, fear based policy. We should deal with social ills—such as, child neglect, poverty, unemployment, overcrowding and the like— because these are evils in their own right.

How the present may affect the future

Like the hip bone to the thigh bone, the past is connected to the future by the sinews of the present. But the lessons of the present will take a long time to be learned in the field of criminal justice. The feedback of information about the effects of decisions which might guide policy is almost entirely lacking. The data which do exist are most unreliable. There is no efficient way for the system to learn by its mistakes; indeed, there is a very strong tendency to deny that mistakes are made. Where the processes are so ill-adjusted to learning, the probability of adaptation to change seems remote. Yet, the pressures of crime and public reactions to it are likely always to be strong and to grow stronger. Thus, something will have to be done; what will be done, more often than not, will be reactionary. The past times were better: there were fewer problems then; if we cannot return to yesterday's problems, we can return to yesterday's solutions—and our politicians will!

It is also possible to persuade the public that the problems which are troubling them are yesterday's problems; thus, they welcome outdated remedies for the wrong problems. What does threaten us today? Is it street crime? How dangerous is it to carry out desired activities? Who are the enemies of society? What kinds of crime will characterize the future, and how should we be preparing our social defense? It is possible to put the threats and fears of contemporary society into perspective, but only with considerable difficulty.

Let us consider an example which may indicate what I mean. Suppose that the parents of a son or daughter between the ages of ten and fourteen received a message that their child was dangerously ill in a hospital. The informant, after being asked quickly what happened, says that he does not have any idea, but the parent is to come at once. On the way one would be trying to think what could have happened. What would be the guesses in such a situation? Would the greatest fear be that the cause of the trouble was a crime or a car accident? (How should I write that last word; with or without quotation marks: an "accident" or an accident?) In any event, what would be a reasonable strategy of social action? If car accidents cause, say, ten times more damage than do events which we now call crime, would it not be reasonable to devote ten times the amount of money we spend on crime to attempt to reduce accidents? If this would not be seen as a rational strategy—and it apparently is not so regarded—what are the reasons for this?

KEEPING CRIME VISIBLE

There seems to be a need to keep crime visible—to personalize it in terms of the criminal. The criminal is somebody whom we can fear and, hence, hate. Conversely, we are grateful when some white knight slays the dragon, but this dragon has to be visible. Making roads safer does not have the symbolic appeal of bringing a villain to justice. In England, they are very defensive about the idea of parliamentary government; every Fifth of November children burn in effigy a certain Guy Fawkes, who once, in the seventeenth century, attempted to destroy the government. While the cellers of the House of Commons are being searched for the physical form of Guy Fawkes, we cannot be as concerned with what might be going on in the committee rooms upstairs. While we attempt to detect the gunpowder treason and plot,[14] we will have less concern for the gentlemanly ploys and strategies which subvert the very nature of the democratic process: the one villain can be identified, the collective villains can hide. There is little chance but that the public will continue to be persuaded more by symbols of harm which they can see, than by discussions of harms which are invisible.

Our ideas of property must, and will, change; only if this happens can we hope to protect our concepts of human dignity. Private companies now hold much more information about individuals than do official bodies. What are their rights to this property? To what extent does the disturbance of the coating on a computer tape represent a property? The tape exists in the same form, whether it contains no information or very different forms of information. How can juries deal with these kinds of evidence? What constitutes the theft of information? We are working towards some concepts to deal with these issues, but largely concepts which were current generations ago.

Our physiological reactions to threats are still the same as they were in cave-dwelling days—the level of adrenalin rises when we hear a sudden loud noise. But, sounds are no longer prognostic of the same threats as those for which additional adrenalin flow was useful. The things or conditions which are most threatening to us today are invisible, although some may be seen by the use of a microscope. Perhaps the most serious kinds of threats to the continuance of the human race cannot be foreseen by the use of any current or probable aids. These events which could destroy us can only be inferred by means of sophisticated statistical analysis. One such threat is the possibility of error in our defense systems; another is, of course, the ecological balance problem. A single offender may make a decision to commit a crime against us and be held responsible, in much the same way as in the past. But, who makes the decisions of the large corporate enterprises? Applications of current legal philosophies can, in these kinds of cases, be extremely dysfunctional.[15] How can we develop and put into effect a rational view of collective responsibility and collective guilt? The Neuremberg Trials did not provide a very satisfactory doctrine for these issues. Perhaps, we should not even try developing collective guilt, but rather seek some other ethical basis for our protection.

Conclusion

What is probable and what is desirable are different things. If what is probable is not seen as desirable, we can do something about it—if, but only if, we are aware of the probability. There is a strong tendency to believe that what is desirable is the more probable; while there may be no direct reason why this should be so, there is little doubt that possible developments which are seen as desirable tend to gain in their levels of probability.[16] We are inventing the future now; we must make that process a conscious and rational one. We must accept the idea that the idea of relevance must be future oriented.

Present day values, expressed in terms of immediate relevance, may pave the way towards disaster. Higher levels of abstraction may be more relevant than more concrete considerations. Research investigations which are focused on contemporary problems may have dangerously little pay-off. Research takes time; times change, and they are changing very fast. Thus, we have an interesting paradox: making research more relevant can result in findings that are irrelevant. Research on today's problems—unless, by chance, those problems have an element of generality—would seem to be poor strategy. In the immediate future—and perhaps for at least the next six or seven years—most research expenditure in the social field, and particularly in crime related areas, will be influenced by short term political considerations. In present times there is no sign of any degree of detachment of research funding from local and national governmental interests. Too strong pressure to be relevant —the relevance being determined by specific, local, immediate or bureaucratic considerations—will direct research away from findings which have a high degree of generality; thus, millions of dollars will be wasted.

Questions and answers

Q: Shouldn't we look to the causes of this increase in crime in the climate of modern society? Would you have any suggestions of changes in our economic, social, political and religious life which would remove the causes of crime?

A: I think we should deal with social problems because they are social problems and not because we think they are causes of crime. That's where we've gotten ourselves into a mess. It's because we have been able to point the finger of blame at "them" and worked on that, that we have gone down the wrong road. If a thing is wrong, it's undesirable for society; if poverty is bad, deal with it because it's bad, not because it is believed to be a cause of crime.

Q: It seems to me that the question of crime and criminal justice is one that requires policy leadership and policy statement. We have yet to hear a codified policy statement on crime and criminal justice. I note that the House Select Committee on Crime has been removed. We have yet to have a criminal justice representative on the Cabinet. My question is, what do you see as the major stumbling blocks for a national policy on criminal justice?

A: Want a simple answer? The stumbling blocks are ignorance and prejudice.

Yet, I think this is one of the interesting points. When it comes to other technical issues, the president has advisors, on economics, trade and so on. But in the highly technical area of crime there are no longer the advisors that once were around, in previous administrations. I must say I place some of the blame for this on the way in which politics, morals and law have become confused. The idea of running a functional society and the idea of political constraints have not been spelled out separately; crime has come to be seen as a political platform issue, rather than a technical problem.

It's probably much easier to integrate people against something, than to integrate them for something. One of the cheapest and easiest ways of integrating people against something is to frighten them. So, if you can get people to be afraid of crime—if you so can persuade them—you get them running with you. It's a very useful political tool, and we have, I think, the spectacle of a technical problem being dealt with in terms of propaganda. One couldn't imagine other social problems being dealt with in quite the same way.

This is really the tragedy of it. One has to be very careful about using fear as an integratcng force as, indeed, the advertisers know quite well.

I rather think that the administrations, both in England and in this country, have, perhaps, overcapitalized on fear of crime, and it's going to bounce back. Then we might see a more rational approach to dealing with social problems of that kind.

Q: I am involved with the National Advisory Council on Adult Education. I was appointed as a chairman to do special research, relating to education in the penal and corrective institutions, and to study those individuals who are repeaters. Have you any information that could be useful to me on this project?

A: There have been a very large number of studies of recidivists. The only thing we can say is: we get the best results from doing as little as possible. That's really quite true. Put a person on probation rather than in prison; you get better results that way. The less you bug them, by and large, the better the result.

Q: What I mean is, would you give those people more academic education or more spiritual education to convince them that crime does not pay?

A: I wouldn't force treat anybody, personally; I don't think it is possible. Why should not facilities be available on a voluntary basis? What is achieved by taking the view: thou shalt learn? When people meet me and occasionally say, "You're a teacher?" I say, "I try not to be. I try to create a learning environment." And there is a difference. I think we might do more towards developing learning environments in many sectors.

Q: How would you motivate those individuals not to become involved in crimes again?

A: I would certainly not approve of any form of forced learning, although I would make learning facilities available. I would make conditions humanitarian and institutional routine much more simple. If a person is going to be punished, let's honestly punish him and not kid ourselves that we're treating him.

Q: A single question, and I would be satisfied with a brief answer. Your entire discussion would be enlightened if you would give us some kind of a working definition of "law," even if not a formal definition.

A: One simple definition is: law is what legislators legislate. But I think we have used law to solve a lot of problems which are not really amenable to solution by law. I think there are other kinds of problems for which the legal method of solving problems might be better than other methods of problem solving. One certainly doesn't solve drug addiction by blaming the addict. The drug addiction problem is economic, more than anything else. One has, by the creation of law, created an extra product: that of risk. The value of the product plus the risk, makes a useful commodity for certain illicit enterprises to work in. If we had not created the risk and the inflated price by the misuse of law, we would have had an entirely different drug problem, to say the least.

Q: A few years ago the National Council on Crime and Delinquency (NCCD) was advising correctional personnel on how to build bigger and better prisons. I noticed that last year they came out with a policy statement that said there should be no more prisons built in this country. I was wondering whether you, as chairman of NCCD, could explain how the thinking evolved from "bigger and better prisons," to "no prisons at all."

A: Professor Wolfgang was Chairman then.

A: (M. WOLFGANG): The National Council on Crime and Delinquency, as well as other organizations and agencies in the United States, finally came to recognize—after a series of systematic studies and a kind of anthropological observation—that our prisons simply have not worked. As Professor Wilkins said, they have failed to rehabilitate or to reduce recidivism, and they have been breeding grounds for crime. We have educated more criminals within the confines of that small life-space we call "prisons," than we ever have in society. So it was, I think, quite appropriate that the NCCD recognized this formally and suggested that no more large scale prisons should be built.

Q: The kinds of crimes that most people in America today are most concerned about are crimes of violence. I'd like to ask you, in your projections of the future, if you think there would be any alteration in this concern? If so, what are the kinds of crimes that are likely to be of major concern between now and the end of this century?

A: I think we shall have to get around to gun control. We shall have to recognize that, in addition to the victim and the offender, the implements and the situation are also concerned in crime. These should be properly looked at and dealt with.

I rather hope, too, that we shall see a change in the policy with regard to drugs. Anybody who knows drug addicts, knows that they are not able to commit crimes while they are under the influence of drugs. The reason that they commit crimes, of course, is the economic factor: namely, the price inflated by the risk element. The peddler, in fact, is acting as a sort of insurance broker, covering the risk.

I rather hope that violence will resume its long term trend which has been downhill over, say, more than one hundred years. I've seen data of violent crimes from various countries, and this is generally true.

What has happened should not be seen in terms of the number of persons accused of violent crimes. We are taking a rather dimmer view of the violent situation: if Joe hits Bill now, we consider it more serious than we used to. This is evident from the data of the statistics in countries where serious violence is separated from less serious violence. What has happened is that the number of offenses of serious violence has increased, whereas the number of less serious ones has gone down. This doesn't mean that if Joe hits Bill now, he hits him harder than he used to; it merely means that the perception of what is tolerable violence has changed considerably. The long term trend will probably be resumed once we get rid of the artificial situation of the law trying to deal with a medical problem.

In terms of the future, the most serious crimes are going to be those relating to information, rather than to tangible things, and to the collective responsibility crimes. These are crimes which can threaten the continuity of the human race. It's going to be extremely difficult to handle the idea of theft of information, when you can't even see that information. All you have is a tape with ferrous oxide on it, arranged in different patterns. It can be very difficult to handle those concepts under the current kinds of contraints of law and procedure.

Q: Should we not legalize gambling to deprive organized crime of a lucrative source of income?

A: Yes, and probably a number of other things too. I would take a very large number of operations from the legal jurisdiction of the criminal code and try to have these dealt with by codes analogous to civil codes. Denmark is moving quite rapidly in this direction; it is even considering removing shoplifting from the criminal code. England never has had incarceration for check fraud that this country insists on. What happens here is that credit—your credit and my credit ratings—are supported by people being locked up in prison. That is really what is happening. Some years ago in California, some 15 percent to 20 percent of people in prison were locked up for check frauds. And that fact meant that you and I could very easily cash a check in California. In England, it is not so easy to cash a check, because if the businessman accepts a dud check, he has got to take civil proceedings; he cannot get that person locked up in jail. Thus, the businessman is a lot more careful, and it's not so easy for you, the honest citizen, to cash a check.

These are the ways in which controls work. People always used to try to draw cause or control diagrams, with arrows. It's nonsense. You cannot draw a diagram showing a simple one-way relationship between things in the social world; all effects are at least two dimensional.

Notes

1   On this most futurists agree. Some of the features of accelerating change are discussed by Margaret Mead. See, for example, Margaret Mead, "The Future: Prefigurative Cultures and Unknown Children," in A. Toffler, ed., *The Futurists* (New York: Random House, 1972).

2   Most authorities would argue that this was not only a correct assessment, but that it was a necessary and appropriate feature of law. Barbara Wooton, *Crime and the Criminal Law* (London: Stevens and Sons, 1963) has some interesting comments on the problems of crime preventive methods and law.

3   Many critics of current criminal policy have put forward this viewpoint. Perhaps the best evidence in support of this and other similar claims is to be found in the supporting statements made by any criminal justice agency, which accompany requests for budget increases.

4   T. Platt, *The Politics of Riot Commissions* (New York: Collier Books, 1971) provides ample evidence of local breakdowns in social control and the means employed to deal with the situations.

5   Kai T. Erikson, *Wayward Puritans: A Study in the Sociology of Deviance* (New York: John Wiley, 1966).

6   Although it is difficult to compare data regarding the disposal of offenders in different countries, the differences in the proportions of the population who are, at any time, incarcerated in penal institutions varies widely. A comment on this issue is given in Nils Christie, "Changes in Penal Values," *Scandinavian Studies in Criminology* (Oslo, Norway: Scandinavian University Books, 1968), vol. 2.

7   Erich Jantsch, "Technological Forecasting in Perspective," Publication of the Organization for Economic Co-operation and Development, no. 21, 931 (Paris: 1967), especially pp. 42–44.

8   Eric Trist, "Urban North America" (Paper presented at the World Congress on Mental Health, Edinburgh, England, 1969).

9   Stafford Beer, "The Law and the Profits: The Sixth Frank Newsam Memorial Lecture" (Paper presented at the Police College in Bramshill, England, Oct. 29, 1970). He notes, "[Sir Charles] Goodeve proposed that we should try to produce an eudemonic measure . . . [the complexity] of each of the two conditions is too great for analysis, the only thing left to measure is the difference between them . . . [a] difference *in potential*."

10   Donald Schon, *Displacement of Concepts* (London: Tavistock Publications, 1959).

11   There is little doubt that Charles Dickens, through the medium of his novels, had a very considerable impact upon prison reform. The television "investigative reporter" has had a very considerable impact, where this medium is widely used. Among contemporary authors, the novelist, Arthur Hailey, has highlighted current problems of social control and technology, in his novels, *Airport*, *Wheels* and *Hotel*.

12   Trist, "Urban North America."

13   R. Jeffrey, *Crime Control through Environmental Design* (London: Sage, 1971).

14 The children's rhyme—somewhat akin to some Christmas jingles—runs thus: "Be pleased to remember/The Fifth of November/The gun-powder treason and plot/ . . . Penny for the Guy, Mister?"

15 When railway workers, airport controllers or others work by the rules, the system breaks down. This breakdown is not due to a failure of law or a failure of those concerned to abide by the law; it arises because the workers are following closely the rule of law. The point is that laws are not necessarily made to facilitate the working of systems, but to exculpate those in high positions in such systems. The laws specify who—at a lower level than the lawmakers—may be blamed if anything goes wrong. A classical analysis of such cases is given by J. Bensman and I. Gerver, "Crime and Punishment in the Factory: A Functional Analysis," in L. Rosenberg, I. Gerver, and F. W. Howston, eds., *Mass Society in Crisis* (New York: Macmillan, 1964).

16 See, for example, F. W. Irwin, "Stated Expectations as Functions of Probability and Desirability of Outcomes," *Journal of Personality* 21 (1953), pp. 329–335, and R. W. Marks, "The Effect of Probability, Desirability and Privilege on the Stated Expectations of Children," *Journal of Personality* 19 (1951), pp. 332–351.

Val Clear
Scott Clear

Horizons in the criminal justice system

Witch drownings and the rock pile were once thought to be enlightened penology. Road gangs and the lash are still used in certain areas but are on the way out. The juvenile court and the indeterminate sentence were revolutionary innovations only a few years ago. Change is a constant in the criminal justice system. What lies just ahead?

Gault, Gideon, Miranda, and other decisions set new rules, and further extensions are now being debated. Use of a public defender supplied by the state to contest charges that originate with the state is being questioned. Discrimination against ex-offenders in employment is being reviewed. Long

Reprinted from *Crime and Delinquency*, January 1974, pp. 25–32, with the permission of the National Council on Crime and Delinquency.

pretrial detention, the injustices of the bail system, inclusion of violations of bureaucratic regulations in the criminal system, decriminalization of drug abuse, victimless crimes, federal minimum wages for prisoners—these and almost a hundred other issues are claiming attention. Changes are imminent.

The rock pile, the road gang, the death penalty for ten-year-olds, and the Salem witch trials are viewed with incredulity by today's youth. Their disbelief in these forms of punishment demonstrates the progress made in the criminal justice system. The wide variation in current practice, ranging from the use of the lash in some states to educational release in others, indicates that much remains to be done. Indeed, when one talks of horizons in the criminal justice system he must look both to the east and to the west.

It is difficult for us to realize that the juvenile court, the curfew, and the reform school were once innovations, that when they first appeared they were improvements over existing practices.[1] We take for granted the probation and parole systems, peer-group therapy such as Alcoholics Anonymous, the indeterminate sentence, and the presentence investigation. They would not come into a discussion of innovations. We even take such recent decisions as *Gault* and *Miranda* for granted.

We recently did an inventory of innovations mentioned in the last two years of criminal justice publications, and we emerged with a list of over 100 different ideas (see Appendix). There will be many institutional changes; some will affect prisoners' rights. It seems certain that the implications of the *Gideon* decision will require the state to make counsel available to anyone whose parole is about to be revoked, and perhaps even at the initial parole hearing itself.[2] Internal disciplinary measures in the institution will probably come under judicial review and perhaps also will require the presence of counsel.[3]

It is likely that the present practice of using a public defender, a person employed by the state to represent a client in opposition to the state, will be successfully challenged. Means will be found to provide the indigent accused with an attorney of his own choice, to be reimbursed from public funds. The eager young lawyers now volunteering in many sensitive spots can be expected to provide some of the talent needed for this function, but eventually someone will challenge even that system on the grounds of fairness since the amount of money paid presumably has a direct and causative

524 **Approaches to solutions**

relationship to the quality of the legal representation the accused can enjoy.[4]

We have become accustomed to freedom from job discrimination on the grounds of race, religion, age, or sex. It seems likely that, before long, ex-offenders will be added to this list of prejudicially treated minorities.[5] In most jurisdictions it is impossible for one with a felony record to conceal that fact regardless of its irrelevance to his suitability for the position he is seeking. Job applications usually ask the question and the applicant must state that he has been convicted of a felony. College students and war-resisters with records will keep calling attention to the absence of a time limit in the offender's payment of his "debt" to society. Already some provision has been made for the annulment of convictions and guilty pleas,[6] and the movement to "expunge the record" will probably accelerate in another year or two, as additional pressures are exerted when the debate over amnesty for draft evaders becomes a major issue. Refugee sons of federal lawmakers have already had an effect.

Everyone is looking for successful alternatives to incarceration. Probation and parole are receiving increasingly favorable public attention. That the taxpayer is in a position to save about $4,000 a year for every person placed on parole is in itself effective leverage in persuading the public of the superiority of the system.[7] A newer approach is "street probation," in which the judge delays pronouncing sentence for about a year; it applies an unusually direct and salutary pressure upon the offender since his conduct during that year becomes a part of the presentence report with unmistakable relevance to the sentence the judge will hand down.[8] This perceptive approach seems likely to find its way into our progressive courts.

A persisting scandal of our judicial system is the log jam that produces incredible delay in bringing the accused to the bench. It has been estimated that 60 per cent of the persons incarcerated in this country are awaiting trial. The sheriff in our county makes the point beautifully by telling persons visiting the county jail, "Seventy-five per cent of the men and women in this jail are not guilty." When they discover that some have been sitting it out for six to nine months before trial, all legally innocent and some undoubtedly innocent in fact, they are incensed with the injustice of the laggard system.

Since the amount of bail bond required seems to have no great correlation to the ultimate appearance of the accused in court, there is reason for reducing the load on the jails by likewise reducing the bail bond demands of the courts.[9] A man on the streets on his own recognizance does not cost the state anything for upkeep, and he is able to continue to hold a job and to support his family. The elimination of the money requirement for bail of persons who are apparently good risks is not yet very common, but the Clement Stone Foundation is trying to get a movement off the ground whereby churches supply the bond for persons unable to provide it. Such a movement is reminiscent of the Good Samaritan who told the innkeeper that he would pick up the tab for the pitiful fellow who had been rolled. It seems only a matter of time until the fine, which obviously discriminates against the poor offender, is challenged. In some states 60 per cent of the persons in jail are there for inability to pay fines.[10] One wag has suggested that, if you can pay taxes by Master Charge (now possible in some states), the next step will be to pay fines by credit card.

Part of the modernization of the criminal justice system involves eliminating certain offenses that had no business being in it in the first place.[11] We sense that the penal system cannot deal with white-collar criminals, so—as in the Agnew case—we usually avoid sending them to prison. Such offenses as income tax evasion, violation of the pure food laws, activities in restraint of trade, and similar offenses could better be handled by bureaucratic measures than by traditional courts and prisons.

Related to this is the imminent redefinition of certain drug offenses. A number of states have already reduced the seriousness of marijuana possession (although one state apparently still has a life sentence possible for the possession of one joint), and there is a growing awareness that drug abuse is more a medical than a criminal problem. Trafficking in illicit drugs will undoubtedly continue to be a criminal consideration, but the mere possession or use of illicit drugs will probably be seen more as a call for treatment than for punishment.

In a bit broader spectrum, laws will probably be modified in most states to remove from the criminal statutes the so-called "victimless" crimes. We have seen this happen in the case of abortion and homosexuality in a few states already, and it seems likely that prostitution, gambling, alcoholism, and drug addiction will be receiving increasing attention. Where crimes do have victims we can expect the state to provide compensation if the criminal cannot.[12]

Prevention of crime is attracting considerable attention, and that makes sense.[13] An unprecedented number of volunteers are being used in all kinds of situations. This not only helps prevent criminal acts from taking place but also provides a significant force of informed and concerned persons who can bring pressure upon legislators, courts, and administrators to modify the system. Experimentation with the development of family tactical police units whose function is more social work than law enforcement responds to a long-felt need.

The hope that some physical cause of criminal behavior might be identified dates back at least to Lombroso, who thought he could recognize criminals by the shapes of their chins and ears. Recent research has attracted attention to the XYY syndrome, which suggests a chromosomal imbalance peculiar to violent persons.[14] We should not hold our breath until that research is finished, in the hope of trading in our judicial system for a genetics laboratory, but it will be interesting to watch the course of the investigation.

Another more promising approach is the recent move by the United States to pay Turkish poppy farmers not to grow the source of heroin. We persuaded millionaire farmers to stop growing cotton with a sizable bribe of this kind; why did we not think sooner of trying the same approach with the Turkish farmers? There will still be illicit poppy fields in the Middle East but the total volume will probably be smaller. Since the development of poppy fields and opium production in the Golden Triangle of Laos, Burma, and Thailand has been sponsored by government officials as a moonlighting enterprise, it seems unlikely that subsidy following the Turkish pattern would have much effect there. More and more will Southeast Asia be the source of heroin—deferred payment we shall be making for the Vietnam War for some time to come.

A decade ago no one would have predicted the emptying of our correctional institutions. We should have taken a cue from what was happening to the mental hospitals, which have experienced a drastic reduction in patients because of the new medications available. In a sense, this is parallel to what has happened in criminal justice. Our new medicines are probation, parole, work release, education release, furlough, etc., and these have reduced the number of persons in correctional institutions in many parts of the country.[15] In California the state subsidy system, which encourages counties financially to expand local probation instead of relying on state penal institutions, has resulted in reducing the population of state institutions for delinquents so much that the state government has canceled plans to construct a $6-million institution.[16]

Alcoholics Anonymous has shown how effective self-help can be when reinforced by persons who have lived the same tragic story.

The Fortune Society, a New York-based organization of ex-prisoners, has expanded its program into the Midwest and the South. It is likely that similarly oriented groups of ex-offenders will be springing up in other urban centers to provide support during the critical re-entry phase.

Formerly a parolee who associated with ex-offenders was violating the terms of his parole. That will probably be changed—perhaps through the use of another promising innovation, the community-based treatment center. Having carefully selected ex-inmates in a community center should help in much the same way that ex-addicts give authentic help in a crashpad or halfway house for drug addicts returning clean to society.

Another far-reaching change in the correctional institutions will involve payment of the federal minimum wage by prison industries. The present prison wage is about 20¢ a day; if the minimum wage rule is made applicable to prison labor, the scale will be at least $1.60 an hour. As a result, laws now restricting the sale of prison products will have to be revised. A new competitive atmosphere in prison industries will emerge, with updated equipment and methods and efficient vocational training.

Change in the institutions is already becoming apparent in some states. The newer prisoners differ from the older ones. Many of them are better educated and more of them come from the middle class and upper class or from the militant rather than the docile segment of the lower class. As members of new groups of activists, they regard themselves as political prisoners and can be expected to behave (or misbehave) differently from their predecessors. Early on their agenda for prison reform will be the right to vote even while in prison.[17] Prisoner participation in running the institution will also become an issue. Should correctional educators get ready for a parent-teacher type of association?

What we have looked at above are specific programmatic changes. Probably more far-reaching than any of these is the change in social climate that seems to be taking place. There is no question that the prisoners themselves are becoming increasingly aware of the inequities built into the system, of their basic disadvantage, and of the avenues they can take to secure more acceptable treatment. The system itself is uncertain, self-conscious, and defensive. It reels under the shock of profound social change and seems unsure of many of the certainties of yesteryear. Past prison reform movements rarely stemmed from professionals; disgruntled ex-prisoners and Quakers were the main tinder igniting the flame of reform. Attica got the public's attention in the same way the Missouri farmer got the mule's attention—with a 2 x 4. But the public *is* now alerted to the danger signals in our correctional systems. The move toward institutional accreditation by the American Correctional Association is most timely and should influence reluctant budget authorities to provide state funds for prison reform.

Most innovations in the past were Band-Aid expedients, dealing with a problem when it surfaced and doing so in a way that masked the sore rather than getting at the source of infection. Changes need to encompass more than that. The *Gideon, Miranda,* and *Gault* decisions make a good start. We have begun to question important patterns we had always taken for granted. As the present effort to combine treatment and revenge has proved unsuccessful, alternatives to incarceration are being favored. Eventually the goal of incarceration will be reform.

The assumptions on which the criminal justice system is erected are going to receive increasing scrutiny from young professionals and from intellectually agile prisoners. Part of the result may be the development of a more closely interconnected system. Police, detention home staff, judges and jurists, probation officers, security persons, correctional teachers, institutional psychologists, classification staff, chaplains, parole officers and board members—in short, everybody who has any role in the criminal justice system— will be subjected to increasingly penetrating examination by the public and can be expected to appreciate the value of unity. The criminal justice system, too long a mélange of disparate functionaries performing their duties as if the rest did not exist, will tend to become a coordinated organism in which the functioning of each part can take place only within the context of the whole system. The strategic allocation of funds by the Law Enforcement Assistance Administration can do more in a year than the old nonsystem did in a decade.

Some have suggested that penal institutions ought to be used only for the purpose of protecting the public.[18] Punitive treatment of human beings is now seriously questioned, and persons in responsible positions are calling for a philosophical change that threatens the assumption on which we built our large and prestigious penal institutions of the past two generations. If we move away from institutionalization as the answer to crime, as it appears we will, the future holds quite a different prospect for us.

There is general agreement that something is critically wrong with the criminal justice system and that changes are long overdue and inevitable. Karl Menninger writes, "I suspect that all the crimes committed by all the jailed criminals do not equal in total social damage that of the crimes committed against them." Dr. Menninger does not speak lightly, and he does not speak for himself alone. A growing coterie of knowledgeable persons whose integrity and competence cannot be questioned agree with that position. Among them are persons whose concern for the criminal justice system is unimpeachable, who have given their lives to it, and who feel that the time has come for profound and comprehensive changes.

So the criminal justice system has two horizons: on the far west, an impressive collection of innovations that in their day were daring and creative but are now obsolete and almost useless because we have moved beyond them; on the horizon ahead of us, a fascinating set of challenges, some of which will prove to be highly productive and others grossly disappointing but all of them demanding the utmost skill from the most able professional people in the system.

Notes

1 Robert M. Mennel, "Origins of the Juvenile Court," *Crime and Delinquency*, January 1972, pp. 68 ff.

2 Eugene Barkin and Clair Cripe, "Looking at the Law," *Federal Probation*, September 1971, p. 54; Alvin W. Cohn, ed., *Problems, Thoughts, and Processes in Criminal Justice Administration* (New York: National Council on Crime and Delinquency, 1969), pp. 232–39; Sol Rubin, "Illusions of Treatment in Sentences and Civil Commitments," *Crime and Delinquency*, January 1970, p. 85.

3 Committee on the Model Act, National Council on Crime and Delinquency, "A Model Act to Provide for Minimum Standards for the Protection of the Rights of Prisoners," *Crime and Delinquency*, January 1972, pp. 4–14.

4 "ABA Launches Program of Correctional Reform," *Federal Probation*, June 1971, p. 87.

5 "Ex-Prisoners: Second Chances," *Economist*, Feb. 20, 1971, pp. 24 ff.; Neil P. Cohen and Dean Hill Rivken, "Civil Disabilities: the Forgotten Punishment," *Federal Probation*, June 1971, pp. 21 ff.

6 "California Law Permits Judges to Withdraw Plea of Guilty on Completion of Probation," *Federal Probation*, December 1971, p. 79.

7 *Federal Probation*, December 1970, p. 90.

8 Carl H. Imlay, "Legislation," *Federal Probation*, September 1971, p. 56.

9 "Crisis in the Courts," *New Statesman*, May 1, 1970, pp. 613 ff.; "To Make the Punishment Fit," *Times Literary Supplement*, Jan. 22, 1970, pp. 69 ff.; Michael Meltsner, "The Future of Correction: A Defense Attorney's View," *Crime and Delinquency*, July 1971, pp. 266–70.

530 **Approaches to solutions**

10 "Avoidance of the Traditional Machinery of Adjudication: A Worldwide Trend?" *Social Research*, Summer 1971, pp. 268–97.

11 Norval Morris and Gordon Hawkins, "Rehabilitation: Rhetoric and Reality," *Federal Probation*, December 1970, p. 17.

12 "Victims Compensated," *NCCD News* (September–October 1971), p. 4; Edmund K. Faltermayer, "Some Here-and-Now Steps to Cut Crime," *Fortune*, January 1970, p. 97.

13 "More States Are Awarding Cash Compensations to Victims of Crimes," *Federal Probation*, December 1970, p. 84; David Hume Harrison, "Criminal Injuries Compensation in Britain," *American Bar Association Journal*, May 1971.

14 Menachem Amir and Yitzchak Berman, "Chromosomal Deviation and Crime," *Federal Probation*, June 1970, pp. 55–62; Nicholas N. Kittrie, "Will the XYY Syndrome Abolish Guilt?" *Federal Probation*, June 1971, pp. 26 ff.

15 *Federal Probation*, December 1971, p. 87; Eleanor Harlow, Fred Cohen, and Robert Weber, "Diversion from the Criminal Justice System" (Rockville, Md.: NIMH Center for Studies of Crime and Delinquency, 1971); Norman Holt, "Temporary Prison Release," *Crime and Delinquency*, October 1971, pp. 414–30; Michael Rougier, "Opening the Gates to New Prison Reform," *Life*, Aug. 13, 1971.

16 *Federal Probation*, December 1971, p. 89; Leslie Wilkins, quoted in Norval Morris and Gordon Hawkins, "Rehabilitation: Rhetoric or Reality," *Federal Probation*, December 1970, p. 11.

17 Rubin, pp. 3–7.

18 "Judges Order Jail Overhaul," *NCCD News*, September–October, 1971, p. 9; Morris and Hawkins, p. 12.

Appendix

On the Western Horizon

Trial by ordeal
Trial by combat
Trial by jury
Pillory
Lady almoner
Rock pile
Road gang
Curfew
Reform school
Juvenile court
Probation and parole
Family court

Police Athletic League
Big Brother/Sister
Peer-group therapy (Alcoholics Anonymous, Alanon, Synanon)
National Addict Rehabilitation Act (NARA)
Indeterminate sentence
Presentence investigation
Meter Maid
Gault
Miranda

On the Eastern Horizon

Civil Rights

Miranda revision (for probationers and parolees)

Gault revision

Preventive detention

No-knock

Stop and frisk

Right to revocation hearing

Right to counsel at parole revocation hearings and to confront witnesses

Right to probation

Judicial review of penal institution policies

Sexual rights of inmates

Ex-offender's rights to a job

Ex-offender's rights to civil participation

Limited grounds for revocation

Elimination of capital punishment

Right to privacy

Procedure

Movement of certain offenses from criminal justice system

Narcotics addiction as medical (not criminal) problem

Computerized parole board decisions

Volunteer lawyers

Crediting time done before sentencing

Disclosure of presentence report

Ombudsman

Courts

Annulment of conviction

Police living on beat

Bifurcated hearings

Street probation before trial

Group sentencing

Crimes without victims (abortion, homosexuality, prostitution, alcoholism, drug addiction, pornography)

Decriminalization of marijuana

Institutionalization only to protect public, not punish

Night and weekend courts

Weekend sentences

Adulthood at eighteen

Bail bond: elimination of money requirement (volunteers to supply bond)

Teen-age jury

Victim compensation

Jury system revision (reduce size, increase remuneration, encourage trial without jury)

Legitimization of negotiated plea

Prevention

Saturation programming

Volunteers

Crisis hot lines for parolees and probationers

Transsexual surgery

XYY syndrome research

Indigenous leadership

Paid foster parents

Family tactical police units

Guaranteed family income

Remuneration for Turkish poppy farmers

Institutions

De-emphasis of institutionalization

Halfway house

Prisoners increasingly middle class, educated

College affiliations with institutions

Prison industries (vocational training, minimum wage law)

In-service training for staff and prisoners

Use of inmate volunteers

Former offenders as staff persons

Community-based centers

Diagnostic center

Early Release

Work furlough
Work release
Educational release
Shock parole
Close-supervision parole
Prerelease furlough
All paroles for set period unrelated to amount of time served

Philosophy

Professionalization of criminal justice system
Minority representation
Diversion of certain offenses from criminal justice to bureaucracy
LEAA—develop master strategy
Resegregation
New morality (contraceptives to teenagers)
Political prisoner concept

Therapy

"Outpatient" approach
Ex-offender on staff
Peer-group subculture (Briswell, Highlands, Provo)
Family-centered treatment (Wiltwyck)
Methadone and nonaddictive substitutes
Conjugal visits
Reality therapy
Victimology
Probation subsidy
Self-help in institutions (Alcoholics Anonymous, Jaycees, Kiwanis)
Behavior modification (Robert F. Kennedy Youth Center)
Human Potential Movement (Encounter groups)
Daytop